English Masterpieces

English
Masterpieces

700 - 1900

Edited by

H. W. HERRINGTON

Professor of English, Syracuse University

REVISED EDITION

I

From the Beginnings Through the
XVIII Century

W · W · NORTON & COMPANY · INC.
PUBLISHERS · NEW YORK

TO MY WIFE
Lydia Sumner Herrington

PREFACE

In spite of dissatisfaction expressed from time to time with the "survey course" as given in American colleges, it seems to have maintained its position firmly as an indispensable part of the curriculum. Only the ways of presenting the course have aroused much discussion, and these ways, if not exactly legion, are numerous enough to lead to heated discussion whenever teachers, or students, or both, get together. The first edition of *English Masterpieces* was prepared in the belief, as then expressed, that students "are best introduced to the riches of English literature through the extensive reading of a limited number of the greatest writers." The experience of the editor has only deepened this conviction; and though he would not quarrel with those who by exhibiting specimen bricks would try to build up an understanding of the architecture of English poetry and prose, he would maintain that a surer knowledge is to be got from the examination of certain massive edifices complete, and the study of the great architects who have formed the national style and taste. The contents of various recent anthologies would seem to corroborate his views.

This revision accordingly continues the plan of the earlier edition, although, in response to requests from those who have used the book, a few writers have been added: the "Wakefield Master," or whoever it was that wrote the famous *Second Shepherds' Play;* Sir Thomas Browne; and Dr. Samuel Johnson. Additions will also be found to the texts given from Bacon, Burns, Blake, and "Minor Eighteenth Century Poetry." Finally, the *Authorized Version of the Bible* has been represented by many selections from both Old and New Testaments. Partially to make space for these works, a few omissions have been made, but none, it is hoped, which will impair the usefulness of the book.

One of the cardinal principles of *English Masterpieces* was that the distinguished subject matter should be presented in an attractive format, with large, readable type in single column. The coöperation of the publishers has produced in the revision a page handsomer and pleasanter to read than in the original.

Particular pains have been taken to assure the authenticity of the texts, either the early editions or the most carefully edited modern reprints having been followed. The translation of the

vii

Beowulf is Professor J. Duncan Spaeth's, by permission of the author and of the Princeton University Press. *Sir Gawain and the Green Knight* is presented in the prose translation of the late Jessie L. Weston, by permission of Miss M. W. Malcolm Wood, executor of her estate. The selections from Chaucer, Spenser, Donne, Herrick, Vaughan, Lovelace, Dryden (essays), Boswell, and Blake, are here reprinted from the Oxford editions, by permission of the Oxford University Press; those from Shakespeare, Milton (poetry), Dryden (poetry), Pope, and Burns, as well as the English and Scottish popular ballads from the Cambridge editions, and those of Herbert from Professor G. H. Palmer's edition, by permission of and by arrangement with the Houghton Mifflin Company. President W. A. Neilson has generously accorded his permission also for the selections from Shakespeare. The selections from Milton's *Areopagitica* and from Swift follow the Bohn Library text, by permission of Messrs. G. Bell & Sons, Ltd., and of Harcourt, Brace, and Company; those from Gray and Collins are the Athenæum Press editions (edited by W. L. Phelps and W. C. Bronson respectively), by permission of Ginn and Company. Mr. Norman Ault's *Elizabethan Lyrics* has been used for the text of that section, by permission of the author and of the publishers, Messrs. Longmans, Green & Co. (John Phillip's *Lullaby* by permission of Messrs. W. W. Greg and R. B. McKerrow, from the Malone Society reprint of *Patient Grissell*). Bacon's essays are from Spedding's edition. May the editor take this occasion to express again to the publishers and scholars mentioned above his thanks for their generous permissions to reprint?

The revision has furnished opportunity for the correction of a number of misprints and errors of fact, for calling attention to which the editor is indebted to his colleagues Messrs. Leonard Brown, H. A. Eaton, A. E. Johnson, Herman Kirchhofer, Warren Shepard, R. R. Snook, A. M. Terhune, Norman Whitney, and William Yerington; to Mr. Gordon Coté; and to Professor Alwin Thaler of the University of Tennessee.

The panorama of London reproduced as an end-paper was drawn by Wenceslaus Hollar for: "Londinopolis; an historicall discourse; or, Perlustration of the city of London, the imperial chamber, and chief emporium of Great Britain . . . By Jam. Howel, esq. London. Printed by J. Streater for H. Twiford, 1657." Since the artist was apparently relying partly on memory and partly on earlier views, his drawing shows substantially the London that Shakespeare knew in his later years, and which continued in much these outlines until many familiar landmarks were wiped out by the great fire of 1666. Striking objects are the Tower; London Bridge with its line of shops and houses; the theaters on the Bankside; and the old Gothic St. Paul's, with its truncated spire, lopped off by fire in 1561. The Harvard University Library, through Mr. W. B. Briggs, Acting Librarian, has kindly given permission for the reproduction of this interesting drawing from their copy of Howell's *Londinopolis*.

H. W. H.

CONTENTS

* before this date

* before this date

ENGLISH MASTERPIECES

Volume I

ENGLISH
MASTERPIECES

Volume I

ANGLO-SAXON LITERATURE

Prior to the fifth century, the ancestors of the English were living on the continent of Europe, in that portion of the present German state adjoining the North Sea, and in the neighboring regions of southern Denmark. England itself was then occupied by the Britons, a people of Celtic stock, who had been looked over by Julius Cæsar (55 B. C.), and later conquered by the Romans. They had been partially Romanized, and were probably developing a Romance language. The Angles, Saxons, and Jutes, the three English tribes, were originally pirates and freebooters, like the later Vikings. First descending on England in the fifth century for booty, as a part of that widespread migration of Germanic peoples into the wealthy Roman Empire, they later came to stay, conquered the Britons, who had been abandoned by the Roman legions, and set up various English kingdoms, which were loosely united under Alfred the Great (d. 901). Civilization developed in England largely under the impetus of Christian culture. In 597 Augustine, sent as a missionary by Pope Gregory, landed in Kent; and about the same time Irish missionaries had penetrated into Northumbria, in the north of England, where a high civilization and an important literature first sprang up.

Here wrote, in the Anglian dialect, the school of Cædmon (seventh century), which produced metrical paraphrases of the gospels, and the school of Cynewulf (eighth century), which wrote chiefly poems based upon the life of Christ and the early saints (*Christ, Juliana, Elene, Andreas,* and the *Phœnix*). In the same region and the same century were written several beautiful and mournful lyrics that have survived, like *Deor's Lament, The Wanderer,* and *The Seafarer,* the great epic poem of *Beowulf,* and the *Ecclesiastical History* of the Venerable Bede (originally in Latin, afterwards translated into the West Saxon dialect of English).

In the ninth century, the center of English life had shifted to Wessex, in the south and southwest. Under the fostering influence of Alfred the Great the Anglo-Saxon Chronicle was started, and many translations were made. He himself translated, or caused to be translated, Orosius's *Universal History,* Bœthius' *Consolations of Philosophy,* and Pope Gregory's *Pastoral Care.* English civilization was much disturbed in this century by the inroads of the Danes, who, like the English tribes before them, descended first in naval raids on unprotected towns and farms, then proceeded to conquer the land in larger military units, and finally settled and brought under their sway all the northern and central portions of England. King Alfred's heroic opposition is simply but eloquently narrated in the *Chronicle.* In the end native and invader merged in a homogeneous society.

The later Anglo-Saxon literature flourished mostly in West Saxon, and reached a peak in the tenth century, the century of the great scholar and theologian Ælfric, who wrote prose homilies and other pious works.

Most of what was written in Anglo-Saxon has doubtless perished. In what remains, especially the poetry, there are qualities of high imagination, emotional

3

fervor, vividness and power; yet on the whole, it must be confessed, it is monotonous in subject-matter, and depressingly gloomy in tone. The Englishman thus early shows his trait of taking himself very seriously, his lack of ingratiating wit and charm. Had there not been an infusion of other forces following the Norman Conquest of 1066, English literature could hardly have been the great instrument it is to-day.

The language in which this literature was composed, the Old English or Anglo-Saxon, has developed by perfectly regular progression into our modern speech. Yet so far-reaching have been the changes of twelve centuries that documents in this oldest form of the Mother Tongue cannot be read without special study. The system of sounds has been greatly modified, many of the words have been lost, and most of the others preserved with much altered appearance, and the comparatively rich inflections of the original reduced to the very simplified grammar of modern English. The ordinary reader must accordingly depend upon translation (like that of the *Beowulf* here presented) for his knowledge of our literature from the beginnings to the eleventh century, or later.

BIBLIOGRAPHY. Nearly the entire corpus of Anglo-Saxon poetry is to be found in four unique manuscripts: (1) the Beowulf MS., referred to below, containing also the *Judith;* (2) the Junian MS., containing some of the Cædmonian material; (3) the Exeter Book (left by Leofric, first Bishop of Exeter, to his church), in which are some of the Cynewulfian poems, and elegies, riddles, and proverbs; and (4) the Vercelli Book, discovered in 1832 in the chapter library at Vercelli, in northern Italy, containing other Cynewulfian poetry. The sources of the prose are more various. Convenient translations of Anglo-Saxon literature are A. S. Cook and C. B. Tinker's *Select Translations of Old English Poetry,* and of *Old English Prose* (Ginn), Cosette Faust and Stith Thompson's *Old English Poems* (Scott Foresman), J. D. Spaeth's *Old English Poetry* (Princeton), and F. B. Gummere's *The Oldest English Epic* (Macmillan). Literary histories: B. Ten Brink's *Early English Literature,* trans. H. M. Kennedy (Holt), Stopford Brooke's *Eng. Lit. from the Beginning to the Norman Conquest* (Macmillan), and A. R. Benham's *Eng. Lit. from Widsith to Death of Chaucer* (Yale).

BEOWULF

Beowulf appears in a unique manuscript, now preserved in the British Museum, where it is known as "Cotton Vitellius A, xv." The manuscript has been damaged by fire, but is still legible in most places. In the opinion of competent scholars the poem was written in the first half of the eighth century by a single poet, obviously one of our greatest writers, whose name is unfortunately not known to us. The existing manuscript is preserved in a later West Saxon version, but the poet lived in the north of England—in Northumbria or Mercia—and wrote in the dialect of that region. He of course based his work upon earlier lays and stories which were familiar to him.

The subject-matter of the poem is Continental, concerning chiefly exploits of the Geats (who may have lived in southern Sweden) and the Danes. Yet the poem is entitled to be called the Anglo-Saxon national epic, because of its presentation of the life, customs, ideals, religion, and ways of thinking of our own ancestors. At least one important character in the poem, Beowulf's king,

Hygelac, was an historical person, who lived at the beginning of the sixth century, and it is likely that the hero himself had a living prototype. In the two centuries before the poem was written, legend and myth had been at work, had magnified the deeds recorded, and imaginatively recreated them.

The translation here presented, that by Professor J. Duncan Spaeth in his *Old English Poetry* (Princeton Univ. Press, 1921), is reproduced by special permission of and arrangement with the author and publisher. It preserves much of the atmosphere of the original, and also copies its verse-form. The Anglo-Saxon poetic line consists of two half-lines of two stresses each, with a varying number of unaccented syllables, bound together by alliteration, as reproduced in translation, the complete line having sometimes two and sometimes three alliterative syllables. The accented syllables bear the alliteration, prefixes being disregarded. Each consonant alliterates only with itself, but all vowels alliterate with all other vowels.

The leading stylistic features of the poem will be got by the reader from Professor Spaeth's admirable translation. There are many speeches (quoted in full), a number of episodes from Germanic myth and story (here mostly omitted), and a good deal of moralizing, in which a Christian veneer is thinly laid over a primitive pagan conception of Wyrd, or Fate. These features sometimes make the poem seem long-winded, and it is true that the actual moments of thrilling action are, in contrast, very briefly presented. In smaller compass will be noticed the constant use of several synonymous statements of the same thing—a trick of several phrases or clauses, one after another in apposition; the characteristic "kennings," or conventional brief metaphors, like "swan's road" and "whale's path" for the sea; and the very striking rhetorical figure of litotes, or understatement, which frequently gives to the text a grim irony.

BIBLIOGRAPHY. Beowulf MS. in photographic facsimile, ed. J. Zupitza (Early Eng. Text Soc.). Eds. of original, with critical apparatus, by Fr. Klaeber (Heath) and A. J. Wyatt and R. W. Chambers (Cambridge). Translations reproducing poetic form of original by F. B. Gummere in *The Oldest English Epic* (Macmillan), by G. H. Gerould (Nelson), and that here reprinted, by Professor Spaeth. The latter, by omitting about one-third of the poem, mainly the episodes, gives an impression of greater unity and rapidity than possessed by the original. Other translations by C. B. Tinker (Holt) in prose, and by Wm. Ellery Leonard (Century), in rhymed couplets.

THE MYTH OF THE SHEAF-CHILD

List to an old-time lay of the Spear-Danes,
Full of the prowess of famous kings,
Deeds of renown that were done by the heroes;
Scyld the Sheaf-Child [1] from scourging foemen,
From raiders a-many their mead-halls wrested.
He lived to be feared, though first as a waif,
Puny and frail he was found on the shore.
He grew to be great, and was girt with power
Till the border-tribes all obeyed his rule,

1 Mythical ancestor of the Danish house.

And sea-folk hardy that sit by the whale-path [2]   10
Gave him tribute, a good king was he.
Many years after, an heir was born to him,
A goodly youth, whom God had sent
To stay and support his people in need.
(Long time leaderless living in woe,
The sorrow they suffered He saw full well.)
The Lord of Glory did lend him honor,
Beowulf's [3] fame afar was borne,
Son of old Scyld in the Scandian lands.
A youthful heir must be open-handed,   20
Furnish the friends of his father with plenty,
That thus in his age, in the hour of battle,
Willing comrades may crowd around him
Eager and true. In every tribe
Honorable deeds shall adorn an earl.
The aged Scyld, when his hour had come,
Famous and praised, departed to God.
His faithful comrades carried him down
To the brink of the sea, as himself had bidden,
The Scyldings' friend, before he fell silent,   30
Their lord beloved who long had ruled them.
Out in the bay a boat was waiting
Coated with ice, 'twas the king's own barge.
They lifted aboard their bracelet-bestower,
And down on the deck their dear lord laid,
Hard by the mast. Heaped-up treasure
Gathered from far they gave him along.
Never was ship more nobly laden
With wondrous weapons and warlike gear.
Swords and corslets covered his breast   40
Floating riches to ride afar with him
Out o'er the waves at the will of the sea.
No less they dowered their lord with treasure,
Things of price, than those who at first
Had launched him forth as a little child
Alone on the deep to drift o'er the billows.
They gave him to boot a gilded banner,
High o'er his head they hung it aloft.
Then set him adrift, let the surges bear him.
Sad were their hearts, their spirits mournful;   50
Man hath not heard, no mortal can say
Who found that barge's floating burden.

---

2 the sea. An example of the "kenning," or conventional brief metaphor—a leading feature of Anglo-Saxon poetic style.

3 Not Beowulf, hero of the poem, but a prince of the same name in the Danish line.

I

THE LINE OF THE DANISH KINGS AND THE BUILDING OF HEOROT

Now Beowulf was king in the burgs of the Scyldings,
Famed among folk. (His father had left
The land of the living). From his loins was sprung
Healfdene the royal, who ruled to old age,
Gray and battlegrim, the bold-hearted Scyldings.
Children four to this chief of the people
Woke unto life, one after another;
Heorogar and Hrothgar, and Halga the brave,   60
And winsome Sigeneow, a Scylfing she wedded;
Saewela's queen they say she became.
To Hrothgar was given such glory in battle,
Such fame he won, that his faithful band
Of youthful warriors waxed amain.
So great had grown his guard of kinsmen,
That it came in his mind to call on his people
To build a mead-hall, mightier far
Than any e'er seen by the sons of men,
Wherein to bestow upon old and young,   70
Gifts and rewards, as God vouchsafed them,
Save folk-share lands and freemen's lives.
Far and wide the work was published;
Many a tribe, the mid-earth round,
Helped to fashion the folk-stead fair.
With speed they built it, and soon 'twas finished,
Greatest of halls. Heorot [4] he named it,
Whose word was law o'er lands afar;
Nor failed in his promise, but freely dealt
Gifts at the feast. The fair hall towered   80
Wide-gabled and high, awaiting its doom,
The sweep of fire; not far was the time
That ancient feuds should open afresh,
And sword-hate sunder sons from fathers.

In the darkness dwelt a demon-sprite,
Whose heart was filled with fury and hate,
When he heard each night the noise of revel
Loud in the hall, laughter and song.
To the sound of the harp the singer chanted
Lays he had learned, of long ago;   90

---

[4] "The Hart," or "The Stag," so called because the gables were adorned with antlers or with decorations resembling them.

How the Almighty had made the earth,
Wonder-bright lands, washed by the ocean;
How he set triumphant, sun and moon
To lighten all men that live on the earth.
He brightened the land with leaves and branches;
Life he created for every being,
Each in its kind, that moves upon earth.
So, happy in hall, the heroes lived,
Wanting naught, till one began
To work them woe, a wicked fiend.   100
The demon grim was Grendel called,
March [5]-stalker huge, the moors he roamed.
The joyless creature had kept long time
The lonely fen, the lairs of monsters,
Cast out from men, an exile accurst.
The killing of Abel, on offspring of Cain
Was justly avenged by the Judge Eternal.
Nought gained by the feud the faithless murderer;
He was banished unblest from abode of men.
And hence arose the host of miscreants,   110
Monsters and elves and eldritch sprites,
Warlocks and giants, that warred against God;
Jotuns [6] and goblins; He gave them their due.

II

THE RAVAGING OF HEOROT HALL BY THE MONSTER GRENDEL

When night had fallen, the fiend crept near
To the lofty hall, to learn how the Danes
In Heorot fared, when the feasting was done.
The aethelings all within he saw
Asleep after revel, not recking of danger,
And free from care. The fiend accurst,
Grim and greedy, his grip made ready;   120
Snatched in their sleep, with savage fury,
Thirty warriors; away he sprang
Proud of his prey, to repair to his home,
His blood-dripping booty to bring to his lair.
At early dawn, when day-break came,
The vengeance of Grendel was revealed to all;
Their wails after wassail were widely heard,
Their morning-woe. The mighty ruler,
The aetheling [7] brave, sat bowed with grief.

---

5 border   6 giants   7 prince

The fate of his followers filled him with sorrow, 130
When they traced the tracks of the treacherous foe,
Fiend accurst. Too fierce was that onset,
Too loathsome and long, nor left them respite.
The very next night, anew he began
To maim and to murder, nor was minded to slacken
His fury of hate, too hardened in crime.
'Twas easy to find then earls who preferred
A room elsewhere, for rest at night,
A bed in the bowers,[8] when they brought this news
Of the hall-foe's hate; and henceforth all 140
Who escaped the demon, kept distance safe.

So Grendel wrongfully ruled the hall,
One against all till empty stood
That lordly mansion, and long remained so.
For the space of twelve winters the Scyldings' Friend [9]
Bore in his breast the brunt of this sorrow,
Measureless woe. In mournful lays
The tale became known; 'twas told abroad
In gleemen's songs, how Grendel had warred
Long against Hrothgar, and wreaked his hate 150
With murderous fury through many a year,
Refusing to end the feud perpetual,
Or decently deal with the Danes in parley,
Take their tribute for treaty of peace;
Nor could their leaders look to receive
Pay from his hands for the harm that he wrought.
The fell destroyer kept feeding his rage
On young and old. So all night long
He prowled o'er the fen and surprised his victims,
Death-shadow dark. (The dusky realms 160
Where the hell-runes'[10] haunt are hidden from men.)
So the exiled roamer his raids continued;
Wrong upon wrong in his wrath he heaped.
In midnights dark he dwelt alone
'Mongst Heorot's trophies and treasures rich.
Great was the grief of the gold-friend of Scyldings,
Vexed was his mood that he might not visit
His goodly throne, his gift-seat proud,
Deprived of joy by the judgment of God.
Many the wise men that met to discover 170
Ways of escape from the scourge of affliction.
Often they came for counsel together;

---

8 smaller buildings apart
from the hall. The two previous lines are an example
of "litotes," or under-
statement—common in the
poem.
9 Hrothgar
10 sorcerers of hell

Often at heathen altars they made
Sacrifice-offerings, beseeching their idols
To send them deliverance from assault of the foe.
Such was their practice, they prayed to the Devil;
The hope of the heathen on hell was fixed,
The mood of their mind. Their Maker they knew not,
The righteous Judge and Ruler on high.
The Wielder of Glory they worshipped not,   180
The Warden of Heaven. Woe be to him
Whose soul is doomed through spite and envy,
In utter despair and agony hopeless
Forever to burn. But blessed is he
Who, after this life, the Lord shall seek,
Eager for peace in the arms of the Father.

III

THE VOYAGE TO THE HALL OF HROTHGAR

Thus boiled with care the breast of Hrothgar;
Ceaselessly sorrowed the son of Healfdene,
None of his chieftains might change his lot.
Too fell was the foe that afflicted the people   190
With wrongs unnumbered, and nightly horrors.
Then heard in his home king Hygelac's thane,[11]
The dauntless Jute,[12] of the doings of Grendel.
In strength he outstripped the strongest of men
That dwell in the earth in the days of this life.
Gallant and bold, he gave command
To get him a boat, a good wave-skimmer.
O'er the swan-road, he said, he would seek the king
Noble and famous, who needed men.
Though dear to his kin, they discouraged him not;   200
The prudent in counsel praised the adventure,
Whetted his valor, awaiting good omens.

So Beowulf chose from the band of the Jutes
Heroes brave, the best he could find;
He with fourteen followers hardy,
Went to embark; he was wise in seamanship,
Showed them the landmarks, leading the way.
Soon they descried their craft in the water,

11 Beowulf
12 In the original, *Geat*.
Professor Spaeth assumes,
with certain scholars, that
the *Geats* of the poem were
the Jutes, living in Jutland (southern Denmark),
and consistently translates
the tribal name thus. The
more orthodox view retains
the name *Geats*, and locates them in southern
Sweden.

At the foot of the cliff. Then climbed aboard
The chosen troop; the tide was churning   210
Sea against sand; they stowed away
In the hold of the ship their shining armor,
War-gear and weapons; the warriors launched
Their well-braced boat on her welcome voyage.

Swift o'er the waves with a wind that favored,
Foam on her breast, like a bird she flew.
A day and a night they drove to seaward,
Cut the waves with the curving prow,
Till the seamen that sailed her sighted the land,
Shining cliffs and coast-wise hills,   220
Headlands bold. The harbor opened,
Their cruise was ended. Then quickly the sailors,
The crew of Weder-folk [13] clambered ashore,
Moored their craft with clank of chain-mail,
And goodly war-gear. God they thanked
That their way was smooth o'er the surging waves.

High on the shore, the Scylding coast-guard
Saw from the cliff where he kept his watch,
Glittering shields o'er the gunwale carried,
Polished weapons. It puzzled him sore,   230
He wondered in mind who the men might be.
Down to the strand on his steed came riding
Hrothgar's thane, with threatening arm
Shook his war-spear and shouted this challenge:
"Who are ye, men, all mailed and harnessed,
That brought yon ship o'er the broad sea-ways,
And hither have come across the water,
To land on our shores? Long have I stood
As coast-guard here, and kept my sea-watch,
Lest harrying foe with hostile fleet   240
Should dare to damage our Danish land.
Armed men never from overseas came
More openly hither. But how do ye know
That law of the land doth give ye leave
To come thus near? I never have seen
Statelier earl upon earth than him,—
Yon hero in harness. No house-carl he,
In lordly array, if looks speak true,
And noble bearing. But now I must learn
Your names and country, ere nearer ye come,   250
Underhand spies, for aught I know,

13 Another name for the Geats (or Jutes)

In Danish land. Now listen ye strangers,
In from the sea, to my open challenge:
Heed ye my words and haste me to know
What your errand and whence ye have come."

IV

BEOWULF'S WORDS WITH THE COAST-GUARD

Him the hero hailed with an answer,
The war-troop's leader, his word-hoard unlocked:
"In truth we belong to the tribe of the Jutes;
We are Hygelac's own hearth-companions.
Far among folk my father was known,   26c
A noble chieftain; his name was Ecgtheow.
Honored by all, he ended his days
Full of winters and famed in the land.
Wise men everywhere well remember him.
Hither we fare with friendly purpose
To seek thy lord, the son of Healfdene,
The land-protector. Instruct us kindly.
Bound on adventure we visit thy lord,
The prince of the Danes. Our purpose is open;
Nought keep we secret; thou surely wilt know   27c
If the tale we were told is true or not:
That among the Scyldings a monster strange
A nameless demon, when nights are dark,
With cruel cunning, for cause unknown,
Works havoc and slaughter. I have in mind
A way to help your wise king Hrothgar,
Your ruler to rid of the ravening foe,
If ever his tide of troubles shall turn,
The billows of care that boil in his breast
Shall cool and subside, and his sorrow be cured; 28
Else, failing my purpose, forever hereafter
He shall suffer distress, while stands on its hill,
Mounting on high, his matchless hall."
Straight answered the coast-guard, astride his horse,
The warrior brave: "Twixt words and deeds
A keen-witted thane, if he thinks aright,
Must well distinguish and weigh the difference.
Your words I believe, that you wish no evil
To the Scylding lord. I will let you bring
Your shields ashore and show you the way.   29
My comrades here shall keep the watch,
From meddling foe defend your craft,

Your fresh-tarred boat, fast by the beach,
And faithfully guard her till again she bear
With curving bow, o'er the bounding main,
Her master well-loved to the Wedermark.
Fortune oft favors the fighter who yields not;
Hero unflinching comes unhurt from the fray."
Landward they hastened, leaving behind them
Fast at her moorings the full-bosomed boat,   300
The ship at anchor. Shone the boar-heads [14]
Gleaming with gold, o'er the guards of their helmets;
Bright and fire-forged the beast kept watch.
Forward they pressed, proud and adventurous,
Fit for the fight, till afar they descried
The high-peaked radiant roof of the hall.
Of houses far-praised 'neath heaven by the people
That inhabit the earth, this house was most famous,
The seat of king Hrothgar; its splendor gleamed bright
O'er many a land. Their leader well-armed   310
Showed them the shining shield-burg of heroes,
And set them right on the road to their goal.
Then, wheeling his steed, he wished them farewell:

" 'Tis time that I leave you; the Lord of Heaven,
The Father Almighty in mercy keep you
Safe on your journey; seaward I turn,
Watch to keep and ward against foe."

V

BEOWULF'S ARRIVAL AT THE HALL AND THE MANNER OF HIS RECEPTION

The street was stone-paved; straight it led
To the goal of their journey. Glistened their byrnies [15]
Stout and strong-linked; sang the rings   320
Of their iron mail as they marched along,
In armor and helmet right up to the hall.
Sea-voyage-sated, they set their shields,
Their linden-woods [16] broad, along the wall.
As they bent to the bench, their byrnies clattered.
They stacked their spears that stood in a row,
Ashwood tipped with iron above;
Well-equipped was the warlike band.
A stately Dane the strangers addressed,

---

14 boar-images on the helmets

15 body-armor
16 shields made of linden wood

Asked who they were and whence they had come: 330
"Whence do ye bear your burnished shields,
Your visored helmets and harness gray
Your heap of spear-shafts? A servant of Hrothgar's
His herald, am I. Hardier strangers,
Nobler in mien, have I never seen.
'Tis clear you come to the court of Hrothgar,
Not outlaws and beggars, but bent on adventure."
To him gave answer the hero brave,
The lord of the Weders these words returned,
Bold 'neath his helmet: "We are Hygelac's men,   340
His board-companions. I am Beowulf called.
Ready am I the ruler to answer,
To say to thy lord, the son of Healfdene,
Why we have come his court to seek,
If he will graciously grant us a hearing."
Wulfgar replied (he was prince of the Wendles,
His noble renown was known to many,
His courage in war, and wisdom in counsel):
"I will carry thy quest to the king of the Danes,
And ask him whether he wishes to grant   350
The boon thou dost ask of the breaker-of-rings,
To speak to himself concerning thy journey;
And straight will I bring thee the answer he sends."
Swiftly he hied him where Hrothgar sat,
White-haired and old, his earls around him.
Stately he strode, till he stood in the presence
Of the king of the Danes,—in courtly ways
Was Wulfgar skilled; he spoke to his lord:
"Hither have fared from a far country,
A band of Jutes o'er the bounding sea.   360
Their leader and chief by his chosen comrades
Is Beowulf called; this boon they ask:
That they may find with thee, my lord,
Favor of speech; refuse them not,
But grant them, Hrothgar, gracious hearing.
In armor clad, they claim respect
Of choicest earls; but chiefly their lord
Who lately hither hath led his comrades."

VI
H<small>ROTHGAR'S</small> W<small>ELCOME TO</small> B<small>EOWULF</small>

Hrothgar spoke, the Scyldings' protector:
"Beowulf I knew in his boyhood days: 370
His aged father was Ecgtheow named.

To him, to take home, did Hrethel give
His only daughter. Their dauntless son
Now comes to my court in quest of a friend.
My sea-faring men whom I sent afar
To the land of the Jutes, with generous gifts,
In token of friendship, have told me this,
That the power of his grip was so great it equalled
The strength of thirty stout-armed thanes.
Him bold in battle, the blessed God   380
Hath sent in his mercy, to save our people
—So I hope in my heart—from the horror of Grendel.
I shall offer him gold for his gallant spirit.
Go now in haste, and greet the strangers;
Bid to the hall the whole of the company;
Welcome with words the warrior band,
To the home of the Danes." To the hall door went
Wulfgar the courtly, and called them in:
"My master commands me this message to give you,
The lord of the Danes your lineage knows;   390
Bids me to welcome you, brave-hearted warriors,
Bound on adventure o'er the billowy main.
Ye may rise now and enter, arrayed in your armor,
Covered with helmets, the king to greet.
But leave your shields, and your shafts of slaughter,
Here by the wall to await the issue."
Then rose the leader, around him his comrades,
Sturdy war-band; some waited without,
Bid by the bold one their battle-gear to guard.
Together they hastened where the herald led them,   400
Under Heorot's roof. The hero went first,
Strode under helmet, till he stood by the hearth.
Beowulf spoke, his byrnie glistened,
His corslet chain-linked by cunning of smithcraft:
"Hail, king Hrothgar! Hygelac's thane
And kinsman am I. Known is the record
Of deeds of renown I have done in my youth.
Far in my home, I heard of this Grendel;
Sea-farers tell the tale of the hall:
How bare of warriors, this best of buildings   410
Deserted stands, when the sun goes down
And twilight deepens to dark in the sky.
By comrades encouraged, I come on this journey.
The best of them bade me, the bravest and wisest,
To go to thy succor, O good king Hrothgar;
For well they approved my prowess in battle,
They saw me themselves come safe from the conflict

When five of my foes I defeated and bound,
Beating in battle the brood of the monsters.
At night on the sea with nicors [17] I wrestled,　　　420
Avenging the Weders, survived the sea-peril,
And crushed in my grip the grim sea-monsters
That harried my neighbors. Now I am come
To cope with Grendel in combat single,
And match my might against the monster, alone.
I pray thee therefore, prince of the Scyldings,
Not to refuse the favor I ask,
Having come so far, O friend of the Shield-Danes,
That I alone with my loyal comrades,
My hardy companions, may Heorot purge.　　　430
Moreover they say that the slaughterous fiend
In wanton mood all weapons despises.
Hence,—as I hope that Hygelac may,
My lord and king, be kind to me,—
Sword and buckler I scorn to bear,
Gold-adorned shield, as I go to the conflict.
With my grip will I grapple the gruesome fiend,
Foe against foe, to fight for our life.
And he that shall fall his faith must put
In the judgment of God. If Grendel wins　　　440
He is minded to make his meal in the hall
Untroubled by fear, on the folk of the Jutes,
As often before he fed on the Danes.
No need for thee then to think of my burial.
If I lose my life, the lonely prowler
My blood-stained body will bear to his den,
Swallow me greedily, and splash with my gore
His lair in the marsh; no longer wilt then
Have need to find me food and sustenance.
To Hygelac send, if I sink in the battle,　　　450
This best of corslets that covers my breast,
Heirloom of Hrethel, rarest of byrnies,
The work of Weland.[18] So Wyrd [19] will be done."

VII

The Feasting in Heorot and the Customs of the Hall

Hrothgar spoke, the Scyldings' defender:
"Thou hast come, dear Beowulf, to bring us help,
For the sake of friendship to fight our battles.

17 the sea-monsters men-　　18 The Germanic Vulcan　　19 Fate
tioned below　　　　　　　　(English form Wayland)

(Hrothgar recounts the exploits of Beowulf's father.)

Sad is my spirit and sore it grieves me
To tell to any the trouble and shame
That Grendel hath brought me with bitter hate,
The havoc he wrought in my ranks in the hall.   460
My war-band dwindles, driven by Wyrd
Into Grendel's grasp; but God may easily
End this monster's mad career.
Full often they boasted, my beer-bold warriors,
Brave o'er their ale-cups, the best of my fighters,
They'd meet in the mead-hall the mighty Grendel,
End his orgies with edge of the sword.
But always the mead-hall, the morning after,
The splendid building, was blood-bespattered;
Daylight dawned on the drippings of swords,   470
Soiled with slaughter were sills and benches.
My liege-men perished, and left me poor.
Sit down to the board; unbend thy thoughts;
Speak to my men as thy mood shall prompt."
For the band of the Jutes a bench was cleared;
Room in the mead-hall was made for them all.
Then strode to their seats the strong-hearted heroes.
The warriors' wants a waiting-thane served;
Held in his hand the highly-wrought ale-cup,
Poured sparkling mead, while the minstrel sang   480
Gaily in Heorot. There was gladness of heroes,
A joyous company of Jutes and of Danes.

VIII

UNFERTH TAUNTS BEOWULF

Then up spoke Unferth, Ecglaf's son,
Who sat at the feet of the Scylding ruler;
He vented his jealousy. The journey of Beowulf,
His sea-adventure, sorely displeased him,
It filled him with envy that any other
Should win among men more war-like glory,
More fame under heaven than he himself:
"Art thou the Beowulf that battled with Brecca,   490
Far out at sea, when ye swam together,
What time you two made trial of the billows,
Risking your lives in reckless folly,
On the open sea? None might dissuade you,
Friend nor foe, from the fool-hardy venture,

When straight from the shore you struck for the open,
Breasted the waves and beat with your arms
The mounting billows, measured the sea-paths
With lusty strokes. Stirred was the ocean
By wintry storms. Seven days and nights   500
Your sea-strife lasted; at length he beat you;
His strength was the better; at break of day
He made the beach where the Battle-Reamas
Dwell by the shore; and straightway returned
To his people beloved in the land of the Brondings,
Where liegemen and towns and treasure were his.
In sooth I say, the son of Beanstan
His boast against thee made good to the full.
But now I ween a worse fate awaits thee
Though thy mettle be proved in many a battle   510
And grim encounter, if the coming of Grendel
Thou darest abide, in the dead of the night."
Beowulf spoke, the son of Ecgtheow:
"What a deal of stuff thou hast talked about Brecca,
Garrulous with drink, my good friend Unferth.
Thou hast lauded his deeds. Now listen to me!
More sea-strength had I, more ocean-endurance
Than any man else, the wide earth round.
'Tis true we planned in the pride of our youth
This ocean-adventure, and vowed we would risk   520
Our lives in the deep, each daring the other.
We were both of us boys, but our boast we fulfilled.
Our naked swords as we swam from the land,
We held in our grasp, to guard against whales.
Not a stroke could he gain on me, strive as he would,
Make swifter speed through the swelling waves,
Nor could I in swimming o'ercome him at sea.
Side by side in the surge we labored
Five nights long. At last we were parted
By furious seas and a freezing gale.   530
Night fell black; the norther wild
Rushed on us ruthless and roughened the sea.
Now was aroused the wrath of the monsters,
But my war-proof ring-mail, woven and hand-locked,
Served me well 'gainst the sea beasts' fury;
The close-linked battle-net covered my breast.
I was dragged to the bottom by a blood-thirsty monster,
Firm in his clutch the furious sea-beast
Helpless held me. But my hand came free,
And my foe I pierced with point of my sword.   540

With my battle-blade good 'twas given me to kill
The dragon of the deep, by dint of my blow."

IX

BEOWULF COMPLETES THE STORY OF HIS SWIMMING ADVENTURE WITH BRECCA. HROTHGAR'S DEPARTURE FROM THE HALL

"Thus sore beset me sea-beasts thronging,
Murderous man-eaters. I met their charges,
Gave them their due with my goodly blade.
They failed of their fill, the feast they expected
In circle sitting on the sea-floor together
With me for their meal. I marred their pleasure.
When morning came, they were cast ashore
By the wash of the waves; their wounds proved fatal;   550
Bloated and dead on the beach they lay.
No more would they cross the course of the ships
In the chop of the channel charge the sailors.
Day broke in the east, bright beacon of God;
The sea fell smooth. I saw bold headlands,
Windy walls; for Wyrd oft saveth
A man not doomed, if he dauntless prove.
My luck did not fail me, my long sword finished
Nine of the nicors. Ne'er have I heard
Of fiercer battle fought in the night,   560
Of hero more harried by horrors at sea.
Yet I saved my life from the sea-beasts' clutch.
Worn with the struggle, I was washed ashore
In the realm of the Finns by the run of the tide,
The heave of the flood. I have failed to hear
Of like adventure laid to thee,
Battle so bitter. Brecca did never,—
Neither of you was known to achieve
Deed so valiant, adventure so daring,
Sword-play so nimble; not that I boast of it,   570
But mark me, Unferth, you murdered [20] your brothers,
Your closest of kin. The curse of hell
For this you will suffer, though sharp be your wit.
In sooth I say to you, son of Ecglaf,
Never had Grendel such grim deeds wrought,
Such havoc in Heorot, so harried your king
With bestial fury, if your boasted courage

[20] He may have merely abandoned them to be killed in the fight—a crime equivalent to murder, in this society. (See Sec. XVII.)

In deeds as well as in words you had proved.
But now he has found he need not fear
Vengeance fierce from the Victory-Scyldings,   580
Ruthless attack in return for his raids.
He takes his toll of your tribe as he pleases,
Sparing none of your spearmen proud.
He ravens and rages and recks not the Dane folk,
Safe from their sword-play. But soon I will teach him
How the Jute-folk fight. Then freely may go
To the mead-hall who likes, when the light of the morning,
The next day's dawn, the dark shall dispel,
And the heaven-bright sun from the south shall shine."

Glad in his heart was the giver of rings,   590
Hoped to have help, the hoar-headed king;
The Shield-Danes' shepherd was sure of relief,
When he found in Beowulf so firm a resolve.
There was laughter of heroes. Loud was their revelry,
Words were winsome as Wealhtheow rose,
Queen of Hrothgar, heedful of courtesy,
Gold-adorned greeted the guests in the hall.
First to her lord, the land-defender,
The high-born lady handed the cup;
Bade him be gleeful and gay at the board,   600
And good to his people. Gladly he took it,
Quaffed from the beaker, the battle-famed king.
Then leaving her lord, the lady of the Helmings
Passed among her people in each part of the hall,
Offered the ale-cup to old and young,
Till she came to the bench where Beowulf sat.
The jewel-laden queen in courteous manner
Beowulf greeted; to God gave thanks,
Wise in her words, that her wish was granted,
That at last in her trouble a trusted hero   610
Had come for comfort. The cup received
From Wealhtheow's hand the hardy warrior,
And made this reply, his mind on the battle;
Beowulf spoke, the son of Ecgtheow:
"I made up my mind when my mates and I
Embarked in our boat, outbound on the sea,
That fully I'd work the will of thy people,
Or fall in the fight, in the clutch of the fiend.
I surely shall do a deed of glory,
Worthy an earl, or end my days,   620
My morning of life, in the mead-hall here."
His words pleased well the wife of Hrothgar,

The Jutish lord's boast. The jewelled queen
Went to sit by the side of her lord.

Renewed was the sound of noisy revel,
Wassail of warriors. Brave words were spoken.
Mirth in the mead-hall mounted high,
Till Healfdêne's son the sign did give
That he wished to retire. Full well he knew
The fiend would find a fight awaiting him,   630
When the light of the sun had left the hall,
And creeping night should close upon them,
And shadowy shapes come striding on
Dim through the dark. The Danes arose.
Hrothgar again gave greeting to Beowulf,
Wished him farewell; the wine-hall lofty
He left in his charge. These last words spoke he:
"Never before have I fully entrusted
To mortal man this mighty hall,
Since arm and shield I was able to lift.   640
To thee alone I leave it now,
To have and to hold it. Thy hardihood prove!
Be mindful of glory; keep watch for the foe!
No reward shalt thou lack if thou live through this fight."

X

BEOWULF'S WATCH IN HEOROT

Then Hrothgar went with his warrior-band,
The Arm-of-the-Scyldings, out of the hall.
Would the war-lord Wealhtheow seek,
The queen for his bed-mate. The best of kings
Had placed in the hall, so heroes report,
A watch gainst Grendel, to guard his house,   650
Deliverance bring to the land of the Danes.
But the lord of the Jutes joyfully trusted
In the might of his arm and the mercy of God.
Off he stripped his iron byrnie,
Helmet from head, and handed his sword,
Choicest of blades, to his body-thane,
And bade him keep the battle armor.
Then made his boast once more the warrior,
Beowulf the bold, ere his bed he sought,
Summoned his spirit; "Not second to Grendel   660
In combat I count me and courage of war.
But not with the sword will I slay this foeman,

Though light were the task to take his life.
Nothing at all does he know of such fighting,
Of hewing of shields, though shrewd be his malice
Ill deeds to contrive. We two in the night
Shall do without swords, if he dare to meet me
In hand to hand battle. May the holy Lord
To one or the other award the victory,
As it seems to Him right, Ruler all-wise."   670
Then he sought his bed. The bolster received
The head of the hero. In the hall about him,
Stretched in sleep, his sailormen lay.
Not one of them thought he would ever return
Home to his country, nor hoped to see
His people again, and the place of his birth.
They had heard of too many men of the Danes
O'ertaken suddenly, slain without warning,
In the royal hall. But the Ruler on High
Through the woof of fate to the Wederfolk gave   680
Friendship and help, their foes to o'ercome,
By a single man's strength to slay the destroyer.
Thus all may learn that the Lord Almighty
Wields for aye the Wyrds of men.

XI

BEOWULF'S FIGHT WITH GRENDEL

Now Grendel came, from his crags of mist
Across the moor; he was curst of God.
The murderous prowler meant to surprise
In the high-built hall his human prey.
He stalked 'neath the clouds, till steep before him
The house of revelry rose in his path,   690
The gold-hall of heroes, the gaily adorned.
Hrothgar's home he had hunted full often,
But never before had he found to receive him
So hardy a hero, such hall-guards there.
Close to the building crept the slayer,
Doomed to misery. The door gave way,
Though fastened with bolts, when his fist fell on it.
Maddened he broke through the breach he had made;
Swoln with anger and eager to slay,
The ravening fiend o'er the bright-paved floor   700
Furious ran, while flashed from his eyes
An ugly glare like embers aglow.

He saw in the hall, all huddled together,
The heroes asleep. Then laughed in his heart
The hideous fiend; he hoped ere dawn
To sunder body from soul of each;
He looked to appease his lust of blood,
Glut his maw with the men he would slay.
But Wyrd had otherwise willed his doom;
Never again should he get a victim 710
After that night. Narrowly watched
Hygelac's thane how the horrible slayer
Forward should charge in fierce attack.
Nor was the monster minded to wait:
Sudden he sprang on a sleeping thane,
Ere he could stir, he slit him open;
Bit through the bone-joints, gulped the blood,
Greedily bolted the body piecemeal.
Soon he had swallowed the slain man wholly,
Hands and feet. Then forward he hastened, 720
Sprang at the hero, and seized him at rest;
Fiercely clutched him with fiendish claw.
But quickly Beowulf caught his forearm,
And threw himself on it with all his weight.
Straight discovered that crafty plotter,
That never in all midearth had he met
In any man a mightier grip.
Gone was his courage, and craven fear
Sat in his heart, yet helped him no sooner.
Fain would he hide in his hole in the fenland, 730
His devil's den. A different welcome
From former days he found that night!
Now Hygelac's thane, the hardy, remembered
His evening's boast, and bounding up,
Grendel he clenched, and cracked his fingers;
The monster tried flight, but the man pursued;
The ravager hoped to wrench himself free,
And gain the fen, for he felt his fingers
Helpless and limp in the hold of his foe.
'Twas a sorry visit the man-devourer 740
Made to the Hall of the Hart that night.
Dread was the din, the Danes were frighted
By the uproar wild of the ale-spilling fray.
The hardiest blenched as the hall-foes wrestled
In terrible rage. The rafters groaned:
'Twas wonder great that the wine-hall stood,
Firm 'gainst the fighters' furious onslaught,
Nor fell to the ground, that glorious building.

With bands of iron 'twas braced and stiffened
Within and without. But off from the sill 750
Many a mead-bench mounted with gold
Was wrung where they wrestled in wrath together.
The Scylding nobles never imagined
That open attack, or treacherous cunning,
Could wreck or ruin their royal hall,
The lofty and antlered, unless the flames
Should some day swallow it up in smoke.
The din was renewed, the noise redoubled;
Each man of the Danes was mute with dread,
That heard from the wall the horrible wail, 760
The gruesome song of the godless foe,
His howl of defeat, as the fiend of hell
Bemoaned his hurt. The man held fast;
Greatest he was in grip of strength,
Of all that dwelt upon earth that day.

XII

THE DEFEAT OF GRENDEL

Loath in his heart was the hero-deliverer
To let escape his slaughterous guest.
Of little use that life he deemed
To human kind. The comrades of Beowulf
Unsheathed their weapons to ward their leader, 770
Eagerly brandished their ancient blades,
The life of their peerless lord to defend.
Little they deemed, those dauntless warriors,
As they leaped to the fray, those lusty fighters,
Laying on boldly to left and to right,
Eager to slay, that no sword upon earth
No keenest weapon could wound that monster:
Point would not pierce, he was proof against iron;
'Gainst victory-blades the devourer was charmed.
But a woful end awaited the wretch, 780
That very day he was doomed to depart,
And fare afar to the fiends' domain.

Now Grendel found, who in former days
So many a warrior had wantonly slain,
In brutish lust, abandoned of God,
That the frame of his body was breaking at last.
Keen of courage, the kinsman of Hygelac
Held him grimly gripped in his hands.

Loath was each to the other alive.
The grisly monster got his death-wound: 790
A huge split opened under his shoulder;
Crunched the socket, cracked the sinews.
Glory great was given to Beowulf.
But Grendel escaped with his gaping wound,
O'er the dreary moor his dark den sought,
Crawled to his lair. 'Twas clear to him then,
The count of his hours to end had come,
Done were his days. The Danes were glad,
The hard fight was over, they had their desire.
Cleared was the hall, 'twas cleansed by the hero   800
With keen heart and courage, who came from afar.
The lord of the Jutes rejoiced in his work,
The deed of renown he had done that night.
His boast to the Danes he bravely fulfilled;
From lingering woe delivered them all;
From heavy sorrow they suffered in heart;
From dire distress they endured so long;
From toil and from trouble. This token they saw:
The hero had laid the hand of Grendel
Both arm and claws, the whole forequarter   810
With clutches huge, 'neath the high-peaked roof.

XIII

The Celebration of the Victory and the Song of the Gleeman

When morning arrived, so runs the report,
Around the gift-hall gathered the warriors;
The folk-leaders fared from far and near,
The wide ways o'er, the wonder to view,
The wild beast's footprints. Not one of them felt
Regret that the creature had come to grief,
When they traced his retreat by the tracks on the moor;
Marked where he wearily made his way,
Harried and beaten, to the haunt of the nicors,   820
Slunk to the water, to save his life.
There they beheld the heaving surges,
Billows abrim with bloody froth,
Dyed with gore, where the gruesome fiend,
Stricken and doomed, in the struggle of death
Gave up his ghost in the gloom of the mere,
His heathen soul for hell to receive it.
Then from the mere the thanes turned back,

Men and youths from the merry hunt,
Home they rode on their horses gray,   830
Proudly sitting their prancing steeds.
Beowulf's prowess was praised by all.
They all agreed that go where you will,
'Twixt sea and sea, at the south or the north,
None better than he, no braver hero,
None worthier honor could ever be found.
(They meant no slight to their master and lord
The good king Hrothgar, their ruler kind.)

Now and again the noble chiefs
Gave rein to their steeds, and spurred them to race,   840
Galloped their grays where the ground was smooth.
Now and again a gallant thane,
Whose mind was stored with many a lay,
With songs of battle and sagas old,
Bound new words in well-knit bars,
Told in verse the valor of Beowulf,
Matched his lines and moulded his lay.

   Here is introduced an episode of the Nibelungen Legend. The gleeman tells
how Sigmund the Volsung with his son and nephew Fitela ranged the forests
and slew wild beasts. Later when Fitela was no longer with him, Sigmund killed
a dragon and won a great treasure.

When the lay was ended they urged once more
Their racers fleet to fly o'er the plain.
As the morning sped, and the sun climbed higher,   850
Many went in, the marvellous sight
More closely to scan. The king himself
With a troop of trusty retainers about him
Strode from his bower; the bestower-of-rings
Came, and with him the queen, in state,
The meadow-path trod, by her maidens attended.

XIV

HROTHGAR'S PRAISE OF BEOWULF, AND BEOWULF'S REPLY

Hrothgar spoke when he reached the hall,
Stood on the step, and stared at the roof
Adorned with gold, and Grendel's hand:
"Prompt be my heart to praise the Almighty   860
For the sight I behold. Much harm have I suffered,
And grief from Grendel, but God still works
Wonder on wonder, the Warden of Glory.

But a little while since, I scarcely dared,
As long as I lived, to look for escape
From my burden of sorrow, when blood-stained stood
And dripping with slaughter, this stately hall.
Wide-spread woe my warriors scattered;
They never hoped this house to rid,
While life should last, this land-mark of people, 870
Of demons and devils. 'Tis done by the hero.
By the might of the Lord this man has finished
The feat that all of us failed to achieve
By wit or by war. And well may she say,
—Whoever she be,—that bore this son,
That the Ancient of Days dealt with her graciously,
And blest her in child-birth. Now Beowulf, hear!
I shall henceforth hold thee, hero beloved,
As child of my own, and cherish thee fondly
In kinship new. Thou shalt never lack 880
Meed of reward that is mine to give.
For deeds less mighty have I many times granted
Fullest reward to warriors feebler,
In battle less brave. Thy boldness and valor
Afar shall be known; thy fame shall live
To be great among men. Now God the Almighty
With honor reward thee, as ever he doth."

Beowulf spoke, the son of Ecgtheow:
"Gladly we fought this good fight through,
Fearlessly faced the foe inhuman, 890
Grappled him gruesome; it grieves me sore
That the man-beast himself you may not see,
Dead in the hall, fordone in the fray.
I meant to master the monster quickly,
To his death-bed pin him by power of my grip,
Hold him hard till my hand could strangle him,
Bringing him low, but he broke away.
In vain I tried to prevent his escape.
The Lord was unwilling; I lost my hold
On the man-destroyer; too strong was the monster, 900
Too swift on his feet. But to save his life
He left behind him the whole of his fore-paw,
Arm and shoulder. 'Twas a useless shift,
Profiting nothing. He ne'er will prolong
His life by the loss, the loathly slayer,
Sunk in sin; but sorrow holds him,
Caught in the grasp of its grip relentless,
In woful bonds to await in anguish,

Guilty wretch, the rest of his doom,
As the Lord Almighty shall mete it to him." 910
More silent seemed the son of Ecglaf [21]
Less boastful in bragging of brave deeds done
When all of them, looking aloft, beheld
The hand on high, where it hung 'neath the roof,
The claw of the fiend; each finger was armed
With a steel-like spur instead of a nail,
The heathen's handspikes, the horrible paw
Of the evil fiend. They all declared
No iron blade could e'er have bit
On the monstrous bulk of the man beast's hide, 920
Or hewn away that woful talon.

XV

THE FEASTING AND GIVING OF TREASURE IN THE HALL

Now orders were given the guest-hall to cleanse,
And furnish it fresh. Forth went hurrying
Men and maids. To the mead-hall they went
And busily worked. Woven tapestries,
Glinting with gold, hung gay on the walls,
Marvellous wonders for men to look upon.
Ruin and wreck had been wrought in the building,
Though braced within by iron bands,
The hinges were wrenched, the roof alone stood 930
Undamaged and sound, when the sin-spotted wretch
The demon destroyer, in despair of his life,
Turned and made off,—not easy it is
To escape from death, essay it who will.
(So each of us all to his end must come
Forced by fate to his final abode
Where his body, stretched on the bier of death,
Shall rest after revel.) Now right was the hour
For Healfdene's heir to enter the hall;
The king himself would come to the feast. 940
I never have heard of nobler bearing
'Mongst ranks of liegemen surrounding their lord
As they took their seats, the trusty comrades,
And fell to feasting. Freely quaffed
Many a mead-cup the mighty kinsmen
Hrothgar and Hrothulf,[22] the high hall within.
Heorot was filled with a friendly host.

[21] Unferth. (See Sec. VIII.)　　　　　　　　[22] Hrothgar's nephew

(Far was the day when the Scylding host
Should treachery plot, betraying each other.)
Then Healfdene's son bestowed on Beowulf 950
A gold-adorned banner for battle-reward,
A rich-broidered standard, breast-plate and helmet.
The swordmen assembled saw the treasures
Borne before the hero. Beowulf drank
The health of Hrothgar, nor had reason to feel
Ashamed before shieldmen to show his reward.
Never were offered by earls that I heard of,
In token of friendship four such treasures,
Never was equalled such ale-bench bounty.
Round the ridge of the helmet a rim of iron 960
Wound with wire, warded the head,
That the offspring of files, with fearful stroke,
The hard-tempered sword-blade, might harm it not,
When fierce in the battle the foemen should join.
At a sign from the king, eight stallions proud
Bitted and bridled were brought into hall.
On the back of one was a wondrous saddle,
Bravely wrought and bordered with jewels,
The battle-seat bold of the best of kings
When Hrothgar himself would ride to the sword-play. 970
(Nor flinched from the foe the famous warrior
In the front of the fight where fell the slain.)
To the hero delivered the lord of the Scyldings
The heir of Ing, both armor and horses,
Gave them to Beowulf, and bade him enjoy them.
Thus royally, the ruler famous,
The heroes' hoard-guard, heaped his bounty;
Repaid the struggle with steeds and trophies,
Praised by all singers who speak the truth.

XVI

The King's Gifts to Beowulf's Men, and the Gleeman's Lay of Finn

The Lord of the earls then added gifts, 980
At the mead-bench remembered the men, each one,
That Beowulf brought o'er the briny deep,
With ancient heirlooms and offered to pay
In gold for the man that Grendel had slain,
As more of them surely the monster had killed
Had not holy God and the hero's courage
Averted their doom. (So daily o'errules

The Father Almighty the fortunes of men.
Therefore is insight ever the best,
And prudence of mind; for much shall suffer   990
Of lief and of loath who long endures
The days of his life in labor and toil.)
Now music and song were mingled together,
In the presence of Hrothgar, ruler in war.
Harp was struck and hero-lays told.
Along the mead-bench the minstrel spread
Cheer in hall when he chanted the lay
Of the sudden assault on the sons of Finn.

> The episode which follows, alludes obscurely to details of a feud between Frisians and Danes. The Finnsburg fragment contains a portion of the same story and one of the heroes, Hnaef, is also mentioned in Widsith.

XVII

THE LAY OF FINN ENDED. THE SPEECH OF THE QUEEN

The lay was ended,
The gleeman's song. Sound of revelry   1000
Rose again. Gladness spread
Along bench and board. Beer-thanes poured
From flagons old the flowing wine.
Wealhtheow the queen walked in state,
Under her crown, where uncle and nephew
Together sat,—they still were friends.
There too sat Unferth, trusted counsellor,
At Hrothgar's feet; though faith he had broken
With his kinsmen in battle, his courage was proved.
Then the queen of the Scyldings spoke these words: 1010
"Quaff of this cup my king and my lord,
Gold-friend of men. To thy guests be kind,
To the men of the Jutes be generous with gifts.
Far and near thou now hast peace.
I have heard thou dost wish the hero for son
To hold as thy own, now Heorot is cleansed,
The jewel-bright hall. Enjoy while thou mayest,
Allotment of wealth, and leave to thy heirs
Kingdom and rule when arrives the hour
That hence thou shalt pass to thy place appointed.   1020
Well I know that my nephew Hrothulf
Will cherish in honor our children dear
If thou leavest before him this life upon earth;
He will surely requite the kindness we showed him,
Faithfully tend our two young sons,

When to mind he recalls our care and affection
How we helped him and housed him when *he* was a child."
She turned to the bench where her two boys sat
Hrethic and Hrothmund, and the rest of the youth,
A riotous band, and right in their midst,   1030
Between the two brothers, Beowulf sat.

XVIII

THE QUEEN'S GIFTS TO BEOWULF

With courteous bow the cup she offered,
Greeted him graciously and gave him to boot
Two armlets rare of twisted gold,
A robe and rings, and the rarest collar;
A better was never known among men,
Since Hama brought to his bright-built hall
The jewelled necklace, the gem of the Brisings.

The following passage interrupts the narrative to tell of the subsequent
history of Wealhtheow's gift; how Beowulf gave it to Hygelac, who wore it on
his famous raid against the Frisians, in which he was slain by the Franks.

Before the warriors Wealhtheow spoke:
"Accept dear Beowulf, this bright-gemmed collar;   1040
Make happy use of this heirloom jewelled,
This ring and robe and royal treasure;
Be brave and bold. My boys instruct
In gentle manners; mine be the praise.
Thou hast done such a deed that in days to come
Men will proclaim thy might and valor
To the ends of the earth where the ocean-wave
Washes the windy walls of the land.
I wish thee joy of thy jewelled treasure,
Long be thy life; enlarge thy prosperity,   1050
Show thee a friend to my sons in deed.
Here each earl to the other is faithful,
True to his liege-lord, loyal and kind.
My warriors obey me, willing and prompt.
The Danes carousing, do as I bid."
She went to her seat, the wine flowed free;
'Twas a glorious feast. The fate that impended,
None of them knew, though near to them all.

When darkness came, the king of the Danes
Went to his rest in the royal bower;   1060
But a throng of his kinsmen kept the hall

As they used to do in the days of old.
They cleared the boards and covered the floor
With beds and bolsters. One beer-thane there
Lay down to sleep with his doom upon him.
They placed by their heads their polished shields,
Their battle-boards bright, on the bench nearby.
Above each earl, within easy reach,
Was his helmet high and his harness of mail
And the spear-shaft keen. 'Twas their custom so,   1070
That always at rest they were ready for war
At home or abroad, where'er they might be,
At what hour soever for aid might call
Their lord and king; they were comrades true.

END OF THE FIRST ADVENTURE

XIX

The Coming of Grendel's Dam to Avenge Her Son

Then sank they to sleep, but sorely paid
One poor wretch for his rest that night.
The same thing fell, as in former days
When Grendel his raids on the gold-hall made,
Before the fiend had found his match,
Caught in his sins. 'Twas seen that night   1080
An avenger survived the villainous fiend
Although they had ceased from their sorrow and care.
'Twas Grendel's mother, a monstrous hag.
She remembered her loss. She had lived in the deep,
In a water-hell cold since Cain had become
The evil slayer of his only brother,
His kin by blood; accursed he fled
Marked by murder from men's delights,
Haunted the wilds; from him there sprung
Ghastly demon-shapes, Grendel was one.   1090

The omitted lines break the narrative to turn back to the Grendel fight.

Now grim and vengeful
His mother set out on her errand of woe,
Damage to wreak for the death of her son.
Arrived at Heorot, the Ring-Danes she found
Asleep in the hall. Soon was to come
Surprise to the earls when into the hall
Burst Grendel's dam. (Less grim was the terror
As terror of woman in war is less,

—The fury of maidens, than full-armed men's,
When the blood-stained war-blade with wire-bound hilt,   1100
Hard and hammer-forged, hurtling through air,
Hews the boar from the helmet's crest.)
Many the swords that were suddenly drawn,
Blades from the benches; buckler and shield
Were tightly grasped; no time for the helmet,
For harness of mail, when the horror was on them.
The monster was minded to make for the open;
Soon as discovered, she sought to escape.
Quickly she seized a sleeping warrior,
Fast in her clutch to the fens she dragged him.   1110
He was to Hrothgar of heroes the dearest,
Most trusted of liegemen between the two seas,
Comrade the nearest, killed in his sleep,
The bravest in battle. Nor was Beowulf there;
They had elsewhere quartered the earl that night,
After the giving of gifts in the hall.
There was shouting in Heorot; the hand she seized,
The bloody talon, she took away.
Sorrow was renewed in the nearby dwellings,
Bad was the bargain that both had made   1120
To pay for their friends with further lives lost.
With grief overcome was the gray-haired king
When he learned that his thane was alive no more,
His dearest comrade by death o'ertaken.
Quick from his bower was Beowulf fetched,
The hero brave. At break of dawn
He with his comrades came to the place
Where the king in sorrow was waiting to see
Whether God the Wielder of All would grant him
A turn in his tide of trouble and woe.   1130
Then entered the room the ready hero;
With his band of brave men the boards resounded.
He eagerly greeted the aged ruler,
Delayed not to ask the lord of the Ingwines [23]
If his night had passed in peace and quiet.

XX

HROTHGAR DESCRIBES THE HAUNT OF THE MONSTER
AND ASKS BEOWULF TO UNDERTAKE A
SECOND ADVENTURE

Hrothgar spoke, the Scylding defender:
"Speak not of peace, for pain is renewed

[23] Another name for the Danes

'Mongst all the Danes. Dead is Æschere,
Elder brother of Irmenlaf,
My comrade true and counsellor trusted,   1140
My right-hand friend when in front of the combat
We stood shoulder to shoulder, when shield-burg broke,
And boar-crests crashed in battle together.
Earls should ever like Æschere be.
On Heorot's floor he was foully slain
By warlock wild. I wot not whither
The prey-proud fury hath fled to cover,
Glutted and gorged. With gruesome claws
And violence fierce she avenged thy deed,
The slaying of Grendel her son last night,   1150
Because too long my loyal thanes
He had hunted and hurt. In the hall he fell;
His life was forfeit. To the fray returned
Another as cruel, her kin to avenge;
Faring from far, the feud re-opened.
Hence many a thane shall mourn and think
Of the giver of gifts with grief renewed
And heart-woe heavy. The hand lies low
That fain would have helped and defended you all.
I have heard my people, the peasant folk   1160
Who house by the border and hold the fens,
Say they have seen two creatures strange,
Huge march-stalkers, haunting the moorland,
Wanderers outcast. One of the two
Seemed to their sight to resemble a woman;
The other manlike, a monster misshapen,
But huger in bulk than human kind,
Trod an exile's track of woe.
The folk of the fen in former days
Named him Grendel. Unknown his father,   1170
Or what his descent from demons obscure.
Lonely and waste is the land they inhabit,
Wolf-cliffs wild and windy headlands,
Ledges of mist, where mountain torrents
Downward plunge to dark abysses,
And flow unseen. Not far from here
O'er the moorland in miles, a mere expands:
Spray-frosted trees o'erspread it, and hang
O'er the water with roots fast wedged in the rocks.
There nightly is seen, beneath the flood,   1180
A marvellous light. There lives not the man
Has fathomed the depth of the dismal mere.
Though the heather-stepper, the strong-horned stag,

Seek this cover, forspent with the chase,
Tracked by the hounds, he will turn at bay,
To die on the brink ere he brave the plunge,
Hide his head in the haunted pool.
Wan from its depths the waves are dashed,
When wicked storms are stirred by the wind,
And from sullen skies descends the rain. 1190
In thee is our hope of help once more.
Not yet thou has learned where leads the way
To the lurking-hole of this hatcher of outrage.
Seek, if thou dare, the dreaded spot!
Richly I pay thee for risking this fight,
With heirlooms golden and ancient rings,
As I paid thee before, if thou come back alive."

XXI

The Arrival of Hrothgar and Beowulf at Grendel's Mere

Beowulf spoke, the son of Ecgtheow:
"Sorrow not gray-beard, nor grieve o'er thy friend!
Vengeance is better than bootless mourning. 1200
To each of us here the end must come
Of life upon earth: let him who may
Win glory ere death. I deem that best,
The lot of the brave, when life is over.
Rise, O realm-ward, ride we in haste,
To track the hag that whelped this Grendel.
I tell thee in truth, she may turn where she will,
No cave of ocean nor cover of wood,
No hole in the ground shall hide her from me.
But one day more thy woe endure, 1210
And nurse thy hope as I know thou wilt."
Sprang to his feet the sage old king,
Gave praise to God for the promise spoken.
And now for Hrothgar a horse was bridled,
A curly-maned steed. The king rode on,
Bold on his charger. A band of shield-men
Followed on foot. Afar they saw
Footprints leading along the forest.
They followed the tracks, and found she had crossed
Over the dark moor, dragging the body 1220
Of the goodliest thane that guarded with Hrothgar
Heorot Hall, and the home of the king.
The well-born hero held the trail;

Up rugged paths, o'er perilous ridges,
Through passes narrow, an unknown way,
By beetling crags, and caves of the nicors.
With a chosen few he forged ahead,
Warriors skilled, to scan the way.
Sudden they came on a cluster of trees
Overhanging a hoary rock,   1230
A gloomy grove; and gurgling below,
A stir of waters all stained with blood.
Sick at heart were the Scylding chiefs,
Many a thane was thrilled with woe,
For there they beheld the head of Æschere
Far beneath at the foot of the cliff.
They leaned and watched the waters boil
With bloody froth. The band sat down,
While the war-horn sang its summons to battle.
They saw in the water sea-snakes a many,   1240
Wave-monsters weird, that wallowed about.
At the base of the cliff lay basking the nicors,
Who oft at sunrise ply seaward their journey,
To hunt on the ship-trails and scour the main,
Sea-beasts and serpents. Sudden they fled,
Wrathful and grim, aroused by the hail
Of the battle-horn shrill. The chief of the Jutes,
With a bolt from his bow a beast did sunder
From life and sea-frolic; sent the keen shaft
Straight to his vitals. Slow he floated,   1250
Upturned and dead at the top of the waves.
Eager they boarded their ocean-quarry;
With barb-hooked boar-spears the beast they gaffed,
Savagely broached him and brought him to shore,
Wave-plunger weird. The warriors viewed
The grisly stranger. But straightway Beowulf
Donned his corslet nor cared for his life. . . .

The narrative is here broken with a description of Beowulf's armor and the
sword Hrunting, lent him by Unferth.

XXII

BEOWULF'S FIGHT WITH GRENDEL'S DAM

To Hrothgar spoke the son of Ecgtheow:
"Remember O honored heir of Healfdene,
Now that I go, thou noble king,   1260
Warriors' gold-friend, what we agreed on,

If I my life should lose in thy cause,
That thou wouldst stand in stead of my father,
Fulfil his office when I was gone.
Be guardian thou, to my thanes and kinsmen,
My faithful friends, if I fail to return.
To Hygelac send, Hrothgar beloved,
The goodly gifts thou gavest to me.
May the lord of the Jutes, when he looks on this treasure,
May Hrethel's son, when he sees these gifts,   1270
Know that I found a noble giver,
And joyed while I lived, in a generous lord.
This ancient heirloom to Unferth give,
To the far-famed warrior, my wondrous sword
Of matchless metal. I must with Hrunting
Glory gain, or go to my death."

After these words the Weder-Jute lord
Sprang to his task, nor staid for an answer.
Swiftly he sank 'neath the swirling flood;
'Twas an hour's time ere he touched the bottom.   1280
Soon the sea-hag, savage and wild,
Who had roamed through her watery realms at will,
For winters a hundred, was 'ware from below,
An earthling had entered her ocean domain.
Quickly she reached and caught the hero;
Grappled him grimly with gruesome claws.
Yet he got no scratch, his skin was whole;
His battle-sark shielded his body from harm.
In vain she tried, with her crooked fingers,
To tear the links of his close-locked mail.   1290
Away to her den the wolf-slut dragged
Beowulf the bold, o'er the bottom ooze.
Though eager to smite her, his arm was helpless.
Swimming monsters swarmed about him,
Dented his mail with dreadful tusks.
Sudden the warrior was 'ware they had come
To a sea-hall strange [24] and seeming hostile,
Where water was not nor waves oppressed,
For the caverned rock all round kept back
The swallowing sea. He saw a light,   1300
A flicker of flame that flashed and shone.
Now first he discerned the sea-hag monstrous,
The water-wife wolfish. His weapon he raised,
And struck with his sword a swinging blow.

24 Perhaps a cavern behind a waterfall (so in the Norse *Grettis Saga,* which tells a similar story).

Sang on her head the hard-forged blade
Its war-song wild. But the warrior found
That his battle-flasher refused to bite, .
Or maim the foe. It failed its master
In the hour of need, though oft it had cloven
Helmets, and carved the casques of the doomed   1310
In combats fierce. For the first time now
That treasure failed him, fallen from honor.
But Hygelac's earl took heart of courage;
In mood defiant he fronted his foe.
The angry hero hurled to the ground,
In high disdain, the hilt of the sword,
The gaudy and jewelled; rejoiced in the strength
Of his arm unaided. So all should do
Who glory would find and fame abiding,
In the crash of conflict, nor care for their lives.   1320
The Lord of the Battle-Jutes braved the encounter;
The murderous hag by the hair he caught;
Down he dragged the dam of Grendel
In his swelling rage, till she sprawled on the floor.
Quick to repay in kind what she got,
On her foe she fastened her fearful clutches;
Enfolded the warrior weary with fighting;
The sure-footed hero stumbled and fell.
As helpless he lay, she leapt on him fiercely;
Unsheathed her hip-knife, shining and broad,   1330
Her so to avenge, her offspring sole.
But the close-linked corslet covered his breast,
Foiled the stroke and saved his life.
All had been over with Ecgtheow's son,
Under the depths of the ocean vast,
Had not his harness availed to help him,
His battle-net stiff, and the strength of God.
The Ruler of battles aright decided it;
The Wielder all-wise awarded the victory:
Lightly the hero leaped to his feet.   1340

XXIII

BEOWULF'S VICTORY AND RETURN TO HEOROT

He spied 'mongst the arms a sword surpassing,
Huge and ancient, a hard-forged slayer,
Weapon matchless and warriors' delight,
Save that its weight was more than another
Might bear into battle or brandish in war;

Giants had forged that finest of blades.
Then seized its chain-hilt the chief of the Scyldings;
His wrath was aroused, reckless his mood,
As he brandished the sword for a savage blow.
Bit the blade in the back of her neck,   1350
Cut the neck-bone, and cleft its way
Clean through her flesh; to the floor she sank;
The sword was gory; glad was the hero.
A light flashed out from the inmost den,
Like heaven's candle, when clear it shines
From cloudless skies. He scanned the cave,
Walked by the wall, his weapon upraised;
Grim in his hand the hilt he gripped.
Well that sword had served him in battle.
Steadily onward he strode through the cave,   1360
Ready to wreak the wrongs untold,
That the man-beast had wrought in the realm of Danes. . . .
He gave him his due when Grendel he found
Stretched as in sleep, and spent with the battle.
But dead was the fiend, the fight at Heorot
Had laid him low. The lifeless body
Sprang from the blows of Beowulf's sword,
As fiercely he hacked the head from the carcass.

But the men who were watching the water with Hrothgar
Suddenly saw a stir in the waves,   1370
The chop of the sea all churned up with blood
And bubbling gore. The gray-haired chiefs
For Beowulf grieved, agreeing together
That hope there was none of his home-returning,
With victory crowned, to revisit his lord.
Most of them feared he had fallen prey
To the mere-wolf dread in the depths of the sea.
When evening came, the Scyldings all
Forsook the headland, and Hrothgar himself
Turned homeward his steps. But sick at heart   1380
The strangers sat and stared at the sea,
Hoped against hope to behold their comrade
And leader again.   Now that goodly sword
Began to melt with the gore of the monster;
In bloody drippings it dwindled away.
'Twas a marvellous sight: it melted like ice,
When fetters of frost the Father unlocks,
Unravels the ropes of the wrinkled ice,
Lord and Master of months and seasons.   1390

Beheld in the hall the hero from Juteland
Treasures unnumbered, but naught he took,
Save Grendel's head, and the hilt of the sword,
Bright and jewelled,—the blade had melted,
Its metal had vanished, so venomous hot
Was the blood of the demon-brute dead in the cave.

Soon was in the sea the slayer of monsters;
Upward he shot through the shimmer of waves;
Cleared was the ocean, cleansed were its waters,
The wolfish water-hag wallowed no more;   1400
The mere-wife had yielded her miserable life.
Swift to the shore the sailors' deliverer
Came lustily swimming, with sea-spoil laden;
Rejoiced in the burden he bore to the land.
Ran to meet him his mailèd comrades,
With thanks to God who gave them their leader
Safe again back and sound from the deep.
Quickly their hero's helmet they loosened,
Unbuckled his breastplate. The blood-stained waves
Fell to a calm 'neath the quiet sky.   1410
Back they returned o'er the tracks with the footprints,
Merrily measured the miles o'er the fen,
Way they knew well, those warriors brave;
Brought from the holm-cliff the head of the monster;
'Twas toil and labor to lift the burden,
Four of their stoutest scarce could carry it
Swung from a spear-pole, a staggering load. . . .

Thus the fourteen of them, thanes adventurous,
Marched o'er the moor to the mead-hall of Hrothgar.
Tall in the midst of them towered the hero;   1420
Strode among his comrades, till they came to the hall.
In went Beowulf, the brave and victorious,
Battle-beast hardy, Hrothgar to greet.
Lifting by the hair the head of Grendel,
They laid it in the hall, where the heroes were carousing,
Right before the king, and right before the queen;
Gruesome was the sight that greeted the Danes.

XXIV XXV

BEOWULF'S STORY OF HIS FIGHT, AND HROTHGAR'S COUNSEL

Beowulf spoke, the son of Ecgtheow:
"Gladly we offer this ocean-booty,

That here thou lookest on, lord of the Scyldings, 1430
For sign of victory, son of Healfdene.
Hard was the fight I fought under water;
That combat nearly cost me my life.
Soon had been ended the ocean-encounter,
Had God in his mercy not given me aid.
No help I got from the good blade Hrunting,
The well-tried weapon worthless proved.
By the grace of God, who guided me friendless,
A splendid old sword I spied on the wall,
Hanging there, huge; by the hilt I grasped it, 1440
And seeing my chance, I struck amain
At the sea-cave's wardens, when sudden the blade
Melted and burned, as the blood gushed out,
The battle-gore hot. The hilt I saved
From the villainous fiends, and avenged their crimes,
The murder of the Danes, as was meet and due.
I promise thee now, in peace thou shalt sleep
In Heorot hall, with the whole of thy band.
Thou and thy thanes may throng within
As ye used of yore, both young and old. 1450
Thou need'st not fear renewal of strife,
Harm to thy folk at the hands of the fiends."
The golden hilt was given to the king;
The jewelled work of the giants of old
Came into hand of the hoary warrior.
On the death of the demons, the Danish lord kept it,
Wondersmiths' work. When the world was rid
Of the evil fiend, the enemy of God,
Guilty of murder, and his mother too,
The trophy passed to the peerless lord, 1460
The goodliest king, that gave out treasure
Between the two seas on Scandia's isle.
Hrothgar gazed on the golden hilt,
Relic of old, where was writ the tale
Of a far-off fight, when the flood o'erwhelmed,
The raging sea, the race of the giants
(They wantonly dared to war against God;
Then rose in his wrath the Ruler Eternal,
'Neath the heaving billows buried them all.)
On the polished gold of the guard of the hilt, 1470
Runes were writ that rightly told,
To him that read them, for whom that weapon,
Finest of sword-blades, first was made,
The splendid hilt with serpents entwined.
All were silent, when the son of Healfdene,

The wise king spoke: "Well may he say,
The aged ruler, who aye upholds
Truth and right, 'mid the ranks of his people,
Whose mind runs back to by-gone days,
This guest is born of a goodly breed. 1480
Thy fame shall fly afar among men,
Beowulf my friend, firmly thou holdest
Both wisdom and might. My word will I keep,
The love that I proffered. Thou shalt prove a deliverer
To thy folk and followers in far-off years,
A help to the heroes. Not Heremod thus
Ecgwela's heir, did offer at need
His strength to the Scyldings; instead, he brought
Slaughter and death on the sons of the Danes.
Swoln with wrath he slew his comrades, 1490
His friends at the board and fled alone,
Ill-famed earl, an outcast from men.
Though God endowed him with gifts of strength,
With boldness and might above all men,
And prospered him greatly, yet he grew to be
Blood-thirsty and cruel. No bracelets he gave
To the Danes as was due, but dwelt in gloom,
Reaped the reward of the woful strife,
And wearisome feud. Take warning from him."

Hrothgar now delivers a long sermon to Beowulf on the dangers of pride, the fickleness of fortune, and the brevity of life, and ends by asking him to sit down to the feast, promising more gifts on the morrow.

Beowulf hastened, happy in mood, 1500
To seek his bench as bid by the king.
Once more, as of old, for the earls in hall,
The famous in battle, the board was set
For feasting anew. When night with its shadows
O'erwhelmed the world, the heroes arose.
The gray-haired ruler his rest would seek,
The Scylding his bed; and Beowulf too,
The lusty warrior, longed for his sleep.
Soon an attendant showed the way
To the stranger from far, spent with his faring. 1510
With courtly custom, he cared for his needs.
All that to warriors, overseas wandering,
Was due in those days, he did for the guest.
High-gabled and gold-decked, the gift-hall towered;
The stout-hearted hero slept soundly within,
Till the raven black, with blithe heart hailed
The bliss of heaven, and bright the sun

Came gliding o'er earth. Then, eager to start,
The warriors wakened; they wished to set out
On their homeward journey. The hero brave   1520
Would board his ship, and back again sail.
The hardy one bade that Hrunting be brought
To the son of Ecglaf: the sword he offered him;
Thanked him for lending the lovely weapon;
Called it a war-friend, keen in the battle;
Not a word in blame of the blade he uttered,
Great-hearted hero. Now hastened the guests,
Eager to part, and armed for their voyage.
Their dauntless leader, beloved of the Danes,
Came to the high-seat, and to Hrothgar the king   1530
The bold-in-battle now bade farewell.

XXVI

Beowulf's Leave-Taking of Hrothgar

Beowulf spoke, the son of Ecgtheow:
"Now we sea-farers would make known our desire;
Far-travelled wanderers, we wish to return
To Hygelac now. A hearty welcome
We here have found, thou hast harbored us well.
If ever on earth I may anywise win,
Master of men, more of thy love
Than now I have won, for another adventure
Of arms and war I am eager and willing.   1540
If ever I hear, o'er the ocean-ways
That neighbor-tribes threaten annoyance or war,
As feud-seeking foemen aforetime assailed thee,
A thousand thanes to thee will I bring,
Heroes to help thee. For Hygelac, I know,
Though young in years will yield me aid;
The people's Shepherd will surely help me
By word and deed to do thee service,
And bring thee spear-shafts to speed thee in battle,
Thy might to strengthen when men thou needest.   1550
If ever Hrethric, heir of thy line,
Should come to sojourn at the court of the Jutes,
A host of friends he will find awaiting him.
Who boasts himself brave, abroad should travel."
The aged Hrothgar answering spoke:
"To utter these words, the All-wise Lord
Hath prompted thy heart; more prudent counsel
From one in years so young as thou,

I never have heard. Thou art hardy in strength,
And sage in spirit, and speakest well.　　　　1560
If ever it happen that Hrethel's heir
Be stricken by spear and slain in battle,
If sickness or sword assail thy lord,
And thou survive him, I think it likely
The Sea-Jutes in vain will seek for a better
As choice for their king, their chief to become
And rule o'er the thanes, if thou be willing
The lordship to hold. The longer I know thee
The better I like thee, Beowulf my friend.
Thou hast brought it about that both our peoples.　1570
Jutes and the Spear-Danes shall be joined in peace.
They shall cease from war, the strife shall be ended,
The feuds of aforetime, so fiercely waged.
While I rule this realm, our riches we share;
Many shall travel with treasure laden,
Each other to greet, o'er the gannet's bath;
O'er the rolling waves the ringèd prow
Tokens of friendship shall freely bring
And bind our people in peace together,
Toward friend and foe, in faith as of old."　　　1580

Still other treasures, twelve in all,
Healfdene's heir in the hall bestowed
On Beowulf brave, and bade him take them
And seek his people, and soon return.
Then kissed the king, of kin renowned,
The thane beloved. The lord of the Scyldings
Fell on his neck. Fast flowed the tears
Of the warrior gray; he weighed both chances,
But held to the hope, though hoary with years,
That each should see the other again,　　　　1590
And meet in the mead-hall. The man was so dear
That he could not restrain the storm in his breast.
Locked in his heart, a hidden longing
For the man he loved so, left him no peace,
And burnt in his blood. But Beowulf went;
The gold-decked hero the grass-way trod
Proud of his booty. The boat awaited
Its owner and master, where at anchor it rode.
As they went on their way, the warriors praised
The bounty of Hrothgar, the blameless king.　　1600
None was his equal till age snatched away
The joy of his manhood,—no mortal it spares.

XXVII

BEOWULF'S RETURN VOYAGE TO HYGELAC

Then came to the coast the comrades brave,
The lusty warriors, wearing their ring-nets,
Their chain-linked corslets. The coast-guard saw them,
The same that at first had spied them coming;
This time he chose not to challenge them harshly,
But gave them his greeting, galloping toward them.
Said the Weder-folk would welcome the sight of them
Boarding their ship in shining armor.   1610
Then by the sands, the seaworthy craft,
The iron-ringed keel, with arms was laden,
With horses and treasure. On high the mast
Towered above the treasures of Hrothgar.
To the man who had waited as watchman aboard,
Beowulf gave a gold-bound sword.
(Oft on the mead-bench that heirloom precious
Its owner would honor.) When all had embarked,
They drove for the deep, from Daneland's shore.
Then soon did the mast its sea-suit wear,   1620
A sail was unfurled, made fast with ropes,
The sea-wood sang as she sped o'er the ocean,
No baffling head-wind hindered her course;
The foamy-necked floater flew o'er the billows,
The sea-craft staunch o'er the salt-sea waves,
Till they came in sight of the cliffs of Jutland
The well known capes, and the wind-driven keel
Grating the sand, stood still on the shore.
Soon was at hand the harbor-watch eager.
Long had he looked for his loved companions   1630
Scanning the sea for their safe return.
The broad-bosomed boat to the beach he moored
With anchor-ropes fast, lest the force of the waves
That comely craft should cast adrift.
Then Beowulf bade them bring ashore
His treasure-cargo of costly gold
And weapons fine; not far was the way
To Hygelac's hall, where at home he dwelt
The king and his comrades, close by the sea.

END OF THE SECOND ADVENTURE

After the death of Hygelac and his son, Beowulf became king of the Jutes, and ruled over them fifty years. In his old age his people were harried by a fire-dragon whom the hero went out to fight. It seems that an outlaw, banished and flying for shelter, had come upon a treasure hid in a deep cave or barrow, guarded by a dragon. Long years before, an earl, the last of his race, had buried the treasure. After his death the dragon, sniffing about the stones, had found it and guarded it three hundred years, until the banished man discovered the place, and carried off one of the golden goblets. In revenge the dragon made nightly raids on Beowulf's realm, flying through the air, spitting fire, burning houses and villages, even Beowulf's hall, the "gift-stool" of the Jutes. Beowulf had an iron shield made against the dragon's fiery breath, and with eleven companions, sought out the hill-vault near the sea. These events are related in Sections XXVIII–XXXV of the Beowulf MS.

XXXV

BEOWULF'S FIGHT WITH THE FIRE-DRAGON

Before attacking the fire-dragon Beowulf once more and for the last time makes his "battle-boast" in the presence of his followers.

Beowulf said to them, brave words spoke he: 1640
"Brunt of battles I bore in my youth:
One fight more I make this day.
I mean to win fame defending my people,
If the grim destroyer will seek me out,
Come at my call from his cavern dark."
Then he greeted his thanes each one,
For the last time hailed his helmeted warriors,
His comrades dear. "I should carry no sword,
No weapon of war 'gainst the worm [25] should bear,
If the foe I might slay by strength of my arm,   1650
As Grendel I slew long since by my hand.
But I look to fight a fiery battle,
With scorching puffs of poisonous breath.
For this I bear both breastplate and shield;
No foot will I flinch from the foe of the barrow.
Wyrd is over us, each shall meet
His doom ordained at the dragon-cliff!
Bold is my mood, but my boast I omit
'Gainst the battle-flier. Abide ye here,
Heroes in harness, hard by the barrow,   1660
Cased in your armor the issue await:
Which of us two his wounds shall survive.
Not yours the attempt, the task is mine.
'Tis meant for no man but me alone
To measure his might 'gainst the monster fierce.
I get you the gold in glorious fight,

25 dragon

Or battle-death bitter shall bear off your lord."
  Uprose with his shield the shining hero,
Bold 'neath his helmet. He bore his harness
In under the cliff; alone he went,   1670
Himself he trusted; no task for faint-heart.
Then saw by the wall the warrior brave,
Hero of many a hard-fought battle,
Arches of stone that opened a way;
From the rocky gate there gushed a stream,
Bubbling and boiling with battle-fire.
So great the heat no hope was there
To come at the hoard in the cavern's depth,
Unscathed by the blast of the scorching dragon.
He let from his breast his battle-cry leap;   1680
Swoln with rage was the royal Jute,
Stormed the stout-heart; strong and clear
Through the gloom of the cave his cry went ringing.
Hate was aroused, the hoard-ward knew
The leader's hail. Too late 'twas now
To parley for peace. The poisonous breath
Of the monster shot from the mouth of the cave,
Reeking hot. The hollow earth rumbled.
The man by the rock upraised his shield,
The lord of the Jutes, 'gainst the loathly dragon.   1690
Now kindled for battle the curled-up beast;
The king undaunted with drawn sword stood,
'Twas an heirloom olden with edge of lightning.
Each was so fierce he affrighted the other.
Towering tall 'neath tilted shield,
Waited the king as the worm coiled back,
Sudden to spring: so stood he and waited.
Blazing he came in coils of fire
Swift to his doom. The shield of iron
Sheltered the hero too short a while,—   1700
Life and limb it less protected
Than he hoped it would, for the weapon he held
First time that day he tried in battle;

        .   .   .   .

XXXVI

WIGLAF'S REPROACH TO HIS COMRADES. BEOWULF
MORTALLY WOUNDED.

The shield-thane beloved, lord of the Scylfings,
Wiglaf was called; 'twas Weohstan's son

Ælfhere's kinsman. When his king he saw
Hard by the heat under helmet oppressed,
He remembered the gifts he had got of old,
Lands and wealth of the Wægmunding line,
The folk-rights all that his father's had been;   1710
He could hold no longer, but hard he gripped
Linden shield yellow and ancient sword. . . .

The intervening lines tell the history of the sword and the feuds in which
it has participated.

For the first time there the faithful thane,
Youthful and stalwart, stood with his leader,
Shoulder to shoulder in shock of battle.
Nor melted his courage, nor cracked his blade,
His war-sword true, as the worm found out
When together they got in grim encounter.

Wiglaf in wrath upbraided his comrades,
Sore was his heart as he spake these words: 1720
"Well I mind when our mead we drank
In the princely hall, how we promised our lord
Who gave us these rings and golden armlets,
That we would repay his war-gifts rich,
Helmets and armor, if haply should come
His hour of peril; us hath he made
Thanes of his choice for this adventure;
Spurred us to glory, and gave us these treasures
Because he deemed us doughty spearmen,
Helmeted warriors, hardy and brave.   1730
Yet all the while, unhelped and alone,
He meant to finish this feat of strength,
Shepherd of men and mightiest lord
Of daring deeds. The day is come,—
Now is the hour he needs the aid
Of spearmen good. Let us go to him now,
Help our hero while hard bestead
By the nimble flames. God knows that I
Had rather the fire should ruthlessly fold
My body with his, than harbor me safe.   1740
Shame it were surely our shields to carry
Home to our lands, unless we first
Slay this foe and save the life
Of the Weder-king. Full well I know
To leave him thus, alone to endure,

Bereft of aid, breaks ancient right.
My helmet and sword shall serve for us both;
Shield and armor we share to-day."

Waded the warrior through welter and reek;
Buckler and helmet he bore to his leader;   1750
Heartened the hero with words of hope:
"Do thy best now, dearest Beowulf.
Years ago, in youth, thou vowedst
Living, ne'er to lose thine honor,
Shield thy life and show thy valor.
I stand by thee to the end!"
After these words the worm came on,
Snorting with rage, for a second charge;
All mottled with fire his foes he sought,
The warriors hated. But Wiglaf's shield   1760
Was burnt to the boss by the billows of fire;
His harness helped not the hero young.
Shelter he found 'neath the shield of his kinsman,
When the crackling blaze had crumbled his own.
But mindful of glory, the mighty hero
Smote amain with his matchless sword.
Down it hurtled, driven by anger,
Till it stuck in the skull then snapped the blade,
Broken was Nægling, Beowulf's sword,
Ancient and gray. 'Twas granted him never   1770
To count on edge of iron in battle;
His hand was too heavy, too hard his strokes,
As I have heard tell, for every blade
He brandished in battle: the best gave way,
And left him helpless and hard bestead.
Now for a third time neared the destroyer;
The fire-drake fierce, old feuds remembering,
Charged the warrior who wavered an instant;
Blazing he came and closed his fangs
On Beowulf's throat; and throbbing spirts   1780
Of life-blood dark o'erdrenched the hero.

XXXVII

THE SLAYING OF THE DRAGON

Then in the hour of utmost peril,
The stripling proved what stock he came of;
Showed his endurance and dauntless courage.

Though burnt was his hand when he backed his kinsman,
With head unguarded the good thane charged,
Thrust from below at the loathly dragon,
Pierced with the point and plunged the blade in,
The gleaming-bright, till the glow abated
Waning low. Ere long the king   1790
Came to himself, and swiftly drew
The warknife that hung at his harness' side,
And cut in two the coilèd monster.
So felled they the foe and finished him bravely,
Together they killed him, the kinsmen two,
A noble pair. So needs must do
Comrades in peril. For the king it proved
His uttermost triumph, the end of his deeds
And work in the world. The wound began,
Where the cave-dragon savage had sunk his teeth,   1800
To swell and fever, and soon he felt
The baleful poison pulse through his blood,
And burn in his breast. The brave old warrior
Sat by the wall and summoned his thoughts,
Gazed on the wondrous work of the giants:
Arches of stone, firm-set on their pillars,
Upheld that hill-vault hoar and ancient.

Now Beowulf's thane, the brave and faithful,
Dashed with water his darling lord,
His comrade and king all covered with blood   1810
And faint with the fight; unfastened his helmet.
Beowulf spoke despite his hurt,
His piteous wound; full well he knew
His years on earth were ended now,
His hours of glad life gone for aye
His days allotted, and death was near:
"Now would I gladly give to a son
These weapons of war, had Wyrd but granted
That heir of my own should after me come,
Sprung from my loins. This land have I ruled   1820
Fifty winters. No folk-king dared,
None of the chiefs of the neighboring tribes,
To touch me with sword or assail me with terror
Of battle-threats. I bided at home,
Held my peace and my heritage kept,
Seeking no feuds nor swearing false oaths.
This gives me comfort, and gladdens me now,
Though wounded sore and sick unto death.

As I leave my life, the Lord may not charge me
With killing of kinsmen. Now quickly go,   1830
Wiglaf beloved, to look at the hoard,
Where hidden it rests 'neath the hoary rock.
For the worm lies still, put asleep by his wound,
Robbed of his riches. Then rise and haste!
Give me to see that golden hoard,
To gaze on the store of glorious gems,
The easier then I may end my life,
Leave my lordship that long I held."

XXXVIII

The Rescue of the Hoard and the Death of Beowulf

Swiftly, 'tis said, the son of Weohstan
Obeyed the words of his bleeding lord,   1840
Maimed in the battle. Through the mouth of the cave
Boldly he bore his battle-net in.
Glad of the victory, he gazed about him;
Many a sun-bright jewel he saw,
Glittering gold, strewn on the ground,
Heaped in the den of the dragon hoary,
Old twilight-flier,—flagons once bright,
Wassail cups wondrous of warriors departed
Stript of their mountings, many a helmet
Ancient and rusted, armlets a many,   1850
Curiously woven. (Wealth so hoarded,
Buried treasure, will taint with pride
Him that hides it, whoever it be.)
Towering high o'er the hoard he saw
A gleaming banner with gold inwoven,
Of broidure rare; its radiance streamed
So bright, he could peer to the bounds of the cave,
Survey its wonders; no worm was seen.
Edge of the sword had ended his life.
Then, as they say, that single adventurer   1860
Plundered the hoard that was piled by the giants;
Gathered together old goblets and platters,
Took what he liked; the towering banner
Brightest of beacons he brought likewise.
The blade of Beowulf, his brave old chief,
With edge of iron had ended the life
Of him that had guarded the golden hoard
For many a year, and at midnight hour

Had spread the terror of surging flames
In front of the den, till death o'ertook him.   1870
So Wiglaf returned with treasure laden.
The high-souled hero hastened his steps,
Anxiously wondered if he should find
The lord of the Weders alive where he left him
Sapped of his strength and stretched on the ground.
As he came from the hill he beheld his comrade,
His lord of bounty, bleeding and faint,
Near unto death. He dashed him once more
Bravely with water, till burden of speech
Broke from his breast, and Beowulf spoke,   1880
Gazing sad at the gold before him:
"For the harvest of gold that here I look on,
To the God of Glory I give my thanks.
To the Ruler Eternal I render praise
That ere I must go, he granted me this,
To leave to my people this priceless hoard.
'Twas bought with my life; now look ye well
To my people's need when I have departed.
No more I may bide among ye here.
Bid the battle-famed build on the foreland   1890
A far-seen barrow when flames have burnt me.
High o'er the headland of whales it shall tower,
A beacon and mark to remind my people.
And sailors shall call it in years to come
Beowulf's Barrow, as bound from afar
Their tall ships stem the storm-dark seas.

       The great-hearted king unclasped from his neck
A collar of gold and gave to his thane,
The brave young warrior, his bright-gilt helmet,
Breastplate and ring. So bade him farewell: 1900
"Thou art the last to be left of our house.
Wyrd hath o'erwhelmed our Wægmunding line,
Swept my kinsmen swift to their doom.
Earls in their prime. I must follow them."
These words were the last that the warrior gray
Found, ere the funeral-flames he chose.
Swift from his bosom his soul departed
To find the reward of the faithful and true.

The narrative here doubles back upon itself to repeat the description of
Beowulf and the dragon lying dead before the cave, and to report Wiglaf's
reproach to the returning deserters.

XL

BEOWULF'S DEATH ANNOUNCED TO THE PEOPLE. THE SPEECH OF THE HERALD

Then Wiglaf bade the battle-work tell
To the sorrowful troop that had sat all day   *1910*
At the sea-cliff's edge, their shields in hand,
In dread and in hope, yet doubtful of either:
Their dear lord's return, or his death in the fight.
The herald that came to the headland riding,
Nought kept back of the news that befell,
But truthfully told them the tidings all:
"Now lies low the lord of the Weders;
The generous giver of gifts to the Jutes,
Sleeps his battle-sleep, slain by the worm.
At his side lies stretched his slaughterous foe,   *1920*
Fordone by the dagger. The dragon fierce
Would take no wound from touch of sword;
Its blade would not bite. At Beowulf's side
Wiglaf sits, the son of Weohstan;
By the hero dead, the hero living
At his head keeps watch with woful heart
O'er friend and foe.

   ·   ·   ·   ·   ·   ·   ·

The Herald now warns of renewed attacks on the Jutes by Franks and Frisians, and alludes to the origin of the feud in the famous raid in which Hygelac was slain. He further warns of renewed attacks by the Swedes, now that Beowulf is dead, and refers to the origin of the wars between Swedes and Jutes and to a famous battle at "Ravenswood." The episodic digression over, the herald returns to present events.

XLI

THE HERALD'S SPEECH CONCLUDED

          'Tis time we hasten
To see where lies our lord and king,
Our giver of bounty, and bear him away   *1930*
To the funeral pyre; of precious gems
Not a few shall melt in the fire with him.
The hoard he won, the wealth untold,
The priceless treasure he purchased so dear,
And bought with his life at the bitter end,
The flame shall enfold it, the fire consume.
No warrior one keepsake shall carry away,

No necklace be worn by winsome maid.
In sorrow rather, and reft of her gold,
Alone she shall tread the track of an exile,   1940
Now our lord lies low, his laughter stilled,
His mirth and revel. Now many a spear
Shall morning-cold be clasped in the hand
And held on high. No harp shall sound
The warriors to wake, but the wan-hued raven
Shall croak o'er the carcass and call to the eagle,
To tell how he fared at the feast after battle
When he and the gray wolf gorged on the slain."
Thus ended his tale, his tidings of woe,
The faithful thane, nor falsely reported   1950
Wyrd or word. The warriors rose;
To the Eagles' Cliff they came in sadness,
With welling tears, the wonder to see.
Lying helpless, their lord they found
Stretched on the ground, the giver-of-rings.
The end had come to him, open-handed
King of the Weders, warrior brave.
That day a fearful death he had found.
A stranger thing they saw near by:
The loathsome monster lying dead   1960
On the field where they fought, the fiery dragon,
The gruesome beast was burnt and charred.
Fifty feet in full he measured
In length, as he lay, along the ground.
'Twas his wont at night to wing aloft
And dip to earth as his den he sought;
Now he lay dead, his night-revels over.
Scattered about were bowls and flagons,
Golden platters, and priceless swords,
With rust eaten through, as though they had lain   1970
Winters a thousand in the womb of the earth.
O'er that heritage huge, the hoard of afore-time,
A spell had been woven to ward off despoilers,
And none might touch the treasure-vault hidden;
Save that God alone, the Lord of victory,
The Guardian of men, might grant the power
To unlock the hoard, and lift the treasure,
To such a hero as to Him seemed meet.

.   .   .   .   .   :   .   .   .   .

XLII

BEOWULF'S BODY CARRIED TO THE FUNERAL PYRE AND THE
DRAGON CAST INTO THE SEA.

Wiglaf spoke, the son of Weohstan:
"Let us go once more to gaze at the marvels 1980
Still left 'neath the rock; I will lead you in
Where your hands may touch great heaps of gold,
Bracelets and rings. Let the bier be ready
When out of the cave we come again,
To bear away the warrior brave,
Our lord beloved, where long he shall bide,
Kept in the sheltering care of God."
The son of Weohstan, warrior brave,
Called on the folk-men, far and wide,
From house and home to hasten and bring 1990
Wood for the pyre of the peerless man,
His funeral pile. "Now fire shall consume,
The wan flame wax o'er the warrior strong,
Who oft stood firm in the iron shower
When the storm of arrows, sent from the bow-string,
Flew o'er the shield-wall, and the fleet-winged shaft,
Feathered behind, pushed home the barb."
Now the wise young warrior, Weohstan's son,
Seven men called, of the king's own thanes,
The best of the band; the bravest he gathered; 2000
Himself the eighth, they sought the den
Of the hateful beast; one bore in his hand
A lighted torch and led the way.
No lots were drawn for the dragon's hoard
When they saw it lying, loose in the cave,
Uncared for, unguarded, unclaimed by a soul;
There was none to hinder as they hurried away,
Laden with spoils and splendid heirlooms.
O'er the edge of the cliff they cast the dragon,
Into the sea, the scaly worm; 2010
Let the waves engulf the gold-hoard's keeper.
On a wagon they loaded the wondrous treasure,
Gold past counting. The gray-haired king
They bore to the pyre, on the Point of Whales.

XLIII

THE BURNING OF BEOWULF'S BODY

Then built for Beowulf the band of the Jutes
A funeral pyre; 'twas firmly based.
They hung it with helmets as he had bidden,
With shining byrnies and battle-shields.
In the midst they laid, with loud lament,
Their lord beloved, their leader brave.   2020
On the brow of the cliff they kindled the blaze,
Black o'er the flames the smoke shot up;
Cries of woe, in the windless air,
Rose and blent with the roar of the blast,
Till the frame of the body burst with the heat
Of the seething heart. In sorrowing mood
They mourned aloud their leader dead.
Joined in the wail a woman old,
With hair upbound for Beowulf grieved,
Chanted a dreary dirge of woe,   2030
Dark forebodings of days to come,
Thick with slaughter and throes of battle,
Bondage and shame. The black smoke rose.
High on the headland they heaped a barrow,
Lofty and broad 'twas built by the Weders,
Far to be seen by sea-faring men.
Ten days long they toiled to raise it,
The battle-king's beacon. They built a wall
To fence the brands of the funeral burning,
The choicest and best their chiefs could devise.   2040
In the barrow they buried the bracelets and rings,
All those pieces of precious treasure
That bold-hearted men had brought from the cave,
Returned to earth the heirloom of heroes,
The gold to the ground, again to become
As useless to men as of yore it had been.

Around the barrow the battle-brave rode,
Twelve in the troop, all true-born æthelings,
To make their lament and mourn for the king;
To chant a lay their lord to honor.   2050
They praised his daring; his deeds of prowess
They mentioned in song. For meet it is
That men should publish their master's praise,
Honor their chieftain, and cherish him dearly
When he leaves this life, released from the body.

Thus joined the men of the Jutes in mourning
Their hero's end. His hearth-companions
Called him the best among kings of the earth,
Mildest of men, and most beloved,
Kindest to kinsmen, and keenest for fame. 2060

END OF BEOWULF

MIDDLE ENGLISH LITERATURE

Even before the coming of William the Norman, the English language was in process of active change. The conquest by the Normans superimposed on English society a ruling class who spoke French, and established French as the language of the law courts, of Parliament, and of such schools as existed. Yet it in no sense extinguished English or even, for the time, seriously modified it. English continued to be spoken (to some extent also written) with only such changes as were already in progress. It was no longer, however, regarded as a literary language by the upper classes, who looked toward France. The spoken language, now the possession of the illiterate classes, denied the conserving forces of culture and a literature, altered more rapidly than before, in particular sloughing off inflections and reducing them to a much simplified system. A simpler grammar is to be noted when English again takes position as a literary language, in the thirteenth century, and thereafter with gradually increasing momentum English writings show also the introduction of French syntax, and of French words—in such great numbers as the thirteenth century passed into the fourteenth, and especially as the fourteenth progressed toward its close, that English became bi-lingual instead of uni-lingual in vocabulary. Imported with the new words were aspects of life hitherto unknown in England or not highly regarded. Manners became a fine art, chivalry flourished, new abstractions brought a more subtle and more profound thought, numerous new terms testified to an increased complexity in legal, political, and social institutions. Not in language alone did new forces flow in from France, but in literary forms and literary themes. Rhyme, regular meters, and fixed stanzas displaced the old free alliterative verse. The whole literary inheritance of southern Europe was thus placed in the hands of the English. Established also was a new delicacy, a new humor, a richer sense of the beauty of the world, and a broader humanity, in place of the Anglo-Saxon's noble and earnest but somewhat restricted and somewhat solemn view of life.

The changes just sketched, in language, literature, and thought, foreign in impetus, were, significantly enough, proceeding most actively at the very time that the dominance of the native tongue had so reëstablished itself with all classes that English was restored in the schools (about 1350), in the law courts (1362), and in Parliament (1399). The influence of the Norman Conquest on the language and literature is thus seen to be not direct but indirect, the result eventually of forces not political, but cultural. The Conquest established French culture in England, and England, after the lapse of centuries, paid the tribute to that culture, superior to its own, of borrowing from its language and imitating its literary art.

Because, after the Conquest, English was no longer regarded as a literary tongue, for some two centuries there was little written in the vernacular. Literature was not lacking in England, but it was almost entirely in Latin and French. From about 1250 on the number of works in the now modified English began to increase, and by the time of Chaucer (latter half of the fourteenth century), a brilliant period was in full swing.

The corpus of Middle English literature up to Chaucer includes tales, in prose and verse; chronicles, some of them rhymed like Layamon's *Brut* (about 1200); homilies, saints' legends, and didactic works; some fresh and charming lyrics, many of them anonymous; but especially a great body of romances, the inspiration of which had come from France. These compositions, sometimes in verse and sometimes in prose, present characteristically themes of chivalric adventure and courtly love. The subject-matter falls chiefly into three cycles, as an old writer noted: the "matter of Rome," including the stories of Troy and of Alexander; the "matter of France," concerning chiefly Charlemagne and his peers; and the "matter of Britain," or tales of King Arthur and the knights of the Round Table, eventually associating with Arthur, by a powerful centripetal force, whole lesser cycles which had originally moved about independent heroes like Tristram, Gawain, Lancelot, and Merlin, or had concerned a great series of episodes like the Quest of the Holy Grail.

In the lifetime of Chaucer there came a richer and more varied literary flowering. The works of the great poet himself include practically all the types that were popular in the Middle Ages (see below). Surrounding him were numerous great, though lesser figures. John Gower was writing his *Confessio Amantis*, a collection of some hundred stories in verse (1383 or 1384). William Langland, or whatever authors contributed to the *Piers Plowman*, with moral earnestness and mordant satire, was laying bare the evils of man and the abuses of society in his day, in a revival of the Old English alliterative measure; and in the west of England, an unknown poet of rare power was writing *Sir Gawain and the Green Knight*, *Patience*, and the *Pearl*.

BIBLIOGRAPHY. W. A. Neilson and K. G. T. Webster: *Chief British Poets of the 14th and 15th Centuries* (Houghton Mifflin). W. H. Schofield: *Eng. Lit. from the Norman Conquest to Chaucer* (Macmillan). C. S. Baldwin: *English Mediæval Lit.* (Longmans). A. R. Benham: *Eng. Lit. from Widsith to Death of Chaucer* (Yale). W. P. Ker: *Epic and Romance*. J. E. Wells: *Manual of the Writings in Middle Eng.* (bibliography) (Yale).

SIR GAWAIN AND THE GREEN KNIGHT

In the "matter of Britain," the most interesting of the romance cycles to Englishmen because of its native material, perhaps the most beautiful extant specimen is *Sir Gawain and the Green Knight*. This romance is found in the British Museum manuscript Cotton Nero A. X + 4, along with three other poems, of which one, the *Pearl*, a dream-vision, also ranks among the treasures of Middle English verse. It is generally believed that all four poems are the work of one author, who should deservedly be called one of the greatest of our early poets. The manuscript, dating from about 1360, is in the West Midland dialect, a form of Middle English so difficult that the average reader can enjoy the poem only in translation. *Sir Gawain* is written in a long stanza of which the first eighteen lines are in alliterative measure (somewhat similar to Anglo-Saxon verse), the last four being a rhyming quatrain. The verse-form thus combines the old and the new methods.

The poem skillfully links together two independent stories, each of which is found separately in many versions—the beheading incident and the chastity test. An elaborate study of the genesis of the poem is to be found in G. L. Kittredge's *A Study of Gawain and the Green Knight* (Harvard). The best edition of the poem is that of Tolkien and Gordon (Oxford). Miss Jessie L. Weston has translated the poem in imitative verse in her *Romance, Vision, and Satire* (Houghton Mifflin), a translation which is still difficult reading. The translation here presented is Miss Weston's prose version. Other translations are by W. A. Neilson and K. G. T. Webster in *Chief British Poets of the 14th and 15th Centuries* (Houghton Mifflin), by G. H. Gerould (Nelson); and by T. H. Banks, Jr., in a verse following the original (Crofts).

I

AFTER the siege and the assault of Troy, when that burg was destroyed and burnt to ashes, and the traitor tried for his treason, the noble Æneas and his kin sailed forth to become princes and patrons of well-nigh all the Western Isles. Thus Romulus built Rome (and gave to the city his own name, which it bears even to this day); and Ticius turned him to Tuscany; and Langobard raised him up dwellings in Lombardy; and Felix Brutus sailed far over the French flood, and founded the kingdom of Britain, wherein have been war and waste and wonder, and bliss and bale, ofttimes since.

And in that kingdom of Britain have been wrought more gallant deeds than in any other; but of all British kings Arthur was the most valiant, as I have heard tell; therefore will I set forth a wondrous adventure that fell out in his time. And if ye will listen to me, but for a little while, I will tell it even as it stands in story stiff and strong, fixed in the letter, as it hath long been known in the land.

King Arthur lay at Camelot upon a Christmas-tide, with many a gallant lord and lovely lady, and all the noble brotherhood of the Round Table. There they held rich revels with gay talk and jest; one while they would ride forth to joust and tourney, and again back to the court to make carols; [1] for there was the feast holden fifteen days with all the mirth that men could devise, song and glee, glorious to hear, in the daytime, and dancing at night. Halls and chambers were crowded with noble guests, the bravest of knights and the loveliest of ladies, and Arthur himself was the comeliest king that ever held a court. For all this fair folk were in their youth, the fairest and most fortunate under heaven, and the king himself of such fame that it were hard now to name so valiant a hero.

Now the New Year had but newly come in, and on that day a double portion was served on the high table to all the noble guests, and thither came the king with all his knights, when the service in the chapel had been sung to an end. And they greeted

[1] round or ring dances accompanied with song

each other for the New Year, and gave rich gifts, the one to the other (and they that received them were not wroth, that may ye well believe!) and the maidens laughed and made mirth till it was time to get them to meat. Then they washed and sat them down to the fasting in fitting rank and order, and Guinevere the queen, gaily clad, sat on the high daïs. Silken was her seat, with a fair canopy over her head, of rich tapestries of Tars, embroidered, and studded with costly gems; fair she was to look upon, with her shining gray eyes, a fairer woman might no man boast himself of having seen.

But Arthur would not eat till all were served, so full of joy and gladness was he, even as a child; he liked not either to lie long, or to sit long at meat, so worked upon him his young blood and his wild brain. And another custom he had also, that came of his nobility, that he would never eat upon an high day till he had been advised of some knightly deed, or some strange and marvelous tale, of his ancestors, or of arms, or of other ventures. Or till some stranger knight should seek of him leave to joust with one of the Round Table, that they might set their lives in jeopardy, one against another, as fortune might favor them. Such was the king's custom when he sat in hall at each high feast with his noble knights; therefore on that New Year tide, he abode, fair of face, on the throne, and made much mirth withal.

Thus the king sat before the high tables, and spake of many things; and there good Sir Gawain was seated by Guinevere the queen, and on her other side Agravain, *à la dure main* [2] both were the king's sister's sons and full gallant knights. And at the end of the table was Bishop Bawdewyn, and Ywain, King Urien's son, sat at the other side alone. These were worthily served on the daïs, and at the lower tables sat many valiant knights. Then they bare the first course with the blast of trumpets and waving of banners, with the sound of drums and pipes, of song and lute, that many a heart was uplifted at the melody. Many were the dainties, and rare the meats; so great was the plenty they might scarce find room on the board to set on the dishes. Each helped himself as he liked best, and to each two were twelve dishes, with great plenty of beer and wine.

Now I will say no more of the service, but that ye may know there was no lack, for there drew near a venture that the folk might well have left their labor to gaze upon. As the sound of the music ceased, and the first course had been fitly served, there came in at the hall door one terrible to behold, of stature greater than any on earth; from neck to loin so

2 of the hard hand

strong and thickly made, and with limbs so long and so great
that he seemed even as a giant. And yet he was but a man,
only the mightiest that might mount a steed; broad of chest
and shoulders and slender of waist, and all his features of like
fashion; but men marveled much at his color, for he rode even
as a knight, yet was green all over.

For he was clad all in green, with a straight coat, and a
mantle above; all decked and lined with fur was the cloth
and the hood that was thrown back from his locks and lay
10 on his shoulders. Hose had he of the same green, and spurs
of bright gold with silken fastenings richly worked; and all his
vesture was verily green. Around his waist and his saddle were
bands with fair stones set upon silken work, 't were too long
to tell of all the trifles that were embroidered thereon—birds
and insects in gay gauds of green and gold. All the trappings
of his steed were of metal of like enamel, even the stirrups that
he stood in stained of the same, and stirrups and saddle-bow
alike gleamed and shone with green stones. Even the steed on
which he rode was of the same hue, a green horse, great and
20 strong, and hard to hold, with broidered bridle, meet for the
rider.

The knight was thus gaily dressed in green, his hair falling
around his shoulders; on his breast hung a beard, as thick and
green as a bush, and the beard and the hair of his head were
clipped all round above his elbows. The lower part of his
sleeves was fastened with clasps in the same wise as a king's
mantle. The horse's mane was crisp and plaited with many a
knot folded in with gold thread about the fair green, here a
twist of the hair, here another of gold. The tail was twined
30 in like manner, and both were bound about with a band of
bright green set with many a precious stone; then they were
tied aloft in a cunning knot, whereon rang many bells of burnished gold. Such a steed might no other ride, nor had such
ever been looked upon in that hall ere that time; and all who
saw that knight spake and said that a man might scarce abide
his stroke.

The knight bore no helm nor hauberk, neither gorget nor
breast-plate, neither shaft nor buckler to smite nor to shield,
but in one hand he had a holly-bough, that is greenest when the
40 groves are bare, and in his other an axe, huge and uncomely,
a cruel weapon in fashion, if one would picture it. The head
was an ell-yard long, the metal all of green steel and gold,
the blade burnished bright, with a broad edge, as well shapen
to shear as a sharp razor. The steel was set into a strong staff,
all bound round with iron, even to the end, and engraved with
green in cunning work. A lace was twined about it, that looped

at the head, and all adown the handle it was clasped with tassels on buttons of bright green richly broidered.

The knight rideth through the entrance of the hall, driving straight to the high daïs, and greeted no man, but looked ever upwards; and the first words he spake were, "Where is the ruler of this folk? I would gladly look upon that hero, and have speech with him." He cast his eyes on the knights, and mustered [3] them up and down, striving ever to see who of them was of most renown.

Then was there great gazing to behold that chief, for each 10 man marveled what it might mean that a knight and his steed should have even such a hue as the green grass; and that seemed even greener than green enamel on bright gold. All looked on him as he stood, and drew near unto him, wondering greatly what he might be; for many marvels had they seen, but none such as this, and phantasm and faërie did the folk deem it. Therefore were the gallant knights slow to answer, and gazed astounded, and sat stone still in a deep silence through that goodly hall, as if a slumber were fallen upon them. I deem it was not all for doubt, but some for courtesy that 20 they might give ear unto his errand.

Then Arthur beheld this adventurer before his high daïs, and knightly he greeted him, for fearful was he never. "Sir," he said, "thou art welcome to this place—lord of this hall am I, and men call me Arthur. Light thee down, and tarry awhile, and what thy will is, that shall we learn after."

"Nay," quoth the stranger, "so help me he that sitteth on high, 't was not mine errand to tarry any while in this dwelling; but the praise of this thy folk and thy city is lifted up on high, and thy warriors are holden for the best and most valiant 30 of those who ride mail-clad to the fight. The wisest and the worthiest of this world are they, and well proven in all knightly sports. And here, as I have heard tell, is fairest courtesy; therefore have I come hither as at this time. Ye may be sure by the branch that I bear here that I come in peace, seeking no strife. For had I willed to journey in warlike guise I have at home both hauberk and helm, shield and shining spear, and other weapons to mine hand, but since I seek no war, my raiment is that of peace. But if thou be as bold as all men tell, thou wilt freely grant me the boon I ask."   40

And Arthur answered, "Sir Knight, if thou cravest battle here thou shalt not fail for lack of a foe."

And the knight answered, "Nay, I ask no fight; in faith here on the benches are but beardless children; were I clad in armor on my steed there is no man here might match me. Therefore

[3] surveyed

I ask in this court but a Christmas jest, for that it is Yule-
tide and New Year, and there are here many fain for sport.
If any one in this hall holds himself so hardy, so bold both
of blood and brain, as to dare strike me one stroke for another,
I will give him as a gift this axe, which is heavy enough, in
sooth, to handle as he may list, and I will abide the first blow,
unarmed as I sit. If any knight be so bold as to prove my
words, let him come swiftly to me here, and take this weapon;
I quit claim to it, he may keep it as his own, and I will abide
10 his stroke, firm on the floor. Then shalt thou give me the right
to deal him another, the respite of a year and a day shall he
have. Now haste, and let see whether any here dare say aught."
    Now if the knights had been astounded at the first, yet stiller
were they all, high and low, when they had heard his words.
The knight on his steed straightened himself in the saddle,
and rolled his eyes fiercely round the hall; red they gleamed
under his green and bushy brows. He frowned and twisted his
beard, waiting to see who should rise, and when none answered
he cried aloud in mockery, "What, is this Arthur's hall, and
20 these the knights whose renown hath run through many
realms? Where are now your pride and your conquests, your
wrath, and anger, and mighty words? Now are the praise and
the renown of the Round Table overthrown by one man's
speech, since all keep silence for dread ere ever they have seen
a blow!"
    With that he laughed so loudly that the blood rushed to the
king's fair face for very shame; he waxed wroth, as did all his
knights, and sprang to his feet, and drew near to the stranger
and said, "Now by heaven, foolish is thy asking, and thy folly
30 shall find its fitting answer. I know no man aghast at thy great
words. Give me here thine axe and I shall grant thee the boon
thou hast asked." Lightly he sprang to him and caught at his
hand, and the knight, fierce of aspect, lighted down from his
charger.
    Then Arthur took the axe and gripped the haft, and swung
it round, ready to strike. And the knight stood before him,
taller by the head than any in the hall; he stood, and stroked
his beard, and drew down his coat, no more dismayed for the
king's threats than if one had brought him a drink of wine.
40   Then Gawain, who sat by the queen, leaned forward to the
king and spake, "I beseech ye, my lord, let this venture be
mine. Would ye but bid me rise from this seat, and stand by
your side, so that my liege lady thought it not ill, then would
I come to your counsel before this goodly court. For I think
it not seemly when such challenges be made in your hall that
ye yourself should undertake it, while there are many bold

knights who sit beside ye, none are there, methinks, of readier
will under heaven, or more valiant in open field. I am the weakest, I wot, and the feeblest of wit, and it will be the less loss   ·
of my life if ye seek sooth. For save that ye are mine uncle,
naught is there in me to praise, no virtue is there in my body
save your blood, and since this challenge is such folly that it
beseems ye not to take it, and I have asked it from ye first,
let it fall to me, and if I bear myself ungallantly, then let all
this court blame me."

Then they all spake with one voice that the king should leave 10
this venture and grant it to Gawain.

Then Arthur commanded the knight to rise, and he rose up
quickly and knelt down before the king, and caught hold of the
weapon; and the king loosed his hold of it, and lifted up his
hand, and gave him his blessing, and bade him be strong both
of heart and hand. "Keep thee well, nephew," quoth Arthur,
"that thou give him but the one blow, and if thou redest [4]
him rightly I trow thou shalt well abide the stroke he may
give thee after."

Gawain stepped to the stranger, axe in hand, and he, never 20
fearing, awaited his coming. Then the Green Knight spake to
Sir Gawain, "Make we our covenant ere we go further. First,
I ask thee, knight, what is thy name? Tell me truly, that I may
know thee."

"In faith," quoth the good knight, "Gawain am I, who give
thee this buffet, let what may come of it; and at this time twelvemonth will I take another at thine hand with whatsoever
weapon thou wilt, and none other."

Then the other answered again, "Sir Gawain, so may I thrive
as I am fain to take this buffet at thine hand," and he quoth 30
further, "Sir Gawain, it liketh me well that I shall take at thy
fist that which I have asked here, and thou hast readily and
truly rehearsed all the covenant that I asked of the king, save
that thou shalt swear me, by thy troth, to seek me thyself
wherever thou hopest that I may be found, and win thee such
reward as thou dealest me to-day, before this folk."

"Where shall I seek thee?" quoth Gawain. "Where is thy
place? By him that made me, I wot never where thou dwellest,
nor know I thee, knight, thy court, nor thy name. But teach
me truly all that pertaineth thereto, and tell me thy name, 40
and I shall use all my wit to win my way thither, and that I
swear thee for sooth, and by my sure troth."

"That is enough in the New Year, it needs no more," quoth
the Green Knight to the gallant Gawain, "if I tell thee truly
when I have taken the blow, and thou hast smitten me; then

4 handlest

will I teach thee of my house and home, and mine own name, then mayest thou ask thy road and keep covenant. And if I waste no words then farest thou the better, for thou canst dwell in thy land, and seek no further. But take now thy toll, and let see how thou strikest."

"Gladly will I," quoth Gawain, handling his axe.

Then the Green Knight swiftly made him ready, he bowed down his head, and laid his long locks on the crown that his bare neck might be seen. Gawain gripped his axe and raised 10 it on high, the left foot he set forward on the floor, and let the blow fall lightly on the bare neck. The sharp edge of the blade sundered the bones, smote through the neck, and clave it in two, so that the edge of the steel bit on the ground, and the fair head fell to the earth that many struck it with their feet as it rolled forth. The blood spurted forth, and glistened on the green raiment, but the knight neither faltered nor fell; he started forward with out-stretched hand, and caught the head, and lifted it up; then he turned to his steed, and took hold of the bridle, set his foot in ·the stirrup, and mounted. His 20 head he held by the hair, in his hand. Then he seated himself in his saddle as if naught ailed him, and he were not headless. He turned his steed about, the grim corpse bleeding freely the while, and they who looked upon him doubted them much for the covenant.

For he held up the head in his hand, and turned the face toward them that sat on the high daïs, and it lifted up the eye-lids and looked upon them and spake as ye shall hear. "Look, Gawain, that thou art ready to go as thou hast promised, and seek loyally till thou find me, even as thou hast sworn in this 30 hall in the hearing of these knights. Come thou, I charge thee, to the Green Chapel; such a stroke as thou hast dealt thou hast deserved, and it shall be promptly paid thee on New Year's morn. Many men know me as the Knight of the Green Chapel, and if thou askest, thou shalt not fail to find me. Therefore it behooves thee to come, or to yield thee as recreant."

With that he turned his bridle, and galloped out at the hall door, his head in his hands, so that the sparks flew from be-neath his horse's hoofs. Whither he went none knew, no more than they wist whence he had come; and the king and Ga-40 wain they gazed and laughed, for in sooth this had proved a greater marvel than any they had known aforetime.

Though Arthur the king was astonished at his heart, yet he let no sign of it be seen, but spake in courteous wise to the fair queen: "Dear lady, be not dismayed, such craft is well suited to Christmas-tide when we seek jesting, laughter, and song, and fair carols of knights and ladies. But now I may well

get me to meat, for I have seen a marvel I may not forget."
Then he looked on Sir Gawain, and said gaily, "Now, fair
nephew, hang up thine axe, since it has hewn enough," and they
hung it on the dossal [5] above the daïs, where all men might look
on it for a marvel, and by its true token tell of the wonder.
Then the twain sat them down together, the king and the good
knight, and men served them with a double portion, as was
the share of the noblest, with all manner of meat and of minstrelsy. And they spent that day in gladness, but Sir Gawain
must well bethink him of the heavy venture to which he had 10
set his hand.

II

This beginning of adventures had Arthur at the New Year;
for he yearned to hear gallant tales, though his words were
few when he sat at the feast. But now had they stern work on
hand. Gawain was glad to begin the jest in the hall, but ye
need have no marvel if the end be heavy. For though a man
be merry in mind when he has well drunk, yet a year runs
full swiftly, and the beginning but rarely matches the end.

For Yule was now over-past, and the year after, each season in its turn following the other. For after Christmas comes 20
crabbed Lent, that will have fish for flesh and simpler cheer.
But then the weather of the world chides with winter; the
cold withdraws itself, the clouds uplift, and the rain falls in
warm showers on the fair plains. Then the flowers come forth,
meadows and grove are clad in green, the birds make ready to
build, and sing sweetly for solace of the soft summer that follows thereafter. The blossoms bud and blow in the hedgerows
rich and rank, and noble notes enough are heard in the fair
woods.

After the season of summer, with the soft winds, when 30
zephyr breathes lightly on seeds and herbs, joyous indeed is
the growth that waxes thereout when the dew drips from the
leaves beneath the blissful glance of the bright sun. But then
comes harvest and hardens the grain, warning it to wax ripe
ere the winter. The drought drives the dust on high, flying over
the face of the land; the angry wind of the welkin wrestles
with the sun; the leaves fall from the trees and light upon
the ground, and all brown are the groves that but now were
green, and ripe is the fruit that once was flower. So the year
passes into many yesterdays, and winter comes again, as it 40
needs no sage to tell us.

When the Michaelmas moon was come in with warnings of

5 an ornamental hanging

winter, Sir Gawain bethought him full oft of his perilous journey. Yet till All Hallows Day he lingered with Arthur, and on
that day they made a great feast for the hero's sake, with much
revel and richness of the Round Table. Courteous knights and
comely ladies, all were in sorrow for the love of that knight,
and though they spake no word of it, many were joyless for
his sake.

And after meat, sadly Sir Gawain turned to his uncle, and
spake of his journey, and said, "Liege lord of my life, leave
10 from you I crave. Ye know well how the matter stands without more words; to-morrow am I bound to set forth in search
of the Green Knight."

Then came together all the noblest knights, Ywain and
Erec, and many another. Sir Dodinel le Sauvage, the Duke of
Clarence, Launcelot and Lionel, and Lucan the Good, Sir
Bors and Bedivere, valiant knights both, and many another
hero, with Sir Mador de la Porte, and they all drew near, heavy
at heart, to take counsel with Sir Gawain. Much sorrow and
weeping was there in the hall to think that so worthy a knight
20 as Gawain should wend his way to seek a deadly blow, and
should no more wield his sword in fight. But the knight made
ever good cheer, and said, "Nay, wherefore should I shrink?
What may a man do but prove his fate?"

He dwelt there all that day, and on the morn he arose and
asked betimes for his armor; and they brought it unto him
on this wise: first, a rich carpet was stretched on the floor
(and brightly did the gold gear glitter upon it), then the knight
stepped upon it, and handled the steel; clad he was in a doublet
of silk, with a close hood, lined fairly throughout. Then they
30 set the steel shoes upon his feet, and wrapped his legs with
greaves, with polished knee-caps, fastened with knots of gold.
Then they cased his thighs in cuisses closed with thongs, and
brought him the byrnie of bright steel rings sewn upon a fair
stuff. Well burnished braces they set on each arm with good
elbow-pieces, and gloves of mail, and all the goodly gear that
should shield him in his need. And they cast over all a rich
surcoat, and set the golden spurs on his heels, and girt him
with a trusty sword fastened with a silken bawdrick. When he
was thus clad his harness was costly, for the least loop or
40 latchet gleamed with gold. So armed as he was he hearkened
Mass and made his offering at the high altar. Then he came
to the king, and the knights of his court, and courteously took
leave of lords and ladies, and they kissed him, and commended
him to Christ.

With that was Gringalet ready, girt with a saddle that
gleamed gaily with many golden fringes, enriched and decked

anew for the venture. The bridle was all barred about with
bright gold buttons, and all the covertures and trappings of
the steed, the crupper and the rich skirts, accorded with the
saddle; spread fair with the rich red gold that glittered and
gleamed in the rays of the sun.

Then the knight called for his helmet, which was well lined
throughout, and set it high on his head, and hasped it behind.
He wore a light kerchief over the ventail,[6] that was broidered
and studded with fair gems on a broad silken ribbon, with
birds of gay color, and many a turtle [7] and true-lover's knot 10
interlaced thickly, even as many a maiden had wrought diligently for seven winters long. But the circlet which crowned
his helmet was yet more precious, being adorned with a device
in diamonds. Then they brought him his shield, which was of
bright red, with the pentangle painted thereon in gleaming gold.
And why that noble prince bare the pentangle I am minded
to tell you, though my tale tarry thereby. It is a sign that
Solomon set ere-while, as betokening truth; for it is a figure
with five points and each line overlaps the other, and nowhere
hath it beginning or end, so that in English it is called "the 20
endless knot." And therefore was it well suiting to this knight
and to his arms, since Gawain was faithful in five and five-fold,
for pure was he as gold, void of all villainy and endowed with
all virtues. Therefore he bare the pentangle on shield and surcoat as truest of heroes and gentlest of knights.

For first he was faultless in his five senses; and his five
fingers never failed him; and all his trust upon earth was in
the five wounds that Christ bare on the cross, as the Creed
tells. And wherever this knight found himself in stress of battle
he deemed well that he drew his strength from the five joys 30
which the Queen of Heaven had of her Child. And for this
cause did he bear an image of Our Lady on the one half of
his shield, that whenever he looked upon it he might not lack
for aid. And the fifth five that the hero used were frankness
and fellowship above all, purity and courtesy that never failed
him, and compassion that surpasses all; and in these five virtues was that hero wrapped and clothed. And all these, five-
fold, were linked one in the other, so that they had no end,
and were fixed on five points that never failed, neither at any
side were they joined or sundered, nor could ye find begin- 40
ning or end. And therefore on his shield was the knot shapen,
red-gold upon red, which is the pure pentangle. Now was Sir
Gawain ready, and he took his lance in hand, and bade them
all farewell, he deemed it had been for ever.

Then he smote the steed with his spurs, and sprang on his

6 visor   7 turtle-dove

way, so that sparks flew from the stones after him. All that saw him were grieved at heart, and said one to the other, "By Christ, 't is great pity that one of such noble life should be lost! I' faith, 't were not easy to find his equal upon earth. The king had done better to have wrought more warily. Yonder knight should have been made a duke; a gallant leader of men is he, and such a fate had beseemed him better than to be hewn in pieces at the will of an elfish man, for mere pride. Who ever knew a king to take such counsel as to risk his knights on
10 a Christmas jest?" Many were the tears that flowed from their eyes when that goodly knight rode from the hall. He made no delaying, but went his way swiftly, and rode many a wild road, as I heard say in the book.

So rode Sir Gawain through the realm of Logres,[8] on an errand that he held for no jest. Often he lay companionless at night, and must lack the fare that he liked. No comrade had he save his steed, and none save God with whom to take counsel. At length he drew nigh to North Wales, and left the isles of Anglesey on his left hand, crossing over the fords by the
20 foreland over at Holyhead, till he came into the wilderness of Wirral,[9] where but few dwell who love God and man of true heart. And ever he asked, as he fared, of all whom he met, if they had heard any tidings of a Green Knight in the country thereabout, or of a Green Chapel? And all answered him, "Nay," never in their lives had they seen any man of such a hue. And the knight wended his way by many a strange road and many a rugged path, and the fashion of his countenance changed full often ere he saw the Green Chapel.

Many a cliff did he climb in that unknown land, where afar
30 from his friends he rode as a stranger. Never did he come to a stream or a ford but he found a foe before him, and that one so marvelous, so foul and fell, that it behooved him to fight. So many wonders did that knight behold, that it were too long to tell the tenth part of them. Sometimes he fought with dragons and wolves; sometimes with wild men that dwelt in the rocks; another while with bulls, and bears, and wild boars, or with giants of the high moorland that drew near to him. Had he not been a doughty knight, enduring, and of well-proved valor, and a servant of God, doubtless he had been
40 slain, for he was oft in danger of death. Yet he cared not so much for the strife; what he deemed worse was when the cold clear water was shed from the clouds, and froze ere it fell on the fallow ground. More nights than enough he slept in his harness on the bare rocks, near slain with the sleet, while the

8 England   9 in Cheshire

stream leapt bubbling from the crest of the hills, and hung in hard icicles over his head.

Thus in peril and pain, and many a hardship, the knight rode alone till Christmas Eve, and in that tide he made his prayer to the Blessed Virgin that she would guide his steps and lead him to some dwelling. On that morning he rode by a hill, and came into a thick forest, wild and drear; on each side were high hills, and thick woods below them of great hoar oaks, a hundred together, of hazel and hawthorn with their trailing boughs intertwined, and rough ragged moss spreading every- 10 where. On the bare twigs the birds chirped piteously, for pain of the cold. The knight upon Gringalet rode lonely beneath them, through marsh and mire, much troubled at heart lest he should fail to see the service of the Lord, who on that self-same night was born of a maiden for the cure of our grief; and therefore he said, sighing, "I beseech thee, Lord, and Mary thy gentle Mother, for some shelter where I may hear Mass, and thy matins at morn. This I ask meekly, and thereto I pray my Paternoster, Ave, and Credo." Thus he rode praying, and lamenting his misdeeds, and he crossed himself, and said, "May 20 the Cross of Christ speed me."

Now that knight had crossed himself but thrice ere he was aware in the wood of a dwelling within a moat, above a lawn, on a mound surrounded by many mighty trees that stood round the moat. 'T was the fairest castle that ever a knight owned; built in a meadow with a park all about it, and a spiked palisade, closely driven, that enclosed the trees for more than two miles. The knight was aware of the hold from the side, as it shone through the oaks. Then he lifted off his helmet, and thanked Christ and Saint Julian that they had courteously 30 granted his prayer, and hearkened to his cry. "Now," quoth the knight, "I beseech ye, grant me fair hostel." Then he pricked Gringalet with his golden spurs, and rode gaily towards the great gate, and came swiftly to the bridge end.

The bridge was drawn up and the gates close shut; the walls were strong and thick, so that they might fear no tempest. The knight on his charger abode on the bank of the deep double ditch that surrounded the castle. The walls were set deep in the water, and rose aloft to a wondrous height; they were of hard hewn stone up to the corbels, which were adorned be- 40 neath the battlements with fair carvings, and turrets set in between with many a loophole; a better barbican Sir Gawain had never looked upon. And within he beheld the high hall, with its tower and many windows with carven cornices, and chalk-white chimneys on the turreted roofs that shone fair in

the sun. And everywhere, thickly scattered on the castle battlements, were pinnacles, so many that it seemed as if it were
all wrought out of paper, so white was it.

The knight on his steed deemed it fair enough, if he might
come to be sheltered within it to lodge there while that the
holyday lasted. He called aloud, and soon there came a porter
of kindly countenance, who stood on the wall and greeted this
knight and asked his errand.

"Good sir," quoth Gawain, "wilt thou go mine errand to
10 the high lord of the castle, and crave for me lodging?"

"Yea, by Saint Peter," quoth the porter. "In sooth I trow
that ye be welcome to dwell here so long as it may like ye."

Then he went, and came again swiftly, and many folk with
him to receive the knight. They let down the great drawbridge,
and came forth and knelt on their knees on the cold earth to
give him worthy welcome. They held wide open the great gates,
and courteously he bade them rise, and rode over the bridge.
Then men came to him and held his stirrup while he dismounted, and took and stabled his steed. There came down
20 knights and squires to bring the guest with joy to the hall.
When he raised his helmet there were many to take it from
his hand, fain to serve him, and they took from him sword and
shield.

Sir Gawain gave good greeting to the noble and the mighty
men who came to do him honor. Clad in his shining armor
they led him to the hall, where a great fire burned brightly on
the floor; and the lord of the household came forth from his
chamber to meet the hero fitly. He spake to the knight, and
said: "Ye are welcome to do here as it likes ye. All that is
30 here is your own to have at your will and disposal."

"Gramercy!" quoth Gawain, "may Christ requite ye."

As friends that were fain each embraced the other; and Gawain looked on the knight who greeted him so kindly, and
thought 't was a bold warrior that owned that burg.

Of mighty stature he was, and of high age; broad and flowing
was his beard, and of a bright hue. He was stalwart of limb, and
strong in his stride, his face fiery red, and his speech free: in
sooth he seemed one well fitted to be a leader of valiant men.

Then the lord led Sir Gawain to a chamber, and commanded
40 folk to wait upon him, and at his bidding there came men
enough who brought the guest to a fair bower. The bedding
was noble, with curtains of pure silk wrought with gold, and
wondrous coverings of fair cloth all embroidered. The curtains
ran on ropes with rings of red gold, and the walls were hung
with carpets of Orient, and the same spread on the floor. There
with mirthful speeches they took from the guest his byrnie and

all his shining armor, and brought him rich robes of the choicest in its stead. They were long and flowing, and became him well, and when he was clad in them all who looked on the hero thought that surely God had never made a fairer knight: he seemed as if he might be a prince without peer in the field where men strive in battle.

Then before the hearth-place, whereon the fire burned, they made ready a chair for Gawain, hung about with cloth and fair cushions; and there they cast around him a mantle of brown samite, richly embroidered and furred within with costly skins 10 of ermine, with a hood of the same, and he seated himself in that rich seat, and warmed himself at the fire, and was cheered at heart. And while he sat thus, the serving men set up a tabl. on trestles, and covered it with a fair white cloth, and set thereon salt-cellar, and napkin, and silver spoons; and the knight washed at his will, and set him down to meat.

The folk served him courteously with many dishes seasoned of the best, a double portion. All kinds of fish were there, some baked in bread, some broiled on the embers, some sodden,[10] some stewed and savored with spices, with all sorts of 20 cunning devices to his taste. And often he called it a feast, when they spake gaily to him all together, and said, "Now take ye this penance, and it shall be for your amendment." Much mirth thereof did Sir Gawain make.

Then they questioned that prince courteously of whence he came; and he told them that he was of the court of Arthur, who is the rich royal king of the Round Table, and that it was Gawain himself who was within their walls, and would keep Christmas with them, as the chance had fallen out. And when the lord of the castle heard those tidings he laughed 30 aloud for gladness, and all men in that keep were joyful that they should be in the company of him to whom belonged all fame, and valor, and courtesy, and whose honor was praised above that of all men on earth. Each said softly to his fellow, "Now shall we see courteous bearing, and the manner of speech befitting courts. What charm lieth in gentle speech shall we learn without asking, since here we have welcomed the fine father of courtesy. God has surely shown us his grace since he sends us such a guest as Gawain! When men shall sit and sing, blithe for Christ's birth, this knight shall bring us to the 40 knowledge of fair manners, and it may be that hearing him we may learn the cunning speech of love."

By the time the knight had risen from dinner it was near nightfall. Then chaplains took their way to the chapel, and rang loudly, even as they should, for the solemn evensong of

10 boiled

the high feast. Thither went the lord, and ·the lady also, and entered with her maidens into a comely closet, and thither also went Gawain. Then the lord took him by the sleeve and led him to a seat, and called him by his name, and told him he was of all men in the world the most welcome. And Sir Gawain thanked him truly, and each kissed the other, and they . sat gravely together throughout the service.

Then was the lady fain to look upon that knight; and she came forth from her closet with many fair maidens. The fair-
10 est of ladies was she in face, and figure, and coloring, fairer even than Guinevere, so the knight thought. She came through the chancel to greet the hero; another lady held her by the left hand, older than she, and seemingly of high estate, with many nobles about her. But unlike to look upon were those ladies, for if the younger were fair, the elder was yellow. Rich red were the cheeks of the one, rough and wrinkled those of the other; the kerchiefs of the one were broidered with manv glistening pearls, her throat and neck bare, and whiter than the snow that lies on the hills; the neck of the other was
20 swathed in a gorget, with a white wimple over her black chin. Her forehead was wrapped in silk with many folds, worked with knots, so that naught of her was seen save her black brows, her eyes, her nose, and her lips, and those were bleared, and ill to look upon. A worshipful lady in sooth one might call her! In figure was she short and broad, and thickly made —far fairer to behold was she whom she led by the hand.

When Gawain beheld that fair lady, who looked at him graciously, with leave of the lord he went towards them, and, bowing low, he greeted the elder, but the younger and fairer
30 he took lightly in his arms, and kissed her courteously, and greeted her in knightly wise. Then she hailed him as friend, and he quickly prayed to be counted as her servant, if she so willed. Then they took him between them, and talking, led him to the chamber, to the hearth, and bade them bring spices, and they brought them in plenty with the good wine that was wont to be drunk at such seasons. Then the lord sprang to his feet and bade them make merry, and took off his hood, and hung it on a spear, and bade him win the worship thereof who should make most mirth that Christmas-tide. "And I shall try,
40 by my faith, to fool it with the best, by the help of my friends, ere I lose my raiment." Thus with gay words the lord made trial to gladden Gawain with jests that night, till it was time to bid them light the tapers, and Sir Gawain took leave of them and gat him to rest.

In the morn when all men call to mind how Christ our Lord was born on earth to die for us, there is joy, for his sake, in all dwellings of the world; and so was there here on that day. For high feast was held, with many dainties and cunningly cooked messes. On the daïs sat gallant men, clad in their best. The ancient dame sat on the high seat with the lord of the castle beside her. Gawain and the fair lady sat together, even in the midst of the board when the feast was served; and so throughout all the hall each sat in his degree, and was served in order. There was meat, there was mirth, there was much joy, so that to tell thereof would take me too long, though peradventure I might strive to declare it. But Gawain and that fair lady had much joy of each other's company through her sweet words and courteous converse. And there was music made before each prince, trumpets and drums, and merry pipings; each man hearkened his minstrel, and they too hearkened theirs.

So they held high feast that day and the next, and the third day thereafter, and the joy on Saint John's Day was fair to hearken, for 't was the last of the feast and the guests would depart in the gray of the morning. Therefore they awoke early, and drank wine, and danced fair carols, and at last, when it was late, each man took his leave to wend early on his way. Gawain would bid his host farewell, but the lord took him by the hand, and led him to his own chamber beside the hearth, and there he thanked him for the favor he had shown him in honoring his dwelling at that high season, and gladdening his castle with his fair countenance. "I wis, sir, that while I live I shall be held the worthier that Gawain has been my guest at God's own feast."

"Gramercy, sir," quoth Gawain, "in good faith, all the honor is yours, may the High King give it you, and I am but at your will to work your behest, inasmuch as I am beholden to you in great and small by rights."

Then the lord did his best to persuade the knight to tarry with him, but Gawain answered that he might in no wise do so. Then the host asked him courteously what stern behest had driven him at the holy season from the king's court, to fare all alone, ere yet the feast was ended?

"Forsooth," quoth the knight, "ye say but the truth: 't is a high quest and a pressing that hath brought me afield, for I am summoned myself to a certain place, and I know not whither in the world I may wend to find it; so help me Christ, I would give all the kingdom of Logres an I might find it by New Year's morn. Therefore, sir, I make request of you that ye tell me truly if ye ever heard word of the Green Chapel, where it may be found, and the Green Knight that keeps it. For I am pledged by solemn compact sworn between us to meet that knight at the New Year if so I were on life; and of

that same New Year it wants but little—i' faith, I would look
on that hero more joyfully than on any other fair sight! Therefore, by your will, it behooves me to leave you, for I have
but barely three days, and I would as fain fall dead as fail
of mine errand."

Then the lord quoth, laughing, "Now must ye needs stay,
for I will show you your goal, the Green Chapel, ere your
term be at an end, have ye no fear! But ye can take your ease,
friend, in your bed, till the fourth day, and go forth on the
10 first of the year and come to that place at mid-morn to do as
ye will. Dwell here till New Year's Day, and then rise and
set forth, and ye shall be set in the way; 't is not two miles
hence."

Then was Gawain glad, and he laughed gaily. "Now I thank
you for this above all else. Now my quest is achieved I will
dwell here at your will, and otherwise do as ye shall ask."

Then the lord took him, and set him beside him, and bade
the ladies be fetched for their greater pleasure, tho' between
themselves they had solace. The lord, for gladness, made merry
20 jest, even as one who wist not what to do for joy; and he cried
aloud to the knight, "Ye have promised to do the thing I bid
ye: will ye hold to this behest, here, at once?"

"Yea, forsooth," said that true knight, "while I abide in
your burg I am bound by your behest."

"Ye have traveled from far," said the host, "and since then
ye have waked with me, ye are not well refreshed by rest and
sleep, as I know. Ye shall therefore abide in your chamber,
and lie at your ease to-morrow at Mass-tide, and go to meat
when ye will with my wife, who shall sit with you, and com-
30 fort you with her company till I return; and I shall rise early
and go forth to the chase." And Gawain agreed to all this
courteously.

"Sir knight," quoth the host, "we will make a covenant.
Whatsoever I win in the wood shall be yours, and whatever
may fall to your share, that shall ye exchange for it. Let us
swear, friend, to make this exchange, however our hap may
be, for worse or for better."

"I grant ye your will," quoth Gawain the good; "if ye list
so to do, it liketh me well."

40 "Bring hither the wine-cup, the bargain is made," so said
the lord of that castle. They laughed each one, and drank of
the wine, and made merry, these lords and ladies, as it pleased
them. Then with gay talk and merry jest they rose, and stood,
and spoke softly, and kissed courteously, and took leave of
each other. With burning torches, and many a serving-man,
was each led to his couch; yet ere they gat them to bed the old

lord oft repeated their covenant, for he knew well how to make
sport.

III

Full early, ere daylight, the folk rose up; the guests who
would depart called their grooms, and they made them ready,
and saddled the steeds, tightened up the girths, and trussed
up their mails. The knights, all arrayed for riding, leapt up
lightly, and took their bridles, and each rode his way as pleased
him best.

The lord of the land was not the last. Ready for the chase,
with many of his men, he ate a sop hastily when he had heard 10
Mass, and then with blast of the bugle fared forth to the field.
He and his nobles were to horse ere daylight glimmered upon
the earth.

Then the huntsmen coupled their hounds, unclosed the ken-
nel door, and called them out. They blew three blasts gaily
on the bugles, the hounds bayed fiercely, and they that would
go a-hunting checked and chastised them. A hundred hunters
there were of the best, so I have heard tell. Then the trackers
gat them to the trysting-place and uncoupled the hounds, and
the forest rang again with their gay blasts.   20

At the first sound of the hunt the game quaked for fear, and
fled, trembling, along the vale. They betook them to the
heights, but the liers in wait turned them back with loud cries;
the harts they let pass them, and the stags with their spreading antlers, for the lord had forbidden that they should be
slain, but the hinds and the does they turned back, and drave
down into the valleys. Then might ye see much shooting of
arrows. As the deer fled under the boughs a broad whistling
shaft smote and wounded each sorely, so that, wounded and
bleeding, they fell dying on the banks. The hounds followed 30
swiftly on their tracks, and hunters, blowing the horn, sped
after them with ringing shouts as if the cliffs burst asunder.
What game escaped those that shot was run down at the outer
ring. Thus were they driven on the hills, and harassed at the
waters, so well did the men know their work, and the grey-
hounds were so great and swift that they ran them down as
fast as the hunters could slay them. Thus the lord passed the
day in mirth and joyfulness, even to nightfall.

So the lord roamed the woods, and Gawain, that good knight,
lay ever a-bed, curtained about, under the costly coverlet, 40
while the daylight gleamed on the walls. And as he lay half
slumbering, he heard a little sound at the door, and he raised
his head, and caught back a corner of the curtain, and waited

to see what it might be. It was the lovely lady, the lord's wife; she shut the door softly behind her, and turned towards the bed; and Gawain was shamed, laid him down softly and made as if he slept. And she came lightly to the bedside, within the curtain, and sat herself down beside him, to wait till he wakened. The knight lay there awhile, and marveled within himself what her coming might betoken; and he said to himself, " 'T were more seemly if I asked her what hath brought her hither." Then he made feint to waken, and turned towards her, 10 and opened his eyes as one astonished, and crossed himself; and she looked on him laughing, with her cheeks red and white, lovely to behold, and small smiling lips.

"Good morrow, Sir Gawain," said that fair lady; "ye are but a careless sleeper, since one can enter thus. Now are ye taken unawares, and lest ye escape me I shall bind you in your bed; of that be ye assured!" Laughing, she spake these words.

"Good morrow, fair lady," quoth Gawain blithely. "I will do your will, as it likes me well. For I yield me readily, and 20 pray your grace, and that is best, by my faith, since I needs must do so." Thus he jested again, laughing. "But an ye would, fair lady, grant me this grace that ye pray your prisoner to rise. I would get me from bed, and array me better, then could I talk with ye in more comfort."

"Nay, forsooth, fair sir," quoth the lady, "ye shall not rise, I will rede [11] ye better. I shall keep ye here, since ye can do no other, and talk with my knight whom I have captured. For I know well that ye are Sir Gawain, whom all the world worships, wheresoever ye may ride. Your honor and your 30 courtesy are praised by lords and ladies, by all who live. Now ye are here and we are alone, my lord and his men are afield; the serving men in their beds, and my maidens also, and the door shut upon us. And since in this hour I have him that all men love I shall use my time well with speech, while it lasts. Ye are welcome to my company, for it behooves me in sooth to be your servant."

"In good faith," quoth Gawain, "I think me that I am not him of whom ye speak, for unworthy am I of such service as ye here proffer. In sooth, I were glad if I might set myself by 40 word or service to your pleasure; a pure joy would it be to me!"

"In good faith, Sir Gawain," quoth the gay lady, "the praise and the prowess that pleases all ladies I lack them not, nor hold them light; yet are there ladies enough who would liever now have the knight in their hold, as I have ye here, to dally

11 advise

with your courteous words, to bring them comfort and to ease
their cares, than much of the treasure and the gold that are
theirs. And now, through the grace of Him who upholds the
heavens, I have wholly in my power that which they all desire!"

Thus the lady, fair to look upon, made him great cheer,
and Sir Gawain, with modest words, answered her again:
"Madam," he quoth, "may Mary requite ye, for in good faith
I have found in ye a noble frankness. Much courtesy have
other folk shown me, but the honor they have done me is 10
naught to the worship of yourself, who knoweth but good."

"By Mary," quoth the lady, "I think otherwise; for were I
worth all the women alive, and had I the wealth of the world
in my hand, and might choose me a lord to my liking, then, for
all that I have seen in ye, Sir Knight, of beauty and courtesy
and blithe semblance, and for all that I have hearkened and
hold for true, there should be no knight on earth to be chosen
before ye."

"Well I wot," quoth Sir Gawain, "that ye have chosen a
better; but I am proud that ye should so prize me, and as your 20
servant do I hold ye my sovereign, and your knight am I,
and may Christ reward ye."

So they talked of many matters till mid-morn was past, and
ever the lady made as though she loved him, and the knight
turned her speech aside. For though she were the brightest
of maidens, yet had he forborne to show her love for the danger that awaited him, and the blow that must be given without delay.

Then the lady prayed her leave from him, and he granted
it readily. And she gave him good-day, with laughing glance, 30
but he must needs marvel at her words:

"Now He that speeds fair speech reward ye this disport;
but that ye be Gawain my mind misdoubts me greatly."

"Wherefore?" quoth the knight quickly, fearing lest he had
lacked in some courtesy.

And the lady spake: "So true a knight as Gawain is holden,
and one so perfect in courtesy, would never have tarried so
long with a lady but he would of his courtesy have craved a
kiss at parting."

Then quoth Gawain, "I wot I will do even as it may please 40
ye, and kiss at your commandment, as a true knight should
who forbears to ask for fear of displeasure."

At that she came near and bent down and kissed the knight,
and each commended the other to Christ, and she went forth
from the chamber softly.

Then Sir Gawain rose and called his chamberlain and chose

his garments, and when he was ready he gat him forth to
Mass, and then went to meat, and made merry all day till
the rising of the moon, and never had a knight fairer lodging
than had he with those two noble ladies, the elder and the
younger.

And ever the lord of the land chased the hinds through holt
and heath till eventide, and then with much blowing of bugles
and baying of hounds they bore the game homeward; and by
the time daylight was done all the folk had returned to that
10 fair castle. And when the lord and Sir Gawain met together,
then were they both well pleased. The lord commanded them
all to assemble in the great hall, and the ladies to descend
with their maidens, and there, before them all, he bade the
men fetch in the spoil of the day's hunting, and he called unto
Gawain, and counted the tale of the beasts, and showed them
unto him, and said, "What think ye of this game, Sir Knight?
Have I deserved of ye thanks for my woodcraft?"

"Yea, I wis," quoth the other, "here is the fairest spoil I
have seen this seven year in the winter season."

20 "And all this do I give ye, Gawain," quoth the host, "for by
accord of covenant ye may claim it as your own."

"That in sooth," quoth the other, "I grant you that same;
and I have fairly won this within walls, and with as good will
do I yield it to you." With that he clasped his hands round the
lord's neck and kissed him as courteously as he might. "Take
ye here my spoils, no more have I won; ye should have it
freely, though it were greater than this."

" 'T is good," said the host, "gramercy thereof. Yet were I
fain to know where ye won this same favor, and if it were by
30 your own wit?"

"Nay," answered Gawain, "that was not in the bond. Ask
me no more: ye have taken what was yours by right, be content with that."

They laughed and jested together, and sat them down to
supper, where they were served with many dainties; and after
supper they sat by the hearth, and wine was served out to
them; and oft in their jesting they promised to observe on the
morrow the same covenant that they had made before, and
whatever chance might betide, to exchange their spoil, be it
40 much or little, when they met at night. Thus they renewed
their bargain before the whole court, and then the night-drink
was served, and each courteously took leave of the other and
gat him to bed.

By the time the cock had crowed thrice the lord of the castle
had left his bed; Mass was sung and meat fitly served. The
folk were forth to the wood ere the day broke, with hound

and horn they rode over the plain, and uncoupled their dogs among the thorns. Soon they struck on the scent, and the hunt cheered on the hounds who were first to seize it, urging them with shouts. The other hastened to the cry, forty at once, and there rose such a clamor from the pack that the rocks rang again. The huntsmen spurred them on with shouting and blasts of the horn; and the hounds drew together to a thicket betwixt the water and a high crag in the cliff beneath the hillside. There where the rough rock fell ruggedly they, the huntsmen, fared to the finding, and cast about round the hill and the thicket be- 10 hind them. The knights wist well what beast was within, and would drive him forth with the bloodhounds. And as they beat the bushes, suddenly over the beaters there rushed forth a wondrous great and fierce boar, long since had he left the herd to roam by himself. Grunting, he cast many to the ground, and fled forth at his best speed, without more mischief. The men hallooed loudly and cried, "Hay! Hay!" and blew the horns to urge on the hounds, and rode swiftly after the boar. Many a time did he turn to bay and tare the hounds, and they yelped, and howled shrilly. Then the men made ready their arrows 20 and shot at him, but the points were turned on his thick hide, and the barbs would not bite upon him, for the shafts shivered in pieces, and the head but leapt again wherever it hit.

But when the boar felt the stroke of the arrows he waxed mad with rage, and turned on the hunters and tare many, so that, affrighted, they fled before him. But the lord on a swift steed pursued him, blowing his bugle; as a gallant knight he rode through the woodland chasing the boar till the sun grew low.

So did the hunters this day, while Sir Gawain lay in his bed 30 lapped in rich gear; and the lady forgat not to salute him, for early was she at his side, to cheer his mood.

She came to the bedside and looked on the knight, and Gawain gave her fit greeting, and she greeted him again with ready words, and sat her by his side and laughed, and with a sweet look she spoke to him:

"Sir, if ye be Gawain, I think it a wonder that ye be so stern and cold, and care not for the courtesies of friendship, but if one teach ye to know them ye cast the lesson out of your mind. Ye have soon forgotten what I taught ye yester- 40 day, by all the truest tokens that I knew!"

"What is that?" quoth the knight. "I trow I know not. If it be sooth that ye say, then is the blame mine own."

"But I taught ye of kissing," quoth the fair lady. "Wherever a fair countenance is shown him, it behooves a courteous knight quickly to claim a kiss."

"Nay, my dear," said Sir Gawain, "cease that speech; that durst I not do lest I were denied, for if I were forbidden I wot I were wrong did I further entreat."

"I' faith," quoth the lady merrily, "ye may not be forbid, ye are strong enough to constrain by strength an ye will, were any so discourteous as to give ye denial."

"Yea, by heaven," said Gawain, "ye speak well; but threats profit little in the land where I dwell, and so with a gift that is given not of good will! I am at your commandment to kiss
10 when ye like, to take or to leave as ye list."

Then the lady bent her down and kissed him courteously.

And as they spake together she said, "I would learn somewhat from ye, an ye would not be wroth, for young ye are and fair, and so courteous and knightly as ye are known to be, the head of all chivalry, and versed in all wisdom of love and war—'t is ever told of true knights how they adventured their lives for their true love, and endured hardships for her favors, and avenged her with valor, and eased her sorrows, and brought joy to her bower; and ye are the fairest knight of your
20 time, and your fame and your honor are everywhere, yet I have sat by ye here twice, and never a word have I heard of love! Ye who are so courteous and skilled in such love ought surely to teach one so young and unskilled some little craft of true love! Why are ye so unlearned who art otherwise so famous? Or is it that ye deemed me unworthy to hearken to your teaching? For shame, Sir Knight! I come hither alone and sit at your side to learn of ye some skill; teach me of your wit, while my lord is from home."

"In good faith," quoth Gawain, "great is my joy and my
30 profit that so fair a lady as ye are should deign to come hither, and trouble ye with so poor a man, and make sport with your knight with kindly countenance, it pleaseth me much. But that I, in my turn, should take it upon me to tell of love and such like matters to ye who know more by half, or a hundred fold, of such craft than I do, or ever shall in all my lifetime, by my troth 't were folly indeed! I will work your will to the best of my might as I am bounden, and evermore will I be your servant, so help me Christ!"

Then often with guile she questioned that knight that she
40 might win him to woo her, but he defended himself so fairly that none might in any wise blame him, and naught but bliss and harmless jesting was there between them. They laughed and talked together till at last she kissed him, and craved her leave of him, and went her way.

Then the knight rose and went forth to Mass, and afterward dinner was served and he sat and spake with the ladies all day. But the lord of the castle rode ever over the land chasing the wild boar, that fled through the thickets, slaying the best of his hounds and breaking their backs in sunder; till at last he was so weary he might run no longer, but made for a hole in a mound by a rock. He got the mound at his back and faced the hounds, whetting his white tusks and foaming at the mouth. The huntsmen stood aloof, fearing to draw nigh him; so many of them had been already wounded that they were loath to be torn with his tusks, so fierce he was and mad with rage. At length the lord himself came up, and saw the beast at bay, 10 and the men standing aloof. Then quickly he sprang to the ground and drew out a bright blade, and waded through the stream to the boar.

When the beast was aware of the knight with weapon in hand, he set up his bristles and snorted loudly, and many feared for their lord lest he should be slain. Then the boar leapt upon the knight so that beast and man were one atop of the other in the water; but the boar had the worst of it, for the man had marked, even as he sprang, and set the point of his brand to the beast's chest, and drove it up to the hilt, 20 so that the heart was split in twain, and the boar fell snarling, and was swept down by the water to where a hundred hounds seized on him, and the men drew him to shore for the dogs to slay.

Then was there loud blowing of horns and baying of hounds, the huntsmen smote off the boar's head, and hung the carcass by the four feet to a stout pole, and so went on their way homewards. The head they bore before the lord himself, who had slain the beast at the ford by force of his strong hand.

It seemed him o'er long ere he saw Sir Gawain in the hall, 30 and he called, and the guest came to take that which fell to his share. And when he saw Gawain the lord laughed aloud, and bade them call the ladies and the household together, and he showed them the game, and told them the tale, how they hunted the wild boar through the woods, and of his length and breadth and height; and Sir Gawain commended his deeds and praised him for his valor, well proven, for so mighty a beast had he never seen before.

Then they handled the huge head, and the lord said aloud, "Now, Gawain, this game is your own by sure covenant, as 40 ye right well know."

" 'T is sooth," quoth the knight, "and as truly will I give ye all I have gained." He took the host round the neck, and kissed him courteously twice. "Now are we quits," he said, "this eventide, of all the covenants that we made since I came hither."

And the lord answered, "By Saint Giles, ye are the best I know; ye will be rich in a short space if ye drive such bargains!"

Then they set up the tables on trestles, and covered them with fair cloths, and lit waxen tapers on the walls. The knights sat and were served in the hall, and much game and glee was there round the hearth, with many songs, both at supper and after; song of Christmas, and new carols, with all the mirth one may think of. And ever that lovely lady sat by the knight,
10 and with still stolen looks made such feint of pleasing him, that Gawain marveled much, and was wroth with himself, but he could not for his courtesy return her fair glances, but dealt with her cunningly, however she might strive to wrest the thing.

When they had tarried in the hall so long as it seemed them good, they turned to the inner chamber and the wide hearth-place, and there they drank wine, and the host proffered to renew the covenant for New Year's Eve; but the knight craved leave to depart on the morrow, for it was nigh to the term
20 when he must fulfil his pledge. But the lord would withhold him from so doing, and prayed him to tarry, and said:

"As I am a true knight I swear my troth that ye shall come to the Green Chapel to achieve your task on New Year's morn, long before prime.[12] Therefore abide ye in your bed, and I will hunt in this wood, and hold ye to the covenant to exchange with me against all the spoil I may bring hither. For twice have I tried ye, and found ye true, and the morrow shall be the third time and the best. Make we merry now while we may, and think on joy, for misfortune may take a man when-
30 soever it wills."

Then Gawain granted his request, and they brought them drink, and they gat them with lights to bed.

Sir Gawain lay and slept softly, but the lord, who was keen on woodcraft, was afoot early. After Mass he and his men ate a morsel, and he asked for his steed; all the knights who should ride with him were already mounted before the hall gates.

'T was a fair frosty morning, for the sun rose red in ruddy vapor, and the welkin was clear of clouds. The hunters scat-
40 tered them by a forest side, and the rocks rang again with the blast of their horns. Some came on the scent of a fox, and a hound gave tongue; the huntsmen shouted, and the pack followed in a crowd on the trail. The fox ran before them, and when they saw him they pursued him with noise and much shouting, and he wound and turned through many a thick

12 probably nine o'clock

grove, often cowering and hearkening in a hedge. At last by a little ditch he leapt out of a spinney, stole away slily by a copse path, and so out of the wood and away from the hounds. But he went, ere he wist, to a chosen tryst, and three started forth on him at once, so he must needs double back, and betake him to the wood again.

Then was it joyful to hearken to the hounds; when all the pack had met together and had sight of their game they made as loud a din as if all the lofty cliffs had fallen clattering together. The huntsmen shouted and threatened, and followed 10 close upon him so that he might scarce escape, but Reynard was wily, and he turned and doubled upon them and led the lord and his men over the hills, now on the slopes, now in the vales, while the knight at home slept through the cold morning beneath his costly curtains.

But the fair lady of the castle rose betimes, and clad herself in a rich mantle that reached even to the ground, left her throat and her fair neck bare, and was bordered and lined with costly furs. On her head she wore no golden circlet, but a network of precious stones, that gleamed and shone through her tresses in 20 clusters of twenty together. Thus she came into the chamber, closed the door after her, and set open a window, and called to him gaily, "Sir Knight, how may ye sleep? The morning is so fair."

Sir Gawain was deep in slumber, and in his dream he vexed him much for the destiny that should befall him on the morrow, when he should meet the knight at the Green Chapel, and abide his blow; but when the lady spake he heard her, and came to himself, and roused from his dream and answered swiftly. The lady came laughing, and kissed him courteously, 30 and he welcomed her fittingly with a cheerful countenance. He saw her so glorious and gaily dressed, so faultless of features and complexion, that it warmed his heart to look upon her.

They spake to each other smiling, and all was bliss and good cheer between them. They exchanged fair words, and much happiness was therein, yet was there a gulf between them, and she might win no more of her knight, for that gallant prince watched well his words—he would neither take her love, nor frankly refuse it. He cared for his courtesy, lest he be 40 deemed churlish, and yet more for his honor lest he be traitor to his host. "God forbid," quoth he to himself, 'that it should so befall." Thus with courteous words did he set aside all the special speeches that came from her lips.

Then spake the lady to the knight, "Ye deserve blame if ye hold not that lady who sits beside ye above all else in the

world, if ye have not already a love whom ye hold dearer, and
like better, and have sworn such firm faith to that lady that ye
care not to loose it—and that am I now fain to believe. And
now I pray ye straitly that ye tell me that in truth, and hide
it not."

And the knight answered. "By Saint John" (and he smiled
as he spake), "no such love have I, nor do I think to have yet
awhile."

"That is the worst word I may hear," quoth the lady, "but
10 in sooth I have mine answer; kiss me now courteously, and I
will go hence; I can but mourn as a maiden that loves much."

Sighing, she stooped down and kissed him, and then she
rose up and spake as she stood, "Now, dear, as our parting
do me this grace, give me some gift, if it were but thy glove,
that I may bethink me of my knight, and lessen my mourning."

"Now, I wis," quoth the knight, "I would that I had here the
most precious thing that I possess on earth that I might leave
ye as love-token, great or small, for ye have deserved forsooth
20 more reward than I might give ye. But it is not to your honor
to have at this time a glove for reward as gift from Gawain,
and I am here on a strange errand, and have no man with
me, nor mails with goodly things—that mislikes me much, lady,
at this time; but each man must fare as he is taken, if for
sorrow and ill."

"Nay, knight highly honored," quoth that lovesome lady,
"though I have naught of yours, yet shall ye have somewhat of
mine." With that she reached him a ring of red gold with a
sparkling stone therein, that shone even as the sun (wit ye well,
30 it was worth many marks); but the knight refused it, and
spake readily.

"I will take no gift, lady, at this time. I have none to give,
and none will I take."

She prayed him to take it, but he refused her prayer, and
sware in sooth that he would not have it.

The lady was sorely vexed, and said, "If ye refuse my ring
as too costly, that ye will not be so highly beholden to me, I
will give you my girdle as a lesser gift." With that she loosened
a lace that was fastened at her side, knit upon her kirtle under
40 her mantle. It was wrought of green silk, and gold, only
braided by the fingers, and that she offered to the knight, and
besought him though it were of little worth that he would take
it, and he said nay, he would touch neither gold nor gear ere
God give him grace to achieve the adventure for which he had
come hither. "And therefore, I pray ye, displease ye not, and
ask me no longer, for I may not grant it. I am dearly beholden

to ye for the favor ye have shown me, and ever, in heat and
cold, will I be your true servant."

"Now," said the lady, "ye refuse this silk, for it is simple in
itself, and so it seems, indeed; lo, it is small to look upon and
less in cost, but whoso knew the virtue that is knit therein he
would, peradventure, value it more highly. For whatever knight
is girded with this green lace, while he bears it knotted about
him there is no man under heaven can overcome him, for he
may not be slain for any magic on earth."

Then Gawain bethought him, and it came into his heart 10
that this were a jewel for the jeopardy that awaited him when
he came to the Green Chapel to seek the return blow—could he
so order it that he should escape unslain, 't were a craft worth
trying. Then he bare with her chiding, and let her say her
say, and she pressed the girdle on him and prayed him to
take it, and he granted her prayer, and she gave it him with
good will, and besought him for her sake never to reveal it
but to hide it loyally from her lord, and the knight agreed
that never should any man know it, save they two alone. He
thanked her often and heartily, and she kissed him for the 20
third time.

Then she took her leave of him, and when she was gone
Sir Gawain rose, and clad him in rich attire, and took the
girdle, and knotted it round him, and hid it beneath his robes.
Then he took his way to the chapel, and sought out a priest
privily and prayed him to teach him better how his soul might
be saved when he should go hence; and there he shrived him,
and showed his misdeeds, both great and small, and besought
mercy and craved absolution; and the priest assoiled [13] him,
and set him as clean as if doomsday had been on the mor- 30
row. And afterwards Sir Gawain made him merry with the
ladies, with carols, and all kinds of joy, as never he did but
that one day, even to nightfall; and all the men marveled at
him, and said that never since he came thither had he been so
merry.

Meanwhile the lord of the castle was abroad chasing the fox;
awhile he lost him, and as he rode through a spinney he heard
the hounds near at hand, and Reynard came creeping through
a thick grove, with all the pack at his heels. Then the lord drew
out his shining brand, and cast it at the beast, and the fox 40
swerved aside for the sharp edge, and would have doubled
back, but a hound was on him ere he might turn, and right
before the horse's feet they all fell on him, and worried him
fiercely, snarling the while.

Then the lord leapt from his saddle, and caught the fox from

13 absolved

the jaws, and held it aloft over his head, and hallooed loudly, and many brave hounds bayed as they beheld it; and the hunters hied them thither, blowing their horns; all that bare bugles blew them at once, and all the others shouted. 'T was the merriest meeting that ever men heard, the clamor that was raised at the death of the fox. They rewarded the hounds, stroking them and rubbing their heads, and took Reynard and stripped him of his coat; then blowing their horns, they turned them homewards, for it was nigh nightfall.

10 The lord was gladsome at his return, and found a bright fire on the hearth, and the knight beside it, the good Sir Gawain, who was in joyous mood for the pleasure he had had with the ladies. He wore a robe of blue, that reached even to the ground, and a surcoat richly furred, that became him well. A hood like to the surcoat fell on his shoulders, and all alike were done about with fur. He met the host in the midst of the floor, and jesting, he greeted him, and said, "Now shall I be first to fulfil our covenant which we made together when there was no lack of wine." Then he embraced the knight, and kissed him thrice,
20 as solemnly as he might.

"Of a sooth," quoth the other, "ye have good luck in the matter of this covenant, if ye made a good exchange!"

"Yet, it matters naught of the exchange," quoth Gawain, "since what I owe is swiftly paid."

"Marry," said the other, "mine is behind, for I have hunted all this day, and naught have I got but this foul fox-skin, and that is but poor payment for three such kisses as ye have here given me."

"Enough," quoth Sir Gawain, "I thank ye, by the Rood."

30 Then the lord told them of his hunting, and how the fox had been slain.

With mirth and minstrelsy, and dainties at their will, they made them as merry as a folk well might till 't was time for them to sever, for at last they must needs betake them to their beds. Then the knight took his leave of the lord, and thanked him fairly.

"For the fair sojourn that I have had here at this high feast may the High King give ye honor. I give ye myself, as one of your servants, if ye so like; for I must needs, as you know, go
40 hence with the morn, and ye will give me, as ye promised, a guide to show me the way to the Green Chapel, an God will suffer me on New Year's Day to deal the doom of my weird." [14]

"By my faith," quoth the host, "all that ever I promised, that shall I keep with good will." Then he gave him a servant to set him in the way, and lead him by the downs, that he should

14 to take the judgment of my fate

have no need to ford the stream, and should fare by the shortest road through the groves; and Gawain thanked the lord for the honor done him. Then he would take leave of the ladies, and courteously he kissed them, and spake, praying them to receive his thanks, and they made like reply; then with many sighs they commended him to Christ, and he departed courteously from that fold. Each man that he met he thanked him for his service and his solace, and the pains he had been at to do his will; and each found it as hard to part from the knight as if he had ever dwelt with him.

Then they led him with torches to his chamber, and brought him to his bed to rest. That he slept soundly I may not say, for the morrow gave him much to think on. Let him rest awhile, for he was near that which he sought, and if ye will but listen to me I will tell ye how it fared with him thereafter.

IV

Now the New Year drew nigh, and the night passed, and the day chased the darkness, as is God's will; but wild weather wakened therewith. The clouds cast the cold to the earth, with enough of the north to slay them that lacked clothing. The snow drave smartly, and the whistling wind blew from the heights, and made great drifts in the valleys. The knight, lying in his bed, listened, for though his eyes were shut, he might sleep but little, and hearkened every cock that crew.

He arose ere the day broke, by the light of a lamp that burned in his chamber, and called to his chamberlain, bidding him bring his armor and saddle his steed. The other gat him up, and fetched his garments, and robed Sir Gawain.

First he clad him in his clothes to keep off the cold, and then in his harness, which was well and fairly kept. Both hauberk and plates were well burnished, the rings of the rich byrnie freed from rust, and all as fresh as at first, so that the knight was fain to thank them. Then he did on each piece, and bade them bring his steed, while he put the fairest raiment on himself; his coat with its fair cognizance, adorned with precious stones upon velvet, with broidered seams, and all furred within with costly skins. And he left not the lace, the lady's gift, that Gawain forgot not, for his own good. When he had girded on his sword he wrapped the gift twice about him, swathed around his waist. The girdle of green silk set gaily and well upon the royal red cloth, rich to behold, but the knight ware it not for pride of the pendants, polished though they were with fair gold that gleamed brightly on the ends, but to save himself from sword and knife, when it behooved him to abide his hurt without question. With that the hero went forth, and thanked that kindly folk full often.

Then was Gringalet ready, that was great and strong, and had been well cared for and tended in every wise; in fair condition was that proud steed, and fit for a journey. Then Gawain went to him, and looked on his coat, and said by his sooth, "There is a folk in this place that thinketh on honor; much joy may they have, and the lord who maintains them, and may all good betide that lovely lady all her life long. Since they for charity
10 cherish a guest, and hold honor in their hands, may he who holds the heaven on high requite them, and also ye all. And if I might live anywhile on earth, I would give ye full reward, readily, if so I might." Then he set foot in the stirrup and bestrode his steed, and his squire gave him his shield, which he laid on his shoulder. Then he smote Gringalet with his golden spurs, and the steed pranced on the stones and would stand no longer.

By that his man was mounted, who bare his spear and lance, and Gawain quoth, "I commend this castle to Christ, may he give it ever good fortune." Then the drawbridge was let down,
20 and the broad gates unbarred and opened on both sides; the knight crossed himself, and passed through the gateway, and praised the porter, who knelt before the prince, and gave him good-day, and commended him to God. Thus the knight went on his way, with the one man who should guide him to that dread place where he should receive rueful payment.

The two went by hedges where the boughs were bare, and climbed the cliffs where the cold clings. Naught fell from the heavens, but 't was ill beneath them; mist brooded over the moor and hung on the mountains; each hill had a cap, a great cloak, of
30 mist. The streams foamed and bubbled between their banks, dashing sparkling on the shores where they shelved downwards. Rugged and dangerous was the way through the woods, till it was time for the sun-rising. Then were they on a high hill; the snow lay white beside them, and the man who rode with Gawain drew rein by his master.

"Sir," he said, "I have brought ye hither, and now ye are not far from the place that ye have sought so specially. But I will tell ye for sooth, since I know ye well, and ye are such a knight as I well love, would ye follow my counsel ye would fare the
40 better. The place whither ye go is accounted full perilous, for he who liveth in that waste is the worst on earth, for he is strong and fierce; and loveth to deal mighty blows; taller he is than any man on earth, and greater of frame than any four in Arthur's court, or in any other. And this is his custom at the Green Chapel; there may no man pass by that place, however proud his arms, but he does him to death by force of his hand, for he is

a discourteous knight, and shows no mercy. Be he churl or chaplain who rides by that chapel, monk or mass-priest, or any man
else, he thinks it as pleasant to slay them as to pass alive himself. Therefore, I tell ye, as sooth as ye sit in saddle, if ye come
there and that knight know it, ye shall be slain, though ye had
twenty lives; trow me that truly! He has dwelt here full long
and seen many a combat; ye may not defend ye against his
blows. Therefore, good Sir Gawain, let the man be, and get ye
away some other road; for God's sake seek ye another land,
and there may Christ speed ye! And I will hie me home again, 10
and I promise ye further that I will swear by God and the saints,
or any other oath ye please, that I will keep counsel faithfully,
and never let any wit the tale that ye fled for fear of any man."
   "Gramercy," quoth Gawain, but ill-pleased. "Good fortune
be his who wishes me good, and that thou wouldst keep faith
with me I will believe; but didst thou keep it never so truly, an
I passed here and fled for fear as thou sayest, then were I a
coward knight, and might not be held guiltless. So I will to the
chapel let chance what may, and talk with that man, even as I
may list, whether for weal or for woe as fate may have it. Fierce 20
though he may be in fight, yet God knoweth well how to save his
servants."
   "Well," quoth the other, "now that ye have said so much that
ye will take your own harm on yourself, and ye be pleased to
lose your life, I will neither let [15] nor keep ye. Have here your
helm and the spear in your hand, and ride down this same road
beside the rock till ye come to the bottom of the valley, and
there look a little to the left hand, and ye shall see in that vale
the chapel, and the grim man who keeps it. Now fare ye well,
noble Gawain; for all the gold on earth I would not go with ye 30
nor bear ye fellowship one step further." With that the man
turned his bridle into the wood, smote the horse with his spurs
as hard as he could, and galloped off, leaving the knight alone.
   Quoth Gawain, "I will neither greet nor moan, but commend
myself to God, and yield me to his will."
   Then the knight spurred Gringalet, and rode adown the path
close in by a bank beside a grove. So he rode through the rough
thicket, right into the dale, and there he halted, for it seemed
him wild enough. No sign of a chapel could he see, but high and
burnt banks on either side and rough rugged crags with great 40
stones above. An ill-looking place he thought it.
   Then he drew in his horse and looked round to seek the chapel,
but he saw none and thought it strange. Then he saw as it were
a mound on a level space of land by a bank beside the stream
where it ran swiftly; the water bubbled within as if boiling. The

15 hinder

knight turned his steed to the mound, and lighted down and tied the rein to the branch of a linden; and he turned to the mound and walked round it, questioning with himself what it might be. It had a hole at the end and at either side, and was overgrown with clumps of grass, and it was hollow within as an old cave or the crevice of a crag; he knew not what it might be.

"Ah," quoth Gawain, "can this be the Green Chapel? Here might the devil say his matins at midnight! Now I wis there is wizardry here. 'Tis an ugly oratory, all overgrown with grass,
10 and 't would well beseem that fellow in green to say his devotions on devil's wise. Now feel I in five wits, 't is the foul fiend himself who hath set me this tryst, to destroy me here! This is a chapel of mischance: ill-luck betide it, 't is the cursedest kirk that ever I came in!"

Helmet on head and lance in hand, he came up to the rough dwelling, when he heard over the high hill beyond the brook, as it were in a bank, a wondrous fierce noise, that rang in the cliff as if it would cleave asunder. 'T was as if one ground a scythe on a grindstone, it whirred and whetted like water on a
20 mill-wheel and rushed and rang, terrible to hear.

"By God," quoth Gawain, "I trow that gear is preparing for the knight who will meet me here. Alas! naught may help me, yet should my life be forfeit, I fear not a jot!" With that he called aloud, "Who waiteth in this place to give me tryst? Now is Gawain come hither: if any man will aught of him let him hasten hither now or never."

"Stay," quoth one on the bank above his head, "and ye shall speedily have that which I promised ye." Yet for a while the noise of whetting went on ere he appeared, and then he came
30 forth from a cave in the crag with a fell weapon, a Danish axe newly dight, wherewith to deal the blow. An evil head it had, four feet large, no less, sharply ground, and bound to the handle by the lace that gleamed brightly. And the knight himself was all green as before, face and foot, locks and beard, but now he was afoot. When he came to the water he would not wade it, but sprang over with the pole of his axe, and strode boldly over the bent that was white with snow.

Sir Gawain went to meet him, but he made no low bow. The other said, "Now, fair sir, one may trust thee to keep tryst. Thou
40 art welcome, Gawain, to my place. Thou hast timed thy coming as befits a true man. Thou knowest the covenant set between us: at this time twelve months agone thou didst take that which fell to thee, and I at this New Year will readily requite thee. We are in this valley, verily alone, here are no knights to sever us, do what we will. Have off thy helm from thine head, and have

here thy pay; make me no more talking than I did then when thou didst strike off my head with one blow."

"Nay," quoth Gawain, "by God that gave me life, I shall make no moan whatever befall me, but make thou ready for the blow and I shall stand still and say never a word to thee, do as thou wilt."

With that he bent his head and showed his neck all bare, and made as if he had no fear, for he would not be thought a-dread.

Then the Green Knight made him ready and grasped his grim weapon to smite Gawain. With all his force he bore it aloft with 10 a mighty feint of slaying him: had it fallen as straight as he aimed he who was ever doughty of deed had been slain by the blow. But Gawain swerved aside as the axe came gliding down to slay him as he stood, and shrank a little with the shoulders, for the sharp iron. The other heaved up the blade and rebuked the prince with many proud words:

"Thou art not Gawain," he said, "who is held so valiant, that never feared he man by hill or vale, but thou shrinkest for fear ere thou feelest hurt. Such cowardice did I never hear of Gawain! Neither did *I* flinch from thy blow, or make strife in King 20 Arthur's hall. My head fell to my feet, and yet I fled not; but thou didst wax faint of heart ere any harm befell. Wherefore must I be deemed the braver knight."

Quoth Gawain, "I shrank once, but so will I no more; though an my head fall on the stones I cannot replace it. But haste, Sir Knight, by thy faith, and bring me to the point, deal me my destiny, and do it out of hand, for I will stand thee a stroke and move no more till thine axe have hit me—my troth on it."

"Have at thee, then," quoth the other, and heaved aloft the axe with fierce mien, as if he were mad. He struck at him fiercely 30 but wounded him not, withholding his hand ere it might strike him.

Gawain abode the stroke, and flinched in no limb, but stood still as a stone or the stump of a tree that is fast rooted in the rocky ground with a hundred roots.

Then spake gaily the man in green, "So now thou hast thine heart whole it behooves me to smite. Hold aside thy hood that Arthur gave thee, and keep thy neck thus bent lest it cover it again."

Then Gawain said angrily, "Why talk on thus? Thou dost 40 threaten too long. I hope thy heart misgives thee."

"Forsooth," quoth the other, "so fiercely thou speakest I will no longer let thine errand wait its reward." Then he braced himself to strike, frowning with lips and brow, 't was no marvel that it pleased but ill him who hoped for no rescue. He lifted the

axe lightly and let fall with the edge of the blade on the bare neck. Though he struck swiftly, it hurt him no more than on the one side where it severed the skin. The sharp blade cut into the flesh so that the blood ran over his shoulder to the ground. And when the knight saw the blood staining the snow, he sprang forth, swift-foot, more than a spear's length, seized his helmet and set it on his head, cast his shield over his shoulder, drew out his bright sword, and spake boldly (never since he was born was he half so blithe), "Stop, Sir Knight, bid me no more blows, I have
10 stood a stroke here without flinching, and if thou give me another, I shall requite thee, and give thee as good again. By the covenant made betwixt us in Arthur's hall but one blow falls to me here. Halt, therefore."

Then the Green Knight drew off from him and leaned on his axe, setting the shaft on the ground, and looked on Gawain as he stood all armed and faced him fearlessly—at heart it pleased him well. Then he spake merrily in a loud voice, and said to the knight, "Bold sir, be not so fierce; no man here hath done thee wrong, nor will do, save by covenant, as we made at Arthur's
20 court. I promised thee a blow and thou hast it—hold thyself well paid! I release thee of all other claims. If I had been so minded I might perchance have given thee a rougher buffet. First I menaced thee with a feigned one, and hurt thee not for the covenant that we made in the first night, and which thou didst hold truly. All the gain didst thou give me as a true man should. The other feint I proffered thee for the morrow: my fair wife kissed thee, and thou didst give me her kisses—for both those days I gave thee two blows without scathe—true man, true return. But the third time thou didst fail, and therefore hadst thou
30 that blow. For 't is *my* weed thou wearest, that same woven girdle, my own wife wrought it, that do I wot for sooth. Now know I well thy kisses, and thy conversation, and the wooing of my wife, for 't was mine own doing. I sent her to try thee, and in sooth I think thou art the most faultless knight that ever trod earth. As a pearl among white peas is of more worth than they, so is Gawain, i' faith, by other knights. But thou didst lack a little, Sir Knight, and wast wanting in loyalty, yet that was for no evil work, nor for wooing neither, but because thou lovedst thy life—therefore I blame thee the less."
40 Then the other stood a great while, still sorely angered and vexed within himself; all the blood flew to his face, and he shrank for shame as the Green Knight spake; and the first words he said were, "Cursed be ye, cowardice and covetousness, for in ye is the destruction of virtue." Then he loosed the girdle, and gave it to the knight. "Lo, take there the falsity, may foul befall it!

For fear of thy blow cowardice bade me make friends with covetousness and forsake the customs of largess and loyalty, which
befit all knights. Now am I faulty and false and have been
afeared: from treachery and untruth come sorrow and care. I
avow to thee, Sir Knight, that I have ill done; do then thy will.
I shall be more wary hereafter."

Then the other laughed and said gaily, "I wot I am whole
of the hurt I had, and thou hast made such free confession of thy
misdeeds, and hast so borne the penance of mine axe edge, that
I hold thee absolved from that sin, and purged as clean as if 10
thou hadst never sinned since thou wast born. And this girdle
that is wrought with gold and green, like my raiment, do I give
thee, Sir Gawain, that thou mayest think upon this chance when
thou goest forth among princes of renown, and keep this for a
token of the adventure of the Green Chapel, as it chanced between chivalrous knights. And thou shalt come again with me to
my dwelling and pass the rest of this feast in gladness." Then
the lord laid hold of him, and said, "I wot we shall soon make
peace with my wife, who was thy bitter enemy."

"Nay, forsooth," said Sir Gawain, and seized his helmet and 20
took it off swiftly, and thanked the knight: "I have fared ill,
may bliss betide thee, and may he who rules all things reward
thee swiftly. Commend me to that courteous lady, thy fair wife,
and to the other my honored ladies, who have beguiled their
knight with skilful craft. But 't is no marvel if one be made a
fool and brought to sorrow by women's wiles, for so was Adam
beguiled by one, and Solomon by many, and Samson all too
soon, for Delilah dealt him his doom; and David thereafter was
wedded with Bathsheba, which brought him much sorrow—if one
might love a woman and believe her not, 't were great gain! And 30
since all they were beguiled by women, methinks 't is the less
blame to me that I was misled! But as for thy girdle, that will I
take with good will, not for gain of the gold, nor for samite, nor
silk, nor the costly pendants, neither for weal nor for worship,
but in sign of my frailty. I shall look upon it when I ride in
renown and remind myself of the fault and faintness of the
flesh; and so when pride uplifts me for prowess of arms, the
sight of this lace shall humble my heart. But one thing would I
pray, if it displease thee not: since thou art lord of yonder land
wherein I have dwelt, tell me what thy rightful name may be, and 40
I will ask no more."

"That will I truly," quoth the other. "Bernlak de Hautdesert
am I called in this land. Morgain le Fay dwelleth in mine house,
and through knowledge of clerkly craft hath she taken many. For
long time was she the mistress of Merlin, who knew well all you

knights of the court. Morgain the goddess is she called therefore, and there is none so haughty but she can bring him low.
She sent me in this guise to yon fair hall to test the truth of the
renown that is spread abroad of the valor of the Round Table.
She taught me this marvel to betray your wits, to vex Guinevere
and fright her to death by the man who spake with his head
in his hand at the high table. That is she who is at home, that
ancient lady, she is even thine aunt, Arthur's half-sister, the
daughter of the Duchess of Tintagel, who afterward married
10 King Uther. Therefore I bid thee, knight, come to thine aunt,
and make merry in thine house; my folk love thee, and I wish
thee as well as any man on earth, by my faith, for thy true
dealing."

But Sir Gawain said nay, he would in no wise do so; so they
embraced and kissed, and commended each other to the Prince
of Paradise, and parted right there, on the cold ground. Gawain
on his steed rode swiftly to the king's hall, and the Green Knight
got him whithersoever he would.

Sir Gawain, who had thus won grace of his life, rode through
20 wild ways on Gringalet; oft he lodged in a house, and oft without, and many adventures did he have and came off victor full
often, as at this time I cannot relate in tale. The hurt that he
had in his neck was healed, he bare the shining girdle as a baldric
bound by his side, and made fast with a knot 'neath his left arm,
in token that he was taken in a fault—and thus he came in safety
again to the court.

Then joy awakened in that dwelling when the king knew that
the good Sir Gawain was come, for he deemed it gain. King
Arthur kissed the knight, and the queen also, and many valiant
30 knights sought to embrace him. They asked him how he had
fared, and he told them all that had chanced to him—the adventure of the chapel, the fashion of the knight, the love of the
lady—at last of the lace. He showed them the wound in the
neck which he won for his disloyalty at the hand of the knight:
the blood flew to his face for shame as he told the tale.

"Lo, lady," he quoth, and handled the lace, "this is the bond
of the blame that I bear in my neck, this is the harm and the
loss I have suffered, the cowardice and covetousness in which I
was caught, the token of my covenant in which I was taken. And
40 I must needs wear it so long as I live, for none may hide his
harm, but undone it may not be, for if it hath clung to thee once,
it may never be severed."

Then the king comforted the knight, and the court laughed
loudly at the tale, and all made accord that the lords and the
ladies who belonged to the Round Table, each hero among them,
should wear bound about him a baldric of bright green for the

sake of Sir Gawain. And to this was agreed all the honor of the Round Table, and he who ware it was honored the more thereafter, as it is testified in the book of romance. That in Arthur's days this adventure befell, the book of Brutus bears witness. For since that bold knight came hither first, and the siege and the assault were ceased at Troy, I wis

> Many a venture herebefore
> Hath fallen such as this:
> May He that bare the crown of thorn
> Bring us unto His bliss.
>
> *Amen.*

GEOFFREY CHAUCER (?1340–1400)

Geoffrey Chaucer was born in London about the year 1340, the son of a prosperous wine-merchant. In his boyhood he was placed as a page in the household of a great noble, and as a young man (1359) he went with the English army to France, where he was taken prisoner, and ransomed by the king for the relatively large sum of 16 *l.* Royal favor was further shown at different times in Chaucer's life by the bestowal of various pensions and grants, and by appointment to important and remunerative offices. He was made Comptroller of Customs for Wools, Skins, and Leather for the port of London (1374), Comptroller of the Petty Customs (1382), Clerk of the King's works at Windsor (1390), and a Commissioner to repair the banks of the Thames between Woolwich and Greenwich (1390). In addition, he was employed on several diplomatic missions, being twice sent to Italy in such capacity, once in 1372–73 and again in 1378; to Flanders in 1377, and in the same year to France, to treat for peace with King Charles V. Although Chaucer suffered reversals of fortune when his patrons were out of power, these numerous appointments to responsible positions show how highly his abilities were regarded.

In such leisure as was left from public employment, Chaucer wrote a large quantity of verse. It is customary to divide his work into a French, an Italian, and an English period, although these divisions should not be pressed too far. In the first period are works imitative of French models, notably a translation of part of the *Romance of the Rose*, a great French allegorical love poem, and the *Book of the Duchess*, an elegy commemorating the death of Blanche, Duchess of Lancaster. After Chaucer's first visit to Italy, he shows acquaintance with the works of Dante, Petrarch, and Boccaccio, from whom he derived a new and larger conception of literary art. In this period he wrote the *House of Fame*, a dream-vision poem, the *Parliament of Fowls*, the *Legend of Good Women*, narrating the stories of women who suffered and died for love, and *Troilus and Criseyde*, a long and very remarkable narrative poem, based upon the *Il Filostrato* of Boccaccio, and telling with psychological power the story of the Trojan maiden, Criseyde, who abandoned her lover, Troilus, for the Greek, Diomed. For the last fifteen years of his life Chaucer was mainly occupied with the *Canterbury Tales*.

THE CANTERBURY TALES

In these his scene and his characters are English. The poet represents himself as one of a company of pilgrims setting out from the Tabard Inn in Southwerk for the shrine of Saint Thomas à Becket at Canterbury. The pilgrims, who are brilliantly described in the *Prologue,* are of varied type, and pursue many characteristic occupations of medieval life. To while away the time on the journey, the host of the Inn proposes that each person shall tell two tales on the journey to Canterbury, and two on the return, the teller of the best tale to be rewarded by a supper at the common expense. Since the number of pilgrims is thirty-one [1] (not counting another who joins them later), Chaucer was planning a very large body of tales, of which he actually completed only twenty-four. These include nearly every kind of story current in Chaucer's day, and are very skillfully fitted in most cases to the character of the narrator. The main prologue, the prologues to the several tales, and various end-links emphasize character or present dramatic conflicts between the pilgrims. The *Canterbury Tales* thus becomes a very remarkable example of a series of stories ingeniously set into a framework.

Chaucer's work is here represented by the *Prologue* and several of the Canterbury Tales, and a few shorter pieces. The selections by no means exhibit his astonishing facility and variety, but they are sufficient to show his humanity, his tolerance, his keen observation, his broad and sympathetic understanding of all sorts and conditions of men, his humor, and his moral soundness. These qualities have endeared him to readers of all the centuries after his own, but from the Elizabethan age to the nineteenth century there could not exist a proper appreciation of his literary art, since the pronunciation of the language in which he wrote had been forgotten, and had to be rediscovered by modern scholarship. When read approximately as he himself spoke his lines, he is revealed as technically one of the very greatest of our poets, a master who handled with finesse diverse metrical forms and commanded the most subtle verbal harmonies—that "divine liquidness of diction . . . divine fluidity of movement" to which Matthew Arnold must perforce bear witness, even though he was not in entire sympathy with the poet. For proper appreciation of these technical aspects of Chaucer's art, a guide to his language is here appended.

CHAUCER'S LANGUAGE

Chaucer's variations from modern English in grammar and syntax are not so serious as to cause much difficulty in reading, and the words, although frequently differing in spelling and form, can with a little practice be identified with their modern English equivalents. Obsolete words are explained in the footnotes. Differences in pronunciation are noted below.

1. Vowels are to be given in general their "Continental" values; that is, the sounds which they have in Latin, German, French, Italian. The long and short vowels are to be sounded respectively as: *a* as in f*a*ther, *ahá*; *e* as in th*e*y, hors*e*s, except that final e is like *a* in Chin*a*, and in general where modern *ea* has developed, the vowel is to be sounded as in th*e*re, regardless of the spelling; *i* (or *y*) as in mach*i*ne, p*i*n; *o* as in n*o*te, *o*ff, except that where in modern Eng-

---

1 Possibly the "three priests" accompanying the Prioress is a mistake, or a later interpolation, and Chaucer planned for only one, thus reducing the number to twenty-nine.

lish the sound is like *u* in *cut*, the vowel is to be pronounced like *oo* in *book* (cf. modern English *love*); *u* (long) as in French *tu* or German *müde, u* (short) like the vowel sound in *book*. Note that doubling merely lengthens the vowel; a double vowel is to be pronounced exactly like a single long vowel.

2. Dipthongs: *ai* (or *ay*) as in pl*ay; au* (or *aw*) like *ow* in h*owl; ei* (or *ey*) as in r*ein; oi* (or *oy*) as in b*oil; ou* (or *ow*) as in s*oup*.

3. Consonants in general as in modern English; except that *gh* has the sound of German *ch* as in *ich, ach;* and initial *k* before *n* is to be sounded, as in *k*night.

4. There are no silent letters. Note especially that every vowel is to be pronounced, except that final *e* is usually elided when the following word begins with a vowel or with *h*. Thus in the opening lines of the *Prologue,*

> Whan that Aprille with his shoures sote
> The droghte of Marche hath perced to the rote,

shoures, sote, perced, and *rote,* are each two syllables, and *Aprille* three, with the accent on the second; on the other hand, *droghte* and *Marche* are monosyllables, since in these cases the final *e* elides. The meter (in all the selections in this volume except *Sir Thopas* iambic pentameter or five-stressed line), if strongly marked in reading, will be a useful guide to the pronunciation.

BIBLIOGRAPHY. The principal manuscripts of the *Canterbury Tales* are reprinted in parallel columns by the Chaucer Society. The Complete Works, ed. by W. W. Skeat in 7 volumes (Oxford) and one volume "Student's Chaucer," by same editor and publisher. Best one volume edition, by F. N. Robinson (Houghton Mifflin). Most of the Canterbury Tales ed., with notes, by J. M. Manly (Holt). Useful commentary in R. K. Root, *The Poetry of Chaucer* (Houghton Mifflin), G. L. Kittredge, *Chaucer and his Poetry* (Harvard), T. R. Lounsbury, *Studies in Chaucer*, 3 vols. (Harpers), and J. M. Manly, *New Light on Chaucer* (Holt). A bibliography of Chaucerian scholarship up to 1908 is E. P. Hammond, *Chaucer: A Bibliographical Manual* (Macmillan).

THE CANTERBURY TALES

THE PROLOGUE

Whan that Aprille with his shoures sote [1]
The droghte of Marche hath perced to the rote,[2]
And bathed every veyne in swich [3] licour,
Of which vertu [4] engendred is the flour; [5]
Whan Zephirus eek with his swete breeth
Inspired hath in every holt [6] and heeth
The tendre croppes,[7] and the yonge sonne
Hath in the Ram his halfe cours y-ronne,[8]

1 showers sweet
2 root
3 such
4 power
5 flower
6 wood
7 shoots

8 run. The sun lies in the zodiacal sign of the Ram during the latter part of March and the earlier part of April. He has run his half course in April accordingly, about the middle of that month. Since the mediaeval calendar began the year on March 25, the sun is now "young."

And smale fowles [9] maken melodye,
That slepen al the night with open yë,   10
(So priketh hem nature in hir corages): [10]
Than longen folk to goon on pilgrimages
(And palmers for to seken straunge strondes)
To ferne halwes,[11] couth [12] in sondry londes;
And specially, from every shires ende
Of Engelond, to Caunterbury they wende,
The holy blisful martir for to seke,
That hem hath holpen, whan that they were seke.
    Bifel that, in that seson on a day,
In Southwerk at the Tabard as I lay   20
Redy to wenden on my pilgrimage
To Caunterbury with ful devout corage,
At night was come in-to that hostelrye
Wel nyne and twenty in a companye,
Of sondry folk, by aventure y-falle [13]
In felawshipe, and pilgrims were they alle,
That toward Caunterbury wolden ryde;
The chambres and the stables weren wyde,
And wel we weren esed atte beste.[14]
And shortly, whan the sonne was to reste,   30
So hadde I spoken with hem everichon,
That I was of hir felawshipe anon,
And made forward [15] erly for to ryse,
To take our wey, ther as I yow devyse.
    But natheless, whyl I have tyme and space,
Er that I ferther in this tale pace,
Me thinketh it acordaunt to resoun,
To telle yow al the condicioun
Of ech of hem, so as it semed me,
And whiche they weren, and of what degree;   40
And eek in what array that they were inne:
And at a knight than wol I first biginne.
    A KNIGHT ther was, and that a worthy man,
That fro the tyme that he first bigan
To ryden out, he loved chivalrye,
Trouthe and honour, fredom and curteisye.
Ful worthy was he in his lordes werre,[16]
And therto hadde he riden (no man ferre) [17]
As wel in Christendom as hethenesse,
And ever honoured for his worthinesse.   50

9 birds
10 hearts
11 distant shrines
12 known
13 by chance fallen
14 entertained in the best fashion
15 agreement
16 war
17 farther

At Alisaundre [18] he was, whan it was wonne;
Ful ofte tyme he hadde the bord bigonne [19]
Aboven alle naciouns in Pruce.
In Lettow hadde he reysed [20] and in Ruce,
No Christen man so ofte of his degree.
In Gernade at the sege eek hadde he be
Of Algezir, and riden in Belmarye.
At Lyeys was he, and at Satalye,
Whan they were wonne; and in the Grete See [21]
At many a noble aryve [22] hadde he be.   60
At mortal batailles hadde he been fiftene,
And foughten for our feith at Tramissene
In listes thryes, and ay slayn his fo.
This ilke worthy knight had been also
Somtyme with the lord of Palatye,
Ageyn another hethen in Turkye:
And evermore he hadde a sovereyn prys.[23]
And though that he were worthy, he was wys,
And of his port as meke as is a mayde.
He never yet no vileinye ne sayde   70
In al his lyf, un-to no maner wight.[24]
He was a verray parfit gentil knight.
But for to tellen yow of his array,
His hors [25] were gode, but he was nat gay.
Of fustian he wered a gipoun [26]
Al bismotered with his habergeoun; [27]
For he was late y-come from his viage,[28]
And wente for to doon his pilgrimage.
   With him ther was his sone, a yong Squyer,
A lovyere, and a lusty bacheler,   80
With lokkes crulle,[29] as they were leyd in presse.
Of twenty yeer of age he was, I gesse.
Of his stature he was of evene lengthe,[30]
And wonderly deliver,[31] and greet of strengthe.
And he had been somtyme in chivachye,[32]
In Flaundres, in Artoys, and Picardye,
And born him wel, as of so litel space,
In hope to stonden in his lady [33] grace.

18 Modern names of the places listed are: Alexandria, Prussia, Lithuania, Russia, Granada, Algeciras, Benmarin (in northern Africa), Ayas, Adalia (both in Asia Minor), Tremeyen (in northern Africa), Palathia (in Asia Minor).

19 the table headed
20 made an expedition
21 Mediterranean
22 disembarkation; variant reading, *armee*, expedition
23 renown
24 person
25 horses (plu.)
26 short doublet
27 stained with his coat of mail
28 voyage
29 curled
30 medium height
31 active
32 cavalry expedition
33 lady's

Embrouded was he, as it were a mede [34]
Al ful of fresshe floures, whyte and rede.   90
Singinge he was, or floytinge,[35] al the day;
He was as fresh as is the month of May.
Short was his goune, with sleves longe and wyde.
Wel coude he sitte on hors, and faire ryde.
He coude songes make and wel endyte,
Juste and eek daunce, and wel purtreye and wryte.
So hote he lovede, that by nightertale [36]
He sleep namore than dooth a nightingale.
Curteys he was, lowly, and servisable,
And carf biforn his fader at the table.   100
    A YEMAN hadde he, and servaunts namo
At that tyme, for him liste ryde so;
And he was clad in cote and hood of grene;
A sheef of pecok-arwes brighte and kene
Under his belt he bar ful thriftily;
(Wel coude he dresse his takel [37] yemanly:
His arwes drouped noght with fetheres lowe),
And in his hand he bar a mighty bowe.
A not-heed [38] hadde he, with a broun visage.
Of wode-craft wel coude he al the usage.   110
Upon his arm he bar a gay bracer,
And by his syde a swerd and a bokeler,
And on that other syde a gay daggere,
Harneised [39] wel, and sharp as point of spere;
A Cristofre [40] on his brest of silver shene.
An horn he bar, the bawdrik [41] was of grene;
A forster was he, soothly, as I gesse.
    Ther was also a Nonne, a PRIORESSE,
That of hir smyling was full simple and coy;
Hir gretteste ooth was but by sëynt Loy: [42]   120
And she was cleped [43] madame Eglentyne.
Ful wel she song the service divyne,
Entuned in hir nose ful semely;
And Frensh she spak ful faire and fetisly,[44]
After the scole of Stratford atte Bowe,[45]
For Frensh of Paris was to hir unknowe.
At mete wel y-taught was she with-alle;
She leet no morsel from hir lippes falle,
Ne wette hir fingres in hir sauce depe.
Wel coude she carie a morsel, and wel kepe,   130

34 meadow
35 fluting
36 night-time
37 equipment
38 cropped head

39 equipped
40 Image of St. Christo-
pher
41 cord
42 By Saint Eligius (a

very mild oath)
43 called
44 elegantly
45 A convent near Lon-
don

That no drope ne fille up-on hir brest.
In curteisye was set ful muche hir lest.[46]
Hir over lippe wyped she so clene,
That in hir coppe was no ferthing sene
Of grece, whan she dronken hadde hir draughte.
Ful semely after hir mete she raughte,[47]
And sikerly [48] she was of greet disport,[49]
And ful plesaunt, and amiable of port,
And peyned hir [50] to countrefete chere [51]
Of court, and been estatlich [52] of manere,   140
And to ben holden digne [53] of reverence.
But, for to speken of hir conscience,
She was so charitable and so pitous,
She wolde wepe, if that she sawe a mous
Caught in a trappe, if it were deed or bledde.
Of smale houndes [54] had she, that she fedde
With rosted flesh, or milk and wastel-breed.[55]
But sore weep she if oon of hem were deed,
Or if men smoot it with a yerde [56] smerte:
And al was conscience and tendre herte.   150
Ful semely hir wimpel pinched [57] was;
Hir nose tretys,[58] hir eyen greye as glas;
Hir mouth ful smal, and ther-to softe and reed;
But sikerly she hadde a fair forheed;
It was almost a spanne brood, I trowe;
For, hardily, she was nat undergrowe.
Ful fetis [59] was hir cloke, as I was war.
Of smal coral aboute hir arm she bar
A peire [60] of bedes, gauded al with grene;
And ther-on heng a broche of gold ful shene,   160
On which ther was first write a crowned A,
And after, *Amor vincit omnia.*[61]
    Another NONNE with hir hadde she,
That was hir chapeleyne, and PREESTES THREE.
    A MONK ther was, a fair for the maistrye,[62]
An out-rydere, that lovede venerye; [63]
A manly man, to been an abbot able.
Ful many a deyntee hors hadde he in stable:
And, when he rood, men mighte his brydel here
Ginglen in a whistling wind as clere,   170
And eek as loude as dooth the chapel-belle

46 pleasure
47 reached
48 surely
49 good humor
50 took pains
51 behavior
52 dignified
53 worthy
54 dogs
55 fine white bread
56 stick
57 pleated
58 well-proportioned
59 handsome
60 string
61 Love conquers all things
62 an exceedingly fine one
63 hunting

Ther as this lord was keper of the celle.
The reule of seint Maure or of seint Beneit [64]
By-cause that it was old and som-del streit,[65]
This ilke monk leet olde thinges pace,
And held after the newe world the space.
He yaf [66] nat of that text a pulled hen,
That seith, that hunters been nat holy men;
Ne that a monk, whan he is cloisterlees,
Is lykned til a fish that is waterless;   180
This is to seyn, a monk out of his cloistre.
But thilke text held he nat worth an oistre;
And I seyde, his opinioun was good.
What sholde he studie, and make him-selven wood,[67]
Upon a book in cloistre alwey to poure,
Or swinken [68] with his handes, and laboure,
As Austin bit? [69] How shal the world be served?
Lat Austin have his swink to him reserved.
Therfore he was a pricasour [70] aright;
Grehoundes he hadde, as swifte as fowel in flight;   190
Of priking [70] and of hunting for the hare
Was al his lust, for no cost wolde he spare.
I seigh his sleves purfiled [71] at the hond
With grys,[72] and that the fyneste of a lond;
And, for to festne his hood under his chin,
He hadde of gold y-wroght a curious pin:
A love-knotte in the gretter ende ther was.
His heed was balled, that shoon as any glas,
And eek his face, as he had been anoint.
He was a lord ful fat and in good point; [73]   200
His eyen stepe,[74] and rollinge in his heed,
That stemed [75] as a forneys of a leed; [76]
His botes souple, his hors in greet estat.
Now certeinly he was a fair prelat;
He was nat pale as a for-pyned [77] goost.
A fat swan loved he best of any roost.
His palfrey was as broun as is a berye.
   A FRERE ther was, a wantown and a merye,
A limitour,[78] a ful solempne [79] man.
In alle the ordres foure [80] is noon that can [81]   210
So muche of daliaunce and fair langage.

64 Benedict
65 strict
66 gave
67 mad
68 work
69 bids
70 hard rider; riding
71 edged

72 gray fur
73 *en bon point*, of a well-fed appearance
74 protruding
75 glowed
76 cauldron
77 wasted away
78 One licensed to beg

within certain limits
79 important
80 Dominican, Franciscan, Carmelite and Austin friars
81 knows

He hadde maad ful many a mariage
Of yonge wommen, at his owne cost.
Un-to his ordre he was a noble post.
Ful wel biloved and famulier was he
With frankeleyns [82] over-al in his contree,
And eek with worthy wommen of the toun:
For he had power of confessioun,
As seyde him-self, more than a curat,
For of his ordre he was licentiat.[83]   220
Ful swetely herde he confessioun,
And plesaunt was his absolucioun;
He was an esy man to yeve [84] penaunce
Ther as he wiste to han a good pitaunce;
For unto a povre ordre for to yive
Is signe that a man is wel y-shrive.
For if he yaf, he dorste make avaunt,[85]
He wiste that a man was repentaunt.
For many a man so hard is of his herte,
He may nat wepe al-thogh him sore smerte.   230
Therfore, in stede of weping and preyeres,
Men moot yeve silver to the povre freres.
His tipet was ay farsed [86] ful of knyves
And pinnes, for to yeven faire wyves.
And certeinly he hadde a mery note;
Wel coude he singe and pleyen on a rote.[87]
Of yeddinges [88] he bar utterly the prys.
His nekke whyt was as the flour-de-lys;
Ther-to he strong was as a champioun.
He knew the tavernes wel in every toun,   240
And everich hostiler and tappestere [89]
Bet than a lazar or a beggestere,[90]
For un-to swich a worthy man as he
Acorded nat, as by his facultee,
To have with seke lazars aqueyntaunce.
It is nat honest, it may nat avaunce
For to delen with no swich poraille,[91]
But al with riche and sellers of vitaille.
And over-al, ther as profit sholde aryse,
Curteys he was, and lowly of servyse.   250
Ther nas no man no-where so vertuous.
He was the beste beggere in his hous;
And yaf a certeyn ferme for the graunt; [92]

82 rich land-owners
83 licensed to hear con-
fessions
84 give
85 boast
86 stuffed
87 fiddle
88 songs
89 barmaid
90 Better than a leper or
a beggar
91 poor people
92 gave a stated sum for
the privilege (of begging)

Noon of his bretheren cam ther in his haunt;
For thogh a widwe hadde noght a sho,
So plesaunt was his *"In principio,"* [93]
Yet wolde he have a ferthing, er he wente.
His purchas [94] was wel bettre than his rente.[95]
And rage he coude, as it were right a whelpe.
In love-dayes [96] ther coude he muchel helpe.   260
For there he was nat lyk a cloisterer,
With a thredbar cope, as is a povre scoler,
But he was lyk a maister or a pope.
Of double worsted was his semi-cope,
That rounded as a belle out of the presse.
Somwhat he lipsed, for his wantownesse,
To make his English swete up-on his tonge;
And in his harping, whan that he had songe,
His eyen twinkled in his heed aright,
As doon the sterres in the frosty night.   270
This worthy limitour was cleped Huberd.
    A MARCHANT was ther with a forked berd,
In mottelee, and hye on horse he sat,
Up-on his heed a Flaundrish bever hat;
His botes clasped faire and fetisly.
His resons he spak ful solempnely,
Souninge [97] alway th'encrees of his winning.
He wolde the see were kept for any thing
Bitwixe Middelburgh and Orewelle.[98]
Wel coude he in eschaunge sheeldes [99] selle.   280
This worthy man ful well his wit bisette;
Ther wiste no wight that he was in dette,
So estatly was he of his governaunce,
With his bargaynes, and with his chevisaunce.[1]
For sothe he was a worthy man with-alle,
But sooth to seyn, I noot [2] how men him calle.
    A CLERK ther was of Oxenford also,
That un-to logik hadde longe y-go.
As lene was his hors as is a rake,
And he nas nat right fat, I undertake;   290
But loked holwe, and ther-to soberly.
Ful thredbar was his overest courtepy; [3]
For he had geten him yet no benefyce,
Ne was so worldly for to have offyce.

93 Beginning of St. John's gospel
94 gettings (from begging)
95 what he paid (the *ferme* above); or legitimate income
96 days appointed for the arbitration of disputes
97 tending
98 He wanted the sea route kept open at any cost between Middleburgh (in Holland) and Orwell (an English port, now Harwich)
99 French coins, *écus*
1 dealing
2 know not
3 short coat

For him was lever have at his beddes heed
Twenty bokes, clad in blak or reed,
Of Aristotle and his philosophye,
Than robes riche, or fithele,[4] or gay sautrye [5]
But al be that he was a philosophre,[6]
Yet hadde he but litel gold in cofre;   300
But al that he mighte of his freendes hente,[7]
On bokes and on lerninge he it spente,
And bisily gan for the soules preye
Of hem that yaf him wher-with to scoleye.
Of studie took he most cure and most hede.
Noght o word spak he more than was nede,
And that was seyd in forme and reverence,
And short and quik, and ful of hy sentence.
Souninge in moral vertu was his speche,
And gladly wolde he lerne, and gladly teche.   310
    A SERGEANT OF THE LAWE, war [8] and wys,
That often hadde been at the parvys,[9]
Ther was also, ful riche of excellence.
Discreet he was, and of greet reverence:
He semed swich, his wordes weren so wyse.
Justyce he was ful often in assyse,
By patente, and by pleyn commissioun;
For his science, and for his heigh renoun
Of fees and robes hadde he many oon.
So greet a purchasour [10] was no-wher noon.   320
Al was fee simple to him in effect,[11]
His purchasing mighte nat been infect.[12]
No-wher so bisy a man as he ther nas,
And yet he semed bisier than he was.
In termes hadde he caas and domes [13] alle,
That from the tyme of king William were falle.
Therto he coude endyte, and make a thing,
Ther coude no wight pinche at [14] his wryting;
And every statut coude he pleyn by rote.
He rood but hoomly in a medlee [15] cote   330
Girt with a ceint [16] of silk, with barres smale;
Of his array telle I no lenger tale.
    A FRANKELEYN [17] was in his companye;
Whyt was his berd, as is the dayesye.

4 fiddle
5 psaltery
6 A play on the sense of one who sought the philosopher's stone which should turn base metals to gold
7 get
8 cautious
9 church porch (especially of St. Paul's Cathedral, where lawyers met clients).
10 conveyancer
11 i. e., he could untie any entail or restriction on land
12 invalidated
13 judgments
14 find fault with
15 of mixed color
16 girdle
17 rich land-owner

Of his complexioun he was sangwyn.
Wel loved he by the morwe a sop in wyn.
To liven in delyt was ever his wone,[18]
For he was Epicurus owne sone,
That heeld opinioun, that pleyn delyt
Was verraily felicitee parfyt.   340
An housholdere, and that a greet, was he;
Seint Julian[19] he was in his contree.
His breed, his ale, was alwey after oon;[20]
A bettre envyned[21] man was no-wher noon.
With-oute bake mete was never his hous,
Of fish and flesh, and that so plentevous,
It snewed in his hous of mete and drinke,
Of alle deyntees that men coude thinke.
After the sondry sesons of the yeer,
So chaunged he his mete and his soper.   350
Ful many a fat partrich hadde he in mewe,
And many a breem and many a luce in stewe.[22]
Wo was his cook, but-if his sauce were
Poynaunt and sharp, and redy al his gere.
His table dormant[23] in his halle alway
Stood redy covered al the longe day.
At sessiouns ther was he lord and sire;
Ful ofte tyme he was knight of the shire.
An anlas[24] and a gipser[25] al of silk
Heng at his girdel, whyt as morne milk.   360
A shirreve hadde he been, and a countour;[26]
Was no-wher such a worthy vavasour.[27]
     An HABERDASSHER and a CARPENTER,
A WEBBE,[28] a DYERE, and a TAPICER,[29]
Were with us eek, clothed in o liveree,
Of a solempne and greet fraternitee.
Ful fresh and newe hir gere apyked[30] was;
Hir knyves were y-chaped[31] noght with bras,
But al with silver, wroght ful clene and weel,
Hir girdles and hir pouches every-deel.   370
Wel semed ech of hem a fair burgeys,
To sitten in a yeldhalle[32] on a deys.
Everich, for the wisdom that he can,
Was shaply for to been an alderman.
For catel[33] hadde they y-nogh and rente,[34]

And eek hir wyves wolde it wel assente;
And elles certein were they to blame.
It is ful fair to been y-clept *"ma dame,"*
And goon to vigilyës [35] al bifore,
And have a mantel royalliche y-bore.   380
   A Cook they hadde with hem for the nones,[36]
To boille the chiknes with the mary-bones,
And poudre-marchant [37] tart, and galingale.[38]
Wel coude he knowe a draughte of London ale.
He coude roste, and sethe, and broille, and frye,
Maken mortreux,[39] and wel bake a pye.
But greet harm was it, as it thoughte me,
That on his shine a mormal [40] hadde he;
For blankmanger,[41] that made he with the beste.
   A Shipman was ther, woning [42] fer by weste: 390
For aught I woot, he was of Dertemouthe.
He rood up-on a rouncy,[43] as he couthe,[44]
In a gowne of falding [45] to the knee.
A daggere hanging on a laas hadde he
Aboute his nekke under his arm adoun.
The hote somer had maad his hewe al broun;
And, certeinly, he was a good felawe.
Ful many a draughte of wyn had he y-drawe
From Burdeux-ward, whyl that the chapman [46] sleep.
Of nyce conscience took he no keep.   400
If that he faught, and hadde the hyer hond,
By water he sente hem hoom [47] to every lond.
But of his craft to rekene wel his tydes,
His stremes and his daungers him bisydes,
His herberwe [48] and his mone, his lode-menage,[49]
Ther nas noon swich from Hulle to Cartage.
Hardy he was, and wys to undertake;
With many a tempest hadde his berd been shake.
He knew wel alle the havenes, as they were,
From Gootlond [50] to the cape of Finistere,   410
And every cryke in Britayne and in Spayne;
His barge y-cleped was the Maudelayne.
   With us ther was a Doctour of Phisyk,
In al this world ne was ther noon him lyk
To speke of phisik and of surgerye;
For he was grounded in astronomye.[51]

---

35 ceremonies on the eves
of festivals
36 nonce
37 a spice
38 a root for flavoring
39 thickened soups
40 sore

41 creamed chicken
42 dwelling
43 hackney
44 as well as he could.
45 coarse cloth
46 merchant
47 "made them walk the

plank"
48 harbor
49 steersmanship
50 in the Baltic
51 astrology

He kepte his pacient a ful greet del
In houres [52] by his magik naturel.
Wel coude he fortunen [53] the ascendent
Of his images [54] for his pacient.   420
He knew the cause of everich maladye,
Were it of hoot or cold, or moiste, or drye,[55]
And where engendred, and of what humour;
He was a verrey parfit practisour.
The cause y-knowe, and of his harm the rote,
Anon he yaf the seke man his bote.[56]
Ful redy hadde he his apothecaries,
To sende him drogges and his letuaries,[57]
For ech of hem made other for to winne;
Hir frendschipe nas nat newe to biginne.   430
Wel knew he th'olde Esculapius,
And Deiscorides, and eek Rufus,
Old Ypocras, Haly, and Galien;
Serapion, Razis, and Avicen;
Averrois, Damascien, and Constantyn;
Bernard, and Gatesden, and Gilbertyn.[58]
Of his diete mesurable was he,
For it was of no superfluitee,
But of greet norissing and digestible.
His studie was but litel on the bible.   440
In sangwin [59] and in pers [60] he clad was al,
Lyned with taffata and with sendal; [61]
And yet he was but esy of dispence; [62]
He kepte that he wan in pestilence.
For gold in phisik is a cordial,[63]
Therfore he lovede gold in special.
   A good WYF was ther of bisyde BATHE,
But she was som-del deef, and that was scathe.[64]
Of clooth-making she hadde swiche an haunt,[65]
She passed hem of Ypres and of Gaunt.[66]   450
In all the parisshe wyf ne was ther noon
That to th' offring bifore hir sholde goon;
And if ther dide, certeyn, so wrooth was she,
That she was out of alle charitee.
Hir coverchiefs [67] ful fyne were of ground;

52 watched for the patient's favorable star
53 predict
54 to be used as a charm
55 In mediaeval physiology, the four elemental qualities of which were composed the body fluids or "humors": blood, phlegm, choler (or bile), and black bile. Disease was caused if the humors were not properly tempered (i e., balanced)
56 remedy
57 lectuaries, syrups
58 Classical and medieval medical authorities
59 red
60 blue
61 light silk
62 expenditure
63 remedy for the heart
64 a pity
65 skill
66 Ghent
67 head-dresses

I dorste swere they weyeden ten pound
That on a Sonday were upon hir heed.
Hir hosen weren of fyn scarlet reed,
Ful streite y-teyd, and shoos ful moiste and newe.
Bold was hir face, and fair, and reed of hewe.   460
She was a worthy womman al hir lyve,
Housbondes at chirche-dore [68] she hadde fyve,
Withouten other companye in youthe;
But therof nedeth nat to speke as nouthe.[69]
And thryes hadde she been at Jerusalem;
She hadde passed many a straunge streem;
At Rome she hadde been, and at Boloigne,
In Galice at seint Jame,[70] and at Coloigne.
She coude muche of wandring by the weye:
Gat-tothed [71] was she, soothly for to seye.   470
Up-on an amblere esily she sat,
Y-wimpled [72] wel, and on hir heed an hat
As brood as is a bokeler or a targe; [73]
A foot-mantel aboute hir hipes large,
And on hir feet a paire of spores sharpe.
In felawschip wel coude she laughe and carpe.
Of remedyes of love she knew perchaunce,
For she coude of that art the olde daunce.
    A good man was ther of religioun,
And was a povre PERSOUN [74] of a toun;   480
But riche he was of holy thoght and werk.
He was also a lerned man, a clerk,
That Cristes gospel trewely wolde preche;
His parisshens devoutly wolde he teche.
Benigne he was, and wonder diligent,
And in adversitee ful pacient;
And swich he was y-preved ofte sythes.[75]
Ful looth were him to cursen for his tythes,
But rather wolde he yeven, out of doute,
Un-to his povre parisshens aboute   490
Of his offring, and eek of his substaunce.
He coude in litel thing han suffisaunce.
Wyd was his parisshe, and houses fer a-sonder,
But he ne lafte nat, for reyn ne thonder,
In siknes nor in meschief, to visyte
The ferreste in his parisshe, muche and lyte,
Up-on his feet, and in his hand a staf.

68 where marriages were   Compostello, Spain   73 shield
formerly celebrated (not at   71 teeth set wide apart,   74 parson, parish priest
the altar)   a sign that one will travel   75 times
  69 at present   72 Head covered with a
  70 a celebrated shrine at wimpel

This noble ensample to his sheep he yaf,
That first he wroghte, and afterward he taughte;
Out of the gospel he tho wordes caughte;   500
And this figure he added eek ther-to,
That if gold ruste, what shal iren do?
For if a preest be foul, on whom we truste,
No wonder is a lewed [76] man to ruste;
And shame it is, if a preest take keep,
A shiten shepherde and a clene sheep.
Wel oghte a preest ensample for to yive,
By his clennesse, how that his sheep shold live.
He sette nat his benefice to hyre,
And leet his sheep encombred in the myre,   510
And ran to London, un-to sëynt Poules,
To seken him a chaunterie for soules,[77]
Or with a bretherhed to been withholde; [78]
But dwelte at hoom, and kepte wel his folde,
So that the wolf ne made it nat miscarie;
He was a shepherde and no mercenarie.
And though he holy were, and vertuous,
He was to sinful man nat despitous,[79]
Ne of his speche daungerous ne digne,[80]
But in his teching discreet and benigne.   520
To drawen folk to heven by fairnesse
By good ensample, was his bisinesse:
But it were any persone obstinat,
What-so he were, of heigh or lowe estat,
Him wolde he snibben [81] sharply for the nones.
A bettre preest, I trowe that nowher noon is.
He wayted after no pompe and reverence,
Ne maked him a spyced conscience,
But Cristes lore, and his apostles twelve,
He taughte, and first he folwed it him-selve.   530
    With him ther was a PLOWMAN, was his brother,
That hadde y-lad [82] of dong ful many a fother,[83]
A trewe swinker [84] and a good was he,
Livinge in pees and parfit charitee.
God loved he best with al his hole herte
At alle tymes, thogh him gamed or smerte,[85]
And thanne his neighebour right as him-selve.
He wolde thresshe, and ther-to dyke and delve,
For Cristes sake, for every povre wight,

76 ignorant
77 An endowment for a priest to say mass (usually for the dead)
78 maintained in retire-ment
79 pitiless
80 overbearing nor haughty
81 rebuke
82 carried
83 load
84 laborer
85 though he was joyful or pained

Withouten hyre, if it lay in his might. 540
His tythes payed he ful faire and wel,
Bothe of his propre swink [86] and his catel.[87]
In a tabard [88] he rood upon a mere.
  Ther was also a Reve [89] and a Millere,
A Somnour [90] and a Pardoner also,
A Maunciple,[91] and my-self; ther were namo.
  The MILLER was a stout carl, for the nones,
Ful big he was of braun, and eek of bones;
That proved wel, for over-al ther he cam,
At wrastling he wolde have alwey the ram.[92] 550
He was short-sholdred, brood, a thikke knarre,[93]
Ther nas no dore that he nolde heve of harre,[94]
Or breke it, at a renning, with his heed.
His berd as any sowe or fox was reed,
And ther-to brood, as though it were a spade.
Up-on the cop right of his nose he hade
A werte, and ther-on stood a tuft of heres,
Reed as the bristles of a sowes eres;
His nose-thirles [95] blake were and wyde.
A swerd and bokeler bar he by his syde; 560
His mouth as greet was as a greet forneys.
He was a janglere [96] and a goliardeys,[97]
And that was most of sinne and harlotryes.
Wel coude he stelen corn, and tollen thryes; [98]
And yet he hadde a thombe of gold,[99] pardee.
A whyt cote and a blew hood wered he.
A baggepype wel coude he blowe and sowne,
And ther-with-al he broghte us out of towne.
  A gentil MAUNCIPLE was ther of a temple,[1]
Of which achatours [2] mighte take exemple 570
For to be wyse in bying of vitaille.
For whether that he payde, or took by taille,[3]
Algate he wayted so in his achat,[4]
That he was ay biforn [5] and in good stat.
Now is nat that of God a ful fair grace,
That swich a lewed [6] mannes wit shal pace [7]
The wisdom of an heep of lerned men?
Of maistres hadde he mo than thryes ten,

86 his own labor
87 property
88 sleeveless jacket
89 steward or bailiff of a manor
90 summoner for an ecclesiastical court
91 steward of a college or inn of court
92 given as a prize
93 knotted fellow
94 off its hinges
95 nostrils
96 loud talker
97 buffoon
98 take his legitimate toll three times over
99 because he could test the fineness of the flour with his thumb
1 inn of court
2 buyers
3 tally (credit)
4 always he watched so in his buying
5 ahead
6 ignorant
7 (sur)pass

That were of lawe expert and curious;
Of which ther were a doseyn in that hous   580
Worthy to been stiwardes of rente and lond
Of any lord that is in Engelond,
To make him live by his propre good,[8]
In honour dettelees, but he were wood,[9]
Or live as scarsly as him list desire;
And able for to helpen al a shire
In any cas that mighte falle or happe;
And yit this maunciple sette hir aller cappe.[10]
    The REVE was a sclendre colerik man,
His berd was shave as ny as ever he can.   590
His heer was by his eres round y-shorn.
His top was dokked lyk a preest biforn. ·
Ful longe were his legges, and ful lene,
Y-lyk a staf, ther was no calf y-sene.
Wel coude he kepe a gerner [11] and a binne;
Ther was noon auditour coude on him winne.
Wel wiste he, by the droghte, and by the reyn,
The yelding of his seed, and of his greyn.
His lordes sheep, his neet,[12] his dayerye,
His swyn, his hors, his stoor,[13] and his pultrye,   600
Was hoolly in this reves governing,
And by his covenaunt yaf the rekening,
Sin that his lord was twenty yeer of age;
Ther coude no man bringe him in arrerage.[14]
Ther nas baillif, ne herde, ne other hyne,[15]
That he ne knew his sleighte and his covyne; [16]
They were adrad of him, as of the deeth.
His woning [17] was ful fair up-on an heeth,
With grene treës shadwed was his place.
He coude bettre than his lord purchace.   610
Ful riche he was astored prively,
His lord wel coude he plesen subtilly,
To yeve and lene him of his owne good,[18]
And have a thank, and yet a cote and hood.
In youthe he lerned hadde a good mister; [19]
He was a wel good wrighte, a carpenter.
This reve sat up-on a ful good stot,[20]
That was al pomely [21] grey, and highte Scot.
A long surcote of pers [22] up-on he hade,

8 own income	13 stock of tools, etc.	18 property
9 mad	14 catch him in arrears	19 trade
10 "cheated them all"	15 servant	20 horse
11 granary	16 deceit	21 dappled
12 (neat) cattle	17 dwelling	22 blue

And by his syde he bar a rusty blade.   620
Of Northfolk was this reve, of which I telle,
Bisyde a toun men clepen Baldeswelle,
Tukked he was, as is a frere, aboute,
And ever he rood the hindreste of our route.
    A SOMNOUR was ther with us in that place,
That hadde a fyr-reed cherubinnes face,
For sawcefleem[23] he was, with eyen narwe.
As hoot he was, and lecherous, as a sparwe;
With scalled browes blake, and piled[24] berd;
Of his visage children were aferd.   630
Ther nas quik-silver, litarge, ne brimstoon,
Boras,[25] ceruce,[26] ne oille of tartre noon,
Ne oynement that wolde clense and byte,
That him mighte helpen of his whelkes whyte,
Nor of the knobbes sittinge on his chekes.
Wel loved he garleek, oynons, and eek lekes,
And for to drinken strong wyn, reed as blood.
Than wolde he speke, and crye as he were wood.[27]
And whan that he wel dronken hadde the wyn,
Than wolde he speke no word but Latyn.   640
A fewe termes hadde he, two or three,
That he had lerned out of som decree;
No wonder is, he herde it al the day;
And eek ye knowen wel, how that a jay
Can clepen "Watte," as well as can the pope.
But who-so coude in other thing him grope,[28]
Thanne hadde he spent al his philosophye;
Ay "Questio quid iuris"[29] wolde he crye.
He was a gentil harlot[30] and a kinde;
A bettre felawe sholde men noght finde.   650
He wolde suffre, for a quart of wyn,
A good felawe to have his concubyn
A twelf-month, and excuse him atte fulle:
Full prively a finch eek coude he pulle.[31]
And if he fond o-wher a good felawe,
He wolde techen him to have non awe,
In swich cas, of the erchedeknes curs,[32]
But-if[33] a mannes soule were in his purs;
For in his purs he sholde y-punisshed be.
"Purs is the erchedeknes helle," seyde he.   660
But well I woot he lyed right in dede;

23 pimply
24 scraggy
25 borax
26 white lead

27 mad
28 test
29 "What is the law on this point?"

30 ribald
31 "rob a greenhorn"
32 *i.e.*, excommunication
33 unless

Of cursing oghte ech gilty man him drede—
For curs wol slee, right as assoilling [34] saveth—
And also war him of a *significavit.* [35]
In daunger [36] hadde he at his owne gyse [37]
The yonge girles [38] of the diocyse,
And knew hir counseil, and was al hir reed. [39]
A gerland hadde he set up-on his heed,
As greet as it were for an ale-stake;
A bokeler hadde he maad him of a cake.   670

    With him ther rood a gentil PARDONER
Of Rouncival, [40] his freend and his compeer,
That streight was comen fro the court of Rome.
Ful loude he song, "Com hider, love, to me."
This somnour bar to him a stif burdoun,
Was never trompe of half so greet a soun.
This pardoner hadde heer as yelow as wex,
But smothe it heng, as dooth a strike of flex;
By ounces [41] henge his lokkes that he hadde,
And ther-with he his shuldres over-spradde;   680
But thinne it lay, by colpons [42] oon and oon;
But hood, for jolitee, ne wered he noon,
For it was trussed up in his walet.
Him thoughte, he rood al of the newe jet; [43]
Dischevele, save his cappe, he rood al bare.
Swiche glaringe eyen hadde he as an hare.
A vernicle [44] hadde he sowed on his cappe.
His walet lay biforn him in his lappe,
Bret-ful of pardoun come from Rome al hoot.
A voys he hadde as smal as hath a goot.   690
No berd hadde he, ne never sholde have,
As smothe it was as it were late y-shave;
I trowe he were a gelding or a mare.
But of his craft, fro Berwik into Ware,
Ne was ther swich another pardoner.
For in his male [45] he hadde a pilwe-beer, [46]
Which that, he seyde, was our lady veyl:
He seyde, he hadde a gobet of the seyl
That sëynt Peter hadde, whan that he wente
Up-on the see, til Jesu Crist him hente. [47]   700
He hadde a croys of latoun, [48] ful of stones,

34 absolving
35 writ of excommuni-
cation
36 influence
37 way
38 young people of either
sex
39 rede, counsel

40 A hospital in London
41 bunches
42 shreds
43 fashion
44 copy of the handker-
chief of St. Veronica on
which the picture of
Christ was supposed to

have been miraculously im-
printed
45 bag
46 pillow-case
47 took
48 cross of metal re-
sembling brass

And in a glas he hadde pigges bones.
But with thise relikes, whan that he fond
A povre person dwelling up-on lond,
Up-on a day he gat him more moneye
Than that the person gat in monthes tweye.
And thus, with feyned flaterye and japes,[49]
He made the person and the peple his apes.
But trewely to tellen, atte laste,
IIe was in chirche a noble ecclesiaste.   710
Wel coude he rede a lessoun or a storie,
But alderbest he song an offertorie;
For wel he wiste, whan that song was songe,
He moste preche, and wel affyle [50] his tonge,
To winne silver, as he ful wel coude;
Therefore he song so meriely and loude.

Now have I told you shortly, in a clause,
Th'estat, th'array, the nombre, and eek the cause
Why that assembled was this companye
In Southwerk, at this gentil hostelrye,   720
That highte the Tabard, faste by the Belle.
But now is tyme to yow for to telle
How that we baren us that ilke night,
Whan we were in that hostelrye alight.
And after wol I telle of our viage,
And al the remenaunt of our pilgrimage.
But first I pray yow, of your curteisye,
That ye n'arette [51] it nat my vileinye,[52]
Thogh that I pleynly speke in this matere,
To telle yow hir wordes and hir chere; [53]   730
Ne thogh I speke hir wordes properly.
For this ye knowen al-so wel as I,
Who-so shal telle a tale after a man,
He moot reherce, as ny as ever he can,
Everich a word, if it be in his charge,
Al speke he never so rudeliche and large; [54]
Or elles he moot telle his tale untrewe,
Or feyne thing, or finde wordes newe.
He may nat spare, al-thogh he were his brother;
He moot as wel seye o word as another.   740
Crist spak him-self ful brode in holy writ,
And wel ye woot, no vileinye is it.
Eek Plato seith who-so that can him rede,
The wordes mote be cosin to the dede.

| 49 tricks | 51 count | 53 behavior |
| 50 sharpen | 52 ill breeding | 54 broad |

Also I prey yow to foryeve it me,
Al [55] have I nat set folk in hir degree
Here in this tale, as that they sholde stonde;
My wit is short, ye may wel understonde.
  Greet chere made our hoste us everichon,
And to the soper sette us anon;   750
And served us with vitaille at the beste.
Strong was the wyn, and wel to drinke us leste.
A semely man our hoste was with-alle
For to han been a marshal in an halle;
A large man he was with eyen stepe,[56]
A fairer burgeys is their noon in Chepe: [57]
Bold of his speche, and wys, and wel y-taught,
And of manhod him lakkede right naught.
Eek therto he was right a mery man,
And after soper pleyen he bigan,   760
And spak of mirthe amonges othere thinges,
Whan that we hadde maad our rekeninges;
And seyde thus: "Now, lordinges, trewely,
Ye been to me right welcome hertely:
For by my trouthe, if that I shal nat lye,
I ne saugh this yeer so mery a companye
At ones in this herberwe [58] as is now.
Fayn wolde I doon yow mirthe, wiste I how.
And of a mirthe I am right now bithoght,
To doon yow ese, and it shal coste noght.   770
  Ye goon to Caunterbury; God yow spede,
The blisful martir quyte yow your mede.[59]
And wel I woot, as ye goon by the weye,
Ye shapen yow to talen [60] and to pleye;
For trewely, confort ne mirthe is noon
To ryde by the weye doumb as a stoon;
And therfore wol I maken yow disport,
As I seyde erst, and doon yow som confort.
And if yow lyketh alle, by oon assent,
Now for to stonden at my jugement,   780
And for to werken as I shal yow seye,
To-morwe, whan ye ryden by the weye,
Now, by my fader soule, that is deed,
But ye be merye, I wol yeve yow myn heed.
Hold up your hond, withouten more speche."
  Our counseil was nat longe for to seche;
Us thoughte it was noght worth to make it wys,[61]

---

55 although
56 big, protruding
57 Cheapside

58 inn
59 give you your reward
60 tell tales

61 deliberate about it

And graunted him withouten more avys,[62]
And bad him seye his verdit, as him leste.
"Lordinges," quod he, "now herkneth for the beste;   790
But tak it not, I prey yow, in desdeyn;
This is the poynt, to speken short and pleyn,
That ech of yow, to shorte with your weye,[63]
In this viage, shal telle tales tweye,
To Caunterbury-ward, I mene it so,
And hom-ward he shal tellen othere two,
Of aventures that whylom han bifalle,
And which of yow that bereth him best of alle,
That is to seyn, that telleth in this cas
Tales of best sentence [64] and most solas,[65]   800
Shal have a soper at our aller cost
Here in this place, sitting by this post,
Whan that we come agayn fro Caunterbury.
And for to make yow the more mery,
I wol my-selven gladly with yow ryde,
Right at myn owne cost, and be your gyde.
And who-so wol my jugement withseye
Shal paye al that we spenden by the weye.
And if ye vouche-sauf that it be so,
Tel me anon, with-outen wordes mo,   810
And I wol erly shape me therfore."
    This thing was graunted, and our othes swore
With ful glad herte, and preyden him also
That he wold vouche-sauf for to do so,
And that he wolde been our governour,
And of our tales juge and reportour,
And sette a soper at a certeyn prys;
And we wold reuled been at his devys,
In heigh and lowe; and thus, by oon assent,
We been acorded to his jugement.   820
And ther-up-on the wyn was fet anon;
We dronken, and to reste wente echon,
With-outen any lenger taryinge.
    A-morwe, whan that day bigan to springe,
Up roos our host, and was our aller cok,[66]
And gadrede us togidre, alle in a flok,
And forth we riden, a litel more than pas,[67]
Un-to the watering of seint Thomas.
And there our host bigan his hors areste,
And seyde; "Lordinges, herkneth, if yow leste.   830

62 consideration   64 meaning   67 a walk
  63 make   the   journey   65 amusement
short   66 cock for us all

Ye woot your forward,[68] and I it yow recorde.
If even-song and morwe-song acorde,
Lat see now who shal telle the firste tale.
As ever mote I drinke wyn or ale,
Who-so be rebel to my jugement
Shal paye for al that by the weye is spent.
Now draweth cut, er that we ferrer twinne; [69]
He which that hath the shortest shal biginne.
"Sire knight," quod he, "my maister and my lord,
Now draweth cut, for that is myn acord.   840
Cometh neer," quod he, "my lady prioresse;
And ye, sir clerk, lat be your shamfastnesse,
Ne studieth noght; ley hond to, every man."
     Anon to drawen every wight bigan,
And shortly for to tellen, as it was,
Were it by aventure, or sort,[70] or cas,[71]
The sothe is this, the cut fil to the knight,
Of which ful blythe and glad was every wight;
And telle he moste his tale, as was resoun,
By forward and by composicioun,[72]   850
As ye han herd; what nedeth wordes mo?
And whan this gode man saugh it was so,
As he that wys was and obedient
To kepe his forward by his free assent,
He seyde: "Sin I shal beginne the game,
What, welcome be the cut, a Goddes name!
Now lat us ryde, and herkneth what I seye."
     And with that word we riden forth our weye;
And he bigan with right a mery chere
His tale anon, and seyde in this manere.   860

THE PRIORESSES PROLOGUE

"Wel seyd, by *corpus dominus*," [73] quod our hoste,
"Now longe moot thou sayle by the coste,
Sir gentil maister, gentil marineer!
God yeve this monk a thousand last quad yeer! [74]
A ha! felawes! beth ware of swiche a jape! [75]
The monk putte in the mannes hood an ape,[76]
And in his wyves eek, by seint Austin!
Draweth no monkes more un-to your in.
     But now passe over, and lat us seke aboute,

---

68 agreement
69 farther depart
70 fate
71 chance
72 compact

73 by the body of the Lord. The remarks which follow apply to the Shipman's Tale, which has just been told.

74 a thousand loads of bad years
75 trick
76 "made a fool of the man"

Who shal now telle first, of al this route,   10
Another tale;" and with that word he sayde,
As curteisly as it had been a mayde,
"My lady Prioresse, by your leve,
So that I wiste I sholde yow nat greve,
I wolde demen that ye tellen sholde
A tale next, if so were that ye wolde.
Now wol ye vouche-sauf, my lady dere?"
    "Gladly," quod she, and seyde as ye shal here.

THE PRIORESSES TALE

Domine, dominus noster [77]

O Lord our lord, thy name how merveillous
Is in this large worlde y-sprad—quod she:—
For noght only thy laude precious
Parfourned [78] is by men of dignitee,
But by the mouth of children thy bountee
Parfourned is, for on the brest soukinge
Som tyme shewen they thyn heryinge.[79]

Wherefor in laude, as I best can or may,
Of thee, and of the whyte lily flour
Which that thee bar, and is a mayde alway,   10
To telle a storie I wol do my labour;
Not that I may encresen hir honour;
For she hir-self is honour, and the rote
Of bountee, next hir sone, and soules bote.[80]—

O moder mayde! o mayde moder free!
O bush unbrent,[81] brenninge in Moyses sighte,
That ravisedest [82] doun fro the deitee,
Thurgh thyn humblesse, the goost that in th'alighte,
Of whos vertu,[83] whan he thyn herte lighte,
Conceived was the fadres sapience,   20
Help me to telle it in thy reverence!

Lady! thy bountee, thy magnificence,
Thy vertu, and thy grete humilitee
Ther may no tonge expresse in no science;[84]
For som-tyme, lady, er men praye to thee,
Thou goost biforn of thy benignitee,

---

77 O Lord, our Lord   80 boot; *i.e.*, salvation   83 power
78 performed   81 unburned   84 knowledge
79 praise   82 didst draw (ravish)

And getest us the light, thurgh thy preyere,
To gyden us un-to thy sone so dere.

My conning is so wayk, o blisful quene,
For to declare thy grete worthinesse,   30
That I ne may the weighte nat sustene,
But as a child of twelf monthe old, or lesse,
That can unnethes [85] any word expresse,
Right so fare I, and therfor I yow preye,
Gydeth my song that I shal of yow seye.

Here Beginneth the Prioresses Tale

Ther was in Asie, in a greet citee,
Amonges Cristen folk, a Jewerye,
Sustened by a lord of that contree
For foule usure and lucre of vilanye,
Hateful to Crist and to his companye;   40
And thurgh the strete men mighte ryde or wende,
For it was free, and open at either ende.

A litel scole of Cristen folk ther stood
Doun at the ferther ende, in which ther were
Children an heep, y-comen of Cristen blood,
That lerned in that scole yeer by yere
Swich [86] maner doctrine as men used there,
This is to seyn, to singen and to rede,
As smale children doon in hir childhede.

Among thise children was a widwes sone,   50
A litel clergeon,[87] seven yeer of age,
That day by day to scole was his wone, [88]
And eek also, wher-as he saugh th'image
Of Cristes moder, hadde he in usage,
As him was taught, to knele adoun and seye
His *Ave Marie,* as he goth by the weye.

Thus hath this widwe hir litel sone y-taught
Our blisful lady, Cristes moder dere,
To worshipe ay, and he forgat it naught,
For sely child wol alday sone lere; [89]   60
But ay, whan I remembre on this matere,
Seint Nicholas stant ever in my presence,
For he so yong to Crist did reverence.

---

85 scarcely   87 scholar   89 for good child will
86 such   88 wont   always soon learn

This litel child, his litel book lerninge,
As he sat in the scole at his prymer,
He *Alma redemptoris* [90] herde singe,
As children lerned hir antiphoner;
And, as he dorste, he drough him ner and ner,
And herkned ay the wordes and the note,
Til he the firste vers coude [91] al by rote. 70

Noght wiste he what this Latin was to seye,
For he so yong and tendre was of age;
But on a day his felaw gan he preye
T'expounden him this song in his langage,
Or telle him why this song was in usage;
This preyde he him to construe and declare
Ful ofte tyme upon his knowes [92] bare.

His felaw, which that elder was than he,
Answerde him thus: "this song, I have herd seye,
Was maked of our blisful lady free, 80
Hir to salue, and eek hir for to preye
To been our help and socour whan we deye.
I can no more expounde in this matere;
I lerne song, I can [93] but smal grammere."

"And is this song maked in reverence
Of Cristes moder?" seyde this innocent;
"Now certes, I wol do my diligence
To conne it al, er Cristemasse is went;
Though that I for my prymer shal be shent,[94]
And shal be beten thryës in an houre, 90
I wol it conne, our lady for to honoure."

His felaw taughte him homward prively,
Fro day to day, til he coude it by rote,
And than he song it wel and boldely
Fro word to word, acording with the note;
Twyës a day it passed thurgh his throte,
To scoleward and homward whan he wente;
On Cristes moder set was his entente.

As I have seyd, thurgh-out the Jewerye
This litel child, as he cam to and fro, 100
Ful merily than wolde he singe, and crye
O Alma redemptoris ever-mo.

90 Gracious Mother of   91 knew   93 know
the Redeemer   92 knees   94 scolded

The swetnes hath his herte perced so
Of Cristes moder, that, to hir to preye,
He can nat stinte of singing by the weye.

Our firste fo, the serpent Sathanas,
That hath in Jewes herte his waspes nest,
Up swal, and seide, "O Hebraik peple, allas!
Is this to yow a thing that is honest,
That swich a boy shal walken as him lest   110
In your despyt, and singe of swich sentence,
Which is agayn your lawes reverence?"

Fro thennes forth the Jewes han conspyred
This innocent out of this world to chace;
An homicyde ther-to han they hyred,
That in an aley hadde a privee place;
And as the child gan for-by for to pace,
This cursed Jew him hente [95] and heeld him faste,
And kitte his throte, and in a pit him caste.

I seye that in a wardrobe [96] they him threwe   120
Wher-as these Jewes purgen hir entraille.
O cursed folk of Herodes al newe,
What may your yvel entente yow availle?
Mordre wol out, certein, it wol nat faille,
And namely ther th'onour of god shal sprede,
The blood out cryeth on your cursed dede.

"O martir, souded to [97] virginitee,
Now maystou singen, folwing ever in oon
The whyte lamb celestial," quod she,
"Of which the grete evangelist, seint John,   130
In Pathmos wroot, which seith that they that goon
Biforn this lamb, and singe a song al newe,
That never, fleshly, wommen they ne knewe."

This povre widwe awaiteth al that night
After hir litel child, but he cam noght;
For which, as sone as it was dayes light,
With face pale of drede and bisy thoght,
She hath at scole and elles-wher him soght,
Til finally she gan so fer espye
That he last seyn was in the Jewerye.   140

With modres pitee in hir brest enclosed,
She gooth, as she were half out of hir minde,

95 seized   96 privy   97 confirmed in

To every place wher she hath supposed
By lyklihede hir litel child to finde;
And ever on Cristes moder meke and kinde
She cryde, and atte laste thus she wroghte,
Among the cursed Jewes she him soghte.

She frayneth [98] and she preyeth pitously
To every Jew that dwelt in thilke place,
To telle hir, if hir child wente oght for-by.   150
They seyde, "nay"; but Jesu, of his grace,
Yaf [99] in hir thought, inwith a litel space,
That in that place after hir sone she cryde,
Wher he was a casten in a pit bisyde.

O grete god, that parfournest [1] thy laude
By mouth of innocents, lo heer thy might!
This gemme of chastitee, this emeraude,
And eek of martirdom the ruby bright,
Ther he with throte y-corven [2] lay upright,
He *"Alma redemptoris"* gan to singe   160
So loude, that al the place gan to ringe.

The Cristen folk, that thurgh the strete wente,
In coomen, for to woundre up-on this thing,
And hastily they for the provost sente;
He cam anon with-outen tarying,
And herieth [3] Crist that is of heven king,
And eek his moder, honour of mankinde,
And after that, the Jewes leet he binde.

This child with pitous lamentacioun
Up-taken was, singing his song alway;   170
And with honour of greet processioun
They carien him un-to the nexte abbay.
His moder swowning by the bere lay;
Unnethe [4] might the peple that was there
This newe Rachel bringe fro his bere.

With torment and with shamful deth echon
This provost dooth thise Jewes for to sterve [5]
That of this mordre wiste, and that anon;
He nolde no swich cursednesse observe.[6]
Yvel shal have, that yvel wol deserve.   180

98 asketh   2 cut   5 die
99 gave   3 praiseth   6 favor
1 performest   4 with difficulty

Therfor with wilde hors he dide hem drawe,
And after that he heng hem by the lawe.

Up-on his bere ay lyth this innocent
Biforn the chief auter,[7] whyl masse laste,
And after that, the abbot with his covent
Han sped hem for to burien him ful faste;
And whan they holy water on him caste,
Yet spak this child, whan spreynd [8] was holy water,
And song—"*O Alma redemptoris mater!*"

This abbot, which that was an holy man   190
As monkes been, or elles oghten be,
This yonge child to conjure he bigan,
And seyde, "o dere child, I halse [9] thee,
In vertu of the holy Trinitee,
Tel me what is thy cause for to singe,
Sith that thy throte is cut, to my seminge?"

"My throte is cut un-to my nekke-boon,"
Seyde this child, "and, as by wey of kinde,[10]
I sholde have deyed, ye, longe tyme agoon,
But Jesu Crist, as ye in bokes finde,   200
Wil that his glorie laste and be in minde;
And, for the worship of his moder dere,
Yet may I singe 'O Alma' loude and clere.

This welle of mercy, Cristes moder swete,
I lovede alwey, as after my conninge;
And whan that I my lyf sholde forlete,[11]
To me she cam, and bad me for to singe
This antem verraily in my deyinge,
As ye han herd, and, whan that I had songe,
Me thoughte, she leyde a greyn up-on my tonge.   210

Wherfor I singe, and singe I moot certeyn
In honour of that blisful mayden free,
Til fro my tonge of-taken is the greyn;
And afterward thus seyde she to me,
'My litel child, now wol I fecche thee
Whan that the greyn is fro thy tonge y-take;
Be nat agast, I wol thee nat forsake.'"

This holy monk, this abbot, him mene I,
His tonge out-caughte, and took a-wey the greyn,

7 altar	9 beseech	11 lose
8 sprinkled	10 nature	

And he yaf up the goost ful softely. 220
And whan this abbot had this wonder seyn,
His salte teres trikled doun as reyn,
And gruf [12] he fil al plat up-on the grounde,
And stille he lay as he had been y-bounde.

The covent eek lay on the pavement
Weping, and herien [13] Cristes moder dere,
And after that they ryse, and forth ben went,
And toke awey this martir fro his bere,
And in a tombe of marbul-stones clere
Enclosen they his litel body swete; 230
Ther he is now, god leve us for to mete.

O yonge Hugh of Lincoln, slayn also
With cursed Jewes, as it is notable,
For it nis but a litel whyle ago;
Preye eek for us, we sinful folk unstable,
That, of his mercy, god so merciable
On us his grete mercy multiplye,
For reverence of his moder Marye. Amen.

PROLOGUE TO SIR THOPAS

Bihold the murye wordes of the Host to Chaucer

Whan seyd was al this miracle, every man
As sobre was, that wonder was to see,
Til that our hoste japen [14] tho bigan,
And than at erst he loked up-on me,
And seyde thus, "what man artow?" quod he;
"Thou lokest as thou woldest finde an hare,
For ever up-on the ground I see thee stare.

Approche neer, and loke up merily.
Now war yow,[15] sirs, and lat this man have place;
He in the waast is shape as wel as I; 10
This were a popet [16] in an arm t'enbrace
For any womman, smal and fair of face.
He semeth elvish [17] by his contenaunce,
For un-to no wight dooth he daliaunce.

Sey now somwhat, sin other folk han sayd;
Tel us a tale of mirthe, and that anoon,"—

12 prone
13 praising
14 jest

15 give way
16 puppet, doll (spoken here ironically of Chau-cer's corpulence)
17 *i.e.*, abstracted

"Hoste," quod I, "ne beth nat yvel apayd,[18]
For other tale certes can I noon,
But of a ryme I lerned longe agoon."
"Ye, that is good," quod he; "now shul we here   20
Som deyntee thing, me thinketh by his chere."

SIR THOPAS

Here biginneth Chaucers Tale of Thopas

Listeth, lordes, in good entent,
And I wol telle verrayment
    Of mirthe and of solas;
Al of a knyght was fair and gent
In bataille and in tourneyment,
    His name was sir Thopas.

Y-born he was in fer contree,
In Flaundres, al biyonde the see,
    At Popering, in the place;[19]
His fader was a man ful free,   10
And lord he was of that contree,
    As it was goddes grace.

Sir Thopas wex a doghty swayn,
Whyt was his face as payndemayn,[20]
    His lippes rede as rose;
His rode [21] is lyk scarlet in grayn,
And I yow telle in good certayn,
    He hadde a semely nose.

His heer, his berd was lyk saffroun,
That to his girdel raughte [22] adoun;   20
    His shoon of Cordewane.[23]
Of Brugges were his hosen broun,
His robe was of ciclatoun,[24]
    That coste many a jane.[25]

He coude hunte at wilde deer,
And ryde an hauking for riveer,
    With grey goshauk on honde;
Ther-to he was a good archeer,
Of wrastling was ther noon his peer,
    Ther any ram shal stonde.[26]   30

18 ill-pleased
19 manor house (indicating he was of bourgeois origin)
20 fine white bread
21 complexion
22 reached
23 Cordovan leather
24 a rich cloth
25 a small coin of Genoa
26 See p. 113, f.n. 92 Wrestling was a bourgeois, not a knightly sport

Ful many a mayde, bright in bour,
They moorne for him, paramour,
    Whan hem were bet to slepe;
But he was chast and no lechour,
And sweet as is the bremble-flour [27]
    That bereth the rede hepe.[28]

And so bifel up-on a day,
For sothe, as I yow telle may,
    Sir Thopas wolde out ryde;
He worth [29] upon his stede gray,   40
And in his honde a launcegay,[30]
    A long swerd by his syde.[31]

·   ·   ·   ·   ·   ·

[The Second Fit.[32]]

Now hold your mouth, *par charitee*,
Bothe knight and lady free,
    And herkneth to my spelle;
Of bataille and of chivalry,
And of ladyes love-drury,[33]
    Anon I wol yow telle.

Men speke of romances of priys,[34]
Of Horn child and of Ypotys,[35]   50
    Of Bevis and sir Gy,
Of sir Libeux and Pleyn-damour;
But sir Thopas, he bereth the flour
    Of royal chivalry.

His gode stede al he bistrood,
And forth upon his wey he glood [36]
    As sparkle out of the bronde;
Up-on his crest he bar a tour,[37]
And ther-in stiked a lily-flour,
    God shilde his cors fro shonde! [38]   60

And for he was a knight auntrous,[39]
He nolde slepen in non hous,
    But liggen in his hode; [40]
His brighte helm was his wonger,[41]

27 flower of the bramble
28 hip
29 got
30 a kind of lance
31 There follow twenty
stanzas narrating how he
goes to the land of Fairy,

where he meets a giant
whom he plans to fight
32 division, or canto
33 passion
34 renown
35 Epictetus—a moralist
here mixed in among

heroes of the romances
36 glided
37 tower
38 body from disgrace
39 adventurous
40 lie in his hood
41 pillow

And by him baiteth [42] his dextrer [43]
Of herbes fyne and gode.

Him-self drank water of the wel,
As did the knight sir Percivel,
  So worthy under wede,[44]
Til on a day—   70

PROLOGUE TO MELIBEUS

"No more of this, for goddes dignitee,"
Quod oure hoste, "for thou makest me
So wery of thy verray lewednesse [45]
That, also wisly god my soule blesse,
Myn eres aken of thy drasty speche;
Now swiche a rym the devel I biteche! [46]
This may wel be rym dogerel," quod he.
  "Why so?" quod I, "why wiltow lette [47] me
More of my tale than another man,
Sin that it is the beste rym I can?"   80
  "By god," quod he, "for pleynly, at a word,
Thy drasty ryming is nat worth a tord;
Thou doost nought elles but despendest tyme,
Sir, at o word, thou shalt no lenger ryme.
Lat see wher thou canst tellen aught in geste,[48]
Or telle in prose somwhat at the leste
In which ther be som mirthe or som doctryne."
  "Gladly," quod I, "by goddess swete pyne,
I wol yow telle a litel thing in prose,
That oghte lyken yow, as I suppose,
Or elles, certes, ye been to daungerous.[49]   90
It is a moral tale vertuous,
Al be it told som-tyme in sondry wyse
Of sondry folk, as I shal yow devyse." [50]

  .   .   .   .

THE NONNE PREESTES TALE

A povre widwe, somdel stape [51] in age,
Was whylom dwelling in a narwe cotage,
Bisyde a grove, stonding in a dale.
This widwe, of which I telle yow my tale,

---

42 feedeth
43 courser
44 weed, garment
45 ignorance

46 "I commit to the devil"
47 hinder, stop
48 romantic tale
49 hard to please

50 Chaucer then tells the very moral prose tale of Melibeus.
*51 advanced

Sin thilke day that she was last a wyf,
In pacience ladde a ful simple lyf,
For litel was hir catel and hir rente; [52]
By housbondrye,[53] of such as God hir sente,
She fond [54] hir-self, and eek hir doghtren two.
Three large sowes hadde she, and namo,   10
Three kyn, and eek a sheep that highte Malle.
Ful sooty was hir bour, and eek hir halle,
In which she eet ful many a sclendre meel.
Of poynaunt sauce hir neded never a deel.
No deyntee morsel passed thurgh hir throte;
Hir dyete was accordant to hir cote.
Repleccioun ne made hir never syk;
Attempree [55] dyete was al hir phisyk,
And exercyse, and hertes suffisaunce.
The goute lette [56] hir no-thing for to daunce,   20
N'apoplexye shente [57] nat hir heed;
No wyn ne drank she, neither whyt ne reed;
Hir bord was served most with whyt and blak,
Milk and broun breed, in which she fond no lak,
Seynd [58] bacoun, and somtyme an ey [59] or tweye,
For she was as it were a maner deye.[60]
   A yerd she hadde, enclosed al aboute
With stikkes, and a drye dich with-oute,
In which she hadde a cok, hight Chauntecleer,
In al the land of crowing nas [61] his peer.   30
His vois was merier than the mery orgon
On messe-dayes that in the chirche gon;
Wel sikerer [62] was his crowing in his logge,[63]
Than is a clokke, or an abbey orlogge.[64]
By nature knew he ech ascencioun
Of equinoxial [65] in thilke toun;
For whan degrees fiftene [66] were ascended,
Thanne crew he, that it mighte nat been amended.
His comb was redder than the fyn coral,
And batailed, as it were a castel-wal.   40
His bile was blak, and as the jeet it shoon;
Lyk asur were his legges, and his toon; [67]
His nayles whytter than the lilie flour,
And lyk the burned gold was his colour.
This gentil cok hadde in his governaunce
Sevene hennes, for to doon al his plesaunce,

---

52 her chattels and her income
53 economy
54 provided for
55 a temperate
56 hindered
57 injured
58 broiled
59 egg
60 a kind of dairy-woman
61 was not
62 surer
63 lodge
64 clock
65 i.e., each hour
66 i.e., an hour
67 toes

Whiche were his sustres and his paramours,
And wonder lyk to him, as of colours.
Of whiche the faireste hewed on hir throte
Was cleped faire damoysele Pertelote.   50
Curteys she was, discreet, and debonaire,
And compaignable, and bar hir-self so faire,
Sin thilke day that she was seven night old,
That trewely she hath the herte in hold
Of Chauntecleer loken in every lith; [68]
He loved hir so, that wel was him therwith.
But such a joye was it to here hem singe,
Whan that the brighte sonne gan to springe,
In swete accord, "my lief is faren [69] in londe."
For thilke tyme, as I have understonde,   60
Bestes and briddes coude speke and singe.
     And so bifel, that in a daweninge,
As Chauntecleer among his wyves alle
Sat on his perche, that was in the halle,
And next him sat this faire Pertelote,
This Chauntecleer gan gronen in his throte,
As man that in his dreem is drecched [70] sore.
And whan that Pertelote thus herde him rore,
She was agast, and seyde, "O herte dere,
What eyleth yow, to grone in this manere?   70
Ye been a verray sleper, fy for shame!"
And he answerde and seyde thus, "madame,
I pray yow, that ye take it nat a-grief:
By god, me mette [71] I was in swich meschief
Right now, that yet myn herte is sore afright.
Now god," quod he, "my swevene recche [72] aright,
And keep my body out of foul prisoun!
Me mette, how that I romed up and doun
Withinne our yerde, wher-as I saugh a beste,
Was lyk an hound, and wolde han maad areste   80
Upon my body, and wolde han had me deed.
His colour was bitwixe yelwe and reed;
And tipped was his tail, and bothe his eres,
With blak, unlyk the remenant of his heres;
His snowte smal, with glowinge eyen tweye.
Yet of his look for fere almost I deye;
This caused me my groning, doutelees."
     "Avoy!" quod she, "fy on yow, hertelees!
Allas!" quod she, "for, by that god above,
Now han ye lost myn herte and al my love;   90

68 limb   70 troubled   72 my dream interpret
69 my love is gone   71 I dreamed

I can nat love a coward, by my feith.
For certes, what so any womman seith,
We alle desyren, if it mighte be,
To han housbondes hardy, wyse, and free,
And secree, and no nigard, ne no fool,
Ne him that is agast of every tool,[73]
Ne noon avauntour,[74] by that god above!
How dorste ye seyn for shame unto your love,
That any thing mighte make yow aferd?
Have ye no mannes herte, and han a berd?   100
Allas! and conne ye been agast of swevenis?
No-thing, god wot, but vanitee, in sweven is.
Swevenes engendren of replecciouns,[75]
And ofte of fume,[76] and of complecciouns,[77]
Whan humours been to habundant in a wight.
Certes this dreem, which ye han met to-night,
Cometh of the grete superfluitee
Of youre rede *colera*,[78] pardee,
Which causeth folk to dreden in here dremes
Of arwes, and of fyr with rede lemes,[79]   110
Of grete bestes, that they wol hem byte,
Of contek,[80] and of whelpes grete and lyte;
Right as the humour of malencolye [81]
Causeth ful many a man, in sleep, to crye,
For fere of blake beres, or boles [82] blake,
Or elles, blake develes wole hem take.
Of othere humours coude I telle also,
That werken many a man in sleep ful wo;
But I wol passe as lightly as I can.
    Lo Catoun,[83] which that was so wys a man,   120
Seyde he nat thus, ne do no fors [84] of dremes?
Now, sire," quod she, "whan we flee fro the bemes,[85]
For Goddes love, as tak som laxatyf;
Up [86] peril of my soule, and of my lyf,
I counseille yow the beste, I wol nat lye,
That bothe of colere and of malencolye
Ye purge yow; and for ye shul nat tarie,
Though in this toun is noon apotecarie,
I shal my-self to herbes techen yow,
That shul ben for your hele, and for your prow; [87]   130
And in our yerd tho herbes shal I finde,

---

73 weapon
74 boaster
75 over-eating
76 vapors arising from the stomach to the brain
77 collection of humors (see p. 110, f.n. 55)
78 choler
79 flames
80 strife
81 black bile
82 bulls
83 Dionysius Cato, a medieval writer
84 pay no attention to
85 rafters
86 upon
87 profit

The whiche han of hir propretee, by kinde,[88]
To purgen yow binethe, and eek above.
Forget not this, for goddes owene love!
Ye been ful colerik of compleccioun.[89]
Ware [90] the sonne in his ascencioun
Ne fynde yow nat repleet of humours hote;
And if it do, I dar wel leye a grote,
That ye shul have a fevere terciane,
Or an agu, that may be youre bane.[91]   140
A day or two ye shul have digestyves
Of wormes, er ye take your laxatyves,
Of lauriol, centaure, and fumetere,
Or elles of ellebor, that groweth there,
Of catapuce, or of gaytres [92] beryis,
Of erbe yve,[93] growing in our yerd, that mery is;
Pekke hem up right as they growe, and ete hem in.
Be mery, housbond, for your fader kin!
Dredeth no dreem; I can say yow namore."
    "Madame," quod he, "graunt mercy of [94] your lore.   150
But nathelees, as touching daun [95] Catoun,
That hath of wisdom such a greet renoun,
Though that he had no dremes for to drede,
By god, men may in olde bokes rede
Of many a man, more of auctoritee
Than ever Catoun was, so mote I thee,[96]
That al the revers seyn of his sentence,
And han wel founden by experience,
That dremes ben significaciouns,
As wel of joye as tribulaciouns   160
That folk enduren in this lyf present.
Ther nedeth make of this noon argument;
The verray preve [97] sheweth it in dede.
    Oon of the gretteste auctours [98] that men rede
Seith thus, that whylom two felawes wente
On pilgrimage, in a ful good entente;
And happed so, thay come into a toun,
Wher-as ther was swich congregacioun
Of peple, and eek so streit of herbergage [99]
That they ne founde as muche as o cotage   170
In which they bothe mighte y-logged be.
Wherfor thay mosten, of necessitee,
As for that night, departen compaignye;

88 nature
89 temperament   (mix-
ture of the humors)
90 take care lest
91 death

92 buckthorn
93 ground ivy
94 many thanks for
95 master   (Lat. domi-
nus)

96 thrive
97 proof
98 Cicero, in De Divina-
tione
99 so little lodging

And ech of hem goth to his hostelrye,
And took his logging as it wolde falle.
That oon of hem was logged in a stalle,
Fer in a yerd, with oxen of the plough;
That other man was logged wel y-nough,
As was his aventure,[1] or his fortune,
That us governeth alle as in commune.   180
   And so bifel, that, longe er it were day,
This man mette[2] in his bed, ther-as[3] he lay,
How that his felawe gan up-on him calle,
   And seyde, 'allas! for in an oxes stalle
This night I shal be mordred ther[3] I lye.
Now help me, dere brother, er I dye;
In alle haste com to me,' he sayde.
This man out of his sleep for fere abrayde;[4]
But whan that he was wakned of his sleep,
He turned him, and took of this no keep;   190
Him thoughte his dreem nas but a vanitee.
Thus twyës in his sleping dremed he.
And atte thridde tyme yet his felawe
Cam, as him thoughte, and seide, 'I am now slawe;[5]
Bihold my blody woundes, depe and wyde!
Arys up erly in the morwe-tyde,
And at the west gate of the toun,' quod he,
'A carte ful of dong ther shaltow see,
In which my body is hid ful prively;
Do thilke carte aresten boldely.   200
My gold caused my mordre, sooth to sayn;'
And tolde him every poynt how he was slayn,
With a ful pitous face, pale of hewe.
And truste wel, his dreem he fond ful trewe;
For on the morwe, as sone as it was day,
To his felawes in[6] he took the way;
And whan that he cam to this oxes stalle,
After his felawe he bigan to calle.
   The hostiler answered him anon,
And seyde, 'sire, your felawe is agon,   210
As sone as day he wente out of the toun.'
This man gan fallen in suspecioun,
Remembring on his dremes that he mette,
And forth he goth, no lenger wolde he lette,[7]
Unto the west gate of the toun, and fond
A dong-carte, as it were to donge lond,

---

1 chance   4 started   7 tarry
2 dreamed   5 slain
3 whereas, where   6 inn

That was arrayed in the same wyse
As ye han herd the dede man devyse;
And with an hardy herte he gan to crye
Vengeaunce and justice of this felonye:—   220
'My felawe mordred is this same night,
And in this carte he lyth gapinge upright.[8]
I crye out on the ministres,' quod he,
'That sholden kepe and reulen this citee;
Harrow! allas! her lyth my felawe slayn!'
What sholde I more un-to this tale sayn?
The peple out-sterte, and caste the cart to grounde,
And in the middel of the dong they founde
The dede man, that mordred was al newe.
     O blisful god, that art so just and trewe!   230
Lo, how that thou biwreyest [9] mordre alway!
Mordre wol out, that see we day by day.
Mordre is so wlatsom [10] and abhominable
To God, that is so just and resonable,
That he ne wol nat suffre it heled [11] be;
Though it abyde a yeer, or two, or three,
Mordre wol out, this my conclusioun.
And right anoon, ministres of that toun
Han hent [12] the carter, and so sore him pyned,[13]
And eek the hostiler so sore engyned,[14]   240
That thay biknewe [15] hir wikkednesse anoon,
And were an-hanged by the nekke-boon.
     Here may men seen that dremes been to drede,
And certes, in the same book I rede,
Right in the nexte chapitre after this
(I gabbe [16] nat, so have I joye or blis),
Two men that wolde han passed over see,
For certeyn cause, in-to a fer contree,
If that the wind ne hadde been contrarie,
That made hem in a citee for to tarie,   250
That stood ful mery upon an havensyde.
But on a day, agayn [17] the even-tyde,
The wind gan chaunge, and blew right as hem leste.
Jolif and glad they wente un-to hir reste,
And casten hem ful erly for to saille;
But to that oo man fil a greet mervaille.
That oon of hem, in sleping as he lay,
Him mette a wonder dreem, agayn [17] the day;
Him thoughte a man stood by his beddes syde,

---

8 mouth open, on his back
9 revealest
10 heinous
11 hidden
12 seized
13 tortured
14 racked
15 acknowledged
16 lie
17 against (towards)

And him comaunded, that he sholde abyde, 260
And seyde him thus, 'if thou to-morwe wende,
Thou shalt be dreynt; [18] my tale is at an ende.'
He wook, and tolde his felawe what he mette.
And preyde him his viage for to lette; [19]
As for that day, he preyde him to abyde.
His felawe, that lay by his beddes syde,
Gan for to laughe, and scorned him ful faste.
'No dreem,' quod he, 'may so myn herte agaste,
That I wol lette for to do my thinges.
I sette not a straw by thy dreminges, 270
For swevenes been but vanitees and japes.
Men dreme al-day of owles or of apes,
And eke of many a mase [20] therwithal;
Men dreme of thing that never was ne shal.
But sith I see that thou wolt heer abyde,
And thus for-sleuthen [21] wilfully thy tyde,
God wot it reweth me; and have good day.'
And thus he took his leve, and wente his way.
But er that he hadde halfe his cours y-seyled,
Noot I nat why, ne what mischaunce it eyled, 280
But casuelly [22] the shippes botme rente,
And ship and man under the water wente
In sighte of othere shippes it byside,
That with hem seyled at the same tyde.
And therfor, faire Pertelote so dere,
By swiche ensamples olde maistow lere, [23]
That no man sholde been to recchelees
Of dremes, for I sey thee, doutelees,
That many a dreem ful sore is for to drede.
Lo, in the lyf of seint Kenelm, I rede, 290
That was Kenulphus sone, the noble king
Of Mercenrike, [24] how Kenelm mette a thing;
A lyte [25] er he was mordred, on a day,
His mordre in his avisioun he say. [26]
His norice [27] him expouned every del
His sweven, and bad him for to kepe him wel
For [28] traisoun; but he nas but seven yeer old,
And therfore litel tale hath he told [29]
Of any dreem, so holy was his herte.
By god, I hadde lever than my sherte 300
That ye had rad his legende, as have I.
Dame Pertelote, I sey yow trewely,

18 drowned
19 delay
20 maze, bewilderment
21 waste in sloth
22 accidentally
23 mayest thou learn
24 Mercia
25 little
26 saw
27 nurse
28 against
29 store hath he set

Macrobeus,[30] that writ th' avisioun
In Affrike of the worthy Cipioun,
Affermeth dremes, and seith that they been
Warning of thinges that men after seen.
   And forther-more, I pray yow loketh wel
In th'olde testament, of Daniel,
If he held dremes any vanitee.
Reed eek of Joseph, and ther shul ye see   310
Wher dremes ben somtyme (I sey nat alle)
Warning of thinges that shul after falle.
Loke of Egipt the king, daun Pharao,
His bakere and his boteler also,
Wher they ne felte noon effect in dremes.
Who-so wol seken actes of sondry remes,[31]
May rede of dremes many a wonder thing.
   Lo Cresus, which that was of Lyde king,
Mette he nat that he sat upon a tree,
Which signified he sholde anhanged be?   320
Lo heer Andromacha, Ectores wyf,
That day that Ector sholde lese his lyf,
She dremed on the same night biforn,
How that the lyf of Ector sholde be lorn,
If thilke day he wente in-to bataille;
She warned him, but it mighte nat availle;
He wente for to fighte nathelees,
But he was slayn anoon of Achilles.
But thilke tale is al to long to telle,
And eek it is ny day, I may nat dwelle.   330
Shortly I seye, as for conclusioun,
That I shal han of this avisioun
Adversitee; and I seye forther-more,
That I ne telle of [32] laxatyves no store,
For they ben venimous, I woot it wel;
I hem defye, I love him never a del.
   Now let us speke of mirthe, and stinte al this;
Madame Pertelote, so have I blis,
Of o thing god hath sent me large grace;
For whan I see the beautee of your face,   340
Ye ben so scarlet-reed about your yën,[33]
It maketh al my drede for to dyen;
For, also siker [34] as *In principio,*
Mulier est hominis confusio; [35]
Madame, the sentence of this Latin is—

30 Latin writer of the fifth century, who anno-tated Cicero's *Somnium Scipionis*

31 realms
32 set by
33 eyes
34 sure

35 In the beginning, woman is man's undoing

Womman is mannes joye and al his blis.
For whan I fele a-night your softe syde,
Al-be-it that I may nat on you ryde,
For that our perche is maad so narwe, alas!
I am so ful of joye and of solas   350
That I defye bothe sweven and dreem."
And with that word he fley doun fro the beem.
For it was day, and eek his hennes alle;
And with a chuk he gan hem for to calle,
For he had founde a corn, lay in the yerd.
Royal he was, he was namore aferd;
He fethered Pertelote twenty tyme,
And trad as ofte, er that it was pryme.[36]
He loketh as it were a grim leoun;
And on his toos he rometh up and doun,   360
Him deyned not to sette his foot to grounde.
He chukketh, whan he hath a corn y-founde,
And to him rennen thanne his wyves alle.
Thus royal, as a prince is in his halle,
Leve I this Chauntecleer in his pasture;
And after wol I telle his aventure.
    Whan that the month in which the world bigan,
That highte March, whan god first maked man,
Was complet, and [y]-passed were also,
Sin March bigan, thritty dayes and two,[37]   370
Bifel that Chauntecleer, in al his pryde,
His seven wyves walking by his syde,
Caste up his eyen to the brighte sonne,
That in the signe of Taurus [38] hadde y-ronne
Twenty degrees and oon, and somwhat more;
And knew by kynde,[39] and by noon other lore,
That it was pryme, and crew with blisful stevene.
"The sonne," he sayde, "is clomben up on hevene
Fourty degrees and oon, and more, y-wis.
Madame Pertelote, my worldes blis,   380
Herkneth thise blisful briddes how they singe,
And see the fresshe floures how they springe;
Ful is myn herte of revel and solas."
But sodeinly him fil a sorweful cas;[40]
For ever the latter ende of joye is wo.
God woot that worldly joye is sone ago;
And if a rethor [41] coude faire endyte,
He in a cronique saufly mighte it wryte,

36 nine o'clock
37 March has passed, and thirty-two days more; i.e., it is May 3.
38 See p. 99, f.n. 8. The sun enters the zodiacal sign of the Bull after that of the Ram.
39 nature
40 happening
41 rhetorician

As for a sovereyn notabilitee.
Now every wys man, lat him herkne me;   390
This storie is al-so trewe, I undertake,
As is the book of Launcelot de Lake,
That wommen holde in ful gret reverence.
Now wol I torne agayn to my sentence.

  A col-fox,[42] ful of sly iniquitee,
That in the grove hadde woned[43] yeres three,
By heigh imaginacioun forn-cast,[44]
The same night thurgh-out the hegges brast[45]
Into the yerd, ther Chauntecleer the faire
Was wont, and eek his wyves, to repaire;   400
And in a bed of wortes stille he lay,
Til it was passed undern[46] of the day,
Wayting his tyme on Chauntecleer to falle,
As gladly doon thise homicydes alle,
That in awayt liggen to mordre men.
O false mordrer, lurking in thy den!
O newe Scariot,[47] newe Genilon![48]
False dissimilour, O Greek Sinon,[49]
That broghtest Troye al outrely to sorwe!
O Chauntecleer, acursed be that morwe,   410
That thou into that yerd flough fro the bemes!
Thou were ful wel y-warned by thy dremes,
That thilke day was perilous to thee.
But what that god forwoot mot nedes[50] be,
After the opinioun of certeyn clerkis.
Witnesse on him, that any perfit clerk is,
That in scole is gret altercacioun
In this matere, and greet disputisoun,
And hath ben of an hundred thousand men.
But I ne can not bulte it to the bren,[51]   420
As can the holy doctour Augustyn,
Or Boëce, or the bishop Bradwardyn,[52]
Whether that goddes worthy forwiting[53]
Streyneth me nedely[54] for to doon a thing,
(Nedely clepe I simple necessitee);
Or elles, if free choys be graunted me
To do that same thing, or do it noght,
Though god forwoot it, er that it was wroght;

42 blackish fox
43 lived
44 premeditated
45 hedges burst
46 late in the morning
47 Judas Iscariot
48 Ganelon, the betrayer
of Roland
49 the "dissembler" who
persuaded the Trojans to
admit the wooden horse
50 foresees must needs
51 bolt it to the bran;
i.e. sift
52 St. Augustine, Boethi-
us, Thomas Bradwardine,
14th Cent. Archbishop of
Canterbury (all great ec-
clesiastical writers who
discuss the famous theo-
logical problem of free will
vs. predestination)
53 foreknowledge
54 constrains me neces-
sarily

Or if his witing streyneth nevere a del
But by necessitee condicionel.   430
I wol not han to do of swich matere;
My tale is of a cok, as ye may here,
That took his counseil of his wyf, with sorwe,
To walken in the yerd upon that morwe
That he had met the dreem, that I yow tolde.
Wommennes counseils been ful ofte colde;
Wommannes counseil broghte us first to wo,
And made Adam fro paradys to go,
Ther-as he was ful mery, and wel at ese.—
But for I moot, to whom it mighte displese,   440
If I counseil of wommen wolde blame,
Passe over, for I seyde it in my game.[55]
Rede auctours, wher they trete of swich matere,
And what thay seyn of wommen ye may here.
Thise been the cokkes wordes, and nat myne;
I can noon harm of no womman divyne.—[56]
   Faire in the sond,[57] to bathe hir merily,
Lyth Pertelote, and alle hir sustres by,
Agayn the sonne; and Chauntecleer so free
Song merier than the mermayde in the see;   450
For Phisiologus [58] seith sikerly,
How that they singen wel and merily.
And so bifel that, as he caste his yë,
Among the wortes, on a boterflye,
He was war of this fox that lay ful lowe.
No-thing ne liste him thanne for to crowe,
But cryde anon, "cok, cok," and up he sterte,
As man that was affrayed in his herte.
For naturelly a beest desyreth flee
Fro his contrarie, if he may it see,   460
Though he never erst [59] had seyn it with his yë.
   This Chauntecleer, whan he gan him espye,
He wolde han fled, but that the fox anon
Seyde, "Gentil sire, allas! wher wol ye gon?
Be ye affrayd of me that am your freend?
Now certes, I were worse than a feend,
If I to yow wolde harm or vileinye.
I am nat come your counseil for t'espye;
But trewely, the cause of my cominge
Was only for to herkne how that ye singe.   470
For trewely ye have as mery a stevene [60]

55 sport
56 declare
57 sand
58 or Bestiary, a popular

medieval work describing
alleged qualities of various
animals, with morals de-
duced therefrom

59 before
60 voice

As eny aungel hath, that is in hevene;
Therwith ye han in musik more felinge
Than hadde Boëce,[61] or any that can singe.
My lord your fader (god his soule blesse!)
And eek your moder, of hir gentilesse,
Han in myn hous y-been, to my gret ese; [62]
And certes, sire, ful fayn wolde I yow plese.
But for men speke of singing, I wol saye,
So mote I brouke [63] wel myn eyen [64] tweye,   480
Save yow, I herde never man so singe,
As dide your fader in the morweninge;
Certes, it was of herte, al that he song.
And for to make his voys the more strong,
He wolde so peyne him,[65] that with bothe his yën [64]
He moste winke, so loude he wolde cryen,
And stonden on his tiptoon ther-with-al,
And strecche forth his nekke long and smal.
And eek he was of swich discrecioun,
That ther nas no man in no regioun   490
That him in song or wisdom mighte passe.
I have wel rad in daun Burnel the Asse,[66]
Among his vers, how that ther was a cok,
For that a preestes sone yaf him a knok
Upon his leg, whyl he was yong and nyce,[67]
He made him for to lese his benefyce.
But certeyn, ther nis no comparisoun
Bitwix the wisdom and discrecioun
Of youre fader, and of his subtiltee.
Now singeth, sire, for seinte [68] Charitee,   500
Let see, conne ye your fader countrefete?"
This Chauntecleer his winges gan to bete,
As man that coude his tresoun nat espye,
So was he ravisshed with his flaterye.

    Allas! ye lordes, many a fals flatour
Is in your courtes, and many a losengeour,[69]
That plesen yow wel more, by my feith,
Than he that soothfastnesse [70] unto yow seith.
Redeth Ecclesiaste [71] of flaterye;
Beth war,[72] ye lordes, of hir trecherye.   510

    This Chauntecleer stood hye up-on his toos,
Strecching his nekke, and heeld his eyen cloos,

---

61 Boethius, the cele-
brated late Roman philos-
opher, wrote a treatise on
music
62 ease, pleasure
63 have the use of
64 eyes

65 take pains
66 a 12th Cent. poem,
"Burnel, or the Mirror of
Fools" by Nigellus Wire-
ker
67 foolish
68 holy

69 flatterer
70 truth
71 Ecclesiasticus (in the
Apocrypha)
72 wary

And gan to crowe loude for the nones;
And daun Russel the fox sterte up at ones
And by the gargat hente [73] Chauntecleer,
And on his bak toward the wode him beer,
For yet ne was ther no man that him sewed.[74]
O destinee, that mayst nat been eschewed!
Allas, that Chauntecleer fleigh fro the bemes!
Allas, his wyf ne roghte [75] nat of dremes!   520
And on a Friday fil al this meschaunce.
O Venus, that art goddesse of plesaunce,
Sin that thy servant was this Chauntecleer,
And in thy service dide al his poweer,
More for delyt, than world to multiplye,
Why woldestow [76] suffre him on thy day " to dye?
O Gaufred,[78] dere mayster soverayn,
That, whan thy worthy king Richard was slayn
With shot, compleynedest his deth so sore,
Why ne hadde I now thy sentence and thy lore,   530
The Friday for to chyde, as diden ye?
(For on a Friday soothly slayn was he.)
Than wolde I shewe yow how that I coude pleyne
For Chauntecleres drede, and for his peyne.
   Certes, swich cry ne lamentacioun
Was never of ladies maad, whan Ilioun
Was wonne, and Pirrus with his streite [79] swerd,
Whan he hadde hent king Priam by the berd,
And slayn him (as saith us Eneydos) [80]
As maden alle the hennes in the clos,[81]   540
Whan they had seyn of Chauntecleer the sighte.
But sovereynly dame Pertelote shrighte,
Ful louder than dide Hasdrubales wyf,
Whan that hir housbond hadde lost his lyf,
And that the Romayns hadde brend Cartage;
She was so ful of torment and of rage,
That wilfully into the fyr she sterte,
And brende hir-selven with a stedfast herte.
O woful hennes, right so cryden ye,
As, whan that Nero brende the citee   550
Of Rome, cryden senatoures wyves,
For that hir housbondes losten alle hir lyves;
Withouten gilt this Nero hath hem slayn.
Now wol I torne to my tale agayn:—
   This sely widwe, and eek hir doghtres two,

---

73 throat seized   77 Friday is Venus' day   on the death of Richard I
74 followed   (Fr. vendredi)   79 drawn
75 recked, cared   78 Geoffrey de Vinsauf,   80 Aeneid
76 wouldst thou   who wrote a lamentation   81 enclosure

Herden thise hennes crye and maken wo,
And out at dores sterten they anoon,
And syen [82] the fox toward the grove goon,
And bar upon his bak the cok away;
And cryden, "Out! harrow! and weylaway!   560
Ha, ha, the fox!" and after him they ran,
And eek with staves many another man;
Ran Colle our dogge, and Talbot, and Gerland,
And Malkin, with a distaf in hir hand;
Ran cow and calf, and eek the verray hogges
So were they fered for berking of the dogges
And shouting of the men and wimmen eke,
They ronne so, hem thoughte hir herte breke.
They yelleden as feendes doon in helle;
The dokes cryden as men wolde hem quelle;   570
The gees for fere flowen over the trees;
Out of the hyve cam the swarm of bees;
So hidous was the noyse, a! *benedicite!*
Certes, he Jakke Straw,[83] and his meynee,[84]
Ne made never shoutes half so shrille,
Whan that they wolden any Fleming kille,
As thilke day was maad upon the fox.
Of bras thay broghten bemes,[85] and of box,
Of horn, of boon, in whiche they blewe and pouped,
And therwithal thay shryked and they houped;   580
It semed as that heven sholde falle.
Now, gode men, I pray yow herkneth alle!
  Lo, how fortune turneth sodeinly
The hope and pryde eek of hir enemy!
This cok, that lay upon the foxes bak,
In al his drede, un-to the fox he spak,
And seyde, "sire, if that I were as ye,
Yet sholde I seyn (as wis god helpe me),
Turneth agayn, ye proude cherles alle!
A verray pestilence up-on yow falle!   590
Now am I come un-to this wodes syde,
Maugree your heed,[86] the cok shal heer abyde;
I wol him ete in fyeith, and that anon."—
The fox answerde, "in feith, it shal be don,"—
And as he spak that word, al sodeinly
This cok brak from his mouth deliverly,[87]
And heighe up-on a tree he fleigh anon.
And whan the fox saugh that he was y-gon,
"Allas!" quod he, "O Chauntecleer, allas!

---

82 saw
83 He led a rebellion in 1381
84 followers
85 trumpets
86 in spite of your head
(*i.e.*, all you can do)
87 nimbly

I have to yow," quod he, "y-doon trespas, 600
In-as-muche as I maked yow aferd,
Whan I yow hente, and broghte out of the yerd;
But, sire, I dide it in no wikke [88] entente;
Com doun, and I shal telle yow what I mente.
I shal seye sooth to yow, god help me so."
"Nay than," quod he, "I shrewe [89] us bothe two,
And first I shrewe my-self, bothe blood and bones,
If thou bigyle me ofter than ones.
Thou shalt na-more, thurgh thy flaterye,
Do me to singe and winke with myn yë. 610
For he that winketh, whan he sholde see,
Al wilfully, god lat him never thee!" [90]
"Nay," quod the fox, "but god yeve him meschaunce,
That is so undiscreet of governaunce,
That jangleth [91] whan he sholde holde his pees."
  Lo, swich it is for to be recchelees,
And necligent, and truste on flaterye.
But ye that holden this tale a folye,
As of a fox, or of a cok and hen,
Taketh the moralitee, good men. 620
For seint Paul seith, that al that writen is,
To our doctryne [92] it is y-write, y-wis.
Taketh the fruyt, and lat the chaf be stille.
  Now, gode god, if that it be thy wille,
As seith my lord,[93] so make us alle good men;
And bringe us to his heighe blisse. Amen.

THE PROLOGUE OF THE PARDONERS TALE

Radix malorum est Cupiditas: Ad Thimotheum, sexto [94]

"LORDINGS," quod he, "in chirches whan I preche,
I peyne me to han an hauteyn [95] speche,
And ringe it out as round as gooth a belle,
For I can [96] al by rote that I telle.
My theme is alwey oon, and ever was—
'*Radix malorum est Cupiditas.*'
  First I pronounce whennes that I come,
And than my bulles shewe I, alle and somme.
Our lige lordes seel on my patente,
That shewe I first, my body to warente, 10
That no man be so bold, ne preest ne clerk,

---

88 wicked
89 beshrew, curse
90 prosper
91 prattleth
92 for our teaching (see

2 Timothy iii. 16)
  93 the Archbishop of
Canterbury, according to
a note in one manuscript
  94 The root of all evil is

greed. i Timothy, vi. 10
  95 lofty
  96 know

Me to destourbe of Cristes holy werk;
And after that than telle I forth my tales,
Bulles of popes and of cardinales,
Of patriarkes, and bishoppes I shewe;
And in Latyn I speke a wordes fewe,
To saffron with [97] my predicacioun,
And for to stire men to devocioun.
Than shewe I forth my longe cristal stones,
Y-crammed ful of cloutes [98] and of bones;   20
Reliks been they, as wenen they echoon.[99]
Than have I in latoun [1] a sholder-boon
Which that was of an holy Jewes shepe.
'Good men,' seye I, 'tak of my wordes kepe;
If that this boon be wasshe in any welle,
If cow, or calf, or sheep, or oxe swelle
That any worm hath ete, or worm [2] y-stonge,
Tak water of that welle, and wash his tonge,
And it is hool anon; and forthermore,
Of pokkes and of scabbe, and every sore   30
Shal every sheep be hool, that of this welle
Drinketh a draughte; tak kepe eek what I telle.
If that the good-man, that the bestes oweth,[3]
Wol every wike,[4] er that the cok him croweth,
Fastinge, drinken of this welle a draughte,
As thilke holy Jewe our eldres taughte,
His bestes and his stoor shal multiplye.
And, sirs, also it heleth jalousye;
For, though a man be falle in jalous rage,
Let maken with this water his potage,   40
And never shal he more his wyf mistriste,
Though he the sooth of hir defaute wiste;
Al had she taken preestes two or three.
    Heer is a miteyn eek, that ye may see.
He that his hond wol putte in this miteyn,
He shal have multiplying of his greyn,
When he hath sowen, be it whete or otes,
So that he offre pens, or elles grotes.
    Good men and wommen, o thing warne I yow,
If any wight be in this chirche now,   50
That hath doon sinne horrible, that he
Dar nat, for shame, of it y-shriven be,
Or any womman, be she yong or old,
That hath y-maad hir housbond cokewold,[5]

97 tinge with saffron;   1 latten; an alloy re-   4 week
i.e., color   sembling brass   5 cuckold
98 rags   2 snake
99 imagine they each one   3 owneth

Swich folk shul have no power ne no grace
To offren to my reliks in this place.
And who-so findeth him out of swich blame,
He wol com up and offre in goddes name,
And I assoille [6] him by the auctoritee
Which that by bulle y-graunted was to me.'   60
    By this gaude [7] have I wonne, yeer by yeer,
An hundred mark sith I was Pardoner.
I stonde lyk a clerk in my pulpet,
And whan the lewed peple is doun y-set,
I preche, so as ye han herd bifore,
And telle an hundred false japes [8] more.
Than peyne I me to strecche forth the nekke,
And est and west upon the peple I bekke,[9]
As doth a dowve sitting on a berne.
Myn hondes and my tonge goon so yerne,[10]   70
That it is joye to see my bisinesse.
Of avaryce and of swich cursednesse
Is al my preching, for to make hem free
To yeve her pens, and namely un-to me.
For my entente is nat but for to winne,
And no-thing for correccioun of sinne.
I rekke never, whan that they ben beried,
Though that her soules goon a-blake-beried! [11]
For certes, many a predicacioun
Comth ofte tyme of yvel entencioun;   80
Som for plesaunce of folk and flaterye,
To been avaunced by ipocrisye,
And som for veyne glorie, and som for hate.
For, whan I dar non other weyes debate,
Than wol I stinge him with my tonge smerte
In preching, so that he shal nat asterte [12]
To been defamed falsly, if that he
Hath trespased to my brethren or to me.
For, though I telle noght his propre name,
Men shal wel knowe that it is the same   90
By signes and by othere circumstances.
Thus quyte I folk that doon us displesances;
Thus spitte I out my venim under hewe
Of holynesse, to seme holy and trewe.
    But shortly myn entente I wol devyse;
I preche of no-thing but for coveityse.
Therfor my theme is yet, and ever was—

6 absolve   9 nod   astray
7 trickery   10 eagerly   12 escape
8 jokes, tricks   11 a-blackberrying; *i. e.*,

'*Radix malorum est cupiditas.*'
Thus can I preche agayn that same vyce
Which that I use, and that is avaryce.   100
But, though my-self be gilty in that sinne,
Yet can I maken other folk to twinne [13]
From avaryce, and sore to repente.
But that is nat my principal entente.
I preche no-thing but for coveityse;
Of this matere it oughte y-nogh suffyse.
   Than telle I hem ensamples many oon
Of olde stories, longe tyme agoon:
For lewed [14] peple loven tales olde;
Swich thinges can they wel reporte and holde.   110
What? trowe ye, the whyles I may preche,
And winne gold and silver for I teche,
That I wol live in povert wilfully?
Nay, nay, I thoghte it never trewely!
For I wol preche and begge in sondry londes;
I wol not do no labour with myn hondes,
Ne make baskettes, and live therby,
Because I wol nat beggen ydelly.
I wol non of the apostles counterfete;
I wol have money, wolle,[15] chese, and whete,   120
Al were it yeven of the povrest page,
Or of the povrest widwe in a village,
Al [16] sholde hir children sterve for famyne.
Nay! I wol drinke licour of the vyne,
And have a joly wenche in every toun.
But herkneth, lordings, in conclusioun;
Your lyking is that I shal telle a tale.
Now, have I dronke a draughte of corny ale,
By god, I hope I shall yow telle a thing
That shal, by resoun, been at your lyking.   130
For, though myself be a ful vicious man,
A moral tale yet I yow telle can,
Which I am wont to preche, for to winne.
Now holde your pees, my tale I wol beginne."

The Pardoners Tale

In Flaunders whylom was a companye
Of yonge folk, that haunteden folye,
As ryot, hasard,[17] stewes,[18] and tavernes,

13 depart   15 wool   17 gambling
14 ignorant   16 although   18 brothels

Wher-as, with harpes, lutes, and giternes,[19]
They daunce and pleye at dees [20] bothe day and night,
And ete also and drinken over hir might,   140
Thurgh which they doon the devel sacrifyse
With-in that develes temple, in cursed wyse,
By superfluitee abhominable;
Hir othes been so grete and so dampnable,
That it is grisly for to here hem swere;
Our blissed lordes body they to-tere; [21]
Hem thoughte Jewes rente him noght y-nough;
And ech of hem at otheres sinne lough.
And right anon than comen tombesteres [22]
Fetys [23] and smale, and yonge fruytesteres,[24]   150
Singers with harpes, baudes, wafereres,[25]
Whiche been the verray develes officeres
To kindle and blowe the fyr of lecherye,
That is annexed un-to glotonye;
The holy writ take I to my witnesse,
That luxurie is in wyn and dronkenesse.
  Lo, how that dronken Loth, unkindely,
Lay by his doghtres two, unwitingly;
So dronke he was, he niste [26] what he wroghte.
  Herodes, (who-so wel the stories soghte),   160
Whan he of wyn was replet at his feste,
Right at his owene table he yaf his heste
To sleen the Baptist John ful giltelees.
  Senek [27] seith eek a good word doutelees;
He seith, he can no difference finde
Bitwix a man that is out of his minde
And a man which that is dronkelewe,[28]
But that woodnesse,[29] y-fallen in a shrewe,[30]
Persevereth lenger than doth dronkenesse.
O glotonye, ful of cursednesse,   170
O cause first of our confusioun,
O original of our dampnacioun,
Til Crist had boght us with his blood agayn!
Lo, how dere, shortly for to sayn,
Aboght was thilke cursed vileinye;
Corrupt was al this world for glotonye!
  Adam our fader, and his wyf also,
Fro Paradys to labour and to wo
Were driven for that vyce, it is no drede;
For whyl that Adam fasted, as I rede,   180

19 guitars   23 dainty   27 Seneca
20 dice   24 female fruit-sellers   28 drunkard
21 tear to pieces   25 confectioners   29 madness
22 female tumblers   26 knew not   30 scoundrel

He was in Paradys; and whan that he
Eet of the fruyt defended [31] on the tree,
Anon he was out-cast to wo and peyne.
O glotonye, on thee wel oghte us pleyne!
O, wiste a man how many maladyes
Folwen of excesse and of glotonyes,
He wolde been the more mesurable
Of his diete, sittinge at his table.
Allas! the shorte throte, the tendre mouth,
Maketh that, Est and West, and North and South,   190
In erthe, in eir, in water men to-swinke [32]
To gete a glotoun deyntee mete and drinke!
Of this matere, o Paul, wel canstow trete,
"Mete un-to wombe,[33] and wombe eek un-to mete,
Shal god destroyen bothe," as Paulus seith,[34]
Allas! a foul thing is it, by my feith,
To seye this word, and fouler is the dede,
Whan man so drinketh of the whyte and rede,
That of his throte he maketh his privee,
Thurgh thilke cursed superfluitee.   200
    The apostel weping seith ful pitously,
"Ther walken many of whiche yow told have I,
I seye it now weping with pitous voys,
[That] they been enemys of Cristes croys,
Of whiche the ende is deeth, wombe is her god." [35]
O wombe! O bely! O stinking cod,[36]
Fulfild of donge and of corrupcioun!
At either ende of thee foul is the soun.
How greet labour and cost is thee to finde! [37]
Thise cokes, how they stampe, and streyne, and grinde,   210
And turnen substaunce in-to accident,[38]
To fulfille al thy likerous talent! [39]
Out of the harde bones knokke they
The mary,[40] for they caste noght a-wey
That may go thurgh the golet softe and swote; [41]
Of spicerye, of leef, and bark, and rote
Shal been his sauce y-maked by delyt,
To make him yet a newer appetyt.
But certes, he that haunteth swich delyces
Is deed, whyl that he liveth in tho vyces.   220
    A lecherous thing is wyn, and dronkenesse
Is ful of stryving and of wrecchednesse.

31 forbidden	36 bag	39 gluttonous appetite
32 labor hard	37 maintain	40 marrow
33 belly	38 outward appearance;	41 sweetly
34 1 Cor. vi. 13	i. e., conceal the true na-	
35 Phil. iii. 18, 19	ture	

O dronke man, disfigured is thy face,
Sour is thy breeth, foul artow to embrace,
And thurgh thy dronke nose semeth the soun
As though thou seydest ay "Sampsoun, Sampsoun";
And yet, god wot, Sampsoun drank never no wyn.
Thou fallest, as it were a stiked swyn;
Thy tonge is lost, and al thyn honest cure; [42]
For dronkenesse is verray sepulture   230
Of mannes wit and his discrecioun.
In whom that drinke hath dominacioun,
He can no conseil kepe, it is no drede.
Now kepe yow fro the whyte and fro the rede,
And namely fro the whyte wyn of Lepe, [43]
That is to selle in Fish-strete or in Chepe. [44]
This wyn of Spayne crepeth subtilly
In othere wynes, growing faste by,
Of which ther ryseth swich fumositee, [45]
That whan a man hath dronken draughtes three, 240
And weneth that he be at hoom in Chepe,
He is in Spayne, right at the toune of Lepe,
Nat at the Rochel, ne at Burdeux toun; [46]
And thanne wol he seye, "Sampsoun, Sampsoun."
    But herkneth, lordings, o word, I yow preye,
That alle the soveieyn actes, dar I seye,
Of victories in th' olde testament,
Thurgh verray god, that is omnipotent,
Were doon in abstinence and in preyere;
Loketh the Bible, and ther ye may it lere.   250
    Loke, Attila, the grete conquerour,
Deyde in his sleep, with shame and dishonour,
Bledinge ay at his nose in dronkenesse;
A capitayn shoulde live in sobrenesse.
And over al this, avyseth [47] yow right wel
What was comaunded un-to Lamuel — [48]
Nat Samuel, but Lamuel, seye I—
Redeth the Bible, and finde it expresly
Of wyn-yeving to hem that han justyse. [49]
Na-more of this, for it may wel suffyse.   260
    And now that I have spoke of glotonye,
Now wol I yow defenden hasardrye. [50]
Hasard is verray moder of lesinges, [51]
And of deceite, and cursed forsweringes,

42 care for honor
43 near Cadiz
44 Cheapside
45 fumes (see p. 133, f.n. 76)
46 The wines of La Ro-chelle and Bordeaux were milder than the heavy, sweet wines of Spain
47 consider
48 Lemuel, in Prov. xxxi. 1-5
49 them that have the administration of justice, to whom wine is forbidden in passage cited
50 forbid gambling
51 lies

Blaspheme of Crist, manslaughtre, and wast also
Of catel [52] and of tyme; and forthermo,
It is repreve [53] and contrarie of honour
For to ben holde a commune hasardour.
And ever the hyër he is of estaat,
The more is he holden desolaat.   270
If that a prince useth hasardrye,
In alle governaunce and policye
He is, as by commune opinioun,
Y-holde the lasse in reputacioun.
    Stilbon,[54] that was a wys embassadour,
Was sent to Corinthe, in ful greet honour,
Fro Lacidomie, to make hir alliaunce.
And whan he cam, him happede, par chaunce,
That alle the grettest that were of that lond,
Pleyinge atte hasard he hem fond.   280
For which, as sone as it mighte be,
He stal him hoom agayn to his contree,
And seyde, "ther wol I nat lese my name;
N'I wol nat take on me so greet defame,
Yow for to allye un-to none hasardours.
Sendeth othere wyse embassadours;
For, by my trouthe, me were lever dye,
Than I yow sholde to hasardours allye.
For ye that been so glorious in honours
Shul nat allyen yow with hasardours   290
As by my wil, ne as by my tretee."
This wyse philosophre thus seyde he.
    Loke eek that, to the king Demetrius
The king of Parthes, as the book seith us,[55]
Sente him a paire of dees of gold in scorn,
For he hadde used hasard ther-biforn;
For which he heeld his glorie or his renoun
At no value or reputacioun.
Lordes may finden other maner pley
Honeste y-nough to dryve the day awey.   300
    Now wol I speke of othes false and grete
A word or two, as olde bokes trete.
Gret swering is a thing abhominable,
And false swering is yet more reprevable.
The heighe god forbad swering at al,
Witnesse on Mathew; [56] but in special
Of swering seith the holy Jeremye,[57]

52 wealth
53 reproach
54 Called Chilon in John
of Salisbury's *Polycraticus,*

bk. I., chap. 5
55 story told by John
of Salisbury in same chapter

56 v. 34
57 iv. 2

"Thou shalt seye sooth thyn othes, and nat lye,
And swere in dome,[58] and eek in rightwisnesse";
But ydel swering is a cursednesse.   310
Bihold and see, that in the firste table
Of heighe goddes hestes [59] honurable,
How that the seconde [60] heste of him is this—
"Tak nat my name in ydel or amis."
Lo, rather [61] he forbedeth swich swering
Than homicyde or many a cursed thing;
I seye that, as by ordre, thus it stondeth;
This knowen, that his hestes understondeth,
How that the second heste of god is that.
And forther over, I wol thee telle al plat,[62]   320
That vengeance shal nat parten from his hous,
That of his othes is to outrageous.
"By goddes precious herte, and by his nayles,
And by the blode of Crist, that it is in Hayles,[63]
Seven is my chaunce, and thyn is cink and treye; [64]
By goddes armes, if thou falsly pleye,
This dagger shal thurgh-out thyn herte go"—
This fruyt cometh of the bicched [65] bones two,
Forswering, ire, falsnesse, homicyde.
Now, for the love of Crist that for us dyde,   330
Leveth your othes, bothe grete and smale;
But, sirs, now wol I telle forth my tale.

THISE ryotoures three, of whiche I telle,
Longe erst er pryme [66] rong of any belle,
Were set hem in a taverne for to drinke;
And as they satte, they herde a belle clinke
Biforn a cors, was caried to his grave;
That oon of hem gan callen to his knave,
"Go bet," [67] quod he, "and axe redily,
What cors is this that passeth heer forby;   340
And look that thou reporte his name wel."
"Sir," quod this boy, "it nedeth never-a-del.
It was me told, er ye cam heer, two houres;
He was, pardee, an old felawe of youres;
And sodeynly he was y-slayn to-night,
For-dronke,[68] as he sat on his bench up-right;
Ther cam a privee theef, men clepeth Deeth,
That in this contree al the peple sleeth,

---

58 judgment
59 commands
60 in numbering now used, third
61 earlier
62 plainly
63 relic possessed by the Abbey of Hailes, Gloucestershire
64 five and three
65 cursed
66 9 A. M.
67 quickly
68 dead drunk

And with his spere he smoot his herte a-two,
And wente his wey with-outen wordes mo.   350
He hath a thousand slayn this pestilence:
And, maister, er ye come in his presence,
Me thinketh that it were necessarie
For to be war of swich an adversarie;
Beth redy for to mete him evermore.
Thus taughte me my dame, I sey na-more."
"By seinte Marie," seyde this taverner,
"The child seith sooth, for he hath slayn this yeer,
Henne [69] over a myle, with-in a greet village,
Both man and womman, child and hyne,[70] and page.   360
I trowe his habitacioun be there;
To been avysed [71] greet wisdom it were,
Er that he dide a man a dishonour."
"Ye, goddes armes," quod this ryotour,
"Is it swich peril with him for to mete?
I shal him seke by wey and eek by strete,
I make avow to goddes digne bones!
Herkneth, felawes, we three been al ones;
Lat ech of us holde up his hond til other,
And ech of us bicomen otheres brother,   370
And we wol sleen this false traytour Deeth;
He shal be slayn, which that so many sleeth,
By goddes dignitee, er it be night."
   Togidres han thise three her trouthes plight,
To live and dyen ech of hem for other,
As though he were his owene y-boren brother.
And up they sterte al dronken, in this rage,
And forth they goon towardes that village,
Of which the taverner had spoke biforn,
And many a grisly ooth than han they sworn,   380
And Cristes blessed body they to-rente—
"Deeth shal be deed, if that they may him hente." [72]
   Whan they han goon nat fully half a myle,
Right as they wolde han troden over a style,
An old man and a povre with hem mette.
This olde man ful mekely hem grette,
And seyde thus, "Now, lordes, god yow see!" [73]
   The proudest of thise ryotoures three
Answerde agayn, "What? carl, with sory grace,
Why artow al forwrapped save thy face?   390
Why livestow so longe in so greet age?"
   This olde man gan loke in his visage,

69 hence   71 forewarned   73 protect
70 servant   72 seize

And seyde thus, "For I ne can nat finde
A man, though that I walked in-to Inde,
Neither in citee nor in no village,
That wolde chaunge his youthe for myn age;
And therfore moot I han myn age stille,
As longe time as it is goddes wille.
    Ne deeth, allas! ne wol nat han my lyf;
Thus walke I, lyk a restelees caityf,   400
And on the ground, which is my modres gate,
I knokke with my staf, bothe erly and late,
And seye, 'Leve [74] moder, leet me in!
Lo, how I vanish, flesh, and blood, and skin!
Allas! whan shul my bones been at reste?
Moder, with yow wolde I chaunge my cheste,[75]
That in my chambre longe tyme hath be,
Ye! for an heyre clout [76] to wrappe me!'
But yet to me she wol nat do that grace,
For which ful pale and welked [77] is my face.   410
    But, sirs, to yow it is no curteisye
To speken to an old man vileinye,
But he trespase in worde, or elles in dede.
In holy writ ye may your-self wel rede,
'Agayns [78] an old man, hoor upon his heed,
Ye sholde aryse;' wherfor I yeve yow reed,[79]
Ne dooth un-to an old man noon harm now,
Na-more than ye wolde men dide to yow
In age, if that ye so longe abyde;
And god be with yow, wher ye go or ryde.   420
I moot go thider as I have to go."
    "Nay, olde cherl, by god, thou shalt nat so,"
Seyde this other hasardour anon;
"Thou partest nat so lightly, by seint John!
Thou spak right now of thilke traitour Deeth,
That in this contree alle our frendes sleeth.
Have heer my trouthe, as thou art his aspye,[80]
Tel wher he is, or thou shalt it abye,[81]
By god, and by the holy sacrament!
For soothly thou art oon of his assent,[82]   430
To sleen us yonge folk, thou false theef!"
    "Now, sirs," quod he, "if that yow be so leef [83]
To finde Deeth, turne up this croked wey,
For in that grove I lafte him, by my fey,
Under a tree, and ther he wol abyde;

74 dear   77 withered   80 spy
75 containing   all   his 78 before (see Levit. xix.   81 rue
earthly belongings   32)   82 conspiracy
76 hair cloth; i. e., shroud 79 counsel   83 eager

Nat for your boost he wol him no-thing hyde.
See ye that ook? right ther ye shul him finde.
God save yow, that boghte agayn mankinde,
And yow amende!"—thus seyde this olde man.
And everich of thise ryotoures ran,   440
Til he cam to that tree, and ther they founde
Of florins fyne of gold y-coyned rounde
Wel ny an eighte busshels, as hem thoughte.
No lenger thanne after Deeth they soughte,
But ech of hem so glad was of that sighte,
For that the florins been so faire and brighte,
That doun they sette hem by this precious hord.
The worste of hem he spake the firste word.
    "Brethren," quod he, "tak kepe what I seye;
My wit is greet, though that I bourde [84] and pleye.   450
This tresor hath fortune un-to us yiven,
In mirthe and jolitee our lyf to liven,
And lightly as it comth, so wol we spende.
Ey! goddes precious dignitee! who wende
To-day, that we sholde han so fair a grace?
But mighte this gold be caried fro this place
Hoom to myn hous, or elles un-to youres—
For wel ye woot that al this gold is oures—
Than were we in heigh felicitee.
But trewely, by daye it may nat be;   460
Men wolde seyn that we were theves stronge,
And for our owene tresor doon us honge.[85]
This tresor moste y-caried be by nighte
As wysly and as slyly as it mighte.
Wherfore I rede [86] that cut among us alle
Be drawe, and lat see wher the cut wol falle;
And he that hath the cut with herte blythe
Shal renne to the toune, and that ful swythe,[87]
And bringe us breed and wyn ful prively.
And two of us shul kepen subtilly   470
This tresor wel; and, if he wol nat tarie,
Whan it is night, we wol this tresor carie
By oon assent, wher-as us thinketh [88] best."
That oon of hem the cut broughte in his fest,[89]
And bad hem drawe, and loke wher it wol falle;
And it fil on the yongeste of hem alle;
And forth toward the toun he wente anon.
And al-so sone as that he was gon,
That oon of hem spak thus un-to that other,

84 jest   86 advise   88 it seems to us
85 have us hanged   87 quickly   89 fist

"Thou knowest wel thou art my sworne brother, 480
Thy profit wol I telle thee anon.
Thou woost wel that our felawe is agon;
And heer is gold, and that ful greet plentee,
That shal departed been among us three.
But natheles, if I can shape it so
That it departed were among us two,
Hadde I nat doon a freendes torn to thee?"
   That other answerde, "I noot how that may be;
He woot how that the gold is with us tweye,
What shal we doon, what shal we to him seye?" 490
   "Shal it be conseil?" seyde the firste shrewe,[90]
"And I shal tellen thee, in wordes fewe,
What we shal doon, and bringe it wel aboute."
   "I graunte," quod that other, "out of doute,
That, by my trouthe, I wol thee nat biwreye." [91]
   "Now," quod the firste, "thou woost wel we be tweye,
And two of us shul strenger be than oon.
Look whan that he is set, and right anoon
Arys, as though thou woldest with him pleye;
And I shal ryve him thurgh the sydes tweye 500
Whyl that thou strogelest with him as in game,
And with thy dagger look thou do the same;
And than shal al this gold departed be,
My dere freend, bitwixen me and thee;
Than may we bothe our lustes al fulfille,
And pleye at dees right at our owene wille."
And thus acorded been thise shrewes tweye
To sleen the thridde, as ye han herd me seye.
   This yongest, which that went un-to the toun,
Ful ofte in herte he rolleth up and doun 510
The beautee of thise florins newe and brighte.
"O lord!" quod he, "if so were that I mighte
Have al this tresor to my-self allone,
Ther is no man that liveth under the trone
Of god, that sholde live so mery as I!"
And atte laste the feend, our enemy,
Putte in his thought that he shold poyson beye,[92]
With which he mighte sleen his felawes tweye;
For-why the feend fond him in swich lyvinge,
That he had leve him to sorwe bringe, 520
For this was outrely his fulle entente
To sleen hem bothe, and never to repente.
And forth he gooth, no lenger wolde he tarie,
Into the toun, un-to a pothecarie,

90 scoundrel   91 betray   92 buy

And preyed him, that he him wolde selle
Som poyson, that he mighte his rattes quelle; [93]
And eek ther was a polcat in his hawe, [94]
That, as he seyde, his capouns hadde y-slawe,
And fayn he wolde wreke [95] him, if he mighte,
On vermin, that detroyed him by nighte.   530
    The pothecarie answerde, "and thou shalt have
A thing that, al-so god my soule save,
In al this world ther nis no creature,
That ete or dronke hath of this confiture [96]
Noght but the mountance [97] of a corn of whete,
That he ne shal his lyf anon forlete; [98]
Ye, sterve [99] he shal, and that in lasse whyle
Than thou wolt goon a paas [1] nat but a myle;
This poyson is so strong and violent."
    This cursed man hath in his hond y-hent [2]   540
This poyson in a box, and sith he ran
In-to the nexte strete, un-to a man,
And borwed [of] him large botels three;
And in the two his poyson poured he;
The thridde he kepte clene for his drinke,
For al the night he shoop [3] him for to swinke [4]
In caryinge of the gold out of that place.
And whan this ryotour, with sory grace,
Had filled with wyn his grete botels three,
To his felawes agayn repaireth he.   550
    What nedeth it to sermone of it more?
For right as they had cast his deeth bifore,
Right so they han him slayn, and that anon.
And whan that this was doon, thus spak that oon,
"Now lat us sitte and drinke, and make us merie,
And afterward we wol his body berie."
And with that word it happed him, par cas, [5]
To take the botel ther the poyson was,
And drank, and yaf his felawe drinke also,
For which anon thy storven [6] bothe two.   560
    But certes, I suppose that Avicen [7]
Wroot never in no canon, [8] ne in no fen, [9]
Mo wonder signes of empoisoning
Than hadde thise wrecches two, er hir ending.
Thus ended been thise homicydes two,

93 kill
94 yard
95 avenge
96 mixture
97 amount
98 lose
99 die

1 at a pace (walk)
2 seized
3 planned
4 labor
5 by chance
6 died
7 Avicenna   (980–1037),

celebrated Arabian physi-
cian
    8 The title of Avicenna's
Treatise
    9 a sub-division thereof

And eek the false empoysoner also.

O cursed sinne, ful of cursednesse!
O traytours homicyde, o wikkednesse!
O glotonye, luxurie, and hasardrye!
Thou blasphemour of Crist with vileinye   570
And othes grete, of usage and of pryde!
Allas! mankinde, how may it bityde,
That to thy creatour which that thee wroghte,
And with his precious herte-blood thee boghte,
Thou art so fals and so unkinde, allas!
    Now, goode men, god forgeve yow your trespas,
And ware yow [10] fro the sinne of avaryce.
Myn holy pardoun may yow alle warycc,[11]
So that ye offre nobles or sterlinges,
Or elles silver broches, spones, ringes.   580
Boweth your heed under this holy bulle!
Cometh up, ye wyves, offreth of your wolle!
Your name I entre heer in my rolle anon;
In-to the blisse of hevene shul ye gon;
I yow assoile,[12] by myn heigh power,
Yow that wol offre, as clene and eek as cleer
As ye were born; and, lo, sirs, thus I preche.
And Jesu Crist, that is our soules leche,
So graunte yow his pardon to receyve;
For that is best; I wol yow nat deceyve.   590
    But sirs, o word forgat I in my tale,
I have relikes and pardon in my male,[13]
As faire as any man in Engelond,
Whiche were me yeven by the popes hond.
If any of yow wol, of devocioun,
Offren, and han myn absolucioun,
Cometh forth anon, and kneleth heer adoun,
And mekely receyveth my pardoun:
Or elles, taketh pardon as ye wende,
Al newe and fresh, at every tounes ende,   600
So that ye offren alwey newe and newe
Nobles and pens, which that be gode and trewe.
It is an honour to everich that is heer,
That ye mowe have a suffisant pardoneer
T'assoille yow, in contree as ye ryde,
For aventures which that may bityde.
Peraventure ther may falle oon or two
Doun of his hors, and breke his nekke atwo.

10 keep you   12 absolve   13 wallet
11 cure

Look which a seuretee is it to yow alle
That I am in your felaweship y-falle,   610
That may assoille yow, bothe more and lasse,
Whan that the soule shal fro the body passe.
I rede that our hoste heer shal biginne,
For he is most envoluped in sinne.
Com forth, sir hoste, and offre first anon,
And thou shalt kisse the reliks everichon,
Ye, for a grote! unbokel anon thy purs."
    "Nay, nay," quod he, "than have I Cristes curs!
Lat be," quod he, "it shal nat be, so thee'ch!" [14]

    This pardoner answerde nat a word;   620
So wrooth he was, no word ne wolde he seye.
    "Now," quod our host, "I wol no lenger pleye
With thee, ne with noon other angry man."
But right anon the worthy Knight bigan,
Whan that he saugh that al the peple lough,
"Na-more of this, for it is right y-nough;
Sir Pardoner, be glad and mery of chere;
And ye, sir host, that been to me so dere,
I prey yow that ye kisse the Pardoner.
And Pardoner, I prey thee, drawe thee neer,   630
And, as we diden, lat us laughe and pleye."
Anon they kiste, and riden forth hir weye.

CHAUCER'S WORDS UNTO ADAM, HIS OWNE SCRIVEYN [15]

ADAM scriveyn, if ever it thee bifalle
Boece or Troilus [16] to wryten newe,
Under thy lokkes [17] thou most have the scalle,[18]
But [19] after my making [20] thou wryte trewe.
So ofte a daye I mot [21] thy werk renewe,
Hit to correcte and eek to rubbe and scrape;
And al is through thy negligence and rape.[22]

TRUTH

Balade de bon conseyl

FLEE fro the prees,[23] and dwelle with sothfastnesse,[24]
Suffyce unto thy good,[25] though hit be smal;

14 as may I thrive
15 scribe
16 Chaucer's prose trans-
lation of Boethius's *Consolations of Philosophy;*
his long narrative poem of

Troilus and Criseyde
17 locks
18 scab
19 unless
20 composition
21 must

22 haste
23 crowd
24 truth
25 be content with your
property

For hord hath hate, and climbing tikelnesse,[26]
Prees hath envye, and wele blent overal; [27]
Savour [28] no more than thee bihove shal;
Werk wel thy-self, that other folk canst rede; [29]
And trouthe shal delivere, hit is no drede.[30]

Tempest [31] thee noght al croked to redresse,
In trust of hir [32] that turneth as a bal:
Gret reste stant [33] in litel besinesse;
And eek be war to sporne ageyn an al; [34]
Stryve noght, as doth the crokke with the wal.
Daunte [35] thy-self, that dauntest otheres dede;
And trouthe shal delivere, hit is no drede.

That thee is sent, receyve in buxumnesse,[36]
The wrastling for this worlde axeth [37] a fal.
Her nis non hoom, her nis but wildernesse:
Forth, pilgrim, forth! Forth, beste, out of thy stal!
Know thy contree, look up, thank God of al;
Hold the hye wey, and lat thy gost thee lede:
And trouthe shal delivere, hit is no drede.

Envoy

Therfore, thou vache,[38] leve thyn old wrecchednesse
Unto the worlde; leve now to be thral;
Crye him mercy, that of his hy goodnesse
Made thee of noght, and in especial
Draw unto him, and pray in general
For thee, and eek for other, hevenlich mede; [39]
And trouthe shal delivere, hit is no drede.

Explicit Le bon counseill de G. Chaucer.

THE COMPLEINT OF CHAUCER TO HIS EMPTY PURSE

To you, my purse, and to non other wight
Compleyne I, for ye be my lady dere!
I am so sory, now that ye be light;
For certes, but ye make me hevy chere,
Me were as leef be leyd up-on my bere;
For whiche un-to your mercy thus I crye:
Beth hevy ageyn, or elles mot [40] I dye!

26 uncertainty
27 prosperity blinds everywhere
28 relish
29 advise
30 doubt
31 vex
32 i. e., Fortune
33 stands
34 kick against an awl
35 master
36 humility
37 asks, invites
38 Sir Philip le Vache, friend of Chaucer's (perhaps with pun on the meaning *cow*)
39 heavenly reward
40 must

Now voucheth sauf this day, or hit be night,
That I of you the blisful soun may here,
Or see your colour lyk the sonne bright,
That of yelownesse hadde never pere.
Ye be my lyf, ye be myn hertes stere,[41]
Quene of comfort and of good companye:
Beth hevy ageyn, or elles mot I dye!

Now purs, that be to me my lyves light,
And saveour, as doun in this worlde here,
Out of this toune help me through your might,
Sin that ye wole nat been my tresorere;
For I am shave as nye [42] as any frere.
But yit I pray un-to your curtesye:
Beth hevy ageyn, or elles mot I dye!

Lenvoy de Chaucer

O conqueror of Brutes Albioun! [43]
Which that by lyne and free eleccioun
Ben verray king, this song to you I sende;
And ye, that mowen al our harm amende,
Have minde up-on my supplicacioun!

THE POPULAR BALLAD

All nations have a large body of traditional customs, beliefs, sayings, tales, and poems, which are usually classified collectively under the general name of folk-lore. The kinds of folk-lore which have the most definite and most striking artistic form are the folk tale (usually called in English "fairy" tale), the folk song, and especially the folk or "popular" ballad. This is a song that tells a story, or—from another point of view—a story told in song. It is, then, a narrative poem, divided into stanzas, adapted for singing to some simple tune, and originally always sung, never recited. As a "literary" form, the ballad is obviously among the most ancient known to man, and much speculation has been aroused over the ultimate origin of ballad singing in the human race. Some scholars believe that the earliest ballads were composed "communally" or collectively by the "homogeneous" dancing throng of savage tribal life. Others hold that even in primitive society such songs were the work of individuals. But all this discussion pertains to a very remote period. Comparatively recent texts, like those below, have been doubtless composed by definite ballad-

41 steersman
42 close
43 the England founded, according to tradition, by

Brute, who fled from Troy. The reference in the envoy is to Henry IV, who became King Sept. 30,

1399. The "supplication" was answered on Oct. 3 by an annual grant of forty marks.

singers,—not by trained writers, through the medium of the pen, but orally, by uneducated people acquainted with ballad singing, and then been transmitted from singer to singer, entirely by word of mouth. The conditions governing the creation and transmission of these productions make them completely impersonal. The original composer follows traditional forms, instead of speaking in an individual style (as do conscious literary artists); feels, accordingly, no sense of ownership in his product; does not interpose himself into his song or story; and so his identity, even if once known, is forgotten. Every new singer or story-teller, moreover, feels free to alter; and, as a result, of most folk productions we have many versions, each of which has full claim to authenticity, since the original can never be recovered. To any extant ballad version, then, it may be said that many have contributed.

England and Scotland were very rich in ballads during the Middle Ages and the Renaissance, hence their inclusion chronologically in this volume at the end of the Middle English period. They have, however, been composed at various times, before and after. Since the scholarly interest in ballads was not aroused until modern times, most of the texts have been collected relatively late. Very few were actually recorded before 1600. A number are preserved in a manuscript of the seventeenth century, a manuscript used by Bishop Percy as the basis of his *Reliques of Ancient English Poetry* (1765), an important document in arousing interest in the ballad. The great majority, however, were taken down from the lips of singers in the eighteenth and nineteenth centuries. It need hardly be remarked that the original composition of many of these ballads is much older, some of them having been sung traditionally for centuries. The advance of civilization and the spread of education has almost put an end to ballad singing, yet even to-day ballads can still be collected in remote parts of the British Isles and America, for example, in our own Southern mountains: while a different type of ballad, produced under altered conditions of culture, is still being created, or was recently, among special groups, like the cowboys and lumbermen.

The selections included in this volume will exhibit most of the characteristics of the popular ballad, excepting the phenomena of varying versions, since only one form of any ballad is here reprinted. The reader will note typical stanzaic and metrical forms, the use of refrain and of "incremental repetition" (the repetition of an element with variations which advance the story), and ballad commonplaces or traditional phraseology. The ballads here selected illustrate the most common kinds of subject-matter: the ballad of domestic tragedy (the largest group of ballads); the ballad of the supernatural; the ballad based upon some historical person or historical event; the ballad of outlawry, with the central figure of Robin Hood.

The quality of these folk productions is obviously very different from that of consciously created literature. Appreciation of them will naturally vary with the tastes of individual readers. The influence of the ballad upon our greater writers, particularly in modern times, should not be forgotten.

BIBLIOGRAPHY. The great scholarly collection of *English and Scottish Popular Ballads* by Francis James Child, in five large volumes, giving all variant versions, and including full critical apparatus (Houghton Mifflin). Admirable condensation of above by Helen Child Sargent and G. L. Kittredge (Houghton Mifflin). Excellent collection: the *Old English Ballads* of F. B. Gummere (Ginn). (The last two volumes contain notable introductions.) For ballad problems: F. B. Gummere's *The Popular Ballad* (Houghton Mifflin), and Louise Pound's *Poetic Origins and the Ballad* (Macmillan).

RIDDLES WISELY EXPOUNDED

1. THERE was a lady of the North Country,
    Lay the bent [1] to the bonny broom
And she had lovely daughters three.
    Fa la la la, fa la la la ra re.

2. There was a knight of noble worth
Which also lived in the North.

3. The knight, of courage stout and brave,
A wife he did desire to have.

4. He knocked at the ladie's gate
One evening when it was late.

5. The eldest sister let him in,
And pinned the door with a silver pin.

6. The second sister she made his bed,
And laid soft pillows under his head.

7. The youngest daughter that same night,
She went to bed to this young knight.

8. And in the morning, when it was day,
These words unto him she did say:

9. "Now you have had your will," quoth she,
"I pray, sir knight, will you marry me?"

10. The young brave knight to her replyed,
"Thy suit, fair maid, shall not be deny'd.

11. "If thou canst answer me questions three,
This very day will I marry thee."

12. "Kind sir, in love, O then," quoth she,
"Tell me what your three questions be."

13. "O what is longer than the way,
Or what is deeper than the sea?

14. "Or what is louder than the horn,
Or what is sharper than a thorn?

1 field covered with a coarse grass

15. "Or what is greener than the grass,
Or what is worse then a woman was?"

16. "O love is longer than the way,
And hell is deeper than the sea.

17. "And thunder is louder than the horn,
And hunger is sharper than a thorn.

18. "And poyson is greener than the grass,
And the Devil is worse than woman was."

19. When she these questions answered had,
The knight beame exceeding glad.

20. And having truly try'd her wit,
He much commended her for it.

21. And after, as it is verifi'd,
He made of her his lovely bride.

22. So now, fair maidens all, adieu,
This song I dedicate to you.

23. I wish that you may constant prove
Unto the man that you do love.

THE TWA SISTERS

1. THERE was twa sisters in a bowr,
Edinburgh, Edinburgh,
There was twa sisters in a bowr,
Stirling for ay.
There was twa sisters in a bowr,
There came a knight to be their wooer;
Bonny Saint Johnston stands upon Tay.

2. He courted the eldest wi glove an ring,
But he lovd the youngest above a' thing.

3. He courted the eldest wi brotch an knife,
But lovd the youngest as his life.

4. The eldest she was vexed sair,
An much envi'd her sister fair.

5. Unto her bowr she could not rest,
   Wi grief an spite she almos brast.

6. Upon a morning fair an clear,
   She cried upon her sister dear:

7. "O sister, come to yon sea stran,
   An see our father's ships come to lan."

8. She 's taen her by the milk-white han,
   And led her down to yon sea stran.

9. The youngest stood upon a stane,
   The eldest came an threw her in.

10. She tooke her by the middle sma,
    An dashd her bonny back to the jaw.

11. "O sister, sister, tak my han,
    An Ise mack you heir to a' my lan.

12. "O sister, sister, tak my middle,
    An yes get my goud ² and my gouden girdle.

13. "O sister, sister, save my life,
    An I swear Ise never be nae man's wife."

14. "Foul fa the han that I should tacke,
    It twin'd ³ me an my wardles make.⁴

15. "Your cherry cheeks an yallow hair
    Gars ⁵ me gae maiden for evermair."

16. Sometimes she sank, an sometimes she swam,
    Till she came down yon bonny mill-dam.

17. O out it came the miller's son,
    An saw the fair maid swimmin in.

18. "O father, father, draw your dam,
    Here's either a mermaid or a swan."

19. The miller quickly drew the dam,
    An there he found a drownd woman.

2 gold
3 separated   4 world's mate   5 makes

20. You coudna see her yallow hair
For gold and pearle that were so rare.

21. You coudna see her middle sma
For gouden girdle that was sae braw.

22. You coudna see her fingers white,
For gouden rings that was sae gryte.[6]

23. An by there came a harper fine,
That harped to the king at dine.

24. When he did look that lady upon,
He sighd and made a heavy moan.

25. He's taen three locks o her yallow hair,
An wi them strung his harp sac fair.

26. The first tune he did play and sing,
Was, "Farewell to my father the king."

27. Th nextin tune that he playd syne,[7]
Was, "Farewell to my mother the queen."

28. The lasten tune that he playd then,
Was, "Wae to my sister, fair Ellen."

THE CRUEL BROTHER

1. There was three ladies playd at the ba,
With a hey ho and a lillie gay,
There came a knight and played oer them a'.
As the primrose spreads so sweetly.

2. The eldest was baith tall and fair,
But the youngest was beyond compare.

3. The midmost had a graceful mien,
But the youngest lookd like beautie's queen.

4. The knight bowd low to a' the three,
But to the youngest he bent his knee.

5. The ladie turned her head aside,
The knight he woo'd her to be his bride.

6 great   7 afterwards

6. The ladie blushd a rosy red,
  And sayd, "Sir knight, I'm too young to wed."

7. "O ladie fair, give me your hand,
  And I'll make you ladie of a' my land."

8. "Sir knight, ere ye my favor win,
  You maun [8] get consent frae a' my kin."

9. He's got consent frae her parents dear,
  And likewise frae her sisters fair.

10. He's got consent frae her kin each one,
  But forgot to spiek to her brother John.

11. Now, when the wedding day was come,
  The knight would take his bonny bride home.

12. And many a lord and many a knight
  Came to behold that ladie bright.

13. And there was nae man that did her see,
  But wishd himself bridegroom to be.

14. Her father dear led her down the stair,
  And her sisters twain they kissd her there.

15. Her mother dear led her thro the closs,
  And her brother John set her on her horse.

16. She leand her oer the saddle-bow,
  To give him a kiss ere she did go.

17. He has taen a knife, baith lang and sharp,
  And stabbd that bonny bride to the heart.

18. She hadno ridden half thro the town,
  Until her heart's blude staind her gown.

19. "Ride softly on," says the best young man,
  "For I think our bonny bride looks pale and wan."

20. "O lead me gently up yon hill,
  And I'll there sit down, and make my will."

8 must

21. "O what will you leave to your father dear?"
    "The silver-shode steed that brought me here."

22. "What will you leave to your mother dear?"
    "My velvet pall and my silken gear."

23. "What will you leave to your sister Anne?"
    "My silken scarf and my gowden [9] fan."

24. "What will you leave to your sister Grace?"
    "My bloody cloaths to wash and dress."

25. "What will you leave to your brother John?"
    "The gallows-tree to hang him on."

26. "What will you leave to your brother John's wife?"
    "The wilderness to end her life."

27. This ladie fair in her grave was laid,
    And many a mass was oer her said.

28. But it would have made your heart right sair,
    To see the bridegroom rive his haire.

LORD RANDAL

1. "O where ha you been, Lord Randal, my son?
   And where ha you been, my handsome young man?"
   "I ha been at the greenwood; mother, mak my bed soon,
   For I'm wearied wi hunting, and fain wad lie down."

2. "An wha met ye there, Lord Randal, my son?
   An wha met you there, my handsome young man?"
   "O I met wi my true-love; mother, mak my bed soon,
   For I'm wearied wi huntin, an fain wad lie down."

3. "And what did she give you, Lord Randal, my son?
   Ad what did she give you, my handsome young man?"
   "Eels fried in a pan; mother, mak my bed soon,
   For I'm wearied wi huntin, an fain wad lie down."

4. "And wha gat your leavins, Lord Randal, my son?
   And wha gat your leavins, my handsome young man?"
   "My hawks and my hounds; mother, mak my bed soon,
   For I'm wearied wi hunting, an fain wad lie down."

9 golden

5. "And what becam of them, Lord Randal, my son?
    And what becam of them, my handsome young man?"
    "They stretched their legs out an died; mother, mak my
        bed soon,
    For I'm wearied wi huntin, an fain wad lie down."

6. "O I fear you are poisoned, Lord Randal, my son!
    I fear you are poisoned, my handsome young man!"
    "O yes, I am poisoned; mother, mak my bed soon,
    For I'm sick at the heart, and I fain wad lie down."

7. "What d'ye leave to your mother, Lord Randal, my son?
    What d'ye leave to your mother, my handsome young
        man?"
    "Four and twenty milk kye; [10] mother, mak my bed soon,
    For I'm sick at the heart, and I fain wad lie down."

8. "What d'ye leave to your sister, Lord Randal, my son?
    What d'ye leave to your sister, my handsome young man?"
    "My gold and my silver; mother, mak my bed soon,
    For I'm sick at the heart, and I fain wad lie down."

9. "What d'ye leave to your brother, Lord Randal, my son?
    What d'ye leave to your brother, my handsome young
        man?"
    "My houses and my lands; mother, mak my bed soon,
    For I'm sick at the heart, and I fain wad lie down."

10. "What d'ye leave to your true-love, Lord Randal, my son?
    What d'ye leave to your true-love, my handsome young
        man?"
    "I leave her hell and fire; mother, mak my bed soon,
    For I'm sick at the heart, and I fain wad lie down."

EDWARD

1. "WHY dois your brand sae drap wi bluid,
                    Edward, Edward,
    Why dois your brand sae drap wi bluid,
        And why sae sad gang yee O?"
    "O I hae killed my hauke sae guid,
                    Mither, mither,
    O I hae killed my hauke sae guid,
        And I had nae mair bot hee O."

10 cows

2. "Your haukis bluid was nevir sae reid,
                  Edward, Edward,
Your haukis bluid was nevir sae reid,
     My deir son I tell thee O."
"O I hae killed my reid-roan steid,
                  Mither, mither,
O I hae killed my reid-roan steid,
     That erst was sae fair and frie O."

3. "Your steid was auld, and ye hae gat mair,
                  Edward, Edward,
Your seid was auld, and ye hae gat mair,
     Sum other dule ye drie [11] O."
"O I hae killed my fadir deir,
                  Mither, mither,
O I hae killed my fadir deir,
     Alas, and wae is mee O!"

4. "And whatten penance wul ye drie for that,
                  Edward, Edward?
And whatten penance will ye drie for that?
     My deir son, now tell me O."
"Ile set my feit in yonder boat,
                  Mither, mither,
Ile set my feit in yonder boat,
     And Ile fare ovir the sea O."

5. "And what wul ye doe wi your towirs and your ha,
                  Edward, Edward?
And what wul ye doe wi your towirs and your ha,
     That were sae fair to see O?"
"Ile let thame stand tul they doun fa,
                  Mither, mither,
Ile let thame stand tul they doun fa,
     For here nevir mair maun I bee O."

6. "And what wul ye leive to your bairns and your wife,
                  Edward, Edward?
And what wul ye leive to your bairns and your wife,
     Whan ye gang ovir the sea O?"
"The warldis room, late them beg thrae life,
                  Mither, mither,
The warldis room, late them beg thrae life,
     For thame nevir mair wul I see O."

11 grief ye suffer

7. "And what wul ye leive to your ain mither deir,
   Edward, Edward?
And what wul ye leive to your ain mither deir?
   My deir son, now tell me O."
"The curse of hell frae me sall ye beir,
   Mither, mither,
The curse of hell frae me sall ye beir,
   Sic counseils ye gave to me O."

THE THREE RAVENS

1. THERE were three ravens sat on a tree,
      Downe a downe, hay down, hay downe,
   There were three ravens sat on a tree,
      With a downe,
   There were three ravens sat on a tree,
   They were as blacke as they might be.
      With a downe derrie, derrie, derrie, downe, downe.

2. The one of them said to his mate,
   "Where shall we our breakefast take?"

3. "Downe in yonder greene field,
   There lies a knight slain under his shield.

4. "His hounds they lie downe at his feete,
   So well they can their master keepe.

5. "His haukes they flie so eagerly,
   There's no fowle dare him come nie."

6. Downe there comes a fallow doe,
   As great with yong as she might goe.

7. She lift up his bloudy hed,
   And kist his wounds that were so red.

8. She got him up upon her backe,
   And carried him to earthen lake.[12]

9. She buried him before the prime,
   She was dead herselfe ere even-song time.

10. God send every gentleman,
    Such haukes, such hounds, and such a leman.[13]

12 pit   13 beloved

KEMP OWYNE [14]

1. HER mother died when she was young,
    Which gave her cause to make great moan;
   Her father married the warst woman
    That ever lived in Christendom.

2. She served her with foot and hand,
    In every thing that she could dee,[15]
   Till once, in an unlucky time,
    She threw her in ower Craigy's sea.

3. Says, "Lie you there, dove Isabel,
    And all my sorrows lie with thee;
   Till Kemp Owyne come ower the sea,
    And borrow [16] you with kisses three,
   Let all the warld do what they will,
    Oh borrowed shall you never be!"

4. Her breath grew strang, her hair grew lang,
    And twisted thrice about the tree,
   And all the people, far and near,
    Thought that a savage beast was she.

5. These news did come to Kemp Owyne,
    Where he lived, far beyond the sea;
   He hasted him to Craigy's sea,
    And on the savage beast lookd he.

6. Her breath was strang, her hair was lang,
    And twisted was about the tree,
   And with a swing she came about:
    "Come to Craigy's sea, and kiss with me.

7. "Here is a royal belt," she cried.
    "That I have found in the green sea;
   And while your body it is on,
    Drawn shall your blood never be;
   But if you touch me, tail or fin,
    I vow my belt your death shall be."

8. He stepped in, gave her a kiss,
    The royal belt he brought him wi;
   Her breath was strang, her hair was lang,

14 Champion Ywain, else-   Arthur's knights   16 ransom
where known as one of   15 do

And twisted twice about the tree,
And with a swing she came about:
"Come to Craigy's sea, and kiss with me.

9. "Here is a royal ring," she said,
    "That I have found in the green sea;
And while your finger it is on,
    Drawn shall your blood never be;
But if you touch me, tail or fin,
    I swear my ring your death shall be."

10. He stepped in, gave her a kiss,
    The royal ring he brought him wi;
Her breath was strang, her hair was lang,
    And twisted ance about the tree,
And with a swing she came about:
    "Come to Craigy's sea, and kiss with me.

11. "Here is a royal brand," she said,
    "That I have found in the green sea;
And while your body it is on,
    Drawn shall your blood never be;
But if you touch me, tail or fin,
    I swear my brand your death shall be."

12. He stepped in, gave her a kiss,
    The royal brand he brought him wi;
Her breath was sweet, her hair grew short,
    And twisted nane about the tree,
And smilingly she came about,
    As fair a woman as fair could be.

THOMAS RYMER [17]

1. TRUE THOMAS lay oer yond grassy bank,
    And he beheld a ladie gay,
A ladie that was brisk and bold,
    Come riding oer the fernie brae.[18]

2. Her skirt was of the grass-green silk,
    Her mantel of the velvet fine,
At ilka tett [19] of her horse's mane
    Hung fifty silver bells and nine.

17 or Thomas of Ercel-   the thirteenth century   19 every lock
doune, a Scottish seer of   18 hillside

3. True Thomas he took off his hat,
   And bowed him low down till his knee:
"All hail, thou mighty Queen of Heaven!
   For your peer on earth I never did see."

4. "O no, O no, True Thomas," she says,
   "That name does not belong to me;
I am but the queen of fair Elfland,
   And I'm come here for to visit thee.

.   .   .   .

5. "But ye maun [20] go wi me now, Thomas,
   True Thomas, ye maun go wi me,
For ye maun serve me seven years,
   Thro weel or wae as may chance to be."

6. She turned about her milk-white steed,
   And took True Thomas up behind,
And aye wheneer her bridle rang,
   The steed flew swifter than the wind.

7. For forty days and forty nights
   He wade thro red blude to the knee,
And he saw neither sun nor moon,
   But heard the roaring of the sea.

8. O they rade on, and further on,
   Until they came to a garden green:
"Light down, light down, ye ladie free,
   Some of that fruit let me pull to thee."

9. "O no, O no, True Thomas," she says,
   "That fruit maun not be touched by thee,
For a' the plagues that are in hell
   Light on the fruit of this countrie.

10. "But I have a loaf here in my lap,
    Likewise a bottle of claret wine,
And now ere we go farther on,
    We'll rest a while, and ye may dine."

11. When he had eaten and drunk his fill,
    "Lay down your head upon my knee,"
The lady sayd, "ere we climb yon hill,
    And I will show you fairlies [21] three.

20 must   21 marvels

12. "O see not ye yon narrow road,
   So thick beset wi thorns and briers?
That is the path of righteousness,
   Tho after it but few enquires.

13. "And see not ye that braid braid road,
   That lies across yon lillie leven? [22]
That is the path of wickedness,
   Tho some call it the road to heaven.

14. "And see not ye that bonny road,
   Which winds about the fernie brae? [23]
That is the road to fair Elfland,
   Where you and I this night maun gae.

15. "But Thomas, ye maun hold your tongue,
   Whatever you may hear or see,
For gin ae word you should chance to speak,
   You will neer get back to your ain countrie."

16. He has gotten a coat of the even cloth,
   And a pair of shoes of velvet green,
And till seven years were past and gone
   True Thomas on earth was never seen.

THE TWA BROTHERS

1. THERE were twa brethren in the north,
   They went to school thegithar;
The one unto the other said,
   Will you try a warsle afore?

2. They wrestled up, they wrestled down,
   Till Sir John fell to the ground,
And there was a knife in Sir Willie's pouch,
   Gied him a deadlie wound.

3. "Oh brither dear, take me on your back,
   Carry me to yon burn [24] clear,
And wash the blood from off my wound,
   And it will bleed nae mair."

4. He took him up upon his back,
   Carried him to yon burn clear,

22 lovely lawn   23 hillside   24 brook

And washd the blood from off his wound,
And aye it bled the mair.

5. "Oh brother dear, take me on your back,
Carry me to yon kirk-yard,
And dig a grave baith wide and deep,
And lay my body there."

6. He's taen him up upon his back,
Carried him to yon kirk-yard,
And dug a grave both deep and wide,
And laid his body there.

7. "But what will I say to my father dear,
Should he chance to say, Willie, whar's John?"
"Oh say that he's to England gone,
To buy him a cask of wine."

8. "And what shall I say to my mother dear,
Should she chance to say, Willie, whar's John?"
"Oh say that he's to England gone,
To buy her a new silk gown."

9. "And what will I say to my sister dear,
Should she chance to say, Willie, whar's John?"
"Oh say that he's to England gone,
To buy her a wedding ring."

10. "What will I say to her you loe dear,
Should she cry, Why tarries my John?"
"Oh tell her I lie in fair Kirk-land,
And home will never come."

SIR PATRICK SPENS

1. THE king sits in Dumferling toune,
Drinking the blude-reid wine:
"O whar will I get guid sailor,
To sail this schip of mine?"

2. Up and spak an eldern knicht,
Sat at the kings richt kne:
"Sir Patrick Spence is the best sailor
That sails upon the se."

3. The king has written a braid letter,
And signd it wi his hand,

And sent it to Sir Patrick Spence,
Was walking on the sand.

4. The first line that Sir Patrick red,
A loud lauch lauched he;
The next line that Sir Patrick red,
The teir blinded his ee.

5. "O wha is this has don this deid,
This ill deid don to me,
To send me out this time o' the yeir,
To sail upon the se!

6. "Mak hast, mak hast, my mirry men all,
Our guid schip sails the morne":
"O say na sae, my master deir,
For I feir a deadlie storme.

7. "Late late yestreen I saw the new moone,
Wi the auld moone in hir arme,
And I feir, I feir, my deir master,
That we will cum to harme."

8. O our Scots nobles wer richt laith
To weet their cork-heild schoone;
Bot lang owre a' the play wer playd,
Their hats they swam aboone.

9. O lang, lang may their ladies sit,
Wi their fans into their hand,
Or eir they se Sir Patrick Spence
Cum sailing to the land.

10. O lang, lang may the ladies stand
Wi their gold kems in their hair,
Waiting for thair ain deir lords,
For they'll se thame na mair.

11. Haf owre, haf owre to Aberdour,
It's fiftie fadom deip,
And thair lies guid Sir Patrick Spence,
Wi the Scots lords at his feit.

THE WIFE OF USHER'S WELL

1. THERE lived a wife at Usher's Well,
   And a wealthy wife was she;
   She had three stout and stalwart sons,
   And sent them oer the sea.

2. They hadna been a week from her,
   A week but barely ane,
   Whan word came to the carline wife [25]
   That her three sons were gane.

3. They hadna been a week from her,
   A week but barely three,
   Whan word came to the carlin wife
   That her sons she'd never see.

4. "I wish the wind may never cease,
   Nor fashes in the flood,
   Till my three sons come hame to me,
   In earthly flesh and blood."

5. It fell about the Martinmass,
   When nights are lang and mirk,
   The carlin wife's three sons came hame,
   And their hats were o the birk. [26]

6. It neither grew in syke [27] nor ditch,
   Nor yet in ony sheugh; [27]
   But at the gates o Paradise,
   That birk grew fair eneugh.

   .   .   .   .

7. "Blow up the fire, my maidens,
   Bring water from the well;
   For a' my house shall feast this night,
   Since my three sons are well."

8. And she has made to them a bed,
   She's made it large and wide,
   And she's taen her mantle her about,
   Sat down at the bed-side.

   .   .   .   .

9. Up then crew the red, red cock,
   And up and crew the gray;

25 old woman   26 birch   27 trench

The eldest to the youngest said,
   'Tis time we were away.

10. The cock he hadna crawd but once,
   And clappd his wings at a',
When the youngest to the eldest said,
   Brother, we must awa.

11. "The cock doth craw, the day doth daw,
   The channerin [28] worm doth chide;
Gin we be mist out o our place,
   A sair pain we maun bide.

12. "Fare ye weel, my mother dear!
   Fareweel to barn and byre! [29]
And fare ye weel, the bonny lass
   That kindles my mother's fire!"

BONNY BARBARA ALLAN

1. IT was in and about the Martinmas time,
   When the green leaves were a falling,
That Sir John Graeme, in the West Country,
   Fell in love with Barbara Allan.

2. He sent his man down through the town,
   To the place where she was dwelling:
"O haste and come to my master dear,
   Gin ye be Barbara Allan."

3. O hooly,[30] hooly rose she up,
   To the place where he was lying,
And when she drew the curtain by,
   "Young man, I think you're dying."

4. "O it's I'm sick, and very, very sick,
   And 't is a' for Barbara Allan:"
"O the better for me ye's never be,
   Tho your heart's blood were a spilling.

5. "O dinna ye mind, young man," said she,
   "When ye was in the tavern a drinking,
That ye made the healths gae round and round,
   And slighted Barbara Allan?"

---

28 fretting   29 cow-house   30 slowly

6. He turnd his face unto the wall,
   And death was with him dealing:
   "Adieu, adieu, my dear friends all,
   And be kind to Barbara Allan."

7. And slowly, slowly raise she up,
   And slowly, slowly left him,
   And sighing said, she coud not stay,
   Since death of life had reft him.

8. She had not gane a mile but twa,
   When she heard the dead-bell ringing,
   And every jow [31] that the dead-bell geid,
   It cry'd, Woe to Barbara Allan!

9. "O mother, mother, make my bed!
   O make it saft and narrow!
   Since my love died for me to-day,
   I'll die for him to-morrow."

ROBIN HOOD AND GUY OF GISBORNE

1. When shawes [32] been sheene, and shradds [33] full fayre,
   And leeves both large and longe,
   Itt is merry, walking in the fayre fforrest,
   To heare the small birds songe.

2. The woodweele [34] sang, and wold not cease,
   Amongst the leaves a lyne: [35]
   And it is by two wight [36] yeomen,
   By deare God, that I meane.

   .   .   .   .

3. "Me thought they did mee beate and binde,
   And tooke my bow mee froe;
   If I bee Robin a-live in this lande,
   I 'le be wrocken [37] on both them towe."

4. "Sweavens [38] are swift, master," quoth John,
   "As the wind that blowes ore a hill;
   Ffor if itt be never soe lowde this night,
   To-morrow it may be still."

5. "Buske [39] yee, bowne [39] yee, my merry men all,
   Ffor John shall goe with mee;

31 stroke	34 woodlark	37 revenged
32 woods	35 of the linden	38 dreams
33 copses	36 strong	39 get ready

For I 'le goe seek yond wight yeomen
In greenwood where the bee."

6. Thé cast on their gowne of greene,
A shooting gone are they,
Untill they came to the merry greenwood,
Where they had gladdest bee;
There were the ware of [a] wight yeoman,
His body leaned to a tree.

7. A sword and a dagger he wore by his side,
Had beene many a mans bane,
And he was cladd in his capull-hyde,[40]
Topp, and tayle, and mayne.

8. "Stand you still, master," quoth Litle John,
"Under this trusty tree,
And I will goe to yond wight yeoman,
To know his meaning trulye."

9. "A, John, by me thou setts noe store,
And that's a ffarley [41] thinge;
How offt send I my men beffore,
And tarry my-selfe behinde?

10. "It is noe cunning a knave to ken,
And a man but heare him speake;
And itt were not for bursting of my bowe,
John, I wold thy head breake."

11. But often words they breeden bale,
That parted Robin and John;
John is gone to Barn[e]sdale,
The gates he knowes eche one.

12. And when hee came to Barnesdale,
Great heavinesse there hee hadd;
He ffound two of his fellowes
Were slaine both in a slade,[42]

13. And Scarlett a ffoote flyinge was,
Over stockes and stone,
For the sheriffe with seven score men
Fast after him is gone.

40 horse-hide   41 strange   42 valley

14. "Yett one shoote I 'le shoote," sayes Litle John,
    "With Crist his might and mayne;
    I 'le make yond fellow that flyes soe fast
    To be both glad and ffaine."

15. John bent up a good ueiwe [43] bow,
    And ffetteled him to shoote;
    The bow was made of a tender boughe,
    And fell downe to his foote.

16. "Woe worth thee, wicked wood," sayd Litle John,
    "That ere thou grew on a tree!
    Ffor this day thou art my bale,
    My boote [44] when thou shold bee!"

17. This shoote it was but looselye shott,
    The arrowe flew in vaine,
    And it mett one of the sheriffes men;
    Good William a Trent was slaine.

18. It had beene better for William a Trent
    To hange upon a gallowe
    Then for to lye in the greenwoode,
    There slaine with an arrowe.

19. And it is sayd, when men be mett,
    Six can doe more then three:
    And they have tane Litle John,
    And bound him ffast to a tree.

20. "Thou shalt be drawen by dale and downe," quoth the
        sheriffe,
    "And hanged hye on a hill:"
    "But thou may ffayle," quoth Litle John,
    "If itt be Christs owne will."

21. Let us leave talking of Litle John,
    For hee is bound fast to a tree,
    And talke of Guy and Robin Hood,
    In the green woode where they bee.

22. How these two yeomen together they mett,
    Under the leaves of lyne,
    To see what marchandise they made
    Even at that same time.

43 yew   44 aid

23. "Good morrow, good fellow," quoth Sir Guy;
    "Good morrow, good ffellow," quoth hee;
    "Methinkes by this bow thou beares in thy hand,
        A good archer thou seems to bee."

24. "I am wilfull of my way," quoth Sir Guye,
    "And of my morning tyde:"
    "I 'le lead thee through the wood," quoth Robin,
    "Good ffellow, I 'le be thy guide."

25. "I seeke an outlaw," quoth Sir Guye,
    "Men call him Robin Hood;
    I had rather meet with him upon a day
        Then forty pound of golde."

26. "If you tow mett, itt wold be seene whether were better
    Afore yee did part awaye;
    Let us some other pastime find,
        Good ffellow, I thee pray.

27. "Let us some other masteryes [45] make,
    And wee will walke in the woods even;
    Wee may chance mee[t] with Robin Hoode
        Att some unsett steven." [46]

28. They cutt them downe the summer shroggs [47]
    Which grew both under a bryar,
    And sett them three score rood in twinn, [48]
        To shoote the prickes [49] full neare.

29. "Leade on, good ffellow," sayd Sir Guye,
    "Lead on, I doe bidd thee:"
    "Nay, by my faith," quoth Robin Hood,
    "The leader thou shalt bee."

30. The first good shoot that Robin ledd
    Did not shoote an inch the pricke ffroe;
    Guy was an archer good enoughe,
        But he cold neere shoote soe.

31. The second shoote Sir Guy shott,
    He shott within the garlande; [50]
    But Robin Hoode shott it better then hee,
        For he clove the good pricke-wande.

45 feats of skill
46 time not previously fixed
47 wands
48 in two's
49 marks
50 wreath or ring (set on wands)

32. "Gods blessing on thy heart!" sayes Guye,
  "Goode ffellow, thy shooting is goode;
  For an thy hart be as good as thy hands,
  Thou were better than Robin Hood.

33. "Tell me thy name, good ffellow," quoth Guy,
  "Under the leaves of lyne:"
  "Nay, by my faith," quoth good Robin,
  "Till thou have told me thine."

34. "I dwell by dale and downe," quoth Guye,
  "And I have done many a curst turne;
  And he that calles me by my right name
  Calles me Guye of good Gysborne."

35. "My dwelling is in the wood," sayes Robin;
  "By thee I set right nought;
  My name is Robin Hood of Barnesdale,
  A ffellow thou has long sought."

36. He that had neither beene a kithe nor kin
  Might have seene a full fayre sight,
  To see how together these yeomen went,
  With blades both browne and bright.

37. To have seene how these yeomen together fought,
  Two howers of a summers day;
  Itt was neither Guy nor Robin Hood
  That ffettled [51] them to flyc away.

38. Robin was reacheles on [52] a roote,
  And stumbled at that tyde,[53]
  And Guy was quicke and nimble withall,
  And hitt him ore the left side.

39. "Ah, deere Lady!" sayd Robin Hoode,
  "Thou art both mother and may! [54]
  I thinke it was never mans destinye
  To dye before his day."

40. Robin thought on Our Lady deere,
  And soone leapt up againe,
  And thus he came with an awkwarde stroke;
  Good Sir Guy hee has slayne.

51 made ready   53 time   54 maid
52 reckless of

41. He tooke Sir Guys head by the hayre,
    And sticked itt on his bowes end:
    "Thou hast beene traytor all thy liffe,
    Which thing must have an ende."

42. Robin pulled forth an Irish kniffe,
    And nicked Sir Guy in the fface,
    That hee was never on a woman borne
    Cold tell who Sir Guye was.

43. Saies, Lye there, lye there, good Sir Guye,
    And with me be not wrothe;
    If thou have had the worse stroakes at my hand,
    Thou shalt have the better cloathe.

44. Robin did off his gowne of greene,
    Sir Guye hee did it throwe;
    And hee put on that capull-hyde,
    That cladd him topp to toe.

45. "The bowe, the arrowes, and litle horne,
    And with me now I 'le beare;
    Ffor now I will goe to Barnesdale,
    To see how my men doe ffare."

46. Robin sett Guyes horne to his mouth,
    A lowd blast in it he did blow;
    That beheard the sheriffe of Nottingham,
    As he leaned under a lowe.[55]

47. "Hearken! hearken!" sayd the sheriffe,
    "I heard noe tydings but good;
    For yonder I heare Sir Guyes horne blowe,
    For he hath slaine Robin Hoode.

48. "For yonder I heare Sir Guyes horne blow,
    Itt blowes soe well in tyde,
    For yonder comes that wighty yeoman,
    Cladd in his capull-hyde.

49. "Come hither, thou good Sir Guy,
    Aske of mee what thou wilt have:"
    "I 'le none of thy gold," sayes Robin Hood,
    "Nor I 'le none of itt have.

50. "But now I have slaine the master," he sayd,
    "Let me goe strike the knave;
This is all the reward I aske,
    Nor noe other will I have."

51. "Thou art a madman," said the shiriffe,
    "Thou sholdest have had a knights ffee;
Seeing thy asking hath beene soe badd,
    Well granted it shall be."

52. But Litle John heard his master speake,
    Well he knew that was his steven; [56]
"Now shall I be loset," quoth Litle John,
    "With Christs might in heaven."

53. But Robin hee hyed him towards Litle John,
    Hee thought hee wold loose him belive;
The sheriffe and all his companye
    Fast after him did drive.

54. "Stand abacke! stand abacke!" sayd Robin;
    "Why draw you mee soe neere?"
Itt was never the use in our countrye
    One's shrift another shold heere."

55. But Robin pulled forth an Irysh kniffe,
    And losed John hand and ffoote,
And gave him Sir Guycs bow in his hand,
    And bade it be his boote. [57]

56. But John tooke Guyes bow in his hand—
    His arrowes were rawstye [58] by the roote;
The sherriffe saw Litle John draw a bow
    And ffettle [59] him to shoote.

57. Towards his house in Nottingam
    He ffled full fast away,
And soe did all his companye,
    Not one behind did stay.

58. But he cold neither soe fast goe,
    Nor away soe fast runn,
But Litle John, with an arrow broade,
    Did cleave his heart in twinn.

56 voice   58 rusty   59 make ready
57 help

ROBIN HOOD'S DEATH

1. WHEN Robin Hood and Little John,
   Down a down a down a down,
   Went oer yon bank of broom,
   Said Robin Hood bold to Little John,
   We have shot for many a pound.
   Hey, *etc.*

2. But I am not able to shoot one shot more,
   My broad arrows will not flee;
   But I have a cousin lives down below,
   Please God, she will bleed me.

3. Now Robin he is to fair Kirkly gone,
   As fast as he can win;
   But before he came there, as we do hear,
   He was taken very ill.

4. And when he came to fair Kirkly-hall,
   He knockd all at the ring,
   But none was so ready as his cousin herself
   For to let bold Robin in.

5. "Will you please to sit down, cousin Robin," she said,
   "And drink some beer with me?"
   "No, I will neither eat nor drink,
   Till I am blooded by thee."

6. "Well, I have a room, cousin Robin," she said,
   "Which you did never see,
   And if you please to walk therein,
   You blooded by me shall be."

7. She took him by the lily-white hand,
   And led him to a private room,
   And there she blooded bold Robin Hood,
   While one drop of blood would run down.

8. She blooded him in a vein of the arm,
   And locked him up in the room;
   Then did he bleed all the live-long day,
   Until the next day at noon.

9. He then bethought him of a casement there,
   Thinking for to get down;

But was so weak he could not leap,
     He could not get him down.

10. He then bethought him of his buglehorn,
     Which hung low down to his knee;
     He set his horn unto his mouth,
     And blew out weak blasts three.

11. Then Little John, when hearing him,
     As he sat under a tree,
     "I fear my master is now near dead,
     He blows so wearily."

12. Then Little John to fair Kirkly is gone,
     As fast as he can dree; [60]
     But when he came to Kirkly-hall,
     He broke locks two or three:

13. Until he came bold Robin to see,
     Then he fell on his knee;
     "A boon, a boon," cries Little John,
     "Master, I beg of thee."

14. "What is that boon," said Robin Hood,
     "Little John, thou begs of me?"
     "It is to burn fair Kirkly-hall,
     And all their nunnery."

15. "Now nay, now nay," quoth Robin Hood,
     "That boon I'll not grant thee;
     I never hurt woman in all my life,
     Nor men in woman's company.

16. "I never hurt fair maid in all my time,
     Nor at mine end shall it be;
     But give me my bent bow in my hand,
     And a broad arrow I'll let flee
     And where this arrow is taken up,
     There shall my grave digged be.

17. "Lay me a green sod under my head,
     And another at my feet;
     And lay my bent bow by my side,
     Which was my music sweet;

60 be able

And make my grave of gravel and green,
Which is most right and meet.

18. "Let me have length and breadth enough,
With a green sod under my head;
That they may say, when I am dead,
Here lies bold Robin Hood."

19. These words they readily granted him,
Which did bold Robin please:
And there they buried bold Robin Hood,
Within the fair Kirkleys.

ROBIN HOOD AND THE CURTAL FRIAR

1. In summer time, when leaves grow green,
And flowers are fresh and gay,
Robin Hood and his merry men
Were disposed to play.

2. Then some would leap, and some would run,
And some would use artillery:
"Which of you can a good bow draw,
A good archer to be?

3. "Which of you can kill a buck?
Or who can kill a do?
Or who can kill a hart of greece,[61]
Five hundred foot him fro?"

4. Will Scadlock he killd a buck,
And Midge he killd a do,
And Little John killd a hart of greece,
Five hundred feet him fro.

5. "God's blessing on thy heart," said Robin Hood,
"That hath shot such a shot for me;
I would ride my horse an hundred miles,
To finde one could match with thee."

6. That causd Will Scadlock to laugh,
He laughed full heartily:
"There lives a curtal[62] frier in Fountains Abby
Will beat both him and thee.

61 a fat hart
62 having charge of the vegetable garden at a monastery

7. "That curtal frier in Fountains Abby
   Well can a strong bow draw;
   He will beat you and your yeomen,
   Set them all on a row."

8. Robin Hood took a solemn oath,
   It was by Mary free,
   That he would neither eat nor drink
   Till the frier he did see.

9. Robin Hood put on his harness good,
   And on his head a cap of steel,
   Broad sword and buckler by his side,
   And they became him weel.

10. He took his bow into his hand,
    It was made of a trusty tree,
    With a sheaf of arrows at his belt,
    To the Fountains Dale went he.

11. And coming unto Fountains Dale,
    No further would he ride;
    There was he aware of a curtal frier,
    Walking by the water-side.

12. The fryer had on a harniss good,
    And on his head a cap of steel,
    Broad sword and buckler by his side,
    And they became him weel.

13. Robin Hood lighted off his horse,
    And tied him to a thorn:
    "Carry me over the water, thou curtal frier,
    Or else thy life's forlorn."

14. The frier took Robin Hood on his back,
    Deep water he did bestride,
    And spake neither good word nor bad,
    Till he came at the other side.

15. Lightly leapt Robin Hood off the frier's back;
    The frier said to him again,
    "Carry me over this water, fine fellow,
    Or it shall breed thy pain."

16. Robin Hood took the frier on's back,
    Deep water he did bestride,

And spake neither good word nor bad,
    Till he came at the other side.

17. Lightly leapt the fryer off Robin Hoods back;
    Robin Hood said to him again,
    "Carry me over this water, thou curtal frier,
    Or it shall breed thy pain."

18. The frier took Robin Hood on's back again,
    And stept up to the knee;
    Till he came at the middle stream,
    Neither good nor bad spake he.

19. And coming to the middle stream,
    There he threw Robin in:
    "And chuse thee, chuse thee, fine fellow,
    Whether thou wilt sink or swim."

20. Robin Hood swam to a bush of broom,
    The frier to a wicker wand;
    Bold Robin Hood is gone to shore,
    And took his bow in hand.

21. One of his best arrows under his belt
    To the frier he let flye;
    The curtal frier, with his steel buckler,
    He put that arrow by.

22. "Shoot on, shoot on, thou fine fellow,
    Shoot on as thou hast begun;
    If thou shoot here a summers day,
    Thy mark I will not shun."

23. Robin Hood shot passing well,
    Till his arrows all were gone;
    They took their swords and steel bucklers,
    And fought with might and maine;

24. From ten oth' clock that day,
    Till four ith' afternoon;
    Then Robin Hood came to his knees,
    Of the frier to beg a boon.

25. "A boon, a boon, thou curtal frier,
    I beg it on my knee;

Give me leave to set my horn to my mouth,
And to blow blasts three."

26. "That will I do," said the curtal frier,
"Of thy blasts I have no doubt;
I hope thou'lt blow so passing well
Till both thy eyes fall out."

27. Robin Hood set his horn to his mouth,
He blew but blasts three;
Half a hundred yeomen, with bows bent,
Came raking over the lee.

28. "Whose men are these," said the frier,
"That come so hastily?"
"These men are mine," said Robin Hood;
"Frier, what is that to thee?"

29. "A boon, a boon," said the curtal frier,
"The like I gave to thee;
Give me leave to set my fist to my mouth,
And to whute [63] whutes three."

30. "That will I do," said Robin Hood,
"Or else I were to blame;
Three whutes in a friers fist
Would make me glad and fain."

31. The frier he set his fist to his mouth,
And whuted whutes three;
Half a hundred good ban-dogs
Came running the frier unto.

32. "Here's for every man of thine a dog,
And I my self for thee":
"Nay, by my faith," quoth Robin Hood,
"Frier, that may not be."

33. Two dogs at once to Robin Hood did go,
The one behind, the other before;
Robin Hoods mantle of Lincoln green
Off from his back they tore.

34. And whether his men shot east or west,
Or they shot north or south,

63 whistle

The curtal dogs, so taught they were,
They kept the arrows in their mouth.

35. "Take up thy dogs," said Little John,
"Frier, at my bidding be";
"Whose man art thou," said the curtal frier,
"Comes here to prate with me?"

36. "I am Little John, Robin Hoods man,
Frier, I will not lie;
If thou take not up thy dogs soon,
I'le take up them and thee."

37. Little John had a bow in his hand,
He shot with might and main;
Soon half a score of the friers dogs
Lay dead upon the plain.

38. "Hold thy hand, good fellow," said the curtal frier,
"Thy master and I will agree;
And we will have new orders taken,
With all the haste that may be."

39. "If thou wilt forsake fair Fountains Dale,
And Fountains Abby free,
Every Sunday throughout the year,
A noble shall be thy fee.

40. "And every holy day throughout the year,
Changed shall thy garment be,
If thou wilt go to fair Nottingham,
And there remain with me."

41. This curtal frier had kept Fountains Dale
Seven long years or more;
There was neither knight, lord, nor earl
Could make him yield before.

SIR HUGH, OR, THE JEW'S DAUGHTER [64]

1. Four and twenty bonny boys
Were playing at the ba,
And by it came him sweet Sir Hugh,
And he playd oer them a'.

[64] Another version of the same legend treated in Chaucer's *Prioress's Tale*.

2. He kicked the ba with his right foot,
   And catchd it wi his knee,
   And throuch-and-thro the Jew's window
   He gard [65] the bony ba flee.

3. He's doen him to the Jew's castell,
   And walkd it round about;
   And thcre he saw the Jew's daughter,
   At the window looking out.

4. "Throw down the ba, ye Jew's daughter,
   Throw down the ba to me!"
   "Never a bit," says the Jew's daughter,
   "Till up to me come ye."

5. "How will I come up? How can I come up?
   How can I come to thee?
   For as ye did to my auld father,
   The same ye'll do to me."

6. She's gane till her father's garden,
   And pu'd an apple red and green;
   'T was a' to wyle him sweet Sir Hugh,
   And to entice him in.

7. She's led him in through ae dark door,
   And sae has she thro nine;
   She's laid him on a dressing-table,
   And stickit him like a swine.

8. And first camc out the thick, thick blood,
   And syne [66] came out the thin,
   And syne came out the bonny heart's blood;
   There was nae mair within.

9. She's rowd him in a cake o lead,
   Bade him lie still and sleep;
   She's thrown him in Our Lady's draw-well,
   Was fifty fathom deep.

10. When bells were rung, and mass was sung,
    And a' the bairns came hame,
    When every lady gat hame her son,
    The Lady Maisry gat nane.

---

65 made   66 afterwards

11. She's taen her mantle her about,
    Her coffer by the hand,
    And she's gane out to seek her son,
    And wanderd oer the land.

12. She's doen her to the Jew's castell,
    Where a' were fast asleep:
    "Gin ye be there, my sweet Sir Hugh,
    I pray you to me speak."

13. She's doen her to the Jew's garden,
    Thought he had been gathering fruit:
    "Gin ye be there, my sweet Sir Hugh,
    I pray you to me speak."

14. She neard Our Lady's deep draw-well,
    Was fifty fathom deep:
    "Whareer ye be, my sweet Sir Hugh,
    I pray you to me speak."

15. "Gae hame, gae hame, my mither dear,
    Prepare my winding sheet,
    And at the back o merry Lincoln
    The morn I will you meet."

16. Now Lady Maisry is gane hame,
    Made him a winding sheet,
    And at the back o merry Lincoln
    The dead corpse did her meet.

17. And a' the bells o merry Lincoln
    Without men's hands were rung,
    And a' the books o merry Lincoln
    Were read without man's tongue,
    And neer was such a burial
    Sin Adam's days begun.

THE BATTLE OF OTTERBURN [67]

1. Yt fell abowght the Lamasse tyde,
    Whan husbondes wynnes [68] ther haye,
    The dowghtye Dowglasse bowynd [69] hym to ryde,
    In Ynglond to take a praye.

---

67 Fought in 1388. An
older version of the ballad
known as "The Hunting

of the Cheviot" or "Chevy
Chase."
68 farmers dry

69 made ready

2. The yerlle of Fyffe, wythowghten stryffe,
    He bowynd hym over Sulway;
    The grete wolde ever to-gether ryde;
    That raysse [70] they may rewe for aye.

3. Over Hoppertope hyll they cam in,
    And so down by Rodclyffe crage;
    Upon Grene Lynton they lyghted dowyn,
    Styrande many a stage.[71]

4. And boldely brente [72] Northomberlond,
    And haryed many a towyn;
    They dyd owr Ynglyssh men grete wrange,
    To batell that were not bowyn.[73]

5. Than spake a berne [74] vpon the bent,[75]
    Of comforte that was not colde,
    And sayd, "We have brente Northomberlond,
    We have all welth in holde.

6. "Now we have haryed all Bamborowe schyre,
    All the welth in the worlde have wee,
    I rede we ryde to Newe Castell,
    So styll and stalworthlye."

7. Upon the morowe, when it was day,
    The standerds schone full bryght;
    To the Newe Castell the toke the waye,
    And thether they cam full ryght.

8. Syr Henry Perssy laye at the New Castell,
    I tell yow wythowtten drede;
    He had byn a march-man [76] all hys dayes,
    And kepte Barwyke upon Twede.

9. To the Newe Castell when they cam,
    The Skottes they cryde on hyght,
    "Syr Hary Perssy, and thou byste within,
    Com to the fylde, and fyght.

10. "For we have brente Northomberlonde,
     Thy erytage good and ryght,
     And syne my logeyng I have take
     Wyth my brande dubbyd many a knyght."

70 raid   73 ready   76 keeper of the marches,
71 stirring many a stag   74 warrior   or border
72 burned   75 field of coarse grass

11. Syr Harry Perssy cam to the walles,
  The Skottysch oste for to se,
 And sayd, "And thou hast brente Northomberlond,
  Full sore it rewyth me.

12. "Yf thou hast haryed all Bamborowe schyre,
  Thow hast done me grete envye;
 For the trespasse thow hast me done,
  The tone of us schall dye."

13. "Where schall I byde the?" sayd the Dowglas,
  "Or where wylte thow com to me?"
 "At Otterborne, in the hygh way,
  Ther mast thow well logeed be.

14. "The roo [77] full rekeles ther sche rinnes,
  To make the game and glee;
 The fawken and the fesaunt both,
  Among the holtes [78] on hye.

15. "Ther mast thow have thy welth at wyll,
  Well looged ther mast be;
 Yt schall not be long or I com the tyll,"
  Sayd Syr Harry Perssye.

16. "Ther schall I byde the," sayd the Dowglas,
  "By the fayth of my bodye:"
 "Thether schall I com," sayd Syr Harry Perssy,
  "My trowth I plyght to the."

17. A pype of wyne he gave them over the walles,
  For soth as I yow saye;
 Ther he mayd the Dowglasse drynke,
  And all hys ost that daye.

18. The Dowglas turnyd hym homewarde agayne,
  For soth withowghten naye;
 He toke hys logeyng at Oterborne,
  Upon a Wednysday.

19. And ther he pyght [79] hys standerd dowyn,
  Hys gettyng more and lesse,[80]
 And syne [81] he warned hys men to goo
  To chose ther geldynges gresse.[82]

---

77 roe   79 fixed   81 afterwards
78 woods   80 all he had got   82 grass

20. A Skottysshe knyght hoved upon the bent,[83]
    A wache I dare well saye;
    So was he ware on the noble Perssy,
    In the dawnyng of the daye.

21. He prycked to hys pavyleon-dore,
    As faste as he myght ronne;
    "Awaken, Dowglas," cryed the knyght,
    For hys love that syttes in trone.

22. "Awaken, Dowglas," cryed the knyght,
    "For thow maste waken wyth wynne;[84]
    Yender have I spyed the prowde Perssye,
    And seven stondardes wyth hym."

23. "Nay by my trowth," the Dowglas sayed,
    "It ys but a fayned taylle;
    He durst not loke on my brede[85] banner
    For all Ynglonde so haylle.

24. "Was I not yesterdaye at the Newe Castell,
    That stondes so fayre on Tyne?
    For all the men the Perssy had,
    He coude not garre me ones to dyne."[86]

25. He stepped owt at his pavelyon-dore,
    To loke and it were lesse:[87]
    "Araye yow, lordynges, one and all,
    For here bygynnes no peysse.

26. "The yerle of Mentaye, thow arte my eme,[88]
    The fowarde I gyve to the:
    The yerlle of Huntlay, cawte[89] and kene,
    He schall be wyth the.

27. "The lorde of Bowghan, in armure bryght,
    On the other hand he schall be;
    Lord Jhontoune and Lorde Maxwell,
    They to schall be wyth me.

28. "Swynton, fayre fylde upon your pryde!
    To batell make yow bowen
    Syr Davy Skotte, Syr Water Stewarde,
    Syr Jhon of Agurstone!

83 field
84 joy
85 broad

86 give me my dinner,
   fill (beat thoroughly)
87 falsehood

88 uncle
89 wary

29. The Perssy cam byfore hys oste,
    Wych was ever a gentyll knyght;
Upon the Dowglas lowde can [90] he crye,
    "I wyll holde that I have hyght.[91]

30. For thou haste brente Northomberlonde,
    And done me grete envye;
For thys trespasse thou hast me done,
    The tone of us schall dye."

31. The Dowglas answerde hym agayne,
    Wyth grett wurdes upon hye,
And sayd, "I have twenty agaynst thy one,
    Byholde, and thou maste see."

32. Wyth that the Perssy was grevyd sore,
    For soth as I yow saye;
He lyghted dowyn upon his foote,
    And schoote [92] hys horsse clene awaye.

33. Every man sawe that he dyd soo,
    That ryall was euer in rowght; [93]
Euery man schoote hys horsse hym froo,
    And lyght hym rowynde abowght.

34. Thus Syr Hary Perssye toke the fylde,
    For soth as I yow saye;
Jhesu Cryste in hevyn on hyght
    Dyd helpe hym well that daye.

35. But nyne thowzand, ther was no moo,
    The cronykle wyll not layne; [94]
Forty thowsande of Skottes and fowre
    That day fowght them agayne.

36. But when the batell byganne to joyne,
    In hast ther cam a knyght;
The letters fayre furth hath he tayne,
    And thus he sayd full ryght:

37. "My lorde your father he gretes yow well,
    Wyth many a noble knyght;
He desyres yow to byde
    That he may see thys fyght.

90 did   92 sent away   94 lie
91 promised   93 kingly among men

38. "The Baron of Grastoke ys com out of the west,
  Wyth hym a noble companye;
All they loge at your fathers thys nyght,
  And the batell fayne wolde they see."

39. "For Jhesus love," sayd Syr Harye Perssy,
  "That dyed for yow and me,
Wende to my lorde my father agayne,
  And saye thow sawe me not wyth yee.[95]

40. "My trowth ys plyght to yonne Skottysh knyght,
  It nedes me not to layne,
That I schulde byde hym upon thys bent,
  And I have hys trowth agayne.

41. "And if that I weynde of [96] thys growende,[97]
  For soth, ofowghten awaye,
He wolde me call but a kowarde knyght
  On hys londe another daye.

42. "Yet had I lever to be rynde [98] and rente,
  By Mary, that mykkel maye,[99]
Then ever my manhood schulde be reprovyd
  Wyth a Skotte another day.

43. "Wherfore schote, archars, for my sake,
  And let scharpe arowes flee;
Mynstrells, playe up for your waryson,[1]
  And well quyt it schall bee.

44. "Every man thynke on hys trewe-love,
  And marke hym to the Trenite;
For to God I make myne avowe
  Thys day wyll I not flee."

45. The blodye harte in the Dowglas armes,
  Hys standerde stode on hye,
That every man myght full well knowe;
  By syde stode starrës thre.

46. The whyte lyon on the Ynglyssh perte,
  For soth as I yow sayne,
The lucettes [2] and the cressawntes both;
  The Skottes faught them agayne.

95 eye   98 flayed   2 pikes (fish)
96 went from   99 powerful maid
97 ground   1 reward

47. Upon Sent Androwe lowde can they crye,
    And thrysse they schowte on hyght,
    And syne merked them one owr Ynglysshe men,
    As I have tolde yow ryght.

48. Sent George the bryght, owr ladyes knyght,
    To name they were full fayne;
    Owr Ynglyssh men they cryde on hyght,
    And thrysse the schowtte agayne.

49. Wyth that scharpe arowes bygan to flee,
    I tell yow in sertayne;
    Men of armes byganne to joyne,
    Many a dowghty man was ther slayne.

50. The Perssy and the Dowglas mette,
    That ether of other was fayne;
    They swapped³ together whyll⁴ that the swette,
    Wyth swordes of fyne collayne:⁵

51. Tyll the bloode from ther bassonnettes⁶ ranne,
    As the roke⁷ doth in the rayne;
    "Yelde the to me," sayd the Dowglas,
    "Or elles thow schalt be slayne.

52. "For I see by thy bryght bassonet,
    Thow arte sum man of myght;
    And so I do by thy burnysshed brande;
    Thow arte an yerle, or elles a knyght."

53. "By my good faythe," sayd the noble Perssye,
    "Now haste thow rede⁸ full ryght;
    Yet wyll I never yelde me to the,
    Whyll I may stonde and fyght."

54. They swapped together whyll that they swette,
    Wyth swordës scharpe and long;
    Ych on other so faste thee beette,
    Tyll ther helmes cam in peyses dowyn.

55. The Perssy was a man of strenghth,
    I tell yow in thys stounde;⁹
    He smote the Dowglas at the swordës length
    That he felle to the grownyde.

3 smote   6 helmets   9 time
4 till   7 vapor
5 of Cologne steel 8 perceived

56. The sworde was scharpe, and sore can byte,
     I tell yow in sertayne;
     To the harte he cowde hym smyte,
     Thus was the Dowglas slayne.

57. The stonderdes stode styll on eke a syde,
     Wyth many a grevous grone;
     Ther the fowght the day, and all the nyght,
     And many a dowghty man was slayne.

58. Ther was no freke [10] that ther wolde flye,
     But styffely in stowre [11] can stond,
     Ychone hewyng on other whyll they myght drye,[12]
     Wyth many a bayllefull bronde.

59. Ther was slayne upon the Skottës syde,
     For soth and sertenly,
     Syr James a Dowglas ther was slayne,
     That day that he cowde [13] dye.

60. The yerlle of Mentaye he was slayne,
     Grysely groned upon the growynd;
     Syr Davy Skotte, Syr Water Stewarde,
     Syr Jhon of Agurstoune.

61. Syr Charllës Morrey in that place,
     That never a fote wold flee;
     Syr Hewe Maxwell, a lorde he was,
     Wyth the Dowglas dyd he dye.

62. Ther was slayne upon the Skottës syde,
     For soth as I yow saye,
     Of fowre and forty thowsande Scottes
     Went but eyghtene awaye.

63. Ther was slayne upon the Ynglysshe syde,
     For soth and sertenlye,
     A gentell knyght, Syr Jhon Fechewe,
     Yt was the more pety.

64. Syr James Hardbottell ther was slayne,
     For hym ther hartes were sore;
     The gentyll Lovell ther was slayne,
     That the Perssys standerd bore.

10 man   12 endure   13 did
11 fight

65. Ther was slayne upon the Ynglyssh perte,
    For soth as I yow saye,
    Of nyne thowsand Ynglyssh men
    Fyve hondert cam awaye.

66. The other were slayne in the fylde;
    Cryste kepe ther sowlles from wo!
    Seyng ther was so fewe fryndes
    Agaynst so many a foo.

67. Then on the morne they made them beerys
    Of byrch and haysell graye;
    Many a wydowe, wyth wepyng teyres,
    Ther makes [14] they fette [15] awaye.

68. Thys fraye bygan at Otterborne,
    Bytwene the nyght and the day;
    Ther the Dowglas lost hys lyffe,
    And the Perssy was lede awaye.

69. Then was ther a Scottysh prisoner tayne,
    Syr Hewe Mongomery was hys name;
    For soth as I yow saye,
    He borowed [16] the Perssy home agayne.

70. Now let us all for the Perssy praye
    To Jhesu most of myght,
    To bryng hys sowlle to the blysse of heven,
    For he was a gentyll knyght.

THE SECOND SHEPHERDS' PLAY

For many centuries after the fall of Rome, there was no regular drama performed in Europe. The culture that fosters the theater and its arts had been
destroyed by the barbarian invasions; the Christian church, moreover, dominant in these centuries, had from the beginning frowned upon all theatric
representation. Ironic it is, then, that the revival of the drama in the later
Middle Ages was stimulated by the church itself, and originated in its services;
in the interpolation of words, or dialogue, into the wordless antiphonal chants
of the mass. Such *tropes*, as they were called, appear first in the Resurrection
liturgy, in the colloquy of the three Marys and the Angel before the tomb
of the risen Christ, and later in the Christmas and other services. Dialogues
of this sort, from their effectiveness in presenting the scripture story, were inevitably expanded and extended; so much so, that the liturgical plays were
felt to be unseemly in the church, were removed outside, were eventually done

---

14 mates   15 fetched   16 ransomed

in the vernacular (instead of the churchly Latin), and handed over to lay actors.

By the end of the Middle Ages, in many places it had become customary to present, on a single occasion in the year, usually the feast of Corpus Christi, falling in the ninth week after Easter, a whole cycle of religious plays, one after the other, based upon the most dramatic incidents in the narrative of both Old and New Testaments. These plays, usually called in England *miracle plays*, were typically acted and produced by the medieval trade guilds, as a matter of civic pride, for a community festival. Though sometimes done on stationary stages, a common mounting was on movable wagons or floats (called *pageants*), which were drawn from place to place in a town, and stopped for performance before the crowds gathered at various vantage points. When the first play was done, its "pageant" was drawn to another point, where the performance was repeated, its place at the first station being taken by a second pageant, and so on, until all the plays had been presented at all the stations announced. Since some of the cycles contained as many as forty-eight plays, the process was a lengthy one. The subjects treated varied in different communities, favorites being such stories as the Creation, Cain and Abel, Noah's Flood, Abraham and Isaac, the Procession of the Prophets (including Balaam on his ass), the Shepherds, the Magi, the Treachery of Judas, the Crucifixion, the Harrowing of Hell, the Resurrection, and the Judgment Day. Each craft (or sometimes two or more together) was responsible for the mounting and acting of one of the plays. Though the assignment of plays to the several guilds had often no significance, an appropriateness (sometimes humorous) may be seen when, for example, the watermen or shipwrights did Noah's Ark, the goldsmiths the Magi, the bakers the Last Supper, and the cooks the Harrowing of Hell.

From old account books and records we know that miracle plays were performed at many places, but English manuscripts of only four complete cycles are extant. Two of these come from Chester and from York respectively. The locale of a third is uncertain (the manuscript states it is to be performed at *N-town*). A fourth, from Wakefield, in southern Yorkshire (sometimes called also the Towneley cycle, from the family formerly owning the manuscript), is for literary merit the most distinguished. The manuscript dates from the latter half of the fifteenth century, but the composition is probably somewhat earlier. The thirty-two plays exhibit several strata, of divergent authorship, but at least five, and perhaps a number of others, were written by a single writer who may have lived in the second quarter of the fifteenth century. This writer's contribution stands out from the rest because of his great skill in characterization, in the invention of dramatic incident, and in the management of the verse, and because of his lively sense of humor. For the anonymous genius, our first great playwright, has been suggested the name, "The Wakefield Master." His masterpiece is the *Second Shepherds' Play*, so called because the Wakefield cycle also contains another, or *first* Shepherds' play on the nativity theme.

The *Second Shepherds' Play* is a spirited, original comedy of three English shepherds, a clever rascal and his cleverer wife, in a thoroughly native setting. Only at the end is its inclusion in a Biblical cycle justified, rather lamely but none the less charmingly, by the appearance of the Angel singing "Gloria in Excelsis," and the visit of the shepherds to the Christ-child in the manger. The reader will not fail to notice the sharply differentiated drawing of all five of the leading characters, the abundant humor (which is sometimes rough fun), the rich background of English weather, English life, and English social conditions of the time, the skillful use of the playwright's bag of tricks—suspense, surprise, dramatic irony, and the rest; yes, and the poet's technical mastery of the remarkable nine-line stanza employed. The version here presented is freely adapted from the original, to eliminate most of the obsolete terms and so promote easier reading, without, however, doing much violence to either rhyme or meter, and none, it is hoped, to the sense.

Although drama is in general outside the scope of the present work, this entertaining medieval masterpiece has nevertheless been included in the belief it will lead to a better understanding of our older literature than would soberer essays or non-dramatic verse from the same period.

Those interested in dramatic origins should also read specimens of the morality play—a sort of dramatized sermon, in which good and evil characters, in allegoric wise, battle for the possession of man's soul. The finest extant play of this type is the well-known *Everyman*.

BIBLIOGRAPHY. Convenient anthologies of miracle and morality plays in J. Q. Adams, *Chief Pre-Shakespearean Dramas* (Houghton Mifflin), J. M. Manly, *Specimens of the Pre-Shakesperean Drama* (Ginn), Vol. I, and (with discussion), in A. W. Pollard, *English Miracle Plays, Morality Plays, and Interludes* (Oxford). Text of the Wakefield plays, ed. G. England, in E. E. T. S. Extra ser., LXXI, 1897. Discussions and apparatus also in E. K. Chambers, *Mediaeval Stage* (Oxford), Vol. II, A. W. Ward, *Hist. of Eng. Dramatic Lit.* (Macmillan), Vol. I, and Karl Young, *Drama of the Medieval Church* (Oxford), 2 vols. Readable account, J. M. Gayley, *Plays of Our Forefathers* (Duffield).

THE SECOND SHEPHERDS' PLAY

[Wakefield]

CHARACTERS

The 1st Shepherd (*sometimes called* COLL)
The 2nd Shepherd (*or* GIB)
The 3rd Shepherd, a boy (DAW)
MAK, the Sheep-stealer
GILL, Mak's wife
The Virgin Mary
The Christ Child
An Angel

[*The pageant or stage was divided into two parts: the fields where the shepherds watched their flocks, and the home of* MAK *and his wife* GILL, *respectively; either at opposite ends, or on an upper and a lower section.*]

[*Enter the* 1st Shepherd.]

1st Shepherd. Lord! How these weathers are cold, and I am ill
        wrapped;
My numb hands scarce hold, so long have I napped.

My legs they fold, my fingers are chapped;
It is not as I would, for I am all lapped
    In sorrow.
In storms and tempest,
Now in the east, now in the west,
Woe is him has never rest
    Midday nor morrow!

But we silly shepherds that walk on the moor,   10
In faith, we are near-hands out of the door;
No wonder, as it stands, if we be poor,
For the tilth of our lands lies fallow as the floor,
    As ye ken.
We are so lamed,
Over-taxed and blamed,
We are made hand-tamed
    By these gentlery-men.[1]

Thus they reave us of our rest; our curses, by Mary!
These men that are lord-fast, they cause the plough tarry.   20
That, men say, is for the best; we find it contrary.
Thus are husbandmen oppressed, in point to miscarry,
    In life.
Thus hold they us under;
Thus they bring us in blunder!
It were great wonder
    If ever should we thrive.

There shall come a swain as proud as a po,[2]
He must borrow my wain, my plough also;
Then I am full fain to grant ere he go.   30
Thus live we in pain, anger, and woe
    By night and day.
He must have it if he langéd,
If I should forgang[3] it.
I were better be hangéd
    Than once say him nay.

For may he get a painted sleeve, or a brooch, now-a-days,
Woe if any shall him grieve, or against him aught says!
Dare no man him reprove, whatever mastery he displays.
And yet may no man believe one word that he says,   40
    No letter.

1 In this and the following three stanzas, the 1st Shepherd complains of 14th–15th century social conditions, particularly oppression of poor husbandmen by the rich land-owners, operating through unprincipled agents.
    2 peacock   3 have to do without

He can make purveyance,
With boasting and insolence;
And all is through maintenance
    Of men that are greater.

It does me good, as I walk thus by mine own,
Of this world for to talk in manner of moan.
To my sheep will I stalk and hearken anon;
There abide on a block, or sit on a stone,
    Full soon.   50
For I trow, pardie,
True men if they be,
We get more company
    Ere it be noon.   [*Steps aside.*]

[*Enter the* 2nd Shepherd. *He does not see the* 1st Shepherd.]

2nd Shep. Ben'ste [4] and Dominus! What may this mean?
Why fares this world thus? Oft have we not seen!
Lord, these weathers are piteous, and the winds full keen;
And the frosts so hideous, they water my een;
    No lie.
Now in dry, now in wet,   60
Now in snow, now in sleet,
When my shoes freeze to my feet,
    It is not all easy.

But, as far as I ken, or yet as I go,
We silly wedded men suffer much woe; [5]
We have sorrow then and then, it falls oft so.
Silly Capel, our hen, both to and fro
    She cackles;
But begin she to croak,
To groan or to cluck,   70
Woe is him, our cock,
    For he is in the shackles.

These men that are wed have not all their will.
When they are full hard bestead, they sigh full still.
God wot they are led full hard and full ill;
In bower nor in bed do they say aught theretill,
    This tide,
My part have I found,

---

4 benedicite ("blessings on us")
5 Complaint of the hen-pecked husband and satire on the married state are familar
medieval motives (or shall we call them perennial?).

I know my lessón!
Woe is him that is bound,   80
    For he must abide.

But now late in our lives,—a marvel to me,
That I think my heart rives such wonders to see,
What that destiny drives, it should so be!—
Some men will have two wives, and some men three
    In store.
Some are woe that has any!
But so far ken I—
Woe is him that has many,
    For he feels sore.   [*Addresses audience.*]   90

But, young men, of wooing, for God that you bought,
Be well ware of wedding, and think in your thought,
"Had I wist" is a thing that serves you naught.
Much still mourning has wedding home brought,
    And griefs,
With many a sharp shower;
For thou may catch in an hour
That shall savor full sour
    As long as thou lives.

For, as ever read I epistle,[6] I have one to my fere,[7]   100
As sharp as a thistle, as rough as a briar;
She is browed like a bristle, with a sour-laden cheer;
Had she once wet her whistle, she could sing full clear
    Her paternoster.
She is as great as a whale;
She has a gallon of gall;
By him that died for us all,
    I would I had run till I had lost her!

                              [1st Shepherd *interrupts him.*]

1st Shep. God! look over the row! full deafly ye stand.
    2nd Shep. Yea, the devil in thy maw—so late and so grand!   110
Saw thou anywhere Daw?
    1st Shep.   Yea, on a lea-land
Heard I him blow. He comes here at hand
    Not far.
Stand still.
    2nd Shep. Why?

---

6 epistle (in the New Testament)   7 mate

1st Shep. For he comes, hope I.
2nd Shep. He will make us both a lie
Unless we beware.

[*Enter* 3rd Shepherd, *a boy. Does not see the others.*]

3rd Shep. Christ's cross me speed, and Saint Nicholas!
Thereof had I need; it is worse than it was.
Whoso knows, take heed, and let the world pass,   120
It is ever in dread and brittle as glass,
          Never blithe.
This world fared never so,
With marvels moe and moe,
Now in weal, now in woe,
          And all things writhe.

Was never since Noah's flood such floods seen,
Winds and rains so rude, and storms so keen!
Some stammered, some stood in doubt, as I ween.
Now God turn all to good! I say as I mean,   130
          For ponder.
These floods so they drown,
Both in fields and in town,
And bear all down;
          And that is a wonder.

We that walk in the nights our cattle to keep,
We see sudden sights when other men sleep.   [*Sees the others.*]
Yet methinks my heart lights; I see rogues peep.
Ye are two tall wights! I will give my sheep
          A turn.   140
But full ill have I meant;
As I walk on this bent,
I may lightly repent,
          My toes if I spurn.   [*The other two advance.*]

Ah, sir, God you save, and master mine!
A drink fain would I have, and somewhat to dine.
     1st Shep. Christ's curse, my knave, thou art a lazy hind!
     2nd Shep. What! the boy likes to rave! Abide for thine
          Till we have made it.
Ill thrift on thy pate!   150
Though the rogue came late,
Yet is he in state
          To dine—if he had it.

3rd Shep. Such servants as I, that sweats and swinks,[8]
Eat our bread full dry, and thereto methinks
We are oft wet and weary when master men winks;
Yet come full lately both dinners and drinks.
   But neatly
Both our dame and our sire,
When we have run in the mire,   160
They can nip at our hire,
   And pay us full lately.

But hear my truth, master: for the fare ye purvey
I shall hereafter work as ye pay;
I shall do a little, sir, and then I shall play;
For never yet my supper in my stomach lay
   In the fields.
Whereto should I weep?
With my staff can I leap;
And men say "Light cheap [9]   170
   But little yields."

1st Shep. Thou were an ill lad, to ride a-wooing
With a man that had but little for spending.
   2nd Shep. Peace, boy! I bade: No more jangling,
Or I shall make thee full 'fraid, by the heaven's king,
   With thy gauds.[10]
Where are our sheep, boy? We scorn.
   3rd Shep. Sir, this same day at morn
I them left in the corn,
   When they rang lauds.[11]   180

They have pasture good, they cannot go wrong.
   1st Shep. That is right. By the rood, these nights are long!
Yet I would, ere we yode,[12] one gave us a song.
   2nd Shep. So I thought as I stood, to mirth us among.
   3rd Shep. I grant.
   1st Shep. Let me sing the tenory.
   2nd Shep. And I the treble so high.
   3rd Shep. Then the mean falls to me.
   Let see how ye chant.   [*They sing.*[13]]

[*Enter* MAK, *with a cloak thrown over his smock.*]

Mak. Now, Lord, for thy names seven, that made both stars
   and moon   190

8 toils   10 tricks   12 went
9 a cheap bargain   11 early morning service
13 the first of several songs indicated (see also ll. 476, 637, 662, 752)

And more than I can neven,[14] oh Lord, grant me a boon.
I am all uneven; my brains they swoon.
Now would to God I were in heaven, where no bairns out of tune
　Weep ever ill.
1st Shep. Who is that pipes so poor?
Mak. Would ye knew what I endure!
Lo, a man that walks on the moor,
　And has not all his will!

2nd Shep. Mak, where hast thou gone? Tell us tidings.
3rd Shep. Is he come? Then everyone take heed to his
　things.　　　　　　　*[Takes the cloak from him.]*　200
Mak. What! I am a yeoman, I tell you, of the king's;
The self and the same, sent from great lordings
　And such.
Fie on you! Go hence!
Out of my presence!
I must have reverence.
　Why, who be ich?[15]

1st Shep. Why make ye it so quaint? Mak, ye do wrong.
2nd Shep. But Mak,—list, ye saint! I trow for that you long.
3rd Shep. I trow the rogue can paint! May the devil him
　hang!　　　　　　　　　　　　　　　　210
Mak. I shall make complaint, and they will flog the whole gang
　At a word,
And tell even how ye doth.
1st Shep. But, Mak, is that truth?
Now take out that southern tooth,
　And set in a turd.

2nd Shep. Mak, the devil in your eye! A stroke would I lend
　you.　　　　　　　　　　　　　*[Strikes him.]*
3rd Shep. Mak, know ye not me? By God, I could rend you.
Mak. God, look you all three! From evil defend you.
Ye are a fair company.
1st Shep. Can ye now pretend, you?　　　　　　220
2nd Shep. Shrewd leap!
Thus late as thou goes,
What will men suppose?
And thou hast an ill noise
　For stealing of sheep.

---

14 name
15 Mak, making a pretense of dignity, adopts (not very consistently) a Southern dialect, in which *I* becomes *ich*, probably in imitation of the "lord-fast swains" complained of in ll. 20–45. The shepherds see his drift. Cf. "southern tooth," l. 215.

Mak. And I am true as steel! all men wot!
But a sickness I feel that holds me full hot;
My belly fares not well, it is out of its state.
3rd Shep. Seldom lies the devil dead by the gate!
Mak. Therefore   230
Full sore am I and ill;
If I stand stone still,
I eat not my fill
    This month and more.

1st Shep. How fares thy wife? By my hood, tell me true.
Mak. Lies weltering, by the rood! by the fire, lo!
And a house full of brood.[16] She drinks well, too;
Ill speed other good that she will do
    But so!
Eats as fast as she can;   240
And every year that comes to man
Adds a brat to our clan,
    And some years two.

But were I not more gracious and richer by far,
I were eaten out of house and of harbor.
Yet she is a foul spouse if ye come near;
There is none that trows nor knows a waur [17]
    Than ken I.
Now will ye see what I proffer?
To give all in my coffer   250
Tomorrow next to offer
    Her head-mass penny.[18]

2nd Shep. I wot so for-waked [19] is none in this shire.
I would sleep, if I taked less to my hire.
3rd Shep. I am cold and naked, and would have a fire.
1st Shep. I am weary, all ached, and run in the mire.
    Watch, thou!
2nd Shep. Nay, I will lie down by,
For I must sleep, truly.
3rd Shep. As good a man's son was I   260
    As any of you.

But, Mak, come hither! Thou shalt lie down between.
Mak. Then might I bother when ye whisper, I ween.[20]

.   .   .   .
                                          [They lie down.]

16 children   17 worse
18 money for a mass for her soul (after her death, of course!)
19 all tired out from staying awake
20 The two lines which should follow are missing in the ms.

Mak. Indeed,
From my top to my toe,
Manus tuas commendo,
Pontio Pilato,[21]
    Christ's cross me speed!

[*Then he rises, the* shepherds *being asleep, and says:*]

Now were time for a man that lacks what he would
To stalk privily then unto a fold,   270
And nimbly to work then, and be not too bold,
For he might rue the bargain, if it were told,
    At the ending.
Now were time it befell;
But he needs good counsel
That fain would fare well,
    And has but little spending.
                              [*Pretends to draw a magic circle.*]

But about you a circle as round as a moon,
Till I have done that I will, and that it be noon,
That ye lie stone still till that I have done.   280
And I shall say theretill of good words soon
    A spell.
Over your heads my hand I lift:
Out go your eyes! Ye see not my drift.
But yet I must make better shift
    If it be well.   [*The* shepherds *snore.*]

Lord, what! They sleep hard, that may ye all hear.
I never was a shepherd, but I will learn here.
If the flock be scared, yet shall I steal near.
                              [*Approaches the sheep.*]
How! Draw hitherward! Now mends our cheer   290
    From sorrow.
A fat sheep, I dare say!
A good fleece, dare I lay!
Repay when I may,
    But this will I borrow.
            [MAK *takes the sheep, and goes to his house.*]
How, Gill, art thou in? Get us some light.
    Wife. Who makes such din this time of the night?
I am set for to spin; I hope not I might
Rise a penny to win. I curse them forthright.
    So fares   300

---

21 "Into thy hands I commend [them], Pontius Pilate." Mak's theology is a little
mixed. (Cf. *Luke*, xxiii, 46)

A housewife that has been,
To be raised thus between!
Here may no work be seen
    For such small chores.

Mak. Good wife, open the heck![22] Seest thou not what I
    bring?
Wife. I may let thee draw the sneck.[23] Ah, come in, my sweet-
    ing!
Mak. Yea, thou dost not reck of my long standing.
Wife. By thy naked neck art thou like for to swing!
Mak.   Go away:
I am worthy of my meat;   310
For in a strait can I get
More than they that swink[24] and sweat
    All the long day.

Thus it fell to my lot, Gill! I had such grace.
                          [*Shows her the sheep.*]
Wife. It were a foul blot to be hanged for the case.
Mak. I have scaped, Gelott, often from as hard a place.
Wife. But so long goes the pot to the water, men says,
    At last
Comes it home broken.
Mak. Well know I the token,   320
But let it never be spoken;
    But come and help fast.

I would he were slain; I list we'll eat.
This twelvemonth was I not so fain of good sheep's meat.
Wife. Should they come ere he be slain, and hear the sheep
    bleat—
Mak. Then might I be ta'en! That were a cold sweat!
                          [*Trembles.*]
    Go bar
The gate door.
Wife.   Yes, Mak,
For and they come at thy back—
Mak. Then might I pay for all the pack!   330
    The devil of them 'ware.

Wife. A good trick have I spied, since thou ken none.
Here shall we him hide till they be gone—
In my cradle abide—let me alone,
And I shall lie beside in childbed, and groan.

22 door   23 latch   24 toil

Mak. Well said!
And I shall say thou was light
Of a male child this night.
   Wife. Now well is my day bright,
     That ever was I bred.   340

This is a good disguise and a far cast!
Yet a woman's advice helps at the last!
I wot never who spies. Again go thou fast.
   Mak. But I come ere they rise, else blows a cold blast!
   I will go sleep.
     [MAK *returns to the* shepherds, *and lies down in his place.*]
Yet sleeps all this company;
And I shall go stalk privily,
As it had never been I
   That carried their sheep.
         [*The* 1st *and* 2nd Shepherds *awake.*]

   1st Shep. Resurrex a mortuis! [25] Have hold of my hand.   350
Judas carnas dominus! I may not well stand;
My foot sleeps, by Jesus, and I'm dry as sand.
I thought that we laid us full near England.
   2nd Shep. Ah, yea!
Lord, but I have slept well.
As fresh as an eel,
As light I me feel
   As leaf on a tree.   [3rd Shepherd *awakes.*]

   3rd Shep. Ben'ste be herein! I feel myself quake.
My heart is out of skin. With fright I shake.   360
Who makes all this din? So my head grows black.
Who has out of door been? Hark, fellows, wake!
   Four we were:
See ye aught of Mak now?
   1st Shep. We were up ere thou.
   2nd Shep. Man, I give God a vow,
     Yet went he nowhere.

   3rd Shep. Methought he was lapped in a wolf's skin.
   1st Shep. So are many happed now—namely, within.
   3rd Shep. When we had long napped, methought with a
     gin [26]   370
A fat sheep he trapped; but he made no din.
   2nd Shep. Be still!

25 "Resurrection from the dead"? This and the next line contain "hog" or mock
Latin.
26 trap or trick

Thy dream makes thee mad;
'Tis but a phantom, by the rood.
  1st Shep. Now God turn all to good,
    If it be his will!   [*They awaken* Mak.]

  2nd Shep. Rise, Mak! For shame! Thou liest right long.
  Mak. Now Christ's holy name be us among!
What is this, by Saint James! I may not well gang!
I trow I be the same. Ah! my neck has lain wrong   380
    Enow.   [*They help* Mak *to his feet.*]
Many thanks! Since yester even,
Now, by Saint Stephen,
I was flayed with a sweven [27]
    That my heart nearly slew.

I thought Gill began to croak and travail full sad,
Well nigh at the first cock, of a young lad
For to mend our flock. Then be I never glad;
I have tow on my rock [28] more than ever I had.
    Ah, my head!   390
A house full of young swains!
The devil knock out their brains!
Too many bairns bring pains,
    When there's little bread!

I must go home, by your leave, to Gill, as I thought.
I pray you look in my sleeve that I steal naught;
I am loath you to grieve or from you take aught.
                              [Mak *leaves them.*]
  3rd Shep. Go forth; thou might us deceive! Now would I we
    sought,
    This morn,
That we had all our store.   400
  1st Shep. But I will go before;
Let us meet.
  2nd Shep. Where?
  3rd Shep.   At the crooked thorn. [*Exeunt* shepherds.]

    [Mak *arrives at his home.*]

  Mak. Undo this door! Who is here? How long shall I stand?
  Wife. Who makes such a stir? Now walk in the waniand! [29]
  Mak. Ah, Gill, what cheer? It is I, Mak, your husband.
  Wife. Then may we see here the devil in a band,
    Sir Guile.

---

27 dream   28 distaff   29 waning of the moon—an unlucky time

Lo, he sings with a note
As were a halter round his throat.³⁰   41c
I may not work for the lout
    A hand-long while.

Mak. Will ye hear what fuss she makes to get her a gloze? ³¹
She does naught but what she likes, and claws her toes.
    Wife. Why, who wanders? Who wakes? Who comes? Who
        goes?
Who brews? Who bakes? Who makes me this hose?
    And then,
It is ruth to behold,
Now in hot, now in cold,
Full woeful is the household   420
    That wants a woman.

But what end has thou made with the herdsmen, Mak?
    Mak. The last word that they said, when I turned my back,
They would look that they had all their sheep in the pack.
I trow they will not be well paid when they their sheep lack.
    Perdie!
But howso the game goes,
'Tis me they'll suppose,
And make a foul noise,
    And cry out upon me.   430

But thou must do as thou hight.³²
    Wife.   I accord me theretill;
I shall swaddle him right in my cradle.
If it were a greater sleight, yet could I help still.
I will lie down straight. Come, wrap me.
    Mak.   I will.
                                        [*Tucks her in bed.*]

    Wife. Behind!
Come Coll's band ere the morrow,
They will nip us full narrow.
    Mak. But I may cry "Out, harrow!"
    The sheep if they find.

    Wife. Hearken aye when they call; they will come anon. 44c
Come and make ready all; and sing by thine own;
Sing lullaby thou shall, for I must groan
And cry out by the wall on Mary and John,
    For sore.
Sing lullaby on fast

---

³⁰ an allusion to hanging   ³¹ excuse   ³² promised

When thou hears at the last;
And but I play a false cast,
    Trust me no more!

[*The* shepherds *return and speak at the other end of the pageant.*]
    3rd Shep. Ah, Coll, good morn! Why sleep thou not?
    1st Shep. Alas, that ever was I born! We have a foul blot.   450
A fat wether have we lorn.
    3rd Shep.   Marry, God forbot! [33]
    2nd Shep. Who should do us that scorn? That were a foul spot.
    1st Shep. Some shrew.
I have sought with my dogs
All Horbury Shrogs, [34]
And of fifteen hogs [35]
    Found I all but one ewe. [36]

    3rd Shep. Now trust me if ye will, by Saint Thomas of Kent,
Either Mak or Gill was at that assent.
    1st Shep. Peace, man; be still! I saw when he went.   460
Thou slanders him ill. Thou ought to repent,
    Good speed.
    2nd Shep. Now as ever thrive we three,
If I should even here die,
I would say it were he
    That did that same deed.

    3rd Shep. Go we thither, where he's fled, and run on our feet.
I shall never eat bread the truth till I wit.
    1st Shep. Nor drink in my head with him till I meet.
    2nd Shep. I will rest in no stead till that I him greet,   470
    My brother!
I vow aright,
Till I see him in sight
Shall I never sleep one night—
    No, not another.

[*They go to* MAK's *house. His* Wife *begins to groan and* MAK,
    sitting by the cradle, begins to sing a lullaby.]
    3rd Shep. Will ye hear how they hack? Our sire tries to croon.
    1st Shep. Heard I never voice crack so clear out of tune!
Call on him.
    2nd Shep.   Mak! Undo your door soon.

---

[33] forbid   [34] Horbury thickets—about four miles from Wakefield
[35] year-old sheep
[36] an inconsistency, since most of the allusions are to a lost ram

Mak. Who is it that spake as it were noon
  Aloft?
Who is that, I say?   480
3rd Shep. Good fellows, were it day.
Mak. [*Opens door.*] As far as ye may,
  Good, speak soft,

Over a sick woman's head that travail knows;
I had liefer be dead ere she suffered more blows.
Wife. Go away instead! I cannot repose.
Each foot that ye tread goes through my nose
    So high!
  1st Shep. Tell us, Mak, if ye may,   490
How fare ye, I say?
  Mak. But are ye in this town today?
  Now how fare ye?

Ye have run in the mire, and are wet yet.
I shall make you a fire if ye will sit.
A nurse would I hire, think ye on it.
Well quit is my hire; my dream—this is it,
    In season.   [*Points to cradle.*]
I have bairns, if ye knew,
Well more than enow.   500
But we must drink as we brew,
  And that is but reason.

I would ye dined ere ye yode.[37] Methinks that ye sweat.
  2nd Shep. Nay, neither mends our mood, drink nor meat.
  Mak. Why, sir, ails you aught but good?
  3rd Shep.   Yea, our sheep that
  we get
Are stolen as they yode.[37] Our loss is great.
  Mak.   Sirs, drink!
Had I been there,
Some should have bought it full sore.
  1st Shep. Marry, some men think that ye were;
  And that makes us think.   510

  2nd Shep. Mak, some men trows that it should be ye.
  3rd Shep. Either ye or your spouse, so say we.
  Mak. Now, if ye suppose it was Gill or me,
Come and rip our house, and then ye may see
  Who had her.
If I any sheep got,

37 went

Any cow or stott,[38]
And Gill, my wife, rose not
   Since here she laid her;

As I am true and leal, to God here I pray   520
That this be the first meal that I shall eat this day.
                                         [Points to cradle.]
   1st Shep. Mak, as have I weal, advise thee, I say;
He learned timely to steal that could not say nay.
                                   [The shepherds *search.]*
   Wife. I swelt![39]
Out, thieves! how ache my bones!
Ye come to rob us, for the nonce.
   Mak. Hear ye not how she groans?
Your hearts should melt.

   Wife. Out, thieves, from my bairn! Go not nigh him there!
   Mak. Wist ye what she had borne, your hearts would be
   sore.   530
Ye do wrong, I you warn, that thus come before
After all she has borne—but I say no more!
   Wife. Ah, my middle!
I pray to God so mild,
If ever I you beguiled,
That I eat this child
   That lies in this cradle.

   Mak. Peace, woman, for God's pain! And cry not so!
Thou racks thy brain, and makes me full of woe.
   2nd Shep. I trow our sheep be slain. What find ye two?   540
   3rd Shep. All work we in vain; as well may we go,
   For all it matters.
I can find no flesh,
Hard nor nesh,
Salt nor fresh,
   But two empty platters.

Live cattle but this, tame nor wild,
None, as have I bliss, so loud ere smelled.
   Wife. No, so God me bless, and give me joy of my child!
   1st Shep. We have marked amiss; I hold us beguiled.   550
   2nd Shep. Sir, done!   *[Speaks to* MAK *at the cradle.]*
Sir, Our Lady him save!
Is your child a knave?[40]

---

38 bullock   39 die   40 boy

Mak. Any lord might him have,
  This child as his son.

When he wakens he skips, that joy is to spy.
  3rd Shep. In good time to his hips! Good fortune be nigh!
But who were his gossips,⁴¹ so soon ready?
  Mak. So fair fall their lips!
  1st Shep. [*Aside.*] Hark now, a lie!
  Mak.   So God them thank,   560
Parkin and Gibbon Waller, I say,
And gentle John Horn, in good fay,
He made heyday
  With the great shank.

  2nd Shep. Mak, friends will we be, for we are all one.
  Mak. We! Now I hold for me, for amends get I none.
Farewell, all three! All glad were ye gone!
  3rd Shep. Fair words may there be, but love there is none
  This year.   [*Exeunt* shepherds.]
  1st Shep. Gave ye the child anything?   570
  2nd Shep. I trow, not one farthing!
  3rd Shep. Fast back will I fling;
  Abide ye me here.   [3rd Shepherd *returns.*]

Mak, take it to no grief, if I come to thy child.
  Mak. Nay, thou thinkst me a thief; and my name hast defiled.
  3rd Shep. The child will it not grieve, little day-star mild.
Mak, with your leave, let me give your child
  But sixpence.
  Mak. Nay, go 'way! He sleeps.
  3rd Shep. Methinks he peeps.   580
  Mak. When he wakens he weeps!
I pray you, go hence!

  3rd Shep. Give me leave him to kiss, and lift up the clout.
        [*Lifts the cover and thinks the child deformed.*]
What the devil is this? He has a long snout!
        [*The other* shepherds *have come in and press forward.*]
  1st Shep. He is marked amiss. We wait ill about.
  2nd Shep. An ill spun weft, ywis, aye comes foul out.⁴²
        [*Looks more closely and sees that it is a sheep.*]
  Aye, so!
He is like to our sheep!
  3rd Shep. How, Gib, may I peep?

---

⁴¹ sponsors at baptism   ⁴² an old proverb

1st Shep. I trow, kind [43] will creep   590
   Where it may not go!
                    [*They lift the sheep out of the cradle.*]

   2nd Shep. This was a quaint gaud [44] and a far cast!
It was a high fraud!
   3rd Shep.   Yea, sirs, was't.
Let's burn this bawd, and bind her fast.
Ah! false scold, hang at the last,
   So shall thou!
Will ye see how they swaddle
His four feet in the middle?
Saw I never in a cradle
   A hornéd lad ere now!   600

   Mak. Peace, bid I! What! Let be your fare!
I am he that him begot, and yon woman him bare.
   1st Shep. After what devil shall he be hatt? [45] "Mak"? Lo, God,
   Mak's heir!
   2nd Shep. Let be all that. Now God give him care,
   I say.
   Wife. A pretty child is he
As sits on a woman's knee;
A dilly-downe, perdie,
   To make a man gay.

   3rd Shep. I know him by the ear-mark; that is a good token! 610
   Mak. I tell you, sirs, hark! His nose was broken;
Later told me a clerk that he was forespoken. [46]
   1st Shep. This is a false work; I would fain be wroken [47]
   Get a weapon!
   Wife. He was taken by an elf, [48]
I saw it myself;
When the clock struck twelve
   Was he misshapen.

   2nd Shep. Ye two are right deft—the same path ye tread.
   3rd Shep. Since they maintain their theft, let's strike them
   dead.   620
   Mak. If I trespass eft, [49] gird off my head!
With you will I be left.

---

43 nature   45 be named   48 *i. e.,* for a fairy changeling
44 trick   46 bewitched   49 again
                       47 avenged

1st Shep.   Sirs, do not as ye said.
  For this trespass
We will neither curse nor smite,
Chide nor fight,
But hold him tight,
  And cast him in canvas.
      [*They toss* MAK *in a sheet, and then return to the fields.*]

  1st Shep. Lord, what! I am sore in point for to burst.
In faith, I may no more; therefore will I rest.
  2nd Shep. As a sheep of seven score he weighed in my fist.   630
For to sleep anywhere methinks that I list.
  3rd Shep. Now I pray you,
Lie down on this green.
  1st Shep. Such thieves I've ne'er seen.
  3rd Shep. Whereto should ye teen? [50]
    Do as I say you!   [*They lie down and fall asleep.*]

  [*An* Angel *sings "Gloria in excelsis," then let him say:*]

  Angel. Rise, herdsmen, attend! For now is he born
That shall take from the fiend what Adam had lorn:
That warlock [51] to end this night is he born;
God is made your friend now at this morn.   640
    He behests
To Bethlehem go ye three,
Where the child ye shall see
In a crib full poorly
    Betwixt two beasts.   [*Exit* Angel.]

  1st Shep. 'Twas as sweet a song even as ever yet I heard.
A marvel to us is given; why be we scared?
  2nd Shep. Of God's son of heaven he spake upward.
Methought the wood riven, and lightning flared
    So clear.
  3rd Shep. He spake of a bairn   650
In Bethlehem, I you warn.
  1st Shep. See yon star brightly burn?
    Let us seek him there.

  2nd Shep. Say, what was his song? Heard ye not how he
    cracked it,
Three breves to a long?

---

50 grieve   **51** wizard (*i. e.*, the devil)

3rd Shep.   Yea, marry, he hacked it;
Was no crotchet wrong, nor nothing that lacked it.
    1st Shep. For to sing us among, right as he knacked it,
    I can.
    2nd Shep. Let's see how ye croon.
Can ye bark at the moon?   660
    3rd Shep. Hold your tongues! Have done!
    1st Shep. Hark after, then!

    2nd Shep. To Bethlehem he bade that we should gang;
I am full 'fraid that we tarry too long.
    3rd Shep. Be merry and not sad; of mirth is our song;
Everlasting glad as we go along
    Without noise.
    1st Shep. Hie we thither, fore-thy,
If we be wet and weary,
To that Child and that Lady!   670
    We have it not to lose.

    2nd Shep. We find by the prophecy—let be your din!—
Of David and Isaiah and more than I ken,
They prophesied by clergy that in a virgin
Should he light and lie, to quench our sin
    And slake it,
Our kind from woe.
For Isaiah said so:
Ecce virgo
    Concipet [52] a child that is naked.   680

    3rd Shep. Full glad may we be, and abide that day
That lovely to see that all creatures obey.
Lord, well were me, for once and for aye,
Might I kneel on my knee some word for to say
    To that child.
But the angel said,
In a crib was he laid;
He was poorly arrayed,
    Both meek and mild.

    1st Shep. Patriarchs that have been, and prophets beforn, 690
They desired to have seen this child that is born.
They are gone full clean; that have they lorn.
We shall see him, I ween, ere it be morn,
    As a token.
When I see him and feel,

[52] behold, a virgin shall conceive

Then wot I full weel
It is true as steel
   That prophets have spoken:

To so poor as we are that he would appear,
First find, and declare by his messenger.   700
  2nd Shep. Go we now, let us fare; the place is us near.
  3rd Shep. I am ready and yare; together go here
    To that bright.
Lord, if thy will it be—
We are poor folk, all three—
Grant us some kind of glee
    To comfort thy wight.

[*They enter the stable. The* 1st Shepherd *kneels before the*
  Babe.]
  1st Shep. Hail, comely and clean! Hail, young Child!
Hail, Maker, as I mean! Of a maiden so mild!
Thou has put down, I ween, the warlock so wild;   710
False beguiler he has been, now goes he beguiled.
    Lo, he merry is!
Lo, he laughs, my sweeting!
A welfare meeting!
Take thou my greeting.
    Have a bob of cherries!   [*The* 2nd Shepherd *kneels.*]

  2nd Shep. Hail, sovereign Savior, for thou hast us sought!
Hail! noble child and flower, that all things has wrought!
Hail, full of favor, that made all of naught!
Hail! I kneel and I cower. A bird have I brought   720
    To my bairn.
Hail, little tiny mop!
Of our creed thou art crop.
I would drink of thy cup,
    Little day-star!   [*The* 3rd Shepherd *kneels.*]

  3rd Shep. Hail, darling dear, full of Godhead!
I pray thee be near when that I have need.
Hail! Sweet is thy cheer! My heart would bleed
To see thee sit here in so poor weed,
    With no pennies.   730
Hail! Put forth thy dall.[53]
I bring thee but a ball:

53 fist

Take and play it withal,
    And go to the tennis.

Mary. The Father of Heaven, God omnipotent,
That set all in days seven, his Son has he sent.
My name could he neven [54] and light ere he went
I conceived him full even, through might as he meant;
    And now he is born.
May he keep you from woe!   740
I shall pray him so.
Tell it, forth as ye go,
    And mind on this morn.

1st Shep. Farewell, lady, so fair to behold,
With thy child on thy knee!
2nd Shep.   But he lies full cold.
Lord, well is me! Now we go, thou behold.
    3rd Shep. Forsooth, already it seems to be told
    Full oft.
1st Shep. What grace we have found!
2nd Shep. Come forth; now are we won!   750
3rd Shep. To sing are we bound:
    Let it ring aloft!   [*They go out singing.*]

EXPLICIT PAGINA PASTORUM

SIR THOMAS MALORY (c. 1394–1471)

So far as English chronology is concerned, the fifteenth century marks the end
of the Middle Ages. The modern world is ushered in by the Renaissance, and the
Renaissance burst upon England at the very beginning of the sixteenth century.
The Middle Ages were not, in England, to expire to the accompaniment of much
literary glory, the fifteenth being in English letters one of the most barren of all
centuries. In it wrote certain followers and imitators of Chaucer, of whom
Thomas Occleve and John Lydgate are now the best remembered; John Skel-
ton, in his earlier work (after 1483); and the unknown authors of the *Flower
and the Leaf* and the *Ploughman's Tale* (at one time attributed to Chaucer)
and of the romance, *The Squire of Low Degree.* The disturbed political conditions incident to the Wars of the Roses, which filled England during most of
the century with the violence of civil strife, are undoubtedly responsible in

54 name or call

part for the dearth of good literature. Scottish literature in this period, by contrast, showed much vitality, two notable names being Robert Henryson, who in the *Testament of Cresseid* presented a new version of Chaucer's story, and William Dunbar, the author of the allegory of the *Golden Targe*, and of the *Dance of the Seven Deadly Sins* (written shortly after 1500).

In 1474 William Caxton printed at Bruges the first English printed book, the *Recuyell of the Histories of Troy*, and two years later set up his press at Westminster, whence he issued in 1477 the first book printed in England, the *Dictes and Sayings of the Philosophers*. The most famous book printed by Caxton was the *Morte d'Arthur* of Sir Thomas Malory (1485).

Of the author little was known until Professor G. L. Kittredge in 1897 identified him as a native of Warwickshire. The recent researches of Mr. Edward Hicks have now given us the material for a biography. Mr. Hicks characterizes his career as "turbulent." He came of a distinguished Warwickshire family. He saw military service with the English forces in France in the days of Joan of Arc. He was a member of Parliament in 1445. The "turbulent" acts were committed in 1451. He was first arrested for a raid made on the monastery of Monks Kirby—a raid which Mr. Hicks suggests was undertaken to recover property taken by the monastery; was committed to the custody of the Sheriff at Coventry; swam the moat and escaped; organized another raid on Coombe Abbey, from which he was accused of removing money and valuables; and was again arrested and tried on this charge, plus various others of extortion, robbery of individuals, and rape! Evidence shows that the last charge is not to be taken seriously; but on the combined counts Malory was sentenced to prison, where he dragged out most of the remainder of his life, principally at Newgate in London. It is probable that he is not to be regarded as an ordinary freebooter, but that he was trying to redress by his own hand, in a common fifteenth century way, wrongs for which the processes of law, directed by powerful interests, gave him no recourse. He died at Newgate in 1471.

It was doubtless while in prison that Malory finished in 1469 the *Morte d'Arthur*. Caxton tells us in his Preface that Malory took the Morte "out of certain books of French, and reduced it to English." His French sources are now largely known; they are various, and lengthy. Malory selected, arranged, and condensed; taking apparently such stories as pleased him most, and giving the whole a kind of unity by grouping the stories around the central figure of Arthur. That the result has any unity at all is a tribute to Sir Thomas's art. His compendium, by gathering together material of diverse origin, becomes thus the final repository of the Arthurian legends in English. His book possesses high story interest, dramatic power, vivid romantic coloring, and poignancy; and swells to a magnificent tragic close in Book XXI, here partially reprinted. The prose in which it is written may seem loose and rambling, when judged by modern standards; but it has for four centuries enjoyed a deservedly high reputation because of its fine cadences, its picturesqueness, and its individual flavor. The importance of the book in English literature is immense. Almost all of the numerous revivals of Arthurian story are based upon it; Tennyson, for example, using it for all but one of his *Idylls*. English literature of the Middle Ages came nobly to an end in the *Morte d'Arthur*.

BIBLIOGRAPHY. Exhaustive scholarly ed. by H. Oskar Sommer. Accessible modern ed. the Globe (Macmillan) and Dent's. Edward Hicks: *Sir Thomas Malory* (Harvard).

LE MORTE D'ARTHUR

Book XXI

CHAPTER I

As Sir Mordred was ruler of all England, he did do make [1] letters as though that they came from beyond the sea, and the letters specified that King Arthur was slain in battle with Sir Launcelot. Wherefore Sir Mordred made a parliament, and called the lords together, and there he made them to choose him king; and so was he crowned at Canterbury, and held a feast there fifteen days; and afterward he drew him unto Winchester, and there he took the Queen Guenever, and said plainly that he would wed her which was his uncle's wife and his father's wife. And so he made ready for the feast, and a day prefixed that they should be wedded; wherefore Queen Guenever was passing heavy. But she durst not discover her heart, but spake fair, and agreed to Sir Mordred's will. Then she desired of Sir Mordred for to go to London, to buy all manner of things that longed unto the wedding. And by cause of her fair speech Sir Mordred trusted her well enough, and gave her leave to go. And so when she came to London she took the Tower of London, and suddenly in all haste possible she stuffed it with all manner of victual, and well garnished it with men, and so kept it. Then when Sir Mordred wist and understood how he was beguiled, he was passing wroth out of measure. And a short tale for to make, he went and laid a mighty siege about the Tower of London, and made many great assaults thereat, and threw many great engines unto them, and shot great guns. But all might not prevail Sir Mordred, for Queen Guenever would never for fair speech nor for foul, would never trust to come in his hands again. Then came the Bishop of Canterbury, the which was a noble clerk and an holy man, and thus he said to Sir Mordred: "Sir, what will ye do? will ye first displease God and sithen shame yourself and all knighthood? Is not King Arthur your uncle, no farther but your mother's brother, and on her himself King Arthur begat you upon his own sister, therefore how may you wed your father's wife? Sir," said the noble clerk, "leave this opinion or I shall curse you with book and bell and candle." "Do thou thy worst," said Sir Mordred, "wit thou well I shall defy thee." "Sir," said the Bishop, "and wit you well I shall not fear me to do that me ought to do. Also where ye noise where my lord

1 have made

Arthur is slain, and that is not so, and therefore ye will make
a foul work in this land." "Peace, thou false priest," said Sir
Mordred, "for an thou chafe me any more I shall make strike
off thy head." So the Bishop departed and did the cursing in
the most orgulist [2] wise that might be done, and then Sir
Mordred sought the Bishop of Canterbury, for to have slain
him. Then the Bishop fled, and took part of his goods with
him, and went nigh unto Glastonbury; and there he was as
priest hermit in a chapel, and lived in poverty and in holy
10 prayers, for well he understood that mischievous war was at
hand. Then Sir Mordred sought on Queen Guenever by letters
and sondes,[3] and by fair means and foul means, for to have
her to come out of the Tower of London; but all this availed
not, for she answered him shortly, openly and privily, that she
had lever slay herself than to be married with him. Then came
word to Sir Mordred that King Arthur had araised the siege
for Sir Launcelot, and he was coming homeward with a great
host, to be avenged upon Sir Mordred; wherefore Sir Mordred
made write writs to all the barony of this land, and much
20 people drew to him. For then was the common voice among
them that with Arthur was none other life but war and strife,
and with Sir Mordred was great joy and bliss. Thus was Sir
Arthur depraved,[4] and evil said of. And many there were that
King Arthur had made up of nought, and given them lands,
might not then say him a good word. Lo ye all Englishmen,
see ye not what a mischief here was! for he that was the most
king and knight of the world, and most loved the fellowship
of noble knights, and by him they were all upholden, now might
not these Englishmen hold them content with him. Lo thus was
30 the old custom and usage of this land; and also men say that
we of this land have not yet lost nor forgotten that custom and
usage. Alas, this is a great default of us Englishmen, for there
may no thing please us no term. And so fared the people at that
time, they were better pleased with Sir Mordred than they were
with King Arthur; and much people drew unto Sir Mordred,
and said they would abide with him for better and for worse.
And so Sir Mordred drew with a great host to Dover, for there
he heard say that Sir Arthur would arrive, and so he thought
to beat his own father from his lands; and the most part of all
40 England held with Sir Mordred, the people were so new fangle.

CHAPTER II

AND so as Sir Mordred was at Dover with his host, there
came King Arthur with a great navy of ships, and galleys, and

2 haughtiest   3 messages   4 slandered

carracks. And there was Sir Mordred ready awaiting upon his landing, to let his own father to lend upon the land that he was king over. Then there was launching of great boats and small, and full of noble men of arms; and there was much slaughter of gentle knights, and many a full bold baron was laid full low, on both parties. But King Arthur was so courageous that there might no manner of knights let him to land, and his knights fiercely followed him; and so they landed maugre [5] Sir Mordred and all his power, and put Sir Mordred aback, that he fled and all his people. So when this battle was done, King Arthur let bury his people that were dead. And then was noble Sir Gawaine found in a great boat, lying more than half dead. When Sir Arthur wist that Sir Gawaine was laid so low, he went unto him; and there the king made sorrow out of measure, and took Sir Gawaine in his arms, and thrice he there swooned. And then when he awaked, he said: "Alas, Sir Gawaine, my sister's son, here now thou liest, the man in the world that I loved most; and now is my joy gone, for now, my nephew Sir Gawaine, I will discover me unto your person: in Sir Launcelot and you I most had my joy, and mine affiance, [6] and now have I lost my joy of you both; wherefore all mine earthly joy is gone from me." "Mine uncle King Arthur," said Sir Gawaine, "wit you well my death day is come, and all is through mine own hastiness and willfulness; for I am smitten upon the old wound the which Sir Launcelot gave me, on the which I feel well I must die; and had Sir Launcelot been with you as he was, this unhappy war had never begun; and of all this am I causer, for Sir Launcelot and his blood, through their prowess, held all your cankered enemies in subjection and danger. And now," said Sir Gawaine, "ye shall miss Sir Launcelot. But alas, I would not accord with him, and therefore," said Sir Gawaine, "I pray you, fair uncle, that I may have paper, pen, and ink, that I may write to Sir Launcelot a cedle [7] with mine own hands." And then when paper and ink was brought, then Gawaine was set up weakly by King Arthur, for he was shriven a little tofore; and then he wrote thus, as the French book maketh mention: "Unto Sir Launcelot, flower of all noble knights that ever I heard of or saw by my days, I, Sir Gawaine, King Lot's son of Orkney, sister's son unto the noble King Arthur, send thee greeting, and let thee have knowledge that the tenth day of May I was smitten upon the old wound that thou gavest me afore the city of Benwick, and through the same wound that thou gavest me I am come to my death day. And I will that all the world wit, that I, Sir Gawaine, knight of the Table Round, sought my death, and not through

5 despite   6 trust   7 note

thy deserving, but it was mine own seeking; wherefore I beseech thee, Sir Launcelot, to return again unto this realm, and see my tomb, and pray some prayer more or less for my soul. And this same day that I wrote this cedle, I was hurt to the death in the same wound, the which I had of thy hand, Sir Launcelot; for of a more nobler man might I not be slain. Also Sir Launcelot, for all the love that ever was betwixt us, make no tarrying, but come over the sea in all haste, that thou mayst with thy noble knights rescue that noble king that made thee
10 knight, that is my lord Arthur; for he is full straitly bestad [8] with a false traitor, that is my half-brother, Sir Mordred; and he hath let crown him king, and would have wedded my lady Queen Guenever, and so had he done had she not put herself in the Tower of London. And so the tenth day of May last past, my lord Arthur and we all landed upon them at Dover; and there we put that false traitor, Sir Mordred, to flight, and there it misfortuned me to be stricken upon thy stroke. And at the date of this letter was written, but two hours and a half afore my death, written with mine own hand, and so subscribed with
20 part of my heart's blood. And I require thee, most famous knight of the world, that thou wilt see my tomb." And then Sir Gawaine wept, and King Arthur wept; and then they swooned both. And when they awaked both, the king made Sir Gawaine to receive his Savior. And then Sir Gawaine prayed the king for to send for Sir Launcelot, and to cherish him above all other knights. And so at the hour of noon Sir Gawaine yielded up the spirit; and then the king let inter him in a chapel within Dover Castle; and there yet all men may see the skull of him, and the same wound is seen that Sir Launcelot gave him in
30 battle. Then was it told the king that Sir Mordred had pyghte a new field upon Barham Down. And upon the morn the king rode thither to him, and there was a great battle betwixt them, and much people was slain on both parties; but at the last Sir Arthur's party stood best, and Sir Mordred and his party fled unto Canterbury.

CHAPTER III

AND then the king let search all the towns for his knights that were slain, and interred them; and salved them with soft salves that so sore were wounded. Then much people drew unto King Arthur. And then they said that Sir Mordred warred
40 upon King Arthur with wrong. And then King Arthur drew him with his host down by the seaside westward toward Salisbury; and there was a day assigned betwixt King Arthur and

8 hard pressed

Sir Mordred, that they should meet upon a down beside Salisbury, and not far from the seaside; and this day was assigned
on a Monday after Trinity Sunday, whereof King Arthur was
passing glad, that he might be avenged upon Sir Mordred. Then
Sir Mordred araised much people about London, for they of
Kent, Southsex, and Surrey, Estsex, and of Southfolk, and of
Northfolk, held the most part with Sir Mordred; and many a
full noble knight drew unto Sir Mordred and to the king: but
they that loved Sir Launcelot drew unto Sir Mordred. So upon
Trinity Sunday at night, King Arthur dreamed a wonderful
dream, and that was this: that him seemed he sat upon a
chaflet [9] in a chair, and the chair was fast to a wheel, and
thereupon sat King Arthur in the richest cloth of gold that
might be made; and the king thought there was under him, far
from him, an hideous deep black water, and therein were all
manner of serpents, and worms, and wild beasts foul and horrible; and suddenly the king thought the wheel turned up so
down, and he fell among the serpents, and every beast took him
by a limb; and then the king cried as he lay in his bed and
slept: Help. And then knights, squires, and yeomen awaked
the king; and then he was so amazed that he wist not where he
was; and then he fell on slumbering again, not sleeping nor
thoroughly waking. So the king seemed verily that there came
Sir Gawaine unto him with a number of fair ladies with him.
And when King Arthur saw him, then he said: "Welcome, my
sister's son; I weened thou hadst been dead, and now I see thee
alive, much am I beholding unto almighty Jesu. O fair nephew
and my sister's son, what be these ladies that hither be come
with you?" "Sir," said Sir Gawaine, "all these be ladies for whom
I have foughten when I was man living, and all these are those
that I did battle for in righteous quarrel; and God hath given
them that grace at their great prayer, by cause I did battle for
them, that they should bring me hither unto you: thus much hath
God given me leave, for to warn you of your death; for an ye
fight as tomorn with Sir Mordred, as ye both have assigned,
doubt ye not ye must be slain, and the most part of your people on both parties. And for the great grace and goodness that
almighty Jesu hath unto you, and for pity of you, and many
more other good men there shall be slain, God hath sent me
to you of his special grace, to give you warning that in no wise
ye do battle as tomorn, but that ye take a treaty for a month
day; and proffer you largely, so as tomorn to be put in a delay.
For within a month shall come Sir Launcelot with all his noble
knights, and rescue you worshipfully, and slay Sir Mordred,
and all that ever will hold with him." Then Sir Gawaine and

9 platform

all the ladies vanished. And anon the king called upon his knights, squires, and yeomen, and charged them wightly [10] to fetch his noble lords and wise bishops unto him. And when they were come, the king told them his avision, what Sir Gawaine had told him, and warned him that if he fought on the morn he should be slain. Then the king commanded Sir Lucan the Butler, and his brother Sir Bedivere, with two bishops with them, and charged them in any wise, an they might, "Take a treaty for a month day with Sir Mordred, and 10 spare not, proffer him lands and goods as much as ye think best." So then they departed, and came to Sir Mordred, where he had a grim host of an hundred thousand men. And there they entreated Sir Mordred long time; and at the last Sir Mordred was agreed for to have Cornwall and Kent, by Arthur's days: after, all England, after the days of King Arthur.

CHAPTER IV

THEN were they condescended that King Arthur and Sir Mordred should meet betwixt both their hosts, and every each of them should bring fourteen persons; and they came with this word unto Arthur. Then said he: "I am glad that this is 20 done:" and so he went into the field. And when Arthur should depart, he warned all his host that an they see any sword drawn: "Look ye come on fiercely, and slay that traitor, Sir Mordred, for I in no wise trust him." In likewise Sir Mordred warned his host that: "An ye see any sword drawn, look that ye come on fiercely, and so slay all that ever before you standeth; for in no wise I will not trust for this treaty, for I know well my father will be avenged on me." And so they met as their appointment was, and so they were agreed and accorded thoroughly; and wine was fetched, and they drank. Right soon 30 came an adder out of a little heath bush, and it stung a knight on the foot. And when the knight felt him stung, he looked down and saw the adder, and then he drew his sword to slay the adder, and thought of none other harm. And when the host on both parties saw that sword drawn, then they blew beams,[11] trumpets, and horns, and shouted grimly. And so both hosts dressed them together. And King Arthur took his horse, and said: "Alas this unhappy day!" and so rode to his party. And Sir Mordred in likewise. And never was there seen a more dolefuller battle in no Christian land; for there was but rushing 40 and riding, foining [12] and striking, and many a grim word was there spoken either to other, and many a deadly stroke. But ever King Arthur rode throughout the battle of Sir Mordred

10 swiftly   11 trumpets   12 thrusting

many times, and did full nobly as a noble king should, and at
all times he fainted never; and Sir Mordred that day put him
in devoir,[13] and in great peril. And thus they fought all the
long day, and never stinted till the noble knights were laid to
the cold earth; and ever they fought still till it was near night,
and by that time was there an hundred thousand laid dead
upon the down. Then was Arthur wood [14] wroth out of measure, when he saw his people so slain from him. Then the king
looked about him, and then was he ware, of all his host and of
all his good knights, were left no more alive but two knights; 10
that one was Sir Lucan the Butler, and his brother Sir Bedivere,
and they were full sore wounded. "Jesu mercy," said the king,
"where are all my noble knights become? Alas that ever I should
see this doleful day, for now," said Arthur, "I am come to mine
end. But would to God that I wist where were that traitor Sir
Mordred, that hath caused all this mischief." Then was King
Arthur ware where Sir Mordred leaned upon his sword among
a great heap of dead men. "Now give me my spear," said
Arthur unto Sir Lucan, "for yonder I have espied the traitor
that all this woe hath wrought." "Sir, let him be," said Sir 20
Lucan, "for he is unhappy; and if ye pass this unhappy day ye
shall be right well revenged upon him. Good lord, remember
ye of your night's dream, and what the spirit of Sir Gawaine
told you this night, yet God of his great goodness hath preserved you hitherto. Therefore for God's sake, my lord, leave
off by this, for blessed be God ye have won the field, for here
we be three alive, and with Sir Mordred is none alive; and if ye
leave off now this wicked day of destiny is past." "Tide me
death, betide me life," saith the king, "now I see him yonder
alone he shall never escape mine hands, for at a better avail 30
shall I never have him." "God speed you well," said Sir Bedivere. Then the king gat his spear in both his hands, and ran
toward Sir Mordred, crying: "Traitor, now is thy death day
come." And when Sir Mordred heard Sir Arthur, he ran until
him with his sword drawn in his hand. And there King Arthur
smote Sir Mordred under the shield, with a foin of his spear,
throughout the body, more than a fathom. And when Sir Mordred felt that he had his death wound he thrust himself with
the might that he had up to the bur of King Arthur's spear.
And right so he smote his father Arthur, with his sword holden 40
in both his hands, on the side of the head, that the sword
pierced the helmet and the brain pan, and therewithal Sir
Mordred fell stark dead to the earth; and the noble Arthur fell
in a swoon to the earth, and there he swooned ofttimes. And
Sir Lucan the Butler and Sir Bedivere ofttimes heaved him up.

13 duty   14 mad

And so weakly they led him betwixt them both, to a little chapel not far from the seaside. And when the king was there he thought him well eased. Then heard they people cry in the field. "Now go thou, Sir Lucan," said the king, "and do me to wit what betokens that noise in the field." So Sir Lucan departed, for he was grievously wounded in many places. And so as he yede,[15] he saw and hearkened by the moonlight, how that pillers and robbers were come into the field, to pill and to rob many a full noble knight of brooches, and beads, of many a
10 good ring, and of many a rich jewel; and who that were not dead all out, there they slew them for their harness and their riches. When Sir Lucan understood this work, he came to the king as soon as he might, and told him all what he had heard and seen. "Therefore by my rede," [16] said Sir Lucan, "it is best that we bring you to some town. " "I would it were so," said the king.

CHAPTER V

"But I may not stand, mine head works so. Ah Sir Launcelot," said King Arthur, "this day have I sore missed thee; alas, that ever I was against thee, for now have I my death, whereof
20 Sir Gawaine me warned in my dream." Then Sir Lucan took up the king the one part, and Sir Bedivere the other part, and in the lifting the king swooned; and Sir Lucan fell in a swoon with the lift, that the part of his guts fell out of his body, and therewith the noble knight's heart brast. And when the king awoke, he beheld Sir Lucan, how he lay foaming at the mouth, and part of his guts lay at his feet. "Alas," said the king, "this is to me a full heavy sight, to see this noble duke so die for my sake, for he would have holpen me, that had more need of help than I. Alas, he would not complain him, his heart was so
30 set to help me: now Jesu have mercy upon his soul!" Then Sir Bedivere wept for the death of his brother. "Leave this mourning and weeping," said the king, "for all this will not avail me, for wit thou well an I might live myself, the death of Sir Lucan would grieve me evermore; but my time hieth fast," said the king. "Therefore," said Arthur unto Sir Bedivere, "take thou Excalibur, my good sword, and go with it to yonder water side, and when thou comest there I charge thee throw my sword in that water, and come again and tell me what thou there seest." "My lord," said Bedivere, "your commandment
40 shall be done, and lightly bring you word again." So Sir Bedivere departed, and by the way he beheld that noble sword, that the pommel and the haft was all of precious stones; and

15 went   16 advice

then he said to himself: "If I throw this rich sword in the water, thereof shall never come good, but harm and loss." And then Sir Bedivere hid Excalibur under a tree. And so, as soon as he might, he came again unto the king, and said he had been at the water, and had thrown the sword in the water. "What saw thou there?" said the king. "Sir," he said, "I saw nothing but waves and winds." "That is untruly said of thee," said the king, "therefore go thou lightly again, and do my commandment; as thou art to me lief and dear, spare not, but throw it in." Then Sir Bedivere returned again, and took the [10] sword in his hand; and then him thought sin and shame to throw away that noble sword, and so eft he hid the sword, and returned again, and told to the king that he had been at the water, and done his commandment. "What saw thou there?" said the king. "Sir," he said, "I say nothing but the waters wap [17] and waves wan." [18] "Ah, traitor untrue," said King Arthur, "now hast thou betrayed me twice. Who would have weened that, thou hast been to me so lief and dear? and thou art named a noble knight, and would betray me for the richness of the sword. But now go again lightly, for thy long tarrying putteth [20] me in great jeopardy of my life, for I have taken cold. And but if thou do now as I bid thee, if ever I may see thee, I shall slay thee with mine own hands; for thou wouldst for my rich sword see me dead." Then Sir Bedivere departed, and went to the sword, and lightly took it up, and went to the water side; and there he bound the girdle about the hilts, and then he threw the sword as far into the water as he might; and there came an arm and an hand above the water and met it, and caught it, and so shook it thrice and brandished, and then vanished away the hand with the sword in the water. So Sir [30] Bedivere came again to the king, and told him what he saw. "Alas," said the king, "help me hence, for I dread me I have tarried over long." Then Sir Bedivere took the king upon his back, and so went with him to that water side. And when they were at the water side, even fast by the bank hoved a little barge with many fair ladies in it, and among them all was a queen, and all they had black hoods, and all they wept and shrieked when they saw King Arthur. "Now put me into the barge," said the king. And so he did softly; and there received him three queens with great mourning; and so they set them [40] down, and in one of their laps King Arthur laid his head. And then that queen said: "Ah, dear brother, why have ye tarried so long from me? alas, this wound on your head hath caught over-much cold." And so then they rowed from the land, and Sir Bedivere beheld all those ladies go from him. Then Sir

17 ripple   18 grow dark

Bedivere cried: "Ah my lord Arthur, what shall become of me, now ye go from me and leave me here alone among mine enemies?" "Comfort thyself," said the king, "and do as well as thou mayest, for in me is no trust for to trust in; for I will into the vale of Avilion to heal me of my grievous wound: and if thou hear never more of me, pray for my soul." But ever the queens and ladies wept and shrieked, that it was pity to hear. And as soon as Sir Bedivere had lost the sight of the barge, he wept and wailed, and so took the forest; and so he went
10 all that night, and in the morning he was ware betwixt two holts hoar, of a chapel and an hermitage.

CHAPTER VI

Then was Sir Bedivere glad, and thither he went; and when he came into the chapel, he saw where lay an hermit groveling on all four, there fast by a tomb was new graven. When the hermit saw Sir Bedivere he knew him well, for he was but little tofore Bishop of Canterbury, that Sir Mordred flemed.[19] "Sir," said Bedivere, "what man is there interred that ye pray so fast for?" "Fair son," said the hermit, "I wot not verily, but by my deeming. But this night, at midnight, here came a number of
20 ladies, and brought hither a dead corpse, and prayed me to bury him; and here they offered an hundred tapers, and they gave me an hundred besants." "Alas," said Sir Bedivere, "that was my lord King Arthur, that here lieth buried in this chapel." Then Sir Bedivere swooned; and when he awoke he prayed the hermit he might abide with him still there, to live with fasting and prayers. "For from hence will I never go," said Sir Bedivere, "by my will, but all the days of my life here to pray for my lord Arthur." "Ye are welcome to me," said the hermit, "for I know ye better than ye ween that I do. Ye are the bold
30 Bedivere, and the full noble duke, Sir Lucan the Butler, was your brother." Then Sir Bedivere told the hermit all as ye have heard tofore. So there bode Sir Bedivere with the hermit that was tofore Bishop of Canterbury, and there Sir Bedivere put upon him poor clothes, and served the hermit full lowly in fasting and in prayers. Thus of Arthur I find never more written in books that be authorized nor more of the very certainty of his death heard I never read, but thus was he led away in a ship wherein were three queens; that one was King Arthur's sister, Queen Morgan le Fay; the other was the Queen of
40 Northgalis; the third was the Queen of the Waste Lands. Also there was Nimue, the chief lady of the lake, that had wedded Pelleas the good knight; and this lady had done much for King

19 put to flight

Arthur, for she would never suffer Sir Pelleas to be in no place where he should be in danger of his life; and so he lived to the uttermost of his days with her in great rest. More of the death of King Arthur could I never find, but that ladies brought him to his burials; and such one was buried there, that the hermit bare witness that sometime was Bishop of Canterbury, but yet the hermit knew not in certain that he was verily the body of King Arthur: for this tale Sir Bedivere, knight of the Table Round, made it to be written.

CHAPTER VII

Yet some men say in many parts of England that King Arthur is not dead, but had by the will of our Lord Jesu into another place; and men say that he shall come again, and he shall win the holy cross. I will not say it shall be so, but rather I will say, here in this world he changed his life. But many men say that there is written upon his tomb this verse: *Hic jacet Arthurus Rex, quondam Rex que futurus.*[20] Thus leave I here Sir Bedivere with the hermit, that dwelled that time in a chapel beside Glastonbury, and there was his hermitage. And so they lived in their prayers, and fastings, and great abstinence. And when Queen Guenever understood that King Arthur was slain, and all the noble knights, Sir Mordred and all the remnant, then the queen stole away, and five ladies with her, and so she went to Almesbury; and there she let make herself a nun, and ware white clothes and black, and great penance she took, as ever did sinful lady in this land, and never creature could make her merry; but lived in fasting, prayers, and almsdeeds, that all manner of people marveled how virtuously she was changed. Now leave we Queen Guenever in Almesbury, a nun in white clothes and black, and there she was abbess and ruler as reason would; and turn we from her, and speak we of Sir Launcelot du Lake.

20 Here lies King Arthur, king formerly and in the future.

THE RENAISSANCE

English literature in the sixteenth century is the literature of England's Renaissance, for that great movement in human history, the progenitor of modern culture, developing in Italy in the fourteenth and fifteenth centuries, penetrated slowly into the north, and attained its full growth in England only in the days of Elizabeth. The name means "re-birth," and it is no violent metaphor to say that in the intellectual quickening of these centuries man was born again. He saw a new heaven and a new earth: literally, in the new conception of the cosmos established by Copernicus (1473–1543) to replace the outworn Ptolemaic cosmogony, and in the sweeping away of the ancient physical boundaries of the world by Columbus, Vasco da Gama, and Magellan through their voyages to the Orient, to America, and around the globe; figuratively, in the new religious freedom hesitatingly advanced by Wycliffe and others from the time of Chaucer on, and then thunderously announced by the hammer-blows of Luther as in 1517 he nailed his ninety-five theses to the church door at Wittenberg; in the new appreciation, likewise, of the beauty of the world and in the new cultivation of the arts. Discoveries and inventions widened man's horizons; he was liberated from ancient bondage and surged into new adventures of the spirit. For its promotion of culture, one of the most important forces was the "revival of learning" following the rediscovery of classic literature, first of the Latin; then, and more significantly, of the Greek. Greek scholars, repulsed by the advance of the Ottoman Turks, fled to Italy with precious manuscripts, and on the fall of Constantinople (1453) came in greater numbers. The moment was propitious. The Italian city-states, such as Florence, Pisa, Genoa, and Venice, enriched by trade with the East, were ruled by great families like the Medici that prided themselves on their munificent patronage of learning and the arts. Under their encouragement, the discovery of a brown Greek manuscript became an event; the writing of a great poem or the painting of a great picture received a splendid reward. The gains of the Renaissance were secured by the discovery of printing. In 1455 Gutenberg printed the Mazarin Bible. In 1476 Caxton returned to England and set up his press at Westminster. Before the end of the century presses in every nation of Europe were pouring forth books, incredibly hastening the advancement of learning, and disseminating culture among classes that had never felt its contacts before.

The first wave of the Renaissance, in the fourteenth century, had brought Italy out of the Middle Ages and into the modern world. The change may be studied in the work of Dante, Boccaccio, and Petrarch. By the end of the fifteenth century, the movement swelled in Italy into magnificent achievement, with special emphasis on the pictorial arts. In the year 1500 Ariosto, Botticelli, Leonardo da Vinci, Michelangelo, Titian, Raphael, all were living, and had either just produced or were about to produce their masterpieces. At the same time in England, the first flowers of the Renaissance were at last about to appear.

The beginnings were scholarly. At the universities the group known as the humanists were introducing the study of Greek. Notable among them were

Linacre, Grocyn, and Colet, the Dean of St. Paul's. Erasmus, the great Dutch scholar, came across and lectured at both universities; and Sir Thomas More, his friend, in the intervals of public life, found time to write his *Utopia* (1516). The next impulse of the Renaissance came direct from Italy, and found expression in the imitation of sonnets and other Italian forms by Sir Thomas Wyatt and the Earl of Surrey (second quarter of the century). In 1557 the first of the miscellanies, Tottel's, showed the new interest in poetry; and in 1558 Queen Elizabeth ascended the throne.

Spontaneity, versatility, enthusiasm—this is Professor Wendell's concise formula for the Elizabethan Age. An enthusiastic new patriotism and national pride developed under the new queen, and spread to all classes. National confidence was established by the successful issue, in the defeat of the Armada (1588), of the contest with the greatest power in Europe, Spain. Men of England, like the men of Italy before them, dared to strive in many fields of endeavor, and the age produced a Raleigh and a Bacon. And the wide range of literary forms testified to the versatility of the people.

The greatest of these forms, the drama, lies outside the scope of the present volume. It was a *genre* which flourished naturally in an age of action, like the Elizabethan. From beginnings in the religious drama of the Middle Ages, from performances and imitations too in school and university of the drama of Rome, arose a new and distinct product. Theaters took shape and multiplied, audiences grew, playwrights sprang up to satisfy the demand. Lyly, Greene, Peele, and Marlowe, writing mostly in the 1580's, developed a great drama, and Shakespeare, beginning his career about 1590, carried dramatic writing to the highest point that the English race has achieved. In lyric poetry, the age produced the numerous spontaneous and beautiful Elizabethan songs (see section below), the sonnet cycles, the interesting verse of Sidney, and the superb and varied work of Spenser. Prose romances, largely Italian in inspiration, flourished with Sidney, Lyly, Greene, Nash, and Lodge. Translations abounded, as was natural in a period which was still borrowing foreign culture. The century saw, for example, versions of the *Aeneid* (Surrey's and Phaer's), of the *Iliad* (the beginning of Chapman's), of Ovid's *Metamorphoses* (Golding's), of the *Orlando Furioso* (Harington's), of the *Jerusalem Delivered* (Fairfax's), of Italian tales in numerous collections (notably Painter's *Palace of Pleasure*), of Plutarch's *Lives* (Sir Thomas North's), of the Bible (Tyndale's and others'), preparing the way for the noblest and most influential of all translations into English, the Authorized Version of 1611; while just beyond the turn of the century Florio translated the *Essays* of Montaigne (1603). During the century the Reformation was accomplished in England, not without the expense of much agony and the shedding of much blood, and amid the rumblings of this mighty change in men's religion were written Latimer's direct and moving sermons, Foxe's eloquent and zealous *Book of Martyrs*, the rolling rhythms of the *Book of Common Prayer*, and Hooker's laboriously reasoned defense of the position of the Church of England, *The Laws of Ecclesiastical Polity*. The interest in history brought forth Holinshed's *Chronicles*, which was to furnish inspiration and source for over a dozen of Shakespeare's plays, and the adventurous life found its record in Hakluyt's *Voyages*. This literature, rich in extent and in quality, was England's answer to the challenge of the Renaissance.

BIBLIOGRAPHY. G. Saintsbury, *Hist. of Elizabethan Lit.* (Macmillan), F. E. Schelling, *Eng. Lit. during the Lifetime of Shakespeare* (Holt), L. Einstein, *Italian Renaissance in Eng.* (Macmillan). On the drama: Schelling, *Elizabethan*

Drama, 2 vols. (Houghton Mifflin), and Tucker Brooke, *Tudor Drama* (Houghton Mifflin). On Elizabethan life: J. D. Wilson, *Life in Shakespeare's Eng.* (Cambridge), Sir Sidney Lee, *Shakespeare's Eng.*, 2 vols. (Oxford). Anthologies of *Elizabethan Drama* by W. A. Neilson (Houghton Mifflin), Brooke and Paradise (Heath), H. Spencer (Little, Brown). G. R. Potter, *Elizabethan Verse and Prose* (Holt), J. W. Hebel and H. H. Hudson, *Poetry of the English Renaissance* (Crofts).

EDMUND SPENSER (?1552–1599)

Edmund Spenser was born in London about 1552. His education was at the Merchant Tailors' School (under the celebrated headmaster Richard Mulcaster), and at Pembroke Hall, Cambridge, which he entered as a sizar, or poor scholar in 1569, and at which he took a B.A. in 1573 and an M.A. in 1576. At Cambridge Spenser formed a lasting friendship with Gabriel Harvey, one of the best-known scholars of the day. Through Harvey he met the famous poet, romancer, and gentleman, Sir Philip Sidney, and also Robert Dudley, Earl of Leicester, who gave him a secretarial position in his household in 1578 or 1579. Harvey, Sidney, and Spenser were three prominent members of a literary club called the Areopagus, which also included Fulke Greville, afterwards biographer of Sidney, and Sir Edward Dyer. The club experimented, among other things, with quantitative measures in English.

In 1580 Spenser went to Ireland as secretary to Lord Grey of Wilton, the Lord Deputy. From this time till his death he lived in Ireland with the exception of three visits to London. In 1588 he was granted an estate of some 3000 acres at Kilcolman, County Cork. In 1594 he married Elizabeth Boyle. In 1598, during a rebellion, his castle was burned to the ground. He escaped with his wife and children, went to London, and in the midst of extreme poverty (according to tradition), died there January 16, 1599. He was buried in the Poets' Corner of Westminster Abbey.

Fortified by the enthusiasm of Sir Walter Raleigh, then a neighbor in Ireland, to whom he had read the earlier parts of the *Faerie Queene,* Spenser came up to London, where he published in 1590 the first three books of his masterpiece, dedicated to Queen Elizabeth. Spenser apparently hoped by his poetry to obtain preferment at court—a hope which was never realized. In 1596, on another visit to London, he published the second three books of the *Faerie Queene.* Aside from this great work, his most important poems are: *The Shepherd's Calendar,* a series of twelve eclogues, one for each month of the year (1579); *Astrophel,* a pastoral elegy upon the death of Sir Philip Sidney (1595); *Amoretti,* a sonnet-cycle, and *Epithalamion,* a marriage poem, both addressed to his wife (1595); *Prothalamion,* written to celebrate the marriage of the two daughters of the Earl of Worcester (1596), and *Four Hymns* (1596).

THE FAERIE QUEENE

The *Faerie Queene* in its inception owes something to the English metrical romances, but more to the example of the Italian poets Ariosto and Tasso. The plan and general intent of the poem Spenser outlined in his letter to Sir Walter Raleigh (reprinted in this edition). The plot, woven from many strands of mediaeval romance, is dilatory and digressive. The allegory, perhaps the most striking feature in the architecture of the poem, is elaborate and difficult to follow, and not all the identifications have ever been satisfactorily worked out. There are several planes of allegory: moral, religious, and political. The Red Cross Knight, for example, represents Holiness and the Church of England, and perhaps also Leicester, the favorite of Queen Elizabeth; Duessa is Falsehood, the Church of Rome, and probably Mary, Queen of Scots; and so on. Some of this allegory the reader must inevitably feel; but a failure to grasp all of it need not mar his enjoyment of the poem, which should rest upon its pictorial splendor, and the perfection of its verbal music. In these qualities Spenser is the greatest of English poets. Inheriting the passionate Renaissance love of beauty, he was able to create an endless succession of beautiful forms, and with an amazing artistic inventiveness and a facility that knew no tiring, molded language in every line into harmonies of haunting loveliness. He uses alliteration freely, the more subtle internal return of consonant sounds, and the even more subtle vowel music. He constantly employs archaisms and rare words when they bring to his verse melodious effects or imaginative connotations. There are poetic inversions, sounding of mute syllables, and the like—in a word, all the license that poetry may possibly be allowed. The result is an unparalleled richness. Poets, who are best able to appreciate the unerring ear and the technical resourcefulness that produce such effects, have especially loved him. He has been properly called "the poets' poet."

The Spenserian stanza, invented by him and used in the *Faerie Queene*, consists of nine lines, rhyming ababbcbcc. The first eight lines are pentameters, the last a hexameter or Alexandrine. The elaborate rhyming, and especially the long and slow last line, prevent rapid narrative movement, but are admirably adapted for a series of pictures, stanza by stanza. Nothing shows Spenser's mastery of his craft more than his creation of thousands of these difficult complex stanzas, all of them good. His metrical skill is also demonstrated by his successful handling of numerous other forms, some of them even more difficult, like the nineteen line stanza of the *Epithalamion*. Only Swinburne among our poets possessed comparable powers as a metrist.

The Spenserian stanza is the most brilliant poetic form invented in England. It has been a great favorite with later English poets, particularly Thomson, Byron, Shelley, and Keats.

BIBLIOGRAPHY. *Complete Works* by A. B. Grosart, 1882–84. Best one volume editions of Spenser's poems by J. C. Smith and E. de Selincourt (Oxford), and by R. E. N. Dodge (Houghton Mifflin). *Life* (somewhat out of date), by R. W. Church in Eng. Men of Letters ser.

THE FAERIE QUEENE

A LETTER OF THE AUTHOR'S,

EXPOUNDING his whole intention in the course of this worke: which, for that it giveth great light to the reader, for the better understanding is hereunto annexed.

To the Right Noble and Valorous SIR WALTER RALEIGH, KNIGHT; Lord Wardein of the Stanneryes, and Her Majesties Liefetenaunt of the County of Cornewayll.

Sir, knowing how doubtfully all allegories may be construed, and this booke of mine, which I have entituled the *Faery Queene*, being a continued allegory,

or darke conceit, I have thought good, as well for avoyding of gealous opinions and misconstructions, as also for your better light in reading thereof (being so by you commanded), to discover unto you the general intention and meaning, which in the whole course thereof I have fashioned, without expressing of any particular purposes, or by-accidents therein occasioned. The generall end therefore of all the booke is to fashion a gentleman or noble person in vertuous and gentle discipline: which for that I conceived shoulde be most plausible and pleasing, being coloured with an historicall fiction, the which the most part of men delight to read, rather for variety of matter than for
10 profite of the ensample, I chose the historye of King Arthure, as most fitte for the excellency of his person, being made famous by many men's former workes, and also furthest from the daunger of envy, and suspition of present time. In which I have followed all the antique Poets historicall: first Homere, who in the Persons of Agamemnon and Ulysses hath ensampled a good governour and a vertuous man, the one in his Ilias, the other in his Odysseis; then Virgil, whose like intention was to doe in the person of Aeneas; after him Ariosto comprised them both in his Orlando: and lately Tasso dissevered them againe, and formed both parts in two persons, namely that part which they in Philosophy call Ethice, or vertues of a private man, coloured in his Rinaldo; the
20 other named Politice in his Godfredo. By ensample of which excellente poets, I labour to pourtraict in Arthure, before he was king, the image of a brave knight, perfected in the twelve private morall vertues, as Aristotle hath devised; the which is the purpose of these first twelve bookes: which if I finde to be well accepted, I may be perhaps encoraged to frame the other part of politicke vertues in his person, after that hee came to be king.

To some, I know, this methode will seeme displeasaunt, which had rather have good discipline delivered plainly in way of precepts, or sermoned at large, as they use, than thus clowdily enwrapped in Allegoricall devises. But such, me seeme, should be satisfide with the use of these dayes, seeing all things
30 accounted by their showes, and nothing esteemed of, that is not delightfull and pleasing to commune sence.[1] For this cause is Xenophon preferred before Plato, for that the one, in the exquisite depth of his judgement, formed a commune welth, such as it should be; but the other in the person of Cyrus, and the Persians, fashioned a governement, such as might best be: so much more profitable and gratious is doctrine by ensample, than by rule. So have I laboured to doe in the person of Arthure: whome I conceive, after his long education by Timon, to whom he was by Merlin delivered to be brought up, so soone as he was borne of the Lady Igrayne, to have seene in a dream or vision the Faery Queen, with whose excellent beauty ravished, he awaking resolved to
40 seeke her out; and so being by Merlin armed, and by Timon throughly instructed, he went to seeke her forth in Faerye Land. In that Faery Queene I meane glory in my generall intention, but in my particular I conceive the most excellent and glorious person of our soveraine the Queene, and her kingdome in Faery Land. And yet, in some places els, I doe otherwise shadow her. For considering she beareth two persons, the one of a most royall queene or empresse, the other of a most vertuous and beautifull Lady, this latter part in some places I doe expresse in Belphœbe, fashioning her name according to your owne excellent conceipt of Cynthia (Phœbe and Cynthia being both names of Diana). So in the person of Prince Arthure I sette forth magnificence in par-
50 ticular, which vertue, for that (according to Aristotle and the rest) it is the

1 *i. e.,* directly to the senses

perfection of all the rest, and conteineth in it them all, therefore in the whole course I mention the deedes of Arthure applyable to that vertue which I write of in that booke. But of the xii. other vertues, I make xii. other knights the patrones, for the more variety of the history: of which these three bookes contayn three.[2] The first of the Knight of the Redcrosse, in whome I expresse Holynes: The seconde of Sir Guyon, in whome I sette forth Temperaunce: The third of Britomartis, a lady knight, in whome I picture Chastity. But, because the beginning of the whole worke seemeth abrupte, and as depending upon other antecedents, it needs that ye know the occasion of these three knights severall adventures. For the methode of a poet historical is not such as of an historiographer. For an historiographer discourseth of affayres orderly as they were donne, accounting as well the times as the actions; but a poet thrusteth into the middest, even where it most concerneth him, and there recoursing to the thinges forepaste, and divining of thinges to come, maketh a pleasing analysis of all.

The beginning therefore of my history, if it were to be told by an historiographer, should be the twelfth booke, which is the last; where I devise that the Faery Queene kept her annuall feaste xii. dayes; upon which xii. severall dayes, the occasions of the xii. severall adventures happed, which, being undertaken by xii. severall knights, are in these xii. books severally handled and discoursed. The first was this. In the beginning of the feast, there presented himselfe a tall clownishe younge man, who, falling before the Queene of Faries, desired a boone (as the manner then was) which during that feast she might not refuse: which was that hee might have the atchievement of any adventure, which during that feaste should happen: that being graunted, he rested him on the floore, unfitte through his rusticity for a better place. Soone after entred a faire ladye in mourning weedes, riding on a white asse, with a dwarfe behind her leading a warlike steed, that bore the armes of a knight, and his speare in the dwarfes hand. Shee, falling before the Queene of Faeries, complayned that her father and mother, an ancient king and queene, had bene by an huge dragon many years shut up in a brasen castle, who thence suffred them not to yssew; and therefore besought the Faery Queene to assygne her some one of her knights to take on him that exployt. Presently that clownish person, upstarting, desired that adventure: whereat the Queene much wondering, and the lady much gaine-saying, yet he earnestly importunted his desire. In the end the lady told him, that unlesse that armour which she brought, would serve him (that is, the armour of a Christian man specified by Saint Paul, vi. Ephes.), that he could not succeed in that enterprise: which being forthwith put upon him with dewe furnitures thereunto, he seemed the goodliest man in al that company, and was well liked of the lady. And eftesoones taking on him knighthood, and mounting on that straunge courser, he went forth with her on that adventure: where beginneth the first booke, viz.,

A gentle knight was pricking on the playne, *etc.*

The second day there came in a palmer, bearing an infant with bloody hands, whose parents he complained to have bene slayn by an enchaunteresse called Acrasia; and therefore craved of the Faery Queene, to appoint him some knight to performe that adventure; which being assigned to Sir Guyon, he presently went forth with that same palmer: which is the beginning of

[2] The first three books, to which this letter was appended when they were published in 1590.

the second booke and the whole subject thereof. The third day there came in a groome, who complained before the Faery Queene, that a vile enchaunter, called Busirane, had in hand a most faire lady, called Amoretta, whom he kept in most grievous torment, because she would not yield him the pleasure of her body. Whereupon Sir Scudamour, the lover of that lady, presently tooke on him that adventure. But being unable to performe it by reason of the hard enchauntments, after long sorrow, in the end met with Britomartis, who succoured him, and reskewed his love.

But by occasion hereof many other adventures are intermedled, but rather
10 as accidents then intendments: as the love of Britomart, the overthrow of Marinell, the misery of Florimell, the vertuousness of Belphœbe, the lasciviousnes of Hellenora, and many the like.

Thus much, Sir, I have briefly overronne, to direct your understanding to the welhead of the history, that from thence gathering the whole intention of the conceit ye may, as in a handfull, gripe al the discourse, which otherwise may happily seeme tedious and confused. So, humbly craving the continuance of your honourable favour towards me, and th' eternall establishment of your happines, I humbly take leave.

23 January, 1589.
Yours most humbly affectionate,
ED. SPENSER.

THE FIRST BOOKE OF THE FAERIE QUEENE

CONTAYNING
THE LEGENDE OF THE KNIGHT OF THE RED CROSSE,
OR OF HOLINESSE

I

Lo I the man, whose Muse whilome did maske,
As time her taught, in lowly Shepheards weeds,[3]
Am now enforst a far unfitter taske,
For trumpets sterne to chaunge mine Oaten reeds,
And sing of Knights and Ladies gentle deeds;
Whose prayses having slept in silence long,
Me, all too meane, the sacred Muse areeds [4]
To blazon broad emongst her learned throng:
Fierce warres and faithfull loves shall moralize my song.

2

Helpe then, O holy Virgin chiefe of nine,[5]
Thy weaker Novice to performe thy will,
Lay forth out of thine everlasting scryne [6]
The antique rolles, which there lye hidden still,

3 Spenser refers to his   4 counsels   of heroic poetry
Shepherd's Calendar (1579)   5 probably Calliope, Muse   6 chest

Of Faerie knights and fairest *Tanaquill*,[7]
Whom that most noble Briton Prince [8] so long
Sought through the world, and suffered so much ill,
That I must rue his undeservèd wrong:
O helpe thou my weake wit, and sharpen my dull tong.

3

And thou most dreaded impe of highest *Jove*,
Faire *Venus* sonne, that with thy cruell dart
At that good knight so cunningly didst rove,
That glorious fire it kindled in his hart,
Lay now thy deadly Heben [9] bow apart,
And with thy mother milde come to mine ayde:
Come both, and with you bring triumphant *Mart*,[10]
In loves and gentle jollities arrayd,
After his murdrous spoiles and bloudy rage allayd.

4

And with them eke, O Goddesse heavenly bright,[11]
Mirrour of grace and Majestie divine,
Great Lady of the greatest Isle, whose light
Like *Phœbus* lampe throughout the world doth shine,
Shed thy faire beames into my feeble eyne,[12]
And raise my thoughts too humble and too vile,
To thinke of that true glorious type of thine,
The argument of mine afflicted stile:
The which to heare, vouchsafe, O dearest dred [13] a-while.

CANTO I

The Patron of true Holinesse,
Foule Errour doth defeate:
Hypocrisie him to entrappe,
Doth to his home entreate.

I

A Gentle Knight was pricking [14] on the plaine,
Y-clad in mightie armes and silver shielde,
Wherein old dints of deepe wounds did remaine,

7 A British princess, daughter of Oberon, king of Fairyland; in the allegory representing Queen Elizabeth

8 Arthur
9 ebony
10 Mars
11 Queen Elizabeth
12 eyes

13 object of reverence
14 riding

The cruell markes of many' a bloudy fielde;
Yet armes till that time did he never wield:
His angry steede did chide his foming bitt,
As much disdayning to the curbe to yield:
Full jolly [15] knight he seemd, and faire did sitt,
As one for knightly giusts [16] and fierce encounters fitt.

2

But on his brest a bloudie Crosse he bore,
The deare remembrance of his dying Lord,
For whose sweete sake that glorious badge he wore,
And dead as living ever him ador'd:
Upon his shield the like was also scor'd,
For soveraine hope, which in his helpe he had:
Right faithfull true he was in deede and word,
But of his cheere [17] did seeme too solemne sad;
Yet nothing did he dread, but ever was ydrad.[18]

3

Upon a great adventure he was bond,
That greatest *Gloriana* [19] to him gave,
That greatest Glorious Queene of *Faerie* lond,
To winne him worship, and her grace to have,
Which of all earthly things he most did crave;
And ever as he rode, his hart did earne [20]
To prove his puissance in battell brave
Upon his foe, and his new force to learne;
Upon his foe, a Dragon horrible and stearne.[21]

4

A lovely Ladie [22] rode him faire beside,
Upon a lowly Asse more white then snow,
Yet she much whiter, but the same did hide
Under a vele, that wimpled was full low,
And over all a blacke stole she did throw,
As one that inly mournd: so was she sad,
And heavie sat upon her palfrey slow;
Seemed in heart some hidden care she had,
And by her in a line [23] a milke white lambe she lad.

15 gallant
16 jousts
17 countenance
18 dreaded

19 Queen Elizabeth
20 yearn
21 typifying the devil
(or sin)

22 Una, or Truth
23 by a cord

5

So pure and innocent, as that same lambe,
She was in life and every vertuous lore,
And by descent from Royall lynage came
Of ancient Kings and Queenes, that had of yore
Their scepters stretcht from East to Westerne shore,
And all the world in their subjection held;
Till that infernall feend with foule uprore
Forwasted [24] all their land, and them expeld:
Whom to avenge, she had this Knight from far compeld.

6

Behind her farre away a Dwarfe [25] did lag,
That lasie seemd in being ever last,
Or wearièd with bearing of her bag
Of needments at his backe. Thus as they past,
The day with cloudes was suddeine overcast,
And angry _Jove_ an hidcous storme of raine
Did poure into his Lemans [26] lap so fast,
That every wight to shrowd [27] it did constrain,
And this faire couple eke to shroud themselves were fain.

7

Enforst to seeke some covert nigh at hand,
A shadie grove not far away they spide,
That promist ayde the tempest to withstand:
Whose loftie trees yclad with sommers pride,
Did spred so broad, that heavens light did hide,
Not perceable with power of any starre:
And all within were pathes and alleies wide,
With footing worne, and leading inward farre:
Faire harbour that them seemes; so in they entred arre.

8

And foorth they passe, with pleasure forward led,
Joying to heare the birdes sweete harmony,
Which therein shrouded from the tempest dred,
Seemd in their song to scorne the cruell sky.
Much can they prayse the trees so straight and hy,
The sayling [28] Pine, the Cedar proud and tall,

24 utterly laid waste   26 loved one's; _i. e._, the   27 shelter
25 typifying Prudence   earth's   28 used for ship timbers

The vine-prop Elme, the Poplar never dry,[29]
The builder Oake, sole king of forrests all,
The Aspine good for staves, the Cypresse funerall.[30]

9

The Laurell, meed of mightie Conquerours
And Poets sage, the Firre that weepeth still,[31]
The Willow worne of forlorne Paramours,
The Eugh [32] obedient to the benders will,
The Birch for shaftes, the Sallow for the mill,
The Mirrhe sweete bleeding in the bitter wound,[33]
The warlike Beech,[34] the Ash for nothing ill,
The fruitful Olive, and the Platane round,
The carver Holme,[35] the Maple seeldom inward sound.

10

Led with delight, they thus beguile the way,
Untill the blustring storme is overblowne;
When weening to returne, whence they did stray,
They cannot finde that path, which first was showne,
But wander too and fro in wayes unknowne,
Furthest from end then, when they neerest weene,
That makes them doubt, their wits be not their owne:
So many pathes, so many turnings seene,
That which of them to take, in diverse doubt they been.

11

At last resolving forward still to fare,
Till that some end they finde or in or out,
That path they take, that beaten seemd most bare,
And like to lead the labyrinth about; [36]
Which when by tract they hunted had throughout,
At length it brought them to a hollow cave,
Amid the thickest woods. The Champion stout
Eftsoones dismounted from his courser brave,
And to the Dwarfe awhile his needlesse spere he gave.

12

Be well aware, quoth then that Ladie milde,
Least suddaine mischiefe ye too rash provoke:

29 because° growing best in a moist soil
30 emblematic of death
31 exuding a resin
32 yew
33 Myrrha was wounded by her father and changed into a tree, the Arabian myrtle, which exudes a fragrant though bitter gum
34 used for making lances, etc.
35 a kind of oak used for wood-carvings
36 out of

The danger hid, the place unknowne and wilde,
Breedes dreadfull doubts: Oft fire is without smoke,
And perill without show: therefore your stroke
Sir knight with-hold, till further triall made.
Ah Ladie (said he) shame were to revoke
The forward footing for an hidden shade: [37]
Vertue gives her selfe light, through darkenesse for to wade. [38]

13

Yea but (quoth she) the perill of this place
I better wot then you, though now too late,
To wish you backe returne with foule disgrace,
Yet wisedome warnes, whilest foot is in the gate,
To stay the steppe, ere forcèd to retrate.
This is the wandring wood, this *Errours den,*
A monster vile, whom God and man does hate:
Therefore I read [39] beware. Fly fly (quoth then
The fearefull Dwarfe:) this is no place for living men.

14

But full of fire and greedy hardiment,
The youthfull knight could not for ought be staide,
But forth unto the darksome hole he went,
And lookèd in: his glistring armor made
A little glooming light, much like a shade,
By which he saw the ugly monster plaine,
Halfe like a serpent horribly displaide,
But th'other halfe did womans shape retaine,
Most lothsom, filthie, foule, and full of vile disdaine.

15

And as she lay upon the durtie ground,
Her huge long taile her den all overspred,
Yet was in knots and many boughtes [40] upwound,
Pointed with mortall sting. Of her there bred
A thousand yong ones, which she dayly fed,
Sucking upon her poisonous dugs, eachone
Of sundry shapes, yet all ill favorèd:
Soone as that uncouth light upon them shone,
Into her mouth they crept, and suddain all were gone.

37 to turn back for an   38 walk, go   40 coils
unseen danger   39 advise

16

Their dam upstart, out of her den effraide,
And rushèd forth, hurling her hideous taile
About her cursèd head, whose folds displaid
Were stretcht now forth at length without entraile.[41]
She lookt about, and seeing one in mayle
Armèd to point, sought backe to turne againe;
For light she hated as the deadly bale,
Ay wont in desert darknesse to remaine,
Where plaine none might her see, nor she see any plaine.

17

Which when the valiant Elfe [42] perceiv'd, he lept
As Lyon fierce upon the flying pray,
And with his trenchand blade her boldly kept
From turning backe, and forcèd her to stay:
Therewith enrag'd she loudly gan to bray,
And turning fierce, her speckled taile advaunst,
Threatning her angry sting, him to dismay:
Who nought aghast, his mightie hand enhaunst: [43]
The stroke down from her head unto her shoulder glaunst.

18

Much daunted with that dint, her sence was dazd,
Yet kindling rage, her selfe she gathered round,
And all attonce her beastly body raizd
With doubled forces high above the ground:
Tho wrapping up her wrethed [44] sterne arownd,
Lept fierce upon his shield, and her huge traine
All suddenly about his body wound,
That hand or foot to stirre he strove in vaine:
God helpe the man so wrapt in *Errours* endlesse traine.

19

His Lady sad to see his sore constraint,
Cride out, Now now Sir Knight, shew what ye bee,
Add faith unto your force, and be not faint:
Strangle her, else she sure will strangle thee.
That when he heard, in great perplexitie,
His gall did grate for griefe and high disdaine,[45]

41 fold, coil   43 raised   by pain and great disgust
42 the knight (because   44 twisted
born of elf or fairy)   45 his anger was aroused

And knitting all his force got one hand free,
Wherewith he grypt her gorge [46] with so great paine,
That soone to loose her wicked bands did her constraine.

20

Therewith she spewd out of her filthy maw
A floud of poyson horrible and blacke,
Full of great lumpes of flesh and gobbets raw,
Which stunck so vildly, that it forst him slacke
His grasping hold, and from her turne him backe:
Her vomit full of bookes and papers was,[47]
With loathly frogs and toades, which eyes did lacke,
And creeping sought way in the weedy gras:
Her filthy parbreake [48] all the place defilèd has.

21

As when old father *Nilus* gins to swell
With timely pride above the *Ægyptian* vale,
His fattie waves do fertile slime outwell,
And overflow each plaine and lowly dale:
But when his later spring gins to avale,[49]
Huge heapes of mudd he leaves, wherein there breed
Ten thousand kindes of creatures, partly male
And partly female of his fruitfull seed;
Such ugly monstrous shapes elsewhere may no man reed.[50]

22

The same so sore annoyèd has the knight,
That welnigh chokèd with the deadly stinke,
His forces faile, ne can no longer fight.
Whose corage when the feend perceiv'd to shrinke,
She pourèd forth out of her hellish sinke
Her fruitfull cursèd spawne of serpents small,
Deformèd monsters, fowle, and blacke as inke,
Which swarming all about his legs did crall,
And him encombred sore, but could not hurt at all.

23

As gentle Shepheard in sweete even-tide,
When ruddy *Phœbus* gins to welke [51] in west,

46 throat
47 pamphlets written by Catholics against Protestantism
48 vomit
49 subside
50 perceive
51 wane

High on an hill, his flocke to vewen wide,
Markes which do byte their hasty supper best;
A cloud of combrous gnattes do him molest,
All striving to infixe their feeble stings,
That from their noyance he no where can rest,
But with his clownish hands their tender wings
He brusheth oft, and oft doth mar their murmurings.

24

Thus ill bestedd,[52] and fearefull more of shame,
Then of the certaine perill he stood in,
Halfe furious unto his foe he came,
Resolv'd in minde all suddenly to win,
Or soone to lose, before he once would lin;[53]
And strooke at her with more then manly force,
That from her body full of filthie sin
He raft her hateful head without remorse;
A streame of cole black bloud forth gushèd from her corse.

25

Her scattred brood, soone as their Parent deare
They saw so rudely falling to the ground,
Groning full deadly, all with troublous feare,
Gathred themselves about her body round,
Weening their wonted entrance to have found
At her wide mouth: but being there withstood
They flockèd all about her bleeding wound,
And suckèd up their dying mothers blood,
Making her death their life, and eke her hurt their good.

26

That detestable sight him much amazde,
To see th'unkindly [54] Impes of heaven accurst,
Devoure their dam; on whom while so he gazd,
Having all satisfide their bloudy thurst,
Their bellies swolne he saw with fulnesse burst,
And bowels gushing forth: well worthy end
Of such as drunke her life, the which them nurst;
Now needeth him no lenger labour spend,
His foes have slaine themselves, with whom he should contend.

27

His Ladie seeing all, that chaunst, from farre
Approcht in hast to greet his victorie,

---

[52] situated   [53] cease   [54] unnatural

And said, Faire knight, borne under happy starre,
Who see your vanquisht foes before you lye:
Well worthy be you of that Armorie,[55]
Wherein ye have great glory wonne this day,
And proov'd your strength on a strong enimie,
Your first adventure: many such I pray,
And henceforth ever wish, that like succeed it may.

28

Then mounted he upon his Steede againe,
And with the Lady backward sought to wend;
That path he kept, which beaten was most plaine.
Ne ever would to any by-way bend,
But still did follow one unto the end,
The which at last out of the wood them brought.
So forward on his way (with God to frend)
He passeth forth, and new adventure sought;
Long way he travellèd, before he heard of ought.

29

At length they chaunst to meet upon the way
An agèd Sire,[56] in long blacke weedes yclad,
His feete all bare, his beard all hoarie gray,
And by his belt his booke he hanging had;
Sober he seemde, and very sagely sad,
And to the ground his eyes were lowly bent,
Simple in shew, and voyde of malice bad,
And all the way he prayèd, as he went,
And often knockt his brest, as one that did repent.

30

He faire the knight saluted, louting [57] low,
Who faire him quited,[58] as that courteous was:
And after askèd him, if he did know
Of straunge adventures, which abroad did pas.
Ah my deare Sonne (quoth he) how should, alas,
Silly [59] old man, that lives in hidden cell,
Bidding [60] his beades all day for his trespas,
Tydings of warre and worldly trouble tell?
With holy father sits [61] not with such things to mell.[62]

55 armor
56 Archimago, typifying
hypocrisy

57 bending
58 requited
59 simple

60 telling (counting)
61 befits
62 meddle

31

But if of daunger which hereby doth dwell,
And homebred evill ye desire to heare,
Of a straunge man I can you tidings tell,
That wasteth all this countrey farre and neare.
Of such (said he) I chiefly do inquere,
And shall you well reward to shew the place,
In which that wicked wight his dayes doth weare:
For to all knighthood it is foule disgrace,
That such a cursèd creature lives so long a space.

32

Far hence (quoth he) in wastfull wildernesse
His dwelling is, by which no living wight
May ever passe, but thorough great distresse.
Now (sayd the Lady) draweth toward night,
And well I wote, that of your later fight
Ye all forwearied be: for what so strong,
But wanting rest will also want of might?
The Sunne that measures heaven all day long,
At night doth baite [63] his steedes the *Ocean* waves emong.

33

Then with the Sunne take Sir, your timely rest,
And with new day new worke at once begin:
Untroubled night they say gives counsell best.
Right well Sir knight ye have advisèd bin,
(Quoth then that aged man); the way to win
Is wisely to advise: now day is spent;
Therefore with me ye may take up your In [64]
For this same night. The knight was well content:
So with that godly father to his home they went.

34

A little lowly Hermitage it was,
Downe in a dale, hard by a forests side,
Far from resort of people, that did pas
In travell to and froe: a little wyde [65]
There was an holy Chappell edifyde,[66]
Wherein the Hermite dewly wont to say

63 feed
64 dwelling   65 a little way off   66 built

His holy things each morne and eventyde:
Thereby a Christall streame did gently play,
Which from a sacred fountaine wellèd forth alway.

35

Arrivèd there, the little house they fill,
Ne looke for entertainement, where none was:
Rest is their feast, and all things at their will;
The noblest mind the best contentment has.
With faire discourse the evening so they pas:
For that old man of pleasing wordes had store,
And well could file his tongue as smooth as glas;
He told of Saintes and Popes, and evermore
He strowd an *Ave-Mary* after and before.

36

The drouping Night thus creepeth on them fast,
And the sad humour [67] loading their eye liddes,
As messenger of *Morpheus* on them cast
Sweet slombring deaw, the which to sleepe them biddes.
Unto their lodgings then his guestes he riddes:
Where when all drownd in deadly sleepe he findes,
He to his study goes, and there amiddes
His Magick bookes and artes of sundry kindes,
He seekes out mighty charmes, to trouble sleepy mindes.

37

Then choosing out few wordes most horrible,
(Let none them read) thereof did verses frame,
With which and other spelles like terrible,
He bad awake blacke *Plutoes* griesly Dame,[68]
And cursèd heaven, and spake reprochful shame
Of highest God, the Lord of life and light;
A bold bad man, that dar'd to call by name
Great *Gorgon*, Prince of darknesse and dead night,
At which *Cocytus* quakes, and *Styx* is put to flight.[69]

38

And forth he cald out of deepe darknesse dred
Legions of Sprights, the which like little flyes
Fluttring about his ever damnèd hed,

---

67 heavy moisture   68 Proserpine   69 Two rivers of hell

A-waite whereto their service he applyes,
To aide his friends, or fray [70] his enimies:
Of those he chose out two, the falsest twoo,
And fittest for to forge true-seeming lyes;
The one of them he gave a message too,
The other by him selfe staide other worke to doo.

39

He making speedy way through spersèd [71] ayre,
And through the world of waters wide and deepe,
To *Morpheus* house doth hastily repaire.
Amid the bowels of the earth full steepe,
And low, where dawning day doth never peepe,
His dwelling is; there *Tethys* [72] his wet bed
Doth ever wash, and *Cynthia* [73] still doth steepe
In silver deaw his ever-drouping hed,
Whiles sad Night over him her mantle black doth spred.

40

Whose double gates he findeth lockèd fast,
The one faire fram'd of burnisht Yvory,
The other all with silver overcast;
And wakefull dogges before them farre do lye,
Watching to banish Care their enimy,
Who oft is wont to trouble gentle sleepe.
By them the Sprite doth passe in quietly,
And unto *Morpheus* comes, whom drownèd deepe
In drowsie fit he findes: of nothing he takes keepe.

41

And more, to lulle him in his slumber soft,
A trickling streame from high rocke tumbling downe
And ever-drizling raine upon the loft,
Mixt with a murmuring winde, much like the sowne
Of swarming Bees, did cast him in a swowne:
No other noyse, nor peoples troublous cryes,
As still [74] are wont t'annoy the wallèd towne,
Might there be heard: but carelesse Quiet lyes,
Wrapt in eternall silence farre from enemyes.

42

The messenger approching to him spake,
But his wast wordes returnd to him in vaine:

70 frighten   72 the ocean   74 ever
71 dispersed   73 the moon

So sound he slept, that nought mought him awake.
Then rudely he him thrust, and pusht with paine,
Whereat he gan to stretch: but he againe
Shooke him so hard, that forcèd him to speake.
As one then in a dreame, whose dryer braine [75]
Is tost with troubled sights and fancies weake,
He mumbled soft, but would not all his silence breake.

43

The Sprite then gan more boldly him to wake,
And threatned unto him the dreaded name
Of *Hecate:* [76] whereat he gan to quake,
And lifting up his lumpish head, with blame
Halfe angry askèd him, for what he came.
Hither (quoth he) me *Archimago* sent,
He that the stubborne Sprites can wisely tame,
He bids thee to him send for his intent
A fit false dreame, that can delude the sleepers sent.

44

The God obayde, and calling forth straight way
A diverse dreame out of his prison darke,
Delivered it to him, and downe did lay
His heavie head, devoide of carefull carke, [77]
Whose sences all were straight benumbd and starke.
He backe returning by the Yvorie dore,
Remounted up as light as chearefull Larke,
And on his litle winges the dreame he bore
In hast unto his Lord, where he him left afore.

45

Who all this while with charmes and hidden artes,
Had made a Lady of that other Spright,
And fram'd of liquid ayre her tender partes
So lively, and so like in all mens sight,
That weaker sence it could have ravisht quight:
The maker selfe for all his wondrous witt,
Was nigh beguilèd with so goodly sight:
Her all in white he clad, and over it
Cast a blacke stole, most like to seeme for *Una* fit.

[75] a too dry brain pro-
duced troubled sleep   [76] An underworld goddess of magic and witchery   [77] sorrow full of care

46

Now when that ydle dreame was to him brought,
Unto that Elfin knight he bad him fly,
Where he slept soundly void of evill thought,
And with false shewes abuse his fantasy,
In sort as he him schoolèd privily:
And that new creature borne without her dew,[78]
Full of the makers guile, with usage sly
He taught to imitate that Lady trew,
Whose semblance she did carrie under feignèd hew.

47

Thus well instructed, to their worke they hast,
And comming where the knight in slomber lay,
The one upon his hardy head him plast,
And made him dreame of loves and lustfull play,
That nigh his manly hart did melt away,
Bathèd in wanton blis and wicked joy:
Then seemèd him his Lady by him lay,
And to him playnd, how that false wingèd boy,[79]
Her chast hart had subdewd, to learne Dame pleasures toy.

48

And she her selfe of beautie soveraigne Queene,
Faire Venus seemde unto his bed to bring
Her, whom he waking evermore did weene,
To be the chastest flowre, that ay did spring
On earthly braunch, the daughter of a king,
Now a loose Leman to vile service bound:
And eke the *Graces* seemèd all to sing,
Hymen Iö Hymen,[80] dauncing all around,
Whilst freshest *Flora* [81] her with Yvie girlond crownd.

49

In this great passion of unwonted lust,
Or wonted feare of doing ought amis,
He started up, as seeming to mistrust,
Some secret ill, or hidden foe of his:
Lo there before his face his Lady is,
Under blake stole hyding her bayted hooke,

---

[78] born unnaturally   [80] Hymen was the god   [81] Goddess of flowers
[79] Cupid   of marriage

And as halfe blushing offred him to kis,
With gentle blandishment and lovely looke,
Most like that virgin true, which for her knight him took.

50

All cleane dismayd to see so uncouth sight,
And halfe enragèd at her shamelesse guise,
He thought have slaine her in his fierce despight:
But hasty heat tempring with sufferance wise,
He stayde his hand, and gan himselfe advise
To prove his sense,[82] and tempt [83] her faignèd truth.
Wringing her hands in wemens pitteous wise,
Tho [84] can she weepe, to stirre up gentle ruth,
Both for her noble bloud, and for her tender youth.

51

And said, Ah Sir, my liege Lord and my love,
Shall I accuse the hidden cruell fate,
And mightie causes wrought in heaven above,
Or the blind God, that doth me thus amate,[85]
For hopèd love to winne me certaine hate?
Yet thus perforce he bids me do, or die.
Die is my dew: yet rew my wretched state
You, whom my hard avenging destinie
Hath made judge of my life or death indifferently.

52

Your owne deare sake forst me at first to leave
My Fathers kingdome, There she stopt with teares;
Her swollen hart her speach seemd to bereave,
And then againe begun, My weaker yeares
Captiv'd to fortune and frayle worldly feares,
Fly to your faith for succour and sure ayde:
Let me not dye in languor and long teares.
Why Dame (quoth he) what hath ye thus dismayd?
What frayes ye, that were wont to comfort me affrayd?

53

Love of your selfe, she said, and deare constraint
Lets me not sleepe, but wast the wearie night

82 evidence of his senses   84 then   85 dismay
83 test

In secret anguish and unpittied plaint,
Whiles you in carelesse sleepe are drownèd quight.
Her doubtfull words made that redoubted knight
Suspect her truth: yet since no'untruth he knew,
Her fawning love with foule disdainefull spight
He would not shend,[86] but said, Deare dame I rew,
That for my sake unknowne such griefe unto you grew.

54

Assure your selfe, it fell not all to ground;
For all so deare as life is to my hart,
I deeme your love, and hold me to you bound;
Ne let vaine feares procure your needlesse smart,
Where cause is none, but to your rest depart.
Not all content, yet seemd she to appease
Her mournefull plaintes, beguilèd of [87] her art,
And fed with words, that could not chuse but please,
So slyding softly forth, she turnd as to her ease.

55

Long after lay he musing at her mood,
Much griev'd to thinke that gentle Dame so light,
For whose defence he was to shed his blood.
At last dull wearinesse of former fight
Having yrockt a sleepe his irkesome spright,[88]
That troublous dreame gan freshly tosse his braine,
With bowres, and beds, and Ladies deare delight:
But when he saw his labour all was vaine,
With that misformèd spright he backe returnd againe.

CANTO II

The guilefull great Enchaunter parts
The Redcrosse Knight from Truth:
Into whose stead faire falshood steps,
And workes him wofull ruth.

I

By this the Northerne wagoner [89] had set
His sevenfold teme [90] behind the stedfast starre,[91]
That was in Ocean waves yet never wet,

86 reproach
87 disappointed in
88 tired spirit

89 Constellation Boötes
90 The Dipper, or
Charles's Wain (in the

constellation of the Great
Bear)
91 polar star

But firme is fixt, and sendeth light from farre
To all, that in the wide deepe wandring arre:
And chearefull Chaunticlere with his note shrill
Had warnèd once, that *Phœbus* fiery carre [92]
In hast was climbing up the Easterne hill,
Full envious that night so long his roome did fill.

2

When those accursèd messengers of hell,
That feigning dreame, and that faire-forgèd Spright
Came to their wicked maister, and gan tell
Their bootelesse paines, and ill succeeding night:
Who all in rage to see his skilfull might
Deluded so, gan threaten hellish paine
And sad *Proserpines* wrath, them to affright.
But when he saw his threatning was but vaine,
He cast about, and searcht his balefull bookes againe.

3

Eftsoones he tooke that miscreated faire,
And that false other Spright, on whom he spred
A seeming body of the subtile aire,
Like a young Squire, in loves and lusty-hed
His wanton dayes that ever loosely led,
Without regard of armes and dreaded fight:
Those two he tooke, and in a secret bed,
Covered with darknesse and misdeeming night,
Them both together laid, to joy in vaine delight.

4

Forthwith he runnes with feignèd faithfull hast
Unto his guest, who after troublous sights
And dreames, gan now to take more sound repast,
Whom suddenly he wakes with fearefull frights,
As one aghast with feends or damnèd sprights,
And to him cals, Rise rise unhappy Swaine,
That here wex old in sleepe, whiles wicked wights
Have knit themselves in *Venus* shamefull chaine;
Come see, where your false Lady doth her honour staine.

92 the sun

5

All in amaze he suddenly up start
With sword in hand, and with the old man went;
Who soone him brought into a secret part,
Where that false couple were full closely ment [93]
In wanton lust and lewd embracèment:
Which when he saw, he burnt with gealous fire,
The eye of reason was with rage yblent,
And would have slaine them in his furious ire,
But hardly was restreinèd of that agèd sire.

6

Returning to his bed in torment great,
And bitter anguish of his guiltie sight,
He could not rest, but did his stout heart eat,
And wast his inward gall with deepe despight,
Yrkesome [94] of life, and too long lingring night.
At last faire *Hesperus* [95] in highest skie
Had spent his lampe, and brought forth dawning light,
Then up he rose, and clad him hastily;
The Dwarfe him brought his steed: so both away do fly.

7

Now when the rosy-fingred Morning faire,
Weary of agèd *Tithones* [96] saffron bed,
Had spred her purple robe through deawy aire,
And the high hils *Titan* [97] discoverèd,
The royall virgin shooke off drowsy-hed,
And rising forth out of her baser bowre,
Lookt for her knight, who far away was fled,
And for her Dwarfe, that wont to wait each houre;
Then gan she waile and weepe, to see that woefull stowre.

8

And after him she rode with so much speede
As her slow beast could make, but all in vaine;
For him so far had borne his light-foot steede,
Prickèd with wrath and fiery fierce disdaine,
That him to follow was but fruitlesse paine;
Yet she her weary limbes would never rest,

93 mingled
94 weary
95 the evening star

96 Aurora, who loved
Tithonus, won for him im-
mortality but not youth.

97 the sun-god
98 distress

But every hill and dale, each wood and plaine
Did search, sore grievèd in her gentle brest,
He so ungently left her, whom she lovèd best.

9

But subtill *Archimago*, when his guests
He saw divided into double parts,
And *Una* wandring in woods and forrests,
Th'end of his drift,[99] he praisd his divelish arts,
That had such might over true meaning harts;
Yet rests not so, but other meanes doth make,
How he may worke unto her further smarts:
For her he hated as the hissing snake,
And in her many troubles did most pleasure take.

10

He then devisde himselfe how to disguise;
For by his mightie science [1] he could take
As many formes and shapes in seeming wise,
As ever *Proteus* [2] to himselfe could make:
Sometime a fowle, sometime a fish in lake,
Now like a foxe, now like a dragon fell,
That of himselfe he oft for feare would quake,
And oft would flie away. O who can tell
The hidden power of herbes, and might of Magicke spell?

11

But now seemde best, the person to put on
Of that good knight, his late beguilèd guest:
In mighty armes he was yclad anon:
And silver shield: upon his coward brest
A bloudy crosse, and on his craven crest
A bounch of haires discolourd diversly:
Full jolly [3] knight he seemde, and well addrest,
And when he sate upon his courser free,
Saint George himself ye would have deemèd him to be.

12

But he the knight, whose semblaunt he did beare,
The true *Saint George* was wandred far away,

99 the end he aimed at   2 a sea-god   3 handsome
1 skill

Still flying from his thoughts and gealous feare;
Will was his guide, and griefe led him astray.
At last him chaunst to meete upon the way
A faithlesse Sarazin [4] all arm'd to point,
In whose great shield was writ with letters gay
Sans foy: [5] full large of limbe and every joint
He was, and carèd not for God or man a point.

13

He had a faire companion of his way,
A goodly Lady [6] clad in scarlot red,
Purfled [7] with gold and pearle of rich assay,
And like a *Persian* mitre [8] on her hed
She wore, with crownes and owches [9] garnishèd,
The which her lavish lovers to her gave;
Her wanton palfrey all was overspred
With tinsell trappings, woven like a wave,
Whose bridle rung with golden bels and bosses brave.

14

With faire disport and courting dalliaunce
She intertainde her lover all the way:
But when she saw the knight his speare advaunce,
She soone left off her mirth and wanton play,
And bad her knight addresse him to the fray:
His foe was nigh at hand. He, prickt with pride
And hope to winne his Ladies heart that day,
Forth spurrèd fast: adowne his coursers side
The red bloud trickling staind the way, as he did ride.

15

The knight of the *Redcrosse* when him he spide,
Spurring so hote with rage dispiteous,[10]
Gan fairely couch his speare, and towards ride:
Soone meete they both, both fell and furious,
That daunted with their forces hideous,
Their steeds do stagger, and amazèd stand,
And eke themselves too rudely rigorous,

---

4 Saracen (for pagan in general)
5 Faithless
6 Duessa (or Falsehood) who calls herself Fidessa (Faithful). Probably typifying the Church of Rome and perhaps also Mary Queen of Scots (or Mary Tudor)
7 decorated with an ornamental border
8 Probably allusion the Pope's crown
9 jewels
10 cruel

Astonied with the stroke of their owne hand,
Do backe rebut, and each to other yeeldeth land.

16

As when two rams stird with ambitious pride,
Fight for the rule of the rich fleecèd flocke,
Their hornèd fronts so fierce on either side
Do meete, that with the terrour of the shocke
Astonied both, stand sencelesse as a blocke,
Forgetfull of the hanging victory:
So stood these twaine, unmovèd as a rocke,
Both staring fierce, and holding idely,
The broken reliques of their former cruelty.

17

The *Sarazin* sore daunted with the buffe
Snatcheth his sword, and fiercely to him flies;
Who well it wards, and quyteth cuff with cuff:
Each others equall puissaunce envies,[11]
And through their iron sides with cruel spies
Does seeke to perce: repining courage yields
No foote to foe. The flashing fier flies
As from a forge out of their burning shields,
And streames of purple bloud new dies the verdant fields.

18

Curse on that Crosse (quoth then the *Sarazin*)
That keepes thy body from the bitter fit;[12]
Dead long ygoe I wote thou haddest bin,
Had not that charme from thee forwarnèd it:
But yet I warne thee now assurèd sitt,
And hide thy head. Therewith upon his crest
With rigour so outrageous he smitt,
That a large share it hewd out of the rest,
And glauncing downe his shield, from blame him fairely blest.[13]

19

Who thereat wondrous wroth, the sleeping spark
Of native vertue gan eftsoones revive,
And at his haughtie helmet making mark,

11 vies with   12 death agony   13 fairly preserved him
                                              from harm

So hugely stroke, that it the steele did rive,
And cleft his head. He tumbling downe alive,
With bloudy mouth his mother earth did kis,
Greeting his grave: his grudging ghost did strive
With the fraile flesh; at last it flitted is,
Whither the soules do fly of men, that live amis.

20

The Lady when she saw her champion fall,
Like the old ruines of a broken towre,
Staid not to waile his woefull funerall,
But from him fled away with all her powre;
Who after her as hastily gan scowre,
Bidding the Dwarfe with him to bring away
The *Sarazins* shield, signe of the conqueroure.
Her soone he overtooke, and bad to stay,
For present cause was none of dread her to dismay.

21

She turning backe with ruefull countenaunce,
Cride, Mercy mercy Sir vouchsafe to show
On silly [14] Dame, subject to hard mischaunce,
And to your mighty will. Her humblesse low
In so ritch weedes and seeming glorious show,
Did much emmove his stout heroïcke heart,
And said, Deare dame, your suddein overthrow
Much rueth me; but now put feare apart,
And tell, both who ye be, and who that tooke your part.

22

Melting in teares, then gan she thus lament;
The wretched woman, whom unhappy howre
Hath now made thrall to your commandement,
Before that angry heavens list to lowre,
And fortune false betraide me to your powre,
Was (O what now availeth that I was!)
Borne the sole daughter of an Emperour,
He that the wide West under his rule has,
And high hath set his throne, where *Tiberis* [15] doth pas.

23

He in the first flowre of my freshest age,
Betrothèd me unto the onely haire

14 innocent   15 River Tiber

Of a most mighty king, most rich and sage;
Was never Prince so faithfull and so faire,
Was never Prince so meeke and debonaire;
But ere my hopèd day of spousall shone,
My dearest Lord fell from high honours staire,
Into the hands of his accursèd fone,
And cruelly was slaine, that shall I ever mone.

24

His blessèd body spoild of lively breath,
Was afterward, I know not how, convaid
And from me hid: of whose most innocent death
When tidings came to me unhappy maid,
O how great sorrow my sad soule assaid.
Then forth I went his woefull corse to find,
And many yeares throughout the world I straid,
A virgin widow, whose deepe wounded mind
With love, long time did languish as the striken hind.

25

At last it chauncèd this proud *Sarazin,*
To meete me wandring, who perforce me led
With him away, but yet could never win
The Fort, that Ladies hold in soveraigne dread.
There lies he now with foule dishonour dead,
Who whiles he liv'de, was callèd proud *Sans foy,*
The eldest of three brethren, all three bred
Of one bad sire, whose youngest is *Sans joy,*[16]
And twixt them both was borne the bloudy bold *Sans loy.*[17]

26

In this sad plight, friendlesse, unfortunate,
Now miserable I *Fidessa* dwell,
Craving of you in pitty of my state,
To do none ill, if please ye not do well.
He in great passion all this while did dwell,
More busying his quicke eyes, her face to view,
Then his dull eares, to heare what she did tell;
And said, faire Lady hart of flint would rew
The undeservèd woes and sorrowes, which ye shew.

16 without happiness   17 lawless

27

Henceforth in safe assuraunce may ye rest,
Having both found a new friend you to aid,
And lost an old foe, that did you molest:
Better new friend then an old foe is said.
With chaunge of cheare [18] the seeming simple maid
Let fall her eyen, as shamefast to the earth,
And yeelding soft, in that she nought gain-said,
So forth they rode, he feining seemely merth,
And she coy lookes: so dainty [19] they say maketh derth.[20]

28

Long time they thus together traveilèd,
Till weary of their way, they came at last,
Where grew too goodly trees, that faire did spred
Their armes abroad, with gray mosse overcast,
And their greene leaves trembling with every blast,
Made a calme shadow far in compasse round:
The fearefull Shepheard often there aghast
Under them never sat, ne wont there sound
His mery oaten pipe, but shund th'unlucky ground.

29

But this good knight soone as he them can spie,
For the coole shade him thither hastly got:
For golden *Phœbus* now ymounted hie,
From fiery wheeles of his faire chariot
Hurlèd his beame so scorching cruell hot,
That living creature mote it not abide;
And his new Lady it endurèd not.
There they alight, in hope themselves to hide
From the fierce heat, and rest their weary limbs a tide.

30

Faire seemely pleasaunce each to other makes,
With goodly purposes there as they sit:
And in his falsèd fancy he her takes
To be the fairest wight, that livèd yit;
Which to expresse, he bends his gentle wit,
And thinking of those braunches greene to frame
A girlond for her dainty forehead fit,

18 countenance   19 fastidiousness   20 doth rarity make

He pluckt a bough: out of whose rift there came
Small drops of gory bloud, that trickled downe the same.

31

Therewith a piteous yelling voyce was heard,
Crying, O spare with guilty hands to teare
My tender sides in this rough rynd embard,[21]
But fly, ah fly far hence away, for feare
Least to you hap, that happened to me heare,
And to this wretched Lady, my deare love,
O too deare love, love bought with death too deare.
Astond he stod, and up his haire did hove,
And with that suddein horror could no member move.

32

At last whenas the dreadfull passion
Was overpast, and manhood well awake,
Yet musing at the straunge occasion,
And doubting much his sence, he thus bespake;
What voyce of damnèd Ghost from *Limbo* [22] lake,
Or guilefull spright wandring in empty aire,
Both which fraile men do oftentimes mistake,
Sends to my doubtfull eares these speaches rare,[23]
And ruefull plaints, me bidding guiltlesse bloud to spare?

33

Then groning deepe, Nor damnèd Ghost (quoth he),
Nor guilefull sprite to thee these wordes doth speake,
But once a man *Fradubio*,[24] now a tree,
Wretched man, wretched tree; whose nature weake,
A cruell witch her cursèd will to wreake,
Hath thus transformd, and plast in open plaines,
Where *Boreas* [25] doth blow full bitter bleake,
And scorching Sunne does dry my secret vaines:
For though a tree I seeme, yet cold and heat me paines.

34

Say on *Fradubio* then, or man, or tree,
Quoth then the knight, by whose mischievous arts
Art thou misshapèd thus, as now I see?

21 imprisoned
22 the region bordering
on Hell
23 thin
24 "Brother Doubtful"
25 the north wind

He oft finds med'cine, who his griefe imparts;
But double griefs afflict concealing harts,
As raging flames who striveth to suppresse.
The author then (said he) of all my smarts,
Is one *Duessa* a false sorceresse,
That many errant knights hath brought to wretchednesse.

35

In prime of youthly yeares, when corage hot
The fire of love and joy of chevalree
First kindled in my brest, it was my lot
To love this gentle Lady, whom ye see,
Now not a Lady, but a seeming tree;
With whom as once I rode accompanyde,
Me chauncèd of a knight encountred bee,
That had a like faire Lady by his syde,
Like a faire Lady, but did fowle *Duessa* hyde.

36

Whose forgèd beauty he did take in hand,[26]
All other Dames to have exceeded farre;
I in defence of mine did likewise stand,
Mine, that did then shine as the Morning starre:
So both to battell fierce arraungèd arre,
In which his harder fortune was to fall
Under my speare: such is the dye of warre:
His Lady left as a prise martiall,
Did yield her comely person, to be at my call.

37

So doubly lov'd of Ladies unlike faire,
Th'one seeming such, the other such indeede,
One day in doubt I cast for to compare,
Whether [27] in beauties glorie did exceede;
A Rosy girlond was the victors meede:
Both seemde to win, and both seemde won to bee,
So hard the discord was to be agreede.
Frælissa [28] was as faire, as faire mote bee,
And ever false *Duessa* seemde as faire as shee.

38

The wicked witch now seeing all this while
The doubtfull ballaunce equally to sway,

---

26 maintain   **27** which   **28** "True   Faith   in
Doubt"

What not by right, she cast to win by guile,
And by her hellish science raisd streight way
A foggy mist, that overcast the day,
And a dull blast, that breathing on her [29] face,
Dimmèd her former beauties shining ray,
And with foule ugly forme did her disgrace:
Then was she [30] faire alone, when none was faire in place.

39

Then cride she out, Fye, fye, deformèd wight,
Whose borrowed beautie now appeareth plaine
To have before bewitchèd all mens sight;
O leave her soone, or let her soone be slaine.
Her loathly visage viewing with disdaine,
Eftsoones I thought her such, as she me told,
And would have kild her; but with faignèd paine,
The false witch did my wrathfull hand withhold;
So left her, where she now is turnd to treen mould.[31]

40

Thens forth I tooke *Duessa* for my Dame,
And in the witch unweening joyd long time,
Ne ever wist, but that she was the same,
Till on a day (that day is every Prime,
When Witches wont do penance for their crime)
I chaunst to see her in her proper hew,
Bathing her selfe in origane [32] and thyme:
A filthy foule old woman I did vew,
That ever to have toucht her, I did deadly rew.

41

Her neather partes misshapen, monstruous,
Were hidd in water, that I could not see,
But they did seeme more foule and hideous,
Then womans shape man would beleeve to bee.
Thens forth from her most beastly companie
I gan refraine, in minde to slip away,
Soone as appeard safe opportunitie:
For danger great, if not assur'd decay
I saw before mine eyes, if I were knowne to stray.

---

29 Fraelissa's   31 the shape of a tree
30 Duessa   32 probably wild marjoram

42

The divelish hag by chaunges of my cheare [33]
Perceiv'd my thought, and drownd in sleepie night,
With wicked herbes and ointments did besmeare
My bodie all, through charmes and magicke might,
That all my senses were bereavèd quight:
Then brought she me into this desert waste,
And by my wretched lovers side me pight,[34]
Where now enclosd in wooden wals full faste,
Banisht from living wights, our wearie dayes we waste.

43

But how long time, said then the Elfin knight,
Are you in this misformèd house to dwell?
We may not chaunge (quoth he) this evil plight,
Till we be bathèd in a living well;
That is the terme prescribèd by the spell.
O how, said he, mote I that well out find,
That may restore you to your wonted well? [35]
Time and suffisèd fates to former kynd [36]
Shall us restore, none else from hence may us unbynd.

44

The false *Duessa,* now *Fidessa* hight,
Heard how in vaine *Fradubio* did lament,
And knew well all was true. But the good knight
Full of sad feare and ghastly dreriment,
When all this speech the living tree had spent,
The bleeding bough did thrust into the ground,
That from the bloud he might be innocent,
And with fresh clay did close the wooden wound:
Then turning to his Lady, dead with feare her found.

45

Her seeming dead he found with feignèd feare,
As all unweeting of that well she knew,
And paynd himselfe with busie care to reare
Her out of carelesse swowne. Her eylids blew
And dimmèd sight with pale and deadly hew
At last she up gan lift: with trembling cheare

33 countenance   35 well-being   36 nature
34 placed

Her up he tooke, too simple and too trew,
And oft her kist. At length all passèd feare,
He set her on her steede, and forward forth did beare.

CANTO III

Forsaken Truth long seekes her love,
And makes the Lyon mylde,
Marres blind Devotions mart, and fals
In hand of leachour vylde.

I

Nought is there under heav'ns wide hollownesse,
That moves more deare compassion of mind,
Then beautie brought t'unworthy wretchednesse
Through envies snares or fortunes freakes [37] unkind:
I, whether lately through her brightnesse blind,
Or through alleageance and fast fealtie,
Which I do owe unto all woman kind,
Feele my heart perst with so great agonie,
When such I see, that all for pittie I could die.

2

And now it is empassionèd so deepe,
For fairest *Unaes* sake, of whom I sing,
That my fraile eyes these lines with teares do steepe,
To thinke how she through guileful handeling,
Though true as touch,[38] though daughter of a king,
Though faire as ever living wight was faire,
Though nor in word nor deede ill meriting,
Is from her knight divorcèd in despaire
And her due loves deriv'd to that vile witches share.

3

Yet she most faithfull Ladie all this while
Forsaken, wofull, solitarie mayd
Farre from all peoples prease,[39] as in exile,
In wildernesse and wastfull deserts strayd,
To seeke her knight; who subtilly betrayd
Through that late vision, which th'Enchaunter wrought,
Had her abandond. She of nought affrayd,

---

[37] tricks   [38] touchstone, by which   [39] press
gold was tested

Through woods and wastnesse wide him daily sought;
Yet wishèd tydings none of him unto her brought.

4

One day nigh wearie of the yrkesome way,
From her unhastie beast she did alight,
And on the grasse her daintie limbes did lay
In secret shadow, farre from all mens sight:
From her faire head her fillet she undight,[40]
And laid her stole aside. Her angels face
As the great eye of heaven shynèd bright,
And made a sunshine in the shadie place;
Did never mortall eye behold such heavenly grace.

5

It fortunèd out of the thickest wood
A ramping Lyon [41] rushèd suddainly,
Hunting full greedie after salvage blood;
Soone as the royall virgin he did spy,
With gaping mouth at her ran greedily,
To have attonce devour'd her tender corse:
But to the pray when as he drew more ny,
His bloudie rage asswagèd with remorse,
And with the sight amazd, forgat his furious forse.

6

In stead thereof he kist her wearie feet,
And lickt her lilly hands with fawning tong,
As he her wrongèd innocence did weet.[42]
O how can beautie maister the most strong,
And simple truth subdue avenging wrong?
Whose yeelded pride and proud submission,
Still dreading death, when she had markèd long,
Her hart gan melt in great compassion,
And drizling teares did shed for pure affection.

7

The Lyon Lord of every beast in field
Quoth she, his princely puissance doth abate,
And mightie proud to humble weake does yield,

40 unloosed   41 raging lion, probably   42 know
                     typifying Reason

Forgetfull of the hungry rage, which late
Him prickt, in pittie of my sad estate:
But he my Lyon, and my noble Lord
How does he find in cruell hart to hate
Her that him lov'd, and ever most adord,
As the God of my life? why hath he me abhord?

8

Redounding teares did choke th'end of her plaint,
Which softly ecchoed from the neighbour wood;
And sad to see her sorrowfull constraint
The kingly beast upon her gazing stood;
With pittie calmd, downe fell his angry mood.
At last in close hart shutting up her paine,
Arose the virgin borne of heavenly brood,
And to her snowy Palfrey got againe,
To seeke her strayèd Champion, if she might attaine.

9

The Lyon would not leave her desolate,
But with her went along, as a strong gard
Of her chest person, and a faithfull mate
Of her sad troubles and misfortunes hard:
Still when she slept, he kept both watch and ward,
And when she wakt, he waited diligent,
With humble service to her will prepard:
From her faire eyes he tooke commaundement,
And ever by her lookes conceivèd her intent.

10

Long she thus traveilèd through deserts wyde,
By which she thought her wandring knight shold pas,
Yet never shew of living wight espyde;
Till that at length she found the troden gras,
In which the tract of peoples footing was,
Under the steepe foot of a mountaine hore; [43]
The same she followes, till at last she has
A damzell spyde [44] slow footing her before,
That on her shoulders sad [45] a pot of water bore.

---

43 hoar   44 Abessa, or Supersti-   45 firm
                 tion

11

To whom approching she to her gan call,
To weet, if dwelling place were nigh at hand;
But the rude wench her answer'd nought at all,
She could not heare, nor speake, nor understand;
Till seeing by her side the Lyon stand,
With suddaine feare her pitcher downe she threw,
And fled away: for never in that land
Face of faire Ladie she before did vew,[46]
And that dread Lyons looke her cast in deadly hew.[47]

12

Full fast she fled, ne ever lookt behynd,
As if her life upon the wager lay,
And home she came, whereas her mother blynd [48]
Sate in eternall night: nought could she say,
But suddaine catching hold, did her dismay
With quaking hands, and other signes of feare:
Who full of ghastly fright and cold affray,
Gan shut the dore. By this arrivèd there
Dame *Una,* wearie Dame, and entrance did requere.[49]

13

Which when none yeelded, her unruly Page
With his rude clawes the wicket open rent,
And let her in; where of his cruell rage
Nigh dead with feare, and faint astonishment,
She found them both in darkesome corner pent;
Where that old woman day and night did pray
Upon her beades devoutly penitent;
Nine hundred *Pater nosters* [50] every day,
And thrise nine hundred *Aves* [51] she was wont to say.

14

And to augment her painefull pennance more,
Thrise every weeke in ashes she did sit,
And next her wrinkled skin rough sackcloth wore,
And thrise three times did fast from any bit: [52]
But now for feare her beads she did forget.

46 She is frightened by
Truth, whom she has never
before beheld.
47 made her pale as death

48 Corceca, or Blind De-
votion
49 ask

50 Our   Father   (the
Lord's Prayer)
51 prayers to the Virgin
52 bite of food

Whose needlesse dread for to remove away,
Faire *Una* framèd words and count'nance fit:
Which hardly doen,[53] at length she gan them pray,
That in their cotage small, that night she rest her may.

15

The day is spent, and commeth drowsie night,
When every creature shrowded is in sleepe;
Sad *Una* downe her laies in wearie plight,
And at her feet the Lyon watch doth keepe:
In stead of rest, she does lament, and weepe
For the late losse of her deare lovèd knight,
And sighes, and grones, and evermore does steepe
Her tender brest in bitter teares all night,
All night she thinks too long, and often lookes for light.

16

Now when *Aldeboran* [54] was mounted hie
Above the shynie *Cassiopeias* [55] chaire,
And all in deadly sleepe did drownèd lie,
One [56] knockèd at the dore, and in would fare;
He knockèd fast, and often curst, and sware,
That readie entrance was not at his call:
For on his backe a heavy load he bare
Of nightly stelths [57] and pillage severall,
Which he had got abroad by purchase criminall.[58]

17

He was to weet a stout and sturdie thiefe,
Wont to robbe Churches of their ornaments,
And poore mens boxes of their due reliefe,
Which given was to them for good intents;
The holy Saints of their rich vestiments
He did disrobe, when all men carelesse slept,
And spoild the Priests of their habiliments,
Whiles none the holy things in safety kept;
Then he by cunning sleights in at the window crept.

18

And all that he by right or wrong could find,
Unto this house he brought, and did bestow

---

53 done with difficulty   55 a constellation   57 thefts
54 a bright star in the   56 Kirkrapine, or   58 acquiring   criminal;
constellation Taurus   Church-robber   *i. e.*, robbery

Upon the daughter of this woman blind,
Abessa daughter of *Corceca* slow,
With whom he whoredome usd, that few did know,
And fed her fat with feast of offerings,
And plentie, which in all the land did grow;
Ne sparèd he to give her gold and rings:
And now he to her brought part of his stolen things.

19

Thus long the dore with rage and threats he bet,
Yet of those fearefull women none durst rize,
The Lyon frayèd them, him in to let:
He would no longer stay him to advize,
But open breakes the dore in furious wize,
And entring is; when that disdainfull beast
Encountring fierce, him suddaine doth surprize,
And seizing cruell clawes on trembling brest,
Under his Lordly foot him proudly hath supprest.

20

Him booteth [59] not resist, nor succour call,
His bleeding hart is in the vengers hand,
Who streight him rent in thousand peeces small,
And quite dismembred hath: the thirstie land
Drunke up his life; his corse left on the strand.
His fearefull friends weare out the wofull night,
Ne dare to weepe, nor seeme to understand
The heavie hap, which on them is alight,
Affraid, least to themselves the like mishappen might.

21

Now when broad day the world discoverèd has,
Up *Una* rose, up rose the Lyon eke,
And on their former journey forward pas,
In wayes unknowne, her wandring knight to seeke,
With paines farre passing that long wandring *Greeke*,[60]
That for his love refusèd deitie; [61]
Such were the labours of this Lady meeke,
Still seeking him, that from her still did flie,
Then furthest from her hope, when most she weenèd nie.

59 it avails him   his wife Penelope rather   (*Odyssey,* Book V).
60 Ulysses   than accept the immortal-
61 He chose to return to   ity offered by Calypso

22

Soone as she parted thence, the fearefull twaine,
That blind old woman and her daughter deare
Came forth, and finding *Kirkrapine* there slaine,
For anguish great they gan to rend their heare,
And beat their brests, and naked flesh to teare.
And when they both had wept and wayld their fill,
Then forth they ranne like two amazèd deare,
Halfe mad through malice, and revenging will,
To follow her, that was the causer of their ill.

23

Whom overtaking, they gan loudly bray,
With hollow howling, and lamenting cry,
Shamefully at her rayling all the way,
And her accusing of dishonesty,[62]
That was the flowre of faith and chastity;
And still amidst her rayling, she did pray,
That plagues, and mischiefs, and long misery
Might fall on her, and follow all the way,
And that in endlesse error she might ever stray.

24

But when she saw her prayers nought prevaile,
She backe returnèd with some labour lost;
And in the way as she did weepe and waile,
A knight her met in mighty armes embost,[63]
Yet knight was not for all his bragging bost,
But subtill *Archimag,* that *Una* sought
By traynes [64] into new troubles to have tost:
Of that old woman tydings he besought,
If that of such a Ladie she could tellen ought.

25

Therewith she gan her passion to renew,
And cry, and curse, and raile, and rend her heare,
Saying, that harlot she too lately knew,
That causd her shed so many a bitter teare,
And so forth told the story of her feare:
Much seemèd he to mone her haplesse chaunce,
And after for that Ladie did inquere;

---

62 dishonor   63 arrayed   64 wiles

Which being taught, he forward gan advaunce
His faire enchaunted steed, and eke his charmèd launce.

26

Ere long he came, where *Una* traveild slow,
And that wilde Champion wayting her besyde:
Whom seeing such, for dread he durst not show
Himselfe too nigh at hand, but turnèd wyde [65]
Unto an hill; from whence when she him spyde,
By his like seeming shield, her knight by name
She weend it was, and towards him gan ryde:
Approching nigh, she wist it was the same,
And with faire fearefull humblesse towards him shee came.

27

And weeping said, Ah my long lackèd Lord,
Where have ye bene thus long out of my sight?
Much fearèd I to have bene quite abhord,
Or ought [66] have done, that ye displeasen might,
That should as death unto my deare hart light:
For since mine eye your joyous sight did mis,
My chearefull day is turnd to chearelesse night,
And eke my night of death the shadow is;
But welcome now my light, and shining lampe of blis.

28

He thereto meeting said, My dearest Dame,
Farre be it from your thought, and fro my will,
To thinke that knighthood I so much should shame,
As you to leave, that have me lovèd still,[67]
And chose in Faery court of meere [68] goodwill,
Where noblest knights were to be found on earth:
The earth shall sooner leave her kindly [69] skill
To bring forth fruit, and make eternall derth,
Then I leave you, my liefe,[70] yborne of heavenly berth.

29

And sooth to say, why I left you so long,
Was for to seeke adventure in strange place,
Where *Archimago* said a felon strong

---

65 aside   67 always   69 natural
66 aught   68 absolute   70 dear

To many knights did daily worke disgrace;
But knight he now shall never more deface:
Good cause of mine excuse; that mote ye please
Well to accept, and evermore embrace
My faithfull service, that by land and seas
Have vowd you to defend, now then your plaint appease.

30

His lovely words her seemd due recompence
Of all her passèd paines: one loving howre
For many yeares of sorrow can dispence:
A dram of sweet is worth a pound of sowre:
She has forgot, how many a wofull stowre [71]
For him she late endur'd; she speakes no more
Of past: true is, that true love hath no powre
To looken backe; his eyes be fixt before.
Before her stands her knight, for whom she toyld so sore.

31

Much like, as when the beaten marinere,
That long hath wandred in the *Ocean* wide,
Oft soust in swelling *Tethys* [72] saltish teare,
And long time having tand his tawney hide
With blustring breath of heaven, that none can bide,
And scorching flames of fierce *Orions* hound,[73]
Soone as the port from farre he has espide,
His chearefull whistle merrily doth sound,
And *Nereus* [74] crownes with cups; [75] his mates him
pledg around.

32

Such joy made *Una*, when her knight she found;
And eke th'enchaunter joyous seemd no lesse,
Then the glad marchant, that does vew from ground
His ship farre come from watrie wildernesse,
He hurles out vowes, and *Neptune* oft doth blesse:
So forth they past, and all the way they spent
Discoursing of her dreadfull late distresse,
In which he askt her, what the Lyon ment:
Who told her all that fell [76] in journey as she went.

---

[71] peril
[72] a sea-goddess
[73] Sirius, the dog star

[74] the sea-god
[75] salutes with cups of wine

[76] Should probably be emended to "all that her fell" (befell)

33

They had not ridden farre, when they might see
One pricking towards them with hastie heat,
Full strongly armd, and on a courser free,
That through his fiercenesse fomèd all with sweat,
And the sharpe yron did for anger eat,
When his hot ryder spurd his chauffèd [77] side;
His looke was sterne, and seemèd still to threat
Cruell revenge, which he in hart did hyde,
And on his shield *Sans loy* in bloudie lines was dyde.

34

When nigh he drew unto this gentle payre
And saw the Red-crosse, which the knight did beare,
He burnt in fire, and gan eftsoones prepare
Himselfe to battell with his couchèd speare.
Loth was that other, and did faint through feare,
To taste th'untryèd dint of deadly steele;
But yet his Lady did so well him cheare,
That hope of new good hap he gan to feele;
So bent his speare, and spurnd his horse with yron heele.

35

But that proud Paynim forward came so fierce,
And full of wrath, that with his sharp-head speare
Through vainely crossèd shield he quite did pierce,
And had his staggering steede not shrunke for feare,
Through shield and bodie eke he should him beare:
Yet so great was the puissance of his push,
That from his saddle quite he did him beare:
He tombling rudely downe to ground did rush,
And from his gorèd wound a well of bloud did gush.

36

Dismounting lightly from his loftie steed,
He to him lept, in mind to reave his life,
And proudly said, Lo there the worthie meed
Of him, that slew *Sansfoy* with bloudie knife;
Henceforth his ghost freed from repining strife,
In peace may passen over *Lethe* lake,[78]
When mourning altars purgd with enemies life,

77 chafed   78 the river of forgetfulness in Hades

The blacke infernall *Furies* [79] doen aslake:
Life from *Sansfoy* thou tookst, *Sansloy* shall from thee take.

37

Therewith in haste his helmet gan unlace,
Till *Una* cride, O hold that heavie hand,
Deare Sir, what ever that thou be in place:
Enough is, that thy foe doth vanquisht stand
Now at thy mercy: Mercie not withstand:
For he is one the truest knight alive,
Though conquered now he lie on lowly land,
And whilest him fortune favourd, faire did thrive
In bloudie field: therefore of life him not deprive.

38

Her piteous words might not abate his rage,
But rudely rending up his helmet, would
Have slaine him straight: but when he sees his age,
And hoarie head of *Archimago* old,
His hastie hand he doth amazèd hold,
And halfe ashamèd, wondred at the sight:
For the old man well knew he, though untold,
In charmes and magicke to have wondrous might,
Ne ever wont in field, ne in round lists [80] to fight.

39

And said, Why *Archimago*, lucklesse syre,
What doe I see? what hard mishap is this,
That hath thee hither brought to taste mine yre?
Or thine the fault, or mine the error is,
In stead of foe to wound my friend amis?
He answered nought, but in a traunce still lay,
And on those guilefull dazèd eyes of his
The cloud of death did sit. Which doen away,
He left him lying so, ne would no lenger stay.

40

But to the virgin comes, who all this while
Amasèd stands, her selfe so mockt to see

[79] they punished guilty souls—here demanding vengeance for the slain before the soul could pass   [80] tournaments

By him, who has the guerdon of his guile,
For so misfeigning her true knight to bee:
Yet is she now in more perplexitie,
Left in the hand of that same Paynim bold,
From whom her booteth not at all to flie;
Who by her cleanly garment catching hold,
Her from her Palfrey pluckt, her visage to behold.

41

But her fierce servant full of kingly awe
And high disdaine, when as his soveraine Dame
So rudely handled by her foe he sawe,
With gaping jawes full greedy at him came,
And ramping on his shield, did weene the same
Have reft away with his sharpe rending clawes:
But he was stout, and lust did now inflame
His corage more, that from his griping pawes
He hath his shield redeem'd, and foorth his swerd he drawes.

42

O then too weake and feeble was the forse
Of salvage beast, his puissance to withstand:
For he was strong, and of so mightie corse,
As ever wielded speare in warlike hand,
And feates of armes did wisely understand.
Eftsoones he percèd through his chaufèd chest
With thrilling [81] point of deadly yron brand,
And launcht [82] his Lordly hart: with death opprest
He roar'd aloud, whiles life forsooke his stubborne brest.

43

Who now is left to keepe the forlorne maid
From raging spoile of lawlesse victors will?
Her faithfull gard remov'd, her hope dismaid,
Her selfe a yeelded pray to save or spill. [83]
He now Lord of the field, his pride to fill,
With foule reproches, and disdainfull spight
Her vildly entertaines, and will or nill,
Beares her away upon his courser light:
Her prayers nought prevaile, his rage is more of might.

81 piercing   82 pierced   83 destroy

44

And all the way, with great lamenting paine,
And piteous plaints she filleth his dull eares,
That stony hart could riven have in twaine,
And all the way she wets with flowing teares:
But he enrag'd with rancor, nothing heares.
Her servile beast yet would not leave her so,
But followes her farre off, ne ought he feares,
To be partaker of her wandring woe,
More mild in beastly kind,[84] then that her beastly foe.

The above three cantos give a fair idea of Book I. In the succeeding nine cantos the Red Cross Knight and Una face further perils, and have numerous other adventures with many new figures, while Duessa remains a sinister force throughout the book. Arthur comes to their aid; the Red Cross Knight finally slays the "old dragon" which had been devastating the kingdom of Una's parents (Canto xi.); and the book ends with the betrothal of knight and lady.

EPITHALAMION [85]

Ye learnèd sisters,[86] which have oftentimes
Beene to me ayding, others to adorne,
Whom ye thought worthy of your gracefull rymes,
That even the greatest did not greatly scorne
To heare theyr names sung in your simple layes,
But joyèd in theyr prayse;
And when ye list your owne mishaps to mourne,
Which death, or love, or fortunes wreck did rayse,
Your string could soone to sadder tenor turne,
And teach the woods and waters to lament   10
Your dolefull dreriment:
Now lay those sorrowfull complaints aside,
And having all your heads with girland crownd,
Helpe me mine owne loves prayses to resound;
Ne let the same of any be envide:
So Orpheus did for his owne bride:
So I unto my selfe alone will sing;
The woods shall to me answer, and my eccho ring.

Early, before the worlds light giving lampe
His golden beame upon the hils doth spred,
Having disperst the nights unchearefull dampe,   20
Doe ye awake, and, with fresh lustyhed,
Go to the bowre of my belovèd love,

84 in his nature as a beast
85 "a song celebrating a wedding—" written for
Spenser's own marriage in 1594
86 the muses

My truest turtle dove:
Bid her awake; for Hymen [87] is awake,
And long since ready forth his maske to move,
With his bright tead [88] that flames with many a flake,
And many a bachelor to waite on him,
In theyr fresh garments trim.
Bid her awake therefore, and soone her dight,   30
For lo! the wishèd day is come at last,
That shall, for al the paynes and sorrowes past,
Pay to her usury of long delight:
And whylest she doth her dight,
Doe ye to her of joy and solace sing,
That all the woods may answer, and your eccho ring.

Bring with you all the nymphes that you can heare,
Both of the rivers and the forrests greene,
And of the sea that neighbours to her neare,
Al with gay girlands goodly wel beseene.[89]   40
And let them also with them bring in hand
Another gay girland,
For my fayre love, of lillyes and of roses,
Bound truelove wize with a blew silke riband.
And let them make great store of bridale poses,
And let them eeke bring store of other flowers,
To deck the bridale bowers.
And let the ground whereas her foot shall tread,
For feare the stones her tender foot should wrong,
Be strewed with fragrant flowers all along,
And diapred [90] lyke the discolored mead.   50
Which done, doe at her chamber dore awayt,
For she will waken strayt;
The whiles doe ye this song unto her sing,
The woods shall to you answer, and your eccho ring.

Ye nymphes of Mulla,[91] which with carefull heed
The silver scaly trouts doe tend full well,
And greedy pikes which use therein to feed,
(Those trouts and pikes all others doo excell)
And ye likewise which keepe the rushy lake,   60
Where none doo fishes take,
Bynd up the locks the which hang scatterd light,
And in his waters, which your mirror make,
Behold your faces as the christall bright,

87 god of marriage   90 variegated   Spenser's residence in Ire-
88 torch   91 probably   the   River   land
89 arrayed   Awbeg,   near   Kilcolman,

That when you come whereas [92] my love doth lie,
No blemish she may spie.
And eke ye lightfoot mayds which keepe the deere
That on the hoary mountayne use to towre,
And the wylde wolves, which seeke them to devoure,
With your steele darts doo chace from comming neer,   70
Be also present heere,
To helpe to decke her, and to help to sing,
That all the woods may answer, and your eccho ring.

Wake now, my love, awake! for it is time:
The rosy Morne long since left Tithones bed,
All ready to her silver coche to clyme,
And Phœbus gins to shew his glorious hed.
Hark how the cheerefull birds do chaunt theyr laies,
And carroll of loves praise!
The merry larke hir mattins sings aloft,   80
The thrush replyes, the mavis descant playes,
The ouzell shrills, the ruddock warbles soft,
So goodly all agree, with sweet consent,[93]
To this dayes merriment.
Ah! my deere love, why doe ye sleepe thus long,
When meeter were that ye should now awake,
T'awayt the comming of your joyous make,[94]
And hearken to the birds love-learnèd song,
The deawy leaves among?
For they of joy and pleasance to you sing,   90
That all the woods them answer, and theyr eccho ring.

My love is now awake out of her dreame,
And her fayre eyes, like stars that dimmèd were
With darksome cloud, now shew theyr goodly beams
More bright then Hesperus, his head doth rere.
Come now, ye damzels, daughters of delight,
Helpe quickly her to dight.
But first come ye, fayre Houres, which were begot,
In loves sweet paradice, of Day and Night,
Which doe the seasons of the year allot,   100
And al that ever in this world is fayre
Do make and still repayre.
And ye three handmayds [95] of the Cyprian Queene,
The which doe still [96] adorne her beauties pride,
Helpe to addorne my beautifullest bride:
And as ye her array, still throw betweene

92 where   94 mate   96 always
93 harmony   95 the Graces

Some graces to be seene:
And as ye use to Venus, to her sing,
The whiles the woods shal answer, and your eccho ring.

Now is my love all ready forth to come: 110
Let all the virgins therefore well awayt,
And ye fresh boyes, that tend upon her groome,
Prepare your selves, for he is comming strayt.
Set all your things in seemely good aray,
Fit for so joyfull day,
The joyfulst day that ever sunne did see.
Faire Sun, shew forth thy favourable ray,
And let thy lifull heat not fervent be,
For feare of burning her sunshyny face,
Her beauty to disgrace.   120
O fayrest Phœbus, father of the Muse,
If ever I did honour thee aright,
Or sing the thing that mote [97] thy mind delight,
Doe not thy servants simple boone refuse,
But let this day, let this one day be myne,
Let all the rest be thine.
Then I thy soverayne prayses loud wil sing,
That all the woods shal answer, and theyr eccho ring.

Harke how the minstrels gin to shrill aloud
Their merry musick that resounds from far,   130
The pipe, the tabor,[98] and the trembling croud,[99]
That well agree withouten breach or jar,
But most of all the damzels doe delite,
When they their tymbrels smyte,
And thereunto doe daunce and carrol sweet,
That all the sences they do ravish quite,
The whyles the boyes run up and downe the street,
Crying aloud with strong confusèd noyce,
As if it were one voyce.
Hymen, Iö Hymen, Hymen,[1] they do shout,   140
That even to the heavens theyr shouting shrill
Doth reach, and all the firmament doth fill;
To which the people, standing all about,
As in approvance doe thereto applaud,
And loud advaunce her laud,
And evermore they Hymen, Hymen sing,
That al the woods them answer, and theyr eccho ring.

Loe! where she comes along with portly pace,
Lyke Phœbe, from her chamber of the east,

97 may
98 drum

99 fiddle
1 The refrain of a Ro-

man nuptial song. Hymen
is the god of marriage.

Arysing forth to run her mighty race,   150
Clad all in white, that seemes a virgin best.
So well it her beseemes, that ye would weene
Some angell she had beene.
Her long loose yellow locks lyke golden wyre,
Sprinckled with perle, and perling flowres atweene,
Doe lyke a golden mantle her attyre,
And being crownèd with a girland greene,
Seeme lyke some mayden queene.
Her modest eyes, abashèd to behold
So many gazers as on her do stare,   160
Upon the lowly ground affixèd are;
Ne dare lift up her countenance too bold,
But blush to heare her prayses sung so loud,
So farre from being proud.
Nathlesse [2] doe ye still loud her prayses sing;
That all the woods may answer, and your eccho ring.

Tell me, ye merchants daughters, did ye see
So fayre a creature in your towne before,
So sweet, so lovely, and so mild as she,
Adornd with beautyes grace and vertues store?   170
Her goodly eyes lyke saphyres shining bright,
Her forehead yvory white,
Her cheekes lyke apples which the sun hath rudded,
Her lips lyke cherryes charming men to byte,
Her brest like to a bowle of creame uncrudded,[3]
Her paps lyke lyllies budded,
Her snowie necke lyke to a marble towre,
And all her body like a pallace fayre,
Ascending uppe, with many a stately stayre,
To honors seat and chastities sweet bowre.   180
Why stand ye still, ye virgins, in amaze,
Upon her so to gaze,
Whiles ye forget your former lay to sing,
To which the woods did answer, and your eccho ring.

But if ye saw that which no eyes can see,
The inward beauty of her lively spright,[4]
Garnisht with heavenly guifts of high degree,
Much more then would ye wonder at that sight,
And stand astonisht lyke to those which red [5]
Medusaes mazeful hed.[6]   190
There dwels sweet Love and constant Chastity,
Unspotted Fayth, and comely Womanhood,

2 nevertheless   5 saw   covered with writhing ser-
3 uncurdled   6 Medusa's   head   was   pents
4 spirit

Regard of Honour, and mild Modesty;
There Vertue raynes as queene in royal throne,
And giveth lawes alone,
The which the base affections doe obay,
And yeeld theyr services unto her will;
Ne thought of thing uncomely ever may
Thereto approch to tempt her mind to ill.
Had ye once seene these her celestial threasures,   200
And unrevealèd pleasures,
Then would ye wonder, and her prayses sing,
That al the woods should answer, and your echo ring.

Open the temple gates unto my love,
Open them wide that she may enter in,
And all the postes adorne as doth behove,
And all the pillours deck with girlands trim,
For to receyve this saynt with honour dew,
That commeth in to you.
With trembling steps and humble reverence,   210
She commeth in before th' Almighties vew:
Of her, ye virgins, learne obedience,
When so ye come into those holy places,
To humble your proud faces.
Bring her up to th' high altar, that she may
The sacred ceremonies there partake,
The which do endlesse matrimony make
And let the roring organs loudly play
The praises of the Lord in lively notes,
The whiles with hollow throates   220
The choristers the joyous antheme sing,
That al the woods may answere, and their eccho ring.

Behold, whiles she before the altar stands,
Hearing the holy priest that to her speakes,
And blesseth her with his two happy hands,
How the red roses flush up in her cheekes,
And the pure snow with goodly vermill stayne,
Like crimsin dyde in grayne: [7]
That even th' angels, which continually
About the sacred altare doe remaine,   230
Forget their service and about her fly,
Ofte peeping in her face, that seemes more fayre,
The more they on it stare.
But her sad [8] eyes, still fastened on the ground,
Are governèd with goodly modesty,
That suffers not one looke to glaunce awry,

7 in scarlet dye   8 sober

Which may let in a little thought unsownd.
Why blush ye, love, to give to me your hand,
The pledge of all our band? [9]
Sing, ye sweet angels, Alleluya sing,   240
That all the woods may answere, and your eccho ring.

Now al is done; bring home the bride againe,
Bring home the triumph of our victory,
Bring home with you the glory of her gaine,
With joyance bring her and with jollity.
Never had man more joyfull day then this,
Whom heaven would heape with blis.
Make feast therefore now all this live long day;
This day for ever to me holy is;
Poure out the wine without restraint or stay,   250
Poure not by cups, but by the belly full,
Poure out to all that wull,
And sprinkle all the postes and wals with wine,
That they may sweat, and drunken be withall.
Crowne ye God Bacchus with a coronall.
And Hymen also crowne with wreathes of vine;
And let the Graces daunce unto the rest,
For they can doo it best:
The whiles the maydens doe theyr carroll sing,
The which the woods shal answer, and theyr eccho ring. 260

Ring ye the bels, ye yong men of the towne,
And leave your wonted labors for this day:
This day is holy; doe ye write it downe,
That ye for ever it remember may.
This day [10] the sunne is in his chiefest hight,
With Barnaby the bright,
From whence declining daily by degrees,
He somewhat loseth of his heat and light,
When once the Crab [11] behind his back he sees.
But for this time it ill ordainèd was,   270
To chose the longest day in all the yeare,
And shortest night, when longest fitter weare:
Yet never day so long, but late would passe.
Ring ye the bels, to make it weare away,
And bonefiers make all day,
And daunce about them, and about them sing:
That all the woods may answer, and your eccho ring.

Ah when will this long weary day have end,
And lende me leave to come unto my love?

9 tie
10 St. Barnabas' day, June 11, was, according to the old calendar, the sum- mer solstice.
11 a sign of the zodiac

How slowly do the houres theyr numbers spend! 280
How slowly does sad Time his feathers move!
Haste thee, O fayrest planet,[12] to thy home
Within the westerne fome:
Thy tyrèd steedes long since have need of rest.
Long though it be, at last I see it gloome,
And the bright evening star with golden creast
Appeare out of the east.
Fayre childe of beauty, glorious lampe of love,
That all the host of heaven in rankes doost lead,
And guydest lovers through the nightès dread, 290
How chearefully thou lookest from above,
And seemst to laugh atweene thy twinkling light,
As joying in the sight
Of these glad many, which for joy doe sing,
That all the woods them answer, and their echo ring!

Now ceasse, ye damsels, your delights forepast;
Enough is it that all the day was youres:
Now day is doen, and night is nighing fast:
Now bring the bryde into the brydall boures.
The night is come, now soone her disaray, 300
And in her bed her lay;
Lay her in lillies and in violets,
And silken courteins over her display,
And odourd sheetes, and Arras coverlets.
Behold how goodly my faire love does ly
In proud humility!
Like unto Maia, when as Jove her tooke
In Tempe, lying on the flowry gras,
Twixt sleepe and wake, after she weary was
With bathing in the Acidalian broke, 310
Now it is night, ye damsels may be gon,
And leave my love alone,
And leave likewise your former lay to sing:
The woods no more shal answere, nor your echo ring.

Now welcome, night! thou night so long expected,
That long daies labour doest at last defray,
And all my cares, which cruell Love collected,
Hast sumd in one, and cancellèd for aye:
Spread thy broad wing over my love and me,
That no man may us see, 320
And in thy sable mantle us enwrap,
From feare of perrill and foule horror free.

12 the sun

Let no false treason seeke us to entrap,
Nor any dread disquiet once annoy
The safety of our joy:
But let the night be calme and quietsome,
Without tempestuous storms or sad afray:
Lyke as when Jove with fayre Alcmena lay,
When he begot the great Tirynthian groome: [13]
Or lyke as when he with thy selfe did lie,   330
And begot Majesty.
And let the mayds and yongmen cease to sing:
Ne let the woods them answer, nor theyr eccho ring.

Let no lamenting cryes, nor dolefull teares,
Be heard all night within, nor yet without:
Ne let false whispers, breeding hidden feares,
Breake gentle sleepe with misconceivèd dout.
Let no deluding dreames, nor dreadful sights,
Make sudden sad affrights;
Ne let housefyres, nor lightnings helpelesse [14] harmes,   340
Ne let the Pouke,[15] nor other evill sprights,
Ne let mischivous witches with theyr charmes,
Ne let hob goblins, names whose sence we see not,
Fray us with things that be not.
Let not the shriech oule, nor the storke be heard,
Nor the night raven that still deadly yels,
Nor damnèd ghosts cald up with mighty spels,
Nor griesly vultures make us once affeard:
Ne let th' unpleasant quyre of frogs still croking
Make us to wish theyr choking.   350
Let none of these theyr drery accents sing;
Ne let the woods them answer, nor theyr eccho ring.

But let stil Silence trew night watches keepe,
That sacred Peace may in assurance rayne,
And tymely Sleep, when it is tyme to sleepe,
My poure his limbs forth on your pleasant playne,
The whiles an hundred little wingèd loves,
Like divers fethered doves,
Shall fly and flutter round about your bed,
And in the secret darke that none reproves,   360
Their prety stealthes shall worke, and snares shal spread
To filch away sweet snatches of delight,
Conceald through covert night.
Ye sonnes of Venus, play your sports at will:

---

13 Hercules   14 without help   15 The Puck, or Robin
                                                      Goodfellow

For greedy Pleasure, careless of your toyes,
Thinks more upon her paradise of joyes,
Then what ye do, albe it good or ill.
All night therefore attend your merry play,
For it will soone be day:
Now none doth hinder you, that say or sing,   370
Ne will the woods now answer, nor your eccho ring.

Who is the same which at my window peepes?
Or whose is that faire face that shines so bright?
Is it not Cinthia,[16] she that never sleepes,
But walkes about high heaven al the night?
O fayrest goddesse, do thou not envy
My love with me to spy:
For thou likewise didst love, though now unthought,
And for a fleece of woll, which privily
The Latmian shephard [17] once unto thee brought,   380
His pleasures with thee wrought.
Therefore to us be favorable now;
And sith of wemens labours thou hast charge,
And generation goodly dost enlarge,
Encline thy will t' effect our wishfull vow,
And the chaste wombe informe with timely seed,
That may our comfort breed:
Till which we cease our hopefull hap to sing,
Ne let the woods us answere, nor our eccho ring.

And thou, great Juno, which with awful might   390
The lawes of wedlock still dost patronize,
And the religion of the faith first plight
With sacred rites hast taught to solemnize,
And eeke for comfort often callèd art
Of women in their smart,
Eternally bind thou this lovely band,
And all thy blessings unto us impart.
And thou, glad Genius, in whose gentle hand
The bridale bowre and geniall bed remaine,
Without blemish or staine,   400
And the sweet pleasures of theyr loves delight
With secret ayde doest succour and supply,
Till they bring forth the fruitfull progeny,
Send us the timely fruit of this same night.
And thou, fayre Hebe, and thou, Hymen free,
Grant that it may so be.

---

16 the moon   17 Endymion

Til which we cease your further prayse to sing,
Ne any woods shal answer, nor your eccho ring.

And ye high heavens, the temple of the gods,
In which a thousand torches flaming bright   410
Doe burne, that to us wretched earthly clods
In dreadful darknesse lend desirèd light,
And all ye powers which in the same remayne,
More then we men can fayne,[18]
Poure out your blessing on us plentiously,
And happy influence upon us raine,
That we may raise a large posterity,
Which from the earth, which they may long possesse
With lasting happinesse,
Up to your haughty pallaces may mount,   420
And for the guerdon [19] of theyr glorious merit,
May heavenly tabernacles there inherit,
Of blessèd saints for to increase the count.
So let us rest, sweet love, in hope of this,
And cease till then our tymely joyes to sing:
The woods no more us answer, nor our eccho ring.

Song, made in lieu of many ornaments
With which my love should duly have bene dect,
Which cutting off through hasty accidents,
Ye would not stay your dew time to expect,[20]   430
But promist both to recompens,
Be unto her a goodly ornament,
And for short time an endlesse moniment.

ELIZABETHAN LYRICS

It seems no accident that many of the best of the sixteenth century lyrics
are anonymous, for the writing of song, sonnet, or roundelay was in that
age one of the accomplishments of the cultivated gentleman, and he had no
thought of printing them for fame or profit. The typical songs, indeed,
whether signed or unsigned (except that one may note here and there a finer
artistic gift), were written in a dominant tradition, and bear a striking
similarity to each other. They impress us most by their sheer singing quality,
their musical lilt, their unstudied artlessness—above all by their spontaneity.
These Elizabethan song-writers sang as the bird sings—without premedita-
tion, from pure joy in singing.

An exception should be made in the case of the sonnet. This form, invented
in Italy and carried to perfection by Petrarch and by the French sonneteers,
was imported into England by Wyatt and Surrey in the days of Henry VIII,

18 imagine   19 reward   20 await

and soon attained a tremendous vogue. Cycles by the score were written, of which the most famous are Sidney's, Spenser's and Shakespeare's sonnets, Daniel's *Delia* and Drayton's *Idea*. Petrarch's long-deceased woes were told over and over, and every possible change wrought on the themes of the cruel mistress and the disappointed lover, and on such abstractions as death, sleep, and fame. Italian and French sonnets were translated, adapted, and imitated; with here and tnere an individual note struck by some poet of more daring or more power than his fellows.

Two repositories of the lyric should be mentioned. One is the popular miscellany, or collection of poems by various hands. Of these *Tottel's Miscellany* (1557) is the first and most famous, notable also as preserving for us the poetry of those early experimenters and pioneers, Wyatt and Surrey. But a collection even more beautiful and representative is to be found in *England's Helicon* (1600), and more popular still was the *Paradise of Dainty Devices*, first published in 1576 and thereafter in numerous editions. Other lyrics are to be found in large numbers in contemporary song-books—books of airs, madrigals, and what not, presented with music for the voice, and frequently for accompaniment by lute or viol. Unlike many popular songs to-day, the words are often as charming as the tunes. The gems of song scattered throughout the dramas—inserted in response to that insistent craving of the Elizabethans for music—should also be remembered.

The selections here reprinted from these various sources of the sixteenth century lyric are meant to be representative, not in the least inclusive. A word or two each about the best-known writers is here appended: Sir Thomas Wyatt (1503?–1542) was a courtier and diplomat. He introduced from Italy the sonnet and various lyric forms. Henry Howard, Earl of Surrey (1517?–1547) was a member of a famous English noble family. He held various honorary positions at court, and was beheaded on a charge of conspiracy. Following in the wake of Wyatt, he developed more lyric grace than his predecessor. He is noted for his sonnets and lyrics and for the first blank verse in English, employed in his translation of the *Aeneid*. John Lyly (1554?–1606) is known especially as the author of the *Euphues*, a kind of novel and compendium of elegant manners, written in a fantastic rhetorical prose, and as a writer of graceful comedies, based chiefly on classic story, of which *Campaspe* and *Endymion* are typical. His songs are found in his plays. Robert Greene (1560?–1592), was a dramatist (*Friar Bacon and Friar Bungay*), writer of prose romances, and of journalistic pamphlets about contemporary roguery. Sir Edward Dyer (1545?–1607), minor poet, is best known for the single lyric here presented. Christopher Marlowe (1564–1593) is the most brilliant of Shakespeare's predecessors in the drama (*Tamburlaine, Doctor Faustus, Jew of Malta, Edward II*). He also began a richly beautiful narrative poem (*Hero and Leander*). All his work exhibits the highest poetic powers. He was killed in a tavern brawl at the age of twenty-nine. Sir Walter Raleigh (1552?–1618), one of the most distinguished men of his time, was soldier, adventurer, colonizer, statesman, historian, and poet—a man of great and varied abilities. Thomas Lodge (1558?–1625) is best known as a writer of prose romances, one of which was used by Shakespeare as the source of his *As You Like It*. George Peele (1558?–1597?), a poet of fine lyric gifts, was drawn into the drama in the effort to make a living by his pen (*Old Wives Tale*). Nicholas Breton (1545?–1626?) attained a reputation as a poet and a writer of romances. Robert Southwell (1561?–1595), a devout Catholic and a Jesuit, was imprisoned in the Tower for three years, tortured, and finally executed. Richard Barnfield (1574–1627) was a writer of lyrics and pastoral verse. Sir John Davies (1569–1626), lawyer and poet, is best known as the author of the poems *Orchestra* and *Nosce Teipsum* (Know Thyself), characterized by their ingenious thought and form. Thomas Campion (1575–1620) was physician, poet, and musician. His lyrics appear, often to his own music, in several song-books. Thomas Heywood (d. 1650?) was a facile and prolific practical play-wright, whose lyrics appear in his plays. Michael Drayton (1563–1631), dis-tinguished poet, wrote patriotic descriptive and narrative verse (*Polyolbion*, *The Wars of the Barons, England's Heroical Epistles*), a sonnet cycle (*Idea*), and various lyrics.

BIBLIOGRAPHY. Most satisfying anthology, *Elizabethan Lyrics*, by Norman Ault (Longmans). F. E. Schelling, *A Book of Elizabethan Lyrics* (Ginn).

THE LOVER COMPLAINETH THE UNKINDNESS OF HIS LOVE

My lute, awake! perform the last
Labor that thou and I shall waste,
    And end that I have now begun;
For when this song is sung and past,
    My lute, be still, for I have done.

As to be heard where ear is none,
As lead to grave [1] in marble stone,
    My song may pierce her heart as soon.
Should we then sigh, or sing, or moan?
    No, no, my lute, for I have done.   10

The rocks do not so cruelly
Repulse the waves continually,
    As she my suit and affection;
So that I am past remedy,
    Whereby my lute and I have done.

Proud of the spoil that thou hast got
Of simple hearts through Love's shot,
    By whom unkind thou hast them won,
Think not he hath his bow forgot,
    Although my lute and I have done.   20

Vengeance shall fall on thy disdain
That makest but game on earnest pain.
    Think not alone under the sun
Unquit [2] to cause thy lovers plain, [3]
    Although my lute and I have done.

1 engrave   2 without punishment   3 lament

Perchance thee lie withered and old
The winter nights that are so cold,
    Plaining in vain unto the moon;
Thy wishes then dare not be told.
    Care then who list, for I have done.   30

And then may chance thee to repent
The time that thou hast lost and spent
    To cause thy lovers sigh and swoon;
Then shalt thou know beauty but lent,
    And wish and want as I have done.

Now cease, my lute! this is the last
Labor that thou and I shall waste,
    And ended is that we begun.
Now is the song both sung and past—
    My lute, be still, for I have done.   40
          —*Sir Thomas Wyatt*

THE MEANS TO ATTAIN HAPPY LIFE

My friend, the things that do attain
    The happy life be these, I find:
The riches left, not got with pain;
    The fruitful ground, the quiet mind;

The equal friend; no grudge, no strife;
    No charge of rule, no governance;
Without disease the healthy life;
    The household of continuance;

The mean [4] dièt, no dainty fare;
    Wisdom joinèd with simpleness;   10
The night dischargèd of all care,
    Where wine the wit may not oppress;

The faithful wife, without debate;
    Such sleeps as may beguile the night:
Content thyself with thine estate,
    Neither wish death, nor fear his might.
        —*Henry Howard, Earl of Surrey*

4 moderate

BACK AND SIDE GO BARE

(from *Gammer Gurton's Needle*)

Chorus

BACK and side go bare, go bare,
　Both foot and hand go cold;
But, belly, God send thee good ale enough,
　Whether it be new or old.

I cannot eat but little meat,
　My stomach is not good;
But sure I think that I can drink
　With him that wears a hood.
Though I go bare, take ye no care,
　I am nothing a-cold;　　　　　　　　　10
I stuff my skin so full within
　Of jolly good ale and old.

I love no roast but a nutbrown toast,
　And a crab[5] laid in the fire;
A little bread shall do me stead,
　Much bread I not desire.
No frost nor snow, no wind, I trow,
　Can hurt me if I would,
I am so wrapped and thoroughly lapped
　Of jolly good ale and old.　　　　　　20

And Tib my wife, that as her life
　Loveth well good ale to seek,
Full oft drinks she, till ye may see
　The tears run down her cheek.
Then doth she troll[6] to me the bowl,
　Even as a maltworm should,
And saith "Sweetheart, I took my part
　Of this jolly good ale and old."

Now let them drink till they nod and wink,
　Even as good fellows should do;　　　　30
They shall not miss to have the bliss
　Good ale doth bring men to.
And all poor souls that have scoured bowls,
　Or have them lustily trolled,
God save the lives of them and their wives,
　Whether they be young or old.

—*William Stevenson* (?)

5 crab-apple　　　　　6 pass

LULLABY

LULLABY baby, lullaby baby,
Thy nurse will tend thee, as duly as may be.

Be still, my sweet sweeting, no longer do cry;
Sing lullaby, lullaby, lullaby baby:
Let dolors be fleeting, I fancy thee, I,
    To rock and to lull thee, I will not delay me.
    Lullaby baby, . . .

What creature now living would hasten thy woe?
Sing lullaby, lullaby, lullaby baby:
See for thy relieving, the time I bestow
    To dance and to prance thee, as prett'ly ~s may be.
    Lullaby baby, . . .

The gods be thy shield, and comfort in need;
Sing lullaby, lullaby, lullaby baby:
They give thee good fortune, and well for to speed,
    And this to desire, I will not delay me.
    Lullaby baby, lullaby baby,
    Thy nurse will tend thee, as duly as may be.
                                    —*John Phillip*

LOVE ME LITTLE, LOVE ME LONG

LOVE me little, love me long,
    Is the burden of my song.
Love that is too hot and strong
    Burneth soon to waste:
Still, I would not have thee cold,
Not too backward, nor too bold;
Love that lasteth till 'tis old
    Fadeth not in haste.
        Love me little, love me long,
        Is the burden of my song.   10

If thou lovest me too much,
It will not prove as true as touch;
Love me little, more than such,
    For I fear the end:
I am with little well content,
And a little from thee sent
Is enough, with true intent

To be steadfast friend.
Love me little, love me long, . . .

Say thou lov'st me while thou live;   20
I to thee my love will give,
Never dreaming to deceive
Whiles that life endures:
Nay, and after death, in sooth,
I to thee will keep my truth,
As now, when in my May of youth;
This my love assures.
Love me little, love me long, . . .

Constant love is moderate ever,
And it will through life persèver: 30
Give me that, with true endeavor
I will it restore.
A suit of durance let it be
For all weathers that for me,
For the land or for the sea,
Lasting evermore.
Love me little, love me long, . . .

Winter's cold, or summer's heat,
Autumn's tempests, on it beat,
It can never know defeat,   40
Never can rebel:
Such the love that I would gain,
Such the love, I tell thee plain,
Thou must give, or woo in vain:
So to thee, farewell!
Love me little, love me long,
Is the burden of my song.

—Anon.

APELLES' SONG

(from *Campaspe*)

CUPID and my Campaspe played
At cards for kisses; Cupid paid.
He stakes his quiver, bows and arrows,
His mother's doves and team of sparrows;
Loses them too; then down he throws
The coral of his lip, the rose
Growing on's cheek (but none knows how);
With these, the crystal of his brow,

And then the dimple of his chin:
All these did my Campaspe win.
At last he set her both his eyes;
She won, and Cupid blind did rise.
O Love, has she done this to thee?
What shall, alas, become of me?

—John Lyly

NEW BROOMS

New brooms, green brooms, will you buy any?
Come, maidens, come quickly, let me take a penny.

My brooms are not steepèd,
But very well bound:
My brooms be not crooked,
But smooth-cut and round.
I wish it should please you
To buy of my broom,
Then would it well ease me
If market were done.

Have you any old boots,
Or any old shoon,
Pouch-rings, or buskins,
To cope for new broom?
If so you have, maidens,
I pray you bring hither,
That you and I friendly
May bargain together.

New brooms, green brooms, will you buy any?
Come, maidens, come quickly, let me take a penny.

—Robert Wilson

TICHBORNE'S ELEGY, WRITTEN IN THE TOWER BEFORE HIS EXECUTION, 1586

My prime of youth is but a frost of cares;
My feast of joy is but a dish of pain;
My crop of corn is but a field of tares,
And all my good is but vain hope of gain.
The day is past, and yet I saw no sun;
And now I live, and now my life is done.

My tale was heard, and yet it was not told;
My fruit is fallen, and yet my leaves are green;

My youth is spent, and yet I am not old;
I saw the world, and yet I was not seen.
My thread is cut, and yet it is not spun,
And now I live, and now my life is done.

I sought my death, and found it in my womb;
I looked for life, and saw it was a shade;
I trod the earth, and knew it was my tomb;
And now I die, and now I was but made.
My glass is full, and now my glass is run;
And now I live, and now my life is done.

—*Chidiock Tichborne*

SWEET ARE THE THOUGHTS THAT SAVOR OF CONTENT

Sweet are the thoughts that savor of content;
The quiet mind is richer than a crown;
Sweet are the nights in careless slumber spent;
The poor estate scorns fortune's angry frown:
Such sweet content, such minds, such sleep, such bliss,
Beggars enjoy, when princes oft do miss.

The homely house that harbors quiet rest;
The cottage that affords no pride nor care;
The mean that 'grees with country music best;
The sweet consort of mirth and music's fare;
Obscurèd life sets down a type of bliss:
A mind content both crown and kingdom is.

—*Robert Greene*

MY MIND TO ME A KINGDOM IS

My mind to me a kingdom is;
Such present joys therein I find
That it excels all other bliss
That earth affords or grows by kind.[7]
Though much I want which most would have,
Yet still my mind forbids to crave.

No princely pomp, no wealthy store,
No force to win the victory,
No wily wit to salve a sore,
No shape to feed a loving eye;
To none of these I yield as thrall:
For why? My mind doth serve for all.

10

7 nature

I see how plenty surfeits oft,
    And hasty climbers soon do fall;
I see that those which are aloft
    Mishap doth threaten most of all;
They get with toil, they keep with fear:
Such cares my mind could never bear.

Content to live, this is my stay—
    I seek no more than may suffice;   20
I press to bear no haughty sway;
    Look, what I lack my mind supplies:
Lo! thus I triumph like a king,
Content with that my mind doth bring.

Some have too much, yet still do crave;
    I little have, and seek no more.
They are but poor, though much they have,
    And I am rich with little store:
They poor, I rich; they beg, I give;
They lack, I leave; they pine, I live.   30

I laugh not at another's loss;
    I grudge not at another's gain;
No worldly waves my mind can toss;
    My state at one doth still remain:
I fear no foe, I fawn no friend;
I loathe not life, nor dread my end.

Some weigh their pleasure by their lust,
    Their wisdom by their rage of will;
Their treasure is their only trust;
    A cloakèd craft their store of skill: 40
But all the pleasure that I find
Is to maintain a quiet mind.

My wealth is health and perfect ease,
    My conscience clear my chief defence;
I neither seek by bribes to please,
    Nor by deceit to breed offence:
Thus do I live; thus will I die;
Would all did so as well as I!
                                        —*Sir Edward Dyer*

THE PASSIONATE SHEPHERD TO HIS LOVE

COME live with me and be my love,
And we will all the pleasures prove

That valleys, groves, hills, and fields,
Woods, or steepy mountains yields.

And we will sit upon the rocks
Seeing the shepherds feed their flocks,
By shallow rivers, to whose falls
Melodious birds sing madrigals.

And I will make thee beds of roses
And a thousand fragrant posies,
A cap of flowers, and a kirtle
Embroidered all with leaves of myrtle;

A gown made of the finest wool
Which from our pretty lambs we pull;
Fair linèd slippers for the cold,
With buckles of the purest gold;

A belt of straw and ivy buds
With coral clasps and amber studs:
And if these pleasures may thee move,
Come live with me and be my love.

The shepherd swains shall dance and sing
For thy delight each May morning:
If these delights thy mind may move,
Then live with me and be my love.
                    —*Christopher Marlowe*

THE NYMPH'S REPLY TO THE SHEPHERD

IF all the world and love were young,
And truth in every shepherd's tongue,
These pretty pleasures might me move
To live with thee and be thy love.

Time drives the flocks from field to fold
When rivers rage and rocks grow cold,
And Philomel becometh dumb;
The rest complains of cares to come.

The flowers do fade, and wanton fields
To wayward winter reckoning yields.
A honey tongue, a heart of gall
Is fancy's spring, but sorrow's fall.

Thy gowns, thy shoes, thy beds of roses,
Thy cap, thy kirtle, and thy posies
Soon break, soon wither, soon forgotten,
In folly ripe, in reason rotten.

Thy belt of straw and ivy buds,
Thy coral clasps and amber studs,
All these in me no means can move
To come to thee and be thy love.

But could youth last, and love still breed,
Had joys no date, nor age no need,
Then these delights my mind might move
To live with thee and be thy love.
                    —*Sir Walter Raleigh* (?)

ROSALIND'S MADRIGAL

Love in my bosom like a bee
    Doth suck his sweet;
Now with his wings he plays with me,
    Now with his feet.
Within mine eyes he makes his nest,
His bed amidst my tender breast;
My kisses are his daily feast,
And yet he robs me of my rest:
    Ah, wanton, will ye?

And if I sleep, then percheth he
    With pretty flight,
And makes his pillow of my knee
    The livelong night.
Strike I my lute, he tunes the string;
He music plays if so I sing;
He lends me every lovely thing;
Yet cruel he my heart doth sting:
    Whist, wanton, still ye!—

Else I with roses every day
    Will whip you hence,
And bind you, when you long to play,
    For your offence.
I'll shut mine eyes to keep you in,
I'll make you fast it for your sin,
I'll count your power not worth a pin,—

Alas! what hereby shall I win
 If he gainsay me?

What if I beat the wanton boy
 With many a rod?
He will repay me with annoy,
 Because a god.
Then sit thou safely on my knee,
And let thy bower my bosom be;
Lurk in mine eyes, I like of thee.
O Cupid, so thou pity me,
 Spare not, but play thee!

—Thomas Lodge

WHENAS THE RYE REACH TO THE CHIN

(From *The Old Wives Tale*)

WHENAS the rye reach to the chin,
And chopcherry, chopcherry ripe within,
Strawberries swimming in the cream,
And schoolboys playing in the stream;
Then oh, then oh, then oh, my true love said,
Till that time come again
She could not live a maid.

—George Peele

HIS GOLDEN LOCKS TIME HATH TO SILVER TURNED

His golden locks time hath to silver turned;
 O time too swift, O swiftness never ceasing!
His youth 'gainst time and age hath ever spurned,
 But spurned in vain; youth waneth by increasing:
Beauty, strength, youth, are flowers but fading seen;
Duty, faith, love, are roots, and ever green.

His helmet now shall make a hive for bees;
 And, lovers' sonnets turned to holy psalms,
A man-at-arms must now serve on his knees,
 And feed on prayers, which are age's alms:
But though from court to cottage he depart,
His saint is sure of his unspotted heart.

And when he saddest sits in homely cell,
 He'll teach his swains this carol for a song,—

"Blest be the hearts that wish my sovereign well,
Curst be the souls that think her any wrong."
Goddess, allow this aged man his right,
To be your beadsman now that was your knight.
—*George Peele*

PHYLLIDA AND CORYDON

In the merry month of May,
In a morn by break of day,
Forth I walked by the woodside,
Whenas May was in his pride.
There I spièd all alone
Phyllida and Corydon.
Much ado there was, God wot,
He would love and she would not.
She said, never man was true;
He said, none was false to you.   10
He said, he had loved her long;
She said, love should have no wrong.
Corydon would kiss her then;
She said, maids must kiss no men
Till they did for good and all.
Then she made the shepherd call
All the heavens to witness truth,
Never loved a truer youth.
Thus with many a pretty oath,
Yea and nay, and faith and troth,   20
Such as silly shepherds use
When they will not love abuse;
Love, which had been long deluded,
Was with kisses sweet concluded.
And Phyllida with garlands gay
Was made the Lady of the May.
—*Nicholas Breton*

THE BURNING BABE

As I in hoary winter's night stood shivering in the snow,
Surprised I was with sudden heat which made my heart to
    glow;
And lifting up a fearful eye to view what fire was near,
A pretty Babe all burning bright did in the air appear,
Who scorchèd with excessive heat such floods of tears did
    shed,

As though his floods should quench his flames which with his
    tears were bred;
"Alas!" quoth he, "but newly born, in fiery heats I fry,
Yet none approach to warm their hearts or feel my fire but I.
My faultless breast the furnace is, the fuel wounding thorns;
Love is the fire and sighs the smoke, the ashes shames and
    scorns;   10
The fuel Justice layeth on, and Mercy blows the coals,
The metal in this furnace wrought are men's defilèd souls,
For which, as now on fire I am, to work them to their good,
So will I melt into a bath, to wash them in my blood."
With this he vanished out of sight, and swiftly shrunk away,
And straight I callèd unto mind that it was Christmas day.
                               —*Robert Southwell*

AN ODE

As it fell upon a day
In the merry month of May,
Sitting in a pleasant shade
Which a grove of myrtles made,
Beasts did leap and birds did sing,
Trees did grow and plants did spring;
Every thing did banish moan
Save the nightingale alone.
She, poor bird, as all forlorn,
Leaned her breast against a thorn,   10
And there sung the dolefull'st ditty
That to hear it was great pity.
Fie, fie, fie, now would she cry;
Teru, teru, by and by:
That to hear her so complain
Scarce I could from tears refrain;
For her griefs so lively shown
Made me think upon mine own.
Ah, thought I, thou mourn'st in vain,
None takes pity on thy pain: 20
Senseless trees, they cannot hear thee,
Ruthless beasts, they will not cheer thee;
King Pandion, he is dead,
All thy friends are lapped in lead:
All thy fellow birds do sing
Careless of thy sorrowing:
Even so, poor bird, like thee
None alive will pity me.
                             —*Richard Barnfield*

MAN

I KNOW my body's of so frail a kind,
    As force without, fevers within, can kill;
I know the heavenly nature of my mind,
    But 'tis corrupted both in wit and will.

I know my soul hath power to know all things,
    Yet is she blind and ignorant in all;
I know I am one of nature's little kings,
    Yet to the least and vilest things am thrall.

I know my life's a pain, and but a span;
    I know my sense is mocked with everything;
And, to conclude, I know myself a man,
    Which is a proud, and yet a wretched thing.
                    —Sir John Davies

FOLLOW THY FAIR SUN

FOLLOW thy fair sun, unhappy shadow,
    Though thou be black as night,
    And she made all of light,
Yet follow thy fair sun, unhappy shadow.

Follow her whose light thy light depriveth,
    Though here thou liv'st disgraced,
    And she in heaven is placed,
Yet follow her whose light the world reviveth.

Follow those pure beams whose beauty burneth,
    That so have scorchèd thee,
    As thou still black must be,
Till her kind beams thy black to brightness turneth.

Follow her while yet her glory shineth:
    There comes a luckless night,
    That will dim all her light;
And this the black unhappy shade divineth.

Follow still, since so thy fates ordainèd;
    The Sun must have his shade,
    Till both at once do fade,
The Sun still proud, the shadow still disdainèd.
                    —Thomas Campion

CORINNA

WHEN to her lute Corinna sings,
Her voice revives the leaden strings,
And doth in highest notes appear
As any challenged echo clear.
But when she doth of mourning speak,
Even with her sighs the strings do break.

And as her lute doth live or die,
Led by her passion, so must I.
For when of pleasure she doth sing
My thoughts enjoy a sudden spring;
But if she doth of sorrow speak,
Even from my heart the strings do break.

—*Thomas Campion*

WHEN THOU MUST HOME

WHEN thou must home to shades of underground,
And there arrived, a new admirèd guest,
The beauteous spirits do engirt thee round,
White Iope, blithe Helen, and the rest,
To hear the stories of thy finished love
From that smooth tongue whose music hell can move;

Then wilt thou speak of banqueting delights,
Of masques and revels which sweet youth did make,
Of tourneys and great challenges of knights,
And all these triumphs for thy beauty's sake:
When thou hast told these honors done to thee,
Then tell, O tell, how thou didst murder me!

—*Thomas Campion*

THERE IS A GARDEN IN HER FACE

THERE is a garden in her face
  Where roses and white lilies grow;
A heavenly paradise is that place,
  Wherein all pleasant fruits do flow.
There cherries grow, which none may buy
Till "Cherry-ripe" themselves do cry.

Those cherries fairly do enclose
  Of orient pearl a double row,
Which when her lovely laughter shows,

They look like rosebuds filled with snow,
Yet them nor peer nor prince can buy
Till "Cherry-ripe" themselves do cry.

Her eyes like angels watch them still;
  Her brows like bended bows do stand,
Threatening with piercing frowns to kill
  All that attempt, with eye or hand,
Those sacred cherries to come nigh
Till "Cherry-ripe" themselves do cry.
              —*Thomas Campion*

PHYLLIDA FLOUTS ME

OH, what a plague is love! How shall I bear it?
She will unconstant prove, I greatly fear it.
She so molests my mind that my wit faileth.
She wavers with the wind, as the ship saileth,
  Please her the best I may,
  She looks another way.
  Alack and well-a-day!
    Phyllida flouts me.

At the fair, yesterday, she would not see me,
But turned another way, when she came nigh me.   10
Dick had her in to dine; he might intreat her.
Will had her to the wine; I could not get her.
  With Daniel did she dance;
  At me she looked askance.
  O thrice unhappy chance!
    Phyllida flouts me.

I cannot work and sleep, both at all season:
Love wounds my heart so deep, without all reason.
I do consume, alas! with care and sorrow,
Even like a sort of beasts pinde [8] in a meadow.   20
  I shall be dead, I fear,
  Within this thousand year;
  And all for very care!
    Phyllida flouts me.

She hath a clout of mine, wrought with good coventry,[9]
Which she keeps for a sign of my fidelity;
But, in faith, if she flinch, she shall not wear it;
To Tib, my t'other wench, I mean to bear it.

8 enclosed   9 blue embroidery

Yet it will kill my heart
So quickly to depart.   30
Death, kill me with thy dart!
    Phyllida flouts me.

Yesternight, very late, as I was walking,
I saw one in the gate, with my Love talking.
Every word that she spoke, he gave her kissing,
Which she as kindly took as mother's blessing.
    But when I come to kiss,
    She very dainty is.
    Oh, what a hell is this!
        Phyllida flouts me.   4c

Fair maid, be not so coy, never disdain me!
I am my mother's boy; sweet, entertain me!
She'll give me, when she dies, all things befitting:
Her poultry and her bees, with her goose sitting,
    A pair of mattress beds,
    A barrel full of shreds,—
    And yet, for all my goods,
        Phyllida flouts me.

I saw my face, of late, in a fair fountain;
I know there's none so feat in all the mountain.   50
Lasses do leave their sheep and flock above me,
And for my love do weep, and fain would have me.
    Maidens in every place
    Strives to behold my face;
    And yet—O heavy case!—
        Phyllida flouts me.

Maiden, look what you do, and in time take me!
I can have other two, if you forsake me:
For Doll, the dairy-maid, laughed on me lately,
And wanton Winifred favors me greatly.   6c
    One threw milk on my clothes;
    T'other plays with my nose:
    What loving signs be those!
        Phyllida flouts me.

Come to me, pretty peat,[10] let me embrace thee!
Though thou be fair and feat, do not disgrace me;
For I will constant prove (make no denial!)
And be thy dearest Love—proof maketh trial.

10 pet

If ought do breed thy pain,
I can procure thy gain;   70
Yet, bootless, I complain—
    Phyllida flouts me.

Thou shalt eat curds and cream, all the year lasting;
And drink the crystal stream, pleasant in tasting;
Whig and whey whilst thou burst, and bramble-berries,
Pie-lids and pasty-crust, pears, plums, and cherries.
    Thy garments shall be thin,
    Made of a wether's skin—
    Yet all not worth a pin!
    Phyllida flouts me.   80

I found a stock-dove's nest, and thou shalt have it.
The cheese-cake, in my chest, for thee I save it.
I will give thee rush-rings, key-knobs, and cushnets,[11]
Pence, purse, and other things, bells, beads, and bracelets,
    My sheep-hook, and my dog,
    My bottle, and my bag—
    Yet all not worth a rag!
    Phyllida flouts me.

Thy glorious beauty's gleam dazzles my eyesight,
Like the sun's brightest beam shining at midnight.   90
O my heart! O my heels! Fie on all wenches!
Pluck up thy courage, Giles; bang him that flinches!
    Back to thy sheep again,
    Thou silly shepherd's swain;
    Thy labor is in vain!
    Phyllida flouts me.
                                        —*Anon.*

PACK, CLOUDS, AWAY

PACK, clouds, away, and welcome day,
    With night we banish sorrow;
Sweet air, blow soft; mount, lark, aloft
    To give my Love good-morrow!
Wings from the wind, to please her mind,
    Notes from the lark I'll borrow;
Bird, prune thy wing; nightingale, sing,
    To give my Love good-morrow!
    To give my Love good-morrow
    Notes from them all I'll borrow.

11 pin-cushions

Wake from thy nest, robin-redbreast,
Sing, birds, in every furrow;
And from each bill, let music shrill
Give my fair Love good-morrow!
Blackbird and thrush in every bush,
Stare, linnet, and cock-sparrow,
You pretty elves, amongst yourselves
Sing my fair Love good-morrow!
To give my Love good-morrow
Sing, birds, in every furrow!
                                    —*Thomas Heywood*

SINCE THERE'S NO HELP

SINCE there's no help, come, let us kiss and part—
Nay, I have done, you get no more of me;
And I am glad, yea, glad, with all my heart,
That thus so cleanly I myself can free.
Shake hands for ever, cancel all our vows,
And when we meet at any time again,
Be it not seen in either of our brows,
That we one jot of former love retain.
Now at the last gasp of Love's latest breath,
When, his pulse failing, Passion speechless lies,
When Faith is kneeling by his bed of death,
And Innocence is closing up his eyes—
Now, if thou wouldst, when all have given him over,
From death to life thou might'st him yet recover!
                                    —*Michael Drayton*

WILLIAM SHAKESPEARE (1564–1616)

A proper consideration of the life of the great dramatist, so closely bound up in the London theater, should accompany the study of his plays which is outside the scope of the present volume. Only a brief survey of the chief incidents in his career is, therefore, attempted here.

He was born in Stratford-on-Avon, Warwickshire, in 1564, the son of John Shakespeare, at various times described as a glover, tanner, and dealer in wool, malt, and other farm products. Of his early years we know nothing. It is guessed that he attended the free grammar school at Stratford, where he would have studied Latin grammar, and that he was withdrawn and put to work when his father, hitherto prosperous, suffered business reverses (from 1577 on). In 1582, when only eighteen years old, he married Agnes or Anne Hathaway, of the neighboring village of Shottery, a woman eight years older than himself, under conditions which have given rise to much speculation.

William and Anne, instead of being married in the usual way by thrice asking of the banns, obtained a license of the bishop—an unusual procedure resorted to when haste was desired. There is extant a bond, indemnifying the bishop against any suit that might be brought against him, and signed, not by the bridegroom's father, but by friends of the bride. From these premises, and the additional fact that a daughter, Susanna, was born to the couple in six months, some have drawn the conclusion that this was a forced marriage; but recent biographers, like Mr. J. Q. Adams, from an examination of sixteenth century marriage customs, have argued that no stain necessarily rests on the couple. Less than two years after their first child the twins, Hamnet and Judith, were born. Shakespeare was not yet twenty-one, and he had a family to support. No further motive is needed to explain his departure from Stratford for the greater opportunities of the metropolis, yet there is a piquant interest in the tradition, recorded about a century later, that the youth had to flee the town because he was caught poaching on the preserves of Sir Thomas Lucy, a gentleman with an estate in the vicinity.

We do not know what work Shakespeare did on his coming up to London. Tradition has it that his first money was made holding horses for gentlemen who had ridden to the theater. Whatever his start, he got attached to theatrical companies, and by 1592 was well known as both actor and playwright. His work thereafter for twenty years is one of the greatest glories of English drama and English poetry. He wrote thirty-seven plays (and perhaps collaborated in others), which remain the highest achievement of the English stage; two long narrative poems, *Venus and Adonis* and *The Rape of Lucrece*, published, with dedications to the Earl of Southampton, in 1593 and 1594; and 154 sonnets, circulated by the poet in manuscript, and printed in 1609 apparently without his authorization, by "T. T.," identified as a disreputable publisher, Thomas Thorpe.

The years of Shakespeare's poetic and dramatic composition were years of growing prosperity. He invested in real estate in London; bought (in 1597) New Place, the largest and handsomest mansion in his native town; and made other shrewd business deals, the most lucrative being his purchase in 1605 of the lease of a portion of the tithes, or tax-collections, of Stratford. The source of the funds for these investments should be no mystery. Shakespeare was enjoying an excellent income in his triple capacity as actor, playwright, and especially as one of the owners of the theaters (those in which the Burbages, father and son, were the most active spirits) with which he had finally cast his lot. An interesting venture of these years was his application to the Heralds' College, in the name of his father, for a coat-of-arms. The application, first made and apparently rejected on a technicality in 1596, was renewed and granted in 1599. Henceforth Shakespeare and his family were entitled to the appellation of "gentlemen."

In 1611 or 1612 Shakespeare seems to have retired from London and from the profession of playwriting, which he had pursued with such brilliant artistic and pecuniary success for twenty years, and for the rest of his life resided at New Place in Stratford, where he died on April 23, 1616. He is buried in the church at Stratford, beneath a flagstone that bears the inscription:

"Good frend for Iesus sake forbeare,
To digg the dvst encloased heare:
Bleste be ye man yt spares thes stones,
And cvrst be he yt moves my bones."

Shakespeare had a genial nature that inspired affection among his associates; "sweet" and "gentle" are terms often applied to him. He loved wit and good fellowship, and had some convivial tastes. The traditional conception of a poet, his "eye in a fine frenzy rolling," glancing "from heaven to earth, from earth to heaven," and utterly unable to adjust himself to the practical world, must be completely reversed in the case of Shakespeare. His capacity for friendship, his acquisition of wealth, the satisfaction with which he rose in social prestige, and his desire, as shown in his will, to be the founder of a landed family, all show the possession in a high degree of the ability to get along with people, and a conformity to the ideals of the society in which he lived. No better illustration can be found of the sanity of true genius.

If Shakespeare had written only his narrative and lyric poems, his position would have been an important one in English letters. The *Venus and Adonis* and the *Rape of Lucrece* are specimens of the voluptuous, gorgeously ornamented Renaissance love poetry, of which Marlowe's *Hero and Leander* is an even more conspicuous example. Shakespeare's songs, of which the best are here given, occur in his various plays. They are Elizabethan, and yet timeless; they have spontaneity, grace, singing quality, and variety (although the deeper notes are seldom touched). The sonnets are among the greatest in English. Rejecting the difficult Petrarchan interlacing, Shakespeare followed the more natural English form of three quatrains with alternating rhymes and a concluding couplet, and adapted his music to this scheme, the last two lines setting off the preceding twelve by way of contrast or conclusion. There are plentiful examples of the conceits which appear as well in the *Venus*, the *Lucrece*, and the earlier plays, and the several sonnets are uneven in quality, but most of them are powerful and memorable, full of the just and beautiful imagery which only a great poet could conceive. We have no idea that the order in which T. T. printed them would have been that chosen by Shakespeare, and indeed they tell no continuous story. The first hundred and twenty-six seem to be addressed to a friend of the poet, a man young, beautiful, noble, and unmarried, in all probability that Earl of Southampton who was Shakespeare's only known patron, since the "Mr. W. H." to whom T. T. dedicated his edition is probably a friend of the publisher's, not the writer's, and the reference to him as the *"begetter* of these ensuing sonnets" doubtless means procurer (or less gently stealer) rather than inspirer. The last twenty-eight sonnets tell a story of intrigue. The key sonnet in this section is No. 144, which mentions the "dark lady" who jilted the poet in favor of his fair-haired friend. Lacking intimate biographical details about Shakespeare, and confronted by the baffling impersonality of his plays, readers have endeavored to find in the sonnets the history of his emotional and spiritual life, and have even inferred that his disillusion and despair over the "dark lady" was the cause of the gloom settling over him about 1599, from the depths of which emerged the great tragedies *Hamlet, Lear, Othello,* and *Macbeth.* Others have argued that Shakespeare here, as in his plays, puts only imagined sentiments into the mouths of created characters. Wordsworth, an adherent of the first view, remarked of the sonnets, "with this key Shakespeare unlocked his heart"; to which Browning, himself a poet who could project himself into the souls of other characters and so understood the operations of the dramatist's mind, retorted, "Did he? Then the less Shakespeare he."

BIBLIOGRAPHY. Convenient one vol. eds. of Shakespeare's work: the Kittredge, ed. G. L. Kittredge (Ginn), the Cambridge, ed. W. A. Neilson (Houghton Mif-

flin), and the Oxford, ed. by Craig. Ed. of the *Sonnets* by Tucker Brooke.
Handbooks: *The Facts about Shakespeare*, by W. A. Neilson and A. H. Thorn-
dike (Macmillan), *Shakespeare of Stratford*, ed. Tucker Brooke (Yale).
Biographies: Sir Sidney Lee (Macmillan) and J. Q. Adams (Houghton Mifflin).

SONGS FROM THE PLAYS

WHEN DAISIES PIED

WHEN daisies pied and violets blue,
    And lady-smocks all silver-white,
And cuckoo-buds of yellow hue
    Do paint the meadows with delight,
The cuckoo then, on every tree,
Mocks married men; for thus sings he,
        "Cuckoo!
Cuckoo, cuckoo!"—O word of fear,
Unpleasing to a married ear!

When shepherds pipe on oaten straws,
    And merry larks are ploughmen's clocks,
When turtles [1] tread, and rooks, and daws,
    And maidens bleach their summer smocks,
The cuckoo then, on every tree,
Mocks married men; for thus sings he,
        "Cuckoo!
Cuckoo, cuckoo!"—O word of fear,
Unpleasing to a married ear!
              —*Love's Labor's Lost*

WHEN ICICLES HANG BY THE WALL

When icicles hang by the wall,
    And Dick the shepherd blows his nail,
And Tom bears logs into the hall,
    And milk comes frozen home in pail,
When blood is nipped and ways be foul,
Then nightly sings the staring owl,
"Tu-whit, tu-who!"—a merry note,
While greasy Joan doth keel [2] the pot.

When all aloud the wind doth blow,
    And coughing drowns the parson's saw,
And birds sit brooding in the snow,
    And Marian's nose looks red and raw,

1 doves   2 cool

When roasted crabs [3] hiss in the bowl,
Then nightly sings the staring owl,
"Tu-whit, tu-who!"—a merry note,
While greasy Joan doth keel the pot.
                    —*Love's Labor's Lost*

WHO IS SYLVIA?

Who is Sylvia? What is she,
    That all our swains commend her?
Holy, fair, and wise is she;
    The heaven such grace did lend her,
That she might admirèd be.

Is she kind as she is fair?
    For beauty lives with kindness.
Love doth to her eyes repair
    To help him of his blindness,
And, being helped, inhabits there.

Then to Sylvia let us sing,
    That Sylvia is excelling;
She excels each mortal thing
    Upon the dull earth dwelling.
To her let us garlands bring.
                    —*Two Gentlemen of Verona*

OVER HILL, OVER DALE

Over hill, over dale,
    Thorough bush, thorough brier,
Over park, over pale,
    Thorough flood, thorough fire,
I do wander everywhere,
Swifter than the moon's sphere;
And I serve the fairy Queen,
To dew her orbs upon the green.
The cowslips tall her pensioners [4] be;
In their gold coats spots you see;
Those be rubies, fairy favors,
In those freckles live their savors.
                    —*A Midsummer Night's Dream*

TELL ME, WHERE IS FANCY BRED

Tell me, where is fancy bred,
Or in the heart, or in the head?

3 crab-apples   4 body-guard of gentlemen

How begot, how nourishèd?
Reply, reply.
It is engendered in the eyes,
With gazing fed; and fancy dies
In the cradle where it lies.
Let us all ring fancy's knell;
I'll begin it—Ding, dong, bell.
Ding, dong, bell.
—*Merchant of Venice*

SIGH NO MORE

Sigh no more, ladies, sigh no more!
Men were deceivers ever,
One foot in sea and one on shore,
To one thing constant never.
Then sigh not so, but let them go,
And be you blithe and bonny,
Converting all your sounds of woe
Into Hey nonny, nonny!

Sing no more ditties, sing no moe
Of dumps so dull and heavy!
The fraud of men was ever so,
Since summer first was leafy.
Then sigh not so, but let them go,
And be you blithe and bonny,
Converting all your sounds of woe
Into Hey nonny, nonny!
—*Much Ado About Nothing*

UNDER THE GREENWOOD TREE

Under the greenwood tree
Who loves to lie with me,
And turn his merry note
Unto the sweet bird's throat,
Come hither, come hither, come hither!
Here shall he see
No enemy
But winter and rough weather.

Who doth ambition shun
And loves to live i' the sun,
Seeking the food he eats
And pleased with what he gets,

Come hither, come hither, come hither!
Here shall he see
No enemy
But winter and rough weather.
—*As You Like It*

Blow, Blow, Thou Winter Wind

Blow, blow, thou winter wind!
Thou art not so unkind
As man's ingratitude;
Thy tooth is not so keen,
Because thou art not seen,
Although thy breath be rude.

Heigh ho! sing, heigh ho! unto the green holly.
Most friendship is feigning, most loving mere folly.
Then, heigh ho, the holly!
This life is most jolly.

Freeze, freeze, thou bitter sky,
That dost not bite so nigh
As benefits forgot;
Though thou the waters warp,
Thy sting is not so sharp
As friend remembered not.

Heigh ho! sing, heigh ho! *etc.*
—*As You Like It*

It Was a Lover and His Lass

It was a lover and his lass,
With a hey, and a ho, and a hey nonino,
That o'er the green corn-field did pass
In the spring time, the only pretty ring time,
When birds do sing, hey ding a ding, ding;
Sweet lovers love the spring.

Between the acres of the rye,
With a hey, and a ho, and a hey nonino,
These pretty country folks would lie,
In spring time, &c.

This carol they began that hour,
With a hey, and a ho, and a hey nonino,

How that a life was but a flower
    In spring time, &c.

And therefore take the present time,
    With a hey, and a ho, and a hey nonino;
For love is crowned with the prime
    In spring time, &c.

—As You Like It

O MISTRESS MINE

O Mistress mine, where are you roaming?
O, stay and hear; your true love's coming,
    That can sing both high and low.
Trip no further, pretty sweeting;
Journeys end in lovers meeting,
    Every wise man's son doth know.

What is love? 't is not hereafter.
Present mirth hath present laughter;
    What's to come is still unsure.
In delay there lies no plenty;
Then come kiss me, sweet and twenty,
    Youth's a stuff will not endure.

—Twelfth Night

COME AWAY, COME AWAY, DEATH

Come away, come away, death,
    And in sad cypress let me be laid.
Fly away, fly away, breath;
    I am slain by a fair cruel maid.
My shroud of white, stuck all with yew,
    O, prepare it!
My part of death, no one so true
    Did share it.

Not a flower, not a flower sweet,
    On my black coffin let there be strown.
Not a friend, not a friend greet
    My poor corpse, where my bones shall be thrown.
A thousand thousand sighs to save,
    Lay me, O, where
Sad true lover never find my grave,
    To weep there!

—Twelfth Night

Take, O, Take Those Lips Away

Take, O, take those lips away,
    That so sweetly were forsworn;
And those eyes, the break of day,
    Lights that do mislead the morn;
But my kisses bring again, bring again;
Seals of love, but sealed in vain, sealed in vain.

—Measure for Measure

Hark, Hark! the Lark

Hark, hark! the lark at heaven's gate sings,
    And Phœbus 'gins arise,
His steeds to water at those springs
    On chaliced flowers that lies;
And winking Mary-buds begin
    To ope their golden eyes;
With every thing that pretty is,
    My lady sweet, arise!
        Arise, arise!

—Cymbeline

Fear no More the Heat o' the Sun

Fear no more the heat o' the sun,
    Nor the furious winter's rages;
Thou thy worldly task hast done,
    Home art gone, and ta'en thy wages.
Golden lads and girls all must,
As chimney-sweepers, come to dust.

Fear no more the frown o' the great;
    Thou art past the tyrant's stroke.
Care no more to clothe and eat;
    To thee the reed is as the oak.
The scepter, learning, physic, must
All follow this, and come to dust.

Fear no more the lightning-flash,
    Nor the all-dreaded thunder-stone;
Fear not slander, censure rash;
    Thou hast finished joy and moan.
All lovers young, all lovers must
Consign to thee, and come to dust.

No exorciser harm thee!
  Nor no witchcraft charm thee!
Ghost unlaid forbear thee!
  Nothing ill come near thee!
Quiet consummation have,
And renownèd be thy grave!

—Cymbeline

Lawn as White as Driven Snow

Lawn as white as driven snow;
Cypress black as e'er was crow;
Gloves as sweet as damask roses;
Masks for faces and for noses;
Bugle bracelet, necklace amber,
Perfume for a lady's chamber;
Golden quoifs and stomachers
For my lads to give their dears;
Pins and poking-sticks of steel;
What maids lack from head to heel.
Come buy of me, come; come buy, come buy;
Buy, lads, or else your lasses cry.
Come buy.

—Winter's Tale

Come Unto These Yellow Sands

Come unto these yellow sands,
  And then take hands.
Curtsied when you have, and kissed
  The wild waves whist,
Foot it featly here and there,
And, sweet sprites, the burden bear.
    Hark, hark!
      Bow-wow.
The watch-dogs bark!
      Bow-wow.
Hark, hark! I hear
The strain of strutting chanticleer
Cry, "Cock-a-diddle-dow."

—The Tempest

Full Fathom Five Thy Father Lies

Full fathom five thy father lies;
  Of his bones are coral made;

Those are pearls that were his eyes;
Nothing of him that doth fade
But doth suffer a sea-change
Into something rich and strange.
Sea-nymphs hourly ring his knell;
          Ding-dong!
Hark! now I hear them,—ding-dong, bell.
                    —*The Tempest*

WHERE THE BEE SUCKS

Where the bee sucks, there suck I.
In a cowslip's bell I lie;
There I couch when owls do cry.
On the bat's back I do fly
After summer merrily.
Merrily, merrily shall I live now
Under the blossom that hangs on the bough.
                    —*The Tempest*

SONNETS

TO THE ONLY BEGETTER OF
THESE INSUING SONNETS
MR. W. H. ALL HAPPINESSE
AND THAT ETERNITIE
PROMISED
BY
OUR EVER-LIVING POET
WISHETH
THE WELL-WISHING
ADVENTURER IN
SETTING
FORTH
T. T.

2

When forty winters shall besiege thy brow,
And dig deep trenches in thy beauty's field,
Thy youth's proud livery, so gazed on now,
Will be a tattered weed, of small worth held.
Then being asked where all thy beauty lies,
Where all the treasure of thy lusty days,
To say, within thine own deep-sunken eyes,
Were an all-eating shame and thriftless praise.

How much more praise deserved thy beauty's use
If thou couldst answer, "This fair child of mine
Shall sum my count and make my old excuse,"
Proving his beauty by succession thine!
　　This were to be new made when thou art old,
　　And see thy blood warm when thou feel'st it cold.

12

When I do count the clock that tells the time,
And see the brave day sunk in hideous night;
When I behold the violet past prime,
And sable curls all silvered o'er with white;
When lofty trees I see barren of leaves
Which erst from heat did canopy the herd,
And summer's green all girded up in sheaves
Borne on the bier with white and bristly beard;
Then of thy beauty do I question make,
That thou among the wastes of time must go,
Since sweets and beauties do themselves forsake
And die as fast as they see others grow;
　　And nothing 'gainst Time's scythe can make defence
　　Save breed, to brave him when he takes thee hence.

15

When I consider everything that grows
Holds in perfection but a little moment,
That this huge stage presenteth nought but shows
Whereon the stars in secret influence comment;
When I perceive that men as plants increase,
Cheered and checked even by the self-same sky;
Vaunt in their youthful sap, at height decrease,
And wear their brave state out of memory;
Then the conceit [5] of this inconstant stay
Sets you most rich in youth before my sight,
Where wasteful Time debateth with Decay,
To change your day of youth to sullied night;
　　And all in war with Time for love of you,
　　As he takes from you, I engraft you new.

17

Who will believe my verse in time to come,
If it were filled with your most high deserts?

5 thought

Though yet, heaven knows, it is but as a tomb
Which hides your life and shows not half your parts.
If I could write the beauty of your eyes
And in fresh numbers number all your graces,
The age to come would say, "This poet lies;
Such heavenly touches ne'er touched earthly faces."
So should my papers, yellowed with their age,
Be scorned like old men of less truth than tongue,
And your true rights be termed a poet's rage
And stretchèd meter of an antique song:
    But were some child of yours alive that time,
    You should live twice, in it and in my rhyme.

18

Shall I compare thee to a summer's day?
Thou art more lovely and more temperate:
Rough winds do shake the darling buds of May,
And summer's lease hath all too short a date;
Sometime too hot the eye of heaven shines,
And often is his gold complexion dimmed;
And every fair from fair sometime declines,
By chance or nature's changing course untrimmed:
But thy eternal summer shall not fade
Nor lose possession of that fair thou ow'st;
Nor shall Death brag thou wand'rest in his shade,
When in eternal lines to time thou grow'st;
    So long as men can breathe or eyes can see,
    So long lives this and this gives life to thee.

22

My glass shall not persuade me I am old,
So long as youth and thou are of one date;
But when in thee time's furrows I behold,
Then look I death my days should expiate.
For all that beauty that doth cover thee
Is but the seemly raiment of my heart,
Which in thy breast doth live, as thine in me:
How can I then be elder than thou art?
O, therefore, love, be of thyself so wary
As I, not for myself, but for thee will;
Bearing thy heart, which I will keep so chary
As tender nurse her babe from faring ill.
    Presume not on thy heart when mine is slain;
    Thou gav'st me thine, not to give back again.

23

As an unperfect actor on the stage
Who with his fear is put beside his part,
Or some fierce thing replete with too much rage,
Whose strength's abundance weakens his own heart,
So I, for fear of trust, forget to say
The perfect ceremony of love's rite,
And in mine own love's strength seem to decay,
O'ercharged with burden of mine own love's might.
O, let my books be then the eloquence
And dumb presagers of my speaking breast,
Who plead for love and look for recompense
More than that tongue that more hath more expressed.
    O, learn to read what silent love hath writ:
    To hear with eyes belongs to love's fine wit.

25

Let those who are in favor with their stars
Of public honor and proud titles boast,
Whilst I, whom fortune of such triumph bars,
Unlooked for joy in that I honor most.
Great princes' favorites their fair leaves spread
But as the marigold at the sun's eye,
And in themselves their pride lies burièd,
For at a frown they in their glory die.
The painful warrior famousèd for fight,
After a thousand victories once foiled,
Is from the book of honor razèd quite,
And all the rest forgot for which he toiled.
    Then happy I, that love and am beloved
    Where I may not remove nor be removed.

29

When, in disgrace with Fortune and men's eyes,
I all alone beweep my outcast state,
And trouble deaf heaven with my bootless cries,
And look upon myself and curse my fate,
Wishing me like to one more rich in hope,
Featured like him, like him with friends possessed,
Desiring this man's art, and that man's scope,
With what I most enjoy contented least;
Yet in these thoughts myself almost despising,
Haply I think on thee; and then my state,

Like to the lark at break of day arising
From sullen earth, sings hymns at heaven's gate;
  For thy sweet love remembered such wealth brings
  That then I scorn to change my state with kings.

30

When to the sessions of sweet silent thought
I summon up remembrance of things past,
I sigh the lack of many a thing I sought,
And with old woes new wail my dear time's waste;
Then can I drown an eye, unused to flow,
For precious friends hid in death's dateless night,
And weep afresh love's long since canceled woe,
And moan the expense of many a vanished sight:
Then can I grieve at grievances foregone,
And heavily from woe to woe tell [6] o'er
The sad account of fore-bemoanèd moan,
Which I new pay as if not paid before.
  But if the while I think on thee, dear friend,
  All losses are restored and sorrows end.

32

If thou survive my well-contented day,
When that churl Death my bones with dust shall cover,
And shalt by fortune once more re-survey
These poor rude lines of thy deceasèd lover,
Compare them with the bett'ring of the time,
And though they be outstripped by every pen,
Reserve them for my love, not for their rhyme,
Exceeded by the height of happier men.
O, then vouchsafe me but this loving thought:
"Had my friend's Muse grown with this growing age,
A dearer birth than this his love had brought,
To march in ranks of better equipage;
  But since he died and poets better prove,
  Theirs for their style I'll read, his for his love."

33

Full many a glorious morning have I seen
Flatter the mountain tops with sovereign eye,
Kissing with golden face the meadows green,
Gilding pale streams with heavenly alchemy;

6 count

Or what strong hand can hold his swift foot back?
Or who his spoil of beauty can forbid?
   O, none, unless this miracle have might,
   That in black ink my love may still shine bright.

71

No longer mourn for me when I am dead
Than you shall hear the surly sullen bell
Give warning to the world that I am fled
From this vile world, with vilest worms to dwell.
Nay, if you read this line, remember not
The hand that writ it; for I love you so
That I in your sweet thoughts would be forgot
If thinking on me then should make you woe.
O, if, I say, you look upon this verse
When I perhaps compounded am with clay,
Do not so much as my poor name rehearse,
But let your love even with my life decay,
   Lest the wise world should look into your moan
   And mock you with me after I am gone.

73

That time of year thou mayst in me behold
When yellow leaves, or none, or few, do hang
Upon those boughs which shake against the cold,
Bare ruined choirs where late the sweet birds sang.
In me thou see'st the twilight of such day
As after sunset fadeth in the west,
Which by and by black night doth take away,
Death's second self, that seals up all in rest.
In me thou see'st the glowing of such fire
That on the ashes of his youth doth lie,
As the death-bed whereon it must expire,
Consumed with that which it was nourished by.
   This thou perceiv'st, which makes thy love more strong,
   To love that well which thou must leave ere long.

78

So oft have I invoked thee for my Muse
And found such fair assistance in my verse
As every alien pen hath got my use
And under thee their poesy disperse.
Thine eyes, that taught the dumb on high to sing,

And heavy ignorance aloft to fly,
Have added feathers to the learned's wing
And given grace a double majesty.
Yet be most proud of that which I compile,
Whose influence is thine and born of thee:
In others' works thou dost but mend the style,
And arts with thy sweet graces graced be;
   But thou art all my art and dost advance
   As high as learning my rude ignorance.

79

Whilst I alone did call upon thy aid,
My verse alone had all thy gentle grace,
But now my gracious numbers are decayed
And my sick Muse doth give another place.
I grant, sweet love, thy lovely argument
Deserves the travail of a worthier pen,
Yet what of thee thy poet doth invent
He robs thee of and pays it thee again.
He lends thee virtue and he stole that word
From thy behavior; beauty doth he give
And found it in thy cheek; he can afford
No praise to thee but what in thee doth live.
   Then thank him not for that which he doth say,
   Since what he owes thee thou thyself dost pay.

85

My tongue-tied Muse in manners holds her still,
While comments of your praise, richly compiled,
Reserve their character with golden quill
And precious phrase by all the Muses filed.
I think good thoughts whilst other write good words,
And like unlettered clerk still cry "Amen"
To every hymn that able spirit affords
In polished form of well-refinèd pen.
Hearing you praised, I say, " 'Tis so, 'tis true,"
And to the most of praise add something more;
But that is in my thought, whose love to you,
Though words come hindmost, holds his rank before.
   Then others for the breath of words respect,
   Me for my dumb thoughts, speaking in effect.

Then, in the blazon of sweet beauty's best,
Of hand, of foot, of lip, of eye, of brow,
I see their antique pen would have expressed
Even such a beauty as you master now.
So all their praises are but prophecies
Of this our time, all you prefiguring;
And, for they looked but with divining eyes,
They had not skill enough your worth to sing:
    For we, which now behold these present days,
    Have eyes to wonder, but lack tongues to praise.

107

Not mine own fears, nor the prophetic soul
Of the wide world, dreaming on things to come,
Can yet the lease of my true love control,
Supposed as forfeit to a confined doom.
The mortal moon hath her eclipse endured,
And the sad augurs mock their own presage;
Incertainties now crown themselves assured,
And peace proclaims olives of endless age.
Now with the drops of this most balmy time
My love looks fresh, and Death to me subscribes,
Since, spite of him, I'll live in this poor rhyme,
While he insults o'er dull and speechless tribes:
    And thou in this shalt find thy monument
    When tyrants' crests and tombs of brass are spent.

109

O, never say that I was false of heart,
Though absence seemed my flame to qualify.
As easy might I from myself depart
As from my soul, which in thy breast doth lie.
That is my home of love; if I have ranged,
Like him that travels I return again,
Just to the time, not with the time exchanged,
So that myself bring water for my stain.
Never believe, though in my nature reigned
All frailties that besiege all kinds of blood,
That it could so preposterously be stained,
To leave for nothing all thy sum of good;
    For nothing this wide universe I call,
    Save thou, my rose; in it thou art my all.

land, not published till 1662, a book containing unsystematic but delightful biographical and antiquarian material.

In 1602 Shakespeare wrote his *Hamlet;* in 1642 the Puritans, at last in the saddle, passed an act of Parliament which closed the theaters—formally at least—for eighteen years. The first of the four intervening decades saw the greatest work of the Elizabethan-Jacobean drama: all the later plays of Shakespeare, the masterpieces of Ben Jonson (*Volpone, The Alchemist*), the later work of Thomas Dekker (his *Shoemakers' Holiday* had already been produced in 1599), the greatest play of Thomas Heywood, the fine domestic tragedy *A Woman Killed with Kindness,* and the earlier work of Beaumont and Fletcher (*Knight of the Burning Pestle, Philaster, A Maid's Tragedy*). In the subsequent three decades the drama seems less inspired; some would trace through these years a gradual decay. The drama appealed less to the whole people, more to the court classes; it showed less consistent character portrayal; it stressed sexual themes; it became highly sensational in treatment. These changes are already actively under way in the plays of Beaumont and Fletcher, and proceed apace in John Webster's *Duchess of Malfi,* powerful, somber, and morbid, in John Ford's *'Tis Pity She's a Whore* and *The Broken Heart,* finely poetical, but abnormal and strained; while the work of Philip Massinger (*A New Way to Pay Old Debts*), and of James Shirley, writing mostly in the 1630's, though displaying an able craftsmanship, present nothing that is new. The great dramatic literature, therefore, of the Elizabethan and Stuart epochs, shows a rise, a magnificent climacteric achievement, and a decline.

In 1660, the English nation, sick of civil strife and disgusted with Puritanism, welcomed back the "merry monarch," Charles II. Common-sense replaced fanaticism; wit, grim earnestness; an acceptance of the world as it was, the search for impossible ideals. The new code may be seen amusingly displayed in the *Diary* of Samuel Pepys, written between 1660 and 1669. In these same years Milton, blind, solitary, and unreconciled, wrote the belated epic of Puritanism, *Paradise Lost,* and John Bunyan, for his persistence in preaching the dissenting faith, was spending his time in Bedford jail, from which there later emerged the final statement of the Puritan spirit in his immortal prose allegory, *Pilgrim's Progress* (pub. 1678). But the dominant temper is to be seen rather in the ridicule of the Puritan in Butler's *Hudibras* (1663, 1664); and in the satires of Dryden and others. The drama, responding to the taste of the time, produced the artificial "heroic" plays and at least one enduring tragedy transcending them, the *Venice Preserved* of Thomas Otway (1682). Even more symptomatic were witty but nasty comedies of manners, like those of Etherege and Wycherley, rising to the finer achievement of Congreve (*The Way of the World,* 1700). The literary giant of these years was John Dryden, who excelled in all the kinds of literature which the time approved—comedy, heroic play, satire, prose criticism. French and classic principles prevailed; men distrusted enthusiasm and romantic license, and tried more and more to accept the rule of reason for their guide. Such a temper was favorable to the advance of science and of abstract thought, and the Restoration saw the establishment of the Royal Society (for scientific investigation), and produced a Newton (*Principia,* 1687), and a Locke (*Essay concerning the Human Understanding,* 1690). The contrast of Puritan and Restoration ways is to be observed in two revolutions. The violent and bloody acts of the Puritans had been ineffective and transitory; it was the swift and (to give an example) being variously translated *apparel, raiment, clothing, garments,* etc., whichever fitted best in the sentence at hand. In the examples quoted above it is to be noted that the language of the Authorized Version is pleasantly archaic—archaic, indeed, even for its own time—following as it did translations and traditional interpretations of an elder day. A few years later, in a period of rapidly changing standards, the language would have been much more modern in tone and structure, and the flavor of another world, which undeniably lends charm to Biblical style, would have gone as "the wind passeth."

In all the respects mentioned above the King James Bible has profoundly affected our literature. Therefore, writes Professor Gardiner, "certainly an intimate acquaintance with the English Bible is the best possible preparation for a study of English literature, or for the matter of that, of any literature." One might add, without much fear of contradiction, for the writing, likewise, of English poetry and prose.

The selections below aim to indicate something of the variety of the work in both Old and New Testaments. A highly composite collection of books by various writers, many of them unknown, ranging in time from fragments older than a millennium before Christ down to the second century A. D., the Bible contains the most diverse material: for example, folk-lore, narrative and chronicle, the "law" or ethical and moral codes, prophecy rising at times to impassioned rhapsody, proverbs and collections of gnomic wisdom, poetry including hymns, philosophic drama, and in the New Testament pastoral letters. Most of these literary forms are represented in the selections. The artificial division into verses has been discarded, the punctuation modernized, and the literature arranged as it would be today. The titles prefixed are the editor's.

BIBLIOGRAPHY. A few of the numerous books on the Bible as literature: A. S. Cook, *The Bible and English Prose Style* (Heath), also "The Authorized Version and Its Influence" in *Camb. Hist. of Eng. Lit.,* Vol. IV. (Putnam, Macmillan); R. G. Moulton, *The Literary Study of the Bible* (Heath); J. H. Gardiner, *The Bible as English Literature* (Scribners); Laura H. Wild, *A Literary Guide to the Bible,* also *The Romance of the English Bible* (Doubleday Doran). For reading, Moulton's *Modern Reader's Bible* (Macmillan); and E. S. Bates, *The Bible Designed to be Read as Living Literature* (Simon and Schuster).

RUTH

The Book of Ruth has been called a pastoral idyl. To many generations of readers has appealed the quiet charm of this skilfully told, albeit somewhat saccharine tale, in which long suffering is turned to joy, in which virtue is rewarded, and all turns out well. *Ruth* may also be regarded as a protest against the Jewish policy, following the return from the exile, of forbidding racial intermarriage, since the writer shows that great King David was descended from such a union. The background of the story is the system of levirate marriage, by which a surviving brother (or nearest male relative) married a widow, the son of the union inheriting the name and estates of the dead (*Deut.* xxv). Ruth gleaned "after the reapers" according to a Jewish custom by which a part of the harvest was left to the poor (*Levit.* xix, 9).

And see the reward of the wicked.
Because thou hast made the Lord, which is my refuge, 90
Even the Most High, thy habitation;
There shall no evil befall thee,
Neither shall any plague come nigh thy dwelling.
For He shall give His angels charge over thee,
To keep thee in all thy ways.
They shall bear thee up in their hands,
Lest thou dash thy foot against a stone.
Thou shalt tread upon the lion and adder;
The young lion and the serpent shalt thou trample under feet.
"Because he hath set his love upon Me, therefore will I deliver
    him: 100
I will set him on high, because he hath known My name.
He shall call upon Me, and I will answer him.
I will be with him in trouble;
I will deliver him, and honor him.
With long life will I satisfy him,
And show him My salvation."

THE VOICE OUT OF THE WHIRLWIND
ANSWERS JOB

(*Job*, xxxviii–xlii)

The Book of *Job* is a philosophical drama or series of dramatic monologues debating the problems of sin and suffering. There is a prologue, in which Satan is allowed by God to afflict Job with adversities and disease, and an epilogue, in which Job is restored to prosperity and health. In the intervening sections, Job's three friends, Eliphaz the Temanite, Bildad the Shuhite, and Zophar the Naamathite, debate with him, and a young man, Elihu (perhaps a later interpolation) joins in the argument. In the magnificent concluding chapters God answers Job out of the whirlwind.

THE VOICE OUT OF THE WHIRLWIND. Who is this that darkeneth counsel
By words without knowledge?
Gird up now thy loins like a man;
For I will demand of thee, and answer thou me.
Where wast thou when I laid the foundations of the earth?
Declare, if thou hast understanding.
Who hath laid the measures thereof, if thou knowest?
Or who hath stretched the line upon it?
Whereupon are the foundations thereof fastened?
Or who laid the corner-stone thereof; 10
When the morning stars sang together,
And all the sons of God shouted for joy?
Or who shut up the sea with doors, when it brake forth,

He taketh it with his eyes;   180
His nose pierceth through snares.

Canst thou draw out leviathan [18] with an hook?
Or his tongue with a cord which thou lettest down?
Canst thou put an hook into his nose?
Or bore his jaw through with a thorn?
Will he make many supplications unto thee?
Will he speak soft words unto thee?
Will he make a covenant with thee?
Wilt thou take him for a servant for ever?
Wilt thou play with him as with a bird?   190
Or wilt thou bind him for thy maidens?
Shall the companions make a banquet of him?
Shall they part him among the merchants?
Canst thou fill his skin with barbed irons?
Or his head with fish spears?
Lay thine hand upon him,
Remember the battle, do no more.
Behold, the hope of him is in vain:
Shall not one be cast down even at the sight of him?
None is so fierce that dare stir him up: 200
Who then is able to stand before me?
Who hath prevented me, that I should repay him?
Whatsoever is under the whole heaven is mine.
I will not conceal his parts,
Nor his power, nor his comely proportion.
Who can discover the face of his garment?
Or who can come to him with his double bridle?
Who can open the doors of his face?
His teeth are terrible round about.
His scales are his pride,   210
Shut up together as with a close seal.
One is so near to another,
That no air can come between them.
They are joined one to another,
They stick together, that they cannot be sundered.
By his neesings [19] a light doth shine,
And his eyes are like the eyelids of the morning.
Out of his mouth go burning lamps,
And sparks of fire leap out.
Out of his nostrils goeth smoke,   220
As out of a seething pot or caldron.
His breath kindleth coals,

18 the crocodile? Formerly interpreted as *whale*
19 sneezings (blowing forth of spray?)

And a flame goeth out of his mouth.
In his neck remaineth strength,
And sorrow is turned to joy before him.
The flakes of his flesh are joined together:
They are firm in themselves; they cannot be moved.
His heart is as firm as a stone;
Yea, as hard as a piece of the nether millstone.
When he raiseth up himself, the mighty are afraid: 230
By reason of breakings they purify themselves.[20]
The sword of him that layeth at him cannot hold:
The spear, the dart, nor the habergeon.[21]
He esteemeth iron as straw,
And brass as rotten wood.
The arrow cannot make him flee;
Slingstones are turned with him into stubble.
Darts are counted as stubble;
He laugheth at the shaking of a spear.
Sharp stones are under him;   240
He spreadeth sharp pointed things upon the mire.[22]
He maketh the deep to boil like a pot:
He maketh the sea like a pot of ointment.
He maketh a path to shine after him;
One would think the deep to be hoary.
Upon earth there is not his like,
Who is made without fear.
He beholdeth all high things: [23]
He is a king over all the children of pride.

JOB. I know that thou canst do every thing,   250
And that no thought can be withholden from thee.
Who is he that hideth counsel without knowledge?
Therefore have I uttered that I understood not;
Things too wonderful for me, which I knew not.
Hear, I beseech thee, and I will speak:
I will demand of thee, and declare thou unto me.
I have heard of thee by the hearing of the ear;
But now mine eye seeth thee.
Wherefore I abhor myself,
And repent in dust and ashes.   260

20 Revised version: "by reason of consternation they are beside themselves."
21 coat of mail
22 impressions of his scales ("sharp stones") left in the mud
23 looketh above all great creatures

COMFORT YE, COMFORT YE, MY PEOPLE

(*Isaiah,* xl)

Chapters xl–lxvi of the book of *Isaiah* are not by the prophet of that
name, but by some later, unknown writer of the period of the Exile, variously
referred to by scholars as "the second Isaiah," the "Deutero-Isaiah," or "the
Isaiah of the Exile." In the ecstatic rhapsodies of this unknown poet and seer
the prophetic literature of the Old Testament soars to magnificent heights,
both in the grand doctrines developed of triumph through suffering and of
vicarious sacrifice, and in the lyric splendor of the lines.

"Comfort ye, comfort ye my people,"
  Saith your God.
"Speak ye comfortably to Jerusalem,
  And cry unto her
That her warfare is accomplished,
  That her iniquity is pardoned:
For she hath received of the Lord's hand
  Double for all her sins."

The voice of him that crieth in the wilderness,
"Prepare ye the way of the Lord,   10
Make straight in the desert a highway for our God.
Every valley shall be exalted,
And every mountain and hill shall be made low;
And the crooked shall be made straight,
And the rough places plain;
And the glory of the Lord shall be revealed,
And all flesh shall see it together:
For the mouth of the Lord hath spoken it."

The voice said, "Cry."
And he said, "What shall I cry?   20
All flesh is grass,
And all the goodliness thereof is as the flower of the field:
The grass withereth, the flower fadeth,
Because the spirit of the Lord bloweth upon it;
Surely the people is grass.
The grass withereth, the flower fadeth;
But the word of our God shall stand for ever."
O Zion, that bringest good tidings,
  Get thee up into the high mountain;
O Jerusalem, that bringest good tidings,   30

Lift up thy voice with strength;
Lift it up, be not afraid;
Say unto the cities of Judah,
"Behold your God!"
Behold, the Lord God will come with strong hand,
  And his arm shall rule for him;
Behold, his reward is with him,
  And his work before him.
He shall feed his flock like a shepherd;
He shall gather the lambs with his arm, and carry them in his
  bosom,   40
And shall gently lead those that are with young.

Who hath measured the waters in the hollow of his hand,
And meted out heaven with the span,
And comprehended the dust of the earth in a measure,
And weighed the mountains in scales, and the hills in a balance?
Who hath directed the spirit of the Lord,
Or being his counsellor hath taught him?
With whom took he counsel, and who instructed him,
And taught him in the path of judgment, and taught him knowl-
  edge,
And showed to him the way of understanding?   50
Behold, the nations are as a drop of a bucket,
And are counted as the small dust of the balance.
Behold, he taketh up the isles as a very little thing.
And Lebanon is not sufficient to burn,
Nor the beasts thereof sufficient for a burnt offering.
All nations before him are as nothing;
And they are counted to him less than nothing, and vanity.

To whom then will ye liken God?
Or what likeness will ye compare unto him?
The workman melteth a graven image,   60
And the goldsmith spreadeth it over with gold, and casteth silver
  chains.
He that is so impoverished that he hath no oblation
  Chooseth a tree that will not rot;
He seeketh unto him a cunning workman to prepare a graven
  image
  That shall not be moved.
Have ye not known? Have ye not heard?
Hath it not been told you from the beginning?
Have ye not understood from the foundations of the earth?
It is he that sitteth upon the circle of the earth,
And the inhabitants thereof are as grasshoppers;   70

it shall vanish away. For we know in part, and we prophesy in part. But when that which is perfect is come, then that which is in part shall be done away. When I was a child, I spake as a child, I understood as a child, I thought as a child; but when I became a man, I put away childish things. For now we see through a glass, darkly, but then face to face; now I know in part, but then shall I know even as also I am known. And now abideth faith, hope, and charity, these three; but the greatest of these is charity.

DEATH AND THE RESURRECTION OF THE DEAD

(*1 Corinthians*, xv)

10   MOREOVER, brethren, I declare unto you the gospel which I preached unto you, which also ye have received, and wherein ye stand; by which also ye are saved, if ye keep in memory what I preached unto you, unless ye have believed in vain. For I delivered unto you first of all that which I also received, how that Christ died for our sins according to the scriptures; and that he was buried, and that he rose again the third day according to the scriptures; and that he was seen of Cephas, then of the twelve: after that, he was seen of above five hundred brethren at once; of whom the greater part remain unto this present,
20   but some are fallen asleep. After that, he was seen of James; then of all the apostles. And last of all he was seen of me also, as of one born out of due time. For I am the least of the apostles, that am not meet to be called an apostle, because I persecuted the church of God. But by the grace of God I am what I am, and his grace which was bestowed upon me was not in vain, but I labored more abundantly than they all; yet not I, but the grace of God which was with me. Therefore whether it were I or they, so we preach, and so ye believed.

Now if Christ be preached that he rose from the dead, how
30   say some among you that there is no resurrection of the dead? But if there be no resurrection of the dead, then is Christ not risen; and if Christ be not risen, then is our preaching vain, and your faith is also vain. Yea, and we are found false witnesses of God, because we have testified of God that he raised up Christ; whom he raised not up, if so be that the dead rise not. For if the dead rise not, then is not Christ raised, and if Christ be not raised, your faith is vain; ye are yet in your sins. Then they also which are fallen asleep in Christ are perished. If in this life only we have hope in Christ, we are of all men most
40   miserable.

But now is Christ risen from the dead, and become the first fruits of them that slept. For since by man came death, by man came also the resurrection of the dead. For as in Adam all die, even so in Christ shall all be made alive. But every man in his own order: Christ the first fruits; afterwards they that are Christ's at his coming. Then cometh the end, when he shall have delivered up the kingdom to God, even the Father; when he shall have put down all rule and all authority and power. For he must reign till he hath put all enemies under his feet. The last enemy that shall be destroyed is death. For he hath put all things under his feet. But when he saith all things are put under him, it is manifest that he is excepted which did put all things under him. And when all things shall be subdued unto him, then shall the Son also himself be subject unto him that put all things under him, that God may be all in all.

Else what shall they do which are baptized for the dead, if the dead rise not at all? Why are they then baptized for the dead? And why stand we in jeopardy every hour? I protest by your rejoicing which I have in Christ Jesus our Lord, I die daily. If after the manner of men I have fought with beasts at Ephesus, what advantageth it me if the dead rise not? Let us eat and drink, for tomorrow we die. Be not deceived: evil communications corrupt good manners. Awake to righteousness, and sin not, for some have not the knowledge of God; I speak this to your shame.

But some man will say, "How are the dead raised up? And with what body do they come?" Thou fool, that which thou sowest is not quickened, except it die; and that which thou sowest, thou sowest not that body that shall be, but bare grain, it may chance of wheat, or of some other grain: but God giveth it a body as it hath pleased him, and to every seed his own body. All flesh is not the same flesh; but there is one kind of flesh of men, another flesh of beasts, another of fishes, and another of birds. There are also celestial bodies, and bodies terrestrial; but the glory of the celestial is one, and the glory of the terrestrial is another. There is one glory of the sun, and another glory of the moon, and another glory of the stars; for one star differeth from another star in glory. So also is the resurrection of the dead. It is sown in corruption; it is raised in incorruption. It is sown in dishonor; it is raised in glory. It is sown in weakness; it is raised in power. It is sown a natural body; it is raised a spiritual body. There is a natural body, and there is a spiritual body. And so it is written, the first man Adam was made a living soul; the last Adam was made a quickening spirit. Howbeit that was not first which is spiritual, but that which is natural; and afterward that which is spiritual. The first man is of the earth, earthy; the second man is the Lord from heaven. As is the earthy, such are they also that are earthy; and as is the heavenly, such are they also that are heavenly. And as we have borne the image of the earthy, we shall also bear the image of the heavenly.

Now this I say, brethren, that flesh and blood cannot inherit the kingdom of God; neither doth corruption inherit incorruption. Behold, I show you a mystery: we shall not all sleep, but we shall all be changed, in a moment, in the twinkling of an
10 eye, at the last trump; for the trumpet shall sound, and the dead shall be raised incorruptible, and we shall be changed. For this corruptible must put on incorruption, and this mortal must put on immortality. So when this corruptible shall have put on incorruption, and this mortal shall have put on immortality, then shall be brought to pass the saying that is written, "Death is swallowed up in victory." O death, where is thy sting? O grave, where is thy victory? The sting of death is sin, and the strength of sin is the law. But thanks be to God, which giveth us the victory through our Lord Jesus Christ.
20   Therefore, my beloved brethren, be ye steadfast, unmovable, always abounding in the work of the Lord, forasmuch as ye know that your labor is not in vain in the Lord.

THE NEW JERUSALEM

(Revelation, xxi, 1–14, 22–27)

The counterpart to the prophecy of the Old Testament is the Book of *Revelation* in the new. The series of grandiose visions, compact with elaborate allegory and symbolism, sweeps on to the conception of the New Jerusalem of Chapter xxi.

AND I saw a new heaven and a new earth, for the first heaven and the first earth were passed away; and there was no more sea. And I, John, saw the holy city, new Jerusalem, coming down from God out of heaven, prepared as a bride adorned for her husband. And I heard a great voice out of heaven saying, "Behold, the tabernacle of God is with men, and he will dwell with them, and they shall be his people, and God himself shall
30 be with them and be their God. And God shall wipe away all tears from their eyes; and there shall be no more death, neither sorrow, nor crying, neither shall there be any more pain: for the former things are passed away."

And he that sat upon the throne said, "Behold, I make all

things new." And he said unto me, "Write, for these words are
true and faithful." And he said unto me, "It is done. I am Alpha
and Omega, the beginning and the end. I will give unto him that
is athirst of the fountain of the water of life freely. He that
overcometh shall inherit all things; and I will be his God, and
he shall be my son. But the fearful, and unbelieving, and the
abominable, and murderers, and whoremongers, and sorcerers,
and idolaters, and all liars, shall have their part in the lake which
burneth with fire and brimstone: which is the second death."

And there came unto me one of the seven angels which had 10
the seven vials full of the seven last plagues, and talked with
me, saying, "Come hither, I will show thee the bride, the
Lamb's wife."

And he carried me away in the spirit to a great and high
mountain, and showed me that great city, the holy Jerusalem,
descending out of heaven from God, having the glory of God;
and her light was like unto a stone most precious, even like a
jasper stone, clear as crystal; and had a wall great and high, and
had twelve gates, and at the gates twelve angels, and names
written thereon which are the names of the twelve tribes of the 20
children of Israel: on the east three gates; on the north three
gates; on the south three gates; and on the west three gates.
And the wall of the city had twelve foundations, and in them
the names of the twelve apostles of the Lamb. . . .

And I saw no temple therein, for the Lord God Almighty and
the Lamb are the temple of it. And the city had no need of the
sun, neither of the moon, to shine in it; for the glory of God
did lighten it, and the Lamb is the light thereof. And the nations
of them which are saved shall walk in the light of it; and the
kings of the earth do bring their glory and honor into it. And 30
the gates of it shall not be shut at all by day, for there shall be
no night there. And they shall bring the glory and honor of the
nations into it. And there shall in no wise enter into it any
thing that defileth, neither whatsoever worketh abomination, or
maketh a lie; but they which are written in the Lamb's book
of life.

FRANCIS BACON (1561–1626)

Francis Bacon was literally born into the English ruling class. His father
was Sir Nicholas Bacon, Keeper of the Great Seal, and his uncle Lord
Burghley, Queen Elizabeth's most trusted minister. He attended Trinity
College, Cambridge, and Gray's Inn, being called to the Bar in 1582. Two
years later he entered Parliament, where he served many terms. His abilities

as a lawyer were early recognized, but his ambition to hold important posi-
tions in the state received very limited encouragement under Queen Elizabeth.
After the accession of King James, however, he rose rapidly, being made in
succession solicitor-general, attorney-general, lord keeper, and lord chancellor.
High title was also bestowed upon him. He was knighted in 1603, created
Baron Verulam in 1618, and in 1621 Viscount St. Albans. In the latter year
his public life came to an abrupt end, in a great scandal. He was tried in the
Lords on the charge of accepting gifts from suitors. He denied that these
had influenced his decisions, but admitted the fact, pleading pathetically,
"I beseech your lordships to be merciful to a broken reed." He was condemned
to pay the enormous fine of £40,000; to be imprisoned at the King's pleasure; and to be incapable henceforth of holding public office. The fine was
promptly remitted by the King, and he was released after only a few days'
imprisonment; but the third penalty stood. During the rest of his life Bacon
lived in private, devoting himself to study and writing. In his will he left
his name and memory "to men's charitable speeches, and to foreign nations,
and to the next ages."

The confidence of this statement is characteristic. As a young man he
had boldly asserted, "I have taken all knowledge to be my province." Possessed of a mind at once brilliant and far-reaching, he had planned a vast
analysis of human knowledge, and had expected by his own efforts to increase the body of such knowledge. In the intervals left from public office and
his ceaseless efforts to establish himself in high position and great fortune, he
nevertheless managed to complete portions of his grand scheme, which gave
him a distinguished place as philosopher, scientist, and man of letters. His
magnum opus was to be his *Instauratio Magna*, announced and sketched in
1620. The first part of this comprehensive work was to survey the divisions
of human knowledge. The second part, or *Novum Organum*, defined the "new
instrument" for the study of the sciences; to wit, the experimental or induc-
tive method, as superseding the deductive or syllogistic reasoning. The four
later sections of the *Instauratio* are frankly fragmentary, or else mere outlines
for the great work which Bacon had hoped to write. They were to include an
extensive natural history and a whole library of experimental science. At the
immensity of the whole scheme, which would have required many lives, one
stands aghast, while admiring the boldness that plotted it. Bacon's actual
achievements in science are slight and disappointing; yet his "new instrument"
is profound in significance, and its indirect results great. It points the way
which modern science was to go, and announces the break with the sterile
methods of antiquity. Bacon did not overrate his own achievement. He said,
"I only sound the clarion; but I enter not the battle."

All of Bacon's work which he considered of first importance he wrote in
Latin, the language of scholarship. He considered that to write in English
would be "to play the bankrupt with books." Yet his works in the vernacular
give him high rank as an English stylist; classify him, indeed, as one of the
most forceful writers who ever wielded the mother tongue. The most notable
of the English works include *The Advancement of Learning* (1605), in its
original form; *The New Atlantis* (1613), his imaginary commonwealth of
scientists; the *History of Henry VII* (1622), an important historical work;
and especially the celebrated *Essays*, appearing in successive editions, each
much enlarged over its predecessors, in 1597, 1612, and 1625 respectively. Ben
Jonson, writing of Bacon's public addresses and legal arguments, said, "No

man ever spake more pressly, more weightily, or suffered less emptiness, less idleness, in what he uttered. . . . His hearers could not cough, or look aside from him, without loss." The same qualities mark his essays. Their tremendous compression, their pointed and pregnant diction, their terse, perfectly phrased apothegms and aphorisms, are everywhere notable; while their antitheses and balanced structure, their abundant illustrations, and their apt figures of speech, show Bacon a great rhetorician. To look in them for the fluent ease and flexibility of certain later writers is to inquire too curiously.

The subject-matter of the essays is largely concerned with man in his social and public relations. From them one gets the picture of a man governing his life by reason and the practical wisdom of the world—keen, shrewd, but somewhat hard, deficient perhaps in tender emotion and in human love, his idealism tempered by the demands of the society in which he lived. The life of the man reënforces this impression. The greatest thinker of his time devoted his best energies to the acquirement of rank and wealth, lived magnificently and ostentatiously, spent great fortunes and plunged in debts as great, adapted himself to the customs of his time in accepting bribes, and seems to have made gratitude and friendship subordinate to his career, in that he prosecuted the Earl of Essex after having enjoyed his confidence and having received from him rich gifts. His defence is that he was merely doing as others of his time did; but one expects higher aims of the philosopher. The remark of Pope concerning him is often quoted: "The wisest, brightest, meanest of mankind."

There is something splendid in the manner of his dying. Desiring to experiment on the effect of cold in preserving flesh, he purchased a fowl and stuffed it with snow. The exposure incurred in this act brought on a chill from which he died (April 9, 1626). His death may be regarded as a sacrifice for the cause of science.

BIBLIOGRAPHY. *Complete Works* by Spedding, Ellis, and Heath, and *Letters and Life* by Spedding (monumental). Brief biography by R. W. Church in Eng. Men of Letters ser. The Essays in innumerable eds.

LETTER TO LORD BURGHLEY

(Written in 1592)

In this famous letter Bacon makes declaration of his aims and purposes in the pursuit of knowledge.

MY LORD—With as much confidence as mine own honest and faithful devotion unto your service and your honorable correspondence unto me and my poor estate can breed in a man, do I commend myself unto your Lordship. I wax now somewhat ancient; one-and-thirty years is a great deal of sand in the hour-glass. My health, I thank God, I find confirmed; and I do not fear that action shall impair it, because I account my ordinary course of study and meditation to be more painful than most parts of action are. I ever bare in mind (in some middle place that I could discharge) to serve her Majesty, not as a man born under Sol, that loveth honor, nor under Jupiter, that loveth business (for the contemplative planet carrieth me away wholly), but as a man born under an excellent sovereign that deserveth the dedication of all men's abilities. Besides, I do not find in myself so much self-love but that the greater parts of my thoughts are to deserve well (if I be able) of my friends, and namely of your Lordship; who, being the Atlas of this commonwealth, the honor of my house, and the second founder of my poor estate, I am tied by all duties, both of a good patriot, and of an unworthy kinsman, and of an obliged servant, to employ whatsoever I am to do you service. Again, the meanness of my estate doth somewhat move me; for though I cannot accuse myself that I am either prodigal or slothful, yet my health is not to spend, nor my course to get. Lastly, I confess that I have as vast contemplative ends as I have moderate civil ends; for I have taken all knowledge to be my province; and if I could purge it of two sorts of rovers, whereof the one with frivolous disputations, confutations, and verbosities, the other with blind experiments and auricular traditions and impostures, hath committed so many spoils, I hope I should bring in industrious observations, grounded conclusions, and profitable inventions and discoveries: the best state of that province. This, whether it be curiosity or vainglory, or nature, or (if one take it favorably) *philanthropia,* is so fixed in my mind as it cannot be removed. And I do easily see that place of any reasonable countenance doth bring commandment of more wits than a man's own; which is the thing I greatly affect. And for your Lordship, perhaps you shall not find more strength and less encounter in any other. And if your Lordship shall find now, or at any other time, that I do seek or affect any place whereunto any that is nearer unto your Lordship shall be concurrent, say then that I am a most dishonest man. And if your Lordship will not carry me on, I will not do as Anaxagoras did, who reduced himself with contemplation unto voluntary poverty, but this I will do—I will sell the inheritance I have, and purchase some lease of quick revenue, or some office of gain that shall be executed by deputy, and so give over all care of service, and become some sorry book-maker, or a true pioneer in that mine of truth which (he said) lay so deep. This which I have writ unto your Lordship is rather thoughts than words, being set down without all art, disguising, or reservation. Wherein I have done honor both to your Lordship's wisdom, in judging that that will be best believed of your Lordship which is truest, and to your Lordship's good nature, in retaining nothing from you. And even so I wish your Lordship all happiness, and to myself means and

occasions to be added to my faithful desire to do you service.
From my lodgings at Gray's Inn.

ESSAYS OR COUNSELS

CIVIL AND MORAL

1.—OF TRUTH

"WHAT is truth?" said jesting Pilate,[1] and would not stay
for an answer. Certainly there be that delight in giddiness,
and count it a bondage to fix a belief; affecting free-will in
thinking, as well as in acting. And though the sects of philosophers of that kind be gone,[2] yet there remain certain discoursing wits which are of the same veins, though there be
not so much blood in them as was in those of the ancients.
But it is not only the difficulty and labor which men take in
finding out of truth, nor again that when it is found it im-
poseth upon men's thoughts, that doth bring lies in favor; but 10
a natural though corrupt love of the lie itself. One of the later
school of the Grecians examineth the matter, and is at a stand
to think what should be in it, that men should love lies, where
neither they make for pleasure, as with poets; nor for advantage, as with the merchant; but for the lie's sake. But I
cannot tell: this same truth is a naked and open day-light,
that doth not show the masques and mummeries and triumphs
of the world half so stately and daintily as candle-lights. Truth
may perhaps come to the price of a pearl, that showeth best
by day; but it will not rise to the price of a diamond or car- 20
buncle, that showeth best in varied lights. A mixture of a lie
doth ever add pleasure. Doth any man doubt, that if there
were taken out of men's minds vain opinions, flattering hopes,
false valuations, imaginations as one would, and the like, but
it would leave the minds of a number of men poor shrunken
things, full of melancholy and indisposition, and unpleasing to
themselves? One of the fathers, in great severity, called poesy
vinum dæmonum,[3] because it filleth the imagination, and yet
it is but with the shadow of a lie. But it is not the lie that passeth
through the mind, but the lie that sinketh in and settleth in 30
it, that doth the hurt, such as we spake of before. But howso-
ever these things are thus in men's depraved judgments and
affections, yet truth, which only doth judge itself, teacheth that
the inquiry of truth, which is the love-making or wooing of
it, the knowledge of truth, which is the presence of it, and the
belief of truth, which is the enjoying of it, is the sovereign good

1 John xviii. 38   2 the skeptics   3 devil's wine

of human nature. The first creature of God in the works of the days was the light of the sense; the last was the light of reason; and his sabbath work ever since is the illumination of his Spirit. First he breathed light upon the face of the matter or chaos; then he breathed light into the face of man; and still he breatheth and inspireth light into the face of his chosen. The poet that beautified the sect [4] that was otherwise inferior to the rest, saith yet excellently well: "It is a pleasure to stand upon the shore and to see ships tossed upon the sea; a pleasure to stand in the window of a castle, and to see a battle and the adventures thereof below: but no pleasure is comparable to the standing upon the vantage ground of truth" (a hill not to be commanded, and where the air is always clear and serene), "and to see the errors, and wanderings, and mists, and tempests, in the vale below"; so always that this prospect be with pity, and not with swelling or pride. Certainly it is heaven upon earth to have a man's mind move in charity, rest in providence, and turn upon the poles of truth.

To pass from theological and philosophical truth to the truth of civil business, it will be acknowledged, even by those that practise it not, that clear and round dealing is the honor of man's nature; and that mixture of falsehood is like alloy in coin of gold and silver, which may make the metal work the better, but it embaseth it. For these winding and crooked courses are the goings of the serpent; which goeth basely upon the belly, and not upon the feet. There is no vice that doth so cover a man with shame as to be found false and perfidious. And therefore Montaigne saith prettily, when he inquired the reason why the word of the lie should be such a disgrace and such an odious charge. Saith he: "If it be well weighed, to say that a man lieth, is as much to say as that he is brave towards God and a coward towards men." For a lie faces God, and shrinks from man. Surely the wickedness of falsehood and breach of faith cannot possibly be so highly expressed, as in that it shall be the last peal to call the judgments of God upon the generations of men; it being foretold that when Christ cometh, "he shall not find faith upon the earth." [5]

5.—OF ADVERSITY

It was a high speech of Seneca (after the manner of the Stoics), "That the good things which belong to prosperity are to be wished; but the good things that belong to adversity are to be admired." *Bona rerum secundarum optabilia, adversarum mirabilia.* Certainly, if miracles be the command over nature,

4 Lucretius, one of the Epicureans   5 Luke xviii. 8

they appear most in adversity. It is yet a higher speech of his than the other (much too high for a heathen), "It is true greatness to have in one the frailty of a man, and the security of a god." *Vere magnum, habere fragilitatem hominis, securitatem dei.* This would have done better in poesy, where transcendences are more allowed. And the poets indeed have been busy with it; for it is in effect the thing which is figured in that strange fiction of the ancient poets, which seemeth not to be without mystery; nay, and to have some approach to the state of a Christian: that "Hercules, when he went to unbind Prometheus (by whom human nature is represented), sailed the length of the great ocean in an earthen pot or pitcher": lively describing Christian resolution, that saileth in the frail bark of the flesh through the waves of the world. But to speak in a mean.[6] The virtue of prosperity is temperance; the virtue of adversity is fortitude; which in morals is the more heroical virtue. Prosperity is the blessing of the Old Testament; adversity is the blessing of the New; which carrieth the greater benediction, and the clearer revelation of God's favor. Yet even in the Old Testament, if you listen to David's harp, you shall hear as many hearse-like airs as carols; and the pencil of the Holy Ghost hath labored more in describing the afflictions of Job than the felicities of Solomon. Prosperity is not without many fears and distastes; and adversity is not without comforts and hopes. We see in needleworks and embroideries, it is more pleasing to have a lively work upon a sad and solemn ground, than to have a dark and melancholy work upon a lightsome ground: judge therefore of the pleasure of the heart by the pleasure of the eye. Certainly virtue is like precious odors, most fragrant when they are incensed or crushed: for prosperity doth best discover vice, but adversity doth best discover virtue.

7.—Of Parents and Children

The joys of parents are secret, and so are their griefs and fears: they cannot utter the one, nor they will not utter the other. Children sweeten labors, but they make misfortunes more bitter: they increase the cares of life, but they mitigate the remembrance of death. The perpetuity by generation is common to beasts; but memory, merit, and noble works are proper to men. And surely a man shall see the noblest works and foundations have proceeded from childless men, which have sought to express the images of their minds, where those of their bodies have failed. So the care of posterity is most in them

6 temperately

that have no posterity. They that are the first raisers of their houses are most indulgent towards their children; beholding them as the continuance not only of their kind but of their work; and so both children and creatures.

The difference in affection of parents towards their several children is many times unequal, and sometimes unworthy, especially in the mother; as Solomon saith: "A wise son rejoiceth the father, but an ungracious son shames the mother." [7] A man shall see, where there is a house full of children, one or two
10 of the eldest respected, and the youngest made wantons; [8] but in the midst some that are as it were forgotten, who many times nevertheless prove the best. The illiberality of parents in allowance towards their children is an harmful error; makes them base; acquaints them with shifts; makes them sort with mean company; and makes them surfeit more when they come to plenty. And therefore the proof is best, when men keep their authority towards their children, but not their purse. Men have a foolish manner (both parents and schoolmasters and servants) in creating and breeding an emulation between broth-
20 ers during childhood, which many times sorteth to discord when they are men, and disturbeth families. The Italians make little difference between children and nephews or near kinsfolks; but so they be of the lump, they care not though they pass not through their own body. And, to say truth, in nature it is much a like matter; insomuch that we see a nephew sometimes resembleth an uncle or a kinsman more than his own parent, as the blood happens. Let parents choose betimes the vocations and courses they mean their children should take; for then they are most flexible; and let them not too much apply
30 themselves to the disposition of their children, as thinking they will take best to that which they have most mind to. It is true, that if the affection or aptness of the children be extraordinary, then it is good not to cross it; but generally the precept is good. *Optimum elige, suave et facile illud faciet consuetudo.* [9] Younger brothers are commonly fortunate, but seldom or never where the elder are disinherited.

8.—OF MARRIAGE AND SINGLE LIFE

He that hath wife and children hath given hostages to fortune; for they are impediments to great enterprises, either of virtue or mischief. Certainly the best works, and of greatest
40 merit for the public, have proceeded from the unmarried or childless men, which both in affection and means have mar-

---

7 Proverbs x. 1   8 spoiled children   will make it pleasant and
                       9 Choose the best; habit   easy.

ried and endowed the public. Yet it were great reason that those that have children should have greatest care of future times; unto which they know they must transmit their dearest pledges. Some there are, who though they lead a single life, yet their thoughts do end with themselves, and account future times impertinences. Nay, there are some other that account wife and children but as bills of charges. Nay more, there are some foolish rich covetous men that take a pride in having no children, because they may be thought so much the richer. For perhaps they have heard some talk, "Such an one is a great rich man," and another except to it, "Yea, but he hath a great charge of children"; as if it were an abatement to his riches. But the most ordinary cause of a single life is liberty, especially in certain self-pleasing and humorous [10] minds, which are so sensible of every restraint, as they will go near to think their girdles and garters to be bonds and shackles. Unmarried men are best friends, best masters, best servants; but not always best subjects, for they are light to run away; and almost all fugitives are of that condition. A single life doth well with churchmen; for charity will hardly water the ground where it must first fill a pool. It is indifferent for judges and magistrates; for if they be facile and corrupt, you shall have a servant five times worse than a wife. For soldiers, I find the generals commonly in their hortatives put men in mind of their wives and children; and I think the despising of marriage amongst the Turks maketh the vulgar soldier more base. Certainly wife and children are a kind of discipline of humanity; and single men, though they be many times more charitable, because their means are less exhaust, yet, on the other side, they are more cruel and hard-hearted (good to make severe inquisitors), because their tenderness is not so oft called upon. Grave natures, led by custom, and therefore constant, are commonly loving husbands; as was said of Ulysses, *Vetulam suam prætulit immortalitati.*[11] Chaste women are often proud and froward, as presuming upon the merit of their chastity. It is one of the best bonds both of chastity and obedience in the wife, if she think her husband wise; which she will never do if she find him jealous. Wives are young men's mistresses; companions for middle age; and old men's nurses. So as a man may have a quarrel [12] to marry when he will. But yet he [13] was reputed one of the wise men, that made answer to the question, when a man should marry? "A young man not yet, an elder man not at all." It is often seen that bad husbands have very good wives; whether it be that it raiseth the

10 capricious
11 He preferred his aged wife to immortality.
12 reason
13 Thales, the Greek philosopher of sixth and
seventh century B. C.

price of their husband's kindness when it comes; or that the
wives take a pride in their patience. But this never fails, if
the bad husbands were of their own choosing, against their
friends' consent; for then they will be sure to make good their
own folly.

10.—OF LOVE

The stage is more beholding to love than the life of man.
For as to the stage, love is ever matter of comedies, and now
and then of tragedies: but in life it doth much mischief; sometimes like a siren, sometimes like a fury. You may observe,
10 that amongst all the great and worthy persons (whereof the
memory remaineth, either ancient or recent), there is not one
that hath been transported to the mad degree of love; which
shows that great spirits and great business do keep out this
weak passion. You must except, nevertheless, Marcus Antonius, the half partner of the empire of Rome, and Appius
Claudius,[14] the decemvir and lawgiver: whereof the former
was indeed a voluptuous man, and inordinate; but the latter
was an austere and wise man: and therefore it seems (though
rarely) that love can find entrance not only into an open heart,
20 but also into a heart well fortified, if watch be not well kept.
It is a poor saying of Epicurus, *Satis magnum alter alteri
theatrum sumus:*[15] as if man, made for the contemplation
of heaven and all noble objects, should do nothing but kneel
before a little idol, and make himself a subject, though not of
the mouth (as beasts are), yet of the eye, which was given
him for higher purposes. It is a strange thing to note the excess of this passion, and how it braves the nature and value
of things, by this, that the speaking in a perpetual hyperbole
is comely in nothing but in love. Neither is it merely in the
30 phrase; for whereas it hath been well said that the arch-
flatterer, with whom all the petty flatterers have intelligence,
is a man's self, certainly the lover is more. For there was never
proud man thought so absurdly well of himself as the lover
doth of the person loved; and therefore it was well said, "That
it is impossible to love and to be wise." Neither doth this weakness appear to others only, and not to the party loved, but to
the loved most of all, except the love be reciproque. For it is a
true rule that love is ever rewarded either with the reciproque [16]
or with an inward and secret contempt. By how much the
40 more men ought to beware of this passion, which loseth not
only other things, but itself. As for the other losses, the poet's

14 celebrated   as   the   Virginia respectively   spectacle to each other
lovers of Cleopatra and of   15 We are a big enough   16 reciprocal

he had not the power to deny the nature. The Indians of the West have names for their particular gods, though they have no name for God: as if the heathens should have had the names Jupiter, Apollo, Mars, *etc.*, but not the word *Deus;* which shows that even those barbarous people have the notion, though they have not the latitude and extent of it. So that against atheists the very savages take part with the very subtlest philosophers. The contemplative atheist is rare: a Diagoras, a Bion, a Lucian perhaps, and some others; and yet they seem to be more than they are, for that all that impugn a re- [10] ceived religion, or superstition, are, by the adverse part, branded with the name of atheists. But the great atheists indeed are hypocrites; which are ever handling holy things, but without feeling; so as they must needs be cauterized in the end. The causes of atheism are: divisions in religion, if they be many; for any one main division addeth zeal to both sides, but many divisions introduce atheism. Another is, scandal of priests; when it is come to that which St. Bernard saith: *Non est jam dicere, ut populus, sic sacerdos, quia nec sic populus, ut sacerdos.*[37] A third is, custom of profane scoffing in holy [20] matters, which doth by little and little deface the reverence of religion. And lastly, learned times, specially with peace and prosperity; for troubles and adversities do more bow men's minds to religion. They that deny a God destroy man's nobility; for certainly man is of kin to the beasts by his body, and if he be not of kin to God by his spirit, he is a base and ignoble creature. It destroys likewise magnanimity, and the raising of human nature; for take an example of a dog, and mark what a generosity and courage he will put on when he finds himself maintained by a man, who to him is in stead of a god, or [30] *melior natura;*[38] which courage is manifestly such as that creature, without that confidence of a better nature than his own, could never attain. So man, when he resteth and assureth himself upon divine protection and favor, gathereth a force and faith which human nature in itself could not obtain. Therefore, as atheism is in all respects hateful, so in this, that it depriveth human nature of the means to exalt itself above human frailty. As it is in particular persons, so it is in nations: never was there such a state for magnanimity as Rome. Of this state hear what Cicero saith: *Quam volumus licet, patres conscripti, nos* [40] *amemus, tamen nec numero Hispanos, nec robore Gallos, nec calliditate Pœnos, nec artibus Græcos, nec denique hoc ipso hujus gentis et terræ domestico nativoque sensu Italos ipsos et*

---

37 It is not now to be said, as the people so the priest; for the people are not now like the priest (the priest being worse). 38 better nature

Latinos; sed pietate, ac religione, atque hac und sapientia, quod Deorum immortalium numine omnia regi gubernarique perspeximus, omnes gentes nationesque superavimus.[39]

23.—Of Wisdom for a Man's Self

An ant is a wise creature for itself, but it is a shrewd [40] thing in an orchard or garden. And certainly men that are great lovers of themselves waste the public. Divide with reason between self-love and society; and be so true to thyself, as thou be not false to others, specially to thy king and country. It is a poor center of a man's actions, himself. It is right
10 earth. For that only stands fast upon his own center; whereas all things that have affinity with the heavens move upon the center of another,[41] which they benefit. The referring of all to a man's self is more tolerable in a sovereign prince; because themselves are not only themselves, but their good and evil is at the peril of the public fortune. But it is a desperate evil in a servant to a prince, or a citizen in a republic. For whatsoever affairs pass such a man's hands, he crooketh them to his own ends; which must needs be often eccentric to the ends of his master or state. Therefore let princes, or states, choose
20 such servants as have not this mark; except they mean their service should be made but the accessary. That which maketh the effect more pernicious is that all proportion is lost. It were disproportion enough for the servant's good to be preferred before the master's; but yet it is a greater extreme, when a little good of the servant shall carry things against a great good of the master's. And yet that is the case of bad officers, treasurers, ambassadors, generals, and other false and corrupt servants; which set a bias upon their bowl,[42] of their own petty ends and envies, to the overthrow of their master's great and im
30 portant affairs. And for the most part, the good such servants receive is after the model of their own fortune; but the hurt they sell for that good is after the model of their master's fortune. And certainly it is the nature of extreme self-lovers, as they will set an house on fire, and it were but to roast their eggs; and yet these men many times hold credit with their masters, because their study is but to please them and profit

---

[39] We may plume ourselves as much as we please, conscript fathers, yet neither in numbers are we superior to the Spaniards, nor in bodily strength to the Gauls, nor in cunning to the Carthaginians, nor in arts to the Greeks, nor lastly to the Italians and Latins themselves in the inborn and native sense of this race and land; but by our devotion and piety, and this sole true wisdom, that we have perceived that all things are ruled and governed by the power of the immortal gods, have we surpassed all races and nations.
[40] mischievous
[41] *i. e.*, the earth, center of the universe in the Ptolemaic astronomy
[42] weight placed in a bowling ball to make it travel in a curve

themselves; and for either respect they will abandon the good
of their affairs.

Wisdom for a man's self is, in many branches thereof, a depraved thing. It is the wisdom of rats, that will be sure to
leave a house somewhat before it fall. It is the wisdom of
the fox, that thrusts out the badger, who digged and made
room for him. It is the wisdom of crocodiles, that shed tears
when they would devour. But that which is specially to be
noted is, that those which (as Cicero says of Pompey) are *sui
amantes sine rivali*,[43] are many times unfortunate. And whereas
they have all their time sacrificed to themselves, they become
in the end themselves sacrifices to the inconstancy of fortune,
whose wings they thought by their self-wisdom to have pin-
ioned.

27.—OF FRIENDSHIP

It had been hard for him that spake it to have put more
truth and untruth together in a few words, than in that
speech: "Whosoever is delighted in solitude is either a wild
beast or a god."[44] For it is most true that a natural and secret
hatred and aversation towards society, in any man, hath somewhat of the savage beast; but it is most untrue that it should
have any character at all of the divine nature; except it proceed, not out of a pleasure in solitude, but out of a love and
desire to sequester a man's self for a higher conversation: such
as is found to have been falsely and feignedly in some of the
heathen; as Epimenides the Candian, Numa the Roman, Em-
pedocles the Sicilian, and Apollonius of Tyana; and truly and
really in divers of the ancient hermits and holy fathers of the
church. But little do men perceive what solitude is, and how
far it extendeth. For a crowd is not company, and faces are
but a gallery of pictures, and talk but a tinkling cymbal, where
there is no love. The Latin adage meeteth with it a little,
Magna civitas, magna solitudo;[45] because in a great town
friends are scattered; so that there is not that fellowship, for
the most part, which is in less neighborhoods. But we may go
further and affirm most truly, that it is a mere and miserable
solitude to want true friends, without which the world is but
a wilderness; and even in this sense also of solitude, whosoever in the frame of his nature and affections is unfit for friendship, he taketh it of the beast, and not from humanity.

A principal fruit of friendship is the ease and discharge of
the fullness and swellings of the heart, which passions of all

43 lovers of themselves   44 Aristotle in his *Poli-*   45 A great city is a great
without rival   *tics*   solitude.

kinds do cause and induce. We know diseases of stoppings and suffocations are the most dangerous in the body; and it is not much otherwise in the mind; you may take sarza [46] to open the liver, steel to open the spleen, flower of sulphur for the lungs, castoreum for the brain; but no receipt openeth the heart, but a true friend, to whom you may impart griefs, joys, fears, hopes, suspicions, counsels, and whatsoever lieth upon the heart to oppress it, in a kind of civil shrift or confession.

It is a strange thing to observe how high a rate great kings and monarchs do set upon this fruit of friendship whereof we speak: so great, as they purchase it many times at the hazard of their own safety and greatness. For princes, in regard of the distance of their fortune from that of their subjects and servants, cannot gather this fruit, except (to make themselves capable thereof) they raise some persons to be as it were companions and almost equals to themselves, which many times sorteth to inconvenience. The modern languages give unto such persons the name of favorites, or *privadoes;* as if it were matter of grace, or conversation. But the Roman name attaineth the true use and cause thereof, naming them *participes curarum;* [47] for it is that which tieth the knot. And we see plainly that this hath been done, not by weak and passionate princes only, but by the wisest and most politic that ever reigned; who have oftentimes joined to themselves some of their servants, whom both themselves have called friends, and allowed others likewise to call them in the same manner, using the word which is received between private men.

L. Sylla, when he commanded Rome, raised Pompey (after surnamed the Great) to that height, that Pompey vaunted himself for Sylla's overmatch. For when he had carried the consulship for a friend of his, against the pursuit of Sylla, and that Sylla did a little resent thereat, and began to speak great, Pompey turned upon him again, and in effect bade him be quiet, "for that more men adored the sun rising than the sun setting." With Julius Cæsar, Decimus Brutus had obtained that interest, as he set him down in his testament for heir in remainder after his nephew. And this was the man that had power with him to draw him forth to his death. For when Cæsar would have discharged the senate, in regard of some ill presages, and specially a dream of Calpurnia, this man lifted him gently by the arm out of his chair, telling him he hoped he would not dismiss the senate till his wife had dreamt a better dream. And it seemeth his favor was so great, as Antonius, in a letter which is recited *verbatim* in one of Cicero's

46 sarsaparilla   47 partners in cares

Philippics, calleth him *venefica,* "witch"; as if he had enchanted Cæsar. Augustus raised Agrippa (though of mean
birth) to that height, as, when he consulted with Mæcenas
about the marriage of his daughter Julia, Mæcenas took the
liberty to tell him, "that he must either marry his daughter
to Agrippa, or take away his life; there was no third way,
he had made him so great." With Tiberius Cæsar, Sejanus had
ascended to that height, as they two were termed and reckoned as a pair of friends. Tiberius in a letter to him saith, *Hæc
pro amicitiâ nostrâ non occultavi,*[48] and the whole senate dedi- 10
cated an altar to Friendship, as to a goddess, in respect of the
great dearness of friendship between them two. The like or
more was between Septimius Severus and Plautianus. For he
forced his eldest son to marry the daughter of Plautianus; and
would often maintain Plautianus in doing affronts to his son;
and did write also in a letter to the senate by these words: "I
love the man so well, as I wish he may over-live me." Now
if these princes had been as a Trajan, or a Marcus Aurelius,
a man might have thought that this had proceeded of an
abundant goodness of nature; but being men so wise, of 20
such strength and severity of mind, and so extreme lovers of
themselves, as all these were, it proveth most plainly that they
found their own felicity (though as great as ever happened
to mortal men) but as an half piece, except they might have a
friend to make it entire: and yet, which is more, they were
princes that had wives, sons, nephews; and yet all these could
not supply the comfort of friendship.
It is not to be forgotten, what Comineus observeth of his
first master, Duke Charles the Hardy; namely, that he would
communicate his secrets with none; and least of all, those se- 30
crets which troubled him most. Whereupon he goeth on and
saith, that towards his latter time "that closeness did impair
and a little perish his understanding." Surely Comineus might
have made the same judgment also, if it had pleased him, of
his second master, Lewis the Eleventh, whose closeness was
indeed his tormentor. The parable of Pythagoras is dark, but
true; *Cor ne edito,* "Eat not the heart." Certainly, if a man
would give it a hard phrase, those that want friends to open
themselves unto are cannibals of their own hearts. But one
thing is most admirable (wherewith I will conclude this first 40
fruit of friendship), which is, that this communicating of a
man's self to his friend works two contrary effects; for it re-
doubleth joys, and cutteth griefs in halves. For there is no man
that imparteth his joys to his friend, but he joyeth the more;
and no man that imparteth his griefs to his friend, but he

[48] On account of our friendship I have not concealed these things from you.

grieveth the less. So that it is in truth of operation upon a man's mind, of like virtue as the alchemists use to attribute to their stone for man's body; that it worketh all contrary effects, but still to the good and benefit of nature. But yet, without praying in aid [49] of alchemists, there is a manifest image of this in the ordinary course of nature. For in bodies, union strengtheneth and cherisheth any natural action; and, on the other side, weakeneth and dulleth any violent impression; and even so is it of minds.

10 The second fruit of friendship is healthful and sovereign for the understanding, as the first is for the affections. For friendship maketh indeed a fair day in the affections, from storm and tempests; but it maketh daylight in the understanding, out of darkness and confusion of thoughts. Neither is this to be understood only of faithful counsel, which a man receiveth from his friend; but before you come to that, certain it is that whosoever hath his mind fraught with many thoughts, his wits and understanding do clarify and break up, in the communicating and discoursing with another: he tosseth his 20 thoughts more easily; he marshaleth them more orderly; he seeth how they look when they are turned into words; finally, he waxeth wiser than himself; and that more by an hour's discourse than by a day's meditation. It was well said by Themistocles to the king of Persia, "that speech was like cloth of Arras, opened and put abroad; whereby the imagery doth appear in figure; whereas in thoughts they lie but as in packs." [50] Neither is the second fruit of friendship, in opening the understanding, restrained only to such friends as are able to give a man counsel: (they indeed are best); but even with- 30 out that, a man learneth of himself, and bringeth his own thoughts to light, and whetteth his wits as against a stone, which itself cuts not. In a word, a man were better relate himself to a statue or picture, than to suffer his thoughts to pass in smother.

Add now, to make this second fruit of friendship complete, that other point, which lieth more open, and falleth within vulgar observation; which is faithful counsel from a friend. Heraclitus saith well in one of his enigmas: "Dry light is ever the best." And certain it is that the light that a man receiveth 40 by counsel from another is drier and purer than that which cometh from his own understanding and judgment; which is ever infused and drenched in his affections and customs. So as there is as much difference between the counsel that a friend giveth, and that a man giveth himself, as there is between the counsel of a friend and of a flatterer. For there is no such flat-

49 calling in aid   50 in stacks or piles; not opened out

terer as is a man's self; and there is no such remedy against
flattery of a man's self as the liberty of a friend. Counsel is of
two sorts; the one concerning manners, the other concerning
business. For the first, the best preservative to keep the mind
in health is the faithful admonition of a friend. The calling
of a man's self to a strict account is a medicine, sometime,
too piercing and corrosive. Reading good books of morality is
a little flat and dead. Observing our faults in others is sometimes unproper for our case. But the best receipt (best, I say,
to work, and best to take) is the admonition of a friend. It 10
is a strange thing to behold what gross errors and extreme
absurdities many (especially of the greater sort) do commit,
for want of a friend to tell them of them, to the great damage
both of their fame and fortune. For as St. James saith, they
are as men "that look sometimes into a glass, and presently
forget their own shape and favor." [51] As for business, a man
may think, if he will, that two eyes see no more than one;
or that a gamester seeth always more than a looker-on; or that
a man in anger is as wise as he that hath said over the four
and twenty letters; [52] or that a musket may be shot off as 20
well upon the arm as upon a rest; and such other fond and
high imaginations, to think himself all in all. But when all is
done, the help of good counsel is that which setteth business
straight. And if any man think that he will take counsel, but
it shall be by pieces; asking counsel in one business of one
man, and in another business of another man; it is well (that
is to say, better perhaps than if he asked none at all); but
he runneth two dangers. One, that he shall not be faithfully
counseled; for it is a rare thing except it be from a perfect
and entire friend to have counsel given, but such as shall be 30
bowed and crooked to some ends which he hath that giveth
it. The other, that he shall have counsel given, hurtful and
unsafe (though with good meaning), and mixed partly of mischief and partly of remedy: even as if you would call a physician, that is thought good for the cure of the disease you complain of, but is unacquainted with your body; and therefore
may put you in way for a present cure, but overthroweth your
health in some other kind; and so cure the disease and kill
the patient. But a friend that is wholly acquainted with a man's
estate will beware, by furthering any present business, how he 40
dasheth upon other inconvenience. And therefore rest not upon
scattered counsels; they will rather distract and mislead than
settle and direct.

After these two noble fruits of friendship (peace in the af-

51 James i. 23, 24
52 One that has taken the
familiar advice, "When in
anger, say over the alpha-
bet before speaking." *I* and
V formerly did duty for *J*
and *U* respectively.

fections, and support of the judgment) followeth the last fruit, which is like the pomegranate, full of many kernels; I mean aid and bearing a part in all actions and occasions. Here the best way to represent to life the manifold use of friendship is to cast and see how many things there are which a man cannot do himself; and then it will appear that it was a sparing speech of the ancients, to say "that a friend is another himself"; for that a friend is far more than himself. Men have their time, and die many times in desire of some things which they
10 principally take to heart; the bestowing of a child, the finishing of a work, or the like. If a man have a true friend, he may rest almost secure that the care of those things will continue after him. So that a man hath as it were two lives in his desires. A man hath a body, and that body is confined to a place; but where friendship is, all offices of life are as it were granted to him and his deputy. For he may exercise them by his friend. How many things are there which a man cannot, with any face or comeliness, say or do himself! And man can scarce allege his own merits with modesty, much less extol
20 them; a man cannot sometimes brook to supplicate or beg; and a number of the like. But all these things are graceful in a friend's mouth, which are blushing in a man's own. So again, a man's person hath many proper relations which he cannot put off. A man cannot speak to his son but as a father; to his wife but as a husband; to his enemy but upon terms: whereas a friend may speak as the case requires, and not as it sorteth with the person. But to enumerate these things were endless. I have given the rule, where a man cannot fitly play his own part; if he have not a friend, he may quit the stage.

28.—Of Expense

30 Riches are for spending, and spending for honor and good actions. Therefore extraordinary expense must be limited by the worth of the occasion; for voluntary undoing may be as well for a man's country as for the kingdom of heaven. But ordinary expense ought to be limited by a man's estate; and governed with such regard, as it be within his compass; and not subject to deceit and abuse of servants; and ordered to the best show, that the bills may be less than the estimation abroad. Certainly, if a man will keep but of even hand,[53] his ordinary expenses ought to be but to the half of his receipts;
40 and if he think to wax rich, but to the third part. It is no baseness for the greatest to descend and look into their own estate.

53 his accounts balanced

Some forbear it, not upon negligence alone, but doubting to bring themselves into melancholy, in respect they shall find it broken. But wounds cannot be cured without searching.[54] He that cannot look into his own estate at all, had need both choose well those whom he employeth, and change them often; for new are more timorous and less subtle. He that can look into his estate but seldom, it behoveth him to turn all to certainties. A man had need, if he be plentiful in some kind of expense, to be as saving again in some other. As, if he be plentiful in diet, to be saving in apparel; if he be plenti- 10 ful in the hall, to be saving in the stable; and the like. For he that is plentiful in expenses of all kinds will hardly be preserved from decay. In clearing of a man's estate, he may as well hurt himself in being too sudden, as in letting it run on too long. For hasty selling is commonly as disadvantageable as interest. Besides, he that clears at once will relapse; for finding himself out of straits, he will revert to his customs: but he that cleareth by degrees induceth a habit of frugality, and gaineth as well upon his mind as upon his estate. Certainly, who hath a state to repair may not despise small things; 20 and commonly it is less dishonorable to abridge petty charges, than to stoop to petty gettings. A man ought warily to begin charges which once begun will continue; but in matters that return not he may be more magnificent.

32.—OF DISCOURSE

Some in their discourse desire rather commendation of wit, in being able to hold all arguments, than of judgment, in discerning what is true; as if it were a praise to know what might be said, and not what should be thought. Some have certain commonplaces and themes wherein they are good, and want variety; which kind of poverty is for the most part tedious, 30 and, when it is once perceived, ridiculous. The honorablest part of talk is to give the occasion; and again to moderate and pass to somewhat else; for then a man leads the dance. It is good, in discourse, and speech of conversation, to vary and intermingle speech of the present occasion with arguments; tales with reasons; asking of questions with telling of opinions; and jest with earnest: for it is a dull thing to tire, and, as we say now, to jade any thing too far. As for jest, there be certain things which ought to be privileged from it; namely, religion, matters of state, great persons, any man's present business of 40 importance, and any case that deserveth pity. Yet there be

54 probing

some that think their wits have been asleep, except they dart out somewhat that is piquant and to the quick: that is a vein which would be bridled:

Parce, puer, stimulis, et fortius utere loris.[55]

And generally, men ought to find the difference between saltness and bitterness. Certainly, he that hath a satirical vein, as he maketh others afraid of his wit, so he had need be afraid of others' memory. He that questioneth much, shall learn much, and content much; but especially if he apply his ques-
10 tions to the skill of the persons whom he asketh: for he shall give them occasion to please themselves in speaking, and himself shall continually gather knowledge. But let his questions not be troublesome; for that is fit for a poser.[56] And let him be sure to leave other men their turns to speak. Nay, if there be any that would reign and take up all the time, let him find means to take them off and to bring others on; as musicians use to do with those that dance too long galliards. If you dissemble sometimes your knowledge of that you are thought to know, you shall be thought another time to know that you
20 know not. Speech of a man's self ought to be seldom, and well chosen. I knew one was wont to say in scorn, "He must needs be a wise man, he speaks so much of himself": and there is but one case wherein a man may commend himself with good grace, and that is in commending virtue in another, especially if it be such a virtue whereunto himself pretendeth. Speech of touch towards [57] others should be sparingly used; for discourse ought to be as a field, without coming home to any man. I knew two noblemen, of the west part of England, whereof the one was given to scoff, but kept ever royal cheer in his house; the
30 other would ask of those that had been at the other's table, "Tell truly, was there never a flout or dry blow [58] given?" To which the guest would answer, "Such and such a thing passed." The lord would say, "I thought he would mar a good dinner." Discretion of speech is more than eloquence; and to speak agreeably to him with whom we deal, is more than to speak in good words or in good order. A good continued speech, without a good speech of interlocution, shows slowness; and a good reply or second speech, without a good settled speech, showeth shallowness and weakness. As we see in beasts, that
40 those that are weakest in the course, are yet nimblest in the turn; as it is betwixt the greyhound and the hare. To use too many circumstances, ere one come to the matter, is wearisome; to use none at all, is blunt.

---

55 Spare the whip, boy, and hold the reins more   tightly. (Ovid)
56 examiner
57 hits at
58 insult or hard knock

34.—OF RICHES

I cannot call riches better than the baggage of virtue. The Roman word is better, *impedimenta*. For as the baggage is to an army, so is riches to virtue. It cannot be spared nor left behind, but it hindereth the march; yea, and the care of it sometimes loseth or disturbeth the victory. Of great riches there is no real use, except it be in the distribution; the rest is but conceit. So saith Solomon: "Where much is, there are many to consume it; and what hath the owner but the sight of it with his eyes?" [59] The personal fruition in any man cannot reach to feel great riches: there is a custody of them; or a power of dole and donative of them; or a fame of them; but no solid use to the owner. Do you not see what feigned prices are set upon little stones and rarities? and what works of ostentation are undertaken, because there might seem to be some use of great riches? But then you will say, they may be of us to buy men out of dangers or troubles. As Solomon saith: "Riches are as a stronghold, in the imagination of the rich man." [60] But this is excellently expressed, that it is in imagination, and not always in fact. For certainly great riches have sold more men than they have bought out. Seek not proud riches, but such as thou mayest get justly, use soberly, distribute cheerfully, and leave contentedly. Yet have no abstract nor friarly contempt of them. But distinguish, as Cicero saith well of Rabirius Posthumus: *In studio rei amplificandæ apparebat non avaritiæ prædam sed instrumentum bonitati quæri.*[61] Hearken also to Solomon, and beware of hasty gathering of riches: *Qui festinat ad divitias non erit insons.*[62] The poets feign that when Plutus (which is Riches) is sent from Jupiter, he limps and goes slowly; but when he is sent from Pluto, he runs and is swift of foot: meaning, that riches gotten by good means and just labor pace slowly; but when they come by the death of others (as by the course of inheritance, testaments, and the like), they come tumbling upon a man. But it might be applied likewise to Pluto, taking him for the devil. For when riches come from the devil (as by fraud and oppression and unjust means), they come upon speed. The ways to enrich are many, and most of them foul. Parsimony is one of the best, and yet is not innocent; for it withholdeth men from works of liberality and charity. The improvement of the ground is the most natural obtaining of riches; for it is our great mother's blessing, the earth's; but it is slow. And yet,

59 Eccl. v. 11
60 Proverbs xviii. 11
61 In his desire to increase his fortune it was evident that he sought not the spoils of avarice but the means of doing good.
62 He that maketh haste to be rich shall not be innocent. (Proverbs xxviii. 20)

where men of great wealth do stoop to husbandry, it multiplieth riches exceedingly. I knew a nobleman in England, that had the greatest audits of any man in my time: a great grazier, a great sheep-master, a great timber man, a great collier, a great cornmaster, a great lead-man, and so of iron, and a number of the like points of husbandry: so as the earth seemed a sea to him, in respect of the perpetual importation. It was truly observed by one, that himself came very hardly to a little riches, and very easily to great riches. For when a man's stock is come to that, that he can expect the prime of markets, and overcome [63] those bargains which for their greatness are few men's money, and be partner in the industries of younger men, he cannot but increase mainly. The gains of ordinary trades and vocations are honest, and furthered by two things chiefly: by diligence, and by a good name for good and fair dealing. But the gains of bargains are of a more doubtful nature; when men shall wait upon others' necessity, broke [64] by servants and instruments to draw them on, put off others cunningly that would be better chapmen,[65] and the like practices, which are crafty and naught. As for the chopping of bargains, when a man buys, not to hold, but to sell over again, that commonly grindeth double, both upon the seller and upon the buyer. Sharings do greatly enrich, if the hands be well chosen that are trusted. Usury is the certainest means of gain, though one of the worst; as that whereby a man doth eat his bread *in sudore vultûs alieni,*[66] and besides, doth plough upon Sundays. But yet, certain though it be, it hath flaws; for that the scriveners and brokers do value unsound men, to serve their own turn. The fortune in being the first in an invention, or in a privilege, doth cause sometimes a wonderful overgrowth in riches; as it was with the first sugar man in the Canaries. Therefore if a man can play the true logician, to have as well judgment as invention, he may do great matters; especially if the times be fit. He that resteth upon gains certain, shall hardly grow to great riches, and he that puts all upon adventures, doth oftentimes break and come to poverty; it is good therefore to guard adventures with certainties that may uphold losses. Monopolies, and coemption of wares [67] for re-sale, where they are not restrained, are great means to enrich; especially if the party have intelligence what things are like to come into request, and so store himself beforehand. Riches gotten by service, though it be of the best rise, yet when they are gotten by flattery, feeding humors, and other servile conditions, they

---

63 wait for the most favorable markets, and take advantage of
64 negotiate (*cf. broker*)
65 traders
66 in the sweat of another's brow
67 buying up all of a commodity

may be placed amongst the worst. As for fishing for testaments and executorships (as Tacitus saith of Seneca, *testamenta et orbos tanquam indagine capi* [68]) it is yet worse; by how much men submit themselves to meaner persons than in service. Believe not much them that seem to despise riches; for they despise them that despair of them; and none worse, when they come to them. Be not penny-wise; riches have wings, and sometimes they fly away of themselves, sometimes they must be set flying to bring in more. Men leave their riches either to their kindred, or to the public; and moderate portions prosper best in both. A great state left to an heir, is as a lure to all the birds of prey round about to seize on him, if he be not the better stablished in years and judgment. Likewise glorious gifts and foundations are like sacrifices without salt; and but the painted sepulchers of alms, which soon will putrefy and corrupt inwardly. Therefore measure not thine advancements [69] by quantity, but frame them by measure, and defer not charities till death; for certainly, if a man weigh it rightly, he that doth so is rather liberal of another man's than of his own.

42.—Of Youth and Age

A man that is young in years may be old in hours, if he have lost no time. But that happeneth rarely. Generally, youth is like the first cogitations, not so wise as the second. For there is a youth in thoughts as well as in ages. And yet the invention of young men is more lively than that of old; and imaginations stream into their minds better, and, as it were, more divinely. Natures that have much heat, and great and violent desires and perturbations, are not ripe for action till they have passed the meridian of their years; as it was with Julius Cæsar, and Septimius Severus. Of the latter of whom it is said, *Juventutem egit erroribus, imo furoribus, plenam.* [70] And yet he was the ablest emperor, almost, of all the list. But reposed natures may do well in youth. As it is seen in Augustus Cæsar, Cosmus, Duke of Florence, [71] Gaston de Foix, [72] and others. On the other side, heat and vivacity in age is an excellent composition for business. Young men are fitter to invent than to judge; fitter for execution than for counsel; and fitter for new projects than for settled business. For the experience of age, in things that fall within the compass of it, directeth them; but in new things, abuseth them. The errors

68 bequests and wardships were caught as in a net
69 gifts
70 He passed his youth full of errors, yea of mad acts.
71 Cosimo de' Medici
72 Duc de Nemours, celebrated French general, 1489-1512

of young men are the ruin of business; but the errors of aged
men amount but to this, that more might have been done, or
sooner. Young men, in the conduct and manage of actions,
embrace more than they can hold; stir more than they can
quiet; fly to the end, without consideration of the means and
degrees; pursue some few principles which they have chanced
upon absurdly; care [73] not to innovate, which draws unknown
inconveniences; use extreme remedies at first; and, that which
doubleth all errors, will not acknowledge or retract them; like
10 an unready horse, that will neither stop nor turn. Men of
age object too much, consult too long, adventure too little,
repent too soon, and seldom drive business home to the full
period, but content themselves with a mediocrity of success.
Certainly, it is good to compound employments of both; for
that will be good for the present, because the virtues of either
age may correct the defects of both; and good for succession, that young men may be learners, while men in age are
actors; and, lastly, good for extern accidents, because authority followeth old men, and favor and popularity youth. But
20 for the moral part, perhaps youth will have the pre-eminence,
as age hath for the politic. A certain rabbin, upon the text,
"Your young men shall see visions, and your old men shall
dream dreams," [74] inferreth that young men are admitted
nearer to God than old, because vision is a clearer revelation
than a dream. And certainly, the more a man drinketh of the
world, the more it intoxicateth, and age doth profit rather in
the powers of understanding than in the virtues of the will
and affections. There be some have an over-early ripeness in
their years, which fadeth betimes. These are, first, such as
30 have brittle wits, the edge whereof is soon turned; such as
was Hermogenes the rhetorician, whose books are exceeding
subtle, who afterwards waxed stupid. A second sort is of those
that have some natural dispositions which have better grace in
youth than in age; such as is a fluent and luxuriant speech,
which becomes youth well, but not age: so Tully saith of Hor-
tensius, *Idem manebat, neque idem decebat.*[75] The third is of
such as take too high a strain at the first, and are magnanimous
more than tract of years can uphold. As was Scipio Africanus,
of whom Livy saith in effect, *Ultima primis cedebant.*[76]

43.—OF BEAUTY

40   Virtue [77] is like a rich stone, best plain set; and surely virtue
is best in a body that is comely, though not of delicate features,

73 hesitate
74 Joel ii. 28
75 He remained the same

when the same was not be-
coming.
76 His last acts were not

equal to his first.
77 excellence in general;
ability

and that hath rather dignity of presence than beauty of aspect. Neither is it always seen that very beautiful persons are otherwise of great virtue, as if nature were rather busy not to err, than in labor to produce excellency; and therefore they prove accomplished, but not of great spirit, and study rather behavior than virtue. But this holds not always; for Augustus Cæsar, Titus Vespasianus, Philip le Bel of France, Edward the Fourth of England, Alcibiades of Athens, Ismael the Sophy of Persia, were all high and great spirits, and yet the most beautiful men of their times. In beauty, that of favor [78] is more than that of color; and that of decent and gracious motion, more than that of favor. That is the best part of beauty, which a picture cannot express; no, nor the first sight of life. There is no excellent beauty that hath not some strangeness in the proportion. A man cannot tell whether Apelles or Albert Durer were the more trifler; whereof the one would make a personage by geometrical proportions; the other, by taking the best parts out of divers faces to make one excellent. Such personages, I think, would please nobody but the painter that made them. Not but I think a painter may make a better face than ever was; but he must do it by a kind of felicity (as a musician that maketh an excellent air in music), and not by rule. A man shall see faces that, if you examine them part by part, you shall find never a good, and yet altogether do well. If it be true that the principal part of beauty is in decent motion, certainly it is no marvel, though persons in years seem many times more amiable; 'Pulchrorum autumnus pulcher;" [79] for no youth can be comely but by pardon,[80] and considering the youth as to make up the comeliness. Beauty is as summer fruits, which are easy to corrupt, and cannot last; and for the most part it makes a dissolute youth, and an age a little out of countenance; but yet certainly again, if it light well, it maketh virtue shine, and vices blush.

46.—Of Gardens

God Almighty first planted a garden; and, indeed, it is the purest of human pleasures. It is the greatest refreshment to the spirits of man; without which buildings and palaces are but gross handiworks; and a man shall ever see that, when ages grow to civility and elegancy, men come to build stately, sooner than to garden finely; as if gardening were the greater perfection. I do hold it, in the royal ordering of gardens, there ought to be gardens for all the months in the year, in which,

78 feature   79 The autumn of the beautiful is beautiful.   80 by making allowances

severally, things of beauty may be then in season. For December and January, and the latter part of November, you must take such things as are green all winter: holly, ivy, bays, juni-* per, cypress trees, yew, pineapple [81] trees; fir trees, rosemary, lavender; periwinkle, the white, the purple, and the blue; germander, flags, orange trees, lemon trees, and myrtles, if they be stoved,[82] and sweet marjoram, warm set. There followeth, for the latter part of January and February, the mezereon tree, which then blossoms; crocus vernus, both the yellow and 10 the gray; primroses, anemones, the early tulip, hyacinthus orientalis, chamaïris, fritellaria. For March, there come violets, especially the single blue, which are the earliest; the yellow daffodil, the daisy, the almond tree in blossom, the peach tree in blossom, the cornelian tree in blossom, sweetbrier. In April follow the double white violet, the wallflower, the stock-gillyflower, the cowslip, flower-de-luces, and lilies of all natures; rosemary flowers, the tulip, the double peony, the pale daffodil, the French honeysuckle, the cherry tree in blossom, the damascene [83] and plum trees in blossom, the white thorn in leaf, the lilac tree. In 20 May and June come pinks of all sorts, especially the blush pink; roses of all kinds, except the musk, which comes later, honeysuckles, strawberries, bugloss, columbine, the French marigold, flos Africanus, cherry tree in fruit, ribes,[84] figs in fruit, rasps, vine-flowers, lavender in flowers, the sweet satyrian with the white flowers; herba muscaria, lilium convallium,[85] the apple tree in blossom. In July come gillyflowers of all varieties, musk-roses, the lime tree in blossom, early pears and plums in fruit, genitings, codlins. In August come plums of all sorts in fruit, pears, apricots, barberries, filberts, musk-melons, monkshoods of all 30 colors. In September come grapes, apples, poppies of all colors, peaches, melocotones, nectarines, cornelians, wardens, quinces. In October and the beginning of November come services, medlars, bullaces, roses cut or removed to come late, hollyoaks, and such like. These particulars are for the climate of London; but my meaning is perceived, that you may have "ver perpetuum," [86] as the place affords.

And because the breath of flowers is far sweeter in the air (where it comes and goes, like the warbling of music) than in the hand, therefore nothing is more fit for that delight, than to 40 know what be the flowers and plants that do best perfume the air. Roses, damask and red, are fast flowers of their smell [87] so that you may walk by a whole row of them, and find nothing of their sweetness; yea, though it be in a morning's dew. Bays, likewise, yield no smell as they grow, rosemary little,

81 pine	83 damson (Damascus)	85 lily of the valley
82 kept warm by stove (as in a greenhouse)	plum	86 perpetual spring
	84 currant	87 keeping their perfume

nor sweet marjoram. That which above all others yields the
sweetest smell in the air, is the violet, specially the white double
violet, which comes twice a year, about the middle of April, and
about Bartholomew tide. Next to that is the musk-rose; then
the strawberry leaves dying with a most excellent cordial smell;
then the flower of the vines, it is a little dust like the dust of a
bent,[88] which grows upon the cluster in the first coming forth;
then sweetbrier, then wall-flowers, which are very delightful to
be set under a parlor or lower chamber window; then pinks and
gillyflowers, specially the matted pink and clove gillyflower; then 10
the flowers of the lime tree; then the honeysuckles, so they be
somewhat afar off. Of bean-flowers I speak not, because they are
field flowers; but those which perfume the air most delightfully,
not passed by as the rest, but being trodden upon and crushed,
are three; that is, burnet, wild thyme, and water mints: therefore you are to set whole alleys of them, to have the pleasure
when you walk or tread.

For gardens (speaking of those which are indeed prince-
like, as we have done of buildings), the contents ought not well
to be under thirty acres of ground, and to be divided into 20
three parts: a green in the entrance, a heath, or desert, in
the going forth, and the main garden in the midst, besides alleys on both sides; and I like well that four acres of ground
be assigned to the green, six to the heath, four and four to
either side, and twelve to the main garden. The green hath
two pleasures: the one, because nothing is more pleasant to the
eye than green grass kept finely shorn; the other, because it
will give you a fair alley in the midst, by which you may go
in front upon a stately hedge, which is to inclose the garden.
But because the alley will be long, and in great heat of the 30
year, or day, you ought not to buy the shade in the garden
by going in the sun through the green; therefore you are, of
either side the green, to plant a covert alley upon carpenter's
work, about twelve foot in height, by which you may go in
shade into the garden. As for the making of knots or figures
with divers colored earths, that they may lie under the windows
of the house on that side which the garden stands, they be but
toys; you may see as good sights many times in tarts. The
garden is best to be square, encompassed on all the four sides
with a stately arched hedge; the arches to be upon pillars of 40
carpenter's work, of some ten foot high and six foot broad,
and the spaces between of the same dimension with the breadth
of the arch. Over the arches let there be an entire hedge of
some four foot high, framed also upon carpenter's work; and
upon the upper hedge, over every arch a little turret, with a

88 a grass

belly enough to receive a cage of birds; and over every space between the arches some other little figure, with broad plates of round colored glass gilt for the sun to play upon; but this hedge I intend to be raised upon a bank, not steep, but gently slope, of some six foot, set all with flowers. Also, I understand that this square of the garden should not be the whole breadth of the ground, but to leave on either side ground enough for diversity of side alleys, unto which the two covert alleys of the green may deliver [89] you; but there must be no alleys with hedges at either end of this great inclosure; not at the hither end, for letting [90] your prospect upon this fair hedge from the green; nor at the further end for letting your prospect from the hedge through the arches upon the heath.

For the ordering of the ground within the great hedge, I leave it to variety of device; advising, nevertheless, that whatsoever form you cast it into first, it be not too bushy, or full of work; wherein I, for my part, do not like images cut out in juniper or other garden stuff; they be for children. Little low hedges, round like welts, with some pretty pyramids, I like well; and in some places fair columns upon frames of carpenter's work. I would also have the alleys spacious and fair. You may have closer alleys upon the side grounds, but none in the main garden. I wish also in the very middle a fair mount, with three ascents and alleys, enough for four to walk abreast; which I would have to be perfect circles, without any bulwarks or embossments; and the whole mount to be thirty foot high; and some fine banqueting-house, with some chimneys neatly cast, and without too much glass.

For fountains, they are a great beauty and refreshment; but pools mar all, and make the garden unwholesome, and full of flies and frogs. Fountains I intend to be of two natures: the one that sprinkleth or spouteth water; the other a fair receipt of water, of some thirty or forty foot square, but without fish, or slime, or mud. For the first, the ornaments of images, gilt or of marble, which are in use, do well; but the main matter is so to convey the water as it never stay, either in the bowls or in the cistern; that the water be never by rest discolored green, or red, or the like, or gather any mossiness or putrefaction; besides that, it is to be cleansed every day by the hand; also, some steps up to it, and some fine pavement about it, doth well. As for the other kind of fountain, which we may call a bathing pool, it may admit much curiosity and beauty, wherewith we will not trouble ourselves; as, that the bottom be finely paved, and with images; the sides likewise; and withal, embellished with colored glass and such things of luster; encompassed also with fine rails of low statues. But the main point is the same which we mentioned in the former kind, of fountain; which is, that the water be in perpetual motion, fed by a water higher than the pool, and delivered into it by fair spouts, and then discharged away under ground by some equality of bores, that it stay little; and for fine devices, of arching water without spilling, and making it rise in several forms (of feathers, drinking glasses, canopies, and the like), they be pretty things to look on, but nothing to health and sweetness.

For the heath, which was the third part of our plot, I wish it to be framed as much as may be to a natural wildness. Trees I would have none in it, but some thickets made only of sweetbrier and honeysuckle, and some wild vine amongst; and the ground set with violets, strawberries, and primroses; for these are sweet, and prosper in the shade, and these to be in the heath here and there, not in any order. I like also little heaps in the nature of molehills (such as are in wild heaths), to be set, some with wild thyme, some with pinks, some with germander, that gives a good flower to the eye; some with periwinkle, some with violets, some with strawberries, some with cowslips, some with daisies, some with red roses, some with lilium convallium,[91] some with sweet-williams red, some with bear's-foot and the like low flowers, being withal sweet and sightly; part of which heaps to be with standards of little bushes pricked upon their top, and part without; the standards to be roses, juniper, holly, barberries (but here and there, because of the smell of their blossoms), red currants, gooseberries, rosemary, bays, sweetbrier, and such like; but these standards to be kept with cutting, that they grow not out of course.

For the side grounds, you are to fill them with variety of alleys, private, to give a full shade; some of them wheresoever the sun be. You are to frame some of them likewise for shelter, that when the wind blows sharp you may walk as in a gallery: and those alleys must be likewise hedged at both ends to keep out the wind; and these closer alleys must be ever finely graveled, and no grass, because of going wet. In many of these alleys, likewise, you are to set fruit trees of all sorts, as well upon the walls as in ranges;[92] and this should be generally observed, that the borders wherein you plant your fruit trees be fair, and large, and low, and not steep; and set with fine flowers, but thin and sparingly, lest they deceive[93] the trees. At the end of both

91 lilies of the valley   92 rows   93 deprive (of nourishment) by stealth

the side grounds I would have a mount of some pretty height, leaving the wall of the inclosure breast high, to look abroad into the fields.

For the main garden, I do not deny but there should be some fair alleys ranged on both sides with fruit trees, and some pretty tufts of fruit trees and arbors with seats, set in some decent order; but these to be by no means set too thick, but to leave the main garden so as it be not too close, but the air open and free. For as for shade, I would have you rest upon the alleys of 10 the side grounds, there to walk, if you be disposed, in the heat of the year or day; but to make account that the main garden is for the more temperate parts of the year, and in the heat of summer for the morning and the evening or overcast days.

For aviaries, I like them not, except they be of that largeness as they may be turfed, and have living plants and bushes set in them; that the birds may have more scope and natural nestling, and that no foulness appear in the floor of the aviary. So I have made a platform of a princely garden, partly by precept, partly by drawing; not a model, but some general lines of 20 it; and in this I have spared for no cost. But it is nothing for great princes, that, for the most part, taking advice with workmen, with no less cost set their things together, and sometimes add statues and such things for state and magnificence, both nothing to the true pleasure of a garden.

47.—OF NEGOTIATING

It is generally better to deal by speech than by letter; and by the mediation of a third than by a man's self. Letters are good, when a man would draw an answer by letter back again; or when it may serve for a man's justification afterwards to produce his own letter; or where it may be danger to be inter-30 rupted, or heard by pieces To deal in person is good, when a man's face breedeth regard, as commonly with inferiors; or in tender cases, where a man's eye upon the countenance of him with whom he speaketh may give him a direction how far to go; and generally, where a man will reserve to himself liberty either to disavow or to expound. In choice of instruments, it is better to choose men of a plainer sort, that are like to do that that is committed to them, and to report back again faithfully the success, than those that are cunning to contrive out of other men's business somewhat to grace themselves, and will help the 40 matter in report for satisfaction sake. Use also such persons as affect [94] the business wherein they are employed, for that quickeneth much; and such as are fit for the matter, as bold men for

94 are fond of

expostulation, fair-spoken men for persuasion, crafty men for inquiry and observation, forward and absurd men for business that doth not well bear out itself. Use also such as have been lucky and prevailed before in things wherein you have employed them; for that breeds confidence, and they will strive to maintain their prescription.[95] It is better to sound a person with whom one deals afar off, than to fall upon the point at first; except you mean to surprise him by some short question. It is better dealing with men in appetite,[96] than with those that are where they would be. If a man deal with another upon condi- 10 tions, the start or first performance is all; which a man cannot reasonably demand, except either the nature of the thing be such which must go before; or else a man can persuade the other party that he shall still need him in some other thing; or else that he be counted the honester man. All practice [97] is to discover, or to work. Men discover themselves in trust; in passion; at unawares; and of necessity, when they would have somewhat done and cannot find an apt pretext. If you would work any man, you must either know his nature and fashions, and so lead him; or his ends, and so persuade him; or his weak- 20 ness and disadvantages, and so awe him; or those that have interest in him, and so govern him. In dealing with cunning persons, we must ever consider their ends, to interpret their speeches; and it is good to say little to them, and that which they least look for. In all negotiations of difficulty, a man may not look to sow and reap at once; but must prepare business, and so ripen it by degrees.

50.—Of Studies

Studies serve for delight, for ornament, and for ability. Their chief use for delight is in privateness and retiring; for ornament, is in discourse; and for ability, is in the judgment 30 and disposition of business. For expert men can execute, and perhaps judge of particulars, one by one; but the general counsels, and the plots and marshaling of affairs, come best from those that are learned. To spend too much time in studies is sloth; to use them too much for ornament is affectation; to make judgment wholly by their rules is the humor of a scholar. They perfect nature, and are perfected by experience; for natural abilities are like natural plants, that need pruning by study; and studies themselves do give forth directions too much at large, except they be bounded in by experience. Crafty men 40 contemn studies; simple men admire them; and wise men use

95 reputation   96 ambitious   97 dealing

them: for they teach not their own use; but that is a wisdom without them and above them, won by observation. Read not to contradict and confute; nor to believe and take for granted; nor to find talk and discourse; but to weigh and consider. Some books are to be tasted, others to be swallowed, and some few to be chewed and digested: that is, some books are to be read only in parts; others to be read, but not curiously; [98] and some few to be read wholly, and with diligence and attention. Some books also may be read by deputy, and extracts made of them 10 by others; but that would be only in the less important arguments, and the meaner sort of books; else distilled books are like common distilled waters, flashy [99] things. Reading maketh a full man; conference a ready man; and writing an exact man. And therefore, if a man write little, he had need have a great memory; if he confer little, he had need have a present wit; and if he read little, he had need have much cunning, to seem to know that he doth not. Histories make men wise; poets witty; the mathematics subtle; natural philosophy deep; moral grave; logic and rhetoric able to content. *Abeunt studia in* 20 *mores*.[1] Nay, there is no stond [2] or impediment in the wit, but may be wrought out by fit studies; like as diseases of the body may have appropriate exercises. Bowling is good for the stone and reins; [3] shooting for the lungs and breast; gentle walking for the stomach; riding for the head; and the like. So if a man's wit be wandering, let him study the mathematics; for in demonstrations, if his wit be called away never so little, he must begin again. If his wit be not apt to distinguish or find differences, let him study the schoolmen; for they are *cymini sectores*.[4] If he be not apt to beat over matters, and to call 30 one thing to prove and illustrate another, let him study the lawyers' cases. So every defect of the mind may have a special receipt.

JOHN DONNE (1573–1631)

John Donne was the son of a well-to-do ironmonger, of a prominent Catholic family. He was born in London in 1573, received his early education of tutors, later attended Oxford and Cambridge, and then studied law. He did much reading in the points of controversy between Catholics and Protestants, with the result that he joined the Church of England. He served under the Earl of Essex in the expedition to Cadiz (1596). We have it on the authority of Izaak Walton that his youth was wild; yet these early years produced his amazing poems, the best of which, says Jonson in his conversations with Drummond of Hawthornden, were written before he was twenty-five. In 1597 he was made secretary to Sir Thomas Egerton, the Lord Keeper. In the

98 carefully
99 insipid

1 Studies develop into manners (Ovid).
2 hindrance

3 kidneys
4 hair-splitters

latter's house he met and fell in love with Anne More, the niece of Sir Thomas's wife, and secretly married her in 1601, when she was only seventeen. Sir George More, her father, indignant at what he regarded as the imprudent match, managed to have Donne dismissed and imprisoned. Donne in a bitter pun commented thus to his wife on their misfortunes: "John Donne, Anne Donne, Un-done." He devotedly loved her throughout his life.

During the next dozen years, Donne was striving unsuccessfully for political preferment, and living precariously on his friends and his wife's relatives. He was finally persuaded to take holy orders (1615), on which he rose rapidly as a divine, enjoying a reputation as the most eloquent preacher of his time, and being given in 1621 the important Deanship of St. Paul's. Walton's famous *Life* mostly concerns the devout Donne of these later years—years when, according to Jonson, he repented highly and would have destroyed all his poems. The thought of death came to have for him more and more a morbid fascination. During his last illness he had himself swathed in a winding-sheet, and stood, with closed eyes, his own model for the making of his monument which stands to-day in St. Paul's Cathedral.

The best contemporary criticism of Donne is that of Ben Jonson. Among other comments, Ben declared, with his usual bluntness, "that Donne, for not keeping of accent, deserved hanging," and that "for not being understood [he] would perish"; yet he esteemed him "the first poet of the world in some things," and critics of succeeding generations have concurred. Donne's poetry is emphatic, original, and perverse. He discarded alike the Italianate mellifluousness of Spenser, and the classic balance of Jonson, and though indebted to the decadent schools of conceit of the Renaissance, spoke with a strikingly individual voice. Vehemence and passion are there, and an intense intellectual energy that led him to create ingenious metaphors based upon the processes of the mind rather than upon the senses. The thought is often so involved and subtle as to defy clear expression. The language may be tortured, the verse harsh. The result is that obscurity that Ben Jonson mentions, in spite of which he has not perished. Dr. Samuel Johnson, with these qualities in view, characterized Donne and his school as "metaphysical poets."

Although Donne's poems, with a few exceptions, were in his lifetime known only from manuscript circulation, he exerted on his own and the succeeding generation a powerful influence. He is generally esteemed to-day one of the great voices of his time and one of the most interesting and brilliant of English poets, after the few finished artists of the first rank are excepted. He has had a notable revival in our own time.

BIBLIOGRAPHY. *Poetical Works*, ed. H. J. C. Grierson, 2 vols., Oxford (standard, in old spelling). Muses' Lib. ed., ed. E. K. Chambers, 2 vols. Complete *Works* in 1 vol. (Random House). Sel. of Donne's Sermons by L. P. Smith (Oxford). Izaak Walton's *Life*. Edmund Gosse's *Life and Letters of John Donne*, 2 vols. Dr. Samuel Johnson's *Life of Cowley* in his *Lives of the Poets* (famous commentary). Numerous recent studies.

SONG

Go and catch a falling star,
Get with child a mandrake root,[1]
Tell me where all past years are,
Or who cleft the devil's foot;

1 It has a shape resembling the human body—the basis of many folk beliefs.

Teach me to hear mermaids [2] singing,
  Or to keep off envy's stinging,
    And find
    What wind
Serves to advance an honest mind.

If thou beest born to strange sights,
  Things invisible to see,
Ride ten thousand days and nights
  Till age snow white hairs on thee;
Thou, when thou return'st, wilt tell me
All strange wonders that befell thee,
    And swear
    No where
Lives a woman true and fair.

If thou find'st one, let me know;
  Such a pilgrimage were sweet.
Yet do not; I would not go,
  Though at next door we might meet.
Though she were true when you met her,
And last till you write your letter,
    Yet she
    Will be
False, ere I come, to two or three.

THE INDIFFERENT

I CAN love both fair and brown;
Her whom abundance melts, and her whom want betrays;
Her who loves loneness best, and her who masks and plays;
Her whom the country formed, and whom the town;
Her who believes, and her who tries;
Her who still weeps with spongy eyes,
And her who is dry cork and never cries.
I can love her, and her, and you, and you;
I can love any, so she be not true.

Will no other vice content you?
Will it not serve your turn to do as did your mothers?
Or have you all old vices spent and now would find out others?
Or doth a fear that men are true torment you?
Oh we are not; be not you so;
Let me—and do you—twenty know.

2 probably confused with sirens

Rob me, but bind me not, and let me go.
Must I, who came to travel thorough you,
Grow your fixed subject because you are true?

Venus heard me sigh this song,
And by love's sweetest part, variety, she swore
She heard not this till now; and that it should be so no more.
She went; examined, and returned ere long,
And said, "Alas! some two or three
Poor heretics in love there be,
Which think to stablish dangerous constancy.
But I have told them, 'Since you will be true,
You shall be true to them who're false to you.' "

THE CANONIZATION

For God's sake hold your tongue, and let me love;
    Or chide my palsy, or my gout;
    My five gray hairs, or ruined fortune flout:
With wealth your state, your mind with arts improve;
    Take you a course, get you a place,
    Observe his Honor, or his Grace;
Or the king's real, or his stamped face
    Contemplate; what you will, approve,
    So you will let me love.

Alas, alas! who's injured by my love?
    What merchant's ships have my sighs drowned?
    Who says my tears have overflowed his ground?
When did my colds a forward spring remove?
    When did the heats which my veins fill
    Add one more to the plaguy bill? [3]
Soldiers find wars, and lawyers find out still
    Litigious men, which quarrels move,
    Though she and I do love.

Call us what you will, we are made such by love;
    Call her one, me another fly;
    We're tapers too, and at our own cost die,
And we in us find th'eagle and the dove.
    The phoenix riddle hath more wit
    By us; we two being one, are it;
So, to one neutral thing both sexes fit.

3 bulletin of numbers dying by the plague

We die and rise the same, and prove
Mysterious by this love.

We can die by it, if not live by love,
And if unfit for tombs and hearse,
Our legend be, it will be fit for verse;
And if no piece of chronicle we prove,
We'll build in sonnets pretty rooms;
As well a well-wrought urn becomes
The greatest ashes, as half-acre tombs,
And by these hymns all shall approve
Us canonized for love;

And thus invoke us: "You, whom reverend love
Made one another's hermitage;
You, to whom love was peace, that now is rage;
Who did the whole world's soul contract, and drove
Into the glasses of your eyes;
So made such mirrors, and such spies,
That they did all to you epitomize,
Countries, towns, courts, beg from above
A pattern of your love."

A VALEDICTION FORBIDDING MOURNING

As virtuous men pass mildly away,
And whisper to their souls, to go,
Whilst some of their sad friends do say,
"The breath goes now," and some say, "No,"

So let us melt, and make no noise,
No tear-floods nor sigh-tempests move;
'Twere profanation of our joys
To tell the laity our love.

Moving of the earth [4] brings harms and fears,
Men reckon what it did and meant,
But trepidation [5] of the spheres,
Though greater far, is innocent.[6]

Dull sublunary [7] lovers' love,
Whose soul is sense, cannot admit
Absence, because it doth remove
Those things which elemented [8] it.

10

4 earthquake
5 In Ptolemaic system, an oscillation of the heavenly
sphere assumed to account for certain astronomic variations.
6 non-harming.
7 earthly
8 constituted its essence

But we, by a love so much refined
That ourselves know not what it is,
Inter-assurèd of the mind,
Care less eyes, lips, and hands to miss. 20

Our two souls therefore, which are one,
Though I must go, endure not yet
A breach, but an expansion,
Like gold to airy thinness beat.

If they be two, they are two so
As stiff twin compasses are two;
Thy soul, the fixed foot, makes no show
To move, but doth if the other do.

And though it in the center sit,
Yet when the other far doth roam, 30
It leans, and hearkens after it,
And grows erect, as that comes home.

Such wilt thou be to me, who must
Like the other foot, obliquely run;
Thy firmness makes my circle just,
And makes me end where I begun.

THE ECSTASY [9]

WHERE, like a pillow on a bed,
A pregnant bank swelled up, to rest
The violet's reclining head,
Sat we two, one another's best.
Our hands were firmly cemented
With a fast balm, which thence did spring;
Our eye-beams twisted, and did thread
Our eyes upon one double string.
So to entergraft our hands as yet
Was all the means to make us one, 10
And pictures in our eyes to get
Was all our propagation.
As, 'twixt two equal armies, fate
Suspends uncertain victory,
Our souls—which, to advance their state,
Were gone out—hung 'twixt her and me.
And whilst our souls negotiate there,

9 State of rapture in which the body was supposed to be incapable of sensation
while the soul was engaged in the contemplation of divine things.

We like sepulchral statues lay;
All day, the same our postures were,
    And we said nothing, all the day.   20
If any, so by love refined
    That he soul's language understood,
And by good love were grown all mind,
    Within convenient distance stood,
He, though he knew not which soul spake
    Because both meant, both spake the same,
Might then a new concoction [10] take,
    And part far purer than he came.
This ecstasy doth unperplex,
    We said, and tell us what we love;   30
We see by this, it was not sex;
    We see, we saw not what did move:
But as all several souls contain
    Mixture of things, they know not what,
Love these mixed souls doth mix again,
    And makes both one, each this and that.
A single violet transplant,
    The strength, the color, and the size,
(All which before was poor and scant)
    Redoubles still, and multiplies.   40
When love with one another so
    Interinanimates two souls,
That abler soul, which thence doth flow,
    Defects of loneliness controls.[11]
We then, who are this new soul, know
    Of what we are composed and made,
For the atomies of which we grow
    Are souls, whom no change can invade.
But O alas! so long, so far
    Our bodies why do we forbear?   50
They are ours, though they are not we. We are
    The intelligences, they the sphere.[12]
We owe them thanks, because they thus
    Did us to us at first convey,
Yielded their forces, sense, to us,
    Nor are dross to us, but allay.[13]
On man heaven's influence [14] works not so
    But that it first imprints the air;
So soul into the soul may flow,
    Though it to body [15] first repair.   60

10 purification   spheres   term)
11 overmasters   13 alloy   15 medium for influence
12 as angels direct move- 14 power flowing from of soul, as the air is for
ments of the heavenly   the stars (astrological influence of stars

As our blood labors to beget
　　Spirits,[16] as like souls as it can,
Because such fingers need to knit
　　That subtle knot that makes us man;
So must pure lovers' souls descend
　　To affections, and to faculties
Which sense may reach and apprehend,
　　Else a great prince in prison lies.
To our bodies turn we then, that so
　　Weak men on love revealed may look;　　70
Love's mysteries in souls do grow,
　　But yet the body is his book.
And if some lover, such as we,
　　Have heard this dialogue of one,
Let him still mark us, he shall see
　　Small change, when we are to bodies gone.

LOVE'S DEITY

I long to talk with some old lover's ghost
　　Who died before the god of love was born.
I cannot think that he who then loved most
　　Sunk so low as to love one which did scorn.
But since this god produced a destiny,
And that vice-nature, custom, lets it be,
　　I must love her that loves not me.

Sure they which made him god, meant not so much,
　　Nor he in his young godhead practised it.
But when an even flame two hearts did touch,
　　His office was indulgently to fit
Actives to passives. Correspondency
Only his subject was; it cannot be
　　Love, till I love her that loves me.

But every modern god will now extend
　　His vast prerogative as far as Jove.
To rage, to lust, to write to, to commend,
　　All is the purlieu of the god of love.
O, were we wakened by this tyranny
To ungod this child again, it could not be
　　I should love her who loves not me.

Rebel and atheist too, why murmur I,
　　As though I felt the worst that love could do?

16 the active part of the blood, a kind of middle nature, between soul and body,
whose function is to apply the faculties of soul to the organs of the body

Love might make me leave loving, or might try
A deeper plague, to make her love me too;
Which, since she loves before, I'm loth to see.
Falsehood is worse than hate; and that must be,
If she whom I love, should love me.

THE WILL

BEFORE I sigh my last gasp, let me breathe,
Great Love, some legacies: Here I bequeath
Mine eyes to Argus,[17] if mine eyes can see;
If they be blind, then Love, I give them thee;
My tongue to fame; to ambassadors mine ears;
    To women, or the sea, my tears.
Thou, Love, hast taught me heretofore,
By making me serve her who had twenty more,
That I should give to none but such as had too much before.

My constancy I to the planets [18] give;   10
My truth to them who at the court do live;
Mine ingenuity and openness
To Jesuits; [19] to buffoons my pensiveness;
My silence to any who abroad have been;
    My money to a Capuchin.[20]
Thou, Love, taught'st me, by appointing me
To love there, where no love received can be,
Only to give to such as have an incapacity.

My faith I give to Roman Catholics;
All my good works unto the Schismatics [21]   20
Of Amsterdam; my best civility
And courtship, to an university;
My modesty I give to soldiers bare;
    My patience let gamesters share.
Thou, Love, taughst me, by making me
Love her that holds my love disparity,
Only to give to those that count my gifts indignity.

I give my reputation to those
Which were my friends; mine industry to foes;
To schoolmen [22] I bequeath my doubtfulness;   30
    My sickness to physicians, or excess;

17 the hundred-eyed
18 the ever-moving, not fixed stars
19 reputed very subtle
20 who had taken a vow of poverty
21 who would reject his orthodox "good works"
22 the mediaeval scholastic philosophers, engaged in quibbling disputations

To Nature, all that I in rhyme have writ;
   And to my company my wit.
Thou, Love, by making me adore
Her, who begot this love in me before,
Taughtst me to make as though I gave, when I did but restore.

To him for whom the passing bell next tolls
   I give my physic books; my written rolls
Of moral counsels, I to Bedlam [23] give;
My brazen medals, unto them which live   40
   In want of bread; to them which pass among
   All foreigners, mine English tongue.
Thou, Love, by making me love one
Who thinks her friendship a fit portion
For younger lovers, dost my gifts thus disproportion.

Therefore I'll give no more; but I'll undo
   The world by dying, because love dies too.
Then all your beauties will be no more worth
Than gold in mines where none do draw it forth;
And all your graces no more use shall have   50
   Than a sun-dial in a grave.
Thou, Love, taughst me, by making me
Love her, who doth neglect both me and thee,
To invent, and practise this one way to annihilate all three.

THE FUNERAL

Whoever comes to shroud me, do not harm
   Nor question much
That subtle wreath of hair which crowns my arm;
The mystery, the sign you must not touch,
   For 'tis my outward soul,
Viceroy to that which, unto heaven being gone,
   Will leave this to control
And keep these limbs, her provinces, from dissolution.

For if the sinewy thread my brain lets fall
   Through every part
Can tie those parts, and make me one of all;
These hairs which upward grew, and strength and art
   Have from a better brain,
Can better do't: except she meant that I
   By this should know my pain,
As prisoners then are manacled, when they're condemned to die.

23 the insane asylum

Whate'er she meant by 't, bury it with me;
  For since I am
Love's martyr, it might breed idolatry
If into other hands these relics came;
  As 'twas humility
To afford to it all that a soul can do,
  So 'tis some bravery
That, since you would have none of me, I bury some of you.

ROBERT HERRICK (1591–1674)

Robert Herrick was born in London in August, 1591, the son of a gold-smith, and was apprenticed to the same trade. He attended Trinity College, Cambridge, taking his B.A. in 1616, seems thereafter to have lived for some dozen years a convivial life in London, then took holy orders, and was presented by Charles I to the living of Dean Prior, in Devonshire, where he lived (with the exception of the period of the Commonwealth, when he was temporarily ejected) till his death in 1674. He loved good living and good fellowship, and yet became much attached to his country home, and was not lacking in devout feeling. As a young man he sat at the feet of Ben Jonson (*q. v.*), and was proud to call himself one of the "tribe of Ben." From his master he acquired that sense of classic propriety, of even and graceful expression, which characterizes the poetry of both, but his work shows also the independent influence of Anacreon, Horace, and Catullus, and he stands easily at the head of this school in English. His subjects are light, his emotions never profound, but he excels in lyric quality, in neat and deft phrasing, and in the finish and polish of his verses. The intellectual vigor and depth of a Donne or a Milton are not here present, but in their stead is the perfect technique of the consummate artist. Practically all of his work was published in the *Hesperides* and *Noble Numbers* of 1648. Editions: Oxford, ed. F. W. Moorman; Canterbury Poets ser., ed. H. P. Horne, with a biography by Ernest Rhys; Muses' Lib., 2 vols., ed. A. Pollard with preface by A. C. Swinburne.

THE ARGUMENT OF HIS BOOK

I sing of brooks, of blossoms, birds and bowers,
Of April, May, of June and July-flowers;
I sing of may-poles, hock-carts, wassails, wakes,[1]
Of bridegrooms, brides, and of their bridal cakes;
I write of youth, of love, and have access
By these to sing of cleanly wantonness;
I sing of dews, of rains, and, piece by piece,
Of balm, of oil, of spice and ambergris;
I sing of times trans-shifting, and I write
How roses first came red and lilies white;

1 the last cart loaded at harvest; drinking bouts; parish holidays

I write of groves, of twilights, and I sing
The court of Mab, and of the Fairy King;
I write of hell; I sing (and ever shall)
Of heaven, and hope to have it after all.

UPON THE LOSS OF HIS MISTRESSES

I HAVE lost, and lately, these
Many dainty mistresses:
Stately Julia, prime of all;
Sapho next, a principal;
Smooth Anthea, for a skin
White and heaven-like crystalline;
Sweet Electra, and the choice
Myrha, for the lute and voice.
Next, Corinna, for her wit,
And the graceful use of it;
With Perilla: all are gone,
Only Herrick's left alone,
For to number sorrow by
Their departures hence, and die.

DISCONTENTS IN DEVON

MORE discontents I never had
Since I was born, than here;
Where I have been, and still am sad,
In this dull Devonshire.
Yet justly too I must confess
I ne'er invented such
Ennobled numbers for the press
Than where I loathed so much.

CHERRY-RIPE

CHERRY-RIPE, ripe, ripe, I cry,
Full and fair ones; come and buy!
If so be you ask me where
They do grow, I answer, there,
Where my Julia's lips do smile;
There's the land, or cherry-isle,
Whose plantations fully show
All the year where cherries grow.

HIS REQUEST TO JULIA

JULIA, if I chance to die
Ere I print my poetry,

I most humbly thee desire
To commit it to the fire.
Better 'twere my book were dead
Than to live not perfected.

DELIGHT IN DISORDER

A SWEET disorder in the dress
Kindles in clothes a wantonness.
A lawn about the shoulders thrown
Into a fine distraction;
An erring lace, which here and there
Enthralls the crimson stomacher;
A cuff neglectful, and thereby
Ribbons to flow confusedly;
A winning wave (deserving note)
In the tempestuous petticoat;
A careless shoe-string, in whose tie
I see a wild civility;—
Do more bewitch me than when art
Is too precise in every part.

CORINNA'S GOING A-MAYING

GET up, get up for shame, the blooming morn
Upon her wings presents the god unshorn.
    See how Aurora throws her fair
    Fresh-quilted colors through the air:
    Get up, sweet slug-a-bed, and see
    The dew bespangling herb and tree.
Each flower has wept and bowèd toward the east
Above an hour since: yet you not dressed;
    Nay! not so much as out of bed?
    When all the birds have matins said   10
And sung their thankful hymns, 'tis sin,
    Nay, profanation, to keep in,
Whenas a thousand virgins on this day
Spring, sooner than the lark, to fetch in May.

Rise, and put on your foliage, and be seen
To come forth, like the spring-time, fresh and green,
    And sweet as Flora.[2] Take no care
    For jewels for your gown or hair:
    Fear not; the leaves will strew
    Gems in abundance upon you: 20
Besides, the childhood of the day has kept,

2 goddess of flowers

Against you come,[3] some orient pearls unwept;
  Come and receive them while the light
  Hangs on the dew-locks of the night:
  And Titan [4] on the eastern hill
  Retires himself, or else stands still
Till you come forth. Wash, dress, be brief in praying:
Few beads [5] are best when once we go a-Maying.

Come, my Corinna, come; and coming, mark
How each field turns a street, each street a park
  Made green and trimmed with trees; see how
  Devotion gives each house a bough
  Or branch: each porch, each door ere this
  An ark, a tabernacle is,
Made up of white-thorn, neatly interwove;
As if here were those cooler shades of love.
  Can such delights be in the street
  And open fields and we not see 't?
  Come, we'll abroad; and let's obey
  The proclamation made for May:
And sin no more, as we have done, by staying;
But, my Corinna, come, let's go a-Maying.

There's not a budding boy or girl this day
But is got up, and gone to bring in May.
  A deal of youth, ere this, is come
  Back, and with white-thorn laden home.
  Some have despatched their cakes and cream
  Before that we have left to dream:
And some have wept, and wooed, and plighted troth,
And chose their priest, ere we can cast off sloth:
  Many a green-gown [6] has been given;
  Many a kiss, both odd and even:
  Many a glance too has been sent
  From out the eye, love's firmament;
Many a jest told of the keys betraying
This night, and locks picked, yet we're not a-Maying.

Come, let us go while we are in our prime;
And take the harmless folly of the time.
  We shall grow old apace, and die
  Before we know our liberty.
  Our life is short, and our days run
  As fast away as does the sun;

30

40

50

60

3 for your arrival   5 prayers   6 tumble on the grass
4 the sun

And, as a vapor or a drop of rain,
Once lost, can ne'er be found again,
So when or you or I are made
A fable, song, or fleeting shade,
All love, all liking, all delight
Lies drowned with us in endless night.
Then while time serves, and we are but decaying,
Come, my Corinna, come let's go a-Maying.   70

TO THE VIRGINS TO MAKE MUCH OF TIME

GATHER ye rosebuds while ye may,
  Old Time is still a-flying;
And this same flower that smiles to-day,
  To-morrow will be dying.

The glorious lamp of heaven, the sun,
  The higher he's a-getting,
The sooner will his race be run,
  And nearer he's to setting.

That age is best which is the first,
  When youth and blood are warmer;
But being spent, the worse and worst
  Times still succeed the former.

Then be not coy, but use your time,
  And while ye may, go marry;
For, having lost but once your prime,
  You may forever tarry.

HIS POETRY HIS PILLAR

ONLY a little more
  I have to write;
  Then I'll give o'er,
And bid the world good-night.

Tis but a flying minute
  That I must stay,
  Or linger in it;
And then I must away.

O time that cut'st down all!
  And scarce leav'st here
  Memorial
Of any men that were.

How many lie forgot
In vaults beneath,
And piecemeal rot
Without a fame in death?

Behold this living stone
I rear for me,
Ne'er to be thrown
Down, envious Time, by thee.

Pillars let some set up
(If so they please)
Here is my hope,
And my pyramidës.

TO ANTHEA, WHO MAY COMMAND HIM ANYTHING

Bid me to live, and I will live
Thy protestant to be:
Or bid me love, and I will give
A loving heart to thee.

A heart as soft, a heart as kind,
A heart as sound and free
As in the whole world thou canst find,
That heart I'll give to thee.

Bid that heart stay, and it will stay,
To honor thy decree:
Or bid it languish quite away,
And 't shall do so for thee.

Bid me to weep, and I will weep,
While I have eyes to see:
And having none, yet I will keep
A heart to weep for thee.

Bid me despair, and I'll despair,
Under that cypress tree:
Or bid me die, and I will dare
E'en death, to die for thee.

Thou art my life, my love, my heart,
The very eyes of me,
And hast command of every part,
To live and die for thee.

UPON A CHILD THAT DIED

HERE she lies, a pretty bud,
Lately made of flesh and blood:
Who as soon fell fast asleep,
As her little eyes did peep.
Give her strewings, but not stir
The earth that lightly covers her.

TO DAFFODILS

FAIR Daffodils, we weep to see
　　You haste away so soon;
As yet the early rising sun
　　Has not attained his noon.
　　　Stay, stay,
　　Until the hasting day
　　　　Has run
　　But to the even-song;
And, having prayed together, we
　　Will go with you along.

We have short time to stay, as you,
　　We have as short a spring;
As quick a growth to meet decay,
　　As you, or anything.
　　　We die
　　As your hours do, and dry
　　　　Away,
　　Like to the summer's rain;
Or as the pearls of morning's dew,
　　Ne'er to be found again.

TO ENJOY THE TIME

WHILE fates permit us, let's be merry:
Pass all we must the fatal ferry;
And this our life too whirls away
With the rotation of the day.

TO BLOSSOMS

FAIR pledges of a fruitful tree,
　　Why do ye fall so fast?
　　Your date is not so past;
But you may stay yet here a while,

To blush and gently smile;
And go at last.

What, were ye born to be
An hour or half's delight,
And so to bid good-night?
'Twas pity Nature brought ye forth
Merely to show your worth,
And lose you quite.

But you are lovely leaves, where we
May read how soon things have
Their end, though ne'er so brave;
And after they have shown their pride,
Like you a while, they glide
Into the grave.

HIS WINDING-SHEET

Come thou, who art the wine and wit
Of all I've writ;
The grace, the glory, and the best
Piece of the rest.
Thou art, of what I did intend,
The all and end;
And what was made, was made to meet
Thee, thee, my sheet.
Come then, and be to my chaste side
Both bed and bride.   10
We two, as relics left, will have
One rest, one grave;
And, hugging close, we will not fear
Lust ent'ring here,
Where all desires are dead, or cold
As is the mold,
And all affections are forgot,
Or trouble not.
Here, here the slaves and pris'ners be
From shackles free,   20
And weeping widows, long oppressed,
Do here find rest.
The wrongèd client ends his laws
Here, and his cause;
Here those long suits of chancery lie
Quiet, or die,
And all star-chamber bills do cease,

Or hold their peace.
Here needs no court for our request,
    Where all are best;   30
All wise, all equal, and all just,
    Alike i' th' dust;
Nor need we here to fear the frown
    Of court, or crown;
Where fortune bears no sway o'er things,
    There all are kings.
In this securer place we'll keep,
    As lulled asleep;
Or for a little time we'll lie,
    As robes laid by,   40
To be another day re-worn,—
    Turned, but not torn:
Or like old testaments engrossed,
    Locked up, not lost:
And for a while lie here concealed,
    To be revealed
Next at that great Platonic year,[7]
    And then meet here.

ART ABOVE NATURE. TO JULIA

WHEN I behold a forest spread
With silken trees upon thy head,
And when I see that other dress
Of flowers set in comeliness;
When I behold another grace
In the ascent of curious lace,
Which like a pinnacle doth show
The top, and the top-gallant too;
Then, when I see thy tresses bound
Into an oval, square, or round,   10
And knit in knots far more than I
Can tell by tongue, or true-love tie;
Next, when those lawny films I see
Play with a wild civility,
And all those airy silks to flow,
Alluring me, and tempting so:
I must confess, mine eye and heart
Dotes less on nature than on art.

[7] the year in which everything will return to its original state

THE PRIMROSE

Ask me why I send you here
This sweet infanta of the year?
Ask me why I send to you
This primrose, thus bepearled with dew?
I will whisper to your ears,
The sweets of love are mixed with tears.

Ask me why this flower does show
So yellow-green, and sickly too?
Ask me why the stalk is weak
And bending, yet it doth not break?
I will answer, these discover
What fainting hopes are in a lover.

HIS PRAYER TO BEN JONSON

When I a verse shall make,
Know I have prayed thee,
For old religion's sake,
Saint Ben, to aid me.

Make the way smooth for me,
When I, thy Herrick,
Honoring thee, on my knee
Offer my lyric.

Candles I'll give to thee,
And a new altar;
And thou, Saint Ben, shalt be
Writ in my psalter.

THE NIGHT-PIECE, TO JULIA

Her eyes the glow-worm lend thee,
The shooting stars attend thee;
And the elves also,
Whose little eyes glow
Like the sparks of fire, befriend thee.

No Will-o'-th'-Wisp mis-light thee,
Nor snake or slow-worm bite thee;
But on, on thy way,

Not making a stay,
Since ghost there's none to affright thee.

Let not the dark thee cumber;
What though the moon does slumber?
    The stars of the night
    Will lend thee their light,
Like tapers clear without number.

Then, Julia, let me woo thee,
Thus, thus, to come unto me;
    And when I shall meet
    Thy silvery feet
My soul I'll pour into thee.

TO ELECTRA

I DARE not ask a kiss;
    I dare not beg a smile;
Lest having that or this,
    I might grow proud the while.

No, no, the utmost share
    Of my desire shall be,
Only to kiss that air
    That lately kissèd thee.

UPON JULIA'S CLOTHES

WHENAS in silks my Julia goes,
Then, then, methinks, how sweetly flows
That liquefaction of her clothes.

Next, when I cast mine eyes and see
That brave vibration each way free;
O, how that glittering taketh me!

UPON PRUE HIS MAID

IN this little urn is laid
Prudence Baldwin, once my maid;
From whose happy spark here let
Spring the purple violet.

AN ODE FOR BEN JONSON

Ah, Ben!
Say how or when

Shall we, thy guests,
Meet at those lyric feasts,
Made at the Sun,
The Dog, the Triple Tun; [8]
Where we such clusters had,
As made us nobly wild, not mad?
And yet each verse of thine
Out-did the meat, out-did the frolic wine.

My Ben!
Or come again,
Or send to us
Thy wit's great overplus;
But teach us yet
Wisely to husband it,
Lest we that talent spend;
And having once brought to an end
That precious stock, the store
Of such a wit the world should have no more.

HIS PRAYER FOR ABSOLUTION

For those my unbaptizèd rhymes,
Writ in my wild unhallowed times;
For every sentence, clause, and word
That's not inlaid with Thee, my Lord,
Forgive me, God, and blot each line
Out of my book that is not Thine.
But if, 'mongst all, thou find'st here one
Worthy thy benediction,
That one of all the rest shall be
The glory of my work and me.

HIS LITANY TO THE HOLY SPIRIT

In the hour of my distress,
When temptations me oppress,
And when I my sins confess,
  Sweet Spirit, comfort me!

When I lie within my bed,
Sick in heart, and sick in head,
And with doubts discomforted,
  Sweet Spirit, comfort me!

When the house doth sigh and weep,
And the world is drowned in sleep,

8 London taverns

10

Yet mine eyes the watch doth keep;
   Sweet Spirit, comfort me!

When the artless doctor sees
No one hope, but of his fees,
And his skill runs on the lees,
   Sweet Spirit, comfort me!

When his potion and his pill,
His, or none, or little skill
Meet for nothing but to kill,
   Sweet Spirit, comfort me!   20

When the passing bell doth toll,
And the Furies in a shoal
Come to fright a parting soul,
   Sweet Spirit, comfort me!

When the tapers now burn blue,
And the comforters are few,
And that number more than true,
   Sweet Spirit, comfort me!

When the priest his last hath prayed,
And I nod to what is said,   30
'Cause my speech is now decayed,
   Sweet Spirit, comfort me!

When, God knows, I'm tossed about
Either with despair, or doubt,
Yet before the glass be out,
   Sweet Spirit, comfort me!

When the Tempter me pursu'th
With the sins of all my youth,
And half damns me with untruth,
   Sweet Spirit, comfort me!   40

When the flames and hellish cries
Fright mine ears, and fright mine eyes,
And all terrors me surprise,
   Sweet Spirit, comfort me!

When the Judgment is revealed,
And that opened which was sealed,
When to Thee I have appealed,
   Sweet Spirit, comfort me!

A THANKSGIVING TO GOD FOR HIS HOUSE

Lord, Thou hast given me a cell
   Wherein to dwell,
A little house, whose humble roof
   Is weather-proof;
Under the spars of which I lie
   Both soft and dry;
Where Thou my chamber for to ward
   Hast set a guard
Of harmless thoughts, to watch and keep
   Me, while I sleep.   10
Low is my porch, as is my fate,
   Both void of state;
And yet the threshold of my door
   Is worn by th'poor,
Who thither come, and freely get
   Good words, or meat.
Like as my parlor, so my hall
   And kitchen's small:
A little buttery, and therein
   A little bin   20
Which keeps my little loaf of bread
   Unchipped, unflead.[9]
Some brittle sticks of thorn or briar
   Make me a fire,
Close by whose living coal I sit,
   And glow like it.
Lord, I confess too, when I dine,
   The pulse is thine,
And all those other bits, that be
   There placed by Thee: 30
The worts, the purslain, and the mess
   Of watercress,
Which of Thy kindness thou hast sent;
   And my content
Makes those, and my beloved beet
   To be more sweet.
'Tis thou that crown'st my glittering hearth
   With guiltless mirth;
And giv'st me wassail bowls to drink
   Spiced to the brink.   40
Lord, 'tis thy plenty-dropping hand
   That soils my land,
And giv'st me, for my bushel sown,
   Twice ten for one.

9 the crust not removed

Thou mak'st my teeming hen to lay
   Her egg each day,
Besides my healthful ewes to bear
   Me twins each year;
The while the conduits of my kine
   Run cream, for wine.
All these, and better, Thou dost send   50
   Me, to this end,
That I should render, for my part,
   A thankful heart,
Which, fired with incense, I resign
   As wholly Thine;
But the acceptance, that must be,
   My Christ, by Thee.

ANOTHER GRACE FOR A CHILD

HERE a little child I stand,
Heaving up my either hand;
Cold as paddocks though they be,
Here I lift them up to Thee,
For a benison to fall
On our meat, and on us all. *Amen.*

TO KEEP A TRUE LENT

Is this a fast, to keep
   The larder lean?
     And clean
From fat of veals, and sheep?

Is it to quit the dish
   Of flesh, yet still
     To fill
The platter high with fish?

Is it to fast an hour,
   Or ragg'd to go,
     Or show
A downcast look, and sour?

No: 'tis a fast, to dole
   Thy sheaf of wheat,
     And meat
Unto the hungry soul.

It is to fast from strife,
   From old debate,
     And hate;
To circumcise thy life.

To show a heart grief-rent;
To starve thy sin,
Not bin;
And that's to keep thy Lent.

THIS CROSS-TREE HERE

THIS   Cross-Tree   here
Doth   Jesus   bear,
who   sweetened   first
The   death   accursed.
Here all things ready are, make haste, make haste away;
For, long this work will be, and very short this day.
Why then, go on to act: here's wonders to be done,
Before the last least sand of Thy ninth hour be run;
Or ere dark clouds do dull, or dead the mid-day's sun.
Act   when   thou   wilt,
Blood   will   be   spilt;
Pure   balm,   that   shall
Bring   health   to   all.
Why   then,   begin
To   pour   first   in
Some   drops   of   wine,
Instead   of   brine,
To   search   the   wound,
So   long   unsound:
And   when   that's   done,
Let   oil,   next,   run,
to   cure   the   sore
Sin   made   before.
And   O!   dear   Christ,
E'en   as   Thou   di'st,
Look   down,   and   see
Us   weep   for   Thee.
And though (Love knows)
Thy   dreadful   woes
We   cannot   ease;
Yet   do   Thou   please,
Who   Mercy   art,
T'accept   each   heart,
That   gladly   would
Help,   if   it   could.
Meanwhile,   let   me,
Beneath   this   tree,
This   honor   have,
To   make   my   grave.

SEVENTEENTH CENTURY LYRICS

BEN JONSON (1572?–1637). Ben Jonson's family originated in Annandale, just over the border in southwestern Scotland, but he himself was born in Westminster, probably in 1572. At Westminster School he was taught to love learning by William Camden, the noted antiquary. He was apprenticed to his stepfather's trade of bricklaying, served in English armies in the Low Countries, returned to England, married a woman whom he afterwards described as "a shrew, yet honest," and perhaps by 1595 began play-writing, which was to be the chief business of his life. His contribution to the stage can here be only briefly summarized. He was noted chiefly for the "comedy of humors," of which *Everyman in His Humor* was the earliest example, for satiric and realistic comedies exposing human villainies, and especially the frauds and sharp practice of his day, like *Volpone, The Alchemist*, and *Bartholomew Fair*, and for tragedy, on classic themes, like *Sejanus*, pedantically fortified on every page by reference to his sources. During the reign of James I he was the most distinguished writer of the ornamental and elaborate court masques. Ben had made himself by his own study the best classical scholar of his time, and in the drama championed what he considered classic as opposed to romantic art. He gave somewhat qualified praise to Shakespeare's work—praise which is still generous enough, if we consider his standards; but as to Shakespeare himself, he says (and there is no reason to doubt his word), "I did love the man, and do honor his memory, on this side idolatry, as much as any."

In addition to his dramas, Ben is known for a prose work giving miscellaneous critical judgments and dicta, *Timber*, or *Discoveries*, and for a considerable body of lyrics, some embedded in his plays, most of them in the volumes which he called, continuing his practice of arboreal titles, *The Forest* and *Underwoods*. These poems obviously strive for classic justness of diction and precision of form. They are clear and graceful; have neat turns of phrase; are perhaps conventional in subject and certainly restrained in emotion; and exhibit throughout a studied art, the polish obtained by grinding and rubbing. In these qualities Ben was the founder of a school which came to full flowering in the generation after his death.

In his later years Ben was the admired center of a group of young men who called themselves "the tribe of Ben." Broad-based, broad-fronted, he dogmatically maintained the superiority of his own standards to all others whatsoever, and his tribe were probably willing to believe that he was not so far wrong when, in regard to a certain piece of his work, he had somewhat blasphemously asserted,

"By G—, 'tis good, and if you like't, you may."

WALLER, SUCKLING, and LOVELACE may be grouped together as "Cavalier poets," since they were all royalist in sympathy. Edmund Waller (1606–1687), lawyer and member of Parliament, showed an easy ability to adapt himself to one party or the other, as their fortunes fluctuated during the period of the Civil Wars. He is known to-day chiefly for his lighter pieces, the most famous of which are here reprinted, but he enjoyed in the seventeenth century a reputation as being one of the first writers of smooth heroic couplets. "Our numbers were in their nonage" till he appeared, writes Dryden. Sir John Suckling (1609–1642) came of a distinguished family, inherited great wealth, saw military service in Europe, and became a great favorite at the court of Charles I. He was noted for his wit, his generosity, and a certain spectacular ostentation. At his own expense he gorgeously fitted out a troop for service under Charles—a troop, according to the accounts, more conspicuous for its trappings than for its courage. He was a famous gambler, and invented the game of cribbage. He wrote four plays, but is now chiefly remembered for the lyrics which appear in this volume, which in their gaiety and wit seem thoroughly characteristic of the man. Richard Lovelace (1618–1658) was an amiable and accomplished man; an enthusiastic royalist, who spent his fortune in support of the king, and was twice imprisoned by the Puritans for his political activities. His two most famous lyrics are here reprinted. All of these poets show an inheritance of the artistic standards of the school of Ben Jonson. So, in some measure, does George Wither (1588–1667), a fresh and delicate lyricist, who, unlike the men just discussed, adhered to the Puritan side and was imprisoned at the Restoration.

George Herbert (1593–1633) was educated at Westminster School and at Trinity College, Cambridge, where he took his B.A. in 1616. He was favored by James I, and hoped for a time to advance himself politically, but changed his views in 1626, took orders, and in 1630 became Rector of Bemerton, Wiltshire, where he discharged his parish duties diligently and conscientiously. He was an excellent classical scholar and an accomplished musician. His best-known work is *The Temple, or Sacred Poems and Private Ejaculations,* published the year after his death. His style owes much to the example of Donne, but a Donne whose amatory passion is translated into religious ecstasy, while he speaks with an originality and power that mark him as a great individual voice.

Henry Vaughan (1622–1695) was born at Newton-by-Usk, Brecknock, Wales, and called himself, after the ancient Silures, or South Welsh, the "Silurist." He attended Jesus College, Oxford, studied law, then medicine, and finally settled as a physician at his birthplace. His best work is contained in two volumes: *Olor Iscanus* (Swan of Usk), pub. 1651, although written earlier, and especially a volume of "Sacred Poems and Pious Ejaculations" which he entitled *Silex Scintillans* (Sparks from the flint), 1650. Prior to the composition of this latter work, he had become acquainted with the *Temple* of George Herbert, and had determined to model his life and works on Herbert's career and example. There will be noticed in Vaughan's work a certain quality of imagination and especially a mysticism that is not present in his model. With *The Retreat* should be compared Wordsworth's *Ode on the Intimations of Immortality.*

Bibliography. Best plays of Ben Jonson in Mermaid ser. Complete Works by Gifford and Cunningham. New ed. by C. H. Herford and Percy Simpson, in progress (Oxford), first two vols. of which contain best life. Short Life by G. Gregory Smith in Eng. Men of Letters ser. Admirable coll. of *Seventeenth Century Lyrics,* with biographies and notes, by A. C. Judson (Chicago); also *Eng. Poetry of the Seventeenth Century,* ed. R. F. Brinkley (Norton). Definitive ed. of *Poems of George Herbert,* with critical and biog. essays by G. H. Palmer, 2 vols. (Houghton Mifflin). *Works of Suckling,* ed. A. H. Thompson (Dutton). *Works of Vaughan,* ed. L. C. Martin, 2 vols. (Oxford). *Poems of Lovelace,* ed. C. H. Wilkinson, 2 vols. (Oxford).

HYMN TO DIANA

QUEEN and Huntress, chaste and fair,
Now the sun is laid to sleep,
Seated in thy silver chair
State in wonted manner keep:
  Hesperus entreats thy light,
  Goddess excellently bright.

Earth, let not thy envious shade
Dare itself to interpose;
Cynthia's shining orb was made
Heaven to clear when day did close:
  Bless us then with wishèd sight,
  Goddess excellently bright.

Lay thy bow of pearl apart
And thy crystal-shining quiver;
Give unto the flying hart
Space, to breathe, how short soever:
  Thou that mak'st a day of night,
  Goddess excellently bright.

—Ben Jonson

TO CELIA

DRINK to me only with thine eyes,
  And I will pledge with mine;
Or leave a kiss but in the cup,
  And I'll not look for wine.
The thirst that from the soul doth rise
  Doth ask a drink divine;
But might I of Jove's nectar sup,
  I would not change for thine.

I sent thee late a rosy wreath,
  Not so much honoring thee
As giving it a hope, that there
  It could not withered be.
But thou thereon didst only breathe,
  And sent'st it back to me;
Since when it grows, and smells, I swear,
  Not of itself, but thee.

—Ben Jonson

STILL TO BE NEAT

STILL to be neat, still to be dressed,
As you were going to a feast;
Still to be powdered, still perfumed;
Lady, it is to be presumed,
Though art's hid causes are not found,
All is not sweet, all is not sound.

Give me a look, give me a face,
That makes simplicity a grace;
Robes loosely flowing, hair as free:
Such sweet neglect more taketh me
Than all the adulteries of art;
They strike mine eyes, but not my heart.
—*Ben Jonson*

TO THE MEMORY OF MY BELOVED MASTER WILLIAM SHAKESPEARE

To draw no envy, Shakespeare, on thy name,
Am I thus ample to thy book and fame,
While I confess thy writings to be such
As neither man nor Muse can praise too much.
'T is true, and all men's suffrage. But these ways
Were not the paths I meant unto thy praise;
For silliest ignorance on these may light,
Which, when it sounds at best, but echoes right;
Or blind affection, which doth ne'er advance
The truth, but gropes, and urgeth all by chance;   10
Or crafty malice might pretend this praise,
And think to ruin where it seemed to raise.
These are, as some infamous bawd or whore
Should praise a matron. What could hurt her more?
But thou art proof against them, and, indeed,
Above the ill fortune of them, or the need.
I therefore will begin. Soul of the age,
The applause, delight, the wonder of our stage,
My Shakespeare, rise! I will not lodge thee by
Chaucer or Spenser, or bid Beaumont lie   20
A little further to make thee a room:
Thou art a monument without a tomb,
And art alive still while thy book doth live
And we have wits to read and praise to give.
That I not mix thee so, my brain excuses—

I mean with great, but disproportioned Muses;
For if I thought my judgment were of years,
I should commit thee surely with thy peers,
And tell how far thou didst our Lyly outshine,
Or sporting Kyd, or Marlowe's mighty line.   30
And though thou hadst small Latin and less Greek,
From thence to honor thee, I would not seek
For names; but call forth thundering Æschylus,
Euripides, and Sophocles to us;
Pacuvius, Accius,[1] him of Cordova [2] dead,
To life again, to hear thy buskin tread,
And shake a stage; or, when thy socks [3] were on,
Leave thee alone for the comparison
Of all that insolent Greece or haughty Rome
Sent forth, or since did from their ashes come.   40
Triumph, my Britain; thou hast one to show
To whom all scenes of Europe homage owe.
He was not of an age, but for all time!
And all the Muses still were in their prime,
When, like Apollo, he came forth to warm
Our ears, or like a Mercury to charm.
Nature herself was proud of his designs
And joyed to wear the dressing of his lines,
Which were so richly spun, and woven so fit,
As, since, she will vouchsafe no other wit.   50
The merry Greek, tart Aristophanes,
Neat Terence, witty Plautus, now not please;
But antiquated and deserted lie,
As they were not of Nature's family.
Yet must I not give Nature all; thy art,
My gentle Shakespeare, must enjoy a part.
For though the poet's matter nature be,
His art doth give the fashion; and, that he
Who casts to write a living line must sweat,
(Such as thine are) and strike the second heat   60
Upon the Muses' anvil; turn the same
And himself with it, that he thinks to frame,
Or for the laurel he may gain a scorn;
For a good poet's made, as well as born.
And such wert thou: look how the father's face
Lives in his issue; even so the race
Of Shakespeare's mind and manners brightly shines
In his well turnèd, and true filèd lines,

---

1 Roman tragic poets   high boot worn in classical   worn by actors in comedy.
2 Seneca   times by actors in tragedy;
3 The buskin was the   the sock the light shoe

In each of which he seems to shake a lance,
As brandished at the eyes of ignorance.   70
Sweet Swan of Avon! what a sight it were
To see thee in our waters yet appear,
And make those flights upon the banks of Thames,
That so did take Eliza, and our James! [4]
But stay; I see thee in the hemisphere
Advanced, and made a constellation there!
Shine forth, thou star of poets, and with rage
Or influence, chide or cheer the drooping stage,
Which, since thy flight from hence, hath mourned like night,
And despairs day, but for thy volume's light.   80
                                    —*Ben Jonson*

EPITAPH ON ELIZABETH, L. H.

WOULD'ST thou hear what man can say
In a little? reader, stay.
Underneath this stone doth lie
As much beauty as could die;
Which in life did harbor give
To more virtue than doth live.
If at all she had a fault,
Leave it buried in this vault.
One name was Elizabeth;
The other, let it sleep with death:
Fitter, where it died, to tell,
Than that it lived at all. Farewell!
                                    —*Ben Jonson*

EPITAPH ON SALATHIEL PAVY

WEEP with me, all you that read
        This little story:
And know, for whom a tear you shed
        Death's self is sorry.
'T was a child that so did thrive
        In grace and feature,
As heaven and nature seemed to strive
        Which owned the creature.
Years he numbered scarce thirteen
        When fates turned cruel,   10
Yet three filled zodiacs [5] had he been
        The stage's jewel;
And did act, what now we moan,

4 Elizabeth and James I   5 years

Old men so duly,
As, sooth, the Parcæ [6] thought him one,
He played so truly.
So, by error, to his fate
They all consented;
But viewing him since, alas, too late,
They have repented,   20
And have sought, to give new birth,
In baths to steep him;
But being so much too good for earth,
Heaven vows to keep him.

                —*Ben Jonson*

SHALL I, WASTING IN DESPAIR

SHALL I, wasting in despair,
Die, because a woman's fair?
Or make pale my cheeks with care,
'Cause another's rosy are?
Be she fairer than the day,
Or the flowery meads in May,
   If she be not fair to me,
   What care I how fair she be?

Should my heart be grieved or pined,
'Cause I see a woman kind?
Or a well disposèd nature
Joinèd with a lovely feature?
Be she meeker, kinder than
Turtle dove or pelican,
   If she be not so to me,
   What care I how kind she be?

Shall a woman's virtues move
Me to perish for her love?
Or her well deserving known,
Make me quite forget mine own?
Be she with that goodness blest
Which may gain her name of best,
   If she be not such to me,
   What care I how good she be?

'Cause her fortune seems too high,
Shall I play the fool, and die?
Those that bear a noble mind,
Where they want of riches find,

6 the Fates

Think "What, with them, they would do
That, without them, dare to woo."
  And unless that mind I see,
  What care I though great she be?

Great, or good, or kind, or fair,
I will ne'er the more despair!
If she love me (this believe!)
I will die, ere she shall grieve.
If she slight me when I woo,
I can scorn, and let her go!
  For if she be not for me,
  What care I for whom she be?

—*George Wither*

THE COLLAR

I STRUCK the board, and cried, "No more!
  I will abroad.
What! shall I ever sigh and pine?
My lines and life are free; free as the road,
  Loose as the wind, as large as store.[7]
    Shall I be still in suit?
Have I no harvest but a thorn
To let me blood, and not restore
What I have lost with cordial fruit?
    Sure there was wine   10
Before my sighs did dry it; there was corn
  Before my tears did drown it;
Is the year only lost to me?
    Have I no bays to crown it,
No flowers, no garlands gay? all blasted,
    All wasted?
Not so, my heart, but there is fruit,
    And thou hast hands.
Recover all thy sigh-blown age
On double pleasures; leave thy cold dispute   20
Of what is fit and not; forsake thy cage,
    Thy rope of sands
Which petty thoughts have made, and made to thee
  Good cable, to enforce and draw,
    And be thy law,
While thou didst wink and wouldst not see.
    Away! take heed;
    I will abroad.

7 abundance

Call in thy death's head there, tie up thy fears;
    He that forbears   30
To suit and serve his need
    Deserves his load."
But as I raved, and grew more fierce and wild
    At every word,
Methought I heard one calling, "Child";
    And I replied, "My Lord."
                            —*George Herbert*

THE PULLEY

WHEN God at first made man,
Having a glass of blessing standing by;
"Let us," said he, "pour on him all we can:
Let the world's riches, which dispersèd lie,
    Contract into a span."

So strength first made a way;
Then beauty flowed; then wisdom, honor, pleasure.
When almost all was out, God made a stay,
Perceiving that alone, of all his treasure,
    Rest in the bottom lay.

"For if I should," said he,
"Bestow this jewel also on my creature,
He would adore my gifts instead of me,
And rest in Nature, not the God of Nature;
    So both should losers be.

"Yet let him keep the rest,
But keep them with repining restlessness;
Let him be rich and weary, that at least,
If goodness lead him not, yet weariness
    May toss him to my breast."
                            —*George Herbert*

VIRTUE

SWEET day, so cool, so calm, so bright,
    The bridal of the earth and sky!
The dew shall weep thy fall to-night;
    For thou must die.

Sweet rose, whose hue, angry and brave,
    Bids the rash gazer wipe his eye,

Thy root is ever in its grave,
    And thou must die.

Sweet spring, full of sweet days and roses,
    A box where sweets compacted lie,
My music shows ye have your closes,
    And all must die.

Only a sweet and virtuous soul,
    Like seasoned timber, never gives;
But though the whole world turn to coal,
    Then chiefly lives.

                        —*George Herbert*

LOVE

Love bade me welcome; yet my soul drew back,
    Guilty of dust and sin.
But quick-eyed Love, observing me grow slack
    From my first entrance in,
Drew nearer to me, sweetly questioning,
    If I lacked anything.

"A guest," I answered, "worthy to be here":
    Love said, "You shall be he."
"I, the unkind, ungrateful? Ah, my dear,
    I cannot look on thee!"
Love took my hand and smiling did reply,
    "Who made the eyes but I?"

"Truth, Lord; but I have marred them: let my shame
    Go where it doth deserve."
"And know you not," says Love, "who bore the blame?"
    "My dear, then I will serve."
"You must sit down," says Love, "and taste my meat."
    So I did sit and eat.

                        —*George Herbert*

GO, LOVELY ROSE!

Go, lovely Rose!
Tell her that wastes her time and me,
That now she knows,
When I resemble her to thee,
How sweet and fair she seems to be.

Tell her that's young,
And shuns to have her graces spied,
That hadst thou sprung
In deserts, where no men abide,
Thou must have uncommended died.

Small is the worth
Of beauty from the light retired;
Bid her come forth,
Suffer herself to be desired,
And not blush so to be admired.

Then die! that she
The common fate of all things rare
May read in thee;
How small a part of time they share
That are so wondrous sweet and fair!
—*Edmund Waller*

ON A GIRDLE

THAT which her slender waist confined,
Shall now my joyful temples bind;
No monarch but would give his crown,
His arms might do what this has done.

It was my heaven's extremest sphere,
The pale which held that lovely deer,
My joy, my grief, my hope, my love,
Did all within this circle move!

A narrow compass! and yet there
Dwelt all that's good, and all that's fair;
Give me but what this ribband bound,
Take all the rest the sun goes round!
—*Edmund Waller*

THE CONSTANT LOVER

Out upon it! I have loved
    Three whole days together;
And am like to love three more,
    If it prove fair weather.

Time shall molt away his wings
    Ere he shall discover

In the whole wide world again
Such a constant lover.

But the spite on it is, no praise
Is due at all to me:
Love with me had made no stays
Had it any been but she.

Had it any been but she,
And that very face,
There had been at least ere this
A dozen dozen in her place.
—*Sir John Suckling*

WHY SO PALE AND WAN?

WHY so pale and wan, fond lover?
Prithee, why so pale?
Will, when looking well can't move her,
Looking ill prevail?
Prithee, why so pale?

Why so dull and mute, young sinner?
Prithee, why so mute?
Will, when speaking well can't win her,
Saying nothing do 't?
Prithee, why so mute?

Quit, quit for shame; this will not move,
This cannot take her.
If of herself she will not love,
Nothing can make her:
The devil take her!
—*Sir John Suckling*

TO LUCASTA, ON GOING TO THE WARS

TELL me not, sweet, I am unkind,
That from the nunnery
Of thy chaste breast and quiet mind
To war and arms I fly.

True, a new mistress now I chase,
The first foe in the field;
And with a stronger faith embrace
A sword, a horse, a shield.

Yet this inconstancy is such
   As thou too shalt adore;
I could not love thee, dear, so much,
   Loved I not honor more.

                 —Richard Lovelace

TO ALTHEA, FROM PRISON

WHEN Love with unconfinèd wings
   Hovers within my gates,
And my divine Althea brings
   To whisper at the grates;
When I lie tangled in her hair
   And fettered to her eye,
The birds that wanton in the air
   Know no such liberty.

When flowing cups run swiftly round
   With no allaying Thames,
Our careless heads with roses bound,
   Our hearts with loyal flames;
When thirsty grief in wine we steep,
   When healths and draughts go free,
Fishes that tipple in the deep
   Know no such liberty.

When, like committed linnets, I
   With shriller throat will sing
The sweetness, mercy, majesty,
   And glories of my king;
When I shall voice aloud how good
   He is, how great should be,
Enlargèd winds that curl the flood
   Know no such liberty.

Stone walls do not a prison make,
   Nor iron bars a cage;
Minds innocent and quiet take
   That for an hermitage.
If I have freedom in my love
   And in my soul am free,
Angels, alone, that soar above,
   Enjoy such liberty.

                 —Richard Lovelace

THE RETREAT

HAPPY those early days, when I
Shined in my angel-infancy;
Before I understood this place
Appointed for my second race,
Or taught my soul to fancy aught
But a white, celestial thought;
When yet I had not walked above
A mile or two from my first love,
And looking back at that short space,
Could see a glimpse of his bright face;   10
When on some gilded cloud or flower
My gazing soul would dwell an hour,
And in those weaker glories spy
Some shadows of eternity;
Before I taught my tongue to wound
My conscience with a sinful sound,
Or had the black art to dispense
A several sin to every sense,
But felt through all this fleshly dress
Bright shoots of everlastingness.   20
    O, how I long to travel back,
And tread again that ancient track,
That I might once more reach that plain,
Where first I felt my glorious train,
From whence the enlightened spirit sees
That shady city of palm trees.
But ah! my soul with too much stay
Is drunk, and staggers in the way.
Some men a forward motion love;
But I by backward steps would move,   30
And when this dust falls to the urn,
In that state I came, return.
                              —*Henry Vaughan*

THE WORLD

I SAW Eternity the other night,
Like a great ring of pure and endless light,
        All calm as it was bright;
And round beneath it, Time, in hours, days, years,
        Driven by the spheres,
Like a vast shadow moved; in which the world
        And all her train were hurled.

The doting lover in his quaintest strain
    Did there complain;
Near him, his lute, his fancy, and his flights,   10
    Wit's sour delights,
With gloves, and knots, the silly snares of pleasure,
    Yet his dear treasure,
All scattered lay, while he his eyes did pour
    Upon a flower.

The darksome statesman, hung with weights and woe,
Like a thick midnight-fog, moved there so slow,
    He did not stay, nor go;
Condemning thoughts, like sad eclipses, scowl
    Upon his soul,   20
And clouds of crying witnesses without
    Pursued him with one shout.
Yet digged the mole, and lest his ways be found,
    Worked under ground,
Where he did clutch his prey; but one did see
    That policy:
Churches and altars fed him; perjuries
    Were gnats and flies;
It rained about him blood and tears, but he
    Drank them as free.   30

The fearful miser on a heap of rust
Sat pining all his life there, did scarce trust
    His own hands with the dust,
Yet would not place one piece above, but lives
    In fear of thieves.
Thousands there were as frantic as himself,
    And hugged each one his pelf;
The downright epicure placed heaven in sense,
    And scorned pretence;
While others, slipt into a wide excess,   40
    Said little less;
The weaker sort, slight, trivial wares enslave,
    Who think them brave;
And poor, despisèd Truth sat counting by
    Their victory.

Yet some, who all this while did weep and sing,
And sing and weep, soared up into the ring;
    But most would use no wing.
"O fools," said I, "thus to prefer dark night
    Before true light!   50

To live in grots and caves, and hate the day
    Because it shows the way,
The way, which from this dead and dark abode
    Leads up to God;
A way where you might tread the sun, and be
    More bright than he!"
But, as I did their madness so discuss,
    One whispered thus,
"This ring the Bridegroom did for none provide
    But for his bride."   60
                       —Henry Vaughan

THE TIMBER

SURE thou didst flourish once; and many springs,
    Many bright mornings, much dew, many showers,
Passed o'er thy head; many light hearts and wings,
    Which now are dead, lodged in thy living bowers.

And still a new succession sings and flies;
    Fresh groves grow up, and their green branches shoot
Towards the old and still enduring skies,
    While the low violet thrives at their root.

But thou beneath the sad and heavy line
    Of death dost waste, all senseless, cold, and dark;
Where not so much as dreams of light may shine,
    Nor any thought of greenness, leaf, or bark.

And yet—as if some deep hate and dissent,
    Bred in thy growth betwixt high winds and thee,
Were still alive—thou dost great storms resent
    Before they come, and know'st how near they be.

Else all at rest thou liest, and the fierce breath
    Of tempests can no more disturb thy ease;
But this thy strange resentment after death
    Means only those who broke in life thy peace.
                       —Henry Vaughan

DEPARTED FRIENDS

THEY are all gone into the world of light!
    And I alone sit lingering here;
Their very memory is fair and bright,
    And my sad thoughts doth clear.

It glows and glitters in my cloudy breast,
    Like stars upon some gloomy grove,
Or those faint beams in which this hill is drest,
    After the sun's remove.

I see them walking in an air of glory,
    Whose light doth trample on my days;
My days, which are at best but dull and hoary,   10
    Mere glimmering and decays.

O holy hope! and high humility,
    High as the heavens above!
These are your walks, and you have showed them me,
    To kindle my cold love.

Dear, beauteous death! the jewel of the just,
    Shining nowhere but in the dark,
What mysteries do lie beyond thy dust,
    Could man outlook that mark!   20

He that hath found some fledged bird's nest may know
    At first sight if the bird be flown;
But what fair well or grove he sings in now,
    That is to him unknown.

And yet, as angels in some brighter dreams
    Call to the soul, when man doth sleep,
So some strange thoughts transcend our wonted themes,
    And into glory peep.

If a star were confined into a tomb,
    The captive flames must needs burn there;   30
But when the hand that locked her up gives room,
    She'll shine through all the sphere.

O Father of eternal life, and all
    Created glories under Thee,
Resume Thy spirit from this world of thrall
    Into true liberty!

Either disperse these mists, which blot and fill
    My perspective still as they pass;
Or else remove me hence unto that hill,
    Where I shall need no glass.

                        —Henry Vaughan   40

SIR THOMAS BROWNE (1605-1682)

Sir Thomas Browne was born in London in 1605, the son of a mercer. He was educated at Winchester School, and at Broadgates Hall (now Pembroke College), Oxford, taking B.A. and M.A. degrees in 1626 and 1629 respectively. Thereafter he traveled on the Continent, studying medicine at three famous schools, Montpellier, Padua, and Leyden, probably receiving from the last a medical degree. In 1637 Oxford made him a doctor of medicine. During almost all his mature life, he was a practising physician in the city of Norwich, in Norfolk. The Civil War passed over England in his time, but although he was a royalist by conviction, he seems to have taken no active part in the struggle. Instead, he devoted his life to his profession and to the quiet pursuits of a scholar. He was knighted by Charles II. in 1671.

His active and inquiring mind busied itself with all kinds of speculations, many of which would now be regarded as remote and erudite. He was interested in theology and metaphysics, and had a strong bent toward the mystical, while at the same time displaying a scientist's skepticism. By the age of thirty he had written his private confession of faith, the *Religio Medici*, which he circulated among his friends in manuscript, and was persuaded to publish, in 1642, only because garbled copies had got abroad. Even more famous, perhaps, is his *Hydriotaphia*, or *Urn-Burial*, 1658, a series of somber speculations on death, immortality, and the vanity of human life, aroused by the discovery in Norfolk of certain burial urns containing supposedly Roman remains. Two other characteristic works are his *Pseudodoxia Epidemica* or *Vulgar Errors*, 1646, and the *Garden of Cyrus*, or the *Quincuncial Lozenge*, 1658, in which the mystical has got such complete possession as to render the work extremely obscure.

Although hardly one of our greatest writers, Sir Thomas Browne has been included here out of deference to those who believe that certainly in the *Hydriotaphia* he has written the most sustained and gorgeous piece of rhetoric in the language. The subtle verbal harmonies, the haunting, measured cadences, the soaring, majestic accents of this masterpiece are beyond all praise, and have received due tribute from all who love prose as an artistic instrument. Interesting comparisons may be made with Milton's prose, almost contemporary, and with Dryden's, of the next generation. Striving for somewhat similar effects, Milton cannot match Browne's sonorous and polished periods, while with Dryden we are in another world, the world of modern prose, where an easy, flexible, and spontaneous style replaces the carefully contrived rhythms and the stately pomp of the older writer.

BIBLIOGRAPHY. *Complete Works*, ed. Geoffrey Keynes (Rudge), *Religio Medici* and *Hydriotaphia* in one vol. in Everyman's Library (Dutton). Life by Edmund Gosse in Eng. Men of Letters ser. Essays by De Quincey and Pater (both of whom were influenced by him), and by Leslie Stephen in *Hours in a Library*.

ON FAITH

(from *Religio Medici*)

As for those wingy mysteries in divinity, and airy subtleties in religion, which have unhinged the brains of better heads, they

never stretched the *Pia Mater* [1] of mine. Methinks there be not impossibilities enough in religion for an active faith; the deepest mysteries ours contains have not only been illustrated, but maintained, by syllogism and the rule of reason. I love to lose myself in a mystery, to pursue my reason to an *O altitudo!* [2] 'Tis my solitary recreation to pose my apprehension with those involved enigmas and riddles of the Trinity, with Incarnation, and Resurrection. I can answer all the objections of Satan and my rebellious reason with that odd resolution I learned of Tertullian,
10 *Certum est, quia impossibile est.* [3] I desire to exercise my faith in the difficultest point; for to credit ordinary and visible objects is not faith, but persuasion. Some believe the better for seeing Christ's sepulcher; and, when they have seen the Red Sea, doubt not of the miracle. Now, contrarily, I bless myself and am thankful that I lived not in the days of miracles, that I never saw Christ nor His disciples. I would not have been one of those Israelites that pass'd the Red Sea, nor one of Christ's patients on whom He wrought His wonders; then had my faith been thrust upon me, nor should I enjoy that greater blessing pronounced to
20 all that believe and saw not. 'Tis an easy and necessary belief, to credit what our eye and sense hath examined. I believe He was dead, and buried, and rose again; and desire to see Him in His glory, rather than to contemplate Him in His cenotaph or sepulcher. Nor is this much to believe; as we have reason, we owe this faith unto history: *they* only had the advantage of a bold and noble faith, who lived before His coming, who upon obscure prophecies and mystical types could raise a belief, and expect apparent impossibilities.

'Tis true, there is an edge in all firm belief, and with an easy
30 metaphor we may say, the *Sword* of Faith; but in these obscurities I rather use it in the adjunct the apostle gives it, a *Buckler;* under which I conceive a wary combatant may lie invulnerable. Since I was of understanding to know we knew nothing, my reason hath been more pliable to the will of Faith; I am now content to understand a mystery without a rigid definition, in an easy and Platonic [4] description. That allegorical description of Hermes [5] pleaseth me beyond all the metaphysical definitions of divines. Where I cannot satisfy my reason, I love to humor my fancy. . . . And thus I teach my haggard and unreclaimed
40 reason to stoop unto the lure of faith. I believe there was already

---

1 membrane enveloping brain and spinal cord
2 altitude (beyond comprehension by ordinary reason)
3 It is certain because it is impossible (by Quintus Tertullianus, 2d-3d Cent. A. D., an early church father).
4 transcendental (like some of the mystical speculations of Plato)
5 Hermes Trismegistus (fl. 4th Cent. A. D.), alchemist, magician and mystic. His allegorical description is, "A globe whose center is everywhere and whose circumference is nowhere."

a tree whose fruit our unhappy parents tasted, though, in the same chapter when God forbids it, 'tis positively said, the plants of the field were not yet grown, *for God had not caused it to rain upon the earth.* I believe that the Serpent, (if we shall literally understand it) from his proper form and figure, made his motion on his belly before the curse. I find the trial of the pucelage [6] and virginity of women, which God ordained the Jews, is very fallible. Experience and history informs me, that not only many particular women, but likewise whole nations, have escaped the curse of childbirth, which God seems to pronounce upon the whole sex. Yet do I believe that all this is true, which indeed my reason would persuade me to be false; and this I think is no vulgar part of faith, to believe a thing not only above but contrary to reason, and against the arguments of our proper senses.

How shall the dead arise, is no question of my faith; to believe only possibilities, is not faith, but mere philosophy. Many things are true in divinity, which are neither inducible by reason, nor confirmable by sense; and many things in philosophy confirmable by sense, yet not inducible by reason. Thus it is impossible by any solid or demonstrative reasons to persuade a man to believe the conversion of the needle to the north; though this be possible, and true, and easily credible, upon a single experiment unto the sense. I believe that our estranged and divided ashes shall unite again; that our separated dust, after so many pilgrimages and transformations into the parts of minerals, plants, animals, elements, shall at the voice of God return into their primitive shapes, and join again to make up their primary and predestinate forms. As at the creation there was a separation of that confused mass into its species; so at the destruction thereof there shall be a separation into its distinct individuals. As at the creation of the world, all the distinct species that we behold lay involved in one mass, till the fruitful voice of God separated this united multitude into its several species; so at the last day, when those corrupted relics shall be scattered in the wilderness of forms, and seem to have forgot their proper habits, God by a powerful voice shall command them back into their proper shapes, and call them out by their single individuals. Then shall appear the fertility of Adam, and the magic of that sperm that hath dilated into so many millions. I have often beheld as a miracle, that artificial resurrection and revivification of mercury, how being mortified into a thousand shapes, it assumes again its own, and returns into its numerical self. Let us speak naturally and like philosophers, the forms of alterable bodies in these sensible corruptions perish not; nor, as we imagine, wholly quit their

6 virginity

mansions, but retire and contract themselves into their secret and unaccessible parts, where they may best protect themselves from the action of their antagonist. A plant or vegetable consumed to ashes to a contemplative and school-philosopher seems utterly destroyed, and the form to have taken his leave for ever; but to a sensible artist the forms are not perished, but withdrawn into their incombustible part, where they lie secure from the action of that devouring element. This is made good by experience, which can from the ashes of a plant revive the plant, and from its cinders recall it into its stalk and leaves again. What the art of man can do in these inferior pieces, what blasphemy is it to affirm the finger of God cannot do in these more perfect and sensible structures! This is that mystical philosophy, from whence no true scholar becomes an atheist, but from the visible effects of nature grows up a real divine, and beholds not in a dream, as Ezekiel, but in an ocular and visible object, the types of his resurrection.

HYDRIOTAPHIA OR URN-BURIAL

CHAPTER V

Now since these dead bones have already outlasted the living ones of Methuselah, and in a yard under ground, and thin walls of clay, out-worn all the strong and specious buildings above it, and quietly rested under the drums and tramplings of three conquests: what prince can promise such diuturnity [7] unto his relics, or might not gladly say,

Sic ego componi versus in ossa velim? [8]

Time, which antiquates antiquities, and hath an art to make dust of all things, hath yet spared these minor monuments.

In vain we hope to be known by open and visible conservatories,[9] when to be unknown was the means of their continuation, and obscurity their protection. If they died by violent hands, and were thrust into their urns, these bones become considerable, and some old philosophers would honor them, whose souls they conceived most pure, which were thus snatched from their bodies, and to retain a stronger propension unto them; whereas they weariedly left a languishing corpse, and with faint desires of re-union. If they fell by long and aged decay, yet wrapped up in the bundle of time, they fall into indistinction,[10] and make but one blot with infants. If we begin to die when we live, and

---

7 long duration
8 "So when I have become dust, I might wish to be laid to rest." (Tibullus, III. ii. 26)
9 resting places (*i. e.*, tombs)   10 obscurity

long life be but a prolongation of death, our life is a sad composition; we live with death, and die not in a moment. How many pulses made up the life of Methuselah,[11] were work for Archimedes: [12] common counters sum up the life of Moses's man.[13] Our days become considerable, like petty sums, by minute accumulations; where numerous fractions make up but small round numbers; and our days of a span long, make not one little finger.[14]

If the nearness of our last necessity brought a nearer conformity into it, there were a happiness in hoary hairs, and no calamity in half-senses. But the long habit of living indisposeth us for dying; when avarice makes us the sport of death, when even David grew politically cruel and Solomon could hardly be said to be the wisest of men. But many are too early old, and before the date of age. Adversity stretcheth our days, misery makes Alcmena's nights,[15] and time hath no wings unto it. But the most tedious being is that which can unwish itself, content to be nothing, or never to have been, which was beyond the malcontent of Job, who cursed not the day of his life, but his nativity; content to have so far been, as to have a title to future being, although he had lived here but in an hidden state of life, and as it were an abortion.

What song the Sirens [16] sang, or what name Achilles [17] assumed when he hid himself among women, though puzzling questions, are not beyond all conjecture. What time the persons of these ossuaries [18] entered the famous nations of the dead, and slept with princes and counselors, might admit a wide solution. But who were the proprietaries of these bones, or what bodies these ashes made up, were a question above antiquarism; not to be resolved by man, nor easily perhaps by spirits, except we consult the provincial guardians, or tutelary observators.[19] Had they made as good provision for their names, as they have done for their relics, they had not so grossly erred in the art of perpetuation. But to subsist in bones, and be but pyramidally [20] extant, is a fallacy in duration. Vain ashes which in the oblivion of names, persons, times, and sexes, have found unto themselves a fruitless continuation, and only arise unto late posterity, as em-

11 whom the Bible credits with 969 years (*Gen.* v. 27)
12 the famous mathematician of Syracuse, Sicily (287?–212 B. C.)
13 See *Ex.* ii. 12.
14 or 100 years (indicated, by an ancient arithmetical sign, by the bent little finger of the right hand)
15 one night as long as three (like the night, artificially lengthened to the space of three nights, which Jupiter spent with her, for the begetting of Hercules)
16 the fabled sea nymphs, who by their songs lured mariners to their destruction. Ulysses escaped them by filling his mariners' ears with wax and lashing himself to the mast
17 disguised by his mother Thetis in woman's clothes, and hid with women, to prevent his taking part in the Trojan war. Browne says these are questions which Tiberius put to the grammarians.
18 bones   19 guardian spirits   20 in pyramids or tombs

hlems of mortal vanities, antidotes against pride, vain-glory, and madding vices. Pagan vain-glories which thought the world might last for ever, had encouragement for ambition; and, finding no Atropos [21] unto the immortality of their names, were never damped with the necessity of oblivion. Even old ambitions had the advantage of ours, in the attempts of their vain-glories, who acting early, and before the probable meridian of time, have by this time found great accomplishment of their designs, whereby the ancient heroes have already out-lasted their monuments and mechanical preservations. But in this latter scene of time, we cannot expect such mummies unto our memories, when ambition may fear the prophecy of Elias, and Charles the Fifth can never hope to live within two Methuselahs of Hector.[22]

And therefore, restless unquiet for the diuturnity of our memories unto present considerations seems a vanity almost out of date, and superannuated piece of folly. We cannot hope to live so long in our names, as some have done in their persons. One face of Janus [23] holds no proportion unto the other. 'Tis too late to be ambitious. The great mutations of the world are acted, or time may be too short for our designs. To extend our memories by monuments, whose death we daily pray for, and whose duration we cannot hope, without injury to our expectations in the advent of the last day, were a contradiction to our beliefs. We whose generations are ordained in this setting part of time, are providentially taken off from such imaginations; and, being necessitated to eye the remaining particle of futurity, are naturally constituted unto thoughts of the next world, and cannot excusably decline the consideration of that duration, which maketh pyramids pillars of snow, and all that's past a moment.

Circles and right lines limit and close all bodies, and the mortal right-lined circle [24] must conclude and shut up all. There is no antidote against the opium of time, which temporarily considereth all things: our fathers find their graves in our short memories, and sadly tell us how we may be buried in our survivors. Gravestones tell truth scarce forty years.[25] Generations pass while some trees stand, and old families last not three oaks. To be read by bare inscriptions like many in Gruter,[26] to hope for eternity by enigmatical epithets or first letters of our names, to be studied by antiquaries, who we were, and have new names

21 that one of the three Fates who cut the thread of life.
22 Elias, or Elijah, in 1 Kings, xxi, prophesied the death of King Ahab and his wife Jezebel. Charles the Fifth, emperor of Germany (1500-1558). Hector, Trojan hero in the *Iliad*.
23 ancient Roman two-faced god
24 Allusion is to the Greek letter Θ (theta), first letter of Θανατος, death, used by the Greeks as "the character of death," as when judges inscribed the letter on their ballots when voting the death penalty.
25 because, in crowded churchyards, other bodies are placed under them.
26 Jan Gruter or Gruytère (1560-1627), Flemish scholar, author of a book on *Ancient Inscriptions*.

given us like many of the mummies, are cold consolations unto the students of perpetuity, even by everlasting languages.

To be content that times to come should only know there was such a man, not caring whether they knew more of him, was a frigid ambition in Cardan,[27] disparaging his horoscopical inclination and judgment of himself. Who cares to subsist like Hippocrates'[28] patients, or Achilles' horses in Homer, under naked nominations,[29] without deserts and noble acts, which are the balsam[30] of our memories, the *entelechia*[31] and soul of our subsistences? To be nameless in worthy deeds, exceeds an infamous history. The Canaanitish woman[32] lives more happily without a name, than Herodias with one. And who had not rather been the good thief than Pilate?

But the iniquity of oblivion blindly scattereth her poppy, and deals with the memory of men without distinction to merit of perpetuity. Who can but pity the founder of the pyramids? Herostratus lives that burned the temple of Diana;[33] he is almost lost that built it. Time hath spared the epitaph of Adrian's[34] horse, confounded that of himself. In vain we compute our felicities by the advantage of our good names, since bad have equal durations, and Thersites is like to live as long as Agamemnon.[35] Who knows whether the best of men be known, or whether there be not more remarkable persons forgot, than any that stand remembered in the known account of time? Without the favor of the everlasting register, the first man had been as unknown as the last, and Methuselah's long life had been his only chronicle.

Oblivion is not to be hired. The greater part must be content to be as though they had not been, to be found in the register of God, not in the record of man. Twenty-seven names make up the first story,[36] and the recorded names ever since contain not one living century.[37] The number of the dead long exceedeth all that shall live. The night of time far surpasseth the day, and who knows when was the equinox? Every hour adds unto that current arithmetic,[38] which scarce stands one moment. And since death must be the *Lucina*[39] of life, and even Pagans could doubt, whether thus to live were to die; since our longest sun sets at

---

27 Geronimo Cardano (1501–1576), Italian physician, mathematician, and astrologer. He wrote, "I could wish to be recognized because I am. I have no desire that my character should be known."
28 famous Greek physician, fl. 5th–4th century B. C.   29 names
30 for embalming or preserving   31 actual existence
32 perhaps the one who was healed by Jesus (*Mark*, v. 25–34). Herodias, wicked wife of Herod (*Matt.* xiv. 1–12). The "good thief" was crucified with Jesus (*Luke*, xxiii. 40–43), after Pontius Pilate, the Roman governor, had turned him over to the Jews.
33 at Ephesus, in 356 B. C.   34 Roman emperor (76–138 A. D.).
35 Thersites, boaster and coward. Agamemnon, heroic leader of Greek armies in the *Iliad*.
36 before Noah's flood   37 hundred
38 continuously moving record of time   39 goddess of childbirth

right descensions, and makes but winter arches, and therefore it cannot be long before we lie down in darkness, and have our light in ashes; since the brother of death daily haunts us with dying mementos, and time that grows old in itself, bids us hope no long duration;—diuturnity is a dream and folly of expectation.

Darkness and light divided the course of time, and oblivion shares with memory a great part even of our living beings; we slightly remember our felicities, and the smartest strokes of af-
10 fliction leave but short smart upon us. Sense endureth no extremities, and sorrows destroy us or themselves. To weep into stones are fables. Afflictions induce callosities; [40] miseries are slippery, or fall like snow upon us, which notwithstanding is no unhappy stupidity. To be ignorant of evils to come, and forgetful of evils past, is a merciful provision in nature, whereby we digest the mixture of our few and evil days, and, our delivered senses not relapsing into cutting remembrances, our sorrows are not kept raw by the edge of repetitions. A great part of antiquity contented their hopes of subsistency with a transmigration of
20 their souls,—a good way to continue their memories, while having the advantage of plural successions, they could not but act something remarkable in such variety of beings, and enjoying the fame of their passed selves, make accumulation of glory unto their last durations. Others, rather than be lost in the uncomfortable night of nothing, were content to recede into the common being, and make one particle of the public soul of all things, which was no more than to return into their unknown and divine original again. Egyptian ingenuity was more unsatisfied contriving their bodies in sweet consistencies, [41] to attend the return of
30 their souls. But all was vanity, feeding the wind, and folly. The Egyptian mummies, which Cambyses [42] or time hath spared, avarice now consumeth. Mummy is become merchandise, Mizraim cures wounds, and Pharaoh is sold for balsams. [43]

In vain do individuals hope for immortality, or any patent from oblivion, in preservations below the moon; men have been deceived even in their flatteries above the sun, and studied conceits to perpetuate their names in heaven. The various cosmography of that part hath already varied the names of contrived constellations: Nimrod is lost in Orion, and Osiris in the Dog-
40 star. [44] While we look for incorruption in the heavens, we find they are but like the earth—durable in their main bodies, alterable in their parts; whereof, beside comets and new stars, per-

40 calloused or hardened states   41 as of mummies embalmed in spices
42 Persian conqueror, 6th century B. C.
43 Powdered mummy was used in the Middle Ages for medicine. Mizraim, grandson of Noah, whose descendents are supposed to have peopled Egypt. (*Gen.* x. 6, 13)
44 *i. e.*, heroes and gods are transformed into stars and constellations.

spectives [45] begin to tell tales, and the spots that wander about the sun, with Phaëton's [46] favor, would make clear conviction. There is nothing strictly immortal, but immortality. Whatever hath no beginning, may be confident of no end (all others have a dependent being and within the reach of destruction); which is the peculiar of that necessary essence that cannot destroy itself; and the highest strain of omnipotency, to be so powerfully constituted as not to suffer even from the power of itself. But the sufficiency of Christian immortality frustrates all earthly glory, and the quality of either state after death, makes a folly of posthumous memory. God who can only destroy our souls, and hath assured our resurrection, either of our bodies or names hath directly promised no duration. Wherein there is so much of chance, that the boldest expectants have found unhappy frustration; and to hold long subsistence, seems but a scape in oblivion. But man is a noble animal, splendid in ashes, and pompous in the grave, solemnizing nativities and deaths with equal luster, nor omitting ceremonies of bravery in the infamy of his nature.

Life is a pure flame, and we live by an invisible sun within us. A small fire sufficeth for life, great flames seemed too little after death, while men vainly affected precious pyres, and to burn like Sardanapalus; [47] but the wisdom of funeral laws found the folly of prodigal blazes, and reduced undoing fires unto the rule of sober obsequies, wherein few could be so mean as not to provide wood, pitch, a mourner, and an urn.

Five languages secured not the epitaph of Gordianus. [48] The man of God lives longer without a tomb, than any by one, invisibly interred by angels, and adjudged to obscurity, though not without some marks directing human discovery. Enoch and Elias, [49] without either tomb or burial, in an anomalous state of being, are the great examples of perpetuity, in their long and living memory, in strict account being still on this side death, and having a late part yet to act upon this stage of earth. If in the decretory term [50] of the world, we shall not all die but be changed, according to received translation, the last day will make but few graves; at least quick resurrections will anticipate lasting sepultures. Some graves will be opened before they be quite closed, and Lazarus be no wonder. When many that feared to die, shall groan that they can die but once, the dismal state is the second and living death, when life puts despair on the damned;

45 telescopes   46 son of Apollo, the sun god, who on occasion drove the chariot of the sun himself
47 who when Nineveh was about to fall before the Medes, set fire to his palace, and so burned himself and his court (9th cent. B. c?)
48 Roman emperor, 3d cent. A. D.
49 Both translated to heaven direct (*Gen.* v. 24; 2 *Kings* ii. 1-11). The burial place of Moses, the "man of God," is unknown (*Deut.* xxxiv. 6)
50 decreed end, judgment day

when men shall wish the coverings of mountains, not of monuments, and annihilations shall be courted.

While some have studied monuments, others have studiously declined them, and some have been so vainly boisterous, that they durst not acknowledge their graves; wherein Alaricus [51] seems most subtle, who had a river turned to hide his bones at the bottom. Even Sylla,[52] that thought himself safe in his urn, could not prevent revenging tongues, and stones thrown at his monument. Happy are they whom privacy makes innocent, who
10 deal so with men in this world, that they are not afraid to meet them in the next; who, when they die, make no commotion among the dead, and are not touched with that poetical taunt of Isaiah.[53]

Pyramids, arches, obelisks, were but the irregularities of vainglory, and wild enormities of ancient magnanimity. But the most magnanimous resolution rests in the Christian religion, which trampleth upon pride, and sits on the neck of ambition, humbly pursuing that infallible perpetuity, unto which all others must diminish their diameters, and be poorly seen in angles of con
20 tingency.[54]

Pious spirits who passed their days in raptures of futurity, made little more of this world, than the world that was before it, while they lay obscure in the chaos of preordination, and night of their fore-beings. And if any have been so happy as truly to understand Christian annihilation, ecstasies, exolution, liquefaction, transformation, the kiss of the spouse, gustation of God, and ingression into the divine shadow,[55] they have already had an handsome anticipation of heaven; the glory of the world is surely over, and the earth in ashes unto them.

30   To subsist in lasting monuments, to live in their productions, to exist in their names and predicament of chimeras,[56] was large satisfaction unto old expectations, and made one part of their Elysiums.[57] But all this is nothing in the metaphysics of true belief. To live indeed, is to be again ourselves, which being not only an hope, but an evidence in noble believers, 'tis all one to lie in St. Innocents' church-yard,[58] as in the sands of Egypt. Ready to be any thing, in the ecstasy of being ever, and as content with six foot as the *moles* of Adrianus.[59]

—tabesne cadavera solvat,
40   *An rogus, haud refert.*[60]

51 King of the Visigoths, who sacked Rome 410 A. D.
52 Lucius Cornelius Sulla (138–78 B. C.), Roman general.
53 *Is.* xiv. 4–12.   54 thin acute angles   55 "terms and phrases characteristic of the
                                          speculation of Christian mystics." (Browne)
56 condition of ghosts   57 dwelling place of happy souls after death
58 "in Paris, where bodies soon consume" (Browne)
59 Roman tomb of the Emperor Hadrian (76–138 A. D.)
60 Whether rotting in earth or funeral pyre consumes our bodies, matters little.
(Lucan, *Pharsalia*, vii. 809–810)

JOHN MILTON (1608–1674)

Milton's father had broken with his family, who were Catholics, and become a Puritan. Establishing himself in London, he had become a prosperous scrivener (drawer of legal documents). He was a man of fine integrity, who appreciated literature, and loved music. In this favorable atmosphere Milton was born, in a house in Bread Street, London, on December 9, 1608. He was educated at St. Paul's School, and at Christ's College, Cambridge, where his personal beauty and his moral uprightness gained for him the title, "the lady of Christ's." At Cambridge he wrote a number of Latin poems and several in English, the best known being *On the Morning of Christ's Nativity* (1629). Although he found academic discipline irksome, he remained at the university for seven years, finally taking his M.A. in 1632.

There followed a period of six years during which Milton lived quietly amid rural sights at Horton, on the Thames, whither his father had retired, perfecting his powers and preparing himself by contemplation and further study for the great vocation of poet, to which he had dedicated himself. His conception of the moral qualifications for his work was lofty. At a later date he declared, "He who would not be frustrate of his hope to write well hereafter in laudable things ought himself to be a true poem, . . . not presuming to sing high praises of heroic men or famous cities unless he have in himself the experience and practice of all that which is praiseworthy." He believed also that a poet should be a learned man, and no great poet has shown a profounder erudition. These fundamental ideas explain the comparative inaction of the Horton period, when, as he says, he "spent a long holiday turning over the Latin and Greek authors." Yet the products of this holiday, although not numerous, are among the greatest glories of English verse. They include *L'Allegro* and *Il Penseroso; Arcades* and *Comus* (two masques with musical settings by the distinguished composer Henry Lawes); and the elegy *Lycidas*. The freshness and grace of the first two poems, their sensuous delight in that which is beautiful, mark Milton as the last child of the Renaissance, yet even here the mood is contemplative; while the moral earnestness of the later Milton, the Puritan poet, is already present in the praise of chastity which is the central motive of *Comus,* and in the impassioned attack on the corrupt clergy which throbs and burns in *Lycidas*. His acceptance of the great poetical traditions of the past is shown especially in the pastoral machinery of the latter poem.

In 1638 he left Horton to travel to Italy, where he met, among other distinguished men, the blind Galileo. It is characteristic of his high ideals that he cut short his travels on hearing of political troubles in England. He said, "I thought it base to be travelling for amusement abroad, while my fellow-citizens were fighting for liberty at home." On his return he did not, however, join immediately in his countrymen's struggle, but became for some years a schoolmaster. His actual entrance into public life was delayed, indeed, until 1649, when he was appointed Latin Secretary to Cromwell's government, the functions of his office being to write state papers in Latin, and in a more general way to defend the Puritans in book and pamphlet. Milton's leaving of Horton marks the end of his first productive period, that of his early poems. His second period, down to the Restoration, is almost destitute of poetry, the notable exceptions being the series of great sonnets, "alas, too few!" Instead, it is a period of prose composition, mostly in Latin, partly in English, in which Milton, under the stress of his duties to mankind, as he saw them, devoted all his energies to the fight for human freedom, "religious, domestic, and civil." Toward the first end he wrote a series of pamphlets against the authority of the established church, and especially the institution of bishops (1641, 1642, and later). His battle for domestic liberty he prosecuted in three tracts (1643–1645) advocating divorce for "unfitness and contrariety of mind." These treatises followed the collapse of his own marriage. His wife, Mary Powell, the daughter of an Oxfordshire royalist, a girl of seventeen, whom he had married in 1643, had fled back to her family after a month of living with the austere poet. She was, however, persuaded to return in 1645, and three daughters were born of the union. Milton's attitude towards woman as a creature lower than man—an attitude born of his conviction and his experience— is reflected in his portrait of Eve. His first wife died in 1652, and he married twice again, his last wife surviving him for many years. The later marriages seem to have been more satisfactory.

Milton's defense of civil liberty was conducted in a series of tracts of which the most famous are *Eikonoklastes*, or Image-breakers (1649), in reply to the glowing picture of the last days of Charles I presented in Dr. Gauden's *Eikon Basilike; The Tenure of Kings and Magistrates* (1649), defending the execution of the king; the *Pro Populo Anglicano Defensio* (1650), and the second *Defensio* (1654), in which works Milton entered into a violent controversy with the Dutchman, Salmasius. The severe strain on Milton's eyesight, imposed by his labors as Latin Secretary and his writing of the controversial pamphlets, resulted in his becoming totally blind by 1652. He had been warned by physicians to desist, but had grimly forged ahead, so that it may be truthfully said that he sacrificed his eyes to his country and the good fight.

Aside from the three groups of prose works mentioned, Milton composed a *Tractate on Education,* and especially his *Areopagitica,* a speech for the freedom of the press (1644), of all Milton's prose works the one of greatest permanent interest, written in a powerful and resonant style, magnificent in its very involutions and Latinization of vocabulary and structure.

On the Restoration, in 1660, Milton went into retirement, but he was hardly molested by the new government, and was eventually included in the general amnesty. He now set about writing the great work which he had planned from his youth. The subject finally decided upon, after the rejection of many, including the story of Arthur, seemed to him the most important in the world. Dictated, because of his blindness, to amanuenses, *Paradise Lost* was composed between 1660 and 1665 and published in 1667. Milton had now entered upon the third of his productive periods, that of the major poems. The lyric notes of the Horton days had been replaced by organ tones, epic sweep, and grandeur without parallel in English verse, as he sang of cosmic actors, God and his hosts, Satan and his cohort of fallen angels, and the drama of the temptation and fall of man. *Paradise Regained,* generally esteemed less successful, followed in 1671, and *Samson Agonistes,* a drama in the Greek manner, in the same year. The latter is one of Milton's most superb achievements. The subject he doubtless chose partly because of the analogy between Samson and himself, old, blind, betrayed, and fallen into the hands of his enemies. He died on November 8, 1674.

The intellectual distinction, dynamic power, and varied and perfect artistry of Milton must always classify him as among the very first of our poets. Those who are disappointed at not finding in him humor, or breadth of human sympathies, or dramatic ability, are looking for qualities which a very great man simply did not possess. Sometimes one wishes he had had a little less zeal, a little less purity, and a little more toleration and human weakness, although one cannot help admiring, as Macaulay puts it, "the faith which he so sternly kept with his country and with his fame."

BIBLIOGRAPHY. One volume *Complete Works*, ed. William Vaughan Moody in the Cambridge Poets ser. (Houghton Mifflin). *The Poetical Works* in original spelling, H. C. Beeching (Oxford). *The Prose Works*, ed. J. A. St. John, "Bohn Library," 5 vols. (the Latin works being in translation). *Student's Milton*, ed. F. A. Patterson (Crofts), containing the complete verse and selected prose. Complete *Works* being issued by Columbia Univ. Press. *Life of Milton* by David Masson in 7 vols. (standard). Short lives by Mark Pattison in the Eng. Men of Letters, and by Richard Garnett in Great Writers ser. D. Saurat's *Milton, Man and Thinker* (Dial Press). J. H. Hanford's *Milton Handbook* (Crofts).

ON SHAKESPEARE [1]

WHAT needs my Shakespeare, for his honored bones,
The labor of an age in pilèd stones?
Or that his hallowed relics should be hid
Under a star-ypointing pyramid?
Dear son of Memory, great heir of Fame,
What need'st thou such weak witness of thy name?
Thou, in our wonder and astonishment
Hast built thyself a livelong monument.
For whilst, to the shame of slow-endeavoring art,
Thy easy numbers flow, and that each heart
Hath, from the leaves of thy unvalued book,
Those Delphic lines with deep impression took;
Then thou, our fancy of itself bereaving,
Dost make us marble, with too much conceiving;
And, so sepulchred, in such pomp dost lie,
That kings for such a tomb would wish to die.

L'ALLEGRO

HENCE, loathèd Melancholy,
    Of Cerberus and blackest Midnight born
In Stygian cave forlorn
    'Mongst horrid [2] shapes, and shrieks, and sights unholy,
Find out some uncouth [3] cell,
    Where brooding Darkness spreads his jealous wings,
    And the night-raven sings;
    There under ebon shades and low-browed rocks,
As ragged as thy locks,
    In dark Cimmerian desert [4] ever dwell.   10

---

of Shakespeare, 1632
2 terrifying
3 unknown, strange

4 a land perpetually involved in mist and darkness (*Odyssey*, xi. 14)

But come, thou Goddess fair and free,
In heaven yclep'd Euphrosyne,[5]
And by men heart-easing Mirth,
Whom lovely Venus at a birth,
With two sister Graces more
To ivy-crownèd Bacchus bore;
Or whether (as some sager sing)
The frolic wind that breathes the spring,
Zephyr with Aurora playing,
As he met her once a-Maying,   20
There on beds of violets blue,
And fresh-blown roses washed in dew,
Filled her with thee, a daughter fair,
So buxom,[6] blithe, and debonair.
    Haste thee, Nymph, and bring with thee
Jest and youthful Jollity,
Quips and cranks and wanton wiles,
Nods and becks and wreathèd smiles,
Such as hang on Hebe's cheek,
And love to live in dimple sleek;   30
Sport that wrinkled Care derides,
And Laughter holding both his sides.
Come, and trip it as you go,
On the light fantastic toe;
And in thy right hand lead with thee
The mountain-nymph, sweet Liberty;
And, if I give thee honor due,
Mirth, admit me of thy crew,
To live with her, and live with thee,
In unreprovèd pleasures free;   40
To hear the lark begin his flight,
And, singing, startle the dull night,
From his watch-tower in the skies,
Till the dappled dawn doth rise;
Then to come, in spite of [7] sorrow,
And at my window bid good-morrow,
Through the sweet-briar or the vine,
Or the twisted eglantine;
While the cock with lively din
Scatters the rear of darkness thin;   50
And to the stack, or the barn-door,
Stoutly struts his dames before:
Oft listening how the hounds and horn
Cheerly rouse the slumbering morn,

5 typifying innocent pleasure, born of love and wine,   6 lively
or of spring and the dawn   7 to spite

From the side of some hoar hill,
Through the high wood echoing shrill:
Sometime walking, not unseen,
By hedgerow elms, on hillocks green,
Right against the eastern gate
Where the great Sun begins his state, 60
Robed in flames and amber light,
The clouds in thousand liveries dight,
While the ploughman, near at hand,
Whistles o'er the furrowed land,
And the milkmaid singeth blithe,
And the mower whets his scythe,
And every shepherd tells his tale [8]
Under the hawthorn in the dale.
Straight mine eye hath caught new pleasures
Whilst the landscape round it measures: 70
Russet lawns, and fallows gray,
Where the nibbling flocks do stray,
Mountains on whose barren breast
The laboring clouds do often rest;
Meadows trim with daisies pied;
Shallow brooks, and rivers wide;
Towers and battlements it sees
Bosomed high in tufted trees,
Where perhaps some beauty lies,
The cynosure [9] of neighboring eyes. 80
Hard by, a cottage chimney smokes
From betwixt two agèd oaks,
Where Corydon and Thyrsis [10] met
Are at their savory dinner set
Of herbs and other country messes,
Which the neat-handed Phyllis dresses;
And then in haste her bower she leaves,
With Thestylis to bind the sheaves;
Or, if the earlier season lead,
To the tanned haycock in the mead. 90
Sometimes, with secure [11] delight,
The upland hamlets will invite,
When the merry bells ring round,
And the jocund rebecks [12] sound
To many a youth and many a maid
Dancing in the checkered shade,
And young and old come forth to play

[8] takes tally, or count, of his sheep
[9] Constellation of the Lesser Bear, containing the Pole-star, by which the Tyrian sailors steered; hence center of attention
[10] These and the following are conventional names in pastoral poetry.
[11] carefree
[12] fiddles

On a sunshine holiday,
Till the livelong daylight fail:
Then to the spicy nut-brown ale,   100
With stories told of many a feat,
How fairy Mab the junkets eat.
She was pinched and pulled, she said;
And he, by Friar's lantern [13] led,
Tells how the drudging goblin [14] sweat
To earn his cream-bowl duly set,
When in one night, ere glimpse of morn,
His shadowy flail hath threshed the corn
That ten day-laborers could not end;
Then lies him down, the lubber [15] fiend,   110
And, stretched out all the chimney's length,
Basks at the fire his hairy strength,
And crop-full out of doors he flings,
Ere the first cock his matin rings.
Thus done the tales, to bed they creep,
By whispering winds soon lulled asleep.
Towered cities please us then,
And the busy hum of men,
Where throngs of knights and barons bold,
In weeds [16] of peace, high triumphs hold,   120
With store of ladies, whose bright eyes
Rain influence, and judge the prize
Of wit or arms, while both contend
To win her grace whom all commend.
There let Hymen oft appear
In saffron robe, with taper clear,
And pomp, and feast, and revelry,
With mask and antique pageantry;
Such sights as youthful poets dream
On summer eves by haunted stream.   130
Then to the well-trod stage anon,
If Jonson's learnèd sock [17] be on,
Or sweetest Shakespeare, Fancy's child,
Warble his native wood-notes wild.
And ever, against eating cares,
Lap me in soft Lydian airs,
Married to immortal verse,
Such as the meeting soul may pierce,
In notes with many a winding bout [18]
Of linkèd sweetness long drawn out   140

13 Friar Rush, or Will o'   15 clumsy   in comedy
the wisp   16 garments   18 turn
14 Robin Goodfellow   17 slipper worn by actors

With wanton heed and giddy cunning,
The melting voice through mazes running,
Untwisting all the chains that tie
The hidden soul of harmony;
That Orpheus' self may heave his head
From golden slumber on a bed
Of heaped Elysian flowers, and hear
Such strains as would have won the ear
Of Pluto to have quite set free
His half-regained Eurydice.   150
These delights if thou canst give,
Mirth, with thee I mean to live.

IL PENSEROSO

Hence, vain deluding Joys,
    The brood of Folly without father bred!
How little you bested,[19]
    Or fill the fixèd mind with all your toys!
Dwell in some idle brain,
    And fancies fond [20] with gaudy shapes possess,
As thick and numberless
    As the gay motes that people the sunbeams,
Or likest hovering dreams,
    The fickle pensioners [21] of Morpheus' train.   10
But, hail! thou Goddess sage and holy!
Hail, divinest Melancholy!
Whose saintly visage is too bright
To hit the sense of human sight,
And therefore to our weaker view
O'erlaid with black, staid Wisdom's hue;
Black, but such as in esteem
Prince Memnon's [22] sister might beseem,
Or that starred Ethiop queen [23] that strove
To set her beauty's praise above   20
The Sea-Nymphs, and their powers offended.
Yet thou art higher far descended:
Thee bright-haired Vesta long of yore
To solitary Saturn bore; [24]
His daughter she; in Saturn's reign
Such mixture was not held a stain.
Oft in glimmering bowers and glades
He met her, and in secret shades

19 help
20 foolish
21 bodyguard
22 a prince of the Ethi-
opians, in Homer
23 Cassiopeia, trans-
formed into the constellation
24 Melancholy is born of
solitary thought (Saturn)
and purity (Vesta).

Of woody Ida's inmost grove,
Whilst yet there was no fear of Jove.   30
Come, pensive Nun, devout and pure,
Sober, steadfast, and demure,
All in a robe of darkest grain,[25]
Flowing with majestic train,
And sable stole of cypress lawn [26]
Over thy decent shoulders drawn.
Come; but keep thy wonted state,
With even step, and musing gait,
And looks commercing with the skies,
Thy rapt soul sitting in thine eyes: 40
There, held in holy passion still,
Forget thyself to marble, till
With a sad leaden downward cast
Thou fix them on the earth as fast.
And join with thee calm Peace and Quiet,
Spare Fast, that oft with gods doth diet,
And hears the Muses in a ring
Aye round about Jove's altar sing;
And add to these retirèd Leisure,
That in trim gardens takes his pleasure;   50
But, first and chiefest, with thee bring
Him that yon soars on golden wing,
Guiding the fiery-wheelèd throne,
The Cherub Contemplation;
And the mute Silence hist along,
'Less Philomel [27] will deign a song,
In her sweetest saddest plight,
Smoothing the rugged brow of Night,
While Cynthia [28] checks her dragon yoke
Gently o'er the accustomed oak.   60
Sweet bird, that shunn'st the noise of folly,
Most musical, most melancholy!
Thee, chauntress, oft the woods among
I woo, to hear thy even-song;
And, missing thee, I walk unseen
On the dry smooth-shaven green
To behold the wandering moon,
Riding near her highest noon,
Like one that had been led astray
Through the heaven's wide pathless way,   70
And oft, as if her head she bowed,
Stooping through a fleecy cloud.

25 purple or dark blue   27 the nightingale   28 the moon
26 black crape

Oft, on a plat of rising ground,
I hear the far-off curfew sound,
Over some wide-watered shore,
Swinging slow with sullen roar;
Or, if the air will not permit,
Some still removèd place will fit,
Where glowing embers through the room
Teach light to counterfeit a gloom,   80
Far from all resort of mirth,
Save the cricket on the hearth,
Or the bellman's drowsy charm
To bless the doors from nightly harm.
Or let my lamp, at midnight hour,
Be seen in some high lonely tower,
Where I may oft outwatch the Bear,[29]
With thrice great Hermes,[30] or unsphere [31]
The spirit of Plato, to unfold
What worlds or what past regions hold   90
The immortal mind that hath forsook
Her mansion in this fleshly nook;
And of those demons that are found
In fire, air, flood, or underground,
Whose power hath a true consent
With planet or with element.
Sometime let gorgeous Tragedy
In sceptered pall come sweeping by,
Presenting Thebes, or Pelops' line,
Or the tale of Troy divine,   100
Or what (though rare) of later age
Ennobled hath the buskined [32] stage.
But, O sad Virgin! that thy power
Might raise Musæus from his bower;
Or bid the soul of Orpheus sing
Such notes as, warbled to the string,
Drew iron tears down Pluto's cheek,
And made Hell grant what love did seek;
Or call up him [33] that left half-told
The story of Cambuscan bold,   110
Of Camball, and of Algarsife,
And who had Canace to wife,
That owned the virtuous ring and glass,
And of the wondrous horse of brass

29 *i. e.*, sit up till dawn, since in northern latitudes the Great Bear never sets
30 Hermes Trismegistus, reputed author of magic and mystical books
31 call down his spirit from the heavenly sphere which it inhabits
32 wearing the heavy boot of actors in tragedy
33 Chaucer, in his *Squire's Tale*

On which the Tartar king did ride;
And if aught else great bards beside
In sage and solemn tunes have sung,
Of turneys, and of trophies hung,
Of forests, and enchantments drear,
Where more is meant than meets the ear.[34]   120
Thus, Night, oft see me in thy pale career,
Till civil-suited Morn appear,
Not tricked and frounced, as she was wont
With the Attic boy [35] to hunt,
But kerchiefed in a comely cloud,
While rocking winds are piping loud,
Or ushered with a shower still,
When the gust hath blown his fill,
Ending on the rustling leaves,
With minute-drops from off the eaves.   130
And, when the sun begins to fling
His flaring beams, me, Goddess, bring
To archèd walks of twilight groves,
And shadows brown, that Sylvan loves,
Of pine, or monumental oak,
Where the rude axe with heavèd stroke
Was never heard the nymphs to daunt,
Or fright them from their hallowed haunt.
There, in close covert, by some brook,
Where no profaner eye may look,   140
Hide me from day's garish eye,
While the bee with honeyed thigh,
That at her flowery work doth sing,
And the waters murmuring,
With such consort as they keep,
Entice the dewy-feathered Sleep.
And let some strange mysterious dream
Wave at his wings, in airy stream
Of lively portraiture displayed,
Softly on my eyelids laid;   150
And, as I wake, sweet music breathe
Above, about, or underneath,
Sent by some Spirit to mortals good,
Or the unseen Genius of the wood.
But let my due feet never fail
To walk the studious cloister's pale,[36]
And love the high embowèd roof,
With antique pillars massy-proof,

---

34 alluding perhaps to   35 Cephalus, loved by   36 enclosure
Spenser's *Faerie Queene*   Aurora

And storied windows richly dight,
Casting a dim religious light.   160
There let the pealing organ blow,
To the full-voiced quire below,
In service high and anthems clear,
As may with sweetness, through mine ear,
Dissolve me into ecstasies,
And bring all Heaven before mine eyes.
And may at last my weary age
Find out the peaceful hermitage,
The hairy gown and mossy cell,
Where I may sit and rightly spell [37]   170
Of every star that heaven doth shew,
And every herb that sips the dew,
Till old experience do attain
To something like prophetic strain.
These pleasures, Melancholy, give,
And I with thee will choose to live.

LYCIDAS [38]

In this Monody the Author bewails a learned Friend,[39] unfortunately drowned in his passage from Chester on the Irish Seas, 1637; and, by occasion, foretells the ruin of our corrupted clergy, then in their height.

YET once more, O ye laurels, and once more,
Ye myrtles brown, with ivy never sere,
I come to pluck your berries harsh and crude,
And with forced fingers rude
Shatter your leaves before the mellowing year.
Bitter constraint and sad occasion dear
Compels me to disturb your season due; [40]
For Lycidas is dead, dead ere his prime,
Young Lycidas, and hath not left his peer.
Who would not sing for Lycidas? he knew   10
Himself to sing, and build the lofty rhyme.
He must not float upon his watery bier
Unwept, and welter to the parching wind,
Without the meed of some melodious tear.
Begin, then, Sisters of the sacred well [41]
That from beneath the seat of Jove doth spring;
Begin, and somewhat loudly sweep the string.

---

37 read
38 a pastoral name, taken from the Idyls of Theocritus
39 Edward King, a fellow student of Milton's at Christ's College, Cambridge
40 King's death compels Milton to write once more before he feels his poetic powers are ripe.
41 Muses of the Pierian spring

Hence with denial vain and coy excuse:
So may some gentle Muse
With lucky words favor *my* destined urn,   20
And as he passes turn,
And bid fair peace be to my sable shroud!
    For we were nursed upon the self-same hill,
Fed the same flock, by fountain, shade, and rill;
Together both, ere the high lawns appeared
Under the opening eyelids of the Morn,
We drove a-field, and both together heard
What time the gray-fly winds her sultry horn,
Battening [42] our flocks with the fresh dews of night,
Oft till the star that rose at evening bright   30
Toward heaven's descent had sloped his westering wheel.
Meanwhile the rural ditties were not mute;
Tempered to the oaten flute,
Rough Satyrs danced, and Fauns with cloven heel
From the glad sound would not be absent long;
And old Damœtas [43] loved to hear our song.
    But, oh! the heavy change, now thou art gone,
Now thou art gone and never must return!
Thee, Shepherd, thee the woods and desert caves,
With wild thyme and the gadding vine o'ergrown,   40
And all their echoes, mourn.
The willows, and the hazel copses green,
Shall now no more be seen
Fanning their joyous leaves to thy soft lays.
As killing as the canker to the rose,
Or taint-worm to the weanling herds that graze,
Or frost to flowers, that their gay wardrobe wear,
When first the white-thorn blows;
Such, Lycidas, thy loss to shepherd's ear.
    Where were ye, Nymphs, when the remorseless deep   50
Closed o'er the head of your loved Lycidas?
For neither were ye playing on the steep
Where your old bards, the famous Druids, lie,
Nor on the shaggy top of Mona [44] high,
Nor yet where Deva [45] spreads her wizard stream.
Ay me! I fondly [46] dream
"Had ye been there," . . . for what could that have done?
What could the Muse [47] herself that Orpheus bore,
The Muse herself, for her enchanting son,

42 feeding
43 The conventional older shepherd present at song-contests in classical poetry; possibly alluding also to a college tutor.
44 Island of Angelsey (Wales)
45 the River Dee
46 foolishly
47 Calliope. Orpheus was torn to pieces by Thracian women on his refusal to take part in the Bacchic orgies.

Whom universal nature did lament, 60
When, by the rout that made the hideous roar,
His gory visage down the stream was sent,
Down the swift Hebrus to the Lesbian shore?
  Alas! what boots [48] it with uncessant care
To tend the homely, slighted, shepherd's trade,
And strictly meditate the thankless Muse?
Were it not better done, as others use,
To sport with Amaryllis in the shade,
Or with the tangles of Neæra's hair?
Fame is the spur that the clear spirit doth raise 70
(That last infirmity of noble mind)
To scorn delights and live laborious days;
But the fair guerdon when we hope to find,
And think to burst out into sudden blaze,
Comes the blind Fury [49] with the abhorrèd shears,
And slits the thin-spun life. "But not the praise,"
Phœbus replied, and touched my trembling ears:
"Fame is no plant that grows on mortal soil,
Nor in the glistering foil [50]
Set off to the world, nor in broad rumor lies, 80
But lives and spreads aloft by those pure eyes
And perfect witness of all-judging Jove;
As he pronounces lastly on each deed,
Of so much fame in heaven expect thy meed."
  O fountain Arethuse, [51] and thou honored flood,
Smooth-sliding Mincius, [52] crowned with vocal reeds,
That strain I heard was of a higher mood.
But now my oat [53] proceeds,
And listens to the Herald of the Sea,
That came in Neptune's plea. 90
He asked the waves, and asked the felon winds,
What hard mishap hath doomed this gentle swain?
And questioned every gust of rugged wings
That blows from off each beakèd promontory.
They knew not of his story;
And sage Hippotades [54] their answer brings,
That not a blast was from his dungeon strayed:
The air was calm, and on the level brine
Sleek Panope [55] with all her sisters played.
It was that fatal and perfidious bark, 100
Built in the eclipse, and rigged with curses dark,

48 avails
49 Atropos, one of the Fates
50 gold or silver leaf placed behind a gem to

throw it into relief
51 in Sicily, representing Greek pastoral inspiration
52 Virgil's native river, associated with his

Eclogues
53 shepherd's pipe
54 Aeolus, god of winds
55 One of the Nereids

That sunk so low that sacred head of thine.
Next, Camus,[56] reverend sire, went footing slow,
His mantle hairy, and his bonnet sedge,
Inwrought with figures dim, and on the edge
Like to that sanguine flower inscribed with woe.[57]
"Ah! who hath reft," quoth he, "my dearest pledge?"
Last came, and last did go,
The Pilot of the Galilean Lake; [58]
Two massy keys he bore of metals twain   110
(The golden opes, the iron shuts amain).
He shook his mitered locks, and stern bespake:—
"How well could I have spared for thee, young swain,
Enow of such as, for their bellies' sake,
Creep, and intrude, and climb into the fold!
Of other care they little reckoning make
Than how to scramble at the shearers' feast,
And shove away the worthy bidden guest.
Blind mouths! that scarce themselves know how to hold
A sheep-hook, or have learned aught else the least   120
That to the faithful herdman's art belongs!
What recks it them? What need they? They are sped;
And, when they list, their lean and flashy songs [59]
Grate on their scrannel pipes of wretched straw;
The hungry sheep look up, and are not fed,
But, swoln with wind and the rank mist they draw,
Rot inwardly, and foul contagion spread;
Besides what the grim wolf with privy paw
Daily devours apace,[60] and nothing said.
But that two-handed engine [61] at the door   130
Stands ready to smite once, and smite no more."
    Return, Alpheus; [62] the dread voice is past
That shrunk thy streams; return, Sicilian Muse,
And call the vales, and bid them hither cast
Their bells and flowerets of a thousand hues.
Ye valleys low, where the mild whispers use
Of shades, and wanton winds, and gushing brooks,
On whose fresh lap the swart star [63] sparely looks,
Throw hither all your quaint enameled eyes
That on the green turf suck the honeyed showers,   140
And purple all the ground with vernal flowers.

56 personification of the River Cam, at Cambridge
57 the hyacinth, said to be inscribed with the Greek lamentation *ai, ai*
58 St. Peter, keeper of the keys to Heaven and founder of the Church, into which King was to have entered.
59 *i. e.*, trivial and insipid sermons, inculcating false doctrine (rank mist) 60 conversions made by the Catholic Church
61 the sword of God's
vengeance
62 Greek river, signifying return to the pastoral mood
63 the dog-star, Sirius, which brings heat that blackens vegetation

Bring the rathe [64] primrose that forsaken dies,
The tufted crow-toe, and pale jessamine,
The white pink, and the pansy freaked with jet,
The glowing violet,
The musk rose, and the well-attired woodbine,
With cowslips wan that hang the pensive head,
And every flower that sad embroidery wears;
Bid amaranthus all his beauty shed,
And daffadillies fill their cups with tears,   150
To strew the laureate hearse where Lycid lies.
For so, to interpose a little ease,
Let our frail thoughts dally with false surmise.
Ay me! whilst thee the shores and sounding seas
Wash far away, where'er thy bones are hurled;
Whether beyond the stormy Hebrides,
Where thou perhaps under the whelming tide
Visit'st the bottom of the monstrous world; [65]
Or whether thou, to our moist vows denied,
Sleep'st by the fable of Bellerus old,[66]   160
Where the great Vision of the guarded mount [67]
Looks toward Namancos and Bayona's hold.[68]
Look homeward, Angel, now, and melt with ruth:
And, O ye dolphins, waft the hapless youth.
   Weep no more, woeful shepherds, weep no more,
For Lycidas, your sorrow, is not dead,
Sunk though he be beneath the watery floor.
So sinks the day-star in the ocean bed,
And yet anon repairs his drooping head,
And tricks his beams, and with new-spangled ore   170
Flames in the forehead of the morning sky:
So Lycidas sunk low, but mounted high,
Through the dear might of Him that walked the waves,
Where, other groves and other streams along,
With nectar pure his oozy locks he laves,
And hears the unexpressive nuptial song,[69]
In the blest kingdoms meek of joy and love.
There entertain him all the Saints above,
In solemn troops, and sweet societies,
That sing, and singing in their glory move,   180
And wipe the tears for ever from his eyes.
Now, Lycidas, the shepherds weep no more;
Henceforth thou art the Genius of the shore,

64 early
65 world of monsters
66 name invented from
Bellerium (Land's End)

67 St. Michael's Mount,
Cornwall, where the Arch-
angel Michael was said to
have appeared

68 in Spain
69 inexpressible song of
the soul's mystic marriage
with Christ

In thy large recompense, and shalt be good
To all that wander in that perilous flood.

Thus sang the uncouth swain to the oaks and rills,
While the still morn went out with sandals gray:
He touched the tender stops of various quills,
With eager thought warbling his Doric lay: [70]
And now the sun had stretched out all the hills, 190
And now was dropped into the western bay.
At last he rose, and twitched his mantle blue:
To-morrow to fresh woods, and pastures new.

SONNETS

On His Being Arrived to the Age of Twenty-three [71]

How soon hath Time, the subtle thief of youth,
　　Stolen on his wing my three-and-twentieth year!
My hasting days fly on with full career,
　　But my late spring no bud or blossom shew'th.
Perhaps my semblance might deceive the truth
　　That I to manhood am arrived so near;
　　And inward ripeness doth much less appear,
That some more timely-happy [72] spirits endu'th.
Yet, be it less or more, or soon or slow,
　　It shall be still in strictest measure even
　　To that same lot, however mean or high,
Toward which Time leads me, and the will of Heaven;
　　All is, if I have grace to use it so,
　　As ever in my great Task-Master's eye.

When the Assault was Intended to the City [73]

Captain, or colonel, or knight in arms,
　　Whose chance on these defenceless doors may seize,
　　If deed of honor did thee ever please,
Guard them, and him within protect from harms.
He can requite thee, for he knows the charms
　　That call fame on such gentle acts as these;
　　And he can spread thy name o'er lands and seas,
Whatever clime the sun's bright circle warms.
Lift not thy spear against the Muses' bower:
　　The great Emathian conqueror [74] bid spare

70 pastoral song
71 Written just as Milton was leaving Cambridge, 1631
72 fortunate in more seasonable development
73 When the King's forces were about to assault London, November, 1642.
74 Alexander the Great

The house of Pindarus, when temple and tower
Went to the ground; and the repeated air
Of sad Electra's poet [75] had the power
To save the Athenian walls from ruin bare.

To a Virtuous Young Lady

Lady, that in the prime of earliest youth
Wisely hast shunned the broad way and the green,
And with those few art eminently seen
That labor up the hill of heavenly Truth,
The better part with Mary and with Ruth,
Chosen thou hast; and they that overween,
And at thy growing virtues fret their spleen,
No anger find in thee, but pity and ruth.
Thy care is fixed, and zealously attends
To fill thy odorous lamp with deeds of light,
And hope that reaps not shame. Therefore be sure
Thou, when the Bridegroom with his feastful friends
Passes to bliss at the mid-hour of night,
Hast gained thy entrance, Virgin wise and pure.

On the Detraction which Followed upon My Writing Certain Treatises

A book was writ of late called *Tetrachordon*,[76]
And woven close, both matter, form, and style;
The subject new: it walked the town a while,
Numbering good intellects; now seldom pored on.
Cries the stall-reader, "Bless us! what a word on
A title-page is this!"; and some in file
Stand spelling false, while one might walk to Mile-
End Green. Why, is it harder, sirs, than *Gordon,
Colkitto*, or *Macdonnel*, or *Galasp?* [77]
Those rugged names to our like mouths grow sleek,
That would have made Quintilian stare and gasp.
Thy age, like ours, O soul of Sir John Cheek,
Hated not learning worse than toad or asp,
When thou taught'st Cambridge and King Edward Greek.

On the Same

I did but prompt the age to quit their clogs
By the known rules of ancient liberty,

75 Euripides
76 This "four-stringed" pamphlet presented Mil- ton's views on divorce.
77 Scotch names are selected because the Scotch Presbyterians were most scandalized by the divorce pamphlets.

When straight a barbarous noise environs me
Of owls and cuckoos, asses, apes, and dogs;
As when those hinds that were transformed to frogs
Railed at Latona's twin-born progeny,[78]
Which after held the Sun and Moon in fee.
But this is got by casting pearl to hogs,
That bawl for freedom in their senseless mood,
And still revolt when Truth would set them free.
License they mean when they cry Liberty;
For who loves that must first be wise and good:
But from that mark how far they rove we see,
For all this waste of wealth and loss of blood.

TO MR. H. LAWES [79] ON HIS AIRS

Harry, whose tuneful and well-measured song
First taught our English music how to span
Words with just note and accent, not to scan
With Midas' ears,[80] committing short and long,
Thy worth and skill exempts thee from the throng,
With praise enough for Envy to look wan;
To after age thou shalt be writ the man
That with smooth air couldst humor best our tongue.
Thou honor'st verse, and verse must lend her wing
To honor thee, the priest of Phœbus' quire,
That tunest their happiest lines in hymn or story.
Dante shall give Fame leave to set thee higher
Than his Casella, whom he wooed to sing,
Met in the milder shades of Purgatory.

ON THE LORD GENERAL FAIRFAX [81] AT THE SIEGE OF COLCHESTER

Fairfax, whose name in arms through Europe rings,
Filling each mouth with envy or with praise,
And all her jealous monarchs with amaze,
And rumors loud that daunt remotest kings,
Thy firm unshaken virtue ever brings
Victory home, though new rebellions raise
Their Hydra heads, and the false North displays
Her broken league to imp [82] their serpent wings.
O yet a nobler task awaits thy hand

---

78 Apollo and Diana
79 The musician who composed the musical settings to Milton's *Comus*
80 Changed by Apollo to asses' ears when he adjudged Pan the better musician.
81 Commander-in-chief of the Parliamentary for̃es. He besieged Kentish rebels at Colchester in 1648.
82 put new feathers in

No wonder, fallen such a pernicious highth!"
    He scarce had ceased when the superior Fiend
Was moving toward the shore; his ponderous shield,
Ethereal temper, massy, large, and round,
Behind him cast. The broad circumference
Hung on his shoulders like the moon, whose orb
Through optic glass the Tuscan artist [5] views
At evening, from the top of Fesolè,
Or in Valdarno,[6] to descry new lands,   290
Rivers, or mountains, in her spotty globe.
His spear—to equal which the tallest pine
Hewn on Norwegian hills, to be the mast
Of some great ammiral,[7] were but a wand—
He walked with, to support uneasy steps
Over the burning marl, not like those steps
On Heaven's azure; and the torrid clime
Smote on him sore besides, vaulted with fire.
Nathless he so endured, till on the beach
Of that inflamèd sea he stood, and called   300
His legions—Angel Forms, who lay entranced
Thick as autumnal leaves that strow the brooks
In Vallombrosa,[8] where the Etrurian shades
High over-arched embower; or scattered sedge
Afloat, when with fierce winds Orion armed
Hath vexed the Red-Sea coast, whose waves o'erthrew
Busiris [9] and his Memphian chivalry,
While with perfidious hatred they pursued
The sojourners of Goshen, who beheld
From the safe shore their floating carcases   310
And broken chariot-wheels. So thick bestrown,
Abject and lost, lay these, covering the flood,
Under amazement of their hideous change.
He called so loud that all the hollow deep
Of Hell resounded:—"Princes, Potentates,
Warriors, the Flower of Heaven—once yours; now lost,
If such astonishment as this can seize
Eternal Spirits! Or have ye chosen this place
After the toil of battle to repose
Your wearied virtue, for the ease you find   320
To slumber here, as in the vales of Heaven?
Or in this abject posture have ye sworn
To adore the Conqueror, who now beholds
Cherub and Seraph rolling in the flood

5 Galileo, inventor of the   6 Valley of the Arno   8 near **Florence**
telescope, whom Milton   (vicinity of Florence)   9 Pharaoh
met   7 flag-ship of an admiral

Of riot ascends above their loftiest towers,
And injury and outrage; and, when night 500
Darkens the streets, then wander forth the sons
Of Belial, flown [23] with insolence and wine.
Witness the streets of Sodom, and that night
In Gibeah, when the hospitable door
Exposed a matron, to avoid worse rape.
　These were the prime in order and in might:
The rest were long to tell; though far renowned
The Ionian gods—of Javan's [24] issue held
Gods, yet confessed later than Heaven and Earth,
Their boasted parents;—*Titan*, Heaven's first-born, 510
With his enormous brood, and birthright seized
By younger *Saturn:* he from mightier Jove,
His own and Rhea's son, like measure found;
So *Jove* usurping reigned. These, first in Crete
And Ida known, thence on the snowy top
Of cold Olympus ruled the middle air,
Their highest heaven; or on the Delphian cliff,
Or in Dodona, and through all the bounds
Of Doric land; or who with Saturn old
Fled over Adria to the Hesperian fields, 520
And o'er the Celtic roamed the utmost Isles.
　All these and more came flocking; but with looks
Downcast and damp; [25] yet such wherein appeared
Obscure some glimpse of joy to have found their Chief
Not in despair, to have found themselves not lost
In loss itself; which on his countenance cast
Like doubtful hue. But he, his wonted pride
Soon recollecting, with high words, that bore
Semblance of worth, not substance, gently raised
Their fainting courage, and dispelled their fears: 530
Then straight commands that, at the warlike sound
Of trumpets loud and clarions, be upreared
His mighty standard. That proud honor claimed
Azazel as his right, a Cherub tall:
Who forthwith from the glittering staff unfurled
The imperial ensign; which, full high advanced,
Shone like a meteor streaming to the wind,
With gems and golden luster rich emblazed,
Seraphic arms and trophies; all the while
Sonorous metal blowing martial sounds: 540
At which the universal host up-sent
A shout that tore Hell's concave, and beyond

23 flushed　　　　　mythical ancestor of the　　25 depressed
24 Noah's　grandson,　Greeks

Frighted the reign of Chaos and old Night.
All in a moment through the gloom were seen
Ten thousand banners rise into the air,
With orient [26] colors waving: with them rose
A forest huge of spears; and thronging helms
Appeared, and serried shields in thick array
Of depth immeasurable. Anon they move
In perfect phalanx to the Dorian mood [27]   550
Of flutes and soft recorders [28]—such as raised
To highth of noblest temper heroes old
Arming to battle, and instead of rage
Deliberate valor breathed, firm, and unmoved
With dread of death to flight or foul retreat;
Nor wanting power to mitigate and swage
With solemn touches troubled thoughts, and chase
Anguish and doubt and fear and sorrow and pain
From mortal or immortal minds. Thus they,
Breathing united force with fixèd thought,   560
Moved on in silence to soft pipes that charmed
Their painful steps o'er the burnt soil. And now
Advanced in view they stand—a horrid [29] front
Of dreadful length and dazzling arms, in guise
Of warriors old, with ordered spear and shield,
Awaiting what command their mighty Chief
Had to impose. He through the armèd files
Darts his experienced eye, and soon traverse [30]
The whole battalion views—their order due,
Their visages and stature as of gods;   570
Their number last he sums. And now his heart
Distends with pride, and, hardening in his strength,
Glories: for never, since created Man,
Met such embodied force as, named with these,
Could merit more than that small infantry [31]
Warred on by cranes—though all the giant brood
Of Phlegra [32] with the heroic race were joined
That fought at Thebes and Ilium, on each side
Mixed with auxiliar gods; and what resounds
In fable or romance of Uther's son [33]   580
Begirt with British and Armoric knights;
And all who since, baptized or infidel,
Jousted in Aspramont, or Montalban,
Damasco, or Marocco, or Trebisond,
Or whom Biserta sent from Afric shore

26 bright
27 appropriate to martial music
28 kind of flute
29 bristling
30 across
31 the Pygmies (see Iliad, III. 5)
32 where the Giants fought the gods
33 King Arthur

When Charlemagne with all his peerage fell
By Fontarabbia.[34] Thus far these beyond
Compare of mortal prowess, yet observed [35]
Their dread Commander. He, above the rest
In shape and gesture proudly eminent,   590
Stood like a tower. His form had yet not lost
All her original brightness, nor appeared
Less than Archangel ruined, and the excess
Of glory obscured: as when the sun new-risen
Looks through the horizontal misty air
Shorn of his beams, or from behind the moon,
In dim eclipse, disastrous twilight sheds
On half the nations, and with fear of change
Perplexes monarchs. Darkened so, yet shone
Above them all the Archangel: but his face   600
Deep scars of thunder had intrenched, and care
Sat on his faded cheek, but under brows
Of dauntless courage, and considerate [36] pride
Waiting revenge. Cruel his eye, but cast
Signs of remorse and passion,[37] to behold
The fellows of his crime, the followers rather
(Far other once beheld in bliss), condemned
For ever now to have their lot in pain—
Millions of Spirits for his fault amerced [38]
Of Heaven, and from eternal splendors flung   610
For his revolt—yet faithful how they stood,
Their glory withered; as, when heaven's fire
Hath scathed the forest oaks or mountain pines,
With singèd top their stately growth, though bare,
Stands on the blasted heath. He now prepared
To speak; whereat their doubled ranks they bend
From wing to wing, and half enclose him round
With all his peers: Attention held them mute.
Thrice he assayed, and thrice, in spite of scorn,
Tears, such as angels weep, burst forth: at last   620
Words interwove with sighs found out their way:—
    "O myriads of immortal Spirits! O Powers
Matchless, but with the Almighty!—and that strife
Was not inglorious, though the event [39] was dire,
As this place testifies, and this dire change,
Hateful to utter. But what power of mind,
Foreseeing or presaging, from the depth
Of knowledge past or present, could have feared

---

34 At the above places   36 thoughtful   38 punished by loss
Christians fought Saracens.   37 pity and strong emo-   39 outcome
  35 obeyed   tion

How such united force of gods, how such
As stood like these, could ever know repulse? 630
For who can yet believe, though after loss,
That all these puissant legions, whose exile
Hath emptied Heaven, shall fail to re-ascend,
Self-raised, and re-possess their native seat?
For me, be witness all the host of Heaven,
If counsels different, or danger shunned
By me, have lost our hopes. But he who reigns
Monarch in Heaven till then as one secure
Sat on his throne, upheld by old repute,
Consent or custom, and his regal state 640
Put forth at full, but still his strength concealed—
Which tempted our attempt, and wrought our fall.
Henceforth his might we know, and know our own,
So as not either to provoke, or dread
New war provoked: our better part remains
To work in close design, by fraud or guile,
What force effected not; that he no less
At length from us may find, who overcomes
By force hath overcome but half his foe.
Space may produce new Worlds; whereof so rife 650
There went a fame in Heaven that he ere long
Intended to create, and therein plant
A generation whom his choice regard
Should favor equal to the Sons of Heaven.
Thither, if but to pry, shall be perhaps
Our first eruption—thither, or elsewhere;
For this infernal pit shall never hold
Celestial Spirits in bondage, nor the Abyss
Long under darkness cover. But these thoughts
Full counsel must mature. Peace is despaired; 660
For who can think submission? War, then, war
Open or understood, must be resolved."
　He spake; and, to confirm his words, ouflew
Millions of flaming swords, drawn from the thighs
Of mighty Cherubim; the sudden blaze
Far round illumined Hell. Highly they raged
Against the Highest, and fierce with graspèd arms
Clashed on their sounding shields the din of war,
Hurling defiance toward the vault of Heaven.
　There stood a hill not far, whose grisly top 670
Belched fire and rolling smoke; the rest entire
Shone with a glossy scurf—undoubted sign
That in his womb was hid metallic ore,

The work of sulphur.[40] Thither, winged with speed,
A numerous brigad hastened: as when bands
Of pioneers, with spade and pickaxe armed,
Forerun the royal camp, to trench a field,
Or cast a rampart. Mammon led them on—
Mammon, the least erected Spirit that fell
From Heaven; for even in Heaven his looks and thoughts   680
Were always downward bent, admiring more
The riches of Heaven's pavement, trodden gold,
Than aught divine or holy else enjoyed
In vision beatific. By him first
Men also, and by his suggestion taught,
Ransacked the center, and with impious hands
Rifled the bowels of their mother earth
For treasures better hid. Soon had his crew
Opened into the hill a spacious wound,
And digged out ribs of gold. Let none admire [41]   690
That riches grow in Hell; that soil may best
Deserve the precious bane. And here let those
Who boast in mortal things, and wondering tell
Of Babel, and the works of Memphian kings,[42]
Learn how their greatest monuments of fame
And strength, and art, are easily outdone
By Spirits reprobate, and in an hour
What in an age they, with incessant toil
And hands innumerable, scarce perform.
Nigh on the plain, in many cells prepared,   700
That underneath had veins of liquid fire
Sluiced from the lake, a second multitude
With wondrous art founded the massy ore,
Severing each kind, and scummed the bullion-dross.
A third as soon had formed within the ground
A various mold, and from the boiling cells
By strange conveyance filled each hollow nook;
As in an organ, from one blast of wind,
To many a row of pipes the sound-board breathes.
Anon out of the earth a fabric huge   710
Rose like an exhalation, with the sound
Of dulcet symphonies and voices sweet—
Built like a temple, where pilasters round
Were set, and Doric pillars overlaid
With golden architrave; nor did there want
Cornice or frieze, with bossy sculptures graven;
The roof was fretted gold. Not Babylon

40 supposed the forma-   41 wonder   42 the Pyramids
tive element of metals

Nor great Alcairo such magnificence
Equaled in all their glories, to enshrine
Belus or Serapis their gods, or seat   720
Their kings, when Egypt with Assyria strove
In wealth and luxury. The ascending pile
Stood fixed her stately highth; and straight the doors,
Opening their brazen folds, discover, wide
Within, her ample spaces o'er the smooth
And level pavement: from the archèd roof,
Pendent by subtle magic, many a row
Of starry lamps and blazing cressets, fed
With naphtha and asphaltus, yielded light
As from a sky. The hasty multitude   730
Admiring entered; and the work some praise,
And some the architect. His hand was known
In Heaven by many a towered structure high,
Where sceptered Angels held their residence,
And sat as Princes, whom the supreme King
Exalted to such power, and gave to rule,
Each in his hierarchy, the Orders bright.
Nor was his name unheard or unadored
In ancient Greece; and in Ausonian land [43]
Men called him Mulciber; and how he fell   740
From Heaven they fabled, thrown by angry Jove
Sheer o'er the crystal battlements: from morn
To noon he fell, from noon to dewy eve,
A summer's day, and with the setting sun
Dropt from the zenith, like a falling star,
On Lemnos, the Ægæan isle. Thus they relate,
Erring; for he with this rebellious rout
Fell long before; nor aught availed him now
To have built in Heaven high towers; nor did he scape
By all his engines,[44] but was headlong sent,   750
With his industrious crew, to build in Hell.
     Meanwhile the wingèd heralds, by command
Of sovran power, with awful ceremony
And trumpet's sound, throughout the host proclaim
A solemn council forthwith to be held
At Pandemonium,[45] the high capital
Of Satan and his peers. Their summons called
From every band and squarèd regiment
By place or choice the worthiest; they anon
With hundreds and with thousands trooping came   760
Attended. All access was thronged; the gates
And porches wide, but chief the spacious hall

[43] Italy   [44] contrivances   [45] "Hall of all demons"

his audience, transformed, with himself also, suddenly into Serpents, according to his doom given in Paradise; then, deluded with a show of the Forbidden Tree springing up before them, they, greedily reaching to take of the fruit, chew dust and bitter ashes. The proceedings of Sin and Death: God foretells the final victory of his Son over them, and the renewing of all things; but, for the present, commands his Angels to make several alterations in the heavens and elements. Adam, more and more perceiving his fallen condition, heavily bewails, rejects the condolement of Eve; she persists, and at length appeases him: then, to evade the curse likely to fall on their offspring, proposes to Adam violent ways; which he approves not, but, conceiving better hope, puts her in mind of the late promise made them, that her seed should be revenged on the Serpent, and exhorts her, with him, to seek peace of the offended Deity by repentance and supplication.

Book XI

THE ARGUMENT

The Son of God presents to his Father the prayers of our first parents now repenting, and intercedes for them. God accepts them, but declares that they must no longer abide in Paradise; sends Michael with a band of Cherubim to dispossess them, but first to reveal to Adam future things: Michael's coming down. Adam shows to Eve certain ominous signs; he discerns Michael's approach; goes out to meet him: the Angel announces their departure. Eve's lamentation. Adam pleads, but submits: the Angel leads him up to a high hill; sets before him in vision what shall happen till the Flood.

Book XII

THE ARGUMENT

The Angel Michael continues, from the Flood, to relate what shall succeed; then, in the mention of Abraham, comes by degrees to explain who that Seed of the Woman shall be which was promised Adam and Eve in the Fall: his incarnation, death, resurrection, and ascension; the state of the Church till his second coming. Adam greatly satisfied and recomforted by these relations and promises, descends the hill with Michael; wakens Eve, who all this while had slept, but with gentle dreams composed to quietness of mind and submission. Michael in either hand leads them out of Paradise, the fiery Sword waving behind them, and the Cherubim taking their stations to guard the place.

HE ended; and thus Adam last replied:—
"How soon hath thy prediction, Seer blest,
Measured this transient World, the race of Time,
Till Time stands fixed! Beyond is all abyss—
Eternity, whose end no eye can reach.
Greatly instructed I shall hence depart,
Greatly in peace of thought, and have my fill

Of knowledge, what this vessel can contain;
Beyond which was my folly to aspire. 560
Henceforth I learn that to obey is best,
And love with fear the only God, to walk
As in his presence, ever to observe
His providence, and on him sole depend,
Merciful over all his works, with good
Still overcoming evil, and by small
Accomplishing great things—by things deemed weak
Subverting worldly-strong, and worldly-wise
By simply meek; that suffering for Truth's sake
Is fortitude to highest victory, 570
And to the faithful death the gate of life—
Taught this by his example whom I now
Acknowledge my Redeemer ever blest."
      To whom thus also the Angel last replied:—
"This having learned, thou hast attained the sum
Of wisdom; hope no higher, though all the stars
Thou knew'st by name, and all the ethereal powers,
All secrets of the Deep, all Nature's works,
Or works of God in heaven, air, earth, or sea,
And all the riches of this world enjoy'dst, 580
And all the rule, one empire. Only add
Deeds to thy knowledge answerable; add faith;
Add virtue, patience, temperance; add love,
By name to come called Charity, the soul
Of all the rest: then wilt thou not be loath
To leave this Paradise, but shalt possess
A Paradise within thee, happier far.
Let us descend now, therefore, from this top
Of speculation; [59] for the hour precise
Exacts our parting hence; and, see! the guards, 590
By me encamped on yonder hill, expect
Their motion, at whose front a flaming sword,
In signal of remove, waves fiercely round.
We may no longer stay. Go, waken Eve;
Her also I with gentle dreams have calmed,
Portending good, and all her spirits composed
To meek submission: thou, at season fit,
Let her with thee partake what thou hast heard—
Chiefly what may concern her faith to know,
The great deliverance by her seed to come 600
(For by the Woman's Seed) on all mankind—
That ye may live, which will be many days,
Both in one faith unanimous; though sad

59 the mountain from which we have watched; perhaps also in the ordinary sense

With cause for evils past, yet much more cheered
With meditation on the happy end."
　　He ended, and they both descend the hill.
Descended, Adam to the bower where Eve
Lay sleeping, ran before, but found her waked:
And thus with words not sad she him received:—
　　"Whence thou return'st and whither went'st I know;　　610
For God is also in sleep, and dreams advise,
Which he hath sent propitious, some great good
Presaging, since, with sorrow and heart's distress
Wearied, I fell asleep. But now lead on:
In me is no delay; with thee to go
Is to stay here; without thee here to stay
Is to go hence unwilling; thou to me
Art all things under Heaven, all places thou,
Who for my willful crime art banished hence.
This further consolation yet secure　　620
I carry hence: though all by me is lost,
Such favor I unworthy am vouchsafed,
By me the Promised Seed shall all restore."
　　So spake our mother Eve; and Adam heard
Well pleased, but answered not; for now too nigh
The Archangel stood, and from the other hill
To their fixed station, all in bright array,
The Cherubim descended, on the ground
Gliding metéorous, as evening mist
Risen from a river o'er the marish glides,　　630
And gathers ground fast at the laborer's heel
Homeward returning. High in front advanced,
The brandished sword of God before them blazed,
Fierce as a comet; which with torrid heat,
And vapor as the Libyan air adust,[60]
Began to parch that temperate clime; whereat
In either Hand the hastening Angel caught
Our lingering Parents, and to the eastern gate
Led them direct, and down the cliff as fast
To the subjected [61] plain—then disappeared.　　640
They, looking back, all the eastern side beheld
Of Paradise, so late their happy seat,
Waved over by that flaming brand; the gate
With dreadful faces thronged and fiery arms.
Some natural tears they dropped, but wiped them soon;
The world was all before them, where to choose
Their place of rest, and Providence their guide.

60 scorched　　　　　　61 lying beneath

They, hand in hand, with wandering steps and slow,
Through Eden took their solitary way.

AREOPAGITICA

A Speech for the Liberty of Unlicensed Printing, to the Parliament of England

In 1643 Parliament passed an act directing that all books be licensed before publication and providing punishment for offending printers and authors. In the following year Milton urged repeal of the act in his *Areopagitica*, which he cast in the form of a classical oration. It is generally esteemed the noblest plea ever uttered for the freedom of the press, and is certainly the most enduring of all Milton's efforts for human liberty. The condensation here attempted aims to give some appreciation of the scope of Milton's argument, and to present the more notable passages.

[*Milton, in approaching his subject, states his belief that Parliament will listen to the "voice of reason from what quarter soever it be heard speaking," and will be willing to repeal acts already passed.*]

If ye be thus resolved, as it were injury to think ye were not, I know not what should withhold me from presenting ye with a fit instance wherein to show both that love of truth which ye eminently profess, and that uprightness of your judgment which is not wont to be partial to yourselves; by judging over again that order which ye have ordained to regulate printing:—that no book, pamphlet, or paper shall be henceforth printed, unless the same be first approved and licensed by such, or at least one of such, as shall be thereto appointed. For that part which preserves justly every man's copy to himself, or provides for the 10 poor, I touch not, only wish they be not made pretences to abuse and persecute honest and painful men, who offend not in either of these particulars. But that other clause of licensing books, which we thought had died with his brother quadragesimal and matrimonial [62] when the prelates expired,[63] I shall now attend with such a homily, as shall lay before ye, first the inventors of it to be those whom ye will be loth to own; next what is to be thought in general of reading, whatever sort the books be; and that this order avails nothing to the suppressing of scandalous, seditious, and libelous books, which were mainly intended to be 20 suppressed. Last, that it will be primely to the discouragement of all learning, and the stop of truth, not only by disexercising and blunting our abilities in what we know already, but by hindering

62 regulations regarding the eating of food during Lent and regarding marriage licenses   63 The bill for the exclusion of bishops from Parliament, passed 1642

and cropping the discovery that might be yet further made both in religious and civil wisdom.

I deny not, but that it is of greatest concernment in the Church and Commonwealth, to have a vigilant eye how books demean themselves as well as men; and thereafter to confine, imprison, and do sharpest justice on them as malefactors. For books are not absolutely dead things, but do contain a potency of life in them to be as active as that soul was whose progeny they are; nay, they do preserve as in a vial the purest efficacy and extrac-
10 tion of that living intellect that bred them. I know they are as lively, and as vigorously productive, as those fabulous dragon's teeth; and being sown up and down, may chance to spring up armed men.[64] And yet, on the other hand, unless wariness be used, as good almost kill a man as kill a good book. Who kills a man kills a reasonable creature, God's image; but he who destroys a good book, kills reason itself, kills the image of God, as it were in the eye. Many a man lives a burden to the earth; but a good book is the precious life-blood of a master spirit, embalmed and treasured up on purpose to a life beyond life. 'Tis true, no
20 age can restore a life, whereof perhaps there is no great loss; and revolutions of ages do not oft recover the loss of a rejected truth, for the want of which whole nations fare the worse.

We should be wary therefore what persecution we raise against the living labors of public men, how we spill that seasoned life of man, preserved and stored up in books; since we see a kind of homicide may be thus committed, sometimes a martyrdom, and if it extend to the whole impression, a kind of massacre; whereof the execution ends not in the slaying of an elemental life, but strikes at that ethereal and fifth essence,
30 the breath of reason itself, slays an immortality rather than a life.

[*Milton here gives a history of censorship, and cites historical examples to show the necessity of unfettered learning.*]

I conceive, therefore, that when God did enlarge the universal diet of man's body, saving ever the rules of temperance, He then also, as before, left arbitrary the dieting and repasting of our minds; as wherein every mature man might have to exercise his own leading capacity.

How great a virtue is temperance, how much of moment through the whole life of man! Yet God commits the managing so great a trust, without particular law or prescription, wholly
40 to the demeanor of every grown man. And therefore when He Himself tabled the Jews from heaven, that omer, which was every man's daily portion of manna, is computed to have been more than might have well sufficed the heartiest feeder thrice

---

64 familiar in the story of Jason and elsewhere

as many meals. For those actions which enter into a man, rather than issue out of him, and therefore defile not, God uses not to captivate under a perpetual childhood or prescription, but trusts him with the gift of reason to be his own chooser; there were but little work left for preaching, if law and compulsion should grow so fast upon those things which heretofore were governed only by exhortation. Solomon informs us, that much reading is a weariness to the flesh; but neither he nor other inspired author tells us that such or such reading is unlawful; yet certainly had God thought good to limit us herein, it had been much more expedient to have told us what was unlawful than what was wearisome. As for the burning of those Ephesian books by St. Paul's converts; 'tis replied the books were magic, the Syriac so renders them. It was a private act, a voluntary act, and leaves us to a voluntary imitation: the men in remorse burnt those books which were their own; the magistrate by this example is not appointed; these men practised the books, another might perhaps have read them in some sort usefully.

Good and evil we know in the field of this world grow up together almost inseparably; and the knowledge of good is so involved and interwoven with the knowledge of evil, and in so many cunning resemblances hardly to be discerned, that those confused seeds which were imposed upon Psyche as an incessant labor to cull out, and sort asunder, were not more intermixed. It was from out the rind of one apple tasted, that the knowledge of good and evil, as two twins cleaving together, leaped forth into the world. And perhaps this is that doom which Adam fell into of knowing good and evil, that is to say of knowing good by evil. As therefore the state of man now is; what wisdom can there be to choose, what continence to forbear without the knowledge of evil? He that can apprehend and consider vice with all her baits and seeming pleasures, and yet abstain, and yet distinguish, and yet prefer that which is truly better, he is the true wayfaring Christian.

I cannot praise a fugitive and cloistered virtue, unexercised and unbreathed, that never sallies out and sees her adversary, but slinks out of the race, where that immortal garland is to be run for, not without dust and heat. Assuredly we bring not innocence into the world, we bring impurity much rather; that which purifies us is trial, and trial is by what is contrary. That virtue therefore which is but a youngling in the contemplation of evil, and knows not the utmost that vice promises to her followers, and rejects it, is but a blank virtue, not a pure; her whiteness is but excremental whiteness; which was the reason why our sage and serious poet Spenser, whom I dare be known to think a better teacher than Scotus or Aquinas, describing true temper-

ance under the person of Guion, brings him in with his palmer
through the cave of Mammon, and the bower of earthly bliss,
that he might see and know, and yet abstain.

Since therefore the knowledge and survey of vice is in this
world so necessary to the constituting of human virtue, and the
scanning of error to the confirmation of truth, how can we more
safely, and with less danger, scout into the regions of sin and
falsity than by reading all manner of tractates and hearing all
manner of reason? And this is the benefit which may be had of
10 books promiscuously read.

[*Those books "which are likeliest to taint both life and doctrine"
cannot be suppressed without the fall of learning, and of all
ability in disputation. Moreover, the suppression of books alone
is futile.*]

For if they fell upon one kind of strictness, unless their care
were equal to regulate all other things of like aptness to corrupt
the mind, that single endeavor they knew would be but a fond [65]
labor; to shut and fortify one gate against corruption, and be
necessitated to leave others round about wide open.

If we think to regulate printing, thereby to rectify manners,
we must regulate all recreations and pastimes, all that is delightful to man. No music must be heard, no song be set or
sung, but what is grave and Doric. There must be licensing
20 dancers, that no gesture, motion, or deportment be taught our
youth but what by their allowance shall be thought honest;
for such Plato was provided of; it will ask more than the work
of twenty licensers to examine all the lutes, the violins, and the
guitars in every house; they must not be suffered to prattle as
they do, but must be licensed what they may say. And who
shall silence all the airs and madrigals that whisper softness in
chambers? The windows also, and the balconies must be thought
on; there are shrewd books, with dangerous frontispieces, set
to sale; who shall prohibit them, shall twenty licensers? The
30 villages also must have their visitors to inquire what lectures
the bagpipe and the rebeck [66] reads, even to the ballatry [67] and
the gamut of every municipal fiddler, for these are the countryman's Arcadias, and his Monte Mayors.[68]

Next, what more national corruption, for which England
hears ill abroad, than household gluttony? Who shall be the
rectors of our daily rioting? And what shall be done to inhibit
the multitudes that frequent those houses where drunkenness
is sold and harbored? Our garments also should be referred
to the licensing of some more sober workmasters to see them

65 foolish
66 fiddle
67 ballad poetry

68 Sir   Philip   Sidney's   are referred to.
romance and a well-known
Spanish writer of romances

cut into a less wanton garb. Who shall regulate all the mixed
conversation of our youth, male and female together, as is the
fashion of this country? Who shall still appoint what shall be
discoursed, what presumed, and no further? Lastly, who shall
forbid and separate all idle resort, all evil company? These
things will be, and must be; but how they shall be least hurtful,
how least enticing, herein consists the grave and governing
wisdom of a state.

To sequester out of the world into Atlantic and Utopian
polities [69] which never can be drawn into use, will not mend our
condition; but to ordain wisely as in this world of evil, in the
midst whereof God hath placed us unavoidably. Nor is it Plato's
licensing of books will do this, which necessarily pulls along
with it so many other kinds of licensing, as will make us all
both ridiculous and weary and yet frustrate; but those un-
written, or at least unconstraining laws of virtuous education,
religious and civil nurture, which Plato therein mentions as the
bonds and ligaments of the commonwealth, the pillars and the
sustainers of every written statute; these they be which will
bear chief sway in such matters as these, when all licensing
will be easily eluded. Impunity and remissness, for certain, are
the bane of commonwealth; but here the great art lies, to discern in what the law is to bid restraint and punishment and in
what things persuasion only is to work.

If every action which is good or evil in man at ripe years
were to be under pittance and prescription and compulsion, what
were virtue but a name, what praise could be then due to well-
doing, what gramercy [70] to be sober, just, or continent? Many
there be that complain of Divine Providence for suffering Adam
to transgress. Foolish tongues! When God gave him reason, He
gave him freedom to choose, for reason is but choosing; he had
been else a mere artificial Adam, such an Adam as he is in the
motions.[71] We ourselves esteem not of that obedience, or love,
or gift, which is of force. God therefore left him free, set before
him a provoking object, ever almost in his eyes; herein consisted
his merit, herein the right of his reward, the praise of his abstinence. Wherefore did He create passions within us, pleasures
round about us, but that these rightly tempered are the very
ingredients of virtue?

They are not skillful considerers of human things who imagine
to remove sin by removing the matter of sin; for, besides that
it is a huge heap increasing under the very act of diminishing,
though some part of it may for a time be withdrawn from some
persons, it cannot from all, in such a universal thing as books

---

69 the imaginary com-
monwealths of Sir Francis
Bacon's *New Atlantis* and
Sir Thomas More's *Utopia*
70 thanks
71 puppet shows

are; and when this is done, yet the sin remains entire. Though ye take from a covetous man all his treasure, he has yet one jewel left, ye cannot bereave him of his covetousness. Banish all objects of lust, shut up all youth into the severest discipline that can be exercised in any hermitage, ye cannot make them chaste, that came not thither so: such great care and wisdom is required to the right managing of this point.

Suppose we could expel sin by this means; look how much we thus expel of sin, so much we expel of virtue: for the matter
10 of them both is the same; remove that, and ye remove them both alike. This justifies the high providence of God, who, though He commands us temperance, justice, continence, yet pours out before us, even to a profuseness, all desirable things, and gives us minds that can wander beyond all limit and satiety. Why should we then affect a rigor contrary to the manner of God and of nature, by abridging or scanting those means, which books freely permitted are, both to the trial of virtue and the exercise of truth? It would be better done, to learn that the law must needs be frivolous, which goes to restrain things, uncer-
20 tainly and yet equally working to good and to evil. And were I the chooser, a dram of well-doing should be preferred before many times as much the forcible hindrance of evil-doing. For God sure esteems the growth and completing of one virtuous person more than the restraint of ten vicious.

[*The censorship will be a great affront to learned men. It will muzzle teaching, put a stop to advanced thought, rob the world of many great works. It will magnify ecclesiastical abuses. It will be a "step-dame to Truth."*]

Well knows he who uses to consider, that our faith and knowledge thrives by exercise, as well as our limbs and complexion. Truth is compared in Scripture to a streaming fountain; if her waters flow not in a perpetual progression, they sicken into a muddy pool of conformity and tradition. A man
30 may be a heretic in the truth; and if he believe things only because his pastor says so, or the Assembly so determines, without knowing other reason, though his belief be true, yet the very truth he holds becomes his heresy.

There is not any burden that some would gladlier post off to another than the charge and care of their religion. There be—who knows not that there be?—of Protestants and pro-fessors [72] who live and die in as arrant an implicit faith as any lay Papist of Loretto.

A wealthy man, addicted to his pleasure and to his profits,
40 finds religion to be a traffic so entangled, and of so many pid-

---

[72] those who make open profession of religion (applied here to Protestants as opposed to Roman Catholics)

dling accounts, that of all mysteries he cannot skill to keep
a stock going upon that trade. What should he do? fain he
would have the name to be religious, fain he would bear up
with his neighbors in that. What does he therefore, but resolve to give over toiling, and to find himself out some factor,
to whose care and credit he may commit the whole managing
of his religious affairs? some Divine of note and estimation
that must be. To him he adheres, resigns the whole warehouse
of his religion, with all the locks and keys, into his custody;
and indeed makes the very person of that man his religion; 10
esteems his associating with him a sufficient evidence and com-
mendatory of his own piety. So that a man may say his religion is now no more within himself, but is become a dividual
movable, and goes and comes near him, according as that good
man frequents the house. He entertains him, gives him gifts,
feasts him, lodges him; his religion comes home at night, prays,
is liberally supped, and sumptuously laid to sleep, rises, is
saluted, and after the malmsey, or some well-spiced brewage,
and better breakfasted than he whose morning appetite would
have gladly fed on green figs between Bethany and Jerusalem,[73] 20
his religion walks abroad at eight, and leaves his kind enter-
tainer in the shop trading all day without his religion.

Another sort there be who, when they hear that all things
shall be ordered, all things regulated and settled, nothing written
but what passes through the custom-house of certain publicans
that have the tonnaging and poundaging [74] of all free-spoken
truth, will straight give themselves up into your hands, make
'em and cut 'em out what religion ye please; there be delights,
there be recreations and jolly pastimes that will fetch the day
about from sun to sun, and rock the tedious year as in a delight- 30
ful dream. What need they torture their heads with that which
others have taken so strictly and so unalterably into their own
purveying? These are the fruits which a dull ease and cessation
of our knowledge will bring forth among the people. How goodly
and how to be wished were such an obedient unanimity as this,
what a fine conformity would it starch us all into! Doubtless a
staunch and solid piece of framework, as any January could
freeze together. . . .

Truth indeed came once into the world with her Divine
Master, and was a perfect shape most glorious to look on; but 40
when He ascended, and His Apostles after Him were laid asleep,
then straight arose a wicked race of deceivers, who, as that
story goes of the Egyptian Typhon with his conspirators, how
they dealt with the good Osiris, took the virgin Truth, hewed

73 Matt. xxi. 18, 19;   74 duties on exports and
Mark xi. 12, 13   imports

her lovely form into a thousand pieces, and scattered them to the four winds. From that time ever since, the sad friends of Truth, such as durst appear, imitating the careful search that Isis made for the mangled body of Osiris, went up and down gathering up limb by limb, still as they could find them. We have not yet found them all, Lords and Commons, nor ever shall do, till her Master's second coming; He shall bring together every joint and member, and shall mold them into an immortal feature of loveliness and perfection. Suffer not these
10 licensing prohibitions to stand at every place of opportunity, forbidding and disturbing them that continue seeking, that continue to do our obsequies to the torn body of our martyred saint.

[*Division of opinion and active controversy are not to be looked at with alarm. They are a healthy sign. They betoken the vigor of the English nation.*]

Methinks I see in my mind a noble and puissant nation rousing herself like a strong man after sleep, and shaking her invincible locks. Methinks I see her as an eagle mewing her mighty youth, and kindling her undazzled eyes at the full midday beam; purging and unscaling her long-abused sight at the fountain itself of heavenly radiance; while the whole noise of timorous
20 and flocking birds, with those also that love the twilight, flutter about, amazed at what she means, and in their envious gabble would prognosticate a year of sects and schisms.

What would ye do then? should ye suppress all this flowery crop of knowledge and new light sprung up and yet springing daily in this city? should ye set an oligarchy of twenty engrossers over it, to bring a famine upon our minds again, when we shall know nothing but what is measured to us by their bushel? Believe it, Lords and Commons, they who counsel ye to such a suppressing do as good as bid ye suppress yourselves; and I
30 will soon show how.

If it be desired to know the immediate cause of all this free writing and free speaking, there cannot be assigned a truer than your own mild and free and humane government. It is the liberty, Lords and Commons, which your own valorous and happy counsels have purchased us, liberty which is the nurse of all great wits; this is that which hath rarefied and enlightened our spirits like the influence of heaven; this is that which hath enfranchised, enlarged and lifted up our apprehensions degrees above themselves. Ye cannot make us now less capable, less
40 knowing, less eagerly pursuing of the truth, unless ye first make yourselves, that made us so, less the lovers, less the founders of our true liberty. We can grow ignorant again, brutish, formal and slavish, as ye found us; but you then must first

become that which ye cannot be, oppressive, arbitrary and tyrannous, as they were from whom ye have freed us. That our hearts are now more capacious, our thoughts more erected to the search and expectation of greatest and exactest things, is the issue of your own virtue propagated in us; ye cannot suppress that, unless ye reinforce an abrogated and merciless law, that fathers may despatch at will their own children. And who shall then stick closest to ye, and excite others? not he who takes up arms for coat and conduct,[75] and his four nobles [76] of Danegelt.[77] Although I dispraise not the defence of just immunities, yet love my peace better, if that were all. Give me the liberty to know, to utter, and to argue freely according to conscience, above all liberties. [*Let Truth and Falsehood grapple. "Whoever knew Truth put to the worse in a free and open encounter? . . . If it come to prohibiting, there is not aught more likely to be prohibited than Truth itself."*]

JOHN DRYDEN (1631-1700)

John Dryden came of good family on both sides. He was born in the vicarage at Aldwinkle, Northamptonshire, on August 9, 1631. His education was at Westminster School and at Trinity College, Cambridge, where he took his B.A. in 1654. He had come up to London by 1658, in which year he wrote his first important verse, his *Heroic Stanzas* on the death of Oliver Cromwell. Less than two years later he was among the first to welcome the return of Charles II with the poem, *Astraea Redux.* Much has been made of the apparent transfer of loyalty. The impression of time-serving is reënforced by a later shift in religion from Protestantism to Catholicism, at a period when the court was veering in the same direction. To be sure, Dryden, as a man of letters under seventeenth century conditions, for success must needs cater to prevailing sentiment and curry favor with the great, but there is probably more sincerity in his changing faiths, political and religious, than his critics give him credit for. He was not by temperament fixed and unchangeable, like Milton.

Dryden was a professional man of letters—perhaps the first who can be so called. In some forty years of creative life, he did a large quantity of literary work, of a great variety. His productions fall chiefly into the three categories of drama, satiric verse (including, however, some lyric), and critical prose. His plays are twenty-seven in number. Mostly they follow typical Restoration patterns: lascivious comedies, like *Marriage à la Mode* and *The Spanish Friar;* or heroic plays, like *The Conquest of Granada* and *Aurengzebe.* The latter type presents figures greater than life-size. They are torn between the demands of love and honor, and give utterance to their swollen emotions in turgid rhetoric. After a dozen years of handling the heroic couplet in

75 money levied for the clothing and transportation
of the army
76 coin of the value 6s. 8d.
77 a land-tax

these plays, Dryden confessed that he had grown "weary of his long-loved mistress, Rhyme," and his greatest play, *All for Love* (1678), adapted from Shakespeare's *Antony and Cleopatra*, he wrote in blank verse. Modern readers will prefer the older and greater tragedy, but Dryden's play is also splendid, extraordinarily interesting as showing at their finest the heroic standards of its author and his time.

The shift in the ideas and tastes of men at the Restoration had tended to replace, as qualities to be desired, lofty imagination, dogged fanaticism, and preachy morality with common-sense, a practical conformity to workable standards, and wit. In such an era satire flourished, and in this form Dryden, with his keen, dry mind, admirable critical powers, absence of emotionalism, and excellent craftsmanship in verse, was peculiarly fitted to excel, as he was not in the drama. His greatest work in this kind is *Absalom and Achitophel*, a political satire on the plot to depose Charles II in favor of his illegitimate son, the Duke of Monmouth. It was followed by *The Medal*, and then by *MacFlecknoe*, in which he retorted crushingly on Shadwell and others, who had attacked him. Dryden's satire is mostly against public personages and presents his side of important questions. With some exceptions, it is not splenetic and bitterly vindictive. It is thus a higher kind of satire than most of Pope's. The rational bent which directed him toward satire led him also into two argumentative poems, *Religio Laici* and *The Hind and the Panther* (1683, 1687). In the first of these he defends his adherence to the Church of England, in the latter his conversion to Catholicism. If his public conversion was actuated by the desire to gain the favor of the Catholic James II, ironical it is that the next year James was forced out by the Revolution of 1688 and Protestantism restored as the state religion. Yet Dryden did not change his views again. He remained a Catholic to the end of his days, although for his religion he was deprived of the Laureateship (which was bestowed in 1688 on his old enemy Shadwell), and likewise of his pension and state appointments. In all the poems mentioned the rational powers are dominant, rather than the emotional. Dryden never wrote pure lyric, the nearest approach to it being the two splendid odes in varied measure, among the finest of their kind in English, *A Song for Saint Cecilia's Day* and *Alexander's Feast* (1687, 1697). In his old age, his preferment through the court cut off, Dryden turned to translation and adaptation as a source of income, producing, most notably, his *Virgil* (published 1697), and his *Fables* (1700), retold from Chaucer, Boccaccio, Ovid, Homer, and others. All of these works are done in the heroic couplet, which in his hands is a more pleasing, because less rigid, verseform than the hard and brilliant couplets of Pope.

Dryden's command of the heroic couplet is matched by his mastery of English prose. His best criticism is contained in his *Essay of Dramatic Poesy* (1668), and in numerous prefaces to works throughout his entire career, the *Preface to the Fables*, at the end of his life, showing that he had suffered no diminution of his powers through age. As in his political and religious views, so in his critical tenets he frequently changed, lauding heroic plays and then becoming somewhat dubious concerning them, vigorously defending rhyme in drama and then growing tired of it. His standards are in general neo-classical, but with an independence of judgment which became stronger as he grew older. The prose which is the vehicle of his criticism is a remarkable instrument—clear, easy, flexible, and varied, written in the manner of excellent conversation. His is the first modern prose.

If public acknowledgment was denied in his old age of that distinction which he had attained in verse and in that "other harmony of prose," yet private appreciation was not lacking. Around his seat in Will's coffee house thronged younger writers, and in these last years he may be said to have spoken in the tones of a literary dictator. He died on May 1, 1700, and was buried in the Poets' Corner of Westminster Abbey.

The great intellectual powers of Dryden, his industry and facility, his literary skill and his range, command our admiration. A romantic age will naturally not find in his work the same stimulation as does an age that exalts the reason. His limitations were the limitations of his time. So well does he embody in his varied work the best of his own era that the latter part of the seventeenth century is frequently called "the age of Dryden."

BIBLIOGRAPHY. Complete *Works,* ed. Sir Walter Scott, revised by George Saintsbury. Best one volume eds. the Oxford, by John Sargeaunt, and the Cambridge, by G. R. Noyes (Houghton Mifflin), who has also pub. an ed. of the *Plays* (Scott Foresman). Collection of the essays by W. P. Ker (Oxford), 2 vols. Life by G. Saintsbury in Eng. Men of Letters ser.

ABSALOM AND ACHITOPHEL

Si propius stes
Te capiet magis.[1]

Dryden uses a scriptural story (2 Samuel xiii–xviii) to cloak his satire on the attempt of the Earl of Shaftesbury and his party to put on the throne the Duke of Monmouth (l. 18), and to exclude from the succession Charles's brother (afterwards James II), who was a Catholic. The poem was issued about a week before the London grand jury met to consider the charge of high treason against Shaftesbury (November, 1681), but failed to influence their decision, as no indictment was returned.

TO THE READER

'Tis not my intention to make an apology for my poem: some will think it needs no excuse, and others will receive none. The design, I am sure, is honest; but he who draws his pen for one party must expect to make enemies of the other. For wit and fool are consequents of Whig and Tory; and every man is a knave or an ass to the contrary side. There's a treasury of merits in the Fanatic Church, as well as in the Papist; and a pennyworth to be had of saintship, honesty, and poetry, for the lewd, the factious, and the blockheads; but the longest chapter in Deuteronomy has not curses enough for an anti-Bromingham.[2] My comfort is, their manifest prejudice to my cause will render their judgment of less authority against me. Yet if a poem have a genius, it will force its own reception in the world; for there's a sweetness in good verse, which tickles even while it hurts, and no man can be heartily angry with him who pleases him against his will. The commendation of adversaries is the greatest triumph of a writer, because it never comes unless extorted. But I can be satisfied on more easy terms: if I happen to please the more moderate sort, I shall be sure of an honest party, and, in all probability, of the best judges; for the least concerned are commonly the least corrupt. And, I confess, I have laid in for those, by rebating the satire (where justice would allow it) from carrying

---

1 "If you stand nearer, it will attract you more"   2 anti-Whig
(Horace, *Art of Poetry*)

too sharp an edge. They who can criticize so weakly as to imagine I have done my worst, may be convinced, at their own cost, that I can write severely with more ease than I can gently. I have but laughed at some men's follies, when I could have declaimed against their vices; and other men's virtues I have commended, as freely as I have taxed their crimes. And now, if you are a malicious reader, I expect you should return upon me that I affect to be thought more impartial than I am. But if men are not to be judged by their professions, God forgive you commonwealth's-men for professing so plausibly for the government. You cannot be so unconscionable as to charge me for not subscribing of my name; for that would reflect too grossly upon your own party, who never dare, though they have the advantage of a jury to secure them. If you like not my poem, the fault may, possibly, be in my writing (though 'tis hard for an author to judge against himself); but, more probably, 'tis in your morals, which cannot bear the truth of it. The violent, on both sides, will condemn the character of Absalom, as either too favorably or too hardly drawn. But they are not the violent whom I desire to please. The fault on the right hand is to extenuate, palliate, and indulge; and, to confess freely, I have endeavored to commit it. Besides the respect which I owe his birth, I have a greater for his heroic virtues; and David himself could not be more tender of the young man's life than I would be of his reputation. But since the most excellent natures are always the most easy, and, as being such, are the soonest perverted by ill counsels, especially when baited with fame and glory; 'tis no more a wonder that he withstood not the temptations of Achitophel, than it was for Adam not to have resisted the two devils, the serpent and the woman. The conclusion of the story I purposely forbore to prosecute, because I could not obtain from myself to show Absalom unfortunate. The frame of it was cut out but for a picture to the waist, and if the draught be so far true, 'tis as much I designed.

Were I the inventor, who am only the historian, I should certainly conclude the piece with the reconcilement of Absalom to David. And who knows but this may come to pass? Things were not brought to an extremity where I left the story; there seems yet to be room left for a composure; hereafter there may only be for pity. I have not so much as an uncharitable wish against Achitophel, but am content to be accused of a good-natured error, and to hope with Origen, that the Devil himself may at last be saved. For which reason, in this poem, he is neither brought to set his house in order, nor to dispose of his person afterwards as he in wisdom shall think fit. God is infinitely merciful; and his vicegerent is only not so because he is not infinite.

The true end of satire is the amendment of vices by correction. And he who writes honestly is no more an enemy to the offender than the physician to the patient, when he prescribes harsh remedies to an inveterate disease; for those are only in order to prevent the chirurgeon's work of an *ense rescindendum*,[3] which I wish not to my very enemies. To conclude all; if the body politic have any analogy to the natural, in my weak judgment an act of oblivion were as necessary in a hot, distempered state, as an opiate would be in a raging fever.

IN pious times, ere priestcraft did begin,
Before polygamy was made a sin;
When man on many multiplied his kind,
Ere one to one was cursedly confined;

[3] "cutting out with the knife"

When nature prompted, and no law denied
Promiscuous use of concubine and bride;
Then Israel's monarch [4] after Heaven's own heart,
His vigorous warmth did variously impart
To wives and slaves; and, wide as his command,
Scattered his Maker's image through the land.   10
Michal [5] of royal blood, the crown did wear;
A soil ungrateful to the tiller's care:
Not so the rest; for several mothers bore
To godlike David several sons before.
But since like slaves his bed they did ascend,
No true succession could their seed attend.
Of all this numerous progeny was none
So beautiful, so brave, as Absalom: [6]
Whether, inspired by some diviner lust,
His father got him with a greater gust;   20
Or that his conscious destiny made way,
By manly beauty, to imperial sway.
Early in foreign fields he won renown
With kings and states allied to Israel's crown;
In peace the thoughts of war he could remove,
And seemed as he were only born for love.
Whate'er he did, was done with so much ease,
In him alone 't was natural to please:
His motions all accompanied with grace;
And paradise was opened in his face.   30
With secret joy indulgent David viewed
His youthful image in his son renewed:
To all his wishes nothing he denied;
And made the charming Annabel [7] his bride.
What faults he had (for who from faults is free?)
His father could not or he would not see.
Some warm excesses which the law forbore,
Were construed youth that purged by boiling o'er,
And Amnon's murder,[8] by a specious name,
Was called a just revenge for injured fame.   40
Thus praised and loved the noble youth remained,
While David, undisturbed, in Sion [9] reigned.
But life can never be sincerely blest;
Heaven punishes the bad, and proves the best.
The Jews,[10] a headstrong, moody, murmuring race,

4 David—Charles II.
5 Charles II's queen,
Catherine of Portugal, who
was childless
6 The Duke of Mon-
mouth, illegitimate son of

Charles II
7 Anne Scott, Countess of
Buccleuch
8 Probably the assault
(not actually murder) in
December, 1670, upon Sir

John Coventry, who had
made a sarcastic allusion
to the King's amours
9 London
10 the English

As ever tried th' extent and stretch of grace;
God's pampered people, whom, debauched with ease,
No king could govern, nor no God could please
(Gods they had tried of every shape and size,
That god-smiths could produce, or priests devise);   50
These Adam-wits, too fortunately free,
Began to dream they wanted liberty;
And when no rule, no precedent was found,
Of men by laws less circumscribed and bound;
They led their wild desires to woods and caves,
And thought that all but savages were slaves.
They who, when Saul [11] was dead, without a blow,
Made foolish Ishbosheth [12] the crown forego;
Who banished David did from Hebron [13] bring,
And with a general shout proclaimed him king: 60
Those very Jews, who at their very best,
Their humor more than loyalty expressed,
Now wondered why so long they had obeyed
An idol monarch, which their hands had made;
Thought they might ruin him they could create,
Or melt him to that golden calf, a State.
But these were random bolts; no formed design,
Nor interest made the factious crowd to join:
The sober part of Israel, free from stain,
Well knew the value of a peaceful reign;   70
And, looking backward with a wise affright,
Saw seams of wounds, dishonest to the sight:
In contemplation of whose ugly scars
They cursed the memory of civil wars.
The moderate sort of men, thus qualified,
Inclined the balance to the better side;
And David's mildness managed it so well,
The bad found no occasion to rebel.
But when to sin our biased nature leans,
The careful Devil is still at hand with means;   80
And providently pimps for ill desires.
The Good Old Cause, revived, a plot requires.
Plots, true or false, are necessary things,
To raise up commonwealths and ruin kings.
    Th' inhabitants of old Jerusalem
Were Jebusites; [14] the town so called from them;
And theirs the native right.
But when the chosen people [15] grew more strong,

11 Oliver Cromwell
12 Richard Cromwell
13 Scotland, where
Charles II was crowned

in 1651, nearly ten years
before he was crowned in
England. See 2 Samuel v.
4, 5

14 Roman Catholics
15 the Protestants

The rightful cause at length became the wrong;
And very loss the men of Jebus bore,   90
They still were thought God's enemies the more.
Thus worn and weakened, well or ill content,
Submit they must to David's government:
Impoverished and deprived of all command,
Their taxes doubled as they lost their land;
And, what was harder yet to flesh and blood,
Their gods disgraced, and burned like common wood.
This set the heathen priesthood in a flame;
For priests of all religions are the same:
Of whatsoe'er descent their godhead be,   100
Stock, stone, or other homely pedigree,
In his defense his servants are as bold,
As if he had been born of beaten gold.
The Jewish rabbins, though their enemies,
In this conclude them honest men and wise:
For 'twas their duty, all the learned think,
T' espouse his cause, by whom they eat and drink.
From hence began that Plot,[16] the nation's curse,
Bad in itself, but represented worse,
Raised in extremes, and in extremes decried,   110
With oaths affirmed, with dying vows denied,
Not weighed or winnowed by the multitude;
But swallowed in the mass, unchewed and crude.
Some truth there was, but dashed and brewed with lies,
To please the fools, and puzzle all the wise.
Succeeding times did equal folly call,
Believing nothing, or believing all.
Th' Egyptian [17] rites the Jebusites embraced;
Where gods were recommended by their taste.
Such savory deities must needs be good,   120
As served at once for worship and for food.
By force they could not introduce these gods,
For ten to one in former days was odds;
So fraud was used (the sacrificer's trade):
Fools are more hard to conquer than persuade.
Their busy teachers mingled with the Jews,
And raked for converts e'en the court and stews:
Which Hebrew priests the more unkindly took,
Because the fleece accompanies the flock.
Some thought they God's anointed meant to slay   130
By guns, invented since full many a day:

16 the Popish Plot (1678),   and establish Catholicism,   17 French
described   below—alleged   with the aid of France
scheme to kill the King

Our author swears it not; but who can know
How far the Devil and Jebusites may go?
This Plot, which failed for want of common sense,
Had yet a deep and dangerous consequence:
For, as when raging fevers boil the blood,
The standing lake soon floats into a flood,
And every hostile humor, which before
Slept quiet in its channels, bubbles o'er;
So several factions from this first ferment   140
Work up to foam, and threat the government.
Some by their friends, more by themselves thought wise,
Opposed the power to which they could not rise.
Some had in courts been great, and thrown from thence,
Like fiends were hardened in impenitence.
Some, by their monarch's fatal mercy, grown
From pardoned rebels kinsmen to the throne,
Were raised in power and public office high;
Strong bands, if bands ungrateful men could tie.
    Of these the false Achitophel [18] was first;   150
A name to all succeeding ages curst:
For close designs and crooked counsels fit;
Sagacious, bold, and turbulent of wit;
Restless, unfixed in principles and place;
In power unpleased, impatient of disgrace:
A fiery soul, which, working out its way, ⎫
Fretted the pigmy body to decay,   ⎬
And o'er-informed the tenement of clay. ⎭
A daring pilot in extremity;
Pleased with the danger, when the waves went high,   160
He sought the storms; but, for a calm unfit,
Would steer too nigh the sands, to boast his wit.
Great wits are sure to madness near allied,
And thin partitions do their bounds divide;
Else why should he, with wealth and honor blest,
Refuse his age the needful hours of rest?
Punish a body which he could not please;
Bankrupt of life, yet prodigal of ease?
And all to leave what with his toil he won,
To that unfeathered two-legg'd thing, a son;   170
Got, while his soul did huddled notions try
And born a shapeless lump, like anarchy.
In friendship false, implacable in hate;
Resolved to ruin or to rule the State.

18 the Earl of Shaftesbury

To compass this the triple bond [19] he broke,
The pillars of the public safety shook,
And fitted Israel for a foreign yoke;
Then seized with fear, yet still affecting fame,
Usurped a patriot's all-atoning name.
So easy still it proves in factious times,　　　　180
With public zeal to cancel private crimes.
How safe is treason, and how sacred ill,
Where none can sin against the people's will!
Where crowds can wink, and no offense be known,
Since in another's guilt they find their own!
Yet fame deserved no enemy can grudge;
The statesman we abhor, but praise the judge.
In Israel's courts ne'er sat an Abbethdin [20]
With more discerning eyes, or hands more clean;
Unbribed, unsought, the wretched to redress;　　190
Swift of dispatch, and easy of access.
Oh, had he been content to serve the crown,
With virtues only proper to the gown;
Or had the rankness of the soil been freed
From cockle, that oppressed the noble seed;
David for him his tuneful harp had strung,
And Heaven had wanted one immortal song.
But wild Ambition loves to slide, not stand,
And Fortune's ice prefers to Virtue's land.
Achitophel, grown weary to possess　　　　　　200
A lawful fame, and lazy happiness,
Disdained the golden fruit to gather free,
And lent the crowd his arm to shake the tree.
Now, manifest of crimes contrived long since,
He stood at bold defiance with his prince;
Held up the buckler of the people's cause
Against the crown, and skulked behind the laws.
The wished occasion of the Plot he takes;
Some circumstances finds, but more he makes.
By buzzing emissaries fills the ears　　　　　　210
Of list'ning crowds with jealousies and fears
Of arbitrary counsels brought to light,
And proves the king himself a Jebusite.
Weak arguments! which yet he knew full well
Were strong with people easy to rebel.
For, governed by the moon, the giddy Jews

19 The triple alliance of England, Holland, and Sweden (directed against France) was succeeded in 1670 by an alliance of England and France (the "foreign yoke") against Holland. Shaftesbury was not instrumental in the latter.　20 judge

Tread the same track when she the prime renews;
And once in twenty years, their scribes record,
By natural instinct they change their lord.
Achitophel still wants a chief, and none   220
Was found so fit as warlike Absalon:
Not that he wished his greatness to create,
(For politicians neither love nor hate),
But, for he knew his title not allowed,
Would keep him still depending on the crowd,
That kingly power, thus ebbing out, might be
Drawn to the dregs of a democracy.
Him he attempts with studied arts to please,
And sheds his venom in such words as these:
    "Auspicious prince, at whose nativity   230
Some royal planet ruled the southern sky;
Thy longing country's darling and desire;
Their cloudy pillar and their guardian fire:
Their second Moses, whose extended wand
Divides the seas, and shows the promised land;
Whose dawning day in every distant age
Has exercised the sacred prophets' rage;
The people's prayer, the glad diviners' theme,
The young men's vision, and the old men's dream!
Thee, Savior, thee, the nation's vows confess,   240
And, never satisfied with seeing, bless:
Swift unbespoken pomps thy steps proclaim,
And stammering babes are taught to lisp thy name.
How long wilt thou the general joy detain,
Starve and defraud the people of thy reign?
Content ingloriously to pass thy days
Like one of Virtue's fools that feeds on praise;
Till thy fresh glories, which now shine so bright,
Grow stale and tarnish with our daily sight.
Believe me, royal youth, thy fruit must be   250
Or gathered ripe, or rot upon the tree.
Heaven has to all allotted, soon or late,
Some lucky revolution of their fate;
Whose motions if we watch and guide with skill
(For human good depends on human will),
Our fortune rolls as from a smooth descent,
And from the first impression takes the bent;
But, if unseized, she glides away like wind,
And leaves repenting Folly far behind.
Now, now she meets you with a glorious prize,   260
And spreads her locks before her as she flies.
Had thus old David, from whose loins you spring,

Not dared, when Fortune called him, to be king,
At Gath [21] an exile he might still remain,
And Heaven's anointing oil had been in vain.
Let his successful youth your hopes engage;
But shun th' example of declining age:
Behold him setting in his western skies,
The shadows lengthening as the vapors rise.
He is not now, as when on Jordan's sand [22] ⎫ *270*
The joyful people thronged to see him land,   ⎬
Covering the beach, and blackening all the strand;⎭
But, like the Prince of Angels, from his height
Comes tumbling downward with diminished light;
Betrayed by one poor plot to public scorn,
(Our only blessing since his curst return),
Those heaps of people which one sheaf did bind,
Blown off and scattered by a puff of wind.
What strength can he to your designs oppose,
Naked of friends and round beset with foes? *280*
If Pharoah's [23] doubtful succor he should use,
A foreign aid would more incense the Jews:
Proud Egypt would dissembled friendship bring;
Foment the war, but not support the king:
Nor would the royal party e'er unite
With Pharoah's arms t'assist the Jebusite;
Or if they should, their interest soon would break,
And with such odious aid make David weak.
All sorts of men by my successful arts,
Abhorring kings, estrange their altered hearts *290*
From David's rule: and 't is the general cry,
'Religion, commonwealth, and liberty.'
If you, as champion of the public good,
Add to their arms a chief of royal blood,
What may not Israel hope, and what applause
Might such a general gain by such a cause?
Not barren praise alone, that gaudy flower
Fair only to the sight, but solid power;
And nobler is a limited command,
Giv'n by the love of all your native land, *300*
Than a successive title, long and dark,
Drawn from the moldy rolls of Noah's ark."
 What cannot praise effect in mighty minds,
When flattery soothes, and when ambition blinds!
Desire of power, on earth a vicious weed,

21 Brussels
22 Dover. Jordan repre- sents the sea surrounding 23 Louis XIV of France
 England (Egypt)

Yet, sprung from high, is of celestial seed:
In God 't is glory; and when men aspire,
'T is but a spark too much of heavenly fire.
Th' ambitious youth, too covetous of fame,
Too full of angels' metal in his frame,   310
Unwarily was led from virtue's ways,
Made drunk with honor, and debauched with praise.
Half loath, and half consenting to the ill,
(For loyal blood within him struggled still),
He thus replied: "And what pretense have I
To take up arms for public liberty?
My father governs with unquestioned right;
The faith's defender, and mankind's delight;
Good, gracious, just, observant of the laws:
And Heaven by wonders has espoused his cause.   320
Whom has he wronged in all his peaceful reign?
Who sues for justice to his throne in vain?
What millions has he pardoned of his foes,
Whom just revenge did to his wrath expose?
Mild, easy, humble, studious of our good,
Inclined to mercy, and averse from blood;
If mildness ill with stubborn Israel suit,
His crime is God's belovèd attribute.
What could he gain, his people to betray,
Or change his right for arbitrary sway?   330
Let haughty Pharaoh curse with such a reign
His fruitful Nile, and yoke a servile train.
If David's rule Jerusalem displease,
The Dog-star heats their brains to this disease.
Why then should I, encouraging the bad,
Turn rebel and run popularly mad?
Were he a tyrant, who, by lawless might
Oppressed the Jews, and raised the Jebusite,
Well might I mourn; but nature's holy bands
Would curb my spirits and restrain my hands: 340
The people might assert their liberty;
But what was right in them were crime in me.
His favor leaves me nothing to require,
Prevents my wishes, and outruns desire.
What more can I expect while David lives?
All but his kingly diadem he gives:
And that"—But there he paused; then sighing, said—
"Is justly destined for a worthier head.
For when my father from his toils shall rest,
And late augment the number of the blest,   350
His lawful issue shall the throne ascend,

Or the collateral line, where that shall end.
His brother,[24] though oppressed with vulgar spite,
Yet dauntless, and secure of native right,
Of every royal virtue stands possessed,
Still dear to all the bravest and the best.
His courage foes, his friends his truth proclaim;
His loyalty the king, the world his fame.
His mercy ev'n th' offending crowd will find;
For sure he comes of a forgiving kind. 360
Why should I then repine at Heav'n's decree,
Which gives me no pretense to royalty?
Yet O that fate, propitiously inclined,
Had raised my birth, or had debased my mind;
To my large soul not all her treasure lent,
And then betrayed it to a mean descent!
I find, I find my mounting spirits bold,
And David's part disdains my mother's mold.
Why am I scanted by a niggard birth?
My soul disclaims the kindred of her earth; 370
And, made for empire, whispers me within,
'Desire of greatness is a godlike sin.' "
    Him staggering so when hell's dire agent found,
While fainting Virtue scarce maintained her ground,
He pours fresh forces in, and thus replies:
    "Th' eternal God, supremely good and wise,
Imparts not these prodigious gifts in vain:
What wonders are reserved to bless your reign!
Against your will, your arguments have shown,
Such virtue's only given to guide a throne. 380
Not that your father's mildness I contemn;
But manly force becomes the diadem.
'T is true he grants the people all they crave;
And more, perhaps, than subjects ought to have:
For lavish grants suppose a monarch tame,
And more his goodness than his wit proclaim.
But when should people strive their bonds to break,
If not when kings are negligent or weak?
Let him give on till he can give no more,
The thrifty Sanhedrin [25] shall keep him poor; 390
And every shekel which he can receive,
Shall cost a limb of his prerogative.
To ply him with new plots shall be my care;
Or plunge him deep in some expensive war;
Which when his treasure can no more supply,
He must, with the remains of kingship, buy.

24 James, Duke of York (afterwards James II)   25 Parliament

His faithful friends, our jealousies and fears
Call Jebusites, and Pharaoh's pensioners;
Whom when our fury from his aid has torn,
He shall be naked left to public scorn.   400
The next successor, whom I fear and hate,
My arts have made obnoxious to the State;
Turned all his virtues to his overthrow,
And gained our elders to pronounce a foe.
His right, for sums of necessary gold,
Shall first be pawned, and afterwards be sold;
Till time shall ever-wanting David draw,
To pass your doubtful title into law:
If not, the people have a right supreme
To make their kings; for kings are made for them.   410
All empire is no more than power in trust,
Which, when resumed, can be no longer just.
Succession, for the general good designed,
In its own wrong a nation cannot bind;
If altering that the people can relieve,
Better one suffer than a nation grieve.
The Jews well know their power: ere Saul they chose,
God was their king, and God they durst depose.
Urge now your piety, your filial name,
A father's right, and fear of future fame;   420
The public good, that universal call,
To which even Heaven submitted, answers all.
Nor let his love enchant your generous mind;
'T is Nature's trick to propagate her kind.
Our fond begetters, who would never die,
Love but themselves in their posterity.
Or let his kindness by th' effects be tried,
Or let him lay his vain pretense aside.
God said he loved your father; could he bring
A better proof, than to anoint him king?   430
It surely showed he loved the shepherd well,
Who gave so fair a flock as Israel.
Would David have you thought his darling son?
What means he then, to alienate the crown?
The name of godly he may blush to bear;
'T is after God's own heart to cheat his heir.
He to his brother gives supreme command;
To you a legacy of barren land,
Perhaps th' old harp, on which he thrums his lays,
Or some dull Hebrew ballad in your praise.   440
Then the next heir, a prince severe and wise,
Already looks on you with jealous eyes;

Sees through the thin disguises of your arts,
And marks your progress in the people's hearts.
Though now his mighty soul its grief contains
He meditates revenge who least complains;
And, like a lion, slumbering in the way,
Or sleep dissembling, while he waits his prey,
His fearless foes within his distance draws,
Constrains his roaring, and contracts his paws;   450
Till at the last, his time for fury found,
He shoots with sudden vengeance from the ground;
The prostrate vulgar passes o'er and spares,
But with a lordly rage his hunters tears.
Your case no tame expedients will afford:
Resolve on death, or conquest by the sword,
Which for no less a stake than life you draw;
And self-defense is nature's eldest law.
Leave the warm people no considering time;
For then rebellion may be thought a crime.   460
Prevail yourself of what occasion gives,
But try your title while your father lives;
And that your arms may have a fair pretense,
Proclaim you take them in the king's defense;
Whose sacred life each minute would expose
To plots, from seeming friends, and secret foes.
And who can sound the depth of David's soul?
Perhaps his fear his kindness may control.
He fears his brother, though he loves his son,
For plighted vows too late to be undone.   470
If so, by force he wishes to be gained,
Like women's lechery, to seem constrained.
Doubt not: but, when he most affects the frown,
Commit a pleasing rape upon the crown.
Secure his person to secure your cause:
They who possess the prince, possess the laws."
    He said, and this advice above the rest,
With Absalom's mild nature suited best:
Unblamed of life (ambition set aside),
Not stained with cruelty, nor puffed with pride,   480
How happy had he been, if destiny
Had higher placed his birth, or not so high!
His kingly virtues might have claimed a throne,
And blessed all other countries but his own.
But charming greatness since so few refuse,
'T is juster to lament him than accuse.
Strong were his hopes a rival to remove,
With blandishments to gain the public love;

To head the faction while their zeal was hot,
And popularly prosecute the Plot.   490
To further this, Achitophel unites
The malcontents of all the Israelites;
Whose differing parties he could wisely join,
For several ends, to serve the same design:
The best (and of the princes some were such),
Who thought the power of monarchy too much;
Mistaken men, and patriots in their hearts;
Not wicked, but seduced by impious arts.
By these the springs of property were bent,
And wound so high, they cracked the government.   500
The next for interest sought t' embroil the State,
To sell their duty at a dearer rate;
And make their Jewish markets of the throne,
Pretending public good, to serve their own.
Others thought kings an useless heavy load,
Who cost too much, and did too little good.
These were for laying honest David by,
On principles of pure good husbandry.
With them joined all th' haranguers of the throng,
That thought to get preferment by the tongue.   510
Who follow next, a double danger bring,
Not only hating David, but the king:
The Solymæan rout,[26] well-versed of old
In godly faction, and in treason bold;
Cow'ring and quaking at a conqu'ror's sword,
But lofty to a lawful prince restored,
Saw with disdain an Ethnic plot [27] begun,
And scorned by Jebusites to be outdone.
Hot Levites [28] headed these; who, pulled before
From th' ark, which in the Judges' days they bore,   520
Resumed their cant, and with a zealous cry
Pursued their old belov'd Theocracy:
Where Sanhedrin and priest inslaved the nation,
And justified their spoils by inspiration:
For who so fit for reign as Aaron's race,[29]
If once dominion they could found in grace?
These led the pack; though not of surest scent,
Yet deepest mouthed against the government.
A numerous host of dreaming saints succeed,
Of the true old enthusiastic breed: 530

---

26 the London rabble
27 the Popish Plot
28 Presbyterian   clergy-
men, forced out of the
Church of England by the
Act of Uniformity of 1662
29 the clergy

'Gainst form and order they their power employ,
Nothing to build, and all things to destroy.
But far more numerous was the herd of such,
Who think too little, and who talk too much.
These, out of mere instinct, they knew not why,
Adored their fathers' God and property;
And, by the same blind benefit of fate,
The Devil and the Jebusite did hate:
Born to be saved, even in their own despite,
Because they could not help believing right. 540
Such were the tools; but a whole Hydra more
Remains, of sprouting heads too long to score.
Some of their chiefs were princes of the land:
In the first rank of these did Zimri [30] stand;
A man so various, that he seemed to be
Not one, but all mankind's epitome:
Stiff in opinions, always in the wrong;
Was everything by starts, and nothing long;
But, in the course of one revolving moon,
Was chemist, fiddler, statesman, and buffoon: 550
Then all for women, painting, rhyming, drinking,
Besides ten thousand freaks that died in thinking.
Blest madman, who could every hour employ,
With something new to wish, or to enjoy!
Railing and praising were his usual themes;
And both (to show his judgment) in extremes:
So over-violent, or over-civil,
That every man, with him, was God or Devil.
In squandering wealth was his peculiar art:
Nothing went unrewarded but desert. 560
Beggared by fools, whom still he found too late,
He had his jest, and they had his estate.
He laughed himself from court; then sought relief
By forming parties, but could ne'er be chief;
For, spite of him, the weight of business fell
On Absalom and wise Achitophel:
Thus, wicked but in will, of means bereft,
He left no faction, but of that was left.
   Titles and names 't were tedious to rehearse
Of lords, below the dignity of verse. 570
Wits, warriors, commonwealth's-men, were the best;
Kind husbands, and mere nobles, all the rest.
And therefore, in the name of dullness,

---

[30] George Villiers, Duke of Buckingham. His literary farce, *The Rehearsal*, had satirized Dryden.

The well-hung Balaam [31] and cold Caleb free;
And canting Nadab let oblivion damn,
Who made new porridge for the paschal lamb.
Let friendship's holy band some names assure;
Some their own worth, and some let scorn secure.
Nor shall the rascal rabble here have place,
Whom kings no titles gave, and God no grace: 580
Not bull-faced Jonas who could statutes draw
To mean rebellion, and make treason law.
But he, though bad, is followed by a worse,
The wretch who Heaven's anointed dared to curse:
Shimei, whose youth did early promise bring
Of zeal to God and hatred to his king,
Did wisely from expensive sins refrain,
And never broke the Sabbath, but for gain;
Nor ever was he known an oath to vent,
Or curse, unless against the government.   590
Thus heaping wealth, by the most ready way
Among the Jews, which was to cheat and pray,
The city, to reward his pious hate
Against his master, chose him magistrate.
His hand a vare [32] of justice did uphold;
His neck was loaded with a chain of gold.
During his office, treason was no crime;
The sons of Belial had a glorious time;
For Shimei, though not prodigal of pelf,
Yet loved his wicked neighbor as himself.   600
When two or three were gathered to declaim ⎱
Against the monarch of Jerusalem,   ⎬
Shimei was always in the midst of them;   ⎰
And if they cursed the king when he was by,
Would rather curse than break good company.
If any durst his factious friends accuse,
He packed a jury of dissenting Jews;
Whose fellow-feeling in the godly cause
Would free the suffering saint from human laws.
For laws are only made to punish those   610
Who serve the king, and to protect his foes.
If any leisure time he had from power,
(Because 't is sin to misemploy an hour),
His business was, by writing, to persuade
That kings were useless, and a clog to trade;

31 In the following twelve lines Dryden finds scriptural names presenting some parallel to five contemporaries; respectively the Earl of Hunting-don, Lord Grey of Wark; Lord Howard of Esrick, who was said to have taken the communion in "lamb's wool" (ale poured on roasted apples and sugar); Sir William Jones, the attorney-general who prosecuted against the Popish Plot; and Slingsby Bethel, a Whig sheriff of London. 32 wand

And, that his noble style he might refine,
No Rechabite [33] more shunned the fumes of wine.
Chaste were his cellars, and his shrieval board [34]
The grossness of a city feast abhorred:
His cooks, with long disuse, their trade forgot;   620
Cool was his kitchen, though his brains were hot.
Such frugal virtue malice may accuse,
But sure 't was necessary to the Jews;
For towns once burnt such magistrates require
As dare not tempt God's providence by fire.
With spiritual food he fed his servants well,
But free from flesh that made the Jews rebel;
And Moses' laws he held in more account,
For forty days of fasting in the mount.
   To speak the rest, who better are forgot,   630
Would tire a well-breathed witness of the Plot.
Yet, Corah,[35] thou shalt from oblivion pass:
Erect thyself, thou monumental brass,
High as the serpent of thy metal made,
While nations stand secure beneath thy shade.
What though his birth were base, yet comets rise
From earthy vapors, ere they shine in skies.
Prodigious actions may as well be done
By weaver's issue, as by prince's son.
This arch-attestor for the public good   640
By that one deed ennobles all his blood.
Who ever asked the witnesses' high race,
Whose oath with martyrdom did Stephen grace?
Ours was a Levite, and as times went then,
His tribe were God Almighty's gentlemen.
Sunk were his eyes, his voice was harsh and loud,
Sure signs he neither choleric was nor proud:
His long chin proved his wit; his saintlike grace
A church vermilion, and a Moses' face.
His memory, miraculously great,   650
Could plots, exceeding man's belief, repeat;
Which therefore cannot be accounted lies,
For human wit could never such devise.
Some future truths are mingled in his book;
But where the witness failed, the prophet spoke:
Some things like visionary flights appear;
The spirit caught him up, the Lord knows where;
And gave him his rabbinical degree,

---

[33] descendants of Rechab, who drank no wine (Jer. xxxv. 14)   [34] sheriff's table. Bethel's stinginess became proverbial.   [35] Titus Oates, contriver of the Popish Plot

Unknown to foreign university.
His judgment yet his memory did excel;   660
Which pieced his wondrous evidence so well,
And suited to the temper of the times,
Then groaning under Jebusitic crimes.
Let Israel's foes suspect his heavenly call,
And rashly judge his writ apocryphal;
Our laws for such affronts have forfeits made:
He takes his life, who takes away his trade.
Were I myself in witness Corah's place,
The wretch who did me such a dire disgrace,
Should whet my memory, though once forgot,   670
To make him an appendix of my plot.
His zeal to Heaven made him his prince despise,
And load his person with indignities;
But zeal peculiar privilege affords,
Indulging latitude to deeds and words;
And Corah might for Agag's [36] murder call,
In terms as coarse as Samuel used to Saul.
What others in his evidence did join
(The best that could be had for love or coin),
In Corah's own predicament will fall;   680
For *witness* is a common name to all.
   Surrounded thus with friends of every sort,
Deluded Absalom forsakes the court;
Impatient of high hopes, urged with renown,
And fired with near possession of a crown.
Th' admiring crowd are dazzled with surprise,
And on his goodly person feed their eyes.
His joy concealed, he sets himself to show,
On each side bowing popularly low;
His looks his gestures, and his words he frames,   690
And with familiar ease repeats their names.
Thus formed by nature, furnished out with arts,
He glides unfelt into their secret hearts.
Then, with a kind compassionating look,
And sighs, bespeaking pity ere he spoke,
Few words he said; but easy those and fit,
More slow than Hybla-drops,[37] and far more sweet.
   "I mourn, my countrymen, your lost estate;
Though far unable to prevent your fate:
Behold a banished man, for your dear cause   700
Exposed a prey to arbitrary laws!

---

36 Sir Edmund Berry Godfrey, the magistrate before whom Oates made his deposition, was soon thereafter mysteriously murdered. Dryden represents Oates as instigating the deed.

37 honey (from Hybla, Sicily)

Yet oh, that I alone could be undone,
Cut off from empire, and no more a son!
Now all your liberties a spoil are made;
Egypt and Tyrus [38] intercept your trade,
And Jebusites your sacred rites invade.
My father, whom with reverence yet I name,
Charmed into ease, is careless of his fame;
And, bribed with petty sums of foreign gold,
Is grown in Bathsheba's [39] embraces old;   710
Exalts his enemies, his friends destroys;
And all his power against himself employs.
He gives, and let him give, my right away;
But why should he his own and yours betray?
He, only he, can make the nation bleed,
And he alone from my revenge is freed.
Take then my tears (with that he wiped his eyes),
'T is all the aid my present power supplies:
No court-informer can these arms accuse;
These arms may sons against their fathers use: 720
And 't is my wish, the next successor's reign
May make no other Israelite complain."
      Youth, beauty, graceful action seldom fail;
But common interest always will prevail;
And pity never ceases to be shown
To him who makes the people's wrongs his own.
The crowd, that still believe their kings oppress,
With lifted hands their young Messiah bless:
Who now begins his progress to ordain
With chariots, horsemen, and a num'rous train;   730
From east to west his glories he displays,
And, like the sun, the promised land surveys.
Fame runs before him as the morning star,
And shouts of joy salute him from afar:
Each house receives him as a guardian god,
And consecrates the place of his abode.
But hospitable treats did most commend
Wise Issachar,[40] his wealthy western friend.
This moving court, that caught the people's eyes,
And seemed but pomp, did other ends disguise: 740
Achitophel had formed it, with intent
To sound the depths, and fathom, where it went,
The people's hearts; distinguish friends from foes,
And try their strength, before they came to blows.

38 France and Holland   tress of Charles II   entertained Monmouth
39 the Duchess of Ports-   40 Thomas Thynne, a
mouth, the reigning mis- Wiltshire gentleman who

Yet all was colored with a smooth pretense
Of specious love, and duty to their prince.
Religion, and redress of grievances,
Two names that always cheat and always please,
Are often urged; and good King David's life
Endangered by a brother and a wife.   750
Thus in a pageant show a plot is made,
And peace itself is war in masquerade.
O foolish Israel! never warned by ill!
Still the same bait, and circumvented still!
Did ever men forsake their present ease,
In midst of health imagine a disease;
Take pains contingent mischiefs to foresee,
Make heirs for monarchs, and for God decree?
What shall we think! Can people give away,
Both for themselves and sons, their native sway?   760
Then they are left defenseless to the sword
Of each unbounded, arbitrary lord:
And laws are vain, by which we right enjoy,
If kings unquestioned can those laws destroy.
Yet if the crowd be judge of fit and just,
And kings are only officers in trust,
Then this resuming covenant was declared
When kings were made, or is for ever barred.
If those who gave the scepter could not tie
By their own deed their own posterity,   770
How then could Adam bind his future race?
How could his forfeit on mankind take place?
Or how could heavenly justice damn us all,
Who ne'er consented to our father's fall?
Then kings are slaves to those whom they command,
And tenants to their people's pleasure stand.
Add, that the power for property allowed
Is mischievously seated in the crowd;
For who can be secure of private right,
If sovereign sway may be dissolved by might?   780
Nor is the people's judgment always true:
The most may err as grossly as the few;
And faultless kings run down, by common cry,
For vice, oppression, and for tyranny.
What standard is there in a fickle rout,
Which, flowing to the mark, runs faster out?
Nor only crowds, but Sanhedrins may be
Infected with this public lunacy,
And share the madness of rebellious times,
To murder monarchs for imagined crimes.   790

If they may give and take whene'er they please,
Not kings alone (the Godhead's images),
But government itself at length must fall
To nature's state, where all have right to all.
Yet, grant our lords the people kings can make,
What prudent men a settled throne would shake?
For whatsoe'er their sufferings were before,
That change they covet makes them suffer more.
All other errors but disturb a state,
But innovation is the blow of fate.   800
If ancient fabrics nod and threat to fall,
To patch the flaws and buttress up the wall,
Thus far 't is duty: but here fix the mark;
For all beyond it is to touch our ark.
To change foundations, cast the frame anew,
Is work for rebels, who base ends pursue,
At once divine and human laws control,
And mend the parts by ruin of the whole.
The tampering world is subject to this curse,
To physic their disease into a worse.   810
     Now what relief can righteous David bring?
How fatal 't is to be too good a king!
Friends he has few, so high the madness grows:
Who dare be such, must be the people's foes.
Yet some there were, ev'n in the worst of days;
Some let me name, and naming is to praise.
     In this short file Barzillai [11] first appears;
Barzillai, crowned with honor and with years.
Long since, the rising rebels he withstood
In regions waste, beyond the Jordan's flood: 820
Unfortunately brave to buoy the State;
But sinking underneath his master's fate:
In exile with his godlike prince he mourned;
For him he suffered, and with him returned.
The court he practiced, not the courtier's art:
Large was his wealth, but larger was his heart,
Which well the noblest objects knew to choose,
The fighting warrior, and recording Muse.
His bed could once a fruitful issue boast;
Now more than half a father's name is lost.   830
His eldest hope, with every grace adorned,
By me (so Heav'n will have it) always mourned,
And always honored, snatched in manhood's prime
B' unequal fates, and Providence's crime;

41 The Duke of Ormond. By 1681 six of his eight sons were dead, including the
Earl of Ossory, referred to below, a distinguished seaman and soldier

Yet not before the goal of honor won,
All parts fulfilled of subject and of son:
Swift was the race, but short the time to run.
O narrow circle, but of power divine,
Scanted in space, but perfect in thy line!
By sea, by land, thy matchless worth was known,   840
Arms thy delight, and war was all thy own:
Thy force, infused, the fainting Tyrians propped;
And haughty Pharaoh found his fortune stopped.
O ancient honor! O unconquered hand,
Whom foes unpunished never could withstand!
But Israel was unworthy of thy name;
Short is the date of all immoderate fame.
It looks as Heaven our ruin had designed,
And durst not trust thy fortune and thy mind.
Now, free from earth, thy disencumbered soul   850
Mounts up, and leaves behind the clouds and starry pole:
From thence thy kindred legions may'st thou bring,
To aid the guardian angel of thy king.
Here stop, my Muse, here cease thy painful flight;
No pinions can pursue immortal height:
Tell good Barzillai thou canst sing no more,
And tell thy soul she should have fled before:
Or fled she with his life, and left this verse
To hang on her departed patron's hearse?
Now take thy steepy flight from heaven, and see   860
If thou canst find on earth another *he:*
Another *he* would be too hard to find;
See then whom thou canst see not far behind.
Zadoc [42] the priest, whom, shunning power and place,
His lowly mind advanced to David's grace.
With him the Sagan of Jerusalem,
Of hospitable soul, and noble stem;
Him of the western dome, whose weighty sense
Flows in fit words and heavenly eloquence.
The prophets' sons, by such example led,   870
To learning and to loyalty were bred:
For colleges on bounteous kings depend,
And never rebel was to arts a friend.
To these succeed the pillars of the laws:
Who best could plead, and best can judge a cause.
Next them a train of loyal peers ascend;

42 The three churchmen referred to are, respectively, William Sancroft, Archbishop of Canterbury; Henry Compton, Bishop of London; and John Dolben, Dean of Westminster (the "western dome").

Sharp-judging Adriel, [43] the Muses' friend;
Himself a Muse—in Sanhedrin's debate
True to his prince, but not a slave of state:
Whom David's love with honors did adorn,   880
That from his disobedient son were torn.
Jotham of piercing wit, and pregnant thought;
Endued by nature, and by learning taught
To move assemblies, who but only tried
The worse a while, then chose the better side:
Nor chose alone, but turned the balance too;
So much the weight of one brave man can do.
Hushai, the friend of David in distress;
In public storms, of manly steadfastness:
By foreign treaties he informed his youth,   890
And joined experience to his native truth.
His frugal care supplied the wanting throne;
Frugal for that, but bounteous of his own:
'T is easy conduct when exchequers flow,
But hard the task to manage well the low;
For sovereign power is too depressed or high,
When kings are forced to sell, or crowds to buy.
Indulge one labor more, my weary Muse,
For Amiel: who can Amiel's praise refuse?
Of ancient race by birth, but nobler yet   900
In his own worth, and without title great:
The Sanhedrin long time as chief he ruled,
Their reason guided, and their passion cooled:
So dext'rous was he in the crown's defense,
So formed to speak a loyal nation's sense,
That, as their band was Israel's tribes in small,
So fit was he to represent them all.
Now rasher charioteers the seat ascend,
Whose loose careers his steady skill commend:
They, like th' unequal ruler of the day, [44]   910
Misguide the seasons, and mistake the way;
While he withdrawn at their mad labor smiles,
And safe enjoys the sabbath of his toils.
      These were the chief, a small but faithful band ⎫
Of worthies, in the breach who dared to stand, ⎬
And tempt th' united fury of the land. ⎭

---

43 The four "loyal peers" now mentioned are, in order, John Sheffield, Earl of Mulgrave, a poet and critic, and a patron of Dryden; George Savile, Marquis of Halifax, poet and political peacemaker; Laurence Hyde, Earl of Rochester, First Lord of the Treasury; and Edward Seymour, Speaker of the House of Commons, 1673–1679   44 Phaethon, son of Apollo, the sun god, who rashly attempted to drive his father's chariot

With grief they viewed such powerful engines bent,
To batter down the lawful government:
A numerous faction, with pretended frights,
In Sanhedrins to plume [45] the regal rights;   920
The true successor from the court removed;
The Plot, by hireling witnesses, improved.
These ills they saw, and, as their duty bound,
They showed the king the danger of the wound;
That no concessions from the throne would please,
But lenitives fomented the disease;
That Absalom, ambitious of the crown,
Was made the lure to draw the people down;
That false Achitophel's pernicious hate
Had turned the Plot to ruin Church and State;   930
The council violent, the rabble worse;
That Shimei taught Jerusalem to curse.
   With all these loads of injuries oppressed,
And long revolving in his careful breast
Th' event of things, at last, his patience tired,
Thus from his royal throne, by Heav'n inspired,
The godlike David spoke: with awful fear
His train their Maker in their master hear.
   "Thus long have I, by native mercy swayed,
My wrongs dissembled, my revenge delayed: 940
So willing to forgive th' offending age;
So much the father did the king assuage.
But now so far my clemency they slight,
Th' offenders question my forgiving right.
That one was made for many, they contend;
But 'tis to rule; for that's a monarch's end.
They call my tenderness of blood, my fear;
Though manly tempers can the longest bear.
Yet, since they will divert my native course,
'T is time to show I am not good by force.   950
Those heaped affronts that haughty subjects bring,
Are burdens for a camel, not a king.
Kings are the public pillars of the State,
Born to sustain and prop the nation's weight;
If my young Samson will pretend a call
To shake the column, let him share the fall:
But O that yet he would repent and live!
How easy 't is for parents to forgive!
With how few tears a pardon might be won
From nature, pleading for a darling son!   960
Poor pitied youth, by my paternal care

45 pluck out

Raised up to all the height his frame could bear!
Had God ordained his fate for empire born,
He would have given his soul another turn:
Gulled with a patriot's name, whose modern sense
Is one that would by law supplant his prince;
The people's brave, the politician's tool;
Never was patriot yet, but was a fool.
Whence comes it that religion and the laws
Should more be Absalom's than David's cause? 970
His old instructor, ere he lost his place,
Was never thought indued with so much grace.
Good heavens, how faction can a patriot paint!
My rebel ever proves my people's saint.
Would *they* impose an heir upon the throne?
Let Sanhedrins be taught to give their own.
A king's at least a part of government,
And mine as requisite as their consent;
Without my leave a future king to choose,
Infers a right the present to depose. 980
True, they petition me t' approve their choice;
But Esau's hands suit ill with Jacob's voice.
My pious subjects for my safety pray;
Which to secure, they take my power away.
From plots and treasons Heaven preserve my years,
But save me most from my petitioners!
Unsatiate as the barren womb or grave;
God cannot grant so much as they can crave.
What then is left, but with a jealous eye
To guard the small remains of royalty? 990
The law shall still direct my peaceful sway,
And the same law teach rebels to obey:
Votes shall no more established power control—
Such votes as make a part exceed the whole:
No groundless clamors shall my friends remove,
Nor crowds have power to punish ere they prove;
For gods and godlike kings their care express,
Still to defend their servants in distress.
O that my power to saving were confined!
Why am I forced, like Heaven, against my mind, ⎫
To make examples of another kind?   ⎬   1000
Must I at length the sword of justice draw? ⎭
O curst effects of necessary law!
How ill my fear they by my mercy scan!
Beware the fury of a patient man.
Law they require, let Law then show her face;
They could not be content to look on Grace,

Her hinder parts, but with a daring eye
To tempt the terror of her front and die.
By their own arts, 't is righteously decreed,　　1010
Those dire artificers of death shall bleed.
Against themselves their witnesses will swear,
Till viper-like their mother Plot they tear;
And suck for nutriment that bloody gore,
Which was their principle of life before.
Their Belial with their Belzebub will fight;
Thus on my foes, my foes shall do me right.
Nor doubt th' event; for factious crowds engage,
In their first onset, all their brutal rage.
Then let 'em take an unresisted course;　　1020
Retire, and traverse, and delude their force;
But, when they stand all breathless, urge the fight,
And rise upon 'em with redoubled might;
For lawful power is still superior found;
When long driven back, at length it stands the ground."
　　He said. Th' Almighty, nodding, gave consent;
And peals of thunder shook the firmament.
Henceforth a series of new time began,
The mighty years in long procession ran:
Once more the godlike David was restored,　　1030
And willing nations knew their lawful lord.

ALEXANDER'S FEAST

OR, THE POWER OF MUSIC; AN ODE IN HONOR OF ST. CECILIA'S DAY.[46]

I

'T WAS at the royal feast, for Persia won
　　By Philip's warlike son: [47]
　　　Aloft in awful state
　　　The godlike hero sate
　　　On his imperial throne:
　　His valiant peers were placed around;
Their brows with roses and with myrtles bound
　　(So should desert in arms be crowned).
　　The lovely Thais, by his side,
　　Sate like a blooming Eastern bride　　10
In flower of youth and beauty's pride.
　　　Happy, happy, happy pair!

46 St. Cecilia, patron saint of music, and reputed inventress of the organ, was annually celebrated by a London musical society, for whom Dryden wrote this ode as well as his earlier *Song for St. Cecilia's Day*
47 Alexander the Great

None but the brave,
None but the brave,
None but the brave deserves the fair.

CHORUS

Happy, happy, happy pair!
None but the brave,
None but the brave,
None but the brave deserves the fair.

II

Timotheus,[48] placed on high   20
  Amid the tuneful choir,
  With flying fingers touched the lyre:
The trembling notes ascend the sky,
      And heavenly joys inspire.
The song began from Jove,
Who left his blissful seats above
(Such is the power of mighty love).
A dragon's fiery form belied the god:
Sublime on radiant spires he rode,
      When he to fair Olympia pressed;   30
      And while he sought her snowy breast:
Then, round her slender waist he curled,
And stamped an image of himself, a sovereign of the world.
The listening crowd admire the lofty sound;
"A present deity," they shout around;
"A present deity," the vaulted roofs rebound:
      With ravished ears
      The monarch hears,
      Assumes the god,
      Affects to nod,   40
And seems to shake the spheres.

CHORUS

      With ravished ears
      The monarch hears,
      Assumes the god,
      Affects to nod,
And seems to shake the spheres.

48 musician to Alexander

III

The praise of Bacchus then the sweet musician sung,
  Of Bacchus ever fair and ever young:
    The jolly god in triumph comes;
    Sound the trumpets; beat the drums;   50
      Flushed with a purple grace
      He shows his honest face:
Now give the hautboys breath; he comes, he comes.
    Bacchus, ever fair and young,
      Drinking joys did first ordain;
    Bacchus' blessings are a treasure,
    Drinking is the soldier's pleasure:
      Rich the treasure,
      Sweet the pleasure,
      Sweet is pleasure after pain.   60

CHORUS

    Bacchus' blessings are a treasure,
    Drinking is the soldier's pleasure:
      Rich the treasure,
      Sweet the pleasure,
      Sweet is pleasure after pain.

IV

    Soothed with the sound, the king grew vain;
      Fought all his battles o'er again;
And thrice he routed all his foes; and thrice he slew the slain.
    The master saw the madness rise;
    His glowing cheeks, his ardent eyes;   70
    And, while he heaven and earth defied,
    Changed his hand, and checked his pride.
      He chose a mournful Muse,
        Soft pity to infuse:
    He sung Darius [49] great and good,
        By too severe a fate,
    Fallen, fallen, fallen, fallen,
        Fallen from his high estate,
        And weltering in his blood;
    Deserted, at his utmost need,   80
    By those his former bounty fed;
    On the bare earth exposed he lies,
    With not a friend to close his eyes.

49 the Persian King conquered by Alexander

With downcast looks the joyless victor sate,
Revolving in his altered soul
The various turns of chance below;
And, now and then, a sigh he stole;
And tears began to flow.

CHORUS

Revolving in his altered soul
 The various turns of chance below;
And, now and then, a sigh he stole;
 And tears began to flow.
          90

V

• The mighty master smiled, to see   •
That love was in the next degree:
'T was but a kindred sound to move,
For pity melts the mind to love.
 Softly sweet, in Lydian measures,
 Soon he soothed his soul to pleasures.
 "War," he sung, "is toil and trouble;
 Honor, but an empty bubble;   100
  Never ending, still beginning,
 Fighting still, and still destroying:
  If the world be worth thy winning,
 Think, O think it worth enjoying;
  Lovely Thais sits beside thee,
  Take the good the gods provide thee."

The many rend the skies with loud applause;
So Love was crowned, but Music won the cause.
 The prince, unable to conceal his pain,
  Gazed on the fair   .   110
  Who caused his care,
 And sighed and looked, sighed and looked,
 Sighed and looked, and sighed again:
At length, with love and wine at once oppressed,
The vanquished victor sunk upon her breast.

CHORUS

The prince, unable to conceal his pain,
  Gazed on the fair
  Who caused his care,
 And sighed and looked, sighed and looked,

Sighed and looked, and sighed again: 120
At length, with love and wine at once oppressed,
The vanquished victor sunk upon her breast.

VI

Now strike the golden lyre again:
A louder yet, and yet a louder strain.
Break his bands of sleep asunder,
And rouse him, like a rattling peal of thunder.
  Hark, hark, the horrid sound
    Has raised up his head:
    As awaked from the dead,
  And amazed, he stares around. 130
"Revenge, revenge!" Timotheus cries,
  "See the Furies arise!
  See the snakes that they rear,
  How they hiss in their hair,
And the sparkles that flash from their eyes!
  Behold a ghastly band,
  Each a torch in his hand!
Those are Grecian ghosts, that in battle were slain,
    And unburied remain
    Inglorious on the plain: 140
  Give the vengeance due
  To the valiant crew.
Behold how they toss their torches on high,
  How they point to the Persian abodes,
And glittering temples of their hostile gods!"
The princes applaud, with a furious joy;
And the king seized a flambeau with zeal to destroy;
    Thais led the way,
    To light him to his prey,
And, like another Helen, fired another Troy. 150

CHORUS

And the king seized a flambeau with zeal to destroy;
    Thais led the way,
    To light him to his prey,
And, like another Helen, fired another Troy.

VII

    Thus, long ago,
  Ere heaving bellows learned to blow,

While organs yet were mute;
Timotheus, to his breathing flute,
    And sounding lyre,
Could swell the soul to rage, or kindle soft desire.   160
At last, divine Cecilia came,
Inventress of the vocal frame; [50]
The sweet enthusiast, from her sacred store,
    Enlarged the former narrow bounds,
    And added length to solemn sounds,
With nature's mother wit, and arts unknown before.
    Let old Timotheus yield the prize,
        Or both divide the crown;
    He raised a mortal to the skies;
        She drew an angel down.   170

Grand Chorus

At last, divine Cecilia came,
Inventress of the vocal frame;
The sweet enthusiast, from her sacred store,
    Enlarged the former narrow bounds,
    And added length to solemn sounds,
With nature's mother wit, and arts unknown before.
    Let old Timotheus yield the prize,
        Or both divide the crown;
    He raised a mortal to the skies;
        She drew an angel down.   180

PREFACE TO THE FABLES

'Tis with a poet as with a man who designs to build, and is
very exact, as he supposes, in casting up the cost beforehand;
but, generally speaking, he is mistaken in his account, and
reckons short of the expense he first intended. He alters his mind
as the work proceeds, and will have this or that convenience
more, of which he had not thought when he began. So has it happened to me. I have built a house where I intended but a lodge;
yet with better success than a certain nobleman, who, beginning
with a dog-kennel, never lived to finish the palace he had contrived.   10
    From translating the first of Homer's *Iliads* (which I intended
as an essay to the whole work) I proceeded to the translation of
the twelfth book of Ovid's *Metamorphoses*, because it contains,
among other things, the causes, the beginning, and ending of the

50 the organ

Trojan War. Here I ought in reason to have stopped; but the speeches of Ajax and Ulysses lying next in my way, I could not balk 'em. When I had compassed them, I was so taken with the former part of the fifteenth book (which is the masterpiece of the whole *Metamorphoses*) that I enjoined myself the pleasing task of rendering it into English. And now I found, by the number of my verses, that they began to swell into a little volume; which gave me an occasion of looking backward on some beauties of my author, in his former books. There occurred to me the
10 Hunting of the Boar, Cinyras and Myrrha, the good-natured story of Baucis and Philemon, with the rest, which I hope I have translated closely enough, and given them the same turn of verse which they had in the original; and this, I may say without vanity, is not the talent of every poet. He who has arrived the nearest to it is the ingenious and learned Sandys,[51] the best versifier of the former age, if I may properly call it by that name, which was the former part of this concluding century. For Spenser and Fairfax [52] both flourished in the reign of Queen Elizabeth; great masters in our language, and who saw much further
20 into the beauties of our numbers than those who immediately followed them. Milton was the poetical son of Spenser, and Mr. Waller of Fairfax, for we have our lineal descents and clans as well as other families. Spenser more than once insinuates that the soul of Chaucer was transfused into his body, and that he was begotten by him two hundred years after his decease. Milton has acknowledged to me that Spenser was his original, and many besides myself have heard our famous Waller own that he derived the harmony of his numbers from the *Godfrey of Bulloigne*,[53] which was turned into English by Mr. Fairfax.
30 But to return. Having done with Ovid for this time, it came into my mind that our old English poet, Chaucer, in many things resembled him, and that with no disadvantage on the side of the modern author, as I shall endeavor to prove when I compare them; and as I am, and always have been, studious to promote the honor of my native country, so I soon resolved to put their merits to the trial by turning some of the *Canterbury Tales* into our language as it is now refined; for by this means, both the poets being set in the same light and dressed in the same English habit, story to be compared with story, a certain judgment may
40 be made betwixt them by the reader, without obtruding my opinion on him. Or if I seem partial to my countryman and predecessor in the laurel, the friends of antiquity are not few; and besides many of the learned, Ovid has almost all the beaux, and the whole fair sex, his declared patrons. Perhaps I have assumed

---

51 George Sandys, 1578–
1644   52 Edward Fairfax, d.
1635   53 or *Jerusalem Delivered*, by Tasso

somewhat more to myself than they allow me, because I have adventured to sum up the evidence; but the readers are the jury, and their privilege remains entire, to decide according to the merits of the cause, or, if they please, to bring it to another hearing before some other court.

In the meantime, to follow the thread of my discourse (as thoughts, according to Mr. Hobbes,[54] have always some connection), so from Chaucer I was led to think on Boccace,[55] who was not only his contemporary but also pursued the same studies; wrote novels in prose, and many works in verse; particularly is said to have invented the octave rhyme,[56] or stanza of eight lines, which ever since has been maintained by the practice of all Italian writers who are, or at least assume the title of, heroic poets. He and Chaucer, among other things, had this in common, that they refined their mother tongues; but with this difference, that Dante had begun to file their language, at least in verse, before the time of Boccace, who likewise received no little help from his master, Petrarch. But the reformation of their prose was wholly owing to Boccace himself, who is yet the standard of purity in the Italian tongue, though many of his phrases are become obsolete, as in process of time it must needs happen. Chaucer (as you have formerly been told by our learned Mr. Rymer) [57] first adorned and amplified our barren tongue from the Provençal,[58] which was then the most polished of all the modern languages; but this subject has been copiously treated by that great critic, who deserves no little commendation from us his countrymen. For these reasons of time and resemblance of genius in Chaucer and Boccace, I resolved to join them in my present work; to which I have added some original papers of my own, which, whether they are equal or inferior to my other poems, an author is the most improper judge, and therefore I leave them wholly to the mercy of the reader. I will hope the best, that they will not be condemned; but if they should, I have the excuse of an old gentleman, who, mounting on horseback before some ladies, when I was present, got up somewhat heavily, but desired of the fair spectators that they would count fourscore and eight before they judged him. By the mercy of God I am already come within twenty years of his number, a cripple in my limbs; but what decays are in my mind the reader must determine. I think myself as vigorous as ever in the faculties of my soul, excepting only my memory, which is not impaired to any

54 Thomas Hobbes (1588–1679), English philosopher, who stressed the association of ideas
55 Boccaccio (1313–1375), Italian poet and writer of tales, now best known for his *Decameron*
56 The *ottava rima*, an eight line stanza rhyming abababcc
57 Thomas Rymer, 1641–1713
58 The language of Provence (southeastern France), —a mistake, since it was the dialect of Paris which influenced English in Chaucer's day

great degree; and if I lose not more of it, I have no great reason to complain. What judgment I had increases rather than diminishes; and thoughts, such as they are, come crowding in so fast upon me that my only difficulty is to choose or to reject, to run them into verse or to give them the other harmony of prose. I have so long studied and practised both that they are grown into a habit and become familiar to me. In short, though I may lawfully plead some part of the old gentleman's excuse, yet I will reserve it till I think I have greater need, and ask no grains of 10 allowance for the faults of this my present work but those which are given of course to human frailty. I will not trouble my reader with the shortness of time in which I writ it, or the several intervals of sickness: they who think too well of their own performances are apt to boast in their prefaces how little time their works have cost them, and what other business of more importance interfered; but the reader will be as apt to ask the question, why they allowed not a longer time to make their works more perfect, and why they had so despicable an opinion of their judges as to thrust their indigested stuff upon them, as if they 20 deserved no better.

With this account of my present undertaking, I conclude the first part of this discourse: in the second part, as at a second sitting, though I alter not the draught, I must touch the same features over again and change the dead coloring of the whole. In general, I will only say that I have written nothing which savors of immorality or profaneness; at least, I am not conscious to myself of any such intention. If there happen to be found an irreverent expression or a thought too wanton, they are crept into my verses through my inadvertency; if the searchers find 30 any in the cargo, let them be staved or forfeited, like contrabanded goods; at least, let their authors be answerable for them, as being but imported merchandise and not of my own manufacture. On the other side, I have endeavored to choose such fables, both ancient and modern, as contain in each of them some instructive moral; which I could prove by induction, but the way is tedious, and they leap foremost into sight without the reader's trouble of looking after them. I wish I could affirm with a safe conscience that I had taken the same care in all my former writings; for it must be owned that, supposing verses are never 40 so beautiful or pleasing, yet if they contain anything which shocks religion or good manners, they are at best what Horace says of good numbers without good sense, "Versus inopes rerum, nugæque canoræ." [59] Thus far, I hope, I am right in court, without renouncing to my other right of self-defence where I have

---

[59] "Verses devoid of substance, and melodious trifles" (Horace, *De Arte Poetica,* 322)

been wrongfully accused and my sense wire-drawn into blasphemy or bawdry, as it has often been by a religious lawyer [60] in a late pleading against the stage, in which he mixes truth with falsehood, and has not forgotten the old rule of calumniating strongly that something may remain.

I resume the thread of my discourse with the first of my translations, which was the first *Iliad* of Homer. If it shall please God to give me longer life and moderate health, my intentions are to translate the whole *Ilias*, provided still that I meet with those encouragements from the public which may enable me to proceed 10 in my undertaking with some cheerfulness. And this I dare assure the world beforehand, that I have found by trial Homer a more pleasing task than Virgil, though I say not the translation will be less laborious. For the Grecian is more according to my genius than the Latin poet. In the works of the two authors we may read their manners and natural inclinations, which are wholly different. Virgil was of a quiet, sedate temper; Homer was violent, impetuous, and full of fire. The chief talent of Virgil was propriety of thoughts and ornament of words; Homer was rapid in his thoughts, and took all the liberties, both of numbers 20 and of expressions, which his language and the age in which he lived allowed him. Homer's invention was more copious, Virgil's more confined; so that if Homer had not led the way, it was not in Virgil to have begun heroic poetry, for nothing can be more evident than that the Roman poem is but the second part of the *Ilias*—a continuation of the same story, and the persons already formed; the manners of Æneas are those of Hector superadded to those which Homer gave him. The adventures of Ulysses in the *Odysseis* are imitated in the first six books of Virgil's *Æneis;* and though the accidents are not the same (which 30 would have argued him of a servile copying and total barrenness of invention), yet the seas were the same in which both the heroes wandered, and Dido cannot be denied to be the poetical daughter of Calypso. The six latter books of Virgil's poem are the four and twenty *Iliads* contracted—a quarrel occasioned by a lady, a single combat, battles fought, and a town besieged. I say not this in derogation to Virgil, neither do I contradict anything which I have formerly said in his just praise: for his episodes are almost wholly of his own invention; and the form which he has given to the telling makes the tale his own, even 40 though the original story had been the same. But this proves, however, that Homer taught Virgil to design; and if invention be the first virtue of an epic poet, then the Latin poem can only be allowed the second place. Mr. Hobbes, in the preface

60 Jeremy Collier, in his *Short View of the Immorality and Profaneness of the English Stage* (1698)

to his own bald translation of the *Ilias* (studying poetry, as he did mathematics, when it was too late), Mr. Hobbes, I say, begins the praise of Homer where he should have ended it. He tells us that the first beauty of an epic poem consists in diction, that is, in the choice of words and harmony of numbers. Now, the words are the coloring of the work, which in the order of nature is last to be considered: the design, the disposition, the manners, and the thoughts are all before it; where any of those are wanting or imperfect, so much wants or is imperfect in the imitation of human life, which is in the very definition of a poem. Words indeed, like glaring colors, are the first beauties that arise and strike the sight; but if the draught be false or lame, the figures ill-disposed, the manners obscure or inconsistent, or the thoughts unnatural, then the finest colors are but daubing, and the piece is a beautiful monster at the best. Neither Virgil nor Homer were deficient in any of the former beauties; but in this last, which is expression, the Roman poet is at least equal to the Grecian, as I have said elsewhere, supplying the poverty of his language by his musical ear and by his diligence.

But to return: our two great poets, being so different in their tempers, one choleric and sanguine, the other phlegmatic and melancholic, that which makes them excel in their several ways is that each of them has followed his own natural inclination, as well in forming the design as in the execution of it. The very heroes show their authors: Achilles is hot, impatient, revengeful—"Impiger, iracundus, inexorabilis, acer," [61] etc.; Æneas patient, considerate, careful of his people and merciful to his enemies, ever submissive to the will of Heaven—"quo fata trahunt retrahuntque sequamur." [62] I could please myself with enlarging on this subject, but am forced to defer it to a fitter time. From all I have said I will only draw this inference, that the action of Homer being more full of vigor than that of Virgil, according to the temper of the writer, is of consequence more pleasing to the reader. One warms you by degrees; the other sets you on fire all at once, and never intermits his heat. 'Tis the same difference which Longinus [63] makes betwixt the effects of eloquence in Demosthenes and Tully: one persuades, the other commands. You never cool while you read Homer, even not in the second book (a graceful flattery to his countrymen); but he hastens from the ships, and concludes not that book till he has made you an amends by the violent playing of a new machine.[64] From thence he hurries on his action with variety of

61 Horace, *De Arte Poetica*, 121
62 "Where the fates drag us back and forth, let us follow" (*Æneid*, V. 709)
63 Greek rhetorician (213?-273 A. D.), famous for a treatise on the Sublime
64 Probably the supernatural agency or "machinery" of Iris going to rouse the Trojans to battle (Iliad, II. 768 ff.)

events, and ends it in less compass than two months. This vehemence of his, I confess, is more suitable to my temper, and therefore I have translated his first book with greater pleasure than any part of Virgil; but it was not a pleasure without pains. The continual agitations of the spirits must needs be a weakening of any constitution, especially in age; and many pauses are required for refreshment betwixt the heats, the *Iliad* of itself being a third part longer than all Virgil's works together.

This is what I thought needful in this place to say of Homer. I proceed to Ovid and Chaucer, considering the former only in relation to the latter. With Ovid ended the golden age of the Roman tongue; from Chaucer the purity of the English tongue began. The manners of the poets were not unlike: both of them were well-bred, well-natured, amorous, and libertine—at least in their writings, it may be also in their lives. Their studies were the same, philosophy and philology.[65] Both of them were knowing in astronomy, of which Ovid's books of the Roman feasts and Chaucer's treatise of the astrolabe are sufficient witnesses; but Chaucer was likewise an astrologer, as were Virgil, Horace, Persius, and Manilius. Both writ with wonderful facility and clearness. Neither were great inventors; for Ovid only copied the Grecian fables, and most of Chaucer's stories were taken from his Italian contemporaries or their predecessors. Boccace his *Decameron* was first published, and from thence our Englishman has borrowed many of his *Canterbury Tales;* yet that of Palamon and Arcite was written in all probability by some Italian wit in a former age, as I shall prove hereafter. The tale of Grizild [66] was the invention of Petrarch, by him sent to Boccace, from whom it came to Chaucer. *Troilus and Cressida* was also written by a Lombard author,[67] but much amplified by our English translator, as well as beautified, the genius of our countrymen in general being rather to improve an invention than to invent themselves, as is evident, not only in our poetry, but in many of our manufactures. I find I have anticipated already, and taken up from Boccace before I come to him; but there is so much less behind, and I am of the temper of most kings, who love to be in debt, are all for present money, no matter how they pay it afterwards; besides, the nature of a preface is rambling, never wholly out of the way nor in it. This I have learned from the practice of honest Montaigne; and return at my pleasure to Ovid and Chaucer, of whom I have little more to say.

Both of them built on the inventions of other men; yet since

65 including all studies connected with literature
66 Griselda, the heroine of Chaucer's *Clerk's Tale.* Dryden is mistaken, since

Petrarch got the story from Boccaccio, and Chaucer from Petrarch.
67 Another mistake. Chaucer speaks of "myn

auctor Lollius"—a reference which has never been satisfactorily explained. Dryden thought him a Lombard writer.

Chaucer had something of his own, as *The Wife of Bath's Tale,*
The Cock and the Fox,[68] which I have translated, and some
others, I may justly give our countryman the precedence in that
part, since I can remember nothing of Ovid which was wholly
his. Both of them understood the manners, under which name I
comprehend the passions and in a larger sense the descriptions
of persons and their very habits. For an example, I see Baucis
and Philemon as perfectly before me as if some ancient painter
had drawn them; and all the pilgrims in the *Canterbury Tales,*
10 their humors, their features, and the very dress, as distinctly
as if I had supped with them at the Tabard in Southwark. Yet
even there too the figures of Chaucer are much more lively
and set in a better light, which, though I have not time to prove,
yet I appeal to the reader, and am sure he will clear me from
partiality. The thoughts and words remain to be considered in
the comparison of the two poets, and I have saved myself one
half of the labor by owning that Ovid lived when the Roman
tongue was in its meridian, Chaucer in the dawning of our language; therefore that part of the comparison stands not on an
20 equal foot, any more than the diction of Ennius [69] and Ovid, or
of Chaucer and our present English. The words are given up as
a post not to be defended in our poet, because he wanted the
modern art of fortifying. The thoughts remain to be considered,
and they are to be measured only by their propriety, that is,
as they flow more or less naturally from the persons described,
on such and such occasions. The vulgar judges, which are nine
parts in ten of all nations, who call conceits and jingles wit, who
see Ovid full of them and Chaucer altogether without them, will
think me little less than mad for preferring the Englishman to
30 the Roman; yet, with their leave, I must presume to say that
the things they admire are only glittering trifles, and so far
from being witty that in a serious poem they are nauseous because they are unnatural. Would any man who is ready to die
for love describe his passion like Narcissus? Would he think of
"inopem me copia fecit," [70] and a dozen more of such expressions, poured on the neck of one another and signifying all the
same thing? If this were wit, was this a time to be witty, when
the poor wretch was in the agony of death? This is just John
Littlewit in *Bartholomew Fair,*[71] who had a conceit (as he tells
40 you) left him in his misery; a miserable conceit. On these occasions the poet should endeavor to raise pity; but, instead of
this, Ovid is tickling you to laugh. Virgil never made use of such
machines when he was moving you to commiserate the death of

---

68 The Nun's Priest's
Tale
69 early Latin poet, B. C.

239–169
70 "Power has made me
powerless" (Ovid, *Meta-*

morphoses, III. 466)
71 play by Ben Jonson

Dido; he would not destroy what he was building. Chaucer makes Arcite violent in his love and unjust in the pursuit of it; yet when he came to die he made him think more reasonably: he repents not of his love, for that had altered his character, but acknowledges the injustice of his proceedings and resigns Emilia to Palamon. What would Ovid have done on this occasion? He would certainly have made Arcite witty on his death-bed; he had complained he was farther off from possession by being so near, and a thousand such boyisms, which Chaucer rejected as below the dignity of the subject. They who think otherwise 10 would, by the same reason, prefer Lucan and Ovid to Homer and Virgil, and Martial to all four of them. As for the turn of words, in which Ovid particularly excels all poets, they are sometimes a fault and sometimes a beauty, as they are used properly or improperly, but in strong passions always to be shunned, because passions are serious and will admit no playing. The French have a high value for them, and I confess they are often what they call delicate when they are introduced with judgment; but Chaucer writ with more simplicity, and followed nature more closely, than to use them. 20

I have thus far, to the best of my knowledge, been an upright judge betwixt the parties in competition, not meddling with the design nor the disposition of it, because the design was not their own and in the disposing of it they were equal. It remains that I say somewhat of Chaucer in particular.

In the first place, as he is the father of English poetry so I hold him in the same degree of veneration as the Grecians held Homer or the Romans Virgil. He is a perpetual fountain of good sense, learned in all sciences, and therefore speaks properly on all subjects. As he knew what to say, so he knows also 30 when to leave off; a continence which is practised by few writers, and scarcely by any of the ancients, excepting Virgil and Horace. One of our late great poets [72] is sunk in his reputation because he could never forego any conceit which came in his way, but swept, like a drag-net, great and small. There was plenty enough, but the dishes were ill sorted; whole pyramids of sweetmeats for boys and women, but little of solid meat for men. All this proceeded, not from any want of knowledge, but of judgment. Neither did he want that in discerning the beauties and faults of other poets, but only indulged himself in the luxury of writ- 40 ing; and perhaps knew it was a fault but hoped the reader would not find it. For this reason, though he must always be thought a great poet, he is no longer esteemed a good writer; and for ten impressions, which his works have had in so many successive years, yet at present a hundred books are scarcely purchased

72 Abraham Cowley (1618–1667)

once a twelvemonth; for, as my last Lord Rochester said, though
somewhat profanely, "Not being of God, he could not stand."
Chaucer followed nature everywhere, but was never so bold
to go beyond her, and there is a great difference of being *poeta*
and *nimis poeta;* [73] if we believe Catullus, as much as betwixt
a modest behavior and affectation. The verse of Chaucer, I confess, is not harmonious to us; but 'tis like the eloquence of one
whom Tacitus commends, it was "auribus istius temporis ac-
commodata": [74] they who lived with him, and some time after
10 him, thought it musical; and it continues so even in our judgment, if compared with the numbers of Lydgate and Gower, his
contemporaries; there is the rude sweetness of a Scotch tune in
it, which is natural and pleasing though not perfect. 'Tis true
I cannot go so far as he who published the last edition of him,[75]
for he would make us believe the fault is in our ears, and that
there were really ten syllables in a verse where we find but nine;
but this opinion is not worth confuting; 'tis so gross and obvious an error that common sense (which is a rule in everything
but matters of faith and revelation) must convince the reader
20 that equality of numbers in every verse which we call heroic [76]
was either not known or not always practised in Chaucer's age.
It were an easy matter to produce some thousands of his verses
which are lame for want of half a foot and sometimes a whole
one, and which no pronunciation can make otherwise. We can
only say that he lived in the infancy of our poetry, and that
nothing is brought to perfection at the first. We must be children before we grow men. There was an Ennius, and in process
of time a Lucilius and a Lucretius, before Virgil and Horace;
even after Chaucer there was a Spenser, a Harrington, a Fair-
30 fax, before Waller and Denham were in being, and our numbers were in their nonage till these last appeared. I need say
little of his parentage, life, and fortunes: they are to be found
at large in all the editions of his works. He was employed abroad,
and favored by Edward the Third, Richard the Second, and
Henry the Fourth, and was poet, as I suppose, to all three of
them. In Richard's time, I doubt, he was a little dipped in the
rebellion of the Commons; and, being brother-in-law to John
of Gaunt, it was no wonder if he followed the fortunes of that
family, and was well with Henry the Fourth when he had de-
40 posed his predecessor. Neither is it to be admired that Henry,
who was a wise as well as a valiant prince, who claimed by

---

73 "too much a poet"—
from Martial (*Epigrams,*
III. 44), not from Catullus
74 "accommodated to the
ears of that time" (mis-
quoted from Tacitus, *Dia-*

logue on Orators)
75 Thomas Speght. Dry-
den unjustly criticizes
Chaucer's versification because he had a corrupt
text and was ignorant of

the pronunciation of Mid-
dle English
76 the iambic pentameter
couplet

succession, and was sensible that his title was not sound but was rightfully in Mortimer, who had married the heir of York— it was not to be admired, I say, if that great politician should be pleased to have the greatest wit of those times in his interests and to be the trumpet of his praises. Augustus had given him the example, by the advice of Mæcenas, who recommended Virgil and Horace to him; whose praises helped to make him popular while he was alive, and after his death have made him precious to posterity. As for the religion of our poet, he seems to have some little bias towards the opin- 10 ions of Wiclif, after John of Gaunt his patron; somewhat of which appears in the tale of *Piers Plowman*.[77] Yet I cannot blame him for inveighing so sharply against the vices of the clergy in his age: their pride, their ambition, their pomp, their avarice, their worldly interest deserved the lashes which he gave them, both in that and in most of his *Canterbury Tales*. Neither has his contemporary Boccace spared them. Yet both those poets lived in much esteem with good and holy men in orders; for the scandal which is given by particular priests reflects not on the sacred function. Chaucer's Monk, his Canon, 20 and his Friar took not from the character of his Good Parson. A satirical poet is the check of the laymen on bad priests. We are only to take care that we involve not the innocent with the guilty in the same condemnation. The good cannot be too much honored nor the bad too coarsely used; for the corruption of the best becomes the worst. When a clergyman is whipped, his gown is first taken off, by which the dignity of his order is secured. If he be wrongfully accused, he has his action of slander; and 'tis at the poet's peril if he transgress the law. But they will tell us that all kind of satire, though never so well-deserved 30 by particular priests, yet brings the whole order into contempt. Is, then, the peerage of England anything dishonored when a peer suffers for his treason? If he be libelled or any way defamed, he has his *Scandalum Magnatum*[78] to punish the offender. They who use this kind of argument seem to be conscious to themselves of somewhat which has deserved the poet's lash, and are less concerned for their public capacity than for their private; at least there is pride at the bottom of their reasoning. If the faults of men in orders are only to be judged among themselves, they are all in some sort parties; for, since 40 they say the honor of their order is concerned in every member of it, how can we be sure that they will be impartial judges? How far I may be allowed to speak my opinion in this case I

---

77 Not the famous Middle English poem attributed to Wm. Langland, but the spurious *Plowman's*

Tale, printed at the end of the *Canterbury Tales. The Flower and the Leaf,* mentioned on p. 554, is likewise

spurious.
78 "Offence against the great"—a legal term

know not, but I am sure a dispute of this nature caused mischief in abundance betwixt a king of England and an archbishop of Canterbury,[79] one standing up for the laws of his land, and the other for the honor (as he called it) of God's Church, which ended in the murder of the prelate and in the whipping of his Majesty from post to pillar for his penance. The learned and ingenious Dr. Drake [80] has saved me the labor of inquiring into the esteem and reverence which the priests have had of old, and I would rather extend than diminish any part of it; yet
10 I must needs say that when a priest provokes me without any occasion given him, I have no reason, unless it be the charity of a Christian, to forgive him. *Prior læsit* [81] is justification sufficient in the civil law. If I answer him in his own language, self-defence, I am sure, must be allowed me; and if I carry it farther, even to a sharp recrimination, somewhat may be indulged to human frailty. Yet my resentment has not wrought so far but that I have followed Chaucer in his character of a holy man, and have enlarged on that subject with some pleasure, reserving to myself the right, if I shall think fit hereafter, to
20 describe another sort of priests, such as are more easily to be found than the Good Parson, such as have given the last blow to Christianity in this age by a practice so contrary to their doctrine. But this will keep cold till another time. In the meanwhile I take up Chaucer where I left him.

He must have been a man of a most wonderful comprehensive nature, because, as it has been truly observed of him, he has taken into the compass of his *Canterbury Tales* the various manners and humors (as we now call them) of the whole English nation in his age. Not a single character has escaped
30 him. All his pilgrims are severally distinguished from each other, and not only in their inclinations but in their very physiognomies and persons. Baptista Porta [82] could not have described their natures better than by the marks which the poet gives them.

The matter and manner of their tales and of their telling are so suited to their different educations, humors, and callings that each of them would be improper in any other mouth. Even the grave and serious characters are distinguished by their several sorts of gravity: their discourses are such as be-
40 long to their age, their calling, and their breeding, such as are becoming of them and of them only. Some of his persons are vicious and some virtuous; some are unlearned, or (as Chaucer calls them) lewd, and some are learned. Even the ribaldry of

---

79 Henry II (1133–1189) and Thomas à Becket
80 James Drake wrote an answer to Jeremy Collier,
The Ancient and Modern Stages Reviewed, 1699 (see p. 541 f.n. 60)
81 "He hurt (me) first"
82 Italian physiognomist (1543–1615)

the low characters is different: the Reeve, the Miller, and the Cook are several men, and distinguished from each other as much as the mincing Lady Prioress and the broad-speaking, gap-toothed Wife of Bath. But enough of this; there is such a variety of game springing up before me that I am distracted in my choice and know not which to follow. 'Tis sufficient to say, according to the proverb, that here is God's plenty. We have our forefathers and great-grand-dames all before us as they were in Chaucer's days: their general characters are still remaining in mankind, and even in England, though they are called by other names than those of monks and friars and canons and lady abbesses and nuns; for mankind is ever the same, and nothing lost out of nature though everything is altered.

May I have leave to do myself the justice (since my enemies will do me none, and are so far from granting me to be a good poet that they will not allow me so much as to be a Christian or a moral man), may I have leave, I say, to inform my reader that I have confined my choice to such tales of Chaucer as savor nothing of immodesty? If I had desired more to please than to instruct, the Reeve, the Miller, the Shipman, the Merchant, the Summoner, and above all the Wife of Bath, in the prologue to her tale, would have procured me as many friends and readers as there are beaux and ladies of pleasure in the town. But I will no more offend against good manners; I am sensible, as I ought to be, of the scandal I have given by my loose writings, and make what reparation I am able by this public acknowledgment. If anything of this nature or of profaneness be crept into these poems, I am so far from defending it that I disown it. "Totum hoc indictum volo." [83] Chaucer makes another manner of apology for his broad speaking, and Boccace makes the like; but I will follow neither of them. Our countryman, in the end of his characters, before the *Canterbury Tales,* thus excuses the ribaldry, which is very gross in many of his novels:—

"But firste, I pray you of your courtesy,
That ye ne arrete it not my villany,
Though that I plainly speak in this mattere,
To tellen you her words, and eke her chere:
Ne though I speak her words properly,
For this ye knowen as well as I,
Who shall tellen a tale after a man,
He mote rehearse as nye as ever he can:
Everich word of it ben in his charge,
All speke he, never so rudely, ne large.

83 "All this I wish unsaid"

Or else he mote tellen his tale untrue,
Or feine things, or find words new:
He may not spare, altho he were his brother
He mote as well say o word as another.
Christ spake himself full broad in holy writ,
And well I wote no villany is it.
Eke Plato saith, who so can him rede,
The words mote been cousin to the dede."

Yet if a man should have inquired of Boccace or of Chaucer
10 what need they had of introducing such characters where obscene words were proper in their mouths but very indecent
to be heard, I know not what answer they could have made;
for that reason such tales shall be left untold by me. You have
here a specimen of Chaucer's language, which is so obsolete
that his sense is scarce to be understood; and you have likewise
more than one example of his unequal numbers,[84] which were
mentioned before. Yet many of his verses consist of ten syllables, and the words not much behind our present English; as
for example these two lines, in the description of the carpenter's
20 young wife:—

"Wincing she was, as is a jolly colt,
Long as a mast, and upright as a bolt."

I have almost done with Chaucer when I have answered
some objections relating to my present work. I find some people
are offended that I have turned these tales into modern English, because they think them unworthy of my pains, and look
on Chaucer as a dry, old-fashioned wit, not worth reviving.
I have often heard the late Earl of Leicester say that Mr.
Cowley himself was of that opinion; who, having read him
30 over at my lord's request, declared he had no taste of him. I
dare not advance my opinion against the judgment of so great
an author; but I think it fair, however, to leave the decision to
the public. Mr. Cowley was too modest to set up for a dictator; and, being shocked perhaps with his old style, never
examined into the depth of his good sense. Chaucer, I confess,
is a rough diamond, and must first be polished ere he shines. I
deny not, likewise, that, living in our early days of poetry, he
writes not always of a piece, but sometimes mingles trivial
things with those of greater moment. Sometimes, also, though
40 not often, he runs riot like Ovid, and knows not when he has
said enough. But there are more great wits besides Chaucer
whose fault is their excess of conceits, and those ill-sorted. An
author is not to write all he can but only all he ought. Having

84 The verses Dryden quotes are corrupt

observed this redundancy in Chaucer (as it is an easy matter
for a man of ordinary parts to find a fault in one of greater),
I have not tied myself to a literal translation, but have often
omitted what I judged unnecessary or not of dignity enough to
appear in the company of better thoughts. I have presumed
further, in some places, and added somewhat of my own where
I thought my author was deficient and had not given his thoughts
their true luster, for want of words in the beginning of our language. And to this I was the more emboldened because (if I
may be permitted to say it of myself) I found I had a soul con- 10
genial to his and that I had been conversant in the same studies.
Another poet, in another age, may take the same liberty with
my writings; if at least they live long enough to deserve correction. It was also necessary sometimes to restore the sense of
Chaucer, which was lost or mangled in the errors of the press.
Let this example suffice at present: in the story of Palamon and
Arcite, where the temple of Diana is described, you find these
verses in all the editions of our author:—

> "There saw I Danè, turned unto a tree,
> I mean not the goddess Diane,   20
> But Venus daughter, which that hight Danè;"

which, after a little consideration, I knew was to be reformed
into this sense, that Daphne, the daughter of Peneus, was
turned into a tree. I durst not make thus bold with Ovid, lest
some future Milbourn [85] should arise and say I varied from
my author because I understood him not.

But there are other judges who think I ought not to have
translated Chaucer into English, out of a quite contrary notion: they suppose there is a certain veneration due to his
old language, and that it is little less than profanation and sac- 30
rilege to alter it. They are farther of opinion that somewhat
of his good sense will suffer in this transfusion, and much of
the beauty of his thoughts will infallibly be lost, which appear
with more grace in their old habit. Of this opinion was that excellent person, whom I mentioned, the late Earl of Leicester,
who valued Chaucer as much as Mr. Cowley despised him. My
lord dissuaded me from this attempt (for I was thinking of it
some years before his death), and his authority prevailed so far
with me as to defer my undertaking while he lived, in deference
to him; yet my reason was not convinced with what he urged 40
against it. If the first end of a writer be to be understood, then,
as his language grows obsolete, his thoughts must grow obscure:—

85 See p. 602 and note 92.

"Multa renascentur quæ nunc cecidere; cadentque
Quæ nunc sunt in honore vocabula, si volet usus,
Quem penes arbitrium est et jus norma loquendi." [86]

When an ancient word for its sound and significance deserves
to be revived, I have that reasonable veneration for antiquity
to restore it. All beyond this is superstition. Words are not like
landmarks, so sacred as never to be removed; customs are
changed, and even statutes are silently repealed when the reason
ceases for which they were enacted. As for the other part of the
10 argument, that his thoughts will lose of their original beauty by
the innovation of words, in the first place not only their beauty
but their being is lost where they are no longer understood,
which is the present case. I grant that something must be lost
in all transfusion, that is, in all translations; but the sense will
remain, which would otherwise be lost, or at least be maimed,
when it is scarce intelligible and that but to a few. How few
are there who can read Chaucer so as to understand him perfectly? And if imperfectly, then with less profit and no pleasure.
It is not for the use of some old Saxon friends that I have taken
20 these pains with him; let them neglect my version, because
they have no need of it. I made it for their sakes who understand sense and poetry as well as they, when that poetry and
sense is put into words which they understand. I will go farther,
and dare to add that what beauties I lose in some places I give
to others which had them not originally: but in this I may be
partial to myself; let the reader judge, and I submit to his
decision. Yet I think I have just occasion to complain of them
who, because they understand Chaucer, would deprive the
greater part of their countrymen of the same advantage, and
30 hoard him up, as misers do their grandam gold, only to look on
it themselves, and hinder others from making use of it. In sum,
I seriously protest that no man ever had or can have a greater
veneration for Chaucer than myself. I have translated some part
of his works only that I might perpetuate his memory, or at
least refresh it, amongst my countrymen. If I have altered him
anywhere for the better, I must at the same time acknowledge
that I could have done nothing without him. "Facile est inventis
addere" [87] is no great commendation, and I am not so vain to
think I have deserved a greater. I will conclude what I have to
40 say of him singly, with this one remark: A lady of my acquaintance, who keeps a kind of correspondence with some authors
of the fair sex in France, has been informed by them that

86 Horace, *De Arte Po-
etica*, 70–72. In Ben Jonson's translation:
"Much praise that now is
dead shall be revived,

And much shall die that
now is nobly lived,
If custom please; at whose
disposing will
The power and rule of

speaking resteth still."
87 "It is easy to add to
what has already been in-
vented."

Mademoiselle de Scudery,[88] who is as old as Sibyl, and inspired like her by the same god of poetry, is at this time translating Chaucer into modern French. From which I gather that he has been formerly translated into the old Provençal; for how she should come to understand old English, I know not. But the matter of fact being true, it makes me think that there is something in it like fatality that, after certain periods of time, the fame and memory of great wits should be renewed, as Chaucer is both in France and England. If this be wholly chance, 'tis extraordinary, and I dare not call it more for fear of being taxed with superstition.

Boccace comes last to be considered, who, living in the same age with Chaucer, had the same genius and followed the same studies. Both writ novels, and each of them cultivated his mother tongue. But the greatest resemblance of our two modern authors being in their familiar style and pleasing way of relating comical adventures, I may pass it over, because I have translated nothing from Boccace of that nature. In the serious part of poetry the advantage is wholly on Chaucer's side; for though the Englishman has borrowed many tales from the Italian, yet it appears that those of Boccace were not generally of his own making but taken from authors of former ages and by him only modeled, so that what there was of invention in either of them may be judged equal. But Chaucer has refined on Boccace, and has mended the stories which he has borrowed in his way of telling, though prose allows more liberty of thought, and the expression is more easy when unconfined by numbers. Our countryman carries weight, and yet wins the race at disadvantage. I desire not the reader should take my word, and therefore I will set two of their discourses on the same subject, in the same light, for every man to judge betwixt them. I translated Chaucer first, and amongst the rest pitched on *The Wife of Bath's Tale;* not daring, as I have said, to adventure on her Prologue, because 'tis too licentious. There Chaucer introduces an old woman, of mean parentage, whom a youthful knight, of noble blood, was forced to marry, and consequently loathed her. The crone being in bed with him on the wedding night, and finding his aversion, endeavors to win his affection by reason, and speaks a good word for herself (as who could blame her?) in hope to mollify the sullen bridegroom. She takes her topics from the benefits of poverty, the advantages of old age and ugliness, the vanity of youth, and the silly pride of ancestry and titles without inherent virtue, which is the true nobility. When I had closed Chaucer, I returned to Ovid and translated some more of his fables; and by this time had so far forgotten *The Wife of Bath's Tale* that,

88 French novelist (1607–1701)

when I took up Boccace, unawares I fell on the same argument
of preferring virtue to nobility of blood and titles, in the story
of *Sigismonda,* which I had certainly avoided for the resemblance of the two discourses if my memory had not failed me.
Let the reader weigh them both; and if he thinks me partial to
Chaucer, 'tis in him to right Boccace.

I prefer in our countryman, far above all his other stories,
the noble poem of *Palamon and Arcite,*[89] which is of the epic
kind, and perhaps not much inferior to the *Ilias* or the *Æneis.*
The story is more pleasing than either of them, the manners as
perfect, the diction as poetical, the learning as deep and various,
and the disposition full as artful; only it includes a greater length
of time, as taking up seven years at least; but Aristotle has left
undecided the duration of the action, which yet is easily reduced into the compass of a year by a narration of what preceded the return of Palamon to Athens. I had thought for the
honor of our nation, and more particularly for his whose laurel,[90]
though unworthy, I have worn after him, that this story was of
English growth and Chaucer's own, but I was undeceived by
Boccace; for, casually looking on the end of his seventh *Giornata,*
I found Dioneo (under which name he shadows himself) and
Fiametta (who represents his mistress, the natural daughter of
Robert, King of Naples), of whom these words are spoken.
"Dioneo e la Fiametta gran pezza cantarono insieme d'Arcita,
e di Palemone";[91] by which it appears that this story was
written before the time of Boccace; but the name of its author
being wholly lost, Chaucer is now become an original, and I
question not but the poem has received many beauties by passing
through his noble hands. Besides this tale there is another of
his own invention, after the manner of the Provençals, called
The Flower and the Leaf, with which I was so particularly
pleased both for the invention and the moral, that I cannot
hinder myself from recommending it to the reader.

As a corollary to this preface, in which I have done justice
to others, I owe somewhat to myself; not that I think it worth
my time to enter the lists with one M—— and one B——,[92] but
barely to take notice that such men there are who have written
scurrilously against me without any provocation. M——, who is
in orders, pretends amongst the rest this quarrel to me, that
I have fallen foul on priesthood: if I have, I am only to ask
pardon of good priests, and am afraid his part of the reparation
will come to little. Let him be satisfied that he shall not be

---

89 Chaucer's Knight's
Tale
90 Both Chaucer and
Dryden were poets laureate
91 "Dioneo and the

grand lady Fiametta sang
together of Arcite and of
Palamon." Dryden was un-
acquainted with Boccaccio's
Teseide, the immediate

source of the Knight's
Tale.
92 Rev. Luke Milbourn
and Sir Richard Black-
more

able to force himself upon me for an adversary. I contemn him too much to enter into competition with him. His own translations of Virgil have answered his criticisms on mine. If (as they say he has declared in print) he prefers the version of Ogilby to mine, the world has made him the same compliment, for it is agreed on all hands that he writes even below Ogilby. That, you will say, is not easily to be done; but what cannot M—— bring about? I am satisfied, however, that while he and I live together I shall not be thought the worst poet of the age. It looks as if I had desired him underhand to write so ill against me; but, upon my honest word, I have not bribed him to do me this service, and am wholly guiltless of his pamphlet. 'Tis true I should be glad if I could persuade him to continue his good offices and write such another critique on anything of mine; for I find by experience he has a great stroke with the reader, when he condemns any of my poems, to make the world have a better opinion of them. He has taken some pains with my poetry, but nobody will be persuaded to take the same with his. If I had taken to the Church (as he affirms, but which was never in my thoughts), I should have had more sense, if not more grace, than to have turned myself out of my benefice by writing libels on my parishioners. But his account of my manners and my principles are of a piece with his cavils and his poetry; and so I have done with him forever.

As for the City Bard, or Knight Physician, I hear his quarrel to me is that I was the author of *Absalom and Achitophel,* which he thinks is a little hard on his fanatic patrons in London. But I will deal the more civilly with his two poems because nothing ill is to be spoken of the dead, and therefore peace be to the *manes* of his Arthurs.[93] I will only say that it was not for this noble knight that I drew the plan of an epic poem on King Arthur, in my preface to the translation of Juvenal. The guardian angels of kingdoms were machines too ponderous for him to manage; and therefore he rejected them, as Dares did the whirl-bats of Eryx when they were thrown before him by Entellus.[94] Yet from that preface he plainly took his hint; for he began immediately upon the story, though he had the baseness not to acknowledge his benefactor but instead of it to traduce me in a libel.

I shall say the less of Mr. Collier [95] because in many things he has taxed me justly, and I have pleaded guilty to all thoughts and expressions of mine which can be truly argued of obscenity, profaneness, or immorality, and retract them. If he be my enemy, let him triumph; if he be my friend, as I have given him

93 Blackmore's epics, *Prince Arthur* and *King Arthur,* pub. in 1695 and 1697
94 *Æneid,* V. 400 ff.
95 See p. 589 f.n. 60.

no personal occasion to be otherwise, he will be glad of my repentance. It becomes me not to draw my pen in the defence of a bad cause when I have so often drawn it for a good one. Yet it were not difficult to prove that in many places he has perverted my meaning by his glosses, and interpreted my words into blasphemy and bawdry of which they were not guilty. Besides that, he is too much given to horse-play in his raillery, and comes to battle like a dictator from the plough. I will not say the zeal of God's house has eaten him up, but I am sure it has devoured 10 some part of his good manners and civility. It might also be doubted whether it were altogether zeal which prompted him to this rough manner of proceeding. Perhaps it became not one of his function to rake into the rubbish of ancient and modern plays; a divine might have employed his pains to better purpose than in the nastiness of Plautus and Aristophanes, whose examples, as they excuse not me, so it might be possibly supposed that he read them not without some pleasure. They who have written commentaries on those poets, or on Horace, Juvenal, and Martial, have explained some vices which without their in- 20 terpretation had been unknown to modern times. Neither has he judged impartially betwixt the former age and us. There is more bawdry in one play of Fletcher's, called *The Custom of the Country,* than in all ours together. Yet this has been often acted on the stage, in my remembrance. Are the times so much more reformed now than they were five and twenty years ago? If they are, I congratulate the amendment of our morals. But I am not to prejudice the cause of my fellow poets, though I abandon my own defence; they have some of them answered for themselves, and neither they nor I can think Mr. Collier 30 so formidable an enemy that we should shun him. He has lost ground at the latter end of the day by pursuing his point too far, like the Prince of Condé at the battle of Senneph: [96] from immoral plays to no plays, "ab abuso ad usum non valet consequentia." [97] But, being a party, I am not to erect myself into a judge. As for the rest of those who have written against me, they are such scoundrels that they deserve not the least notice to be taken of them. B—— and M—— are only distinguished from the crowd by being remembered to their infamy.

"Demetri, teque, Tigelli,
40   Discipulorum inter jubeo plorare cathedras." [98]

96 The French general's battle with the Dutch, August 11, 1674
97 "From abuse to use is not a valid consequence"
98 "Demetrius, and you, Tigellius, I bid whine among the easy chairs of your disciples" (Horace, *Satires,* I. x. 90–91)

THE EIGHTEENTH CENTURY

The eighteenth century presents at its two ends a sharp contrast in the accepted principles that governed human life, philosophic thought, political and social history, and literature. At the beginning of the century men wished to live in conformity to what had come to be regarded as reasonable standards; the end of the century saw a revolt from these standards, and a reassertion of individual freedom. The earlier eighteenth century is appropriately called "the age of reason." Reason led the men of Queen Anne's day to follow the well-ordered life, and to deprecate unrestrained enthusiasms; to admire culture, civilization, and the rich social contacts of the city, and to care little for the rough and the unpolished (the "Gothic," as they termed it), little for nature (without human embellishments). Reason was best displayed in the ancient classics; and so these, as read by the aid of artificial or "neo-classical" interpretation, became the models to follow. Such writers as Spenser and Shakespeare were romantic, and therefore unsafe guides. In verse, they admired smoothness, decorum, "correctness" (to use their cant term). In practice, this meant the heroic couplet; other forms were frowned upon as "incorrect."

The master of this "Augustan Age" of English literature was Alexander Pope, who wrote between 1709 and 1742. His *Essay on Criticism* is an exposition of neo-classical rules; his *Essay on Man* a statement of the current rational deistic philosophy; his *Dunciad* his own envenomed version of the satire appropriate to an intellectual age; his *Rape of the Lock* the apotheosis of the elegant trifling of drawing-room and court. And all this in the hardest, the most brilliant heroic couplets ever devised. Jonathan Swift, perhaps the most colossal intellect of his day, followed and at the same time transcended a vogue in his tremendous satires in prose, *The Battle of the Books, A Tale of a Tub,* and *Gulliver's Travels.* Meantime Addison and Steele, in the *Tatler* and *Spectator* papers, were seeking to polish the manners, morals, and tastes of the times by their more polite ridicule and more urbane satire. And even John Gay, beloved for his unconventional *Beggars' Opera* (1728), who does not quite fit into the picture, celebrates the sights and incidents of the London streets in his *Trivia.*

Pope remained the great name through the second half of the century, and the standards and practices of the Age of Queen Anne were still the orthodox literary conventions well down into the reign of George III. Dr. Johnson, staunch arbiter of taste, was still satirizing in heroic couplets, still judging, in his *Lives of the Poets,* by neo-classical rules, still uttering moral precepts, in his *Rambler* essays and in the allegorical tale, *Rasselas,* although more heavily and less gracefully than did Addison and Steele. Yet the signs of revolt, which had been noticeable even during the lifetime of Pope, extended until they rather dominated the scene before Dr. Johnson died. As early as 1726 Thomson, in the first of the *Seasons,* had shown an accurate observation of nature and a tender love for her, and in *The Castle of Indolence* (1748) had copied the stanza and the manner of Spenser. Collins, in his *Odes* of 1746, had demonstrated a classic quality that was real and not imitation. Gray's distinguished verse (1751–

605

1768) had celebrated the glory of the humble, had derived from Milton and older writers, and had gone for subject-matter to such barbaric places as Wales and Scandinavia. The prose poems of James Macpherson (1762) which, in a famous hoax, were passed off as translations of a Gaelic bard, Ossian, were mystical and full of cloudy romantic imagery. In 1765 Bishop Percy, with his *Reliques of Ancient English Poetry,* revived the interest in the ballad. Goldsmith, writing in the 1760's and 1770's, presented with warm feeling the humble, the rural, and the picturesque; and in the last two decades of the century Cowper, Burns, and Blake brought back into literature the lyric of personal emotion and simple utterance. None of these writers, except possibly Blake, was thoroughly romantic, nor did the movement become conscious of itself until Wordsworth and Coleridge issued and explained their *Lyrical Ballads* in 1798. Inheritances of the classic age are to be seen in the work of nearly all of these pre-Romantics. In particular, one notices the use of an artificial "poetic diction," in which sheep become "the bleating kind," chickens "the feathered tribes domestic," a farmboy is a "laboring swain," a rural poem presents "the lowly train in life's sequestered scene," and to roll hoop is to "chase the rolling circle's speed"; while personified abstractions like "Chill Penury" and "Black Misfortune's baleful train" are always at hand to disturb the heroes' (and the readers') peace.

It is not accidental but inevitable that the revolution in literary taste should accompany, or rather form a part of a revolution in human thought, most spectacularly displayed in the American and French Revolutions. Voltaire, writing from the 1730's to the 1750's, and especially Rousseau, in the 1760's, had been at the same time symptoms of a new attitude toward the world, and powerful influences in the defining and sharpening of that attitude. The latter, in his *Contrat Social,* had preached that government has validity only as it rests on the consent of the governed and promotes their welfare, and in his *Émile* and *La Nouvelle Héloïse* had exalted the natural instincts, placed the blame for human sufferings on social institutions, and advocated a return to nature as a cure. A somewhat analogous movement in religion, following the preaching of John Wesley and the Methodists (from about 1738), had brought back "enthusiasm" to Christianity, had stressed the importance of personal conversion, and had shown a rare power to stir the common man.

The discussions preceding have dwelt chiefly upon poetry, steadily advancing to the Romantic Movement, and upon the essay, contributed chiefly to the new and important periodical literature. Three other forms should be mentioned. In drama, the age shows a going downhill. In the early years of the century comedies of manners, like Farquhar's *Beaux' Stratagem,* were still being written, but somewhat deodorized and chastened, as befitted a more moral age. The sentimental comedy, as in the plays of Richard Steele and Colley Cibber, and the bourgeois drama, like George Lillo's *George Barnwell, or The London Merchant,* were bathed in emotion and morality. In the latter part of the century, a brilliant but brief revival of witty comedy gave us at least three lasting masterpieces—*She Stoops to Conquer* of Goldsmith, and *The Rivals* and *The School for Scandal* of Sheridan (1773,1775, and 1777), in which the smuttiness of the Restoration is replaced by farcical situation and satire of character. The age showed a notable development in biography and in history, the outstanding works being Boswell's *Life of Johnson* (1791) and Gibbon's *Decline and Fall of the Roman Empire* (1776–1787); and in political thought, as seen in the brilliant speeches of Edmund Burke. The greatest contribution

of the century to literature was, however, the invention and development of
the novel, the most distinguished names being those of Daniel Defoe (*Robinson Crusoe*, 1719, 1720), Samuel Richardson (*Pamela*, 1740, *Clarissa Harlowe*
1748), Henry Fielding (*Joseph Andrews*, 1742, *Tom Jones*, 1749), Laurence
Sterne (*Tristram Shandy*, 1759–1767), and Tobias Smollett (*Roderick Random
Peregrine Pickle*, and *Humphrey Clinker*, 1748, 1751, and 1771). Since these
men wrote the novel has had literally a triumphant career, and it is the special
literary glory of the eighteenth century to have originated the form and produced some of its greatest specimens.

BIBLIOGRAPHY. L. Stephen, *Hist. of Eng. Thought in the Eighteenth Cent.*
(2 vols.), *Eng. Lit. and Society in the Eighteenth Cent.* (Putnams), E. Gosse,
Hist. of Eighteenth Cent. Lit. (Macmillan), J. Dennis, *Age of Pope*, and T. Sec-
combe, *Age of Johnson* (Bell), W. M. Thackeray, *Eng. Humorists of the
Eighteenth Cent.* (some of the judgments superseded), H. A. Beers, *Hist. of
Eng. Romanticism in the Eighteenth Cent.* (Holt), W. L. Cross, *Development
of Eng. Novel* (Macmillan). Anthologies: E. Bernbaum (ed.), *Eng. Poets of
the Eighteenth Cent.* (Scribner's), R. M. Alden, *Readings in Eng. Prose of
Eighteenth Cent.* (Houghton Mifflin), D. H. Stevens, *Types of Eng. Drama*
(Ginn).

JONATHAN SWIFT (1667–1745)

Swift was born in Dublin of English parents. Since he was a posthumous child,
and his mother was left in extreme poverty, he had to depend for his education
on the charity of an uncle. He went to Kilkenny Grammar School and to Trinity College, Dublin, where he displayed no special ability and obtained his
degree only by "special grace." In 1689 he became the secretary of a relative,
Sir William Temple, a well-known diplomat, man of the world, and accomplished
essayist. His relationship with Sir William lasted, with some interruptions, for
ten years. It was at Sir William's house, Moor Park, that he met
his patron's young ward, Esther Johnson ("Stella"), for whom he was to
maintain a lasting and tender affection—on the whole, the most beautiful
thing in his life. During a period of temporary disagreement with Temple, he
went back to Ireland, was ordained priest of the Church of England, obtained
a small living, and wrote the first of his satires, *The Battle of the Books* and
A Tale of a Tub, published together anonymously in 1704. The former is a
brilliant commentary on the then raging literary controversy between the merits
of the ancients and the moderns. The latter, by some regarded as Swift's greatest work, is a vigorous satire on the divisions of the Christian church—Catholic,
Anglican, and Presbyterian.

Swift's middle years were spent in the search for success *via* the route of
government patronage. He left his vicarage at Laracor, Ireland, which had been
bestowed on him in 1699, and spent much of the period from 1701 to 1714 in
London, where he hoped to advance himself by a method common in those
days—that of political writing. At first he adhered to the Whigs, but ultimately
threw in his talents with the Tories, defending them vigorously in a series of
pamphlets from 1710 to 1714. He expected to be made a bishop for his services,
but was forced to be content with the Deanship of St. Patrick's Cathedral,
Dublin, whither he retired on the collapse of the Tory ministry in 1714, and

where he dwelt, with only occasional visits to England, for the rest of his life—an embittered man, his ambitions thwarted, forced to live in a country which he detested. Yet, although he disliked the Irish, he felt so keenly the injustices which they suffered that he wrote much on their behalf. They remember him with affection for his *Drapier's Letters* (1724), written at a time when a scheme was on foot to debase the Irish coinage. The misery and poverty of the Irish people impressed him so profoundly that he wrote his *Modest Proposal*, one of the most terrific satires and consummate pieces of irony in existence. In 1726 he published his most famous work, *Gulliver's Travels*, in which, under the guise of a tale of adventure, he attacks the pettinesses, the coarsenesses, and the bestiality of mankind. Swift's satire is as a rule neither political, like Dryden's, nor personal, like Pope's. It is directed at the human race.

Another side of his nature is revealed in his *Journal to Stella*, written during the years of his rising political power in England (1710 to 1713). It tells intimately of the things which he was doing, the thoughts which he was thinking, the men with whom he conversed, and the public events in which he took part, and reveals also his devotion to her for whom it was written. Swift loved two women, and his relations with them are baffling problems for the psychologist to explain. The second of the two, "Vanessa" (Hester Vanhomrigh), felt a romantic attachment for him which led to the bitterest disappointment when he finally broke with her. The love of Stella was more serene and more unselfish, and she it was who comforted him when shadows began to darken about his path; yet those who feel that he was secretly married to her are probably wrong, and his love for her seems to have been entirely Platonic. After her death in 1728, his life sank more and more into gloom. He had an affection of the labyrinth of the ear which became worse with advancing years. Noises sounded in his ears like the blows of sledge-hammers; he became deaf, and suffered the most intense pain. The disease progressed into cerebral tumors and paralysis, and for the last few years of his life he was helpless and mad. He died on October 19, 1745, leaving by will his fortune, of nearly eleven thousand pounds, to found a hospital for lunatics and idiots. He was buried, by his own direction, in St. Patrick's cathedral beside the body of Stella. There he lies, where, in the words of the Latin epitaph which he himself penned, "fierce indignation can no longer lacerate the heart."

The self-composed epitaph is one of the best commentaries on Swift's character and his life. The apparent heartlessness of much of his work, the hideous "modest proposal" of butchering the Irish infants for the landlords' food, the brutal picture of mankind as the unspeakable Yahoo of the last part of *Gulliver* were cloaks with which a proud, sensitive spirit covered the cruel lacerations of the heart produced by the fierce indignation he felt on contemplating needless human miseries and the pitiless inhumanity of man. This indignation he expressed in the form of satire, perhaps because it was the accepted form of his time, but even more because it was for him the natural medium. As a satirist he is without peer in English, and the engine of irony he wielded with the hand of a master. The countenance, grim and terrible though it be, is never relaxed. The eyes never twinkle, the lip never curls into a smile.

The instrument of his satire is a prose unmatched for sheer force. It is simple, racy, and nervous. It eschews figurative language or ornamentation of any kind. It is perhaps the mightiest prose that any English writer has ever achieved.

BIBLIOGRAPHY. Complete Works, ed. by Temple Scott, in Bohn Library. *A Tale of a Tub* and *Battle of the Books*, ed. A. C. Guthkelch and D. N. Smith

(Oxford). Numerous eds. of *Gulliver's Travels*. Life by Craik. Powerful recent study by Carl Van Doren (Viking Press).

GULLIVER'S TRAVELS

Lemuel Gulliver's *Travels into Several Remote Nations of the World* was published anonymously in 1726. The first part, "A Voyage to Lilliput," is here reprinted. The other voyages are, respectively, II, to Brobdingnag (a land of giants); III, to Laputa, Balnibarbi, Luggnagg, Glubbdubdrib, and Japan (the first being famous for its academy which devoted itself to the elaboration of new projects and schemes, wilder than the South Sea bubble which had burst in England shortly before); IV, to the Country of the Houyhnhnms, where man, a degraded beast called the *Yahoo*, is slave to a race of educated horses. The enduring popularity of *Gulliver's Travels* as a children's book has shown that it may be read with pleasure for its marvelous stories alone; but the adult reader will not fail to perceive the biting satire which Swift wrote into it. That satire is in general directed against the whole human race, its different follies and vices being severally attacked in the various sections. There is also much political satire in the work—most of it obviously to-day unintelligible without such footnotes as those sparingly supplied to Part I, but much more significant to Swift's contemporaries.

THE PUBLISHER TO THE READER

The author of these Travels, Mr. Lemuel Gulliver, is my ancient and intimate friend; there is likewise some relation between us by the mother's side. About three years ago, Mr. Gulliver growing weary of the concourse of curious people coming to him at his house in Redriff, made a small purchase of land, with a convenient house, near Newark, in Nottinghamshire, his native country; where he now lives retired, yet in good esteem among his neighbors.

Although Mr. Gulliver was born in Nottinghamshire, where his father dwelt, yet I have heard him say his family came from Oxfordshire; to confirm which, I have observed in the churchyard at Banbury, in that county, several tombs and monuments of the Gullivers.

Before he quitted Redriff, he left the custody of the following papers in my hands, with the liberty to dispose of them as I should think fit. I have carefully perused them three times: the style is very plain and simple; and the only fault I find is, that the author, after the manner of travelers, is a little too circumstantial. There is an air of truth apparent through the whole; and indeed the author was so distinguished for his veracity, that it became a sort of proverb among his neighbors at Redriff, when any one affirmed a thing, to say it was as true as if Mr. Gulliver had spoke it.

By the advice of several worthy persons, to whom, with the author's permission, I communicated these papers, I now venture to send them into the world, hoping they may be at least, for some time, a better entertainment to our young noblemen, than the common scribbles of politics and party.

This volume would have been at least twice as large, if I had not made bold to strike out innumerable passages relating to the winds and tides, as well as to the variations and bearings in the several voyages; together with the minute descriptions of the management of the ship in storms, in the style of sailors: likewise the account of longitudes and latitudes; wherein I have reason to apprehend that Mr. Gulliver may be a little dissatisfied: but I was resolved to fit the work as much as possible to the general capacity of readers. However, if my own ignorance in sea-affairs shall have led me to commit some mistakes, I alone am answerable for them: and if any traveler hath a curiosity to see the whole work at large, as it came from the hand of the author, I will be ready to gratify him.

As for any further particulars relating to the author, the reader will receive satisfaction from the first pages of the book.

RICHARD SYMPSON.

PART I

A VOYAGE TO LILLIPUT

CHAPTER I

The Author gives some account of himself and family, his first inducements to travel. He is shipwrecked, and swims for his life, gets safe on shore in the country of Lilliput, is made a prisoner, and is carried up country.

MY FATHER had a small estate in Nottinghamshire; I was the third of five sons. He sent me to Emanuel College in Cambridge, at fourteen years old, where I resided three years, and applied myself close to my studies; but the charge of maintaining me (although I had a very scanty allowance) being too great for a narrow fortune, I was bound apprentice to Mr. James Bates, an eminent surgeon in London, with whom I continued four years; and my father now and then sending me small sums of money, I laid them out in learning naviga-
10 tion, and other parts of the mathematics, useful to those who intend to travel, as I always believed it would be some time or other my fortune to do. When I left Mr. Bates, I went down to my father; where, by the assistance of him and my uncle John, and some other relations, I got forty pounds, and a promise of thirty pounds a year to maintain me at Leyden: there I studied physic two years and seven months, knowing it would be useful in long voyages.

Soon after my return from Leyden, I was recommended by my good master, Mr. Bates, to be surgeon to the *Swallow*,
20 Captain Abraham Pannell, commander; with whom I continued three years and a half, making a voyage or two into the Levant, and some other parts. When I came back I resolved to settle in London, to which Mr. Bates, my master, encouraged me, and by him I was recommended to several patients. I took part of a small house in the Old Jury; and being advised to alter my condition, I married Mrs. Mary Burton, second daughter to Mr. Edmund Burton, hosier, in

Newgate-Street, with whom I received four hundred pounds for a portion.

But, my good master Bates dying in two years after, and I having few friends, my business began to fail; for my conscience would not suffer me to imitate the bad practice of too many among my brethren. Having therefore consulted with my wife, and some of my acquaintance, I determined to go again to sea. I was surgeon successively in two ships, and made several voyages, for six years, to the East and West Indies, by which I got some addition to my fortune. My hours of 10 leisure I spent in reading the best authors, ancient and modern, being always provided with a good number of books; and when I was ashore, in observing the manners and dispositions of the people, as well as learning their language, wherein I had a great facility by the strength of my memory.

The last of these voyages not proving very fortunate, I grew weary of the sea, and intended to stay at home with my wife and family. I removed from the Old Jury to Fetter-Lane, and from thence to Wapping, hoping to get business among the sailors; but it would not turn to account. After three years' 20 expectation that things would mend, I accepted an advantageous offer from Captain William Prichard, master of the *Antelope*, who was making a voyage to the South Sea. We set sail from Bristol, May 4, 1699, and our voyage at first was very prosperous.

It would not be proper, for some reasons, to trouble the reader with the particulars of our adventures in those seas; let it suffice to inform him, that in our passage from thence to the East Indies, we were driven by a violent storm to the north-west of Van Diemen's Land. By an observation, we 30 found ourselves in the latitude of 30 degrees 2 minutes south. Twelve of our crew were dead by immoderate labor, and ill food, the rest were in a very weak condition. On the fifth of November, which was the beginning of summer in those parts, the weather being very hazy, the seamen spied a rock, within half a cable's length of the ship; but the wind was so strong, that we were driven directly upon it, and immediately split. Six of the crew, of whom I was one, having let down the boat into the sea, made a shift to get clear of the ship, and the rock. We rowed, by my computation, about three leagues, till 40 we were able to work no longer, being already spent with labor while we were in the ship. We therefore trusted ourselves to the mercy of the waves, and in about half an hour the boat was overset by a sudden flurry from the north. What became of my companions in the boat, as well as of those who escaped on the rock, or were left in the vessel, I cannot tell; but conclude they were all lost. For my own part, I swam as fortune directed me, and was pushed forward by wind and tide. I often let my legs drop, and could feel no bottom: but when I was almost gone, and able to struggle no longer, I found myself within my depth; and by this time the storm was much abated. The declivity was so small, that I walked near a mile before I got to the shore, which I conjectured was about eight o'clock in the evening. I then advanced forward near half a mile, but could not discover any sign of houses or inhabitants; at least 10 I was in so weak a condition, that I did not observe them. I was extremely tired, and with that, and the heat of the weather, and about half a pint of brandy that I drank as I left the ship, I found myself much inclined to sleep. I lay down on the grass, which was very short and soft, where I slept sounder than ever I remember to have done in my life; and, as I reckoned, above nine hours; for when I awaked, it was just day-light. I attempted to rise, but was not able to stir: for as I happened to lie on my back, I found my arms and legs were strongly fastened on each side to the ground; and my hair, 20 which was long and thick, tied down in the same manner. I likewise felt several slender ligatures across my body, from my arm-pits to my thighs. I could only look upwards, the sun began to grow hot, and the light offended my eyes. I heard a confused noise about me, but in the posture I lay, could see nothing except the sky. In a little time I felt something alive moving on my left leg, which advancing gently forward over my breast, came almost up to my chin; when bending my eyes downwards as much as I could, I perceived it to be a human creature not six inches high, with a bow and arrow in his 30 hands, and a quiver at his back. In the mean time, I felt at least forty more of the same kind (as I conjectured) following the first. I was in the utmost astonishment, and roared so loud, that they all ran back in a fright; and some of them as I was afterwards told, were hurt with the falls they got by leaping from my sides upon the ground. However, they soon returned, and one of them, who ventured so far as to get a full sight of my face, lifting up his hands and eyes by way of admiration, cried out in a shrill, but distinct voice, *Hekinah degul:* the others repeated the same words several times, but then I knew 40 not what they meant. I lay all this while, as the reader may believe, in great uneasiness: at length, struggling to get loose, I had the fortune to break the strings, and wrench out the pegs that fastened my left arm to the ground; for, by lifting it up to my face, I discovered the methods they had taken to bind me, and at the same time with a violent pull, which gave me excessive pain, I a little loosened the strings that tied down my hair on the left side, so that I was just able to turn my head about two inches. But the creatures ran off a second time, before I could seize them; whereupon there was a great shout in a very shrill accent, and after it ceased, I heard one of them cry aloud *Tolgo phonac;* when in an instant I felt above an hundred arrows discharged on my left hand, which pricked me like so many needles; and besides, they shot another flight into the air, as we do bombs in Europe, whereof many, I suppose, fell on my body (though I felt them not), and some on my face, which I immediately covered with my left hand. When this shower of arrows was over, I fell a groaning with grief and pain, and then striving again to get loose, they discharged another volley larger than the first, and some of them attempted with spears to stick me in the sides; but, by good luck, I had on a buff jerkin, which they could not pierce. I thought it the most prudent method to lie still, and my design was to continue so till night, when, my left hand being already loose, I could easily free myself: and as for the inhabitants, I had reason to believe I might be a match for the greatest armies they could bring against me, if they were all of the same size with him that I saw. But fortune disposed otherwise of me. When the people observed I was quiet, they discharged no more arrows; but, by the noise I heard, I knew their numbers increased; and about four yards from me, over-against my right ear, I heard a knocking for above an hour, like that of people at work; when turning my head that way, as well as the pegs and strings would permit me, I saw a stage erected, about a foot and a half from the ground, capable of holding four of the inhabitants, with two or three ladders to mount it: from whence one of them, who seemed to be a person of quality, made me a long speech, whereof I understood not one syllable. But I should have mentioned, that before the principal person began his oration, he cried out three times, *Langro dehul san:* (these words and the former were afterwards repeated and explained to me). Whereupon immediately about fifty of the inhabitants came and cut the strings that fastened the left side of my head, which gave me the liberty of turning it to the right, and of observing the person and gesture of him that was to speak. He appeared to be of a middle age, and taller than any of the other three who attended him, whereof one was a page that held up his train, and seemed to be somewhat longer than my middle finger; the other two stood one on each side to support him. He acted every part of an orator, and I could observe many periods of threatenings, and others of promises, pity, and kindness. I answered in a few words, but in the most submissive manner, lifting up my left hand,

and both my eyes to the sun, as calling him for a witness; and
being almost famished with hunger, having not eaten a morsel
for some hours before I left the ship, I found the demands of
nature so strong upon me, that I could not forbear showing
my impatience (perhaps against the strict rules of decency)
by putting my finger frequently on my mouth to signify that
I wanted food. The *Hurgo* (for so they call a great lord, as I
afterwards learned) understood me very well. He descended
from the stage, and commanded that several ladders should be
10 applied to my sides, on which above an hundred of the inhabitants mounted and walked towards my mouth, laden with
baskets full of meat, which had been provided and sent thither
by the King's orders, upon the first intelligence he received
of me. I observed there was the flesh of several animals, but
could not distinguish them by the taste. There were shoulders,
legs, and loins, shaped like those of mutton, and very well
dressed, but smaller than the wings of a lark. I eat them by
two or three at a mouthful, and took three loaves at a time,
about the bigness of musket bullets. They supplied me as fast
20 as they could, showing a thousand marks of wonder and astonishment at my bulk and appetite. I then made another sign
that I wanted drink. They found by my eating, that a small
quantity would not suffice me; and being a most ingenious
people, they slung up with great dexterity one of their largest
hogsheads, then rolled it towards my hand, and beat out the
top; I drank it off at a draught, which I might well do, for it
did not hold half a pint, and tasted like a small wine of
Burgundy, but much more delicious. They brought me a second hogshead, which I drank in the same manner, and made
30 signs for more, but they had none to give me. When I had
performed these wonders, they shouted for joy, and danced
upon my breast, repeating several times as they did at first,
Hekinah degul. They made me a sign that I should throw down
the two hogsheads, but first warning the people below to stand
out of the way, crying aloud, *Borach mivola,* and when they
saw the vessels in the air, there was an universal shout of
Hekinah degul. I confess I was often tempted while they were
passing backwards and forwards on my body, to seize forty
or fifty of the first that came in my reach, and dash them
40 against the ground. But the remembrance of what I had felt,
which probably might not be the worst they could do, and the
promise of honor I made them, for so I interpreted my submissive behavior, soon drove out these imaginations. Besides,
I now considered myself as bound by the laws of hospitality
to a people who had treated me with so much expense and
magnificence. However, in my thoughts, I could not sufficiently

wonder at the intrepidity of these diminutive mortals, who
durst venture to mount and walk upon my body, while one of
my hands was at liberty, without trembling at the very sight
of so prodigious a creature as I must appear to them. After
some time, when they observed that I made no more demands
for meat, there appeared before me a person of high rank from
his Imperial Majesty. His Excellency, having mounted on the
small of my right leg, advanced forwards up to my face, with
about a dozen of his retinue. And producing his credentials
under the Signet Royal, which he applied close to my eyes, 10
spoke about ten minutes, without any signs of anger, but with
a kind of determinate resolution; often pointing forwards,
which, as I afterwards found, was towards the capital city,
about half a mile distant, whither it was agreed by his Majesty
in council that I must be conveyed. I answered in few words,
but to no purpose, and made a sign with my hand that was
loose, putting it to the other (but over his Excellency's head
for fear of hurting him or his train), and then to my own
head and body, to signify that I desired my liberty. It appeared that he understood me well enough, for he shook his 20
head by way of disapprobation, and held his hand in a posture
to show that I must be carried as a prisoner. However, he
made other signs to let me understand that I should have meat
and drink enough, and very good treatment. Whereupon I
once more thought of attempting to break my bonds; but
again, when I felt the smart of their arrows, upon my face and
hands, which were all in blisters, and many of the darts still
sticking in them, and observing likewise that the number of
my enemies increased, I gave tokens to let them know that
they might do with me what they pleased. Upon this, the _Hurgo_ 30
and his train withdrew, with much civility and cheerful counte-
nances. Soon after I heard a general shout, with frequent repetitions of the words, _Peplom selan,_ and I felt great numbers of
people on my left side relaxing the cords to such a degree,
that I was able to turn upon my right, and to ease myself with
making water; which I very plentifully did, to the great astonishment of the people, who conjecturing by my motions
what I was going to do, immediately opened to the right and
left on that side to avoid the torrent which fell with such noise
and violence from me. But before this, they had daubed my 40
face and both my hands with a sort of ointment very pleasant
to the smell, which in a few minutes removed all the smart of
their arrows. These circumstances, added to the refreshment
I had received by their victuals and drink, which were very
nourishing, disposed me to sleep. I slept about eight hours,
as I was afterwards assured; and it was no wonder, for the

physicians, by the Emperor's order, had mingled a sleepy potion in the hogshead of wine.

It seems that upon the first moment I was discovered sleeping on the ground after my landing, the Emperor had early
notice of it by an express; and determined in council that I
should be tied in the manner I have related (which was done
in the night while I slept), that plenty of meat and drink should
be sent to me, and a machine prepared to carry me to the
capital city.

10 This resolution perhaps may appear very bold and dangerous, and I am confident would not be imitated by any prince in
Europe on the like occasion; however, in my opinion, it was
extremely prudent, as well as generous: for supposing these
people had endeavored to kill me with their spears and arrows
while I was asleep, I should certainly have awaked with the
first sense of smart, which might so far have roused my rage
and strength, as to have enabled me to break the strings
wherewith I was tied; after which, as they were not able to
make resistance, so they could expect no mercy.

20 These people are most excellent mathematicians, and arrived
to a great perfection in mechanics, by the countenance and encouragement of the Emperor, who is a renowned patron of
learning. This prince hath several machines fixed on wheels,
for the carriage of trees and other great weights. He often builds
his largest men of war, whereof some are nine foot long, in
the woods where the timber grows, and has them carried on
these engines three or four hundred yards to the sea. Five
hundred carpenters and engineers were immediately set at work
to prepare the greatest engine they had. It was a frame of wood
30 raised three inches from the ground, about seven foot long and
four wide, moving upon twenty-two wheels. The shout I heard
was upon the arrival of this engine, which it seems set out in
four hours after my landing. It was brought parallel to me as
I lay. But the principal difficulty was to raise and place me in
this vehicle. Eighty poles, each of one foot high, were erected
for this purpose, and very strong cords of the bigness of packthread were fastened by hooks to many bandages, which the
workmen had girt round my neck, my hands, my body, and
my legs. Nine hundred of the strongest men were employed
40 to draw up these cords by many pulleys fastened on the poles,
and thus, in less than three hours, I was raised and slung into
the engine, and there tied fast. All this I was told, for, while
the whole operation was performing, I lay in a profound sleep,
by the force of that soporiferous medicine infused into my
liquor. Fifteen hundred of the Emperor's largest horses, each
about four inches and a half high, were employed to draw me

towards the metropolis, which, as I said, was half a mile distant. About four hours after we began our journey, I awaked by a very ridiculous accident; for the carriage being stopped a while to adjust something that was out of order, two or three of the young natives had the curiosity to see how I looked when I was asleep; they climbed up into the engine, and advancing very softly to my face, one of them, an officer in the guards, put the sharp end of his half-pike a good way up into my left nostril, which tickled my nose like a straw, and made 10 me sneeze violently: whereupon they stole off unperceived, and it was three weeks before I knew the cause of my awakening so suddenly. We made a long march the remaining part of that day, and rested at night with five hundred guards on each side of me, half with torches, and half with bows and arrows, ready to shoot me if I should offer to stir. The next morning at sun-rise we continued our march, and arrived within two hundred yards of the city gates about noon. The Emperor, and all his court, came out to meet us; but his great officers would by no means suffer his Majesty to endanger his person by 20 mounting on my body.

At the place where the carriage stopped, there stood an ancient temple, esteemed to be the largest in the whole kingdom; which having been polluted some years before by an unnatural murder, was, according to the zeal of those people, looked upon as profane, and therefore had been applied to common uses, and all the ornaments and furniture carried away. In this edifice it was determined I should lodge. The great gate fronting to the north was about four foot high, and almost two foot wide, through which I could easily creep. On each side 30 of the gate was a small window not above six inches from the ground: into that on the left side, the King's smiths conveyed fourscore and eleven chains, like those that hang to a lady's watch in Europe, and almost as large, which were locked to my left leg with six and thirty padlocks. Over-against this temple, on t'other side of the great highway, at twenty foot distance, there was a turret at least five foot high. Here the Emperor ascended, with many principal lords of his court, to have an opportunity of viewing me, as I was told, for I could not see them. It was reckoned that above an hundred thousand 40 inhabitants came out of the town upon the same errand; and, in spite of my guards, I believe there could not be fewer than ten thousand at several times, who mounted my body by the help of ladders. But a proclamation was soon issued to forbid it upon pain of death. When the workmen found it was impossible for me to break loose, they cut all the strings that

bound me; whereupon I rose up, with as melancholy a disposition as ever I had in my life. But the noise and astonishment of the people at seeing me rise and walk, are not to be
expressed. The chains that held my left leg were about two
yards long, and gave me not only the liberty of walking backwards and forwards in a semicircle; but, being fixed within
four inches of the gate, allowed me to creep in, and lie at my
full length in the temple.

CHAPTER II

*The Emperor of Lilliput, attended by several of the nobility,
comes to see the Author in his confinement. The Emperor's
person and habit described. Learned men appointed to teach
the Author their language. He gains favor by his mild disposition. His pockets are searched, and his sword and pistols
taken from him.*

WHEN I found myself on my feet, I looked about me, and
10 must confess I never beheld a more entertaining prospect.
The country round appeared like a continued garden, and the
inclosed fields, which were generally forty foot square, resembled
so many beds of flowers. These fields were intermingled with
woods of half a stang,[1] and the tallest trees, as I could judge,
appeared to be seven foot high. I viewed the town on my left
hand, which looked like the painted scene of a city in a theater.
I had been for some hours extremely pressed by the neces-
sities of nature; which was no wonder, it being almost two days
since I had last disburdened myself. I was under great diffi-
20 culties between urgency and shame. The best expedient I
could think on, was to creep into my house, which I accordingly did; and shutting the gate after me, I went as far as
the length of my chain would suffer, and discharged my body
of that uneasy load. But this was the only time I was ever
• guilty of so uncleanly an action; for which I cannot but hope
the candid reader will give some allowance, after he hath
maturely and impartially considered my case, and the distress
I was in. From this time my constant practice was, as soon as
I rose, to perform that business in open air, at the full extent
30 of my chain, and due care was taken every morning before
company came, that the offensive matter should be carried
off in wheel-barrows, by two servants appointed for that purpose. I would not have dwelt so long upon a circumstance,
that perhaps at first sight may appear not very momentous, if
I had not thought it necessary to justify my character in point

1 *i. e.,* half a square rod

of cleanliness to the world; which I am told some of my
maligners have been pleased, upon this and other occasions,
to call in question.

When this adventure was at an end, I came back out of my
house, having occasion for fresh air. The Emperor was already
descended from the tower, and advancing on horseback towards
me, which had like to have cost him dear; for the beast, though
very well trained, yet wholly unused to such a sight, which
appeared as if a mountain moved before him, reared up on
his hinder feet: but that prince, who is an excellent horseman, 10
kept his seat, till his attendants ran in, and held the bridle,
while his Majesty had time to dismount. When he alighted, he
surveyed me round with great admiration, but kept beyond
the length of my chain. He ordered his cooks and butlers, who
were already prepared, to give me victuals and drink, which
they pushed forward in a sort of vehicles upon wheels, till I
could reach them. I took these vehicles, and soon emptied them
all; twenty of them were filled with meat, and ten with liquor;
each of the former afforded me two or three good mouthfuls,
and I emptied the liquor of ten vessels, which was contained 20
in earthen vials, into one vehicle, drinking it off at a draught;
and so I did with the rest. The Empress, and young Princes
of the blood of both sexes, attended by many ladies, sat at
some distance in their chairs; but upon the accident that happened to the Emperor's horse, they alighted, and came near
his person, which I am now going to describe. He is taller by
almost the breadth of my nail, than any of his court; which
alone is enough to strike an awe into the beholders. His features are strong and masculine, with an Austrian lip and
arched nose, his complexion olive, his countenance erect, his 30
body and limbs well proportioned, all his motions graceful,
and his deportment majestic. He was then past his prime, being twenty-eight years and three-quarters old, of which he
had reigned about seven, in great felicity, and generally victorious. For the better convenience of beholding him, I lay
on my side, so that my face was parallel to his, and he stood
but three yards off: however, I have had him since many times
in my hand, and therefore cannot be deceived in the description. His dress was very plain and simple, and the fashion of
it between the Asiatic and the European: but he had on his 40
head a light helmet of gold, adorned with jewels, and a plume
on the crest. He held his sword drawn in his hand, to defend
himself, if I should happen to break loose; it was almost
three inches long, the hilt and scabbard were gold enriched
with diamonds. His voice was shrill, but very clear and articu-
late, and I could distinctly hear it when I stood up. The ladies

and courtiers were all most magnificently clad, so that the spot they stood upon seemed to resemble a petticoat spread on the ground, embroidered with figures of gold and silver. His Imperial Majesty spoke often to me, and I returned answers, but neither of us could understand a syllable. There were several of his priests and lawyers present (as I conjectured by their habits) who were commanded to address themselves to me, and I spoke to them in as many languages as I had the least smattering of, which were High and Low Dutch, Latin, French, Spanish, Italian, and. Lingua Franca;[2] but all to no purpose. After about two hours the court retired, and I was left with a strong guard, to prevent the impertinence, and probably the malice of the rabble, who were very impatient to crowd about me as near as they durst, and some of them had the impudence to shoot their arrows at me as I sat on the ground by the door of my house, whereof one very narrowly missed my left eye. But the colonel ordered six of the ringleaders to be seized, and thought no punishment so proper as to deliver them bound into my hands, which some of his soldiers accordingly did, pushing them forwards with the butt-ends of their pikes into my reach; I took them all in my right hand, put five of them into my coat-pocket, and as to the sixth, I made a countenance as if I would eat him alive. The poor man squalled terribly, and the colonel and his officers were in much pain, especially when they saw me take out my pen-knife: but I soon put them out of fear: for, looking mildly, and immediately cutting the strings he was bound with, I set him gently on the ground, and away he ran. I treated the rest in the same manner, taking them one by one out of my pocket, and I observed both the soldiers and people were highly obliged at this mark of my clemency, which was represented very much to my advantage at court.

Towards night I got with some difficulty into my house, where I lay on the ground, and continued to do so about a fortnight; during which time the Emperor gave orders to have a bed prepared for me. Six hundred beds of the common measure were brought in carriages, and worked up in my house; an hundred and fifty of their beds sewn together made up the breadth and length, and these were four double, which however kept me but very indifferently from the hardness of the floor, that was of smooth stone. By the same computation they provided me with sheets, blankets, and coverlets, tolerable enough for one who had been so long inured to hardships as I.

As the news of my arrival spread through the kingdom, it

2 a mixed jargon used around the eastern Mediterranean

brought prodigious numbers of rich, idle, and curious people
to see me; so that the villages were almost emptied, and great
neglect of tillage and household affairs must have ensued, if his
Imperial Majesty had not provided, by several proclamations
and orders of state, against this inconveniency. He directed
that those who had already beheld me should return home,
and not presume to come within fifty yards of my house without license from court; whereby the secretaries of state got
considerable fees.

In the mean time, the Emperor held frequent councils to 10
debate what course should be taken with me; and I was afterwards assured by a particular friend, a person of great quality, who was looked upon to be as much in the secret as any,
that the court was under many difficulties concerning me.
They apprehended my breaking loose, that my diet would be
very expensive, and might cause a famine. Sometimes they
determined to starve me, or at least to shoot me in the face
and hands with poisoned arrows, which would soon dispatch
me; but again they considered, that the stench of so large a
carcass might produce a plague in the metropolis, and probably 20
spread through the whole kingdom. In the midst of these con-
sultations, several officers of the army went to the door of
the great council-chamber; and two of them being admitted,
gave an account of my behavior to the six criminals above
mentioned, which made so favorable an impression in the
breast of his Majesty and the whole board, in my behalf, that
an Imperial Commission was issued out, obliging all the villages nine hundred yards round the city, to deliver in every
morning six beeves, forty sheep, and other victuals for my sustenance; together with a proportionable quantity of bread, and 30
wine, and other liquors; for the due payment of which his
Majesty gave assignments upon his treasury. For this prince
lives chiefly upon his own demesnes, seldom, except upon great
occasions, raising any subsidies upon his subjects, who are
bound to attend him in his wars at their own expense. An establishment was also made of six hundred persons to be my
domestics, who had board-wages allowed for their maintenance, and tents built for them very conveniently on each side
of my door. It was likewise ordered, that three hundred tailors
should make me a suit of clothes after the fashion of the 40
country: that six of his Majesty's greatest scholars should be
employed to instruct me in their language: and, lastly, that the
Emperor's horses, and those of the nobility, and troops of
guards, should be frequently exercised in my sight, to accustom themselves to me. All these orders were duly put in execution, and in about three weeks I made a great progress in

learning their language; during which time, the Emperor frequently honored me with his visits, and was pleased to assist my masters in teaching me. We began already to converse together in some sort; and the first words I learned were to express my desire that he would please give me my liberty, which I every day repeated on my knees. His answer, as I could comprehend it, was, that this must be a work of time, not to be thought on without the advice of his council, and that first I must *Lumos kelmin pesso desmar lon Emposo;* that
10 is, swear a peace with him and his kingdom. However, that I should be used with all kindness; and he advised me to acquire, by my patience and discreet behavior, the good opinion of himself and his subjects. He desired I would not take it ill, if he gave orders to certain proper officers to search me; for probably I might carry about me several weapons, which must needs be dangerous things, if they answered the bulk of so prodigious a person. I said, his Majesty should be satisfied, for I was ready to strip myself, and turn up my pockets before him. This I delivered part in words, and part in signs. He
20 replied, that by the laws of the kingdom I must be searched by two of his officers; that he knew this could not be done without my consent and assistance; that he had so good an opinion of my generosity and justice, as to trust their persons in my hands: that whatever they took from me should be returned when I left the country, or paid for at the rate which I would set upon them. I took up the two officers in my hands, put them first into my coat-pockets, and then into every other pocket about me, except my two fobs, and another secret pocket which I had no mind should be searched, wherein I
30 had some little necessaries that were of no consequence to any but myself. In one of my fobs there was a silver watch, and in the other a small quantity of gold in a purse. These gentlemen, having pen, ink, and paper about them, made an exact inventory of every thing they saw; and when they had done, desired I would set them down, that they might deliver it to the Emperor. This inventory I afterwards translated into English, and is word for word as follows:

Imprimis, In the right coat-pocket of the Great Man-Mountain (for so I interpret the words *Quinbus Flestrin*) after
40 the strictest search, we found only one great piece of coarse cloth, large enough to be a foot-cloth for your Majesty's chief room of state. In the left pocket we saw a huge silver chest, with a cover of the same metal, which we, the searchers, were not able to lift. We desired it should be opened, and one of us stepping into it, found himself up to the mid leg in a sort

of dust, some part whereof flying up to our faces, set us both
a sneezing for several times together. In his right waistcoat-
pocket we found a prodigious bundle of white thin substances,
folded one over another, about the bigness of three men, tied
with a strong cable, and marked with black figures; which
we humbly conceive to be writings, every letter almost half
as large as the palm of our hands. In the left there was a sort
of engine, from the back of which were extended twenty long
poles, resembling the palisadoes before your Majesty's court;
wherewith we conjecture the Man-Mountain combs his head; 10
for we did not always trouble him with questions, because we
found it a great difficulty to make him understand us. In the
large pocket on the right side of his middle cover (so I translate the word *ranfu-lo,* by which they meant my breeches) we
saw a hollow pillar of iron, about the length of a man, fastened to a strong piece of timber, larger than the pillar; and
upon one side of the pillar were huge pieces of iron sticking
out, cut into strange figures, which we know not what to
make of. In the left pocket, another engine of the same kind.
In the smaller pocket on the right side, were several round flat 20
pieces of white and red metal, of different bulk; some of the
white, which seemed to be silver, were so large and heavy,
that my comrade and I could hardly lift them. In the left
pocket were two black pillars irregularly shaped: we could
not, without difficulty, reach the top of them as we stood at
the bottom of his pocket. One of them was covered, and seemed
all of a piece: but at the upper end of the other, there appeared a white round substance, about twice the bigness of
our heads. Within each of these was enclosed a prodigious plate
of steel; which, by our orders, we obliged him to show us, 30
because we apprehended they might be dangerous engines.
He took them out of their cases, and told us, that in his own
country his practice was to shave his beard with one of these,
and cut his meat with the other. There were two pockets which
we could not enter: these he called his fobs; they were two
large slits cut into the top of his middle cover, but squeezed
close by the pressure of his belly. Out of the right fob hung
a great silver chain, with a wonderful kind of engine at the
bottom. We directed him to draw out whatever was fastened
to that chain; which appeared to be a globe, half silver, and 40
half of some transparent metal; for, on the transparent side,
we saw certain strange figures circularly drawn, and thought
we could touch them, till we found our fingers stopped by
that lucid substance. He put this engine to our ears, which
made an incessant noise like that of a water-mill. And we conjecture it is either some unknown animal. or the god that he

worships; but we are more inclined to the latter opinion, because he assured us (if we understood him right, for he expressed himself very imperfectly), that he seldom did anything without consulting it. He called it his oracle, and said it pointed out the time for every action of his life. From the left fob he took out a net almost large enough for a fisherman, but contrived to open and shut like a purse, and served him for the same use: we found therein several massy pieces of yellow metal, which, if they be real gold, must be of immense value.

10 Having thus, in obedience to your Majesty's commands, diligently searched all his pockets, we observed a girdle about his waist made of the hide of some prodigious animal; from which, on the left side, hung a sword of the length of five men; and on the right, a bag or pouch divided into two cells, each cell capable of holding three of your Majesty's subjects. In one of these cells were several globes or balls of a most ponderous metal, about the bigness of our heads, and requiring a strong hand to lift them: the other cell contained a heap of certain black grains, but of no great bulk or weight, for we

20 could hold above fifty of them in the palms of our hands.

This is an exact inventory of what we found about the body of the Man-Mountain, who used us with great civility, and due respect to your Majesty's Commission. Signed and sealed on the fourth day of the eighty-ninth moon of your Majesty's auspicious reign.

CLEFRIN FRELOCK, MARSI FRELOCK.

When this inventory was read over to the Emperor, he directed me, although in very gentle terms, to deliver up the several particulars. He first called for my scimitar, which I took out, scabbard and all. In the mean time he ordered three

30 thousand of his choicest troops (who then attended him) to surround me at a distance, with their bows and arrows just ready to discharge: but I did not observe it, for my eyes were wholly fixed upon his Majesty. He then desired me to draw my scimitar, which, although it had got some rust by the sea-water, was in most parts exceeding bright. I did so, and immediately all the troops gave a shout between terror and surprise; for the sun shone clear, and the reflection dazzled their eyes, as I waved the scimitar to and fro in my hand. His Majesty, who is a most magnanimous prince, was less daunted

40 than I could expect; he ordered me to return it into the scabbard, and cast it on the ground as gently as I could, about six foot from the end of my chain. The next thing he demanded, was one of the hollow iron pillars, by which he meant my pocket-pistols. I drew it out, and at his desire, as well as

I could, expressed to him the use of it; and charging it only with powder, which, by the closeness of my pouch, happened to escape wetting in the sea (an inconvenience against which all prudent mariners take special care to provide), I first cautioned the Emperor not to be afraid, and then I let it off in the air. The astonishment here was much greater than at the sight of my scimitar. Hundreds fell down as if they had been struck dead; and even the Emperor, although he stood his ground, could not recover himself in some time. I delivered up both my pistols in the same manner as I had done my scim- 10 itar, and then my pouch of powder and bullets; begging him that the former might be kept from fire, for it would kindle with the smallest spark, and blow up his imperial palace into the air. I likewise delivered up my watch, which the Emperor was very curious to see, and commanded two of his tallest yeomen of the guards to bear it on a pole upon their shoulders, as draymen in England do a barrel of ale. He was amazed at the continual noise it made, and the motion of the minute-hand, which he could easily discern; for their sight is much more acute than ours: and asked the opinions of his learned 20 men about him, which were various and remote, as the reader may well imagine without my repeating; although indeed I could not very perfectly understand them. I then gave up my silver and copper money, my purse, with nine large pieces of gold, and some smaller ones; my knife and razor, my comb and silver snuff-box, my handkerchief and journal-book. My scimitar, pistols, and pouch, were conveyed in carriages to his Majesty's stores; but the rest of my goods were returned to me.

I had, as I before observed, one private pocket which escaped their search, wherein there was a pair of spectacles 30 (which I sometimes use for the weakness of my eyes), a pocket perspective, and several other little conveniences; which being of no consequence to the Emperor, I did not think myself bound in honor to discover, and I apprehended they might be lost or spoiled if I ventured them out of my possession.

CHAPTER III

The Author diverts the Emperor, and his nobility of both sexes, in a very uncommon manner. The diversions of the court of Lilliput described. The Author has his liberty granted him upon certain conditions.

My gentleness and good behavior had gained so far on the Emperor and his court, and indeed upon the army and people in general, that I began to conceive hopes of getting my liberty in a short time. I took all possible methods to cul-

tivate this favorable disposition. The natives came by degrees to be less apprehensive of any danger from me. I would sometimes lie down, and let five or six of them dance on my hand. And at last the boys and girls would venture to come and play at hide and seek in my hair. I had now made a good progress in understanding and speaking their language. The Emperor had a mind one day to entertain me with several of the country shows, wherein they exceed all nations I have known, both for dexterity and magnificence. I was diverted
10 with none so much as that of the rope-dancers, performed upon a slender white thread, extended about two foot, and twelve inches from the ground. Upon which I shall desire liberty, with the reader's patience, to enlarge a little.

This diversion is only practised by those persons who are candidates for great employments, and high favor, at court. They are trained in this art from their youth, and are not always of noble birth, or liberal education. When a great office is vacant, either by death or disgrace (which often happens), five or six of those candidates petition the Emperor to enter-
20 tain his Majesty and the court with a dance on the rope, and whoever jumps the highest without falling, succeeds in the office. Very often the chief ministers themselves are commanded to show their skill, and to convince the Emperor that they have not lost their faculty. Flimnap,[3] the Treasurer, is allowed to cut a caper on the straight rope, at least an inch higher than any other lord in the whole empire. I have seen him do the summerset several times together upon a trencher fixed on the rope, which is no thicker than a common packthread in England. My friend Reldresal, principal Secretary
30 for Private Affairs, is, in my opinion, if I am not partial, the second after the Treasurer; the rest of the great officers are much upon a par.

These diversions are often attended with fatal accidents, whereof great numbers are on record. I myself have seen two or three candidates break a limb. But the danger is much greater when the ministers themselves are commanded to show their dexterity; for, by contending to excel themselves and their fellows, they strain so far, that there is hardly one of them who hath not received a fall, and some of them two or three.
40 I was assured that a year or two before my arrival, Flimnap would have infallibly broke his neck if one of the King's cushions, that accidentally lay on the ground, had not weakened the force of his fall.[4]

There is likewise another diversion, which is only shown

3 Sir Robert Walpole   Duchess of Kendall, mis-   helped Walpole at a crisis
4 The "cushion" is the   tress of George I, who   in his career.

before the Emperor and Empress, and first minister, upon particular occasions. The Emperor lays on the table three fine silken threads of six inches long. One is blue, the other red, and the third green.[5] These threads are proposed as prizes for those persons whom the Emperor hath a mind to distinguish ·by a peculiar mark of his favor. The ceremony is performed in his Majesty's great chamber of state, where the candidates are to undergo a trial of dexterity very different from the former, and such as I have not observed the least resemblance of in any other country of the old or the new world. The Emperor holds a stick in his hands, both ends parallel to the horizon, while the candidates advancing one by one, sometimes leap over the stick, sometimes creep under it backwards and forwards several times, according as the stick is advanced or depressed. Sometimes the Emperor holds one end of the stick, and his first minister the other; sometimes the minister has it entirely to himself. Whoever performs his part with most agility, and holds out the longest in leaping and creeping, is rewarded with the blue-colored silk; the red is given to the next, and the green to the third, which they all wear girt twice round about the middle; and you see few great persons about this court, who are not adorned with one of these girdles.

The horses of the army, and those of the royal stables, having been daily led before me, were no longer shy, but would come up to my very feet without starting. The riders would leap them over my hand as I held it on the ground, and one of the Emperor's huntsmen, upon a large courser, took my foot, shoe and all; which was indeed a prodigious leap. I had the good fortune to divert the Emperor one day after a very extraordinary manner. I desired he would order several sticks of two foot high, and the thickness of an ordinary cane, to be brought me; whereupon his Majesty commanded the master of his woods to give directions accordingly; and the next morning six woodmen arrived with as many carriages, drawn by eight horses to each. I took nine of these sticks, fixing them firmly in the ground in a quadrangular figure, two foot and a half square. I took four other sticks, and tied them parallel at each corner, about two foot from the ground; then I fastened my handkerchief to the nine sticks that stood erect, and extended it on all sides, till it was tight as the top of a drum; and the four parallel sticks rising about five inches higher than the handkerchief, served as ledges on each side. When I had finished my work, I desired the Emperor to let a troop of his best horse, twenty-four in number, come and ex-

5 the ribbons of the orders of the Garter, the Bath, and the Thistle

ercise upon this plain. His Majesty approved of the proposal, and I took them up, one by one, in my hands, ready mounted and armed, with the proper officers to exercise them. As soon as they got into order, they divided into two parties, performed mock skirmishes, discharged blunt arrows, drew their swords, fled and pursued, attacked and retired, and in short discovered the best military discipline I ever beheld. The parallel sticks secured them and their horses from falling over the stage; and the Emperor was so much delighted that he ordered
10 this entertainment to be repeated several days, and once was pleased to be lifted up and give the word of command; and, with great difficulty, persuaded even the Empress herself to let me hold her in her close chair within two yards of the stage, from whence she was able to take a full view of the whole performance. It was my good fortune that no ill accident happened in these entertainments, only once a fiery horse, that belonged to one of the captains, pawing with his hoof, struck a hole in my handkerchief, and his foot slipping, he overthrew his rider and himself; but I immediately relieved them both,
20 and covering the hole with one hand, I set down the troop with the other, in the same manner as I took them up. The horse that fell was strained in the left shoulder, but the rider got no hurt, and I repaired my handkerchief as well as I could: however, I would not trust to the strength of it any more in such dangerous enterprises.

About two or three days before I was set at liberty, as I was entertaining the court with these kind of feats, there arrived an express to inform his Majesty, that some of his subjects riding near the place where I was first taken up, had seen
30 a great black substance lying on the ground, very oddly shaped, extending its edges round as wide as his Majesty's bedchamber, and rising up in the middle as high as a man; that it was no living creature, as they at first apprehended, for it lay on the grass without motion, and some of them had walked round it several times: that by mounting upon each other's shoulders, they had got to the top, which was flat and even, and stamping upon it they found it was hollow within; that they humbly conceived it might be something belonging to the Man-Mountain; and if his Majesty pleased, they would under-
40 take to bring it with only five horses. I presently knew what they meant, and was glad at heart to receive this intelligence. It seems upon my first reaching the shore after our shipwreck, I was in such confusion, that before I came to the place where I went to sleep, my hat, which I had fastened with a string to my head while I was rowing, and had stuck on all the time I was swimming, fell off after I came to land; the

string, as I conjecture, breaking by some accident which I never observed, but thought my hat had been lost at sea. I entreated his Imperial Majesty to give orders it might be brought to me as soon as possible, describing to him the use and the nature of it: and the next day the wagoners arrived with it, but not in a very good condition; they had bored two holes in the brim, within an inch and half of the edge, and fastened two hooks in the holes; these hooks were tied by a long cord to the harness, and thus my hat was dragged along for above half an English mile; but the ground in that country being extremely smooth and level, it received less damage than I expected.

Two days after this adventure, the Emperor having ordered that part of his army which quarters in and about his metropolis to be in readiness, took a fancy of diverting himself in a very singular manner. He desired I would stand like a Colossus, with my legs as far asunder as I conveniently could. He then commanded his General (who was an old experienced leader, and a great patron of mine) to draw up the troops in close order, and march them under me; the foot by twenty-four in a breast, and the horse by sixteen, with drums beating, colors flying, and pikes advanced. This body consisted of three thousand foot, and a thousand horse. His Majesty gave orders, upon pain of death, that every soldier in his march should observe the strictest decency with regard to my person; which, however, could not prevent some of the younger officers from turning up their eyes as they passed under me. And, to confess the truth, my breeches were at that time in so ill a condition, that they afforded some opportunities for laughter and admiration.

I had sent so many memorials and petitions for my liberty, that his Majesty at length mentioned the matter, first in the cabinet, and then in a full council; where it was opposed by none, except Skyresh Bolgolam, who was pleased, without any provocation, to be my mortal enemy. But it was carried against him by the whole board, and confirmed by the Emperor. That minister was *Galbet,* or Admiral of the Realm, very much in his master's confidence, and a person well versed in affairs, but of a morose and sour complexion. However, he was at length persuaded to comply; but prevailed that the articles and conditions upon which I should be set free, and to which I must swear, should be drawn up by himself. These articles were brought to me by Skyresh Bolgolam in person, attended by two under-secretaries, and several persons of distinction. After they were read, I was demanded to swear to the performance of them; first in the manner of my own country, and afterwards in the method prescribed by their laws; which was to hold my right foot in my left hand, to place the middle finger of my right hand on the crown of my head, and my thumb on the tip of my right ear. But because the reader may be curious to have some idea of the style and manner of expression peculiar to that people, as well as to know the articles upon which I recovered my liberty, I have made a translation of the whole instrument word for word, as near as I was able, which I here offer to the public.

10   GOLBASTO MOMAREM EVLAME GURDILO SHEFIN MULLY ULLY GUE, most mighty Emperor of Lilliput, delight and terror of the universe, whose dominions extend five thousand *blustrugs* (about twelve miles in circumference) to the extremities of the globe; monarch of all monarchs, taller than the sons of men; whose feet press down to the center, and whose head strikes against the sun; at whose nod the princes of the earth shake their knees; pleasant as the spring, comfortable as the summer, fruitful as autumn, dreadful as winter. His most sublime Majesty proposeth to the Man-Mountain, lately
20 arrived to our celestial dominions, the following articles, which by a solemn oath he shall be obliged to perform.

First, the Man-Mountain shall not depart from our dominions, without our license under our great seal.

2d, He shall not presume to come into our metropolis, without our express order; at which time, the inhabitants shall have two hours' warning to keep within their doors.

3rd, The said Man-Mountain shall confine his walks to our principal highroads, and not offer to walk or lie down in a meadow or field of corn.

30   4th, As he walks the said roads, he shall take the utmost care not to trample upon the bodies of any of our loving subjects, their horses, or carriages, nor take any of our subjects into his hands, without their own consent.

5th, If an express requires extraordinary dispatch, the Man-Mountain shall be obliged to carry in his pocket the messenger and horse a six days' journey once in every moon, and return the said messenger back (if so required) safe to our Imperial Presence.

6th, He shall be our ally against our enemies in the Island
40 of Blefuscu,[6] and do his utmost to destroy their fleet, which is now preparing to invade us.

7th, That the said Man-Mountain shall, at his times of leisure, be aiding and assisting our workmen, in helping to raise certain great stones, towards covering the wall of the principal park, and other our royal buildings.

6 probably representing France

8th, That the said Man-Mountain shall, in two moons' time, deliver in an exact survey of the circumference of our dominions by a computation of his own paces round the coast.

Lastly, That upon his solemn oath to observe all the above articles, the said Man-Mountain shall have a daily allowance of meat and drink sufficient for the support of 1728 of our subjects, with free access to our Royal Person, and other marks of our favor. Given at our Palace at Belfaborac the twelfth day of the ninety-first moon of our reign.

I swore and subscribed to these articles with great cheer- 10 fulness and content, although some of them were not so honorable as I could have wished; which proceeded wholly from the malice of Skyresh Bolgolam, the High-Admiral: whereupon my chains were immediately unlocked, and I was at full liberty; the Emperor himself in person did me the honor to be by at the whole ceremony. I made my acknowledgments by prostrating myself at his Majesty's feet; but he commanded me to rise; and after many gracious expressions, which, to avoid the censure of vanity, I shall not repeat, he added, that he hoped I should prove a useful servant, and well deserve 20 all the favors he had already conferred upon me, or might do for the future.

The reader may please to observe, that in the last article for the recovery of my liberty, the Emperor stipulates to allow me a quantity of meat and drink sufficient for the support of 1728 Lilliputians. Some time after, asking a friend at court how they came to fix on that determinate number; he told me that his Majesty's mathematicians, having taken the height of my body by the help of a quadrant, and finding it to exceed theirs in the proportion of twelve to one, they concluded from 30 the similarity of their bodies, that mine must contain at least 1728 of theirs, and consequently would require as much food as was necessary to support that number of Lilliputians. By which, the reader may conceive an idea of the ingenuity of that people, as well as the prudent and exact economy of so great a prince.

CHAPTER IV

Mildendo, the metropolis of Lilliput, described, together with the Emperor's palace. A conversation between the Author and a principal Secretary, concerning the affairs of that empire. The Author's offer to serve the Emperor in his wars.

THE first request I made after I had obtained my liberty, was, that I might have license to see Mildendo, the metropolis;

which the Emperor easily granted me, but with a special charge to do no hurt either to the inhabitants or their houses. The people had notice by proclamation of my design to visit the town. The wall which encompassed it, is two foot and an half high, and at least eleven inches broad, so that a coach and horses may be driven very safely round it; and it is flanked with strong towers at ten foot distance. I stepped over the great Western Gate, and passed very gently, and sideling through the two principal streets, only in my short waistcoat,
10 for fear of damaging the roofs and eaves of the houses with the skirts of my coat. I walked with the utmost circumspection, to avoid treading on any stragglers, that might remain in the streets, although the orders were very strict, that all people should keep in their houses, at their own peril. The garret windows and tops of houses were so crowded with spectators, that I thought in all my travels I had not seen a more populous place. The city is an exact square, each side of the wall being five hundred foot long. The two great streets, which run cross and divide it into four quarters, are five foot wide. The lanes
20 and alleys, which I could not enter, but only viewed them as I passed, are from twelve to eighteen inches. The town is capable of holding five hundred thousand souls. The houses are from three to five stories. The shops and markets well provided.

The Emperor's palace is in the center of the city, where the two great streets meet. It is enclosed by a wall of two foot high, and twenty foot distant from the buildings. I had his Majesty's permission to step over this wall; and the space being so wide between that and the palace, I could easily
30 view it on every side. The outward court is a square of forty foot, and includes two other courts: in the inmost are the royal apartments, which I was very desirous to see, but found it extremely difficult; for the great gates, from one square into another, were but eighteen inches high, and seven inches wide. Now the buildings of the outer court were at least five foot high, and it was impossible for me to stride over them without infinite damage to the pile, though the walls were strongly built of hewn stone, and four inches thick. At the same time the Emperor had a great desire that I should see
40 the magnificence of his palace; but this I was not able to do till three days after, which I spent in cutting down with my knife some of the largest trees in the royal park, about an hundred yards distant from the city. Of these trees I made two stools, each about three foot high, and strong enough to bear my weight. The people having received notice a second

time, I went again through the city to the palace, with my two stools in my hands. When I came to the side of the outer court, I stood upon one stool, and took the other in my hand: this I lifted over the roof, and gently set it down on the space between the first and second court, which was eight foot wide. I then stept over the buildings very conveniently from one stool to the other, and drew up the first after me with a hooked stick. By this contrivance I got into the inmost court; and lying down upon my side, I applied my face to the windows of the middle stories, which were left open on purpose, 10 and discovered the most splendid apartments that can be imagined. There I saw the Empress and the young Princes, in their several lodgings, with their chief attendants about them. Her Imperial Majesty was pleased to smile very graciously upon me, and gave me out of the window her hand to kiss.

But I shall not anticipate the reader with farther descriptions of this kind, because I reserve them for a greater work, which is now almost ready for the press, containing a general description of this empire, from its first erection, through a 20 long series of Princes, with a particular account of their wars and politics, laws, learning, and religion: their plants and animals, their peculiar manners and customs, with other matters very curious and useful; my chief design at present being only to relate such events and transactions as happened to the public, or to myself, during a residence of about nine months in that empire.

One morning, about a fortnight after I had obtained my liberty, Reldresal, principal Secretary (as they style him) of Private Affairs, came to my house attended only by one serv- 30 ant. He ordered his coach to wait at a distance, and desired I would give him an hour's audience; which I readily consented to, on account of his quality and personal merits, as well as the many good offices he had done me during my solicitations at court. I offered to lie down, that he might the more conveniently reach my ear; but he chose rather to let me hold him in my hand during our conversation. He began with compliments on my liberty; said he might pretend to some merit in it: but, however, added, that if it had not been for the present situation of things at court, perhaps I might 40 not have obtained it so soon. For, said he, as flourishing a condition as we may appear to be in to foreigners, we labor under two mighty evils; a violent faction at home, and the danger of an invasion by a most potent enemy from abroad. As to the first, you are to understand, that for about seventy

moons past there have been two struggling parties in this empire, under the names of *Tramecksan* and *Slamecksan*,[7] from the high and low heels on their shoes, by which they distinguish themselves. It is alleged indeed, that the high heels are most agreeable to our ancient constitution; but, however this be, his Majesty hath determined to make use of only low heels in the administration of the government, and all offices in the gift of the Crown, as you cannot but observe; and particularly, that his Majesty's Imperial heels are lower at least by a *drurr*
10 than any of his court (*drurr* is a measure about the fourteenth part of an inch). The animosities between these two parties run so high, that they will neither eat nor drink, nor talk with each other. We compute the *Tramecksan*, or High-Heels, to exceed us in number; but the power is wholly on our side. We apprehend his Imperial Highness, the Heir to the Crown, to have some tendency towards the High-Heels; at least we can plainly discover one of his heels higher than the other, which gives him a hobble in his gait.[8] Now, in the midst of these intestine disquiets, we are threatened with an invasion
20 from the Island of Blefuscu, which is the other great empire of the universe, almost as large and powerful as this of his Majesty. For as to what we have heard you affirm, that there are other kingdoms and states in the world inhabited by human creatures as large as yourself, our philosophers are in much doubt, and would rather conjecture that you dropped from the moon, or one of the stars; because it is certain, that an hundred mortals of your bulk would, in a short time, destroy all the fruits and cattle of his Majesty's dominions. Besides, our histories of six thousand moons make no mention of any
30 other regions, than the two great empires of Lilliput and Blefuscu. Which two mighty powers have, as I was going to tell you, been engaged in a most obstinate war for six and thirty moons past. It began upon the following occasion. It is allowed on all hands, that the primitive way of breaking eggs before we eat them, was upon the larger end: but his present Majesty's grandfather,[9] while he was a boy going to eat an egg, and breaking it according to the ancient practice, happened to cut one of his fingers. Whereupon the Emperor his father published an edict, commanding all his subjects, upon great penal-
40 ties, to break the smaller end of their eggs. The people so highly resented this law, that our histories tell us there have been six rebellions raised on that account; wherein one Emperor lost his life, and another his crown.[10] These civil com-

---

7 Tories and Whigs
8 referring to the intrigues of the Prince of Wales (afterwards George

II) with both parties
9 Henry VIII. The Little-endians are the Protestants, the Big-endians the Roman

Catholics.
10 Charles I and James II respectively

motions were constantly fomented by the monarchs of Blefuscu; and when they were quelled, the exiles always fled for refuge to that empire. It is computed, that eleven thousand persons have, at several times, suffered death, rather than submit to break their eggs at the smaller end. Many hundred large volumes have been published upon this controversy: but the books of the Big-Endians have been long forbidden, and the whole party rendered incapable by law of holding employments. During the course of these troubles, the Emperors of Blefuscu did frequently expostulate by their ambassadors, ac- 10 cusing us of making a schism in religion, by offending against a fundamental doctrine of our great prophet Lustrog, in the fifty-fourth chapter of the Blundecral (which is their Alcoran). This, however, is thought to be a mere strain upon the text: for the words are these; *That all true believers break their eggs at the convenient end:* and which is the convenient end, seems, in my humble opinion, to be left to every man's conscience, or at least in the power of the chief magistrate to determine. Now the Big-Endian exiles have found so much credit in the Emperor of Blefuscu's court, and so much private as- 20 sistance and encouragement from their party here at home, that a bloody war has been carried on between the two empires for six and thirty moons with various success; during which time we have lost forty capital ships, and a much greater number of smaller vessels, together with thirty thousand of our best seamen and soldiers; and the damage received by the enemy is reckoned to be somewhat greater than ours. However, they have now equipped a numerous fleet, and are just preparing to make a descent upon us; and his Imperial Majesty, placing great confidence in your valor and strength, has 30 commanded me to lay this account of his affairs before you.

I desired the Secretary to present my humble duty to the Emperor, and to let him know, that I thought it would not become me, who was a foreigner, to interfere with parties; but I was ready, with the hazard of my life, to defend his person and state against all invaders.

CHAPTER V

The Author, by an extraordinary stratagem, prevents an invasion. A high title of honor is conferred upon him. Ambassadors arrive from the Emperor of Blefuscu, and sue for peace. The Empress's apartment on fire by an accident; the Author instrumental in saving the rest of the palace.

THE Empire of Blefuscu is an island situated to the north north-east side of Lilliput, from whence it is parted only by a channel of eight hundred yards wide. I had not yet seen it, and upon this notice of an intended invasion, I avoided appearing on that side of the coast, for fear of being discovered by some of the enemy's ships, who had received no intelligence of me, all intercourse between the two empires having been strictly forbidden during the war, upon pain of death, and an embargo laid by our Emperor upon all vessels whatsoever. I communicated to his Majesty a project I had formed of seizing the enemy's whole fleet: which, as our scouts assured us, 10 lay at anchor in the harbor ready to sail with the first fair wind. I consulted the most experienced seamen, upon the depth of the channel, which they had often plumbed, who told me, that in the middle at highwater it was seventy *glumgluffs* deep, which is about six foot of European measure; and the rest of it fifty *glumgluffs* at most. I walked towards the north-east coast over against Blefuscu; and lying down behind a hillock, took out my small pocket perspective-glass, and viewed the enemy's fleet at anchor, consisting of about fifty men of war, and a great number of transports: I then came back to my 20 house, and gave order (for which I had a warrant) for a great quantity of the strongest cable and bars of iron. The cable was about as thick as packthread, and the bars of the length and size of a knitting-needle. I trebled the cable to make it stronger, and for the same reason I twisted three of the iron bars together, binding the extremities into a hook. Having thus fixed fifty hooks to as many cables, I went back to the north-east coast, and putting off my coat, shoes, and stockings, walked into the sea in my leathern jerkin, about half an hour before high water. I waited with what haste I could, and swam in the 30 middle about thirty yards till I felt ground; I arrived at the fleet in less than half an hour. The enemy was so frighted when they saw me, that they leaped out of their ships, and swam to shore, where there could not be fewer than thirty thousand souls. I then took my tackling, and fastening a hook to the hole at the prow of each, I tied all the cords together at the end. While I was thus employed, the enemy discharged several thousand arrows, many of which stuck in my hands and face; and besides the excessive smart, gave me much disturbance in my work. My greatest apprehension was for my eyes, which 40 I should have infallibly lost, if I had not suddenly thought of an expedient. I kept among other little necessaries a pair of spectacles in a private pocket, which, as I observed before, had scaped the Emperor's searchers. These I took out and fastened as strongly as I could upon my nose, and thus armed went on boldly with my work in spite of the enemy's arrows, many of which struck against the glasses of my spectacles, but without any other effect, further than a little to discompose them. I had now fastened all the hooks, and taking the knot in my hand, began to pull; but not a ship would stir, for they were all too fast held by their anchors, so that the boldest part of my enterprise remained. I therefore let go the cord, and leaving the hooks fixed to the ships, I resolutely cut with my knife the cables that fastened the anchors, receiving about two hundred shots in my face and hands; then I took up the knotted end of the cables, to which my hooks were tied, and with great ease drew fifty of the enemy's largest men of war after me.   10

The Blefuscudians, who had not the least imagination of what I intended, were at first confounded with astonishment. They had seen me cut the cables, and thought my design was only to let the ships run adrift, or fall foul on each other: but when they perceived the whole fleet moving in order, and saw me pulling at the end, they set up such a scream of grief and despair, that it is almost impossible to describe or conceive. When I had got out of danger, I stopped awhile to pick out the arrows that stuck in my hands and face; and rubbed on some of the same ointment that was given me at my first 20 arrival, as I have formerly mentioned. I then took off my spectacles, and waiting about an hour, till the tide was a little fallen, I waded through the middle with my cargo, and arrived safe at the royal port of Lilliput.

The Emperor and his whole court stood on the shore, expecting the issue of this great adventure. They saw the ships move forward in a large half-moon, but could not discern me, who was up to my breast in water. When I advanced to the middle of the channel, they were yet in more pain, because I was under water to my neck. The Emperor concluded me to 30 be drowned, and that the enemy's fleet was approaching in a hostile manner: but he was soon eased of his fears, for the channel growing shallower every step I made, I came in a short time within hearing, and holding up the end of the cable by which the fleet was fastened, I cried in a loud voice, *Long live the most puissant Emperor of Lilliput!* This great prince received me at my landing with all possible encomiums, and created me a *Nardac* upon the spot, which is the highest title of honor among them.

His Majesty desired I would take some other opportunity 40 of bringing all the rest of his enemy's ships into his ports. And so unmeasurable is the ambition of princes, that he seemed to think of nothing less than reducing the whole empire of Blefuscu into a province, and governing it by a viceroy; of destroying the Big-Endian exiles, and compelling the people to break the smaller end of their eggs, by which he would remain the sole monarch of the whole world. But I endeavored to divert him from this design, by many arguments drawn from the topics of policy as well as justice; and I plainly protested, that I would never be an instrument of bringing a free and brave people into slavery. And when the matter was debated in council, the wisest part of the ministry were of my opinion.

This open bold declaration of mine was so opposite to the schemes and politics of his Imperial Majesty, that he could never forgive it; he mentioned it in a very artful manner at council, where I was told that some of the wisest appeared, at least by their silence, to be of my opinion; but others, who were my secret enemies, could not forbear some expressions, which by a side-wind reflected on me. And from this time began an intrigue between his Majesty and a junto of ministers maliciously bent against me, which broke out in less than two months, and had like to have ended in my utter destruction. Of so little weight are the greatest services to princes, when put into the balance with a refusal to gratify their passions.

About three weeks after this exploit, there arrived a solemn embassy from Blefuscu, with humble offers of a peace; which was soon concluded upon conditions very advantageous to our Emperor, wherewith I shall not trouble the reader. There were six ambassadors, with a train of about five hundred persons, and their entry was very magnificent, suitable to the grandeur of their master, and the importance of their business. When their treaty was finished, wherein I did them several good offices by the credit I now had, or at least appeared to have at court, their Excellencies, who were privately told how much I had been their friend, made me a visit in form. They began with many compliments upon my valor and generosity, invited me to that kingdom in the Emperor their master's name, and desired me to show them some proofs of my prodigious strength, of which they had heard so many wonders; wherein I readily obliged them, but shall not trouble the reader with the particulars.

When I had for some time entertained their Excellencies, to their infinite satisfaction and surprise, I desired they would do me the honor to present my most humble respects to the Emperor their master, the renown of whose virtues had so justly filled the whole world with admiration, and whose royal person I resolved to attend before I returned to my own country: accordingly, the next time I had the honor to see our Emperor, I desired his general license to wait on the Blefuscudian monarch, which he was pleased to grant me, as I could perceive, in a very cold manner; but could not guess the reason, till I had a whisper from a certain person that Flimnap and Bolgolam had represented my intercourse with those ambassadors as a mark of disaffection, from which I am sure my heart was wholly free. And this was the first time I began to conceive some imperfect idea of courts and ministers.

It is to be observed, that these ambassadors spoke to me by an interpreter, the languages of both empires differing as much from each other as any two in Europe, and each nation priding itself upon the antiquity, beauty, and energy of their own tongues, with an avowed contempt for that of their neighbor; yet our Emperor, standing upon the advantage he had got by the seizure of their fleet, obliged them to deliver their credentials, and make their speech in the Lilliputian tongue. And it must be confessed, that from the great intercourse of trade and commerce between both realms, from the continual reception of exiles, which is mutual among them, and from the custom in each empire to send their young nobility and richer gentry to the other, in order to polish themselves by seeing the world, and understanding men and manners; there are few persons of distinction, or merchants, or seamen, who dwell in the maritime parts, but what can hold conversation in both tongues; as I found some weeks after, when I went to pay my respects to the Emperor of Blefuscu, which in the midst of great misfortunes, through the malice of my enemies, proved a very happy adventure to me, as I shall relate in its proper place.

The reader may remember, that when I signed those articles upon which I recovered my liberty, there were some which I disliked upon account of their being too servile, neither could anything but an extreme necessity have forced me to submit. But being now a *Nardac* of the highest rank in that empire, such offices were looked upon as below my dignity, and the Emperor (to do him justice) never once mentioned them to me. However, it was not long before I had an opportunity of doing his Majesty, at least, as I then thought, a most signal service. I was alarmed at midnight with the cries of many hundred people at my door; by which being suddenly awaked, I was in some kind of terror. I heard the word *burglum* repeated incessantly: several of the Emperor's court, making their way through the crowd, entreated me to come immediately to the palace, where her Imperial Majesty's apartment was on fire, by the carelessness of a maid of honor, who fell asleep while she was reading a romance. I got up in an instant; and orders being given to clear the way before me, and it being likewise a moonshine night, I made a shift to get to the Palace without trampling on any of the people. I found

they had already applied ladders to the walls of the apartment, and were well provided with buckets, but the water was at some distance. These buckets were about the size of a large thimble, and the poor people supplied me with them as fast as they could; but the flame was so violent that they did little good. I might easily have stifled it with my coat, which I unfortunately left behind me for haste, and came away only in my leathern jerkin. The case seemed wholly desperate and deplorable; and this magnificent palace would have infallibly
10 been burnt down to the ground, if, by a presence of mind, unusual to me, I had not suddenly thought of an expedient. I had the evening before drunk plentifully of a most delicious wine, called *glimigrim* (the Blefuscudians call it *flunec,* but ours is esteemed the better sort), which is very diuretic. By the luckiest chance in the world, I had not discharged myself of any part of it. The heat I had contracted by coming very near the flames, and by laboring to quench them, made the wine begin to operate by urine; which I voided in such a quantity, and applied so well to the proper places, that in three
20 minutes the fire was wholly extinguished, and the rest of that noble pile, which had cost so many ages in erecting, preserved from destruction.

It was now day-light, and I returned to my house without waiting to congratulate with the Emperor: because, although I had done a very eminent piece of service, yet I could not tell how his Majesty might resent the manner by which I had performed it: for, by the fundamental laws of the realm, it is capital in any person, of what quality soever, to make water within the precincts of the palace. But I was a little
30 comforted by a message from his Majesty, that he would give orders to the Grand Justiciary for passing my pardon in form; which, however, I could not obtain. And I was privately assured, that the Empress, conceiving the greatest abhorrence of what I had done, removed to the most distant side of the court, firmly resolved that those buildings should never be repaired for her use: and, in the presence of her chief confidents could not forbear vowing revenge.[11]

CHAPTER VI

Of the inhabitants of Lilliput; *their learning, laws, and customs, the manner of educating their children. The Author's way of living in that country. His vindication of a great lady.*

ALTHOUGH I intend to leave the description of this empire to a particular treatise, yet in the mean time I am content to

11 This episode perhaps refers to Swift's failure to obtain a bishopric because of his authorship of *A Tale of a Tub.*

gratify the curious reader with some general ideas. As the common size of the natives is somewhat under six inches high, so there is an exact proportion in all other animals, as well as plants and trees: for instance, the tallest horses and oxen are between four and five inches in height, the sheep an inch and a half, more or less: their geese about the bigness of a sparrow, and so the several gradations downwards till you come to the smallest, which, to my sight, were almost invisible; but nature hath adapted the eyes of the Lilliputians to all objects proper for their view: they see with great exactness, but at no great distance. And to show the sharpness of their sight towards objects that are near, I have been much pleased with observing a cook pulling a lark, which was not so large as a common fly; and a young girl threading an invisible needle with invisible silk. Their tallest trees are about seven foot high: I mean some of those in the great royal park, the tops whereof I could but just reach with my fist clinched. The other vegetables are in the same proportion; but this I leave to the reader's imagination.

I shall say but little at present of their learning, which for many ages hath flourished in all its branches among them: but their manner of writing is very peculiar, being neither from the left to the right, like the Europeans; nor from the right to the left, like the Arabians; nor from up to down, like the Chinese; nor from down to up, like the Cascagians; but aslant from one corner of the paper to the other, like ladies in England.

They bury their dead with their heads directly downwards, because they hold an opinion, that in eleven thousand moons they are all to rise again, in which period the earth (which they conceive to be flat) will turn upside down, and by this means they shall, at their resurrection, be found ready standing on their feet. The learned among them confess the absurdity of this doctrine, but the practice still continues, in compliance to the vulgar.

There are some laws and customs in this empire very peculiar; and if they were not so directly contrary to those of my own dear country, I should be tempted to say a little in their justification. It is only to be wished, that they were as well executed. The first I shall mention, relates to informers. All crimes against the state are punished here with the utmost severity; but if the person accused maketh his innocence plainly to appear upon his trial, the accuser is immediately put to an ignominious death; and out of his goods or lands, the innocent person is quadruply recompensed for the loss of his time, for the danger he underwent, for the hardship of his imprisonment, and for all the charges he hath been at in making his defense. Or, if that fund be deficient, it is largely supplied by the Crown. The Emperor does also confer on him some public mark of his favor, and proclamation is made of his innocence through the whole city.

They look upon fraud as a greater crime than theft, and therefore seldom fail to punish it with death; for they allege, that care and vigilance, with a very common understanding, may preserve a man's goods from thieves, but honesty has no fence gainst superior cunning; and since it is necessary that there should be a perpetual intercourse of buying and selling, and dealing upon credit, where fraud is permitted and connived at, or hath no law to punish it, the honest dealer is always undone, and the knave gets the advantage. I remember when I was once interceding with the Emperor for a criminal who had wronged his master of a great sum of money, which he had received by order, and ran away with; and happening to tell his Majesty, by way of extenuation, that it was only a breach of trust; the Emperor thought it monstrous in me to offer, as a defense, the greatest aggravation of the crime: and truly I had little to say in return, farther than the common answer, that different nations had different customs; for, I confess, I was heartily ashamed.

Although we usually call reward and punishment the two hinges upon which all government turns, yet I could never observe this maxim to be put in practice by any nation except that of Lilliput. Whoever can there bring sufficient proof that he hath strictly observed the laws of his country for seventy-three moons, hath a claim to certain privileges, according to his quality and condition of life, with a proportionable sum of money out of a fund appropriated for that use: he likewise acquires the title of *Snilpall*, or Legal, which is added to his name, but does not descend to his posterity. And these people thought it a prodigious defect of policy among us, when I told them that our laws were enforced only by penalties, without any mention of reward. It is upon this account that the image of Justice, in their courts of judicature, is formed with six eyes, two before, as many behind, and on each side one, to signify circumspection; with a bag of gold open in her right hand, and a sword sheathed in her left, to show she is more disposed to reward than to punish.

In choosing persons for all employments, they have more regard to good morals than to great abilities; for, since government is necessary to mankind, they believe that the common size of human understandings is fitted to some station or other, and that Providence never intended to make the management of public affairs a mystery, to be comprehended only by a few persons of sublime genius, of which there seldom are three born in an age: but they suppose truth, justice, temperance, and the like, to be in every man's power; the practice of which virtues, assisted by experience and a good intention, would qualify any man for the service of his country, except where a course of study is required. But they thought the want of moral virtues was so far from being supplied by superior endowments of the mind, that employments could never be put into such dangerous hands as those of persons so quali- 10 fied; and at least, that the mistakes committed by ignorance in a virtuous disposition, would never be of such fatal consequence to the public weal, as the practices of a man whose inclinations led him to be corrupt, and had great abilities to manage, and multiply, and defend his corruptions.

In like manner, the disbelief of a Divine Providence renders a man uncapable of holding any public station; for, since kings avow themselves to be the deputies of Providence, the Lilliputians think nothing can be more absurd than for a prince to employ such men as disown the authority under which he acts. 20

In relating these and the following laws, I would only be understood to mean the original institutions, and not the most scandalous corruptions into which these people are fallen by the degenerate nature of man. For as to that infamous practice of acquiring great employments by dancing on the ropes, or badges of favor and distinction by leaping over sticks and creeping under them, the reader is to observe, that they were first introduced by the grandfather of the Emperor now reigning, and grew to the present height, by the gradual increase of party and faction. 30

Ingratitude is among them a capital crime, as we read it to have been in some other countries: for they reason thus, that whoever makes ill returns to his benefactor, must needs be a common enemy to the rest of mankind, from whom he hath received no obligation, and therefore such a man is not fit to live.

Their notions relating to the duties of parents and children differ extremely from ours. For, since the conjunction of male and female is founded upon the great law of nature, in order to propagate and continue the species, the Lilliputians will 40 needs have it, that men and women are joined together like other animals, by the motives of concupiscence; and that their tenderness towards their young proceeds from the like natural principle: for which reason they will never allow, that a child is under any obligation to his father for begetting him, or to

his mother for bringing him into the world, which, considering the miseries of human life, was neither a benefit in itself, nor intended so by his parents, whose thoughts in their love-encounters were otherwise employed. Upon these, and the like reasonings, their opinion is, that parents are the last of all others to be trusted with the education of their own children; and therefore they have in every town public nurseries, where all parents, except cottagers and laborers, are obliged to send their infants of both sexes to be reared and educated when
10 they come to the age of twenty moons, at which time they are supposed to have some rudiments of docility. These schools are of several kinds, suited to different qualities, and to both sexes. They have certain professors well skilled in preparing children for such a condition of life as befits the rank of their parents, and their own capacities as well as inclinations. I shall first say something of the male nurseries, and then of the female.

The nurseries for males of noble or eminent birth, are provided with grave and learned professors, and their several
20 deputies. The clothes and food of the children are plain and simple. They are bred up in the principles of honor, justice, courage, modesty, clemency, religion, and love of their country; they are always employed in some business, except in the times of eating and sleeping, which are very short, and two hours for diversions, consisting of bodily exercises. They are dressed by men till four years of age, and then are obliged to dress themselves, although their quality be ever so great; and the women attendants, who are aged proportionably to ours at fifty, perform only the most menial offices. They are never
30 suffered to converse with servants, but go together in small or greater numbers to take their diversions, and always in the presence of a professor, or one of his deputies; whereby they avoid those early bad impressions of folly and vice to which our children are subject. Their parents are suffered to see them only twice a year; the visit is to last but an hour. They are allowed to kiss the child at meeting and parting; but a professor, who always stands by on those occasions, will not suffer them to whisper, or use any fondling expressions, or bring any presents of toys, sweetmeats, and the like.
40 The pension from each family for the education and entertainment of a child, upon failure of due payment, is levied by the Emperor's officers.

The nurseries for children of ordinary gentlemen, merchants, traders, and handicrafts, are managed proportionably after the same manner; only those designed for trades, are put out ap-

prentices at eleven years old, whereas those of persons of quality continue in their exercises till fifteen, which answers to one
and twenty with us: but the confinement is gradually lessened
for the last three years.

In the female nurseries, the young girls of quality are educated much like the males, only they are dressed by orderly
servants of their own sex; but always in the presence of a
professor or deputy, till they come to dress themselves, which
is at five years old. And if it be found that these nurses ever
presume to entertain the girls with frightful or foolish stories, 10
or the common follies practised by chambermaids among us,
they are publicly whipped thrice about the city, imprisoned for
a year, and banished for life to the most desolate part of the
country. Thus the young ladies there are as much ashamed
of being cowards and fools, as the men, and despise all personal ornaments beyond decency and cleanliness: neither did
I perceive any difference in their education, made by their
difference of sex, only that the exercises of the females were
not altogether so robust; and that some rules were given them
relating to domestic life, and a smaller compass of learning 20
was enjoined them: for their maxim is, that among people
of quality, a wife should be always a reasonable and agreeable companion, because she cannot always be young. When
the girls are twelve years old, which among them is the mar-
riageable age, their parents or guardians take them home, with
great expressions of gratitude to the professors, and seldom
without tears of the young lady and her companions.

In the nurseries of females of the meaner sort, the children
are instructed in all kinds of works proper for their sex, and
their several degrees: those intended for apprentices, are dis- 30
missed at seven years old, the rest are kept to eleven.

The meaner families who have children at these nurseries,
are obliged, besides their annual pension, which is as low as
possible, to return to the steward of the nursery a small
monthly share of their gettings, to be a portion for the child;
and therefore all parents are limited in their expenses by the
law. For the Lilliputians think nothing can be more unjust,
than for people, in subservience to their own appetites, to bring
children into the world, and leave the burden of supporting
them on the public. As to persons of quality, they give secu- 40
rity to appropriate a certain sum for each child, suitable to
their condition; and these funds are always managed with
good husbandry, and the most exact justice.

The cottagers and laborers keep their children at home, their
business being only to till and cultivate the earth, and there-

fore their education is of little consequence to the public; but the old and diseased among them are supported by hospitals: for begging is a trade unknown in this empire.

And here it may perhaps divert the curious reader, to give some account of my domestic, and my manner of living in this country, during a residence of nine months and thirteen days. Having a head mechanically turned, and being likewise forced by necessity, I had made for myself a table and chair convenient enough, out of the largest trees in the royal park. 10 Two hundred sempstresses were employed to make me shirts, and linen for my bed and table, all of the strongest and coarsest kind they could get; which, however, they were forced to quilt together in several folds, for the thickest was some degrees finer than lawn. Their linen was usually three inches wide, and three foot make a piece. The sempstresses took my measure as I lay on the ground, one standing at my neck, and another at my mid-leg, with a strong cord extended, that each held by the end, while the third measured the length of the cord with a rule of an inch long. Then they measured my right 20 thumb, and desired no more; for by a mathematical computation, that twice round the thumb is once round the wrist, and so on to the neck and the waist, and by the help of my old shirt, which I displayed on the ground before them for a pattern, they fitted me exactly. Three hundred tailors were employed in the same manner to make me clothes; but they had another contrivance for taking my measure. I kneeled down, and they raised a ladder from the ground to my neck; upon this ladder one of them mounted, and let fall a plumb-line from my collar to the floor, which just answered the length of my 30 coat: but my waist and arms I measured myself. When my clothes were finished, which was done in my house, (for the largest of theirs would not have been able to hold them) they looked like the patchwork made by the ladies in England, only that mine were all of a color.

I had three hundred cooks to dress my victuals, in little convenient huts built about my house, where they and their families lived, and prepared me two dishes apiece. I took up twenty waiters in my hand, and placed them on the table: an hundred more attended below on the ground, some with 40 dishes of meat, and some with barrels of wine, and other liquors, slung on their shoulders; all which the waiters above drew up as I wanted, in a very ingenious manner, by certain cords, as we draw the bucket up a well in Europe. A dish of their meat was a good mouthful, and a barrel of their liquor a reasonable draught. Their mutton yields to ours, but their beef is excellent. I have had a sirloin so large, that I have been forced to make three bites of it; but this is rare. My servants were astonished to see me eat it bones and all, as in our country we do the leg of a lark. Their geese and turkeys I usually eat at a mouthful, and I must confess they far exceed ours. Of their smaller fowl I could take up twenty or thirty at the end of my knife.

One day his Imperial Majesty, being informed of my way of living, desired that himself and his Royal Consort, with the young Princes of the blood of both sexes, might have the happiness (as he was pleased to call it) of dining with me. They came accordingly, and I placed them in chairs of state on my table, just over against me, with their guards about them. Flimnap, the Lord High Treasurer, attended there likewise with his white staff; and I observed he often looked on me with a sour countenance, which I would not seem to regard, but eat more than usual, in honor to my dear country, as well as to fill the court with admiration. I have some private reasons to believe, that this visit from his Majesty gave Flimnap an opportunity of doing me ill offices to his master. That minister had always been my secret enemy, though he outwardly caressed me more than was usual to the moroseness of his nature. He represented to the Emperor the low condition of his treasury; that he was forced to take up money at great discount; that exchequer bills would not circulate under nine *per cent.* below par; that in short I had cost his Majesty above a million and a half of *sprugs* (their greatest gold coin, about the bigness of a spangle); and upon the whole, that it would be advisable in the Emperor to take the first fair occasion of dismissing me.

I am here obliged to vindicate the reputation of an excellent lady, who was an innocent sufferer upon my account. The Treasurer took a fancy to be jealous of his wife, from the malice of some evil tongues, who informed him that her Grace had taken a violent affection for my person; and the court-scandal ran for some time, that she once came privately to my lodging. This I solemnly declare to be a most infamous falsehood, without any grounds, farther than that her Grace was pleased to treat me with all innocent marks of freedom and friendship. I own she came often to my house, but always publicly, nor ever without three more in the coach, who were usually her sister and young daughter, and some particular acquaintance; but this was common to many other ladies of the court. And I still appeal to my servants round, whether they at any time saw a coach at my door without knowing what persons were in it. On those occasions, when a servant had given me notice, my custom was to go immediately to

the door; and, after paying my respects, to take up the coach and two horses very carefully in my hands (for, if there were six horses, the postillion always unharnessed four), and place them on a table, where I had fixed a moveable rim quite round, of five inches high, to prevent accidents. And I have often had four coaches and horses at once on my table full of company, while I sat in my chair leaning my face towards them; and when I was engaged with one set, the coachmen would gently drive the others round my table. I have passed many an after-
10 noon very agreeably in these conversations. But I defy the Treasurer, or his two informers (I will name them, and let them make their best of it) Clustril and Drunlo, to prove that any person ever came to me *incognito,* except the secretary Reldresal, who was sent by express command of his Imperial Majesty, as I have before related. I should not have dwelt so long upon this particular, if it had not been a point wherein the reputation of a great lady is so nearly concerned, to say nothing of my own; though I then had the honor to be a *Nardac,* which the Treasurer himself is not; for all the world
20 knows he is only a *Glumglum,* a title inferior by one degree, as that of a Marquis is to a Duke in England, although I allow he preceded me in right of his post. These false informations, which I afterwards came to the knowledge of, by an accident not proper to mention, made Flimnap, the Treasurer, show his lady for some time an ill countenance, and me a worse; and although he were at last undeceived and reconciled to her, yet I lost all credit with him, and found my interest decline very fast with the Emperor himself, who was indeed too much governed by that favorite.

CHAPTER VII

The Author, being informed of a design to accuse him of high treason, makes his escape to Blefuscu. His reception there.

30   Before I proceed to give an account of my leaving this kingdom, it may be proper to inform the reader of a private intrigue which had been for two months forming against me.

I had been hitherto all my life a stranger to courts, for which I was unqualified by the meanness of my condition. I had indeed heard and read enough of the dispositions of great princes and ministers; but never expected to have found such terrible effects of them in so remote a country, governed, as I thought, by very different maxims from those in Europe.

When I was just preparing to pay my attendance on the
40 Emperor of Blefuscu, a considerable person at court (to whom

I had been very serviceable at a time when he lay under the highest displeasure of his Imperial Majesty) came to my house very privately at night in a close chair, and without sending his name, desired admittance. The chairmen were dismissed; I put the chair, with his Lordship in it, into my coat-pocket: and giving orders to a trusty servant to say I was indisposed and gone to sleep, I fastened the door of my house, placed the chair on the table, according to my usual custom, and sat down by it. After the common salutations were over, observing his Lordship's countenance full of concern, and en- 10 quiring into the reason, he desired I would hear him with patience in a matter that highly concerned my honor and my life. His speech was to the following effect, for I took notes of it as soon as he left me.

You are to know, said he, that several Committees of Council have been lately called in the most private manner on your account; and it is but two days since his Majesty came to a full resolution.

You are very sensible that Skyresh Bolgolam (Galbet, or 20 High-Admiral) hath been your mortal enemy almost ever since your arrival. His original reasons I know not; but his hatred is much increased since your great success against Blefuscu, by which his glory, as Admiral, is obscured. This Lord, in conjunction with Flimnap the High-Treasurer, whose enmity against you is notorious on account of his lady, Limtoc the General, Lalcon the Chamberlain, and Balmuff the Grand Justiciary, have prepared articles of impeachment against you, for treason, and other capital crimes.

This preface made me so impatient, being conscious of my 30 own merits and innocence, that I was going to interrupt; when he entreated me to be silent, and thus proceeded.

Out of gratitude for the favors you have done me, I procured information of the whole proceedings, and a copy of the articles, wherein I venture my head for your service.

Articles of Impeachment against Quinbus Flestrin (the Man-Mountain)

ARTICLE I

Whereas, by a statute made in the reign of his Imperial Majesty Calin Deffar Plune, it is enacted, that whoever shall make water within the precincts of the royal palace, shall be liable to the pains and penalties of high treason; notwithstanding, the said Quinbus Flestrin, in open breach of the said law, under color of extinguishing the fire kindled in the apartment of his Majesty's most dear Imperial Consort, did maliciously, traitorously, and devilishly, by discharge of his urine, put out the said fire kindled in the said apartment, lying and being within the precincts of the said royal palace, against the statute in that case provided, etc., against the duty, etc.

That the said Quinbus Flestrin having brought the imperial fleet of Blefuscu into the royal port, and being afterwards commanded by his Imperial Majesty to seize all the other ships of the said empire of Blefuscu, and reduce that empire to a province, to be governed by a viceroy from hence, and to destroy and put to death not only all the Big-Endian exiles, but likewise all the people of that empire, who would not immediately forsake the Big-Endian heresy: He, the said Flestrin, like a false traitor against his most Auspicious, Serene, Imperial Majesty, did petition to be excused from the said service, upon pretence of unwillingness to force the consciences, or destroy the liberties and lives of an innocent people.

ARTICLE III

That, whereas certain ambassadors arrived from the court of Blefuscu, to sue for peace in his Majesty's court: He, the said Flestrin, did, like a false traitor, aid, abet, comfort, and divert the said ambassadors, although he knew them to be servants to a Prince who was lately an open enemy to his Imperial Majesty, and in open war against his said Majesty.

ARTICLE IV

That the said Quinbus Flestrin, contrary to the duty of a faithful subject, is now preparing to make a voyage to the court and empire of Blefuscu, for which he hath received only verbal license from his Imperial Majesty; and under color of the said license, doth falsely and traitorously intend to take the said voyage, and thereby to aid, comfort, and abet the Emperor of Blefuscu, so late an enemy, and in open war with his Imperial Majesty aforesaid.

There are some other articles, but these are the most important, of which I have read you an abstract. In the several debates upon this impeachment, it must be confessed that his Majesty gave many marks of his great lenity, often urging the services you had done him, and endeavoring to extenuate your crimes. The Treasurer and Admiral insisted that you should be put to the most painful and ignominious death, by setting fire on your house at night, and the General was to attend with twenty thousand men armed with poisoned 10 arrows to shoot you on the face and hands. Some of your servants were to have private orders to strew a poisonous juice on your shirts, which would soon make you tear your own flesh, and die in the utmost torture. The General came into the same opinion; so that for a long time there was a majority against you. But his Majesty resolving, if possible, to spare your life, at last brought off the Chamberlain. Upon this incident, Reldresal, principal Secretary for Private Affairs, who always approved himself your true friend, was commanded by the Emperor to deliver his opinion, which he accordingly did; and therein justified the good thoughts you have of him. He allowed your crimes to be great, but that still there was room for mercy, the most commendable virtue in a prince, and for which his Majesty was so justly celebrated. He said, the friendship between you and him was so well known to the world, that perhaps the most honorable board might think him partial: however, in obedience to the command he had received, he would freely offer his sentiments. That if his Majesty, in consideration of your services, and pursuant to his own merciful disposition, would please to spare your life, and only give orders to put out both your eyes, he humbly conceived, that by this expedient, justice might in some measure be satisfied, and all the world would applaud the lenity of the Emperor, as well as the fair and generous proceedings of those who have the honor to be his counselors. That the loss of your eyes would be no impediment to your bodily strength, by which you might still be useful to his Majesty. That blindness is an addition to courage, by concealing dangers from us; that the fear you had for your eyes, was the greatest difficulty in bringing over the enemy's fleet, and it would be sufficient for you to see by the eyes of the ministers, since the greatest princes do no more.

This proposal was received with the utmost disapprobation by the whole board. Bolgolam, the Admiral, could not preserve his temper; but rising up in fury, said, he wondered how the Secretary durst presume to give his opinion for preserving the life of a traitor: that the services you had performed, were, by all true reasons of state, the great aggravation of your crimes; that you, who were able to extinguish the fire, by discharge of urine in her Majesty's apartment (which he mentioned with horror), might, at another time, raise an inundation by the same means, to drown the whole palace; and the same strength which enabled you to bring over the enemy's fleet, might serve, upon the first discontent, to carry it back: that he had good reasons to think you were a Big-Endian in your heart; and as treason begins in the heart, before it appears in overt acts, so he accused you as a traitor on that account, and therefore insisted you should be put to death.

The Treasurer was of the same opinion; he showed to what straits his Majesty's revenue was reduced by the charge of maintaining you, which would soon grow insupportable: that the Secretary's expedient of putting out your eyes was so far from being a remedy against this evil, that it would probably increase it, as it is manifest from the common practice of blinding some kind of fowl, after which they fed the faster, and grew sooner fat: that his sacred Majesty and the Council,

who are your judges, were in their own consciences fully convinced of your guilt, which was a sufficient argument to condemn you to death, without the formal proofs required by the
strict letter of the law.

But his Imperial Majesty, fully determined against capital
punishment, was graciously pleased to say, that since the
Council thought the loss of your eyes too easy a censure, some
other may be inflicted hereafter. And your friend the Secretary
humbly desiring to be heard again, in answer to what the
10 Treasurer had objected concerning the great charge his Majesty was at in maintaining you, said, that his Excellency, who
had the sole disposal of the Emperor's revenue, might easily
provide against that evil, by gradually lessening your establishment; by which, for want of sufficient food, you would grow
weak and faint, and lose your appetite, and consequently decay
and consume in a few months; neither would the stench of
your carcass be then so dangerous, when it should become
more than half diminished; and immediately upon your death,
five or six thousand of his Majesty's subjects might, in two
20 or three days, cut your flesh from your bones, take it away by
cart-loads, and bury it in distant parts to prevent infection,
leaving the skeleton as a monument of admiration to posterity.

Thus by the great friendship of the Secretary, the whole
affair was compromised. It was strictly enjoined, that the project of starving you by degrees should be kept a secret, but the
sentence of putting out your eyes was entered on the books;
none dissenting except Bolgolam the Admiral, who, being a
creature of the Empress, was perpetually instigated by her
Majesty to insist upon your death, she having borne perpetual
30 malice against you, on account of that infamous and illegal
method you took to extinguish the fire in her apartment.

In three days your friend the Secretary will be directed to
come to your house, and read before you the articles of impeachment; and then to signify the great lenity and favor of his
Majesty and Council, whereby you are only condemned to
the loss of your eyes, which his Majesty doth not question you
will gratefully and humbly submit to; and twenty of his
Majesty's surgeons will attend, in order to see the operation
well performed, by discharging very sharp-pointed arrows into
40 the balls of your eyes, as you lie on the ground.

I leave to your prudence what measures you will take; and
to avoid suspicion, I must immediately return in as private a
manner as I came.

His Lordship did so, and I remained alone, under many
doubts and perplexities of mind.

It was a custom introduced by this prince and his ministry

(very different, as I have been assured, from the practices of
former times), that after the court had decreed any cruel execution, either to gratify the monarch's resentment, or the malice
of a favorite, the Emperor always made a speech to his whole
Council, expressing his great lenity and tenderness, as qualities
known and confessed by all the world. This speech was immediately published through the kingdom; nor did any thing
terrify the people so much as those encomiums on his Majesty's
mercy; because it was observed, that the more these praises
were enlarged and insisted on, the more inhuman was the 10
punishment, and the sufferer more innocent. And as to myself,
I must confess, having never been designed for a courtier either
by my birth or education, I was so ill a judge of things, that
I could not discover the lenity and favor of his sentence, but
conceived it (perhaps erroneously) rather to be rigorous than
gentle. I sometimes thought of standing my trial, for although
I could not deny the facts alleged in the several articles, yet I
hoped they would admit of some extenuations. But having in
my life perused many state-trials, which I ever observed to
terminate as the judges thought fit to direct, I durst not rely 20
on so dangerous a decision, in so critical a juncture, and
against such powerful enemies. Once I was strongly bent upon
resistance, for while I had liberty, the whole strength of that
empire could hardly subdue me, and I might easily with stones
pelt the metropolis to pieces; but I soon rejected that project
with horror, by remembering the oath I had made to the Emperor, the favors I received from him, and the high title of
Nardac he conferred upon me. Neither had I so soon learned
the gratitude of courtiers, to persuade myself that his Majesty's
present severities acquitted me of all past obligations. 30

At last I fixed upon a resolution, for which it is probable
I may incur some censure, and not unjustly; for I confess I
owe the preserving my eyes, and consequently my liberty, to
my own great rashness and want of experience: because if I
had then known the nature of princes and ministers, which
I have since observed in many other courts, and their methods
of treating criminals less obnoxious than myself, I should with
great alacrity and readiness have submitted to so easy a punishment. But hurried on by the precipitancy of youth, and
having his Imperial Majesty's license to pay my attendance 40
upon the Emperor of Blefuscu, I took this opportunity, before
the three days were elapsed, to send a letter to my friend the
Secretary, signifying my resolution of setting out that morning
for Blefuscu pursuant to the leave I had got; and without waiting for an answer, I went to that side of the island where our
fleet lay. I seized a large man of war, tied a cable to the prow,

and, lifting up the anchors, I stripped myself, put my clothes (together with my coverlet, which I brought under my arm) into the vessel, and drawing it after me between wading and swimming, arrived at the royal port of Blefuscu, where the people had long expected me: they lent me two guides to direct me to the capital city, which is of the same name. I held them in my hands till I came within two hundred yards of the gate, and desired them to signify my arrival to one of the secretaries, and let him know, I there waited his Majesty's com-
10 mand. I had an answer in about an hour, that his Majesty, attended by the Royal Family, and great officers of the court, was coming out to receive me. I advanced a hundred yards. The Emperor and his train alighted from their horses, the Empress and ladies from their coaches, and I did not perceive they were in any fright or concern. I lay on the ground to kiss his Majesty's and the Empress's hands. I told his Majesty, that I was come according to my promise, and with the license of the Emperor my master, to have the honor of seeing so mighty a monarch, and to offer him any service in my power,
20 consistent with my duty to my own prince; not mentioning a word of my disgrace, because I had hitherto no regular information of it, and might suppose myself wholly ignorant of any such design; neither could I reasonably conceive that the Emperor would discover the secret while I was out of his power: wherein, however, it soon appeared I was deceived.

I shall not trouble the reader with the particular account of my reception at this court, which was suitable to the generosity of so great a prince; nor of the difficulties I was in for want of a house and bed, being forced to lie on the ground, wrapped
30 up in my coverlet.

CHAPTER VIII

The Author, by a lucky accident, finds means to leave Blefuscu: *and, after some difficulties, returns safe to his native country.*

Three days after my arrival, walking out of curiosity to the north-east coast of the island, I observed, about half a league off, in the sea, somewhat that looked like a boat overturned. I pulled off my shoes and stockings, and wading two or three hundred yards, I found the object to approach nearer by force of the tide; and then plainly saw it to be a real boat, which I supposed might, by some tempest, have been driven from a ship; whereupon I returned immediately towards the city, and desired his Imperial Majesty to lend me twenty of the tallest
40 vessels he had left after the loss of his fleet, and three thou-

sand seamen under the command of his Vice-Admiral. This fleet sailed round, while I went back the shortest way to the coast where I first discovered the boat; I found the tide had driven it still nearer. The seamen were all provided with cordage, which I had beforehand twisted to a sufficient strength. When the ships came up, I stripped myself, and waded till I came within an hundred yards of the boat, after which I was forced to swim till I got up to it. The seamen threw me the end of the cord, which I fastened to a hole in the fore-part of the boat, and the other end to a man of war; but I found all 10 my labor to little purpose; for being out of my depth, I was not able to work. In this necessity, I was forced to swim behind, and push the boat forwards as often as I could, with one of my hands; and the tide favoring me, I advanced so far, that I could just hold up my chin and feel the ground. I rested two or three minutes, and then gave the boat another shove, and so on till the sea was no higher than my arm-pits; and now the most laborious part being over, I took out my other cables, which were stowed in one of the ships, and fastening them first to the boat, and then to nine of the vessels which attended 20 me; the wind being favorable, the seamen towed, and I shoved till we arrived within forty yards of the shore; and waiting till the tide was out, I got dry to the boat, and by the assistance of two thousand men, with ropes and engines, I made a shift to turn it on its bottom, and found it was but little damaged.

I shall not trouble the reader with the difficulties I was under by the help of certain paddles, which cost me ten days making, to get my boat to the royal port of Blefuscu, where a mighty concourse of people appeared upon my arrival, full of wonder at the sight of so prodigious a vessel. I told the Em- 30 peror that my good fortune had thrown this boat in my way, to carry me to some place from whence I might return into my native country, and begged his Majesty's orders for getting materials to fit it up, together with his license to depart; which, after some kind expostulations, he was pleased to grant.

I did very much wonder, in all this time, not to have heard of any express relating to me from our Emperor to the court of Blefuscu. But I was afterwards given privately to understand, that his Imperial Majesty, never imagining I had the least notice of his designs, believed I was only gone to Blefuscu 40 in performance of my promise, according to the license he had given me, which was well known at our court, and would return in a few days when that ceremony was ended. But he was at last in pain at my long absence; and after consulting with the Treasurer, and the rest of that cabal, a person of quality was dispatched with the copy of the articles against me. This envoy had instructions to represent to the monarch of Blefuscu, the great lenity of his master, who was content to punish me no farther than with the loss of my eyes; that I had fled from justice, and if I did not return in two hours, I should be deprived of my title of *Nardac,* and declared a traitor. The envoy further added, that in order to maintain the peace and amity between both empires, his master expected that his brother of Blefuscu would give orders to have me sent back to Lilliput, bound hand and foot, to be punished as a traitor.

10   The Emperor of Blefuscu having taken three days to consult, returned an answer consisting of many civilities and excuses. He said, that as for sending me bound, his brother knew it was impossible; that although I had deprived him of his fleet, yet he owed great obligations to me for many good offices I had done him in making the peace. That, however, both their Majesties would soon be made easy; for I had found a prodigious vessel on the shore, able to carry me on the sea, which he had given order to fit up with my own assistance and direction and he hoped in a few weeks both empires would be freed 20 from so insupportable an incumbrance.

With this answer the envoy returned to Lilliput, and the monarch of Blefuscu related to me all that had passed; offering me at the same time (but under the strictest confidence) his gracious protection, if I would continue in his service; wherein although I believed him sincere, yet I resolved never more to put any confidence in princes or ministers, where I could possibly avoid it; and therefore, with all due acknowledgments for his favorable intentions, I humbly begged to be excused. I told him, that since fortune, whether good or evil, 30 had thrown a vessel in my way, I was resolved to venture myself in the ocean, rather than be an occasion of difference between two such mighty monarchs. Neither did I find the Emperor at all displeased; and I discovered by a certain accident, that he was very glad of my resolution, and so were most of his ministers.

These considerations moved me to hasten my departure somewhat sooner than I intended; to which the court, impatient to have me gone, very readily contributed. Five hundred workmen were employed to make two sails to my boat, ac- 40 cording to my directions, by quilting thirteen fold of their strongest linen together. I was at the pains of making ropes and cables, by twisting ten, twenty, or thirty of the thickest and strongest of theirs. A great stone that I happened to find, after a long search, by the sea-shore, served me for an anchor. I had the tallow of three hundred cows for greasing my boat, and other uses. I was at incredible pains in cutting down some of the largest timber-trees for oars and masts, wherein I was, however, much assisted by his Majesty's ship-carpenters, who helped me in smoothing them, after I had done the rough work.

In about a month, when all was prepared, I sent to receive his Majesty's commands, and take my leave. The Emperor and Royal Family came out of the palace; I lay down on my face to kiss his hand, which he very graciously gave me: so did the Empress and young Princes of the blood. His Majesty presented me with fifty purses of two hundred *sprugs* apiece, together with his picture at full length, which I put immediately into one of my gloves, to keep it from being hurt. The ceremonies at my departure were too many to trouble the reader with at this time.

I stored the boat with the carcasses of an hundred oxen, and three hundred sheep, with bread and drink proportionable, and as much meat ready dressed as four hundred cooks could provide. I took with me six cows and two bulls alive, with as many ewes and rams, intending to carry them into my own country, and propagate the breed. And to feed them on board, I had a good bundle of hay, and a bag of corn. I would gladly have taken a dozen of the natives, but this was a thing the Emperor would by no means permit; and besides a diligent search into my pockets, his Majesty engaged my honor not to carry away any of his subjects, although with their own consent and desire.

Having thus prepared all things as well as I was able, I set sail on the twenty-fourth day of September, 1701, at six in the morning; and when I had gone about four leagues to the northward, the wind being at south-east; at six in the evening I descried a small island about half a league to the north-west. I advanced forward, and cast anchor on the lee-side of the island, which seemed to be uninhabited. I then took some refreshment, and went to my rest. I slept well, and as I conjecture at least six hours, for I found the day broke in two hours after I awaked. It was a clear night. I eat my breakfast before the sun was up; and heaving anchor, the wind being favorable, I steered the same course that I had done the day before, wherein I was directed by my pocket-compass. My intention was to reach, if possible, one of those islands, which I had reason to believe lay to the north-east of Van Diemen's Land. I discovered nothing all that day; but upon the next, about three in the afternoon, when I had by my computation made twenty-four leagues from Blefuscu, I descried a sail steering to the south-east; my course was due east. I hailed her, but could get no answer; yet I found I gained upon her, for the wind slackened. I made all the sail I could, and in half an hour she spied me, then hung out her ancient, and discharged a gun. It is not easy to express the joy I was in upon the unexpected hope of once more seeing my beloved country, and the dear pledges I had left in it. The ship slackened her sails, and I came up with her between five and six in the evening, September 26; but my heart leaped within me to see her English colors. I put my cows and sheep into my coat-pockets, and got on board with all my little cargo of provisions. The vessel was an English merchantman returning from Japan by the North and South Seas; the Captain, Mr. John Biddel of Deptford, a very civil man, and an excellent sailor. We were now in the latitude of 30 degrees south; there were about fifty men in the ship; and here I met an old comrade of mine, one Peter Williams, who gave me a good character to the Captain. This gentleman treated me with kindness, and desired I would let him know what place I came from last, and whither I was bound; which I did in a few words, but he thought I was raving, and that the dangers I underwent had disturbed my head; whereupon I took my black cattle and sheep out of my pocket, which, after great astonishment, clearly convinced him of my veracity. I then showed him the gold given me by the Emperor of Blefuscu, together with his Majesty's picture at full length, and some other rarities of that country. I gave him two purses of two hundred *sprugs* each, and promised, when we arrived in England, to make him a present of a cow and a sheep big with young.

I shall not trouble the reader with a particular account of this voyage, which was very prosperous for the most part. We arrived in the Downs on the 13th of April, 1702. I had only one misfortune, that the rats on board carried away one of my sheep; I found her bones in a hole, picked clean from the flesh. The rest of my cattle I got safe on shore, and set them a grazing in a bowling-green at Greenwich, where the fineness of the grass made them feed very heartily, though I had always feared the contrary: neither could I possibly have preserved them in so long a voyage, if the Captain had not allowed me some of his best biscuit, which, rubbed to powder, and mingled with water, was their constant food. The short time I continued in England, I made a considerable profit by showing my cattle to many persons of quality, and others: and before I began my second voyage, I sold them for six hundred pounds. Since my last return, I find the breed is considerably increased, especially the sheep; which I hope will prove much to the advantage of the woolen manufacture, by the fineness of the fleeces.

I stayed but two months with my wife and family; for my insatiable desire of seeing foreign countries would suffer me to continue no longer. I left fifteen hundred pounds with my wife, and fixed her in a good house at Redriff. My remaining stock I carried with me, part in money, and part in goods, in hopes to improve my fortunes. My eldest uncle John had left me an estate in land, near Epping, of about thirty pounds a year; and I had a long lease of the Black Bull in Fetter-Lane, which yielded me as much more; so that I was not in any danger of leaving my family upon the parish. My son Johnny, named so after his uncle, was at the Grammar School, and a towardly child. My daughter Betty (who is now well married, and has children) was then at her needle-work. I took leave of my wife, and boy and girl, with tears on both sides, and went on board the *Adventure*, a merchant-ship of three hundred tons, bound for Surat, Captain John Nicholas, of Liverpool, Commander. But my account of this voyage must be referred to the second part of my Travels.

A MODEST PROPOSAL

For Preventing the Children of Poor People from Being a Burden to Their Parents or Country, and for Making Them Beneficial to the Public

It is a melancholy object to those who walk through this great town [12] or travel in the country, when they see the streets, the roads, and cabin doors, crowded with beggars of the female sex, followed by three, four, or six children, all in rags and importuning every passenger for an alms. These mothers, instead of being able to work for their honest livelihood, are forced to employ all their time in strolling to beg sustenance for their helpless infants, who, as they grow up, either turn thieves for want of work, or leave their dear native country to fight for the Pretender in Spain, or sell themselves to the Barbadoes.

I think it is agreed by all parties that this prodigious number of children in the arms, or on the backs, or at the heels of their mothers, and frequently of their fathers, is in the present deplorable state of the kingdom a very great additional grievance; and therefore whoever could find out a fair, cheap, and easy method of making these children sound, useful members of the commonwealth, would deserve so well of the public as to have his statue set up for a preserver of the nation.

But my intention is very far from being confined to provide

12 Dublin

only for the children of professed beggars; it is of a much greater extent, and shall take in the whole number of infants at a certain age who are born of parents in effect as little able to support them as those who demand our charity in the streets.

As to my own part, having turned my thoughts for many years upon this important subject, and maturely weighed the several schemes of other projectors, I have always found them grossly mistaken in their computation. It is true, a child just
10 dropped from its dam may be supported by her milk for a solar year, with little other nourishment; at most not above the value of two shillings, which the mother may certainly get, or the value in scraps, by her lawful occupation of begging; and it is exactly at one year old that I propose to provide for them in such a manner as instead of being a charge upon their parents or the parish, or wanting food and raiment for the rest of their lives, they shall on the contrary contribute to the feeding, and partly to the clothing, of many thousands.

There is likewise another great advantage in my scheme,
20 that it will prevent those voluntary abortions, and that horrid practice of women murdering their bastard children, alas, too frequent among us, sacrificing the poor innocent babes I doubt more to avoid the expense than the shame, which would move tears and pity in the most savage and inhuman breast.

The number of souls in this kingdom being usually reckoned one million and a half, of these I calculate there may be about two hundred thousand couple whose wives are breeders; from which number I subtract thirty thousand couples who are able to maintain their own children, although I apprehend there
30 cannot be so many under the present distresses of the kingdom; but this being granted, there will remain an hundred and seventy thousand breeders. I again subtract fifty thousand for those women who miscarry, or whose children die by accident or disease within the year. There only remain an hundred and twenty thousand children of poor parents annually born. The question therefore is, how this number shall be reared and provided for, which, as I have already said, under the present situation of affairs, is utterly impossible by all the methods hitherto proposed. For we can neither employ them in
40 handicraft or agriculture; we neither build houses (I mean in the country) nor cultivate land. They can very seldom pick up a livelihood by stealing till they arrive at six years old, except where they are of towardly parts; although I confess they learn the rudiments much earlier, during which time they can however be looked upon only as probationers; as I have been informed by a principal gentleman in the county of Cavan,

who protested to me that he never knew above one or two instances under the age of six, even in a part of the kingdom so renowned for the quickest proficiency in that art.

I am assured by our merchants, that a boy or a girl before twelve years old is no saleable commodity; and even when they come to this age they will not yield above three pounds, or three pounds and half a crown at most on the Exchange; which cannot turn to account either to the parents or the kingdom, the charge of nutriment and rags having been at least four times that value.

I shall now therefore humbly propose my own thoughts, which I hope will not be liable to the least objection.

I have been assured by a very knowing American of my acquaintance in London, that a young healthy child well nursed is at a year old a most delicious, nourishing, and wholesome food, whether stewed, roasted, baked, or boiled; and I make no doubt that it will equally serve in a fricassee or a ragout.

I do therefore humbly offer it to public consideration that of the hundred and twenty thousand children already computed, twenty thousand may be reserved for breed, whereof only one fourth part to be males, which is more than we allow to sheep, black cattle, or swine; and my reason is, that these children are seldom the fruits of marriage, a circumstance not much regarded by our savages, therefore one male will be sufficient to serve four females. That the remaining hundred thousand may at a year old be offered in sale to the persons of quality and fortune through the kingdom; always advising the mother to let them suck plentifully in the last month, so as to render them plump and fat for a good table. A child will make two dishes at an entertainment for friends; and when the family dines alone, the fore or hind quarter will make a reasonable dish, and seasoned with a little pepper or salt will be very good boiled on the fourth day, especially in winter.

I have reckoned upon a medium that a child just born will weigh 12 pounds, and in a solar year if tolerably nursed increaseth to 28 pounds.

I grant this food will be somewhat dear, and therefore very proper for landlords, who, as they have already devoured most of the parents, seem to have the best title to the children.

Infant's flesh will be in season throughout the year, but more plentiful in March, and a little before and after. For we are told by a grave author, an eminent French physician, that fish being a prolific diet, there are more children born in Roman Catholic countries about nine months after Lent than at any other season; therefore, reckoning a year after Lent, the markets will be more glutted than usual, because the number of popish infants is at least three to one in this kingdom; and therefore it will have one other collateral advantage, by lessening the number of papists among us.

I have already computed the charge of nursing a beggar's child (in which list I reckon all cottagers, laborers, and four fifths of the farmers) to be about two shillings per annum, rags included; and I believe no gentleman would repine to give ten shillings for the carcass of a good fat child, which, as I have said, will make four dishes of excellent nutritive meat, when he hath only some particular friend or his own family to dine with him. Thus the squire will learn to be a good landlord, and grow popular among the tenants; the mother will have eight shillings net profit, and be fit for work till she produces another child.

Those who are more thrifty (as I must confess the times require) may flay the carcass; the skin of which artificially dressed will make admirable gloves for ladies, and summer boots for fine gentlemen.

As to our city of Dublin, shambles may be appointed for this purpose in the most convenient parts of it, and butchers we may be assured will not be wanting; although I rather recommend buying the children alive, and dressing them hot from the knife as we do roasting pigs.

A very worthy person, a true lover of his country, and whose virtues I highly esteem, was lately pleased in discoursing on this matter to offer a refinement upon my scheme. He said that many gentlemen of this kingdom, having of late destroyed their deer, he conceived that the want of venison might be well supplied by the bodies of young lads and maidens, not exceeding fourteen years of age nor under twelve; so great a number of both sexes in every country being now ready to starve for want of work and service; and these to be disposed of by their parents, if alive, or otherwise by their nearest relations. But with due deference to so excellent a friend and so deserving a patriot, I cannot be altogether in his sentiments; for as to the males, my American acquaintance assured me from frequent experience that their flesh was generally tough and lean, like that of our schoolboys, by continual exercise, and their taste disagreeable; and to fatten them would not answer the charge. Then as to the females, it would, I think with humble submission, be a loss to the public, because they soon would become breeders themselves: and besides, it is not improbable that some scrupulous people might be apt to censure such a practice (although indeed very unjustly) as a little bordering upon cruelty; which, I confess, has always been with me the strongest objection against any project, however so well intended.

But in order to justify my friend, he confessed that this expedient was put into his head by the famous Psalmanazar, a native of the island Formosa, who came from thence to London above twenty years ago, and in conversation told my friend, that in his country when any young person happened to be put to death, the executioner sold the carcass to persons of quality as a prime dainty; and that in his time the body of a plump girl of fifteen, who was crucified for an attempt to 10 poison the emperor, was sold to his Imperial Majesty's prime minister of state, and other great mandarins of the court, in joints from the gibbet, at four hundred crowns. Neither indeed can I deny, that if the same use were made of several plump young girls in this town, who without one single groat to their fortunes cannot stir abroad without a chair, and appear at the playhouse and assemblies in foreign fineries which they never will pay for, the kingdom would not be the worse.

Some persons of a desponding spirit are in great concern about that vast number of poor people who are aged, diseased, 20 or maimed, and I have been desired to employ my thoughts what course may be taken to ease the nation of so grievous an encumbrance. But I am not in the least pain upon that matter, because it is very well known that they are every day dying and rotting by cold and famine, and filth and vermin, as fast as can be reasonably expected. And as to the younger laborers, they are now in almost as hopeful a condition. They cannot get work, and consequently pine away for want of nourishment, to a degree that if at any time they are accidentally hired to common labor, they have not strength to perform it; 30 and thus the country and themselves are happily delivered from the evils to come.

I have too long digressed, and therefore shall return to my subject. I think the advantages by the proposal which I have made are obvious and many, as well as of the highest importance.

For first, as I have already observed, it would greatly lessen the number of papists, with whom we are yearly overrun, being the principal breeders of the nation as well as our most dangerous enemies; and who stay at home on purpose to deliver the 40 kingdom to the Pretender, hoping to take their advantage by the absence of so many good Protestants, who have chosen rather to leave their country than stay at home and pay tithes against their conscience to an episcopal curate.

Secondly, The poorer tenants will have something valuable of their own, which by law may be made liable to distress, and help to pay their landlord's rent, their corn and cattle being already seized, and money a thing unknown.

Thirdly, Whereas the maintenance of an hundred thousand children, from two years old and upwards, cannot be computed at less than ten shillings a piece per annum, the nation's stock will be thereby increased fifty thousand pounds per annum, besides the profit of a new dish introduced to the tables of all gentlemen of fortune in the kingdom who have any refinement 10 in taste. And the money will circulate among ourselves, the goods being entirely of our own growth and manufacture.

Fourthly, The constant breeders, besides the gain of eight shillings sterling per annum by the sale of their children, will be rid of the charge of maintaining them after the first year.

Fifthly, This food would likewise bring great custom to taverns, where the vintners will certainly be so prudent as to procure the best receipts for dressing it to perfection, and consequently have their houses frequented by all the fine gentlemen, who justly value themselves upon their knowledge in 20 good eating; and a skillful cook, who understands how to oblige his guests, will contrive to make it as expensive as they please.

Sixthly, This would be a great inducement to marriage, which all wise nations have either encouraged by rewards or enforced by laws and penalties. It would increase the care and tenderness of mothers toward their children, when they were sure of a settlement for life to the poor babes, provided in some sort by the public, to their annual profit instead of expense. We should see an honest emulation among the married 30 women, which of them could bring the fattest child to the market. Men would become as fond of their wives during the time of their pregnancy as they are now of their mares in foal, their cows in calf, or sows when they are ready to farrow; nor offer to beat or kick them (as is too frequent a practice) for fear of a miscarriage.

Many other advantages might be enumerated. For instance, the addition of some thousand carcasses in our exportation of barreled beef, the propagation of swine's flesh, and improvement in the art of making good bacon, so much wanted among 40 us by the great destruction of pigs, too frequent at our tables, which are no way comparable in taste or magnificence to a well-grown, fat, yearling child, which roasted whole will make a considerable figure at a lord mayor's feast or any other public entertainment. But this and many others I omit, being studious of brevity.

Supposing that one thousand families in this city would be

constant customers for infants' flesh, besides others who might
have it at merry-meetings, particularly weddings and christen-
ings, I compute that Dublin would take off annually about
twenty thousand carcasses; and the rest of the kingdom (where
probably they will be sold somewhat cheaper) the remaining
eighty thousand.

I can think of no one objection that will possibly be raised
against this proposal, unless it should be urged that the number of people will be thereby much lessened in the kingdom.
This I freely own, and it was indeed one principal design in
offering it to the world. I desire the reader will observe, that
I calculate my remedy for this one individual kingdom of Ireland and for no other that ever was, is, or I think ever can be
upon earth. Therefore let no man talk to me of other expedients: of taxing our absentees at five shillings a pound:
of using neither clothes nor household furniture except what
is of our own growth and manufacture: of utterly rejecting
the materials and instruments that promote foreign luxury:
of curing the expensiveness of pride, vanity, idleness, and gam-
ing in our women: of introducing a vein of parsimony, prudence, and temperance: of learning to love our country, in the
want of which we differ even from LAPLANDERS and the
inhabitants of TOPINAMBOO: of quitting our animosities and
factions, nor acting any longer like the Jews, who were
murdering one another at the very moment their city was
taken: of being a little cautious not to sell our country and
conscience for nothing: of teaching landlords to have at least
one degree of mercy toward their tenants: lastly, of putting a
spirit of honesty, industry, and skill into our shopkeepers;
who, if a resolution could now be taken to buy only our native
goods, would immediately unite to cheat and exact upon us in
the price, the measure, and the goodness, nor could ever yet
be brought to make one fair proposal of just dealing, though
often and earnestly invited to it.

Therefore I repeat, let no man talk to me of these and the
like expedients, till he hath at least some glimpse of hope that
there will ever be some hearty and sincere attempt to put them
in practice.

But as to myself, having been wearied out for many years
with offering vain, idle, visionary thoughts, and at length utterly despairing of success, I fortunately fell upon this proposal; which, as it is wholly new, so it hath something solid
and real, of no expense and little trouble, full in our own power,
and whereby we can incur no danger in disobliging ENG-
LAND. For this kind of commodity will not bear exportation, the flesh being of too tender a consistence to admit a

long continuance in salt, although perhaps I could name a country which would be glad to eat up our whole nation without it.

After all, I am not so violently bent upon my own opinion as to reject any offer proposed by wise men, which shall be found equally innocent, cheap, easy, and effectual. But before something of that kind shall be advanced in contradiction to my scheme, and offering a better, I desire the author or authors will be pleased maturely to consider two points. First, 10 as things now stand, how they will be able to find food and raiment for an hundred thousand useless mouths and backs. And secondly, there being a round million of creatures in human figure throughout this kingdom, whose sole subsistence put into a common stock would leave them in debt two millions of pounds sterling, adding those who are beggars by profession to the bulk of farmers, cottagers, and laborers, with their wives and children who are beggars in effect; I desire those politicians who dislike my overture, and may perhaps be so bold to attempt an answer, that they will first ask 20 the parents of these mortals, whether they would not at this day think it a great happiness to have been sold for food at a year old in the manner I prescribe, and thereby have avoided such a perpetual scene of misfortunes as they have since gone through by the oppression of landlords, the impossibility of paying rent without money or trade, the want of common sustenance, with neither house nor clothes to cover them from the inclemencies of the weather, and the most inevitable prospect of entailing the like or greater miseries upon their breed for ever.

30   I profess, in the sincerity of my heart, that I have not the least personal interest in endeavoring to promote this necessary work, having no other motive than the public good of my country, by advancing our trade, providing for infants, relieving the poor, and giving some pleasure to the rich. I have no children by which I can propose to get a single penny; the youngest being nine years old, and my wife past child-bearing.

JOSEPH ADDISON (1672–1719)
SIR RICHARD STEELE (1672–1729)

The names of Addison and Steele are inseparably connected. They were born in the same year, they were for a while fellows together at school and at college, in mature life they were friends, and they collaborated in the publication of the famous periodicals *Tatler* and *Spectator*.

Addison was born on May 1, 1672, at the small town of Milston, in Wiltshire, where his father was at the time rector. In 1686 he went to the Charterhouse School in London, where he made the acquaintance of Steele. In 1687 he entered Oxford, remaining in various capacities for some twelve years. Coming up to London, he obtained advancement by a means common in the eighteenth century—that of political writing, attaching himself to the Whig party. His fortunes were made by his poem, *The Campaign*, celebrating Marlborough's victory at Blenheim in 1704, and thereafter he was given various important posts, so long as the Whigs were in power. He was in turn an Under-Secretary of State, a member of Parliament, Chief Secretary to the Lord Lieutenant of Ireland, Keeper of the Irish records, a Lord of Trade, and finally full Secretary of State, and was granted a retiring pension on his abandoning public life in 1718.

Meantime he had done a good deal of varied writing. His tragedy of *Cato* (1713), based on classical models, was much admired in its own time, but is now considered frigid and dull. His more enduring fame is based upon his periodical essays. In 1709 Steele had started the *Tatler,* to which Addison contributed about forty papers, and in 1711 and 1712, with a brief revival in 1714, the two friends conducted the famous *Spectator,* with Addison in control. In 1716 he had married the Countess Dowager of Warwick. He is said to have been henpecked. He died at his wife's residence, Holland House, on June 17, 1719.

For two centuries his essay style has been regarded as the ultimate achievement of its kind—a model of urbanity, propriety, and polish. The words of Dr. Johnson are a final criticism on its excellences: "Whoever wishes to attain an English style, familiar but not coarse, and elegant but not ostentatious, must give his days and nights to the volumes of Addison."

In character Addison was shy, retiring, and exceedingly reserved; so much so, that few men felt they knew him intimately and fewer still that they understood him; he seemed unimpassioned and cold. For these reasons his essential magnanimity and kindness were not always appreciated. The charm of his manners and his conversation made him one of the most admired men of his day; yet only to small groups of close friends were these qualities fully revealed.

Very different was warm-hearted, impulsive Richard Steele. He was born in Dublin, in March, 1672, of an English father and an Irish mother. He was sent to Charterhouse School in 1684, to which, somewhat later, came Addison. In 1689 he entered Christ Church College, Oxford, on a Charterhouse exhibition, or scholarship. In 1694 he left Oxford without taking a degree, and enlisted in the Horse Guards. For some ten years he remained in the army, and rose to the rank of captain. A production of these years which has amused many, although doubtless written in all sincerity, is a treatise on morals, *The Christian Hero* (1701). In the same period he wrote several plays, which are identified with the school of sentimental comedy. Since the days of Wycherly and Congreve, a change in public taste had set in—a change of which Steele, with his strong tendency toward moralization, became a leading voice. His plays retain outwardly much of the atmosphere of Restoration comedy, but in them the sympathy is shifted from the reckless rake and debauchee to the victims of his passion. *The Funeral, The Tender Husband,* and *The Lying Lover* (1702, 1703, and 1704) all exhibit these altered standards, and even more strikingly *The Conscious Lovers,* written toward the end of Steele's career (1722). His interest in the theatre, although intermitted in middle life, when other activities engaged his attention, never died. In his later years, he was a patentee of Drury Lane Theater.

Steele's connection with periodical literature began on his appointment in

668 to the SIR RICHARD STEELE

1707 to the office of Gazetteer. By this appointment he became a minor member of the Government, whose duty was the editing of official news. While conducting the *Gazette* he conceived the idea of a more general periodical of news and literature, and the *Tatler* (1709 to 1711) was the result, to be followed by the *Spectator*. At later periods Steele ran the *Guardian* and the *Englishman*, so that his position in the development of periodical literature is one of the greatest importance. The latter magazines were concerned more and more with politics, and less with general literature. His championship of the Whig cause, in these sheets and elsewhere, brought him several political appointments during the earlier years of George I, and knighthood in 1715. He died in 1729.

Steele's manner in the *Tatler* and *Spectator* papers is often contrasted with Addison's. It is less careful, less rhetorical than Addison's; less "correct" and less "elegant" (to use those favorite eighteenth century epithets). It is closer to the level of common speech, more personal, more "journalistic" (to use a familiar epithet of our own time). Yet it has a pleasant informal charm.

It expresses on every page the man—his warm and generous heart, his quick sympathies, and his sincere, if somewhat naïve and sometimes amusing morality. His high professions of conduct he could not himself live up to. He frequently lapsed from grace. He was inconsistent and imprudent; ran through his money (and his wife's), and got into innumerable scrapes; repented and reformed, only to fall again. But in spite of these weaknesses (perhaps because of them) he remains one of the most human and lovable of our writers.

BIBLIOGRAPHY. Collected ed. of Addison's Works in Bohn Lib., 6 vols. Steele's plays in Mermaid ed. (Scribner's) by G. A. Aitken. *Spectator* often reprinted; Everyman's ed. (Dutton) complete and convenient. Excellent sel. in Athenæum Press ser. (Ginn), from Addison by B. Wendell and C. N. Greenough, and from Steele by G. R. Carpenter. Lives in Eng. Men of Letters ser. by W. J. Courthope and by Austin Dobson respectively. G. A. Aitken's *Life of Steele*, 2 vols.

SIR RICHARD STEELE
THE TATLER

PROSPECTUS

No. 1. TUESDAY, APRIL 12, 1709.

Quicquid agunt homines——
nostri est farrago libelli.[1]
—JUV. *Sat.* i. 85, 86.

THOUGH the other papers which are published for the use of the good people of England have certainly very wholesome effects, and are laudable in their particular kinds, they do not seem to come up to the main design of such narrations, which, I humbly presume, should be principally intended for the use

---

1 Whate'er men do, or say, or think, or dream,
Our motley paper seizes for its theme.—Pope.

of politic persons, who are so public-spirited as to neglect their own affairs to look into transactions of state. Now these gentlemen, for the most part, being persons of strong zeal, and weak intellects, it is both a charitable and necessary work to offer something, whereby such worthy and well-affected members of the commonwealth may be instructed, after their reading, what to think; which shall be the end and purpose of this my paper, wherein I shall, from time to time, report and consider all matters of what kind soever that shall occur to me, and publish such my advices and reflections every Tuesday, 10 Thursday, and Saturday in the week, for the convenience of the post. I resolve also to have something which may be of entertainment to the fair sex, in honor of whom I have invented the title of this paper. I therefore earnestly desire all persons, without distinction, to take it in for the present *gratis,* and hereafter at the price of one penny, forbidding all hawkers to take more for it at their peril. And I desire all persons to consider, that I am at a very great charge for proper materials for this work, as well as that, before I resolved upon it, I had settled a correspondence in all parts of the known and know- 20 ing world. And forasmuch as this globe is not trodden upon by mere drudges of business only, but that men of spirit and genius are justly to be esteemed as considerable agents in it, we shall not, upon a dearth of news, present you with musty foreign edicts, or dull proclamations, but shall divide our relation of the passages which occur in action or discourse throughout this town, as well as elsewhere, under such dates of places as may prepare you for the matter you are to expect in the following manner.

All accounts of gallantry, pleasure, and entertainment, shall 30 be under the article of White's Chocolate-house; poetry under that of Will's Coffee-house; learning, under the title of Grecian; foreign and domestic news, you will have from St. James's Coffee-house;[2] and what else I have to offer on any other subject shall be dated from my own Apartment.

I once more desire my reader to consider, that as I cannot keep an ingenious man to go daily to Will's under two-pence each day, merely for his charges; to White's under six-pence; nor to the Grecian, without allowing him some plain Spanish,[3] to be as able as others at the learned table; and that a good 40 observer cannot speak with even Kidney[4] at St. James's without clean linen; I say, these considerations will, I hope, make all persons willing to comply with my humble request (when

2 Steele indicates the types of people who frequented the several houses. These institutions served as informal clubs, and were important in the social, political, and literary life of the period. 3 a wine 4 a waiter

my *gratis* stock is exhausted) of a penny apiece; especially since they are sure of some proper amusement, and that it is impossible for me to want means to entertain them, having, besides the force of my own parts, the power of divination, and that I can, by casting a figure,[5] tell you all that will happen before it comes to pass.

But this last faculty I shall use very sparingly, and speak but of few things until they are passed, for fear of divulging matters which may offend our superiors.[6]

DUELING

No. 25. TUESDAY, JUNE 7, 1709.

WHITE'S CHOCOLATE HOUSE

A letter from a young lady, written in the most passionate terms, wherein she laments the misfortune of a gentleman, her lover, who was lately wounded in a duel, has turned my thoughts to that subject, and inclined me to examine into the causes which precipitate men into so fatal a folly. And as it has been proposed to treat of subjects of gallantry in the article from hence, and no one point in nature is more proper to be considered by the company who frequent this place than that of duels, it is worth our consideration to examine into this chimerical groundless humor, and to lay every other thought aside, until we have stripped it of all its false pretenses to credit and reputation amongst men.

But I must confess, when I consider what I am going about, and run over in my imagination all the endless crowd of men of honor who will be offended at such a discourse, I am undertaking, methinks, a work worthy an invulnerable hero in romance, rather than a private gentleman with a single rapier; but as I am pretty well acquainted by great opportunities with the nature of man, and know of a truth that all men fight against their will, the danger vanishes, and resolution rises upon this subject. For this reason, I shall talk very freely on a custom which all men wish exploded, though no man has courage enough to resist it.

But there is one unintelligible word, which I fear will extremely perplex my dissertation, and I confess to you I find very hard to explain, which is the term "satisfaction." An honest country gentleman had the misfortune to fall into company with two or three modern men of honor, where he hap-

5 horoscope
6 The rest of the essay, here omitted, contains letters from the three coffee-houses and from "my own apartment."

pened to be very ill-treated; and one of the company, being
conscious of his offense, sends a note to him in the morning, and
tells him, he was ready to give him satisfaction. "This is fine
doing," says the plain fellow; "last night he sent me away
cursedly out of humor, and this morning he fancies it would be
a satisfaction to be run through the body."

As the matter at present stands, it is not to do handsome
actions denominates a man of honor; it is enough if he dares
to defend ill ones. Thus you often see a common sharper in
competition with a gentleman of the first rank; though all 10
mankind is convinced that a fighting gamester is only a pick-
pocket with the courage of an highwayman. One cannot with
any patience reflect on the unaccountable jumble of persons
and things in this town and nation, which occasions very frequently that a brave man falls by a hand below that of a common hangman, and yet his executioner escapes the clutches of
the hangman for doing it. I shall therefore hereafter consider
how the bravest men in other ages and nations have behaved
themselves upon such incidents as we decide by combat; and
show, from their practice, that this resentment neither has its 20
foundation from true reason or solid fame; but is an impos-
ture, made of cowardice, falsehood, and want of understanding. For this work, a good history of quarrels would be very
edifying to the public, and I apply myself to the town for
particulars and circumstances within their knowledge, which
may serve to embellish the dissertation with proper cuts.
Most of the quarrels I have ever known have proceeded from
some valiant coxcomb's persisting in the wrong, to defend some
prevailing folly, and preserve himself from the ingenuity of owning a mistake.   30

By this means it is called "giving a man satisfaction" to
urge your offense against him with your sword; which puts me
in mind of Peter's order to the keeper, in *The Tale of a Tub:* [7]
"If you neglect to do all this, damn you and your generation
for ever: and so we bid you heartily farewell." If the contradiction in the very terms of one of our challenges were as
well explained and turned into downright English, would it
not run after this manner?

"SIR,

"Your extraordinary behavior last night, and the liberty 40
you were pleased to take with me, makes me this morning
give you this, to tell you, because you are an ill-bred puppy,
I will meet you in Hyde Park an hour hence; and because you
want both breeding and humanity, I desire you would come
with a pistol in your hand, on horseback, and endeavor to

7 by Swift

shoot me through the head to teach you more manners. If you fail of doing me this pleasure, I shall say, you are a rascal, on every post in town: and so, sir, if you will not injure me more, I shall never forgive what you have done already. Pray, sir, do not fail of getting everything ready; and you will infinitely oblige, sir, your most obedient humble servant, etc." . . .

MEMORIES OF SORROW

No. 181. TUESDAY, JUNE 6, 1710.
—Dies, ni fallor, adest, quem semper acerbum,
Semper honoratum, sic dii voluistis habebo.[8]

VIR. AEN. v. 49.

There are those among mankind who can enjoy no relish of their being except the world is made acquainted with all
10 that relates to them, and think everything lost that passes unobserved; but others find a solid delight in stealing by a crowd, and modeling their life after such a manner as is as much above the approbation as the practice of the vulgar. Life being too short to give instances great enough of true friendship or good will, some sages have thought it pious to preserve a certain reverence for the Manes[9] of their deceased friends; and have withdrawn themselves from the rest of the world at certain seasons to commemorate in their own thoughts such of their acquaintance who have gone before them out
20 of this life. And indeed, when we are advanced in years, there is not a more pleasing entertainment than to recollect in a gloomy moment the many we have parted with that have been dear and agreeable to us, and to cast a melancholy thought or two after those with whom, perhaps, we have indulged ourselves in whole nights of mirth and jollity. With such inclinations in my heart I went to my closet[10] yesterday in the evening, and resolved to be sorrowful; upon which occasion I could not but look with disdain upon myself, that though all the reasons which I had to lament the loss of many of my
30 friends are now as forcible as at the moment of their departure, yet did not my heart swell with the same sorrow which I felt at that time; but I could, without tears, reflect upon many pleasant adventures I have had with some who have long been blended with common earth.

Though it is by the benefit of nature that length of time thus blots out the violence of afflictions; yet with tempers too

8 And now the rising day renews the year,   9 spirits
A day for ever sad, for ever dear.   10 private room

much given to pleasure, it is almost necessary to revive the
old places of grief in our memory; and ponder step by step
on past life, to lead the mind into that sobriety of thought
which poises the heart and makes it beat with due time, without being quickened with desire, or retarded with despair, from
its proper and equal motion. When we wind up a clock that is
out of order to make it go well for the future, we do not immediately set the hand to the present instant, but we make
it strike the round of all its hours before it can recover the
regularity of its time. Such, thought I, shall be my method 10
this evening; and since it is that day of the year which I dedicate to the memory of such in another life as I much delighted
in when living, an hour or two shall be sacred to sorrow and
their memory, while I run over all the melancholy circumstances of this kind which have occurred to me in my whole
life. The first sense of sorrow I ever knew was upon the death
of my father, at which time I was not quite five years of age;
but was rather amazed at what all the house meant than possessed with a real understanding why nobody was willing to
play with me. I remember I went into the room where his 20
body lay, and my mother sat weeping alone by it. I had my
battledore in my hand, and fell a-beating the coffin, and calling papa; for, I know not how, I had some slight idea that
he was locked up there. My mother catched me in her arms,
and, transported beyond all patience of the silent grief she was
before in, she almost smothered me in her embrace; and told
me, in a flood of tears, "Papa could not hear me, and would
play with me no more, for they were going to put him underground, whence he could never come to us again." She was a
very beautiful woman, of a noble spirit, and there was a dig- 30
nity in her grief amidst all the wildness of her transport, which,
methought, struck me with an instinct of sorrow that, before
I was sensible of what it was to grieve, seized my very soul,
and has made pity the weakness of my heart ever since. The
mind in infancy is, methinks, like the body in embryo, and
receives impressions so forcible that they are as hard to be
removed by reason as any mark with which a child is born
is to be taken away by any future application. Hence, it is
that good nature in me is no merit; but having been so frequently overwhelmed with her tears before I knew the cause 40
of any affliction, or could draw defences from my own judgment, I imbibed commiseration, remorse, and an unmanly
gentleness of mind which has since ensnared me into ten thousand calamities; from whence I can reap no advantage, except
it be that in such a humor as I am now in, I can the better
indulge myself in the softnesses of humanity, and enjoy that

sweet anxiety which arises from the memory of past afflictions. We that are very old are better able to remember things which befell us in our distant youth than the passages of later days. For this reason it is that the companions of my strong and vigorous years present themselves more immediately to me in this office of sorrow. Untimely and unhappy deaths are what we are most apt to lament; so little are we able to make it indifferent when a thing happens, though we know it must happen. Thus we groan under life, and bewail those who are

10 relieved from it. Every object that returns to our imagination raises different passions according to the circumstances of their departure. Who can have lived in an army, and in a serious hour reflect upon the many gay and agreeable men that might long have flourished in the arts of peace, and not join with the imprecations of the fatherless and widow on the tyrant to whose ambition they fell sacrifices? But gallant men who are cut off by the sword move rather our veneration than our pity; and we gather relief enough from their own contempt of death to make that no evil which was approached with so much

20 cheerfulness and attended with so much honor. But when we turn our thoughts from the great parts of life on such occasions, and instead of lamenting those who stood ready to give death to those from whom they had the fortune to receive it; I say, when we let our thoughts wander from such noble objects, and consider the havoc which is made among the tender and the innocent, pity enters with an unmixed softness, and possesses all our souls at once.

Here (were there words to express such sentiments with proper tenderness) I should record the beauty, innocence, and

30 untimely death of the first object my eyes ever beheld with love. The beauteous virgin! how ignorantly did she charm, how carelessly excel! Oh, Death! thou hast right to the bold, to the ambitious, to the high, and to the haughty; but why this cruelty to the humble, to the meek, to the undiscerning, to the thoughtless? Nor age, nor business, nor distress can erase the dear image from my imagination. In the same week I saw her dressed for a ball and in a shroud. How ill did the habit of death become the pretty trifler! I still behold the smiling earth— A large train of disasters were coming on to my mem-

40 ory, when my servant knocked at my closet door, and interrupted me with a letter, attended with a hamper of wine, of the same sort with that which is to be put on sale, on Thursday next, at Garraway's coffee-house. Upon the receipt of it, I sent for three of my friends. We are so intimate that we can be company in whatever state of mind we meet and can entertain each other without expecting always to rejoice. The

wine we found to be generous and warming, but with such an heat as moved us rather to be cheerful than frolicsome. It revived the spirits without firing the blood. We commended it until two of the clock this morning; and having to-day met a little before dinner, we found, that though we drank two bottles a man, we had much more reason to recollect than forget what had passed the night before.

[Note—The Spectator, No. 2, given below, is also by Steele.]

JOSEPH ADDISON

THE SPECTATOR

MR. SPECTATOR

No. 1. Thursday, March 1, 1711.

Non fumum ex fulgore, sed ex fumo dare lucem
Cogitat, ut speciosa dehinc miracula promat.[11]
—Horace.

I have observed that a reader seldom peruses a book with pleasure till he knows whether the writer of it be a black or a fair man, of a mild or choleric disposition, married or a bachelor, with other particulars of the like nature that conduce very much to the right understanding of an author. To gratify this curiosity, which is so natural to a reader, I design this paper and my next as prefatory discourses to my following writings, and shall give some account in them of the several persons that are engaged in this work. As the chief trouble of compiling, digesting, and correcting will fall to my share, I must do myself the justice to open the work with my own history.

I was born to a small hereditary estate, which, according to the tradition of the village where it lies, was bounded by the same hedges and ditches in William the Conqueror's time that it is at present, and has been delivered down from father to son whole and entire, without the loss or acquisition of a single field or meadow, during the space of six hundred years. There runs a story in the family, that when my mother was gone with child of me about three months, she dreamt that she was brought to bed of a judge. Whether this might proceed from a lawsuit which was then depending in the family,

---

11 Not smoke from fire his object is to bring,
But fire from smoke, a very different thing.

or my father's being a justice of the peace, I cannot determine; for I am not so vain as to think it presaged any dignity that I should arrive at in my future life, though that was the interpretation which the neighborhood put upon it. The gravity of my behavior at my very first appearance in the world and all the time that I sucked, seemed to favor my mother's dream; for, as she has often told me, I threw away my rattle before I was two months old, and would not make use of my coral till they had taken away the bells from it.

As for the rest of my infancy, there being nothing in it remarkable, I shall pass it over in silence. I find that, during my nonage, I had the reputation of a very sullen youth, but was always a favorite of my schoolmaster, who used to say that *my parts were solid and would wear well.* I had not been long at the University before I distinguished myself by a most profound silence; for during the space of eight years, excepting in the public exercises of the college, I scarce uttered the quantity of an hundred words; and indeed do not remember that I ever spoke three sentences together in my whole life. Whilst I was in this learned body, I applied myself with so much diligence to my studies that there are very few celebrated books, either in the learned or modern tongues, which I am not acquainted with.

Upon the death of my father I was resolved to travel into foreign countries, and therefore left the University with the character of an odd, unaccountable fellow, that had a great deal of learning if I would but show it. An insatiable thirst after knowledge carried me into all the countries of Europe in which there was anything new or strange to be seen; nay, to such a degree was my curiosity raised, that having read the controversies of some great men concerning the antiquities of Egypt, I made a voyage to Grand Cairo, on purpose to take the measure of a pyramid; and as soon as I had set myself right in that particular, returned to my native country with great satisfaction.

I have passed my latter years in this city, where I am frequently seen in most public places, though there are not above half a dozen of my select friends that know me; of whom my next paper shall give a more particular account. There is no place of general resort wherein I do not often make my appearance. Sometimes I am seen thrusting my head into a round of politicians at Will's, and listening with great attention to the narratives that are made in those little circular audiences. Sometimes I smoke a pipe at Child's, and whilst I seem attentive to nothing but *The Postman,* overhear the conversation of every table in the room. I appear on Sunday nights at St. James's Coffee-house, and sometimes join the little committee of politics in the Inner Room, as one who comes there to hear and improve. My face is likewise very well known at the Grecian, the Cocoa-Tree, and in the theaters both of Drury Lane and the Haymarket. I have been taken for a merchant upon the Exchange for above these ten years, and sometimes pass for a Jew in the assembly of stock-jobbers at Jonathan's. In short, wherever I see a cluster of people, I always mix with them, though I never open my lips but in my own club.

Thus I live in the world rather as a SPECTATOR of mankind than as one of the species; by which means I have made myself a speculative statesman, soldier, merchant, and artisan, without ever meddling with any practical part in life. I am very well versed in the theory of a husband or a father, and can discern the errors in the economy, business, and diversion of others better than those who are engaged in them; as standers-by discover blots which are apt to escape those who are in the game. I never espoused any party with violence, and am resolved to observe an exact neutrality between the Whigs and Tories, unless I shall be forced to declare myself by the hostilities of either side. In short, I have acted in all the parts of my life as a looker-on, which is the character I intend to preserve in this paper.

I have given the reader just so much of my history and character as to let him see I am not altogether unqualified for the business I have undertaken. As for other particulars in my life and adventures, I shall insert them in following papers as I shall see occasion. In the meantime, when I consider how much I have seen, read, and heard, I begin to blame my own taciturnity; and since I have neither time nor inclination to communicate the fullness of my heart in speech, I am resolved to do it in writing, and to print myself out, if possible, before I die. I have been often told by my friends that it is a pity so many useful discoveries which I have made should be in the possession of a silent man. For this reason, therefore, I shall publish a sheetful of thoughts every morning for the benefit of my contemporaries; and if I can any way contribute to the diversion or improvement of the country in which I live, I shall leave it, when I am summoned out of it, with the secret satisfaction of thinking that I have not lived in vain.

There are three very material points which I have not spoken to in this paper, and which, for several important reasons, I must keep to myself, at least for some time: I mean, an account of my name, my age, and my lodgings. I must confess, I would gratify my reader in anything that is reasonable; but, as for these three particulars, though I am sensible they might tend very much to the embellishment of my paper, I cannot yet come to a resolution of communicating them to the public. They would indeed draw me out of that obscurity which I have enjoyed for many years, and expose me in public places to several salutes and civilities which have been always very disagreeable to me; for the greatest pain I can suffer is the being talked to and being stared at. It is for this reason, 10 likewise, that I keep my complexion and dress as very great secrets, though it is not impossible but I may make discoveries of both in the progress of the work I have undertaken.

After having been thus particular upon myself, I shall in tomorrow's paper give an account of those gentlemen who are concerned with me in this work; for, as I have before intimated, a plan of it is laid and concerted (as all other matters of importance are) in a club. However, as my friends have engaged me to stand in the front, those who have a mind to correspond with me may direct their letters *To The Spectator,* 20 *at Mr. Buckley's, in Little Britain.* For I must further acquaint the reader that, though our club meets only on Tuesdays and Thursdays, we have appointed a committee to sit every night for the inspection of all such papers as may contribute to the advancement of the public weal.

THE CLUB

[*This number is by Sir Richard Steele*]

No. 2. FRIDAY, MARCH 2, 1711.

——*Ast alii sex*

Et plures uno conclamant ore.[12]

—JUVENAL.

The first of our society is a gentleman of Worcestershire, of ancient descent, a baronet, his name Sir Roger de Coverley. His great-grandfather was inventor of that famous country-dance which is called after him. All who know that shire are very well acquainted with the parts and merits of Sir Roger. 30 He is a gentleman that is very singular in his behavior, but his singularities proceed from his good sense, and are contradictions to the manners of the world only as he thinks the world is in the wrong. However, this humor creates him no enemies, for he does nothing with sourness or obstinacy; and his being

12 Six others and more cry out with one voice

unconfined to modes and forms, makes him but the readier and more capable to please and oblige all who know him. When he is in town, he lives in Soho Square. It is said he keeps himself a bachelor by reason he was crossed in love by a perverse, beautiful widow of the next county to him. Before this disappointment, Sir Roger was what you call a fine gentleman, had often supped with my Lord Rochester and Sir George Etherege, fought a duel upon his first coming to town, and kicked Bully Dawson in a public coffee-house for calling him "youngster." But being ill-used by the above-mentioned widow, he was very serious for a year and a half; and though, his temper being naturally jovial, he at last got over it, he grew careless of himself, and never dressed afterward. He continues to wear a coat and doublet of the same cut that were in fashion at the time of his repulse, which, in his merry humors, he tells us, has been in and out twelve times since he first wore it. 'Tis said Sir Roger grew humble in his desires after he had forgot this cruel beauty, insomuch that it is reported he has frequently offended in point of chastity with beggars and gypsies; but this is looked upon by his friends rather as matter of raillery than truth. He is now in his fifty-sixth year, cheerful, gay, and hearty; keeps a good house both in town and country; a great lover of mankind; but there is such a mirthful cast in his behavior that he is rather beloved than esteemed. His tenants grow rich, his servants look satisfied, all the young women profess love to him, and the young men are glad of his company; when he comes into a house he calls the servants by their names, and talks all the way up stairs to a visit. I must not omit that Sir Roger is a justice of the quorum; that he fills the chair at a quarter-session with great abilities; and, three months ago, gained universal applause by explaining a passage in the Game Act.

The gentleman next in esteem and authority among us is another bachelor, who is a member of the Inner Temple; [13] a man of great probity, wit, and understanding; but he has chosen his place of residence rather to obey the direction of an old humorsome father, than in pursuit of his own inclinations. He was placed there to study the laws of the land, and is the most learned of any of the house in those of the stage. Aristotle and Longinus are much better understood by him than Littleton or Coke.[14] The father sends up, every post, questions relating to marriage-articles, leases, and tenures, in the neighborhood; all which questions he agrees with an attorney to

---

13 one of the "Inns of Court," where law was studied, and where law-yers had their offices, and often their lodgings 14 *i.e.,* understood the rhetoricians better than the writers on law

answer and take care of in the lump. He is studying the passions themselves, when he should be inquiring into the debates among men which arise from them. He knows the argument of each of the orations of Demosthenes and Tully,[15] but not one case in the reports of our own courts. No one ever took him for a fool, but none, except his intimate friends, know he has a great deal of wit. This turn makes him at once both disinterested and agreeable; as few of his thoughts are drawn from business, they are most of them fit for conversation. His
10 taste of books is a little too just for the age he lives in; he has read all, but approves of very few. His familiarity with the customs, manners, actions, and writings of the ancients makes him a very delicate observer of what occurs to him in the present world. He is an excellent critic, and the time of the play is his hour of business; exactly at five he passes through New Inn, crosses through Russell Court, and takes a turn at Will's till the play begins; he has his shoes rubbed and his periwig powdered at the barber's as you go into the Rose. It is for the good of the audience when he is at a play, for the actors have
20 an ambition to please him.

The person of next consideration is Sir Andrew Freeport, a merchant of great eminence in the city of London, a person of indefatigable industry, strong reason, and great experience. His notions of trade are noble and generous, and (as every rich man has usually some sly way of jesting which would make no great figure were he not a rich man) he calls the sea the British Common. He is acquainted with commerce in all its parts, and will tell you that it is a stupid and barbarous way to extend dominion by arms; for true power is to be
30 got by arts and industry. He will often argue that if this part of our trade were well cultivated, we should gain from one nation; and if another, from another. I have heard him prove that diligence makes more lasting acquisitions than valor, and that sloth has ruined more nations than the sword. He abounds in several frugal maxims, among which the greatest favorite is, "A penny saved is a penny got." A general trader of good sense is pleasanter company than a general scholar; and Sir Andrew having a natural unaffected eloquence, the perspicuity of his discourse gives the same pleasure that wit would in
40 another man. He has made his fortunes himself, and says that England may be richer than other kingdoms by as plain methods as he himself is richer than other men; though at the same time I can say this of him, that there is not a point in the compass but blows home a ship in which he is an owner.

Next to Sir Andrew in the club-room sits Captain Sentry

15 Cicero

a gentleman of great courage, good understanding, but invincible modesty. He is one of those that deserve very well, but are very awkward at putting their talents within the observation of such as should take notice of them. He was some years a captain, and behaved himself with great gallantry in several engagements and at several sieges; but having a small estate of his own, and being next heir to Sir Roger, he has quitted a way of life in which no man can rise suitably to his merit who is not something of a courtier as well as a soldier. I have heard him often lament that in a profession where merit is placed in so conspicuous a view, impudence should get the better of modesty. When he has talked to this purpose I never heard him make a sour expression, but frankly confess that he left the world because he was not fit for it. A strict honesty and an even, regular behavior are in themselves obstacles to him that must press through crowds who endeavor at the same end with himself,—the favor of a commander. He will, however, in his way of talk, excuse generals for not disposing according to men's desert, or inquiring into it, "for," says he, "that great man who has a mind to help me, has as many to break through to come at me as I have to come at him"; therefore he will conclude that the man who would make a figure, especially in a military way, must get over all false modesty, and assist his patron against the importunity of other pretenders by a proper assurance in his own vindication. He says it is a civil cowardice to be backward in asserting what you ought to expect, as it is a military fear to be slow in attacking when it is your duty. With this candor does the gentleman speak of himself and others. The same frankness runs through all his conversation. The military part of his life has furnished him with many adventures, in the relation of which he is very agreeable to the company; for he is never overbearing, though accustomed to command men in the utmost degree below him; nor ever too obsequious from an habit of obeying men highly above him.

But that our society may not appear a set of humorists [16] unacquainted with the gallantries and pleasures of the age, we have among us the gallant Will Honeycomb, a gentleman who, according to his years, should be in the decline of his life, but having ever been very careful of his person, and always had a very easy fortune, time has made but very little impression either by wrinkles on his forehead or traces in his brain. His person is well turned and of a good height. He is very ready at that sort of discourse with which men usually entertain women. He has all his life dressed very well, and

16 odd or eccentric fellows

remembers habits as others do men. He can smile when one speaks to him, and laughs easily. He knows the history of every mode, and can inform you from which of the French king's wenches our wives and daughters had this manner of curling their hair, that way of placing their hoods; whose frailty was covered by such a sort of petticoat, and whose vanity to show her foot made that part of the dress so short in such a year. In a word, all his conversation and knowledge has been in the female world. As other men of his age will 10 take notice to you what such a minister said upon such and such an occasion, he will tell you when the Duke of Monmouth danced at court such a woman was then smitten, another was taken with him at the head of his troop in the Park. In all these important relations, he has ever about the same time received a kind glance or a blow of a fan from some celebrated beauty, mother of the present Lord Such-a-one. If you speak of a young commoner that said a lively thing in the House, he starts up: "He has good blood in his veins; Tom Mirabell begot him. The rogue cheated me in that affair; that 20 young fellow's mother used me more like a dog than any woman I ever made advances to." This way of talking of his very much enlivens the conversation among us of a more sedate turn; and I find there is not one of the company but myself, who rarely speak at all, but speaks of him as of that sort of man who is usually called a well-bred, fine gentleman. To conclude his character, where women are not concerned he is an honest, worthy man.

I cannot tell whether I am to account him whom I am next to speak of as one of our company, for he visits us but seldom; 30 but when he does, it adds to every man else a new enjoyment of himself. He is a clergyman, a very philosophic man, of general learning, great sanctity of life, and the most exact good breeding. He has the misfortune to be of a very weak constitution, and consequently cannot accept of such cares and business as preferments in his function would oblige him to; he is therefore among divines what a chamber-counselor is among lawyers. The probity of his mind and the integrity of his life create him followers, as being eloquent or loud advances others. He seldom introduces the subject he speaks upon; but we are 40 so far gone in years that he observes, when he is among us, an earnestness to have him fall on some divine topic, which he always treats with much authority, as one who has no interest in this world, as one who is hastening to the object of all his wishes and conceives hope from his decays and infirmities. These are my ordinary companions.

AIMS OF THE SPECTATOR

No. 10. MONDAY, MARCH 12, 1711.

Non aliter quam qui adverso vix flumine lembum
Remigiis subigit, si brachia forte remisit,
Atque illum in præceps prono rapit alveus amni.[17]

—VIRG.

It is with much satisfaction that I hear this great city inquiring day by day after these my papers, and receiving my morning lectures with a becoming seriousness and attention. My publisher tells me that there are already three thousand of them distributed every day. So that if I allow twenty readers to every paper, which I look upon as a modest computation, I may reckon about three-score thousand disciples in London and Westminster, who I hope will take care to distinguish themselves from the thoughtless herd of their ignorant and unattentive brethren. Since I have raised to myself so great an audience, I shall spare no pains to make their instruction agreeable, and their diversion useful. For which reasons I shall endeavor to enliven morality with wit, and to temper wit with morality, that my readers may, if possible, both ways find their account in the speculation of the day. And to the end that their virtue and discretion may not be short, transient, intermitting starts of thought, I have resolved to refresh their memories from day to day, till I have recovered them out of that desperate state of vice and folly into which the age is fallen. The mind that lies fallow but a single day, sprouts up in follies that are only to be killed by a constant and assiduous culture. It was said of Socrates, that he brought philosophy down from heaven, to inhabit among men; and I shall be ambitious to have it said of me, that I have brought philosophy out of closets and libraries, schools and colleges, to dwell in clubs and assemblies, at tea-tables and in coffee-houses.

I would therefore in a very particular manner recommend these my speculations to all well-regulated families that set apart an hour in every morning for tea and bread and butter; and would earnestly advise them for their good to order this paper to be punctually served up, and to be looked upon as a part of the tea-equipage.

Sir Francis Bacon observes, that a well written book, com-

---

17 Like him who with his oars barely forces the boat against the stream, if he by chance relaxes his arms, the current snatches it headlong down the river. (Georgics, I. 201)

pared with its rivals and antagonists, is like Moses' serpent, that immediately swallowed up and devoured those of the Egyptians. I shall not be so vain as to think that where *The Spectator* appears the other public prints will vanish; but shall leave it to my reader's consideration, whether, is it not much better to be let into the knowledge of one's self, than to hear what passes in Muscovy or Poland; and to amuse ourselves with such writings as tend to the wearing out of ignorance, passion, and prejudice, than such as naturally conduce to in-
10 flame hatreds, and make enmities irreconcilable?

In the next place, I would recommend this paper to the daily perusal of those gentlemen whom I cannot but consider as my good brothers and allies, I mean the fraternity of spectators, who live in the world without having anything to do in it; and either by the affluence of their fortunes or laziness of their dispositions, have no other business with the rest of mankind but to look upon them. Under this class of men are comprehended all contemplative tradesmen, titular physicians, fellows of the Royal Society, Templars that are not given to
20 be contentious, and statesmen that are out of business; in short, every one that considers the world as a theater, and desires to form a right judgment of those who are the actors on it.

There is another set of men that I must likewise lay a claim to, whom I have lately called the blanks of society, as being altogether unfurnished with ideas, till the business and conversation of the day has supplied them. I have often considered these poor souls with an eye of great commiseration, when I have heard them asking the first man they have met with, whether there was any news stirring? and by that means gath-
30 ering together materials for thinking. These needy persons do not know what to talk of till about twelve o'clock in the morning; for by that time they are pretty good judges of the weather, know which way the wind sits, and whether the Dutch mail be come in. As they lie at the mercy of the first man they meet, and are grave or impertinent all the day long, according to the notions which they have imbibed in the morning, I would earnestly intreat them not to stir out of their chambers till they have read this paper, and do promise them that I will daily instil into them such sound and wholesome
40 sentiments as shall have a good effect on their conversation for the ensuing twelve hours.

But there are none to whom this paper will be more useful than to the female world. I have often thought there has not been sufficient pains taken in finding out proper employments and diversions for the fair ones. Their amusements seem con-

trived for them, rather as they are women, than as they are
reasonable creatures; and are more adapted to the sex than
to the species. The toilet is their great scene of business, and
the right adjusting of their hair the principal employment of
their lives. The sorting of a suit of ribbons is reckoned a very
good morning's work; and if they make an excursion to a
mercer's or a toy-shop, so great a fatigue makes them unfit
for anything else all the day after. Their more serious occupations are sewing and embroidery, and their greatest drudgery
the preparation of jellies and sweetmeats. This, I say, is the 10
state of ordinary women; though I know there are multitudes
of those of a more elevated life and conversation, that move
in an exalted sphere of knowledge and virtue, that join all the
beauties of the mind to the ornaments of dress, and inspire
a kind of awe and respect, as well as love, into their male
beholders. I hope to increase the number of these by publishing this daily paper, which I shall always endeavor to make
an innocent if not an improving entertainment, and by that
means at least divert the minds of my female readers from
greater trifles. At the same time, as I would fain give some 20
finishing touches to those which are already the most beautiful pieces in human nature, I shall endeavor to point all those
imperfections that are the blemishes, as well as those virtues
which are the embellishments of the sex. In the meanwhile I
hope these my gentle readers, who have so much time on their
hands, will not grudge throwing away a quarter of an hour
in a day on this paper, since they may do it without any hindrance to business.

I know several of my friends and well-wishers are in great
pain for me, lest I should not be able to keep up the spirit 30
of a paper which I oblige myself to furnish every day: but to
make them easy in this particular, I will promise them faithfully to give it over as soon as I grow dull. This I know will
be matter of great raillery to the small wits; who will frequently put me in mind of my promise, desire me to keep my
word, assure me that it is high time to give over, with many
other little pleasantries of the like nature, which men of a little
smart genius cannot forbear throwing out against their best
friends, when they have such a handle given them of being
witty. But let them remember that I do hereby enter my 40
caveat against this piece of raillery.

WESTMINSTER ABBEY

No. 26. Friday, March 30, 1711.

Pallida mors aequo pulsat pede pauperum tabernas
  Regumque turres. O beata Sexti,
Vitæ summa brevis spem nos vetat inchoare longam.
  Jam te premet nox, fabulæque manes,
Et domus exilis Plutonia.

                                 —Horace.[18]

When I am in a serious humor, I very often walk by myself in Westminster Abbey; where the gloominess of the place, and the use to which it is applied, with the solemnity of the building, and the condition of the people who lie in it, are apt to fill the mind with a kind of melancholy, or rather thoughtfulness, that is not disagreeable. I yesterday passed a whole afternoon in the churchyard, the cloisters, and the church, amusing myself with the tombstones and inscriptions that I met with in those several regions of the dead. Most of them recorded noth-
10 ing else of the buried person but that he was born upon one day and died upon another; the whole history of his life being comprehended in those two circumstances, that are common to all mankind. I could not but look upon these registers of existence, whether of brass or marble, as a kind of satire upon the departed persons, who had left no other memorial of them but that they were born and that they died. They put me in mind of several persons mentioned in the battles of heroic poems, who have sounding names given them for no other reason but that they may be killed, and are celebrated for noth-
20 ing but being knocked on the head.

  Γλαῦκόν τε Μέδοντά τε Θερσίλοχόν τε.—Homer.
  Glaucumque, Medontaque, Thersilochumque.[19]—Virgil

The life of these men is finely described in Holy Writ by *the path of an arrow,* which is immediately closed up and lost.
  Upon my going into the church, I entertained myself with the digging of a grave; and saw in every shovelful of it that was thrown up the fragment of a bone or skull intermixed with a kind of fresh moldering earth that some time or other had a

---

18 With equal foot, rich friend, impartial fate
  Knocks at the cottage, and the palace gate;
  Life's span forbids thee to extend thy cares,
  And stretch thy hopes beyond thy years;
  Night soon will seize, and you must quickly go
  To storied ghosts, and Pluto's house below.—Creech (Horace's Odes, I. iv. 13 ff.)
19 Glaucus, and Medon, and Thersilochus

place in the composition of an human body. Upon this I began
to consider with myself what innumerable multitudes of people lay confused together under the pavement of that ancient
cathedral; how men and women, friends and enemies, priests
and soldiers, monks and prebendaries were crumbled amongst
one another, and blended together in the same common mass;
how beauty, strength, and youth, with old age, weakness, and
deformity lay undistinguished in the same promiscuous heap of
matter.

After having thus surveyed this great magazine of mortality, 10
as it were in the lump, I examined it more particularly by the
accounts which I found on several of the monuments which
are raised in every quarter of that ancient fabric. Some of them
were covered with such extravagant epitaphs that, if it were
possible for the dead person to be acquainted with them, he
would blush at the praises which his friends have bestowed
upon him. There are others so excessively modest that they
deliver the character of the person departed in Greek or Hebrew, and by that means are not understood once in a twelvemonth. In the poetical quarter, I found there were poets who 20
had no monuments and monuments which had no poets. I observed indeed that the present war had filled the church with
many of these uninhabited monuments, which had been erected
to the memory of persons whose bodies were perhaps buried
in the plains of Blenheim,[20] or in the bosom of the ocean.

I could not but be very much delighted with several modern
epitaphs, which are written with great elegance of expression
and justness of thought, and therefore do honor to the living as
well as to the dead. As a foreigner is very apt to conceive an
idea of the ignorance or politeness of a nation from the turn of 30
their public monuments and inscriptions, they should be submitted to the perusal of men of learning and genius before they
are put into execution. Sir Cloudesly Shovel's monument has
very often given me great offence. Instead of the brave, rough
English admiral, which was the distinguishing character of that
plain, gallant man, he is represented on his tomb by the figure
of a beau, dressed in a long periwig, and reposing himself upon
velvet cushions under a canopy of state. The inscription is answerable to the monument; for instead of celebrating the many
remarkable actions he had performed in the service of his coun- 40
try, it acquaints us only with the manner of his death, in which
it was impossible for him to reap any honor.[21] The Dutch,
whom we are apt to despise for want of genius, show an infinitely greater taste of antiquity and politeness in their build-

20 in Bavaria, where the   feated the French in 1704   21 drowned at sea, 1707
Duke of Marlborough de-

ings and works of this nature than what we meet in those of our own country. The monuments of their admirals, which have been erected at the public expense, represent them like themselves, and are adorned with rostral crowns and naval ornaments, with beautiful festoons of seaweed, shells, and coral.

But to return to our subject. I have left the repository of our English kings for the contemplation of another day, when I shall find my mind disposed for so serious an amusement. I know that entertainments of this nature are apt to raise dark
10 and dismal thoughts in timorous minds and gloomy imaginations; but for my own part, though I am always serious, I do not know what it is to be melancholy, and can therefore take a view of nature in her deep and solemn scenes with the same pleasures as in her most gay and delightful ones. By this means I can improve myself with those objects which others consider with terror. When I look upon the tombs of the great, every emotion of envy dies in me; when I read the epitaphs of the beautiful, every inordinate desire goes out; when I meet with the grief of parents upon a tombstone, my heart melts with
20 compassion; when I see the tomb of the parents themselves, I consider the vanity of grieving for those whom we must quickly follow. When I see kings lying by those who deposed them, when I consider rival wits placed side by side, or the holy men that divided the world with their contests and disputes, I reflect with sorrow and astonishment on the little competitions, factions, and debates of mankind. When I read the several dates of the tombs, of some that died yesterday and some six hundred years ago, I consider that great day when we shall all of us be contemporaries, and make our appearance together.

PARTY PATCHES

No. 81. Saturday, June 2, 1711.

*Qualis ubi audito venantum murmure tigris
Horruit in maculas—*[22]

—Statius.

30   About the middle of last winter I went to see an opera at the theater in the Haymarket, where I could not but take notice of two parties of very fine women that had placed themselves in the opposite side-boxes, and seemed drawn up in a kind of battle array one against another. After a short survey of them, I found they were patched differently; the faces on one hand being spotted on the right side of the forehead, and those upon

22 Cowley's translation is quoted in the text.

the other on the left. I quickly perceived that they cast hostile glances upon one another; and that their patches were placed in those different situations as party-signals to distinguish friends from foes. In the middle boxes, between these two opposite bodies, were several ladies who patched indifferently on both sides of their faces, and seemed to sit there with no other intention but to see the opera. Upon inquiry I found that the body of amazons on my right hand were Whigs, and those on my left Tories; and that those who had placed themselves in the middle boxes were a neutral party, whose faces had not yet 10 declared themselves. These last, however, as I afterwards found, diminished daily, and took their party with one side or the other; insomuch that I observed in several of them, the patches, which were before dispersed equally, are now all gone over to the Whig or Tory side of the face. The censorious say that the men whose hearts are aimed at are very often the occasions that one part of the face is thus dishonored, and lies under a kind of disgrace, while the other is so much set off and adorned by the owner; and that the patches turn to the right or to the left, according to the principles of the man who is 20 most in favor. But whatever may be the motives of a few fantastical coquettes, who do not patch for the public good so much as for their own private advantage, it is certain that there are several women of honor who patch out of principle, and with an eye to the interest of their country. Nay, I am informed that some of them adhere so steadfastly to their party, and are so far from sacrificing their zeal for the public to their passion for any particular person, that in a late draft of marriage articles a lady has stipulated with her husband, that, whatever his opinions are, she shall be at liberty to patch on which side she 30 pleases.

I must here take notice that Rosalinda, a famous Whig partisan, has most unfortunately a very beautiful mole on the Tory part of her forehead; which being very conspicuous, has occasioned many mistakes, and given an handle to her enemies to misrepresent her face, as though it had revolted from the Whig interest. But, whatever this natural patch may seem to insinuate, it is well-known that her notions of government are still the same. This unlucky mole, however, has misled several coxcombs; and like the hanging out of false colors, made some 40 of them converse with Rosalinda in what they thought the spirit of her party, when on a sudden she has given them an unexpected fire, that has sunk them all at once. If Rosalinda is unfortunate in her mole, Nigranilla is as unhappy in a pimple, which forces her, against her inclinations, to patch on the Whig side.

I am told that many virtuous matrons, who formerly have
been taught to believe that this artificial spotting of the face
was unlawful, are now reconciled by a zeal for their cause to
what they could not be prompted by a concern for their beauty.
This way of declaring war upon one another, puts me in mind
of what is reported of the tigress, that several spots rise in her
skin when she is angry; or as Mr. Cowley has imitated the
verses that stand as the motto on this paper,

——She swells with angry pride,
10   And calls forth all her spots on every side.

When I was in the theater the time above-mentioned, I had
the curiosity to count the patches on both sides, and found the
Tory patches to be about twenty stronger than the Whig;
but to make amends for this small inequality, I the next morning found the whole puppet-show filled with faces spotted after
the Whiggish manner. Whether or no the ladies had retreated
hither in order to rally their forces I cannot tell; but the next
night they came in so great a body to the opera that they out-
numbered the enemy.

20   This account of party patches will, I am afraid, appear improbable to those who live at a distance from the fashionable
world; but as it is a distinction of a very singular nature, and
what perhaps may never meet with a parallel, I think I should
not have discharged the office of a faithful Spectator had I
not recorded it.

I have, in former papers, endeavored to expose this party-
rage in women, as it only serves to aggravate the hatred and
animosities that reign among men, and in a great measure de-
prives the fair sex of those peculiar charms with which nature
30 has endowed them.

When the Romans and Sabines were at war, and just upon
the point of giving battle, the women, who were allied to both
of them, interposed with so many tears and entreaties, that
they prevented the mutual slaughter which threatened both parties, and united them together in a firm and lasting peace.

I would recommend this noble example to our British ladies,
at a time when their country is torn with so many unnatural
divisions, that if they continue, it will be a misfortune to be
born in it. The Greeks thought it so improper for women to
40 interest themselves in competitions and contentions, that for
this reason, among others, they forbade them, under pain of
death, to be present at the Olympic games, notwithstanding
these were the public diversions of all Greece.

As our English women excel those of all nations in beauty,
they should endeavor to outshine them in all other accomplish-

ments proper to the sex, and to distinguish themselves as tender mothers and faithful wives, rather than as furious partisans. Female virtues are of a domestic turn. The family is the proper province for private women to shine in. If they must be showing their zeal for the public, let it not be against those who are perhaps of the same family, or at least of the same religion or nation, but against those who are the open, professed, undoubted enemies of their faith, liberty and country. When the Romans were pressed with a foreign enemy, the ladies voluntarily contributed all their rings and jewels to assist the government under the public exigence, which appeared so laudable an action in the eyes of their countrymen, that from thenceforth it was permitted by a law to pronounce public orations at the funeral of a woman in praise of the deceased person, which till that time was peculiar to men. Would our English ladies, instead of sticking on a patch against those of their own country, show themselves so truly public-spirited as to sacrifice every one her necklace against the common enemy, what decrees ought not to be made in favor of them?

Since I am recollecting upon this subject such passages as occur to my memory out of ancient authors, I cannot omit a sentence in the celebrated funeral oration of Pericles, which he made in honor of those brave Athenians that were slain in a fight with the Lacedæmonians. After having addressed himself to the several ranks and orders of his countrymen, and shown them how they should behave themselves in the public cause, he turns to the female part of his audience: "And as for you (says he) I shall advise you in very few words: Aspire only to those virtues that are peculiar to your sex; follow your natural modesty, and think it your greatest commendation not to be talked of one way or other."

SIR ROGER AT CHURCH

No. 112. MONDAY, JULY 9, 1711.

'Αθανάτους μὲν πρῶτα θεούς, νόμῳ ὡς διάκειται, Τίμα.[23]

—PYTHAGORAS.

I am always very well pleased with a country Sunday, and think, if keeping holy the seventh day were only a human institution, it would be the best method that could have been thought of for the polishing and civilizing of mankind. It is certain the country people would soon degenerate into a kind of savages and barbarians were there not such frequent returns

23 First reverence the immortal gods, as custom decrees.

of a stated time, in which the whole village meet together with their best faces, and in their cleanliest habits, to converse with one another upon indifferent subjects, hear their duties explained to them, and join together in adoration of the Supreme Being. Sunday clears away the rust of the whole week, not only as it refreshes in their minds the notions of religion, but as it puts both the sexes upon appearing in their most agreeable forms, and exerting all such qualities are are apt to give them a figure in the eye of the village. A country fellow dis-

10 tinguishes himself as much in the churchyard as a citizen does upon the 'Change, the whole parish politics being generally discussed in that place either after sermon or before the bell rings.

My friend Sir Roger, being a good churchman, has beautified the inside of his church with several texts of his own choosing; he has likewise given a handsome pulpit-cloth, and railed in the communion-table at his own expense. He has often told me that, at his coming to his estate, he found his parishioners very irregular; and that, in order to make them kneel and join

20 in the responses, he gave every one of them a hassock and a common-prayer-book, and at the same time employed an itinerant singing-master, who goes about the country for that purpose, to instruct them rightly in the tunes of the Psalms; upon which they now very much value themselves, and indeed outdo most of the country churches that I have ever heard.

As Sir Roger is landlord to the whole congregation, he keeps them in very good order, and will suffer nobody to sleep in it besides himself; for if by chance he has been surprised into a short nap at sermon, upon recovering out of it he stands up and

30 looks about him, and if he sees anybody else nodding, either wakes them himself, or sends his servant to them. Several other of the old knight's particularities break out upon these occasions; sometimes he will be lengthening out a verse in the Singing-Psalms half a minute after the rest of the congregation have done with it; sometimes, when he is pleased with the matter of his devotion, he pronounces "Amen" three or four times to the same prayer; and sometimes stands up when everybody else is upon their knees, to count the congregation, or see if any of his tenants are missing.

40 I was yesterday very much surprised to hear my old friend, in the midst of the service, calling out to one John Matthews to mind what he was about, and not disturb the congregation. This John Matthews, it seems, is remarkable for being an idle fellow, and at that time was kicking his heels for his diversion. This authority of the knight, though exerted in that odd manner

which accompanies him in all circumstances of life, has a very
good effect upon the parish, who are not polite enough to see
anything ridiculous in his behavior; besides that the general
good sense and worthiness of his character makes his friends
observe these little singularities as foils that rather set off than
blemish his good qualities.

As soon as the sermon is finished, nobody presumes to stir
till Sir Roger is gone out of the church. The knight walks down
from his seat in the chancel between a double row of his tenants,
that stand bowing to him on each side, and every now and then 10
inquires how such an one's wife, or mother, or son, or father
do, whom he does not see at church,—which is understood as a
secret reprimand to the person that is absent.

The chaplain has often told me that upon a catechizing day,
when Sir Roger has been pleased with a boy that answers well,
he has ordered a Bible to be given him next day for his encouragement, and sometimes accompanies it with a flitch of
bacon to his mother. Sir Roger has likewise added five pounds a
year to the clerk's place; and, that he may encourage the young
fellows to make themselves perfect in the church service, has 20
promised, upon the death of the present incumbent, who is very
old, to bestow it according to merit.

The fair understanding between Sir Roger and his chaplain,
and their mutual concurrence in doing good, is the more remarkable because the very next village is famous for the differences and contentions that rise between the parson and the
squire, who live in a perpetual state of war. The parson is
always preaching at the squire, and the squire, to be revenged
on the parson, never comes to church. The squire has made all
his tenants atheists and tithe-stealers; while the parson in- 30
structs them every Sunday in the dignity of his order, and
insinuates to them almost in every sermon that he is a better
man than his patron. In short, matters are come to such an
extremity that the squire has not said his prayers either in
public or private this half year; and that the parson threatens
him, if he does not mend his manners, to pray for him in the
face of the whole congregation.

Feuds of this nature, though too frequent in the country,
are very fatal to the ordinary people, who are so used to be
dazzled with riches that they pay as much deference to the 40
understanding of a man of an estate as of a man of learning; and are very hardly brought to regard any truth, how important soever it may be, that is preached to them, when they
know there are several men of five hundred a year who do not
believe it.

SIR ROGER AT THE ASSIZES

No. 122. FRIDAY, JULY 20, 1711.

Comes jucundus in via pro vehiculo est.[24]
—PUBL. SYR.

A man's first care should be to avoid the reproaches of his own heart; his next, to escape the censures of the world. If the last interferes with the former, it ought to be entirely neglected; but otherwise there cannot be a greater satisfaction to an honest mind than to see those approbations which it gives itself seconded by the applauses of the public. A man is more sure of his conduct when the verdict which he passes upon his own behavior is thus warranted and confirmed by the opinion of all that know him.

10   My worthy friend Sir Roger is one of those who is not only at peace within himself but beloved and esteemed by all about him. He receives a suitable tribute for his universal benevolence to mankind in the returns of affection and good-will which are paid him by every one that lives within his neighborhood. I lately met with two or three odd instances of that general respect which is shown to the good old knight. He would needs carry Will Wimble and myself with him to the county assizes. As we were upon the road, Will Wimble joined a couple of plain men who rid before us, and conversed with them for some

20 time, during which my friend Sir Roger acquainted me with their characters.

"The first of them," says he, "that has a spaniel by his side, is a yeoman of about an hundred pounds a year, an honest man. He is just within the Game Act, and qualified to kill an hare or a pheasant. He knocks down a dinner with his gun twice or thrice a week; and by that means lives much cheaper than those who have not so good an estate as himself. He would be a good neighbor if he did not destroy so many partridges; in short he is a very sensible man, shoots flying, and has been

30 several times foreman of the petty-jury.

"The other that rides along with him is Tom Touchy, a fellow famous for taking the law of everybody. There is not one in the town where he lives that he has not sued at a quarter-sessions. The rogue had once the impudence to go to law with the widow. His head is full of costs, damages, and ejectments; he plagued a couple of honest gentlemen so long for a trespass in breaking one of his hedges, till he was forced to sell the

---

24 A pleasant comrade on a journey is as good as a carriage. (Publilius Syrus, *Fragments*)

ground it enclosed to defray the charges of the prosecution. His father left him fourscore pounds a year, but he has cast and been cast [25] so often that he is not now worth thirty. I suppose he is going upon the old business of the willow tree."

As Sir Roger was giving me this account of Tom Touchy, Will Wimble and his two companions stopped short till we came up to them. After having paid their respects to Sir Roger, Will told him that Mr. Touchy and he must appeal to him upon a dispute that arose between them. Will, it seems, had been giving his fellow travelers an account of his angling one day in such a hole; when Tom Touchy, instead of hearing out his story, told him that Mr. Such-an-one, if he pleased, might take the law of him for fishing in that part of the river. My friend Sir Roger heard them both, upon a round trot; and after having paused some time, told them, with an air of a man who would not give his judgment rashly, *that much might be said on both sides.* They were neither of them dissatisfied with the knight's determination, because neither of them found himself in the wrong by it. Upon which we made the best of our way to the assizes.

The court was sat before Sir Roger came; but notwithstanding all the justices had taken their places upon the bench, they made room for the old knight at the head of them; who, for his reputation in the country, took occasion to whisper in the judge's ear that he was glad his lordship had met with so much good weather in his circuit. I was listening to the proceedings of the court with much attention, and infinitely pleased with that great appearance and solemnity which so properly accompanies such a public administration of our laws, when, after about an hour's sitting, I observed to my great surprise, in the midst of a trial, that my friend Sir Roger was getting up to speak. I was in some pain for him, till I found he had acquitted himself of two or three sentences, with a look of much business and great intrepidity.

Upon his first rising the court was hushed, and a general whisper ran among the country people that Sir Roger was up. The speech he made was so little to the purpose that I shall not trouble my readers with an account of it; and I believe was not so much designed by the knight himself to inform the court, as to give him a figure in my eye, and keep up his credit in the country.

I was highly delighted, when the court rose, to see the gentlemen of the country gathering about my old friend, and striving who should compliment him most; at the same time that the ordinary people gazed upon him at a distance, not a little

25 defeated in a law-suit

admiring his courage that was not afraid to speak to the judge. In our return home we met with a very odd accident which I cannot forbear relating, because it shows how desirous all who know Sir Roger are of giving him marks of their esteem. When we were arrived upon the verge of his estate, we stopped at a little inn to rest ourselves and our horses. The man of the house had, it seems, been formerly a servant in the knight's family; and to do honor to his old master, had some time since, unknown to Sir Roger, put him up in a sign-post before the
10 door; so that the knight's head had hung out upon the road about a week before he himself knew anything of the matter. As soon as Sir Roger was acquainted with it, finding that his servant's indiscretion proceeded wholly from affection and good-will, he only told him that he had made him too high a compliment; and when the fellow seemed to think that could hardly be, added, with a more decisive look, that it was too great an honor for any man under a duke; but told him at the same time that it might be altered with a very few touches, and that he himself would be at the charge of it. Accordingly they got a
20 painter, by the knight's directions, to add a pair of whiskers to the face, and by a little aggravation of the features to change it into the Saracen's Head. I should not have known this story had not the inn-keeper, upon Sir Roger's alighting, told him in my hearing that his honor's head was brought back last night with the alterations that he had ordered to be made in it. Upon this my friend, with his usual cheerfulness, related the particulars above mentioned, and ordered the head to be brought into the room. I could not forbear discovering greater expressions of mirth than ordinary upon the appearance of this mon-
30 strous face, under which, notwithstanding it was made to frown and stare in a most extraordinary manner, I could still discover a distant resemblance of my old friend. Sir Roger, upon seeing me laugh, desired me to tell him truly if I thought it possible for people to know him in that disguise. I at first kept my usual silence; but upon the knight's conjuring me to tell him whether it was not still more like himself than a Saracen, I composed my countenance in the best manner I could, and replied that much might be said on both sides.

These several adventures, with the knight's behavior in
40 them, gave me as pleasant a day as ever I met with in any of my travels.

THE VISION OF MIRZAH

No. 159. SATURDAY, SEPTEMBER 1, 1711.

—Omnem, quæ nunc obducta tuenti
Mortales hebetat visus tibi, et humida circum
Caligat, nubem eripiam— [26]

—VIRG.

When I was at Grand Cairo, I picked up several Oriental manuscripts, which I have still by me. Among others I met with one entitled The Visions of Mirzah, which I have read over with great pleasure. I intend to give it to the public when I have no other entertainment for them; and shall begin with the first vision, which I have translated word for word as follows:

"On the fifth day of the moon, which according to the custom of my forefathers I always keep holy, after having washed myself, and offered up my morning devotions, I ascended the high hills of Bagdat, in order to pass the rest of the day in meditation and prayer. As I was here airing myself on the tops of the mountains, I fell into a profound contemplation on the vanity of human life; and passing from one thought to another, 'Surely,' said I, 'man is but a shadow, and life a dream.' Whilst I was thus musing, I cast my eyes towards the summit of a rock that was not far from me, where I discovered one in the habit of a shepherd, with a musical instrument in his hand. As I looked upon him he applied it to his lips, and began to play upon it. The sound of it was exceeding sweet, and wrought into a variety of tunes that were inexpressibly melodious, and altogether different from anything I had ever heard. They put me in mind of those heavenly airs that are played to the departed souls of good men upon their first arrival in Paradise, to wear out the impressions of their last agonies, and qualify them for the pleasures of that happy place. My heart melted away in secret raptures.

"I had been often told that the rock before me was the haunt of a Genius; and that several had been entertained with music who had passed by it, but never heard that the musician had before made himself visible. When he had raised my thoughts by those transporting airs which he played, to taste the pleasures of his conversation, as I looked upon him like one astonished, he beckoned to me, and by the waving of his hand

[26] The cloud, which intercepting the clear light,
Hangs o'er thy eyes, and blunts thy mortal sight,
I will remove . . . (*Æneid*, ii, 604–6)

directed me to approach the place where he sat. I drew near with that reverence which is due to a superior nature; and as my heart was entirely subdued by the captivating strains I had heard, I fell down at his feet and wept. The Genius smiled upon me with a look of compassion and affability that familiarized him to my imagination, and at once dispelled all the fears and apprehensions with which I approached him. He lifted me from the ground, and taking me by the hand, 'Mirzah,' said he, 'I have heard thee in thy soliloquies; follow me.'

10 "He then led me to the highest pinnacle of the rock, and placing me on the top of it, 'Cast thy eyes eastward,' said he, 'and tell me what thou seest.' 'I see,' said I, 'a huge valley, and a prodigious tide of water rolling through it.' 'The valley that thou seest,' said he, 'is the Vale of Misery, and the tide of water that thou seest is part of the great Tide of Eternity.' 'What is the reason,' said I, 'that the tide I see rises out of a thick mist at one end, and again loses itself in a thick mist at the other?' 'What thou seest,' said he, 'is that portion of eternity which is called time, measured out by the sun, and reaching 20 from the beginning of the world to its consummation. Examine now,' said he, 'this sea that is thus bounded with darkness at both ends, and tell me what thou discoverest in it.' 'I see a bridge,' said I, 'standing in the midst of the tide.' 'The bridge thou seest,' said he, 'is Human Life: consider it attentively.' Upon a more leisurely survey of it, I found that it consisted of three-score and ten entire arches, with several broken arches, which added to those that were entire, made up the number about an hundred. As I was counting the arches, the Genius told me that this bridge consisted at first of a thousand arches; but that 30 a great flood swept away the rest, and left the bridge in the ruinous condition I now beheld it. 'But tell me further,' said he, 'what thou discoverest on it.' 'I see multitudes of people passing over it,' said I, 'and a black cloud hanging on each end of it.' As I looked more attentively, I saw several of the passengers dropping through the bridge into the great tide that flowed underneath it; and upon further examination, perceived there were innumerable trap-doors that lay concealed in the bridge, which the passengers no sooner trod upon, but they fell through them into the tide, and immediately disappeared. These 40 hidden pitfalls were set very thick at the entrance of the bridge, so that throngs of people no sooner broke through the cloud, but many of them fell into them. They grew thinner towards the middle, but multiplied and lay closer together towards the end of the arches that were entire.

"There were indeed some persons, but their number was very small, that continued a kind of hobbling march on the broken arches, but fell through one after another, being quite tired and spent with so long a walk.

"I passed some time in the contemplation of this wonderful structure, and the great variety of objects which it presented. My heart was filled with a deep melancholy to see several dropping unexpectedly in the midst of mirth and jollity, and catching at everything that stood by them to save themselves. Some were looking up towards the heavens in a thoughtful posture, and in the midst of a speculation stumbled and fell out of sight. Multitudes were very busy in the pursuit of bubbles that glit- 10 tered in their eyes and danced before them; but often when they thought themselves within the reach of them, their footing failed and down they sunk. In this confusion of objects, I observed some with scimitars in their hands, and others with urinals, who ran to and fro upon the bridge, thrusting several persons on trap-doors which did not seem to lie in their way, and which they might have escaped had they not been thus forced upon them.

"The Genius seeing me indulge myself on this melancholy prospect, told me I had dwelt long enough upon it. 'Take thine 20 eyes off the bridge,' said he, 'and tell me if thou seest anything thou dost not comprehend.' Upon looking up, 'What mean,' said I, 'those great flights of birds that are perpetually hovering about the bridge, and settling upon it from time to time? I see vultures, harpies, ravens, cormorants, and among many other feathered creatures several little winged boys, that perch in great numbers upon the middle arches.' 'These,' said the Genius, 'are Envy, Avarice, Superstition, Despair, Love, with the like cares and passions that infest human life.'

"I here fetched a deep sigh. 'Alas,' said I, 'Man was made in 30 vain! how is he given away to misery and mortality! tortured in life, and swallowed up in death!' The Genius being moved with compassion towards me, bid me quit so uncomfortable a prospect. 'Look no more,' said he, 'on man in the first stage of his existence, in his setting out for eternity; but cast thine eye on that thick mist into which the tide bears the several generations of mortals that fall into it.' I directed my sight as I was ordered, and (whether or no the good Genius strengthened it with any supernatural force, or dissipated part of the mist that was before too thick for the eye to penetrate) I saw the valley 40 opening at the farther end, and spreading forth into an immense ocean, that had a huge rock of adamant running through the midst of it, and dividing it into two equal parts. The clouds still rested on one half of it, insomuch that I could discover nothing in it; but the other appeared to me a vast ocean planted with innumerable islands, that were covered with fruits and flowers, and interwoven with a thousand little shining seas that ran among them. I could see persons dressed in glorious habits with garlands upon their heads, passing among the trees, lying down by the sides of fountains, or resting on beds of flowers; and could hear a confused harmony of singing birds, falling waters, human voices, and musical instruments. Gladness grew in me upon the discovery of so delightful a scene. I wished for the wings of an eagle, that I might fly away to those happy seats; but the Genius told me there was no passage to them, 10 except through the gates of death that I saw opening every moment upon the bridge. 'The islands,' said he, 'that lie so fresh and green before thee, and with which the whole face of the ocean appears spotted as far as thou canst see, are more in number than the sands on the seashore: there are myriads of islands behind those which thou here discoverest, reaching farther than thine eye, or even thine imagination can extend itself. These are the mansions of good men after death, who, according to the degree and kinds of virtue in which they excelled, are distributed among these several islands, which abound with 20 pleasures of different kinds and degrees, suitable to the relishes and perfections of those who are settled in them: every island is a paradise accommodated to its respective inhabitants. Are not these, O Mirzah, habitations worth contending for? Does life appear miserable that gives thee opportunities of earning such a reward? Is death to be feared that will convey thee to so happy an existence? Think not man was made in vain, who has such an eternity reserved for him.' I gazed with inexpressible pleasure on these happy islands. At length said I, 'Show me now, I beseech thee, the secrets that lie hid under those dark 30 clouds which cover the ocean on the other side of the rock of adamant.' The Genius making me no answer, I turned about to address myself to him a second time, but I found that he had left me; I then turned again to the vision which I had been so long contemplating; but instead of the rolling tide, the arched bridge, and the happy islands, I saw nothing but the long hollow valley of Bagdat, with oxen, sheep, and camels grazing upon the sides of it."

PARADISE LOST

No. 267. SATURDAY, JANUARY 5, 1712.

Cedite Romani scriptores, cedite Graii.[27]

—PROPERTIUS

There is nothing in nature so irksome as general discourses, especially when they turn chiefly upon words. For this reason

[27] Let the Roman and Greek writers retire.

I shall waive the discussion of that point which was started some years since, whether Milton's *Paradise Lost* may be called an heroic poem. Those who will not give it that title may call it, if they please, a divine poem. It will be sufficient to its perfection if it has in it all the beauties of the highest kind of poetry; and as for those who allege it is not an heroic poem, they advance no more to the diminution of it, than if they should say Adam is not Æneas, nor Eve Helen.

I shall therefore examine it by the rules of epic poetry, and see whether it falls short of the *Iliad* or *Æneid* in the beauties 10 which are essential to that kind of writing. The first thing to be considered in an epic poem is the fable,[28] which is perfect or imperfect according as the action which it relates is more or less so. This action should have three qualifications in it. First, it should be but one action; secondly, it should be an entire action; and thirdly, it should be a great action. To consider the action of the *Iliad, Æneid,* and *Paradise Lost,* in these three several lights. Homer, to preserve the unity of his action, hastens into the midst of things, as Horace has observed. Had he gone up to Leda's egg, or begun much later, even at the rape of 20 Helen, or the investing of Troy, it is manifest that the story of the poem would have been a series of several actions. He therefore opens his poem with the discord of his princes, and with great art interweaves in the several succeeding parts of it an account of everything material which relates to them, and had passed before that fatal dissension. After the same manner Æneas makes his first appearance in the Tyrrhene seas, and within sight of Italy, because the action proposed to be cele- brated was that of his settling himself in Latium. But because it was necessary for the reader to know what had happened 30 to him in the taking of Troy, and in the preceding parts of his voyage, Virgil makes his hero relate it by way of episode in the second and third books of the *Æneid;* the contents of both which books come before those of the first book in the thread of the story, though, for preserving of this unity of action, they follow them in the disposition of the poem. Milton, in imitation of these two great poets, opens his *Paradise Lost* with an in- fernal council plotting the fall of man, which is the action he proposed to celebrate; and as for those great actions, the battle of the angels and the creation of the world (which would have 40 entirely destroyed the unity of his principal action, had he re- lated them in the same order that they happened), he cast them into the fifth, sixth, and seventh books, by way of episode to this noble poem.

Aristotle himself allows that Homer has nothing to boast of

28 story

as to the unity of his fable, though at the same time that great critic and philosopher endeavors to palliate this imperfection in the Greek poet by imputing it in some measure to the very nature of an epic poem. Some have been of opinion that the *Æneid* labors also in this particular, and has episodes which may be looked upon as excrescences rather than as parts of the action. On the contrary, the poem which we have now under our consideration hath no other episodes than such as naturally arise from the subject, and yet is filled with such a multitude 10 of astonishing incidents that it gives us at the same time a pleasure of the greatest variety and of the greatest simplicity.

I must observe also that as Virgil, in the poem which was designed to celebrate the original of the Roman empire, has described the birth of its great rival, the Carthaginian commonwealth, Milton, with the like art, in his poem on the fall of man has related the fall of those angels who are his professed enemies. Besides the many other beauties in such an episode, its running parallel with the great action of the poem hinders it from breaking the unity so much as another episode would 20 have done, that had not so great an affinity with the principal subject. In short, this is the same kind of beauty which the critics admire in *The Spanish Friar or the Double Discovery*,[29] where the two different plots look like counterparts and copies of one another.

The second qualification required in the action of an epic poem is that it should be an entire action. An action is entire when it is complete in all its parts; or, as Aristotle describes it, when it consists of a beginning, a middle, and an end. Nothing should go before it, be intermixed with it, or follow after it 30 that is not related to it; as, on the contrary, no single step should be omitted in that just and regular process which it must be supposed to take from its original to its consummation. Thus we see the anger of Achilles in its birth, its continuance, and effects; and Æneas's settlement in Italy, carried on through all the oppositions in his way to it both by sea and land. The action in Milton excels (I think) both the former in this particular; we see it contrived in hell, executed upon earth, and punished by Heaven. The parts of it are told in the most distinct manner, and grow out of one another in the most natural 40 method.

The third qualification of an epic poem is its greatness. The anger of Achilles was of such consequence that it embroiled the kings of Greece, destroyed the heroes of Troy, and engaged all the gods in factions. Æneas's settlement in Italy produced the Cæsars, and gave birth to the Roman empire. Milton's

29 play by Dryden

subject was still greater than either of the former; it does not
determine the fate of single persons or nations, but of a whole
species. The united powers of hell are joined together for the
destruction of mankind, which they effected in part, and would
have completed, had not Omnipotence itself interposed. The
principal actors are man in his greatest perfection and woman
in her highest beauty. Their enemies are the fallen angels; the
Messiah their friend, and the Almighty their protector. In
short, everything that is great in the whole circle of being,
whether within the verge of nature or out of it, has a proper
part assigned it in this noble poem.

In poetry, as in architecture, not only the whole, but the
principal members, and every part of them, should be great. I
will not presume to say that the book of games in the Æneid,
or that in the Iliad, are not of this nature, nor to reprehend
Virgil's simile of a top, and many other of the same nature in
the Iliad, as liable to any censure in this particular; but I think
we may say, without derogating from those wonderful performances, that there is an unquestionable magnificence in
every part of Paradise Lost, and indeed a much greater than
could have been formed upon any pagan system.

But Aristotle, by the greatness of the action, does not only
mean that it should be great in its nature, but also in its duration, or in other words, that it should have a due length in it,
as well as what we properly call greatness. The just measure of
the kind of magnitude he explains by the following similitude.
An animal no bigger than a mite cannot appear perfect to the
eye, because the sight takes it in at once, and has only a confused idea of the whole, and not a distinct idea of all its parts;
if on the contrary you should suppose an animal of ten thousand
furlongs in length, the eye would be so filled with a single part
of it that it could not give the mind an idea of the whole. What
these animals are to the eye, a very short or a very long action
would be to the memory. The first would be, as it were, lost
and swallowed up by it, and the other difficult to be contained
in it. Homer and Virgil have shown their principal art in this
particular; the action of the Iliad and that of the Æneid were in
themselves exceeding short, but are so beautifully extended
and diversified by the invention of episodes, and the machinery
of gods, with the like poetical ornaments, that they make
up an agreeable story, sufficient to employ the memory without
overcharging it. Milton's action is enriched with such variety
of circumstances that I have taken as much pleasure in reading the contents of his books as in the best invented story I
ever met with. It is possible that the traditions on which the
Iliad and Æneid were built had more circumstances in them

than the history of the fall of man, as it is related in Scripture. Besides, it was easier for Homer and Virgil to dash the truth with fiction, as they were in no danger of offending the religion of their country by it. But as for Milton, he had not only a very few circumstances upon which to raise his poem, but was also obliged to proceed with the greatest caution in everything that he added out of his own invention. And indeed, notwithstanding all the restraints he was under, he has filled his story with so many surprising incidents, which bear so close an
10 analogy with what is delivered in Holy Writ, that it is capable of pleasing the most delicate reader, without giving offence to the most scrupulous.

The modern critics have collected, from several hints in the *Iliad* and *Æneid,* the space of time which is taken up by the action of each of those poems; but as a great part of Milton's story was transacted in regions that lie out of the reach of the sun and the sphere of day, it is impossible to gratify the reader with such a calculation, which indeed would be more curious than instructive; none of the critics, either ancient or
20 modern, having laid down rules to circumscribe the action of an epic poem with any determined number of years, days, or hours.

This piece of criticism on Milton's *Paradise Lost* shall be carried on in the following Saturday's papers.[30]

CLARINDA'S JOURNAL

No. 323. TUESDAY, MARCH 11, 1712.

Modo vir, modo femina.[31]

—OVID.

The Journal with which I presented my readers on Tuesday last,[32] has brought me in several letters with accounts of many private lives cast into that form. I have the Rake's Journal, the Sot's Journal, the Whoremaster's Journal, and among several others a very curious piece, entitled The Journal of a Mohock.[33]
30 By these instances I find that the intention of my last Tuesday's paper has been mistaken by many of my readers. I did not design so much to expose vice as idleness, and aimed at those persons who pass away their time rather in trifles and impertinence, than in crimes and immoralities. Offences of this

30 For seventeen successive Saturdays Addison continued his critique.
31 Sometimes a man, sometimes a woman (*Metamorphoses,* VI. 280)
32 In No. 317 Addison had presented the journal of a man who was "of greater consequence in his own thoughts than in the eye of the world."
33 one of a band of ruffians who terrorized Londoners at night

latter kind are not to be dallied with, or treated in so ludicrous a manner. In short, my journal only holds up folly to the light, and shows the disagreeableness of such actions as are indifferent in themselves, and blamable only as they proceed from creatures endowed with reason.

My following correspondent, who calls herself Clarinda, is such a journalist as I require. She seems by her letter to be placed in a modish state of indifference between vice and virtue, and to be susceptible of either, were there proper pains taken with her. Had her journal been filled with gallantries, or such 10 occurrences as had shown her wholly divested of her natural innocence, notwithstanding it might have been more pleasing to the generality of readers, I should not have published it; but as it is only the picture of a life filled with a fashionable kind of gaiety and laziness, I shall set down five days of it, as I have received it from the hand of my correspondent.

DEAR MR. SPECTATOR,

You having set your readers an exercise in one of your last week's papers, I have performed mine according to your orders, and herewith send it you enclosed. You must know, Mr. Spec- 20 tator, that I am a maiden lady of a good fortune, who have had several matches offered me for these ten years last past, and have at present warm applications made to me by a very pretty fellow. As I am at my own disposal, I come up to town every winter, and pass my time in it after the manner you will find in the following journal, which I began to write upon the very day after your *Spectator* upon that subject.

TUESDAY *night*. Could not go to sleep till one in the morning for thinking of my journal.

WEDNESDAY. *From Eight till Ten.* Drank two dishes of choco- 30 late in bed, and fell asleep after them.

From Ten to Eleven. Eat a slice of bread and butter, drank a dish of bohea,[34] read *The Spectator.*

From Eleven to One. At my toilette, tried a new head.[35] Gave orders for Veny to be combed and washed. Mem. I look best in blue.

From One till half an hour after Two. Drove to the 'Change. Cheapened a couple of fans.

Till Four. At dinner. Mem. Mr. Froth passed by in his new liveries.

From Four to Six. Dressed, paid a visit to old Lady Blithe
40

---

34 tea.   35 head-dress

and her sister, having before heard they were gone out of town that day.

From Six to Eleven. At basset. Mem. Never set again upon the ace of diamonds.

THURSDAY. *From Eleven at night to Eight in the morning.* Dreamed that I punted to Mr. Froth.

From Eight to Ten. Chocolate. Read two acts in *Aurenzebe* [36] abed.

From Ten to Eleven. Tea-table. Sent to borrow Lady Faddle's Cupid for Veny. Read the play-bills. Received a letter from Mr. Froth. Mem. Locked it up in my strong box.

Rest of the morning. Fontange,[37] the tire-woman, her account of my Lady Blithe's wash. Broke a tooth in my little tortoise-shell comb. Sent Frank to know how my Lady Hectic rested after her monkey's leaping out at window. Looked pale. Fontange tells me my glass is not true. Dressed by Three.

From Three to Four. Dinner cold before I sat down.

From Four to Eleven. Saw company. Mr. Froth's opinion of Milton. His account of the Mohocks. His fancy of a pin-cushion. Picture in the lid of his snuff-box. Old Lady Faddle promises me her woman to cut my hair. Lost five guineas at crimp.

Twelve o'clock at night. Went to bed.

FRIDAY. *Eight in the morning.* Abed. Read over all Mr. Froth's letters. Cupid and Veny.

Ten o'clock. Stayed within all day, not at home.

From Ten to Twelve. In conference with my mantua-maker. Sorted a suit of ribands. Broke my blue china cup.

From Twelve to One. Shut myself up in my chamber, practised Lady Betty Modely's skuttle.

One in the afternoon. Called for my flowered handkerchief. Worked half a violet leaf in it. Eyes ached and head out of order. Threw by my work, and read over the remaining part of *Aurenzebe.*

From Three to Four. Dined.

From Four to Twelve. Changed my mind, dressed, went abroad, and played at crimp till midnight. Found Mrs. Spitely at home. Conversation: Mrs. Brilliant's necklace false stones. Old Lady Loveday going to be married to a young fellow that is not worth a groat. Miss Prue gone into the country. Tom Townley has red hair. Mem. Mrs. Spitely whispered in my ear that she had something to tell me about Mr. Froth; I am sure it is not true.

---

36 Aureng-zebe, heroic play by Dryden   37 a hair-dresser

Between Twelve and One. Dreamed that Mr. Froth lay at my feet, and called me Indamora.[38]

SATURDAY. Rose at eight o'clock in the morning. Sat down to my toilette.

From Eight to Nine. Shifted a patch for half an hour before I could determine it. Fixed it above my left eyebrow.

From Nine to Twelve. Drank my tea, and dressed.

From Twelve to Two. At Chapel. A great deal of good company. Mem. The third air in the new opera. Lady Blithe dressed frightfully.

From Three to Four. Dined. Mrs. Kitty called upon me to go to the opera before I was risen from the table.

From dinner to Six. Drank tea. Turned off a footman for being rude to Veny.

Six o'clock. Went to the opera. I did not see Mr. Froth till the beginning of the second act. Mr. Froth talked to a gentleman in a black wig. Bowed to a lady in the front box. Mr. Froth and his friend clapped Nicolini[39] in the third act. Mr. Froth cried out Ancora.[40] Mr. Froth led me to my chair. I think he squeezed my hand.

Eleven at night. Went to bed. Melancholy dreams. Methought Nicolini said he was Mr. Froth.

SUNDAY. Indisposed.

MONDAY. *Eight o'clock.* Waked by Miss Kitty. *Aurenzebe* lay upon the chair by me. Kitty repeated without book the eight best lines in the play. Went in our mobs to the dumb man, according to appointment. Told me that my lover's name began with a G. Mem. The conjurer was within a letter of Mr. Froth's name, *etc.*

Upon looking back into this my journal, I find that I am at a loss to know whether I pass my time well or ill; and indeed never thought of considering how I did it, before I perused your speculation upon that subject. I scarce find a single action in these five days that I can thoroughly approve of, except the working upon the violet leaf, which I am resolved to finish the first day I am at leisure. As for Mr. Froth and Veny, I did not think they took up so much of my time and thoughts, as I find they do upon my journal. The latter of them I will turn off if you insist upon it; and if Mr. Froth does not bring matters to a conclusion very suddenly, I will not let my life run away in a dream.

Your humble servant,
CLARINDA.

38 heroine of *Aurengzebe*   39 famous Italian singer   40 encore

To resume one of the morals of my first paper, and to confirm Clarinda in her good inclinations, I would have her consider what a pretty figure she would make among posterity, were the history of her whole life published like these five days of it. I shall conclude my paper with an epitaph written by an uncertain author [41] on Sir Philip Sidney's sister, a lady who seems to have been of a temper very much different from that of Clarinda. The last thought of it is so very noble, that I dare say my reader will pardon the quotation.

On the Countess Dowager of Pembroke

Underneath this marble hearse
Lies the subject of all verse,
Sidney's sister, Pembroke's mother;
Death, ere thou hast killed another,
Fair and learn'd and good as she,
Time shall throw a dart at thee.

TASTE

No. 409. THURSDAY, JUNE 19, 1712.

Musaeo contingens cuncta lepore.[42]
—LUCRETIUS.

Gratian very often recommends fine taste as the utmost perfection of an accomplished man. As this word arises very often in conversation, I shall endeavor to give some account of it, and to lay down rules how we may know whether we are possessed of it, and how we may acquire that fine taste of writing which is so much talked of among the polite world.

Most languages make use of this metaphor to express that faculty of the mind which distinguishes all the most concealed faults and nicest perfections in writing. We may be sure this metaphor would not have been so general in all tongues had there not been a very great conformity between that mental taste, which is the subject of this paper, and that sensitive taste which gives us a relish of every different flavor that affects the palate. Accordingly we find there are as many degrees of refinement in the intellectual faculty as in the sense which is marked out by this common denomination.

I knew a person who possessed the one in so great a perfection that, after having tasted ten different kinds of tea, he

41 now attributed to William Browne   42 touching   everything
with the charm of the Muses

would distinguish, without seeing the color of it, the particular
sort which was offered him; and not only so, but any two sorts
of them that were mixed together in an equal proportion. Nay,
he has carried the experiment so far as, upon tasting the composition of three different sorts, to name the parcels from
whence the three several ingredients were taken. A man of a
fine taste in writing will discern, after the same manner, not
only the general beauties and imperfections of an author, but
discover the several ways of thinking and expressing himself
which diversify him from all other authors, with the several ₁₀
foreign infusions of thought and language, and the particular
authors from whom they were borrowed.

After having thus far explained what is generally meant by
a fine taste in writing, and shown the propriety of the metaphor
which is used on this occasion, I think I may define it to be
"that faculty of the soul which discerns the beauties of an
author with pleasure, and the imperfections with dislike." If a
man would know whether he is possessed of this faculty, I
would have him read over the celebrated works of antiquity,
which have stood the test of so many different ages and coun- ₂₀
tries, or those works among the moderns which have the sanction of the politer part of our contemporaries. If, upon the
perusal of such writings, he does not find himself delighted in
an extraordinary manner, or if, upon reading the admired passages in such authors, he finds a coldness and indifference in
his thoughts, he ought to conclude, not—as is too usual among
tasteless readers—that the author wants those perfections
which have been admired in him, but that he himself wants
the faculty of discovering them.

He should, in the second place, be very careful to observe ₃₀
whether he tastes the distinguishing perfections, or—if I may
be allowed to call them so—the specific qualities of the author
whom he peruses; whether he is particularly pleased with Livy
for his manner of telling a story, with Sallust for his entering
into those internal principles of action which arise from the
characters and manners of the persons he describes, or with
Tacitus for displaying those outward motives of safety and
interest which gave birth to the whole series of transactions
which he relates.

He may likewise consider how differently he is affected by ₄₀
the same thought which presents itself in a great writer, from
what he is when he finds it delivered by a person of an
ordinary genius; for there is as much difference in apprehend-
ing a thought clothed in Cicero's language and that of a common author, as in seeing an object by the light of a taper or
by the light of the sun.

It is very difficult to lay down rules for the acquirement of such a taste as that I am here speaking of. The faculty must in some degree be born with us; and it very often happens that those who have other qualities in perfection are wholly void of this. One of the most eminent mathematicians of the age has assured me that the greatest pleasure he took in reading Virgil was in examining Æneas's voyage by the map; as I question not but many a modern compiler of history would be delighted with little more in that divine author than the bare matters of fact.

But, notwithstanding this faculty must in some measure be born in us, there are several methods for cultivating and improving it, and without which it will be very uncertain and of little use to the person that possesses it. The most natural method for this purpose is to be conversant among the writings of the most polite authors. A man who has any relish for fine writing either discovers new beauties or receives stronger impressions from the masterly strokes of a great author every time he peruses him; besides that he naturally wears himself into the same manner of speaking and thinking.

Conversation with men of a polite genius is another method for improving our natural taste. It is impossible for a man of the greatest parts to consider anything in its whole extent and in all its variety of lights. Every man, besides those general observations which are to be made upon an author, forms several reflections that are peculiar to his own manner of thinking; so that conversation will naturally furnish us with hints which we did not attend to, and make us enjoy other men's parts and reflections as well as our own. This is the best reason I can give for the observation which several have made, that men of genius in the same way of writing seldom rise up singly, but at certain periods of time appear together, and in a body; as they did at Rome in the reign of Augustus, and in Greece about the age of Socrates. I cannot think that Corneille, Racine, Molière, Boileau, La Fontaine, Bruyère, Bossuet, or the Daciers would have written so well as they have done, had they not been friends and contemporaries.

It is likewise necessary for a man who would form to himself a finished taste of good writing to be well versed in the works of the best critics, both ancient and modern. I must confess that I could wish there were authors of this kind, who, besides the mechanical rules, which a man of very little taste may discourse upon, would enter into the very spirit and soul of fine writing, and show us the several sources of that pleasure which rises in the mind upon the perusal of a noble work. Thus, although in poetry it be absolutely necessary that the

unities of time, place, and action, with other points of the same
nature, should be thoroughly explained and understood, there
is still something more essential to the art, something that
elevates and astonishes the fancy, and gives a greatness of
mind to the reader, which few of the critics besides Longinus
have considered.

Our general taste in England is for epigram, turns of wit,
and forced conceits, which have no manner of influence either
for the bettering or enlarging the mind of him who reads them,
and have been carefully avoided by the greatest writers, both 10
among the ancients and moderns. I have endeavored, in several of my speculations, to banish this Gothic taste which has
taken possession among us. I entertained the town for a week
together with an essay upon wit, in which I endeavored to
detect several of those false kinds which have been admired
in the different ages of the world, and at the same time to show
wherein the nature of true wit consists. I afterward gave an
instance of the great force which lies in a natural simplicity
of thought to affect the mind of the reader, from such vulgar
pieces as have little else besides this single qualification to 20
recommend them. I have likewise examined the works of the
greatest poet which our nation, or perhaps any other, has produced, and particularized most of those rational and manly
beauties which give a value to that divine work. I shall next
Saturday enter upon an essay on "The Pleasures of the Imagination," which, though it shall consider that subject at
large, will perhaps suggest to the reader what it is that gives
a beauty to many passages of the finest writers both in prose
and verse. As an undertaking of this nature is entirely new, I
question not but it will be received with candor.   30

ALEXANDER POPE (1688–1744)

It was Alexander Pope who was to succeed Dryden as the greatest force in
English poetry, and the lives of the two have an interesting contact. When
Pope was a little child, so he tells us, he was carried to Will's coffee house to
look at the great Dryden, which he did "with veneration." The child prodigy,
who even at a tender age doubtless knew something of his great predecessor,
was the son of a linen merchant in London, where he was born on May 21,
1688. Two conditions determined his development through the impressionable
years. First, his family were Catholics, which meant that they were members of
a more or less ostracized and very limited society, and that their son was denied
the privileges of good schools and the university. For this reason his education,
largely at home, was irregular. His reading was broad, but undisciplined, and
his scholarship always defective. Second, he was afflicted with the most severe
physical infirmities. He was dwarfish in stature, hunchbacked, withered and

shrunken in figure, and subject to severe headaches. Probably it was no exaggeration for him to speak of his life as one "long disease." These disabilities prevented the wholesome contacts of childhood, and the equally important normal relationships with men. His friendships were mostly literary, and often with men much older than himself. He made and kept many friends, among them Swift, Gay, and Dr. Arbuthnot, physician and man of letters. But more often his friendships were undermined by suspicions and jealousies, and he quarreled with those who had at first been well disposed: with Ambrose Phillips, for instance, who had dared to write pastorals which some liked better than his own; with Theobald, who had pointed out the errors in his edition of Shakespeare; with Addison, who had criticized some of his work adversely. In each case he retorted with bitter personal satire. By women he was petted, pampered, and flattered. All of this produced distorted conceptions of life.

Pope tells us that he "lisped in numbers, for the numbers came." Certainly his development was precocious. In early youth he had written epics, which he afterwards destroyed. His *Pastorals*, he says, were written in 1704, at the age of sixteen. These and similar statements of early composition are open to some suspicion, since he persistently cultivated a reputation for prodigiousness. But he wrote his *Essay on Criticism*, in which his style is fully developed, in 1711, and his *Rape of the Lock*, in its earlier form, in 1712. By the age of twenty-five he was famous, generally regarded as the nation's leading poet. When, therefore, in 1713 he issued a prospectus for a translation of the *Iliad*, the announcement was regarded as a national event, and every one of importance subscribed. For ten years he devoted his major energies to this translation, and to that of the *Odyssey*, the latter with the assistance of collaborators. For the two works Pope received nearly £9000, a fortune in those days—the first instance where a man of letters had attained wealth by his pen. The rhymed verse in which he did his Homer was far removed from the epic hexameters of the original. The sophisticated and clever Pope was hardly fitted to reproduce the noble simplicity and splendid swing of his model, yet his *Iliad* is a poem of great vigor, and the brilliant heroic couplets are managed with such mastery that the work has remained one of the classics of the language. The great scholar, Bentley, who knew his Greek, remarked concerning it, "A very pretty poem, Mr. Pope—but do not call it Homer."

The work of Pope's later years consists of satire and philosophic essays in verse. The former are chiefly a product of his literary feuds, and sought to embalm his enemies in innuendo, ridicule, and denunciation. The *Dunciad* (first published in 1728) was meant to dispose of all poetasters and scribblers, with Pope's old antagonist Theobald enthroned as the chief dunce. In fifteen years Pope's quarrels multiplied, and new enemies arose; so that by 1743 he saw fit to depose Theobald and elevate in his stead Colley Cibber, the dramatist, memoir writer, and insignificant poet laureate of his day, to rule over the empire of Dullness. In this kind of personal satire the *Epistle to Dr. Arbuthnot* remains a masterpiece in brief compass. Its most celebrated passage is the attack on Addison under the name of Atticus. The *Essay on Man* (1732–35), in which the poet presents the deistic philosophy of his friend Bolingbroke, is now not important as the epitome of a system of life, but it has given to the language more pithy maxims, in final and perfect phrase, than any comparable work in the whole sweep of English letters.

After the astounding success of the *Iliad* had brought Pope a fortune he leased a house and small estate at Twickenham, on the Thames, his home for the rest of his life. The adornment of his grounds became a hobby with him, his proudest boast being an artificially constructed grotto. At Twickenham he died on May 29, 1744.

For the century after Pope's first successes he was lauded as the greatest of English writers, and English poetry marched in his steps and spoke with his accents for fifty years after his death. The Romantic writers (with Byron a notable exception) despised him and all his works, and their successful revolt was largely a revolt against Popism—its rule of reason (and other rules), its restricted subject-matter, its poetic diction, and especially its rigid verse-form. As this controversy has receded from us, we have become better able to appraise his achievement at its true worth. He had not the higher imaginative powers which we associate with the greatest poetry. His appeal is to the intellect rather than to the emotions. Even in this domain he is not original or profound, repeating stock philosophical ideas of his time or familiar critical dicta. His sympathies, his scope are extremely limited. The restriction of his work to one form —the heroic couplet—forbids varied music, prevents that fine art in which verse responds to thought and mood. As a young man, he had been admonished by Walsh to be *correct;* and correctness, as he himself says, he made his aim: justness of taste, but especially perfection in the one meter which he and his age esteemed "correct." This form he brought to a marvelous precision and polish which cannot be surpassed. His ideal was pointed, condensed, and epigrammatic utterance. In memorable phrase he fixed "what oft was thought, but ne'er so well expressed." No English satire was written with such brilliance as his, while in *The Rape of the Lock*—a subject to which his talents were particularly fitted—he has produced the one English masterpiece of the mock-heroic. The daintier, more graceful, and more elegant aspects of his art there displayed have made this poem more acceptable to succeeding generations than his more didactic and more heavily satiric pieces.

The literary significance of Pope is immense. No writer ever embodied more completely the dominant thought, the standards of conduct, and the artistic canons of an era. If the last half of the seventeenth century is the age of Dryden, so even more surely is the first half of the eighteenth the age of Pope.

BIBLIOGRAPHY. *Works* by W. Elwin and W. J. Courthope (standard). Vol. V. contains the standard *Life.* One-volume eds. of the works, the Cambridge, ed. by H. W. Boynton (Houghton Mifflin), and the Globe, by A. W. Ward (Macmillan). A short biography by Sir Leslie Stephen in the Eng. Men of Letters ser.

AN ESSAY ON CRITICISM

PART I

INTRODUCTION. That it is as great a fault to judge ill as to write ill, and a more dangerous one to the public. That a true taste is as rare to be found as a true genius. That most men are born with some taste, but spoiled by false education. The multitude of critics, and causes of them. That we are to study our own taste, and know the limits of it. Nature the best guide of judgment. Improved by art and rules, which are but methodized nature. Rules derived from the practice of the ancient poets. That therefore the ancients are necessary to be studied by a critic, particularly Homer and Virgil. Of licenses, and the use of them by the ancients. Reverence due to the ancients, and praise of them.

'T is hard to say, if greater want of skill
Appear in writing or in judging ill;
But, of the two less dangerous is th' offense
To tire our patience than mislead our sense.
Some few in that, but numbers err in this,
Ten censure wrong for one who writes amiss;
A fool might once himself alone expose,
Now one in verse makes many more in prose.
    'T is with our judgments as our watches, none
Go just alike, yet each believes his own.   10
In Poets as true genius is but rare,
True Taste as seldom is the Critic's share;
Both must alike from Heaven derive their light,
These born to judge, as well as those to write.
Let such teach others who themselves excel,
And censure freely who have written well.
Authors are partial to their wit, 't is true,
But are not Critics to their judgment too?
    Yet if we look more closely, we shall find
Most have the seeds of judgment in their mind: 20
Nature affords at least a glimmering light;
The lines, though touched but faintly, are drawn right.
But as the slightest sketch, if justly traced, ⎫
Is by ill coloring but the more disgraced, ⎬
So by false learning is good sense defaced: ⎭
Some are bewildered in the maze of schools,
And some made coxcombs Nature meant but fools.
In search of wit these lose their common sense,
And then turn Critics in their own defense:
Each burns alike, who can, or cannot write,   30
Or with a rival's, or an eunuch's spite.
All fools have still an itching to deride,
And fain would be upon the laughing side.
If Mævius [1] scribble in Apollo's spite,
There are who judge still worse than he can write.
    Some have at first for Wits, then Poets passed,
Turned Critics next, and proved plain fools at last.
Some neither can for Wits nor Critics pass,
As heavy mules are neither horse nor ass.
Those half-learn'd witlings, numerous in our isle,   40
As half-formed insects on the banks of Nile;
Unfinished things, one knows not what to call,

[1] an inferior Latin poet who disliked Horace and Virgil

Their generation's so equivocal:
To tell them would a hundred tongues require,
Or one vain wit's, that might a hundred tire.
  But you who seek to give and merit fame,
And justly bear a Critic's noble name,
Be sure yourself and your own reach to know,
How far your genius, taste, and learning go;
Launch not beyond your depth, but be discreet,   50
And mark that point where sense and dullness meet.
  Nature to all things fixed the limits fit,
And wisely curbed proud man's pretending wit.
As on the land while here the ocean gains,
In other parts it leaves wide sandy plains;
Thus in the soul while memory prevails,
The solid power of understanding fails;
Where beams of warm imagination play,
The memory's soft figures melt away.
One science only will one genius fit;   60
So vast is art, so narrow human wit:
Not only bounded to peculiar arts,
But oft in those confined to single parts.
Like kings we lose the conquests gained before,
By vain ambition still to make them more;
Each might his several province well command,
Would all but stoop to what they understand.
  First follow Nature, and your judgment frame
By her just standard, which is still the same;
Unerring Nature, still divinely bright,   70
One clear, unchanged, and universal light,
Life, force, and beauty must to all impart,
At once the source, and end, and test of Art.
Art from that fund each just supply provides,
Works without show, and without pomp presides.
In some fair body thus th' informing soul
With spirits feeds, with vigor fills the whole,
Each motion guides, and every nerve sustains;
Itself unseen, but in th' effects remains.
Some, to whom Heaven in wit has been profuse,   80
Want as much more to turn it to its use;
For wit and judgment often are at strife,
Though meant each other's aid, like man and wife.
'T is more to guide, than spur the Muse's steed,
Restrain his fury than provoke his speed;
The wingèd courser, like a generous horse,
Shows most true mettle when you check his course.
  Those rules of old discovered, not devised,

Are Nature still, but Nature methodized;
Nature, like Liberty, is but restrained   90
By the same laws which first herself ordained.
  Hear how learn'd Greece her useful rules indites
When to repress and when indulge our flights:
High on Parnassus' top her sons she showed,
And pointed out those arduous paths they trod;
Held from afar, aloft, th' immortal prize,
And urged the rest by equal steps to rise.
Just precepts thus from great examples given,
She drew from them what they derived from Heaven.
The generous Critic fanned the Poet's fire,   100
And taught the world with reason to admire.
Then Criticism the Muse's handmaid proved,
To dress her charms, and make her more belov'd:
But following wits from that intention strayed,
Who could not win the mistress, wooed the maid;
Against the Poets their own arms they turned,
Sure to hate most the men from whom they learned.
So modern 'pothecaries, taught the art
By doctors' bills to play the doctor's part,
Bold in the practice of mistaken rules,   110
Prescribe, apply, and call their masters fools.
Some on the leaves of ancient authors prey,
Nor time nor moths e'er spoiled so much as they.
Some dryly plain, without invention's aid,
Write dull receipts how poems may be made.
These leave the sense their learning to display,
And those explain the meaning quite away.
  You then whose judgment the right course would steer,
Know well each ancient's proper character;
His fable, subject, scope in every page;   120
Religion, country, genius of his age:
Without all these at once before your eyes,
Cavil you may, but never criticize.
Be Homer's works your study and delight,
Read them by day, and meditate by night;
Thence form your judgment, thence your maxims bring,
And trace the Muses upward to their spring.
Still with itself compared, his text peruse;
And let your comment be the Mantuan Muse.
  When first young Maro² in his boundless mind   130
A work t' outlast immortal Rome designed,
Perhaps he seemed above the critic's law,
And but from Nature's fountains scorned to draw;

  2 Virgil

But when t' examine every part he came,
Nature and Homer were, he found, the same.
Convinced, amazed, he checks the bold design,
And rules as strict his labored work confine
As if the Stagirite [3] o'erlooked each line.
Learn hence for ancient rules a just esteem;
To copy nature is to copy them.   140
 Some beauties yet no precepts can declare,
For there's a happiness as well as care.
Music resembles poetry, in each
Are nameless graces which no methods teach,
And which a master-hand alone can reach.
If, where the rules not far enough extend
(Since rules were made but to promote their end)
Some lucky license answer to the full
Th' intent proposed, that license is a rule.
Thus Pegasus, a nearer way to take,   150
May boldly deviate from the common track.
Great wits sometimes may gloriously offend,
And rise to faults true Critics dare not mend;
From vulgar bounds with brave disorder part,
And snatch a grace beyond the reach of Art,
Which without passing through the judgment, gains
The heart, and all its end at once attains.
In prospects thus, some objects please our eyes,
Which out of Nature's common order rise,
The shapeless rock, or hanging precipice.   160
But though the ancients thus their rules invade
(As Kings dispense with laws themselves have made)
Moderns, beware! or if you must offend
Against the precept, ne'er transgress its end;
Let it be seldom, and compelled by need;
And have at least their precedent to plead.
The Critic else proceeds without remorse,
Seizes your fame, and puts his laws in force.
 I know there are, to whose presumptuous thoughts
Those freer beauties, ev'n in them, seem faults.   170
Some figures monstrous and mis-shaped appear,
Considered singly, or beheld too near,
Which, but proportioned to their light, or place,
Due distance reconciles to form and grace.
A prudent chief not always must display
His powers in equal ranks and fair array,
But with th' occasion and the place comply,
Conceal his force, nay seem sometimes to fly.

[3] Aristotle, born at Stagira

Those oft are stratagems which errors seem,
Nor is it Homer nods, but we that dream.   180
  Still green with bays each ancient altar stands
Above the reach of sacrilegious hands,
Secure from flames, from Envy's fiercer rage,
Destructive War, and all-involving Age.
See, from each clime the learn'd their incense bring!
Hear in all tongues consenting pæans ring!
In praise so just let every voice be joined,
And fill the general chorus of mankind.
Hail, Bards triumphant! born in happier days,
Immortal heirs of universal praise!   190
Whose honors with increase of ages grow,
As streams roll down, enlarging as they flow;
Nations unborn your mighty names shall sound,
And worlds applaud that must not yet be found!
Oh may some spark of your celestial fire,
The last, the meanest of your sons inspire
(That on weak wings, from far, pursues your flights,
Glows while he reads, but trembles as he writes)
To teach vain Wits a science little known,
T' admire superior sense, and doubt their own!   200

PART II

Causes hindering a true judgment. Pride. Imperfect learning. Judging by parts,
and not by the whole. Critics in wit, language, versification only. Being too
hard to please, or too apt to admire. Partiality—too much love to a sect—to
the ancients or moderns. Prejudice or prevention. Singularity. Inconstancy.
Party spirit. Envy. Against envy, and in praise of good nature. When severity
is chiefly to be used by critics.

  Of all the causes which conspire to blind
Man's erring judgment, and misguide the mind,
What the weak head with strongest bias rules,
Is pride, the never-failing vice of fools.
Whatever Nature has in worth denied,
She gives in large recruits of needful pride;
For as in bodies, thus in souls, we find
What wants in blood and spirits, swelled with wind:
Pride, where wit fails, steps in to our defense,
And fills up all the mighty void of sense.   10
If once right reason drives that cloud away,
Truth breaks upon us with resistless day.
Trust not yourself; but your defects to know,
Make use of every friend—and every foe.
  A little learning is a dangerous thing;

Drink deep, or taste not the Pierian spring.[4]
There shallow draughts intoxicate the brain,
And drinking largely sobers us again.
Fired at first sight with what the Muse imparts,
In fearless youth we tempt the heights of arts,   20
While from the bounded level of our mind
Short views we take, nor see the lengths behind;
But more advanced, behold with strange surprise
New distant scenes of endless science rise!
So pleased at first the towering Alps we try,
Mount o'er the vales, and seem to tread the sky,
Th' eternal snows appear already past,
And the first clouds and mountains seem the last;
But, those attained, we tremble to survey
The growing labors of the lengthened way,   30
Th' increasing prospect tires our wandering eyes,
Hills peep o'er hills, and Alps on Alps arise!
  A perfect judge will read each work of wit
With the same spirit that its author writ:
Survey the whole, nor seek slight faults to find
Where Nature moves, and Rapture warms the mind;
Nor lose, for that malignant dull delight,
The generous pleasure to be charmed with wit.
But in such lays as neither ebb nor flow,
Correctly cold, and regularly low,   40
That, shunning faults, one quiet tenor keep,
We cannot blame indeed——but we may sleep.
In wit, as nature, what affects our hearts
Is not th' exactness of peculiar parts;
'T is not a lip, or eye, we beauty call,
But the joint force and full result of all.
Thus when we view some well-proportioned dome
(The world's just wonder, and ev'n thine, O Rome![5]),
No single parts unequally surprise,
All comes united to th' admiring eyes: 50
No monstrous height, or breadth, or length appear;
The whole at once is bold and regular.
  Whoever thinks a faultless piece to see,
Thinks what ne'er was, nor is, nor e'er shall be.
In every work regard the writer's end,
Since none can compass more than they intend;
And if the means be just, the conduct true,
Applause, in spite of trivial faults, is due.
As men of breeding, sometimes men of wit,

---

4 Pieria in Thessaly was the reputed birthplace of
the Muses.

5 St. Peter's

T' avoid great errors must the less commit,   60
Neglect the rules each verbal critic lays,
For not to know some trifles is a praise.
Most critics, fond of some subservient art,
Still make the whole depend upon a part:
They talk of principles, but notions prize,
And all to one loved folly sacrifice.
  Once on a time La Mancha's Knight,[6] they say,
A certain bard encountering on the way,
Discoursed in terms as just, with looks as sage,
As e'er could Dennis,[7] of the Grecian stage;   70
Concluding all were desperate sots and fools
Who durst depart from Aristotle's rules.
Our author, happy in a judge so nice,
Produced his play, and begged the knight's advice;
Made him observe the subject and the plot,
The manners, passions, unities; what not?
All which exact to rule were brought about,
Were but a combat in the lists left out.
"What! leave the combat out?" exclaims the knight.
"Yes, or we must renounce the Stagirite."   80
"Not so, by Heaven!" he answers in a rage,
"Knights, squires, and steeds must enter on the stage."
"So vast a throng the stage can ne'er contain."
"Then build a new, or act it in a plain."
  Thus critics of less judgment than caprice,
Curious, not knowing, not exact, but nice,
Form short ideas, and offend in arts
(As most in manners), by a love to parts.
  Some to Conceit alone their taste confine,
And glittering thoughts struck out at every line;   90
Please with a work where nothing's just or fit,
One glaring chaos and wild heap of wit.
Poets, like painters, thus unskilled to trace
The naked nature and the living grace,
With gold and jewels cover every part,
And hide with ornaments their want of art.
  True wit is nature to advantage dressed,
What oft was thought, but ne'er so well expressed;
Something whose truth convinced at sight we find,
That gives us back the image of our mind.   100
As shades more sweetly recommend the light,
So modest plainness sets off sprightly wit;
For works may have more wit than does them good,

6 Don Quixote   the critic, who was to be
7 John Dennis (1657–1734),   a life-long foe of Pope's

As bodies perish through excess of blood.
  Others for language all their care express,
And value books, as women men, for dress.
Their praise is still—the style is excellent;
The sense they humbly take upon content.
Words are like leaves; and when they most abound,
Much fruit of sense beneath is rarely found.   110
False eloquence, like the prismatic glass,
Its gaudy colors spreads on every place;
The face of Nature we no more survey,
All glares alike, without distinction gay.
But true expression, like th' unchanging sun, ⎱
Clears and improves whate'er it shines upon; ⎰
It gilds all objects, but it alters none.
Expression is the dress of thought, and still
Appears more decent as more suitable.
A vile conceit in pompous words expressed   120
Is like a clown in regal purple dressed:
For different styles with different subjects sort,
As several garbs with country, town, and court.
Some by old words to fame have made pretence,
Ancients in phrase, mere moderns in their sense.
Such labored nothings, in so strange a style,
Amaze th' unlearn'd, and make the learned smile;
Unlucky as Fungoso [8] in the play, ⎱
These sparks with awkward vanity display ⎰
What the fine gentleman wore yesterday, ⎰   130
And but so mimic ancient wits at best,
As apes our grandsires in their doublets dressed.
In words as fashions the same rule will hold;
Alike fantastic if too new or old:
Be not the first by whom the new are tried,
Nor yet the last to lay the old aside.
  But most by numbers judge a poet's song,
And smooth or rough with them is right or wrong.
In the bright Muse though thousand charms conspire,
Her voice is all these tuneful fools admire;   140
Who haunt Parnassus but to please their ear, ⎱
Not mend their minds; as some to Church repair, ⎰
Not for the doctrine, but the music there. ⎰
These equal syllables alone require,
Though oft the ear the open vowels tire,
While expletives their feeble aid do join,
And ten low words oft creep in one dull line:
While they ring round the same unvaried chimes,

8 character in Ben Jonson's *Every Man out of His Humor*

With sure returns of still expected rhymes;
Where'er you find "the cooling western breeze,"   150
In the next line, it "whispers through the trees;"
If crystal streams "with pleasing murmurs creep,"
The reader's threatened (not in vain) with "sleep;"
Then, at the last and only couplet fraught
With some unmeaning thing they call a thought,
A needless Alexandrine [9] ends the song
That, like a wounded snake, drags its slow length along.
Leave such to tune their own dull rhymes, and know
What 's roundly smooth or languishingly slow;
And praise the easy vigor of a line   160
Where Denham's strength and Waller's sweetnss join.[10]
True ease in writing comes from art, not chance,
As those move easiest who have learned to dance.
'T is not enough no harshness gives offense;
The sound must seem an echo to the sense.
Soft is the strain when Zephyr gently blows,
And the smooth stream in smoother numbers flows;
But when loud surges lash the sounding shore,
The hoarse, rough verse should like the torrent roar.
When Ajax strives some rock's vast weight to throw,   170
The line too labors, and the words move slow;
Not so when swift Camilla scours the plain,
Flies o'er th' unbending corn, and skims along the main.
Hear how Timotheus' varied lays surprise,
And bid alternate passions fall and rise! [11]
While at each change the son of Libyan Jove
Now burns with glory, and then melts with love;
Now his fierce eyes with sparkling fury glow,
Now sighs steal out, and tears begin to flow:
Persians and Greeks like turns of nature found   180
And the world's victor stood subdued by sound!
The power of Music all our hearts allow,
And what Timotheus was is Dryden now.
     Avoid extremes; and shun the fault of such
Who still are pleased too little or too much.
At every trifle scorn to take offense:
That always shows great pride, or little sense.
Those heads, as stomachs, are not sure the best,
Which nauseate all, and nothing can digest.
Yet let not each gay turn thy rapture move;   190
For fools admire, but men of sense approve:

9 exemplified in the suc-
ceeding line
10 English poets of the

17th Century, admired by
Pope for their heroic
couplets

11 See Dryden's *Alexander's Feast.*

As things seem large which we through mists descry,
Dullness is ever apt to magnify.
Some foreign writers, some our own despise;
The ancients only, or the moderns prize.
Thus Wit, like Faith, by each man is applied
To one small sect, and all are damned beside.
Meanly they seek the blessing to confine,
And force that sun but on a part to shine,
Which not alone the southern wit sublimes,   200
But ripens spirits in cold northern climes;
Which from the first has shone on ages past,
Enlights the present, and shall warm the last;
Though each may feel increases and decays,
And see now clearer and now darker days.
Regard not then if wit be old or new,
But blame the false and value still the true.
  Some ne'er advance a judgment of their own,
But catch the spreading notion of the town;
They reason and conclude by precedent,   210
And own stale nonsense which they ne'er invent.
Some judge of authors' names, not works, and then
Nor praise nor blame the writings, but the men.
Of all this servile herd the worst is he
That in proud dullness joins with quality,
A constant critic at the great man's board,
To fetch and carry nonsense for my lord.
What woeful stuff this madrigal would be
In some starved hackney sonneteer or me!
But let a lord once own the happy lines,   220
How the wit brightens! how the style refines!
Before his sacred name flies every fault,
And each exalted stanza teems with thought!
  The vulgar thus through imitation err;
As oft the learn'd by being singular;
So much they scorn the crowd, that if the throng
By chance go right, they purposely go wrong.
So schismatics the plain believers quit,
And are but damned for having too much wit.
Some praise at morning what they blame at night,   230
But always think the last opinion right.
A Muse by these is like a mistress used,
This hour she's idolized, the next abused;
While their weak heads like towns unfortified,
'Twixt sense and nonsense daily change their side.
Ask them the cause; they're wiser still, they say;
And still to-morrow's wiser than to-day.

We think our fathers fools, so wise we grow;
Our wiser sons, no doubt, will think us so.
Once school-divines this zealous isle o'er-spread; 240
Who knew most sentences [12] was deepest read.
Faith, Gospel, all seemed made to be disputed,
And none had sense enough to be confuted.
Scotists and Thomists [13] now in peace remain
Amidst their kindred cobwebs in Duck-lane.[14]
If Faith itself has different dresses worn,
What wonder modes in Wit should take their turn?
Oft, leaving what is natural and fit,
The current folly proves the ready wit;
And authors think their reputation safe, 250
Which lives as long as fools are pleased to laugh.
  Some valuing those of their own side or mind,
Still make themselves the measure of mankind:
Fondly we think we honor merit then,
When we but praise ourselves in other men.
Parties in wit attend on those of state,
And public faction doubles private hate.
Pride, Malice, Folly, against Dryden rose,
In various shapes of parsons, critics, beaux;
But sense survived, when merry jests were past; 260
For rising merit will buoy up at last.
Might he return and bless once more our eyes,
New Blackmores and new Milbourns must arise.[15]
Nay, should great Homer lift his awful head,
Zoilus [16] again would start up from the dead.
Envy will merit, as its shade, pursue,
But like a shadow, proves the substance true;
For envied Wit, like Sol eclipsed, makes known
Th' opposing body's grossness, not its own.
When first that sun too powerful beams displays, 270
It draws up vapors which obscure its rays;
But ev'n those clouds at last adorn its way,
Reflect new glories, and augment the day.
  Be thou the first true merit to befriend;
His praise is lost who stays till all commend.
Short is the date, alas! of modern rhymes,
And 't is but just to let them live betimes.

12 alluding to the *Book of Sentences* of Peter Lombard (1151)
13 disputing followers of Duns Scotus and St. Thomas Aquinas, thirteenth century scholastic philosophers
14 London street where second-hand books were formerly sold
15 Sir Richard Blackmore, physician and poet, and the Rev. Luke Milbourn had both attacked Dryden (see p. 602 f.n. 92).
16 Greek critic of fourth century B. C. who attacked Homer

No longer now that golden age appears,
When patriarch wits survived a thousand years:
Now length of fame (our second life) is lost,   280
And bare threescore is all ev'n that can boast;
Our sons their fathers' failing language see,
And such as Chaucer is shall Dryden be.
So when the faithful pencil has designed
Some bright idea of the master's mind,
Where a new world leaps out at his command,
And ready Nature waits upon his hand;
When the ripe colors soften and unite,
And sweetly melt into just shade and light;
When mellowing years their full perfection give,   290
And each bold figure just begins to live,
The treacherous colors the fair art betray,
And all the bright creation fades away!
　　Unhappy Wit, like most mistaken things,
Atones not for that envy which it brings.
In youth alone its empty praise we boast,
But soon the short-lived vanity is lost;
Like some fair flower the early spring supplies,
That gaily blooms, but ev'n in blooming dies.
What is this Wit, which must our cares employ?   300
The owner's wife, that other men enjoy;
Then most our trouble still when most admired,
And still the more we give, the more required;
Whose fame with pains we guard, but lose with ease,
Sure some to vex, but never all to please;
'T is what the vicious fear, the virtuous shun,
By fools 't is hated, and by knaves undone!
　　If Wit so much from Ignorance undergo,
Ah, let not Learning too commence its foe!
Of old those met rewards who could excel,   310
And such were praised who but endeavored well;
Though triumphs were to generals only due,
Crowns were reserved to grace the soldiers too.
Now they who reach Parnassus' lofty crown
Employ their pains to spurn some others down;
And while self-love each jealous writer rules,
Contending wits become the sport of fools;
But still the worst with most regret commend,
For each ill author is as bad a friend.
To what base ends, and by what abject ways,   320
Are mortals urged through sacred lust of praise!
Ah ne'er so dire a thirst of glory boast,

Nor in the critic let the man be lost!
Good nature and good sense must ever join;
To err is human, to forgive divine.
But if in noble minds some dregs remain
Not yet purged off, of spleen and sour disdain,
Discharge that rage on more provoking crimes,
Nor fear a dearth in these flagitious times.
No pardon vile obscenity should find,   330
Though wit and art conspire to move your mind;
But dullness with obscenity must prove
As shameful sure as impotence in love.
In the fat age of pleasure, wealth, and ease
Sprung the rank weed, and thrived with large increase:
When love was all an easy monarch's care,
Seldom at council, never in a war;
Jilts ruled the state, and statesmen farces writ;
Nay wits had pensions, and young lords had wit;
The fair sat panting at a courtier's play,   340
And not a mask went unimproved away;
The modest fan was lifted up no more,
And virgins smiled at what they blushed before.
The following license of a foreign reign [17]
Did all the dregs of bold Socinus [18] drain;
Then unbelieving priests reformed the nation,
And taught more pleasant methods of salvation;
Where Heaven's free subjects might their rights dispute,
Lest God himself should seem too absolute;
Pulpits their sacred satire learned to spare,   350
And Vice admired to find a flatterer there!
Encouraged thus, Wit's Titans braved the skies,
And the press groaned with licensed blasphemies.
These monsters, Critics! with your darts engage,
Here point your thunder, and exhaust your rage!
Yet shun their fault, who, scandalously nice,
Will needs mistake an author into vice;
All seems infected that th' infected spy,
As all looks yellow to the jaundiced eye.

[17] that of William III. The preceding lines refer to the reign of Charles II. [18] the name of two Italian theologians of the sixteenth century regarded as religious heretics

Trembling begins the sacred rites of Pride.
Unnumbered treasures ope at once, and here
The various offerings of the world appear; 130
From each she nicely culls with curious toil,
And decks the Goddess with the glittering spoil.
This casket India's glowing gems unlocks,
And all Arabia breathes from yonder box.
The tortoise here and elephant unite,
Transformed to combs, the speckled, and the white.
Here files of pins extend their shining rows,
Puffs, powders, patches, bibles, billet-doux.
Now awful Beauty puts on all its arms;
The fair each moment rises in her charms, 140
Repairs her smiles, awakens every grace,
And calls forth all the wonders of her face;
Sees by degrees a purer blush arise,
And keener lightnings quicken in her eyes.
The busy Sylphs surround their darling care,
These set the head, and those divide the hair,
Some fold the sleeve, whilst others plait the gown;
And Betty's [22] praised for labors not her own.

CANTO II

Not with more glories, in th' ethereal plain,
The Sun first rises o'er the purpled main,
Than, issuing forth, the rival of his beams
Launched on the bosom of the silver Thames.
Fair nymphs, and well-dressed youths around her shone,
But every eye was fixed on her alone.
On her white breast a sparkling cross she wore,
Which Jews might kiss, and infidels adore.
Her lively looks a sprightly mind disclose,
Quick as her eyes, and as unfixed as those: 10
Favors to none, to all she smiles extends;
Oft she rejects, but never once offends.
Bright as the sun, her eyes the gazers strike,
And, like the sun, they shine on all alike.
Yet graceful ease, and sweetness void of pride,
Might hide her faults, if belles had faults to hide:
If to her share some female errors fall,
Look on her face, and you'll forget 'em all.
  This nymph, to the destruction of mankind,
Nourished two locks which graceful hung behind 20
In equal curls, and well conspired to deck

22 Belinda's maid

With shining ringlets the smooth ivory neck.
Love in these labyrinths his slaves detains,
And mighty hearts are held in slender chains.
With hairy springes we the birds betray,
Slight lines of hair surprise the finny prey,
Fair tresses man's imperial race ensnare,
And beauty draws us with a single hair.
　　Th' adventurous Baron the bright locks admired;
He saw, he wished, and to the prize aspired.   30
Resolved to win, he meditates the way,
By force to ravish, or by fraud betray;
For when success a lover's toil attends,
Few ask if fraud or force attained his ends.
　　For this, ere Phœbus rose, he had implored
Propitious Heaven, and every power adored,
But chiefly Love—to Love an altar built,
Of twelve vast French romances, neatly gilt.
There lay three garters, half a pair of gloves,
And all the trophies of his former loves;   40
With tender billet-doux he lights the pyre,
And breathes three amorous sighs to raise the fire.
Then prostrate falls, and begs with ardent eyes
Soon to obtain, and long possess the prize:
The powers gave ear, and granted half his prayer,
The rest the winds dispersed in empty air.
　　But now secure the painted vessel glides,
The sunbeams trembling on the floating tides;
While melting music steals upon the sky,
And softened sounds along the waters die;   50
Smooth flow the waves, the zephyrs gently play,
Belinda smiled, and all the world was gay.
All but the Sylph—with careful thoughts oppressed,
Th' impending woe sat heavy on his breast.
He summons straight his denizens of air;
The lucid squadrons round the sails repair:
Soft o'er the shrouds aërial whispers breathe
That seemed but zephyrs to the train beneath.
Some to the sun their insect-wings unfold,
Waft on the breeze, or sink in clouds of gold;   60
Transparent forms too fine for mortal sight,
Their fluid bodies half dissolved in light,
Loose to the wind their airy garments flew,
Thin glittering textures of the filmy dew,
Dipped in the richest tincture of the skies,
Where light disports in ever-mingling dyes,
While every beam new transient colors flings,

Colors that change whene'er they wave their wings.
Amid the circle, on the gilded mast,
Superior by the head was Ariel placed;   70
His purple pinions opening to the sun,
He raised his azure wand, and thus begun:
"Ye Sylphs and Sylphids, to your chief give ear!
Fays, Fairies, Genii, Elves, and Dæmons, hear!
Ye know the spheres and various tasks assigned
By laws eternal to th' aërial kind.
Some in the fields of purest ether play,
And bask and whiten in the blaze of day.
Some guide the course of wandering orbs on high,
Or roll the planets through the boundless sky.   80
Some less refined, beneath the moon's pale light
Pursue the stars that shoot athwart the night,
Or suck the mists in grosser air below,
Or dip their pinions in the painted bow,
Or brew fierce tempests on the wintry main,
Or o'er the glebe distil the kindly rain.
Others on earth o'er human race preside,
Watch all their ways, and all their actions guide:
Of these the chief the care of nations own,
And guard with arms divine the British Throne.   90
    "Our humbler province is to tend the Fair,
Not a less pleasing, though less glorious care;
To save the powder from too rude a gale,
Nor let th' imprisoned essences exhale;
To draw fresh colors from the vernal flowers;
To steal from rainbows e'er they drop in showers
A brighter wash; to curl their waving hairs,
Assist their blushes, and inspire their airs;
Nay oft, in dreams invention we bestow,
To change a flounce, or add a furbelow.   100
    "This day black omens threat the brightest Fair,
That e'er deserved a watchful spirit's care;
Some dire disaster, or by force or slight;
But what, or where, the Fates have wrapped in night.
Whether the nymph shall break Diana's law,
Or some frail China jar receive a flaw;
Or stain her honor or her new brocade,
Forget her prayers, or miss a masquerade,
Or lose her heart, or necklace, at a ball;
Or whether Heaven has doomed that Shock [23] must fall.   110
Haste, then, ye spirits! to your charge repair:
The fluttering fan be Zephyretta's care;

23 Belinda's lap-dog

The drops [24] to thee, Brillante, we consign;
And, Momentilla, let the watch be thine;
Do thou, Crispissa, tend her favorite Lock;
Ariel himself shall be the guard of Shock.
　　"To fifty chosen sylphs, of special note,
We trust th' important charge, the petticoat;
Oft have we known that seven-fold fence to fail,
Though stiff with hoops, and armed with ribs of whale:　　120
Form a strong line about the silver bound,
And guard the wide circumference around.
　　"Whatever spirit, careless of his charge,
His post neglects, or leaves the fair at large,
Shall feel sharp vengeance soon o'ertake his sins,
Be stopped in vials, or transfixed with pins,
Or plunged in lakes of bitter washes lie,
Or wedged whole ages in a bodkin's eye;
Gums and pomatums shall his flight restrain,
While clogged he beats his silken wings in vain,　　130
Or alum styptics with contracting power
Shrink his thin essence like a riveled [25] flower:
Or, as Ixion fixed, the wretch shall feel
The giddy motion of the whirling mill,
In fumes of burning chocolate shall glow,
And tremble at the sea that froths below!"
　　He spoke; the spirits from the sails descend;
Some, orb in orb, around the nymph extend;
Some thread the mazy ringlets of her hair;
Some hang upon the pendants of her ear:　　140
With beating hearts the dire event they wait,
Anxious, and trembling for the birth of Fate.

CANTO III

Close by those meads, for ever crowned with flowers,
Where Thames with pride surveys his rising towers,
There stands a structure of majestic frame,[26]
Which from the neighboring Hampton takes its name.
Here Britain's statesmen oft the fall foredoom
Of foreign tyrants and of nymphs at home;
Here thou, great Anna! whom three realms obey,
Dost sometimes counsel take—and sometimes tea.
　　Hither the heroes and the nymphs resort,
To taste awhile the pleasures of a court;　　10
In various talk th' instructive hours they passed,

24 ear-rings　　　　　　　　　　26 Hampton Court, a royal palace
25 shriveled

E'er felt such rage, resentment, and despair,
As thou, sad Virgin! for thy ravished hair.   10
  For, that sad moment, when the Sylphs withdrew
And Ariel weeping from Belinda flew,
Umbriel, a dusky, melancholy sprite
As ever sullied the fair face of light,
Down to the central earth, his proper scene,
Repaired to search the gloomy cave of Spleen.[31]
  Swift on his sooty pinions flits the Gnome,
And in a vapor reached the dismal dome.
No cheerful breeze this sullen region knows,
The dreaded East is all the wind that blows.   20
Here in a grotto, sheltered close from air,
And screened in shades from day's detested glare,
She sighs for ever on her pensive bed,
Pain at her side, and Megrim [32] at her head.
Two handmaids wait the throne; alike in place,
But differing far in figure and in face.
Here stood Ill-nature like an ancient maid,
Her wrinkled form in black and white arrayed;
With store of prayers for mornings, nights, and noons,
Her hand is filled; her bosom with lampoons.   30
There Affectation, with a sickly mien,
Shows in her cheek the roses of eighteen,
Practised to lisp, and hang the head aside,
Faints into airs, and languishes with pride,
On the rich quilt sinks with becoming woe,
Wrapped in a gown, for sickness and for show.
The fair ones feel such maladies as these,
When each new night-dress gives a new disease.
  A constant vapor o'er the palace flies,
Strange phantoms rising as the mists arise;   40
Dreadful as hermit's dreams in haunted shades,
Or bright as visions of expiring maids.
Now glaring fiends, and snakes on rolling spires,
Pale specters, gaping tombs, and purple fires;
Now lakes of liquid gold, Elysian scenes,
And crystal domes, and angels in machines.[33]
  Unnumbered throngs on every side are seen,
Of bodies changed to various forms by Spleen.
Here living Teapots stand, one arm held out,
One bent; the handle this, and that the spout: 50
A Pipkin there, like Homer's Tripod walks; [34]

---

31 The spleen was regarded as the seat of ill-humor (here personified).

32 sick headache

33 the *deus ex machina*

34 A small jar walks like the self-moving tripods described by Homer (*Iliad*, XVIII. 373–377).

Here sighs a Jar, and there a Goose-pie talks;
Men prove with child, as powerful fancy works,
And maids turned bottles, call aloud for corks.
  Safe passed the Gnome through this fantastic band,
A branch of healing spleenwort in his hand.
Then thus addressed the Power: "Hail, wayward Queen!
Who rule the sex to fifty from fifteen:
Parent of vapors and of female wit,
Who give th' hysteric or poetic fit,   60
On various tempers act by various ways,
Make some take physic, others scribble plays;
Who cause the proud their visits to delay,
And send the godly in a pet to pray.
A nymph there is that all your power disdains,
And thousands more in equal mirth maintains.
But oh! if e'er thy Gnome could spoil a grace,
Or raise a pimple on a beauteous face,
Like citron-waters matrons' cheeks inflame,
Or change complexions at a losing game;   70
If e'er with airy horns I planted heads,
Or rumpled petticoats, or tumbled beds,
Or caused suspicion when no soul was rude,
Or discomposed the head-dress of a prude,
Or e'er to costive lapdog gave disease,
Which not the tears of brightest eyes could ease,
Hear me, and touch Belinda with chagrin:
That single act gives half the world the spleen."
  The Goddess with a discontented air
Seems to reject him though she grants his prayer.   80
A wondrous bag with both her hands she binds,
Like that where once Ulysses held the winds;
There she collects the force of female lungs,
Sighs, sobs, and passions, and the war of tongues.
A vial next she fills with fainting fears,
Soft sorrows, melting griefs, and flowing tears.
The Gnome rejoicing bears her gifts away,
Spreads his black wings, and slowly mounts to day.
  Sunk in Thalestris' [35] arms the nymph he found,
Her eyes dejected and her hair unbound.   90
Full o'er their heads the swelling bag he rent,
And all the Furies issued at the vent.
Belinda burns with more than mortal ire,
And fierce Thalestris fans the rising fire.
"O wretched maid!" she spread her hands, and cried
(While Hampton's echoes, "Wretched maid!" replied),

35 said to be a Mrs. Morley

"Was it for this you took such constant care
The bodkin, comb, and essence to prepare?
For this your locks in paper durance bound,
For this with torturing irons wreathed around? 100
For this with fillets strained your tender head,
And bravely bore the double loads of lead?
Gods! shall the ravisher display your hair,
While the fops envy, and the ladies stare!
Honor forbid! at whose unrivaled shrine
Ease, pleasure, virtue, all our sex resign.
Methinks already I your tears survey,
Already hear the horrid things they say,
Already see you a degraded toast,
And all your honor in a whisper lost! 110
How shall I, then, your helpless fame defend?
'I' will then be infamy to seem your friend!
And shall this prize, th' inestimable prize,
Exposed through crystal to the gazing eyes,
And heightened by the diamond's circling rays,
On that rapacious hand for ever blaze?
Sooner shall grass in Hyde Park Circus grow,
And wits take lodgings in the sound of Bow; 36
Sooner let earth, air, sea, to chaos fall,
Men, monkeys, lapdogs, parrots, perish all!" 120
    She said; then raging to Sir Plume 37 repairs,
And bids her beau demand the precious hairs
(Sir Plume of amber snuff-box justly vain,
And the nice conduct of a clouded cane):
With earnest eyes, and round unthinking face,
He first the snuff-box opened, then the case,
And thus broke out—"My Lord, why, what the devil!
Z—ds! damn the lock! 'fore Gad, you must be civil!
Plague on 't! 't is past a jest—nay prithee, pox!
Give her the hair"—he spoke, and rapped his box. 130
    "It grieves me much," replied the Peer again,
"Who speaks so well should ever speak in vain.
But by this Lock, this sacred Lock I swear
(Which never more shall join its parted hair;
Which never more its honors shall renew,
Clipped from the lovely head where late it grew),
That while my nostrils draw the vital air,
This hand, which won it, shall for ever wear."
He spoke, and speaking, in proud triumph spread

---

36 within sound of the bells of the church of St. Mary le Bow, in Cheap- side, an unfashionable district

37 Sir George Brown, brother of Mrs. Morley. He took offense at the portrait which follows.

The long-contended honors of her head.   140
  But Umbriel, hateful Gnome, forbears not so;
He breaks the vial whence the sorrows flow.
Then see! the nymph in beauteous grief appears,
Her eyes half-languishing, half-drowned in tears;
On her heaved bosom hung her drooping head,
Which with a sigh she raised, and thus she said:
  "For ever cursed be this detested day,
Which snatched my best, my favorite curl away!
Happy! ah, ten times happy had I been,
If Hampton Court these eyes had never seen!   150
Yet am not I the first mistaken maid,
By love of courts to numerous ills betrayed.
O had I rather unadmired remained
In some lone isle, or distant northern land;
Where the gilt chariot never marks the way,
Where none learn Ombre, non e'er taste Bohea! [38]
There kept my charms concealed from mortal eye,
Like roses that in deserts bloom and die.
What moved my mind with youthful lords to roam?
O had I stayed, and said my prayers at home!   160
'T was this the morning omens seemed to tell,
Thrice from my trembling hand the patch-box [39] fell;
The tottering china shook without a wind,
Nay, Poll sat mute, and Shock was most unkind!
A Sylph too warned me of the threats of fate,
In mystic visions, now believed too late!
See the poor remnants of these slighted hairs!
My hands shall rend what e'en thy rapine spares.
These in two sable ringlets taught to break,
Once gave new beauties to the snowy neck;   170
The sister-lock now sits uncouth, alone,
And in its fellow's fate foresees its own;
Uncurled it hangs, the fatal shears demands,
And tempts once more thy sacrilegious hands.
O hadst thou, cruel! been content to seize
Hairs less in sight, or any hairs but these!"

CANTO V

She said: the pitying audience melt in tears.
But Fate and Jove had stopped the Baron's ears.
In vain Thalestris with reproach assails,
For who can move when fair Belinda fails?

38 tea   39 holding patches of court plaster for the face

Not half so fixed the Trojan [40] could remain,
While Anna begged and Dido raged in vain.
Then grave Clarissa graceful waved her fan;
Silence ensued, and thus the nymph began:
   "Say why are beauties praised and honored most,
The wise man's passion, and the vain man's toast?   10
Why decked with all that land and sea afford,
Why angels called, and angel-like adored?
Why round our coaches crowd the white-gloved beaux,
Why bows the side-box from its inmost rows?
How vain are all these glories, all our pains,
Unless good sense preserve what beauty gains;
That men may say when we the front-box grace,
'Behold the first in virtue as in face!'
Oh! if to dance all night, and dress all day,
Charmed the smallpox, or chased old age away;   20
Who would not scorn what housewife's cares produce,
Or who would learn one earthly thing of use?
To patch, nay ogle, might become a saint,
Nor could it sure be such a sin to paint.
But since, alas! frail beauty must decay,
Curled or uncurled, since locks will turn to gray;
Since painted, or not painted, all shall fade,
And she who scorns a man must die a maid;
What then remains but well our power to use,
And keep good humor still whate'er we lose?   30
And trust me, dear, good humor can prevail
When airs, and flights, and screams, and scolding fail.
Beauties in vain their pretty eyes may roll;
Charms strike the sight, but merit wins the soul."
   So spoke the dame, but no applause ensued;
Belinda frowned, Thalestris called her prude.
"To arms, to arms!" the fierce virago cries,
And swift as lightning to the combat flies.
All side in parties, and begin th' attack;
Fans clap, silks rustle, and tough whalebones crack;   40
Heroes' and heroines' shouts confusedly rise,
And bass and treble voices strike the skies.
No common weapons in their hands are found,
Like Gods they fight, nor dread a mortal wound.
   So when bold Homer makes the Gods engage,
And heavenly breasts with human passions rage;
'Gainst Pallas, Mars; Latona, Hermes arms;
And all Olympus rings with loud alarms:
Jove's thunder roars, heaven trembles all around,

40 Æneas

Blue Neptune storms, the bellowing deeps resound: 50
Earth shakes her nodding towers, the ground gives way,
And the pale ghosts start at the flash of day!
   Triumphant Umbriel on a sconce's height
Clapped his glad wings, and sat to view the fight:
Propped on the bodkin spears, the sprites survey
The growing combat, or assist the fray.
   While through the press enraged Thalestris flies,
And scatters death around from both her eyes,
A Beau and Witling perished in the throng,
One died in metaphor, and one in song.   60
"O cruel nymph! a living death I bear,"
Cried Dapperwit, and sunk beside his chair.
A mournful glance Sir Fopling upwards cast,
"Those eyes are made so killing"—was his last.
Thus on Mæander's flowery margin lies
Th' expiring swan, and as he sings he dies.
   When bold Sir Plume had drawn Clarissa down,
Chloe stepped in, and killed him with a frown;
She smiled to see the doughty hero slain,
But, at her smile, the beau revived again.   70
   Now Jove suspends his golden scales in air,
Weighs the men's wits against the lady's hair;
The doubtful beam long nods from side to side;
At length the wits mount up, the hairs subside.
   See, fierce Belinda on the Baron flies,
With more than usual lightning in her eyes;
Nor feared the chief th' unequal fight to try,
Who sought no more than on his foe to die.
But this bold lord with manly strength endued,
She with one finger and a thumb subdued: 80
Just where the breath of life his nostrils drew,
A charge of snuff the wily virgin threw;
The Gnomes direct, to every atom just,
The pungent grains of titillating dust.
Sudden, with starting tears each eye o'erflows,
And the high dome re-echoes to his nose.
   "Now meet thy fate," incensed Belinda cried,
And drew a deadly bodkin from her side.
(The same, his ancient personage to deck,
Her great-great-grandsire wore about his neck,   90
In three seal-rings; which after, melted down,
Formed a vast buckle for his widow's gown:
Her infant grandame's whistle next it grew,
The bells she jingled, and the whistle blew;
Then in a bodkin graced her mother's hairs,

Which long she wore, and now Belinda wears.)
"Boast not my fall," he cried, "insulting foe!
Thou by some other shalt be laid as low.
Nor think to die dejects my lofty mind:
All that I dread is leaving you behind!   100
Rather than so, ah, let me still survive,
And burn in Cupid's flames—but burn alive."
"Restore the Lock!" she cries; and all around
"Restore the Lock!" the vaulted roofs rebound.
Not fierce Othello in so loud a strain
Roared for the handkerchief that caused his pain.
But see how oft ambitious aims are crossed,
And chiefs contend till all the prize is lost!
The lock, obtained with guilt, and kept with pain,
In every place is sought, but sought in vain: 110
With such a prize no mortal must be blessed,
So Heaven decrees! with Heaven who can contest?
  Some thought it mounted to the lunar sphere,
Since all things lost on earth are treasured there.
There heroes' wits are kept in ponderous vases,
And beaux' in snuffboxes and tweezer-cases.
There broken vows and deathbed alms are found,
And lovers' hearts with ends of riband bound,
The courtier's promises, and sick man's prayers,
The smiles of harlots, and the tears of heirs,   120
Cages for gnats, and chains to yoke a flea,
Dried butterflies, and tomes of casuistry.
  But trust the Muse—she saw it upward rise,
Though marked by none but quick, poetic eyes
(So Rome's great founder to the heavens withdrew,
To Proculus alone confessed in view);
A sudden star, it shot through liquid air,
And drew behind a radiant trail of hair.
Not Berenice's locks [41] first rose so bright,
The heavens bespangling with disheveled light.   130
The Sylphs behold it kindling as it flies,
And pleased pursue its progress through the skies.
  This the beau monde shall from the Mall survey,
And hail with music its propitious ray.
This the bless'd lover shall for Venus take,
And send up vows from Rosamonda's lake. [42]
This Partridge [43] soon shall view in cloudless skies,

[41] Dedicated to Venus for her husband's safe return from war, they were transformed into a constellation.

[42] in St. James' Park, London

[43] John Partridge was a ridiculous star-gazer, who in his almanacs every year never failed to predict the downfall of the Pope and the King of France. (Pope's note)

When next he looks through Galileo's eyes;
And hence th' egregious wizard shall foredoom
The fate of Louis, and the fall of Rome.   140
  Then cease, bright Nymph! to mourn thy ravished hair,
Which adds new glory to the shining sphere!
Not all the tresses that fair head can boast,
Shall draw such envy as the Lock you lost.
For, after all the murders of your eye,
When, after millions slain, yourself shall die:
When those fair suns shall set, as set they must,
And all those tresses shall be laid in dust,
This Lock the Muse shall consecrate to fame,
And 'midst the stars inscribe Belinda's name.   150

EPISTLE TO DR. ARBUTHNOT [44]

ADVERTISEMENT

THIS paper is a sort of bill of complaint, begun many years since, and drawn up by snatches, as the several occasions offered. I had no thoughts of publishing it, till it pleased some Persons of Rank and Fortune (the Authors of *Verses to the Imitator of Horace,* and of an *Epistle to a Doctor of Divinity from a Nobleman at Hampton Court*) to attack, in a very extraordinary manner, not only my Writings (of which, being public, the Public is judge), but my Person, Morals, and Family; whereof, to those who know me not, a truer information may be requisite. Being divided between the necessity to say something of myself, and my own laziness to undertake so awkward a task, I thought it the shortest way to put the last hand to this epistle. If it have anything pleasing, it will be that by which I am most desirous to please, the Truth and the Sentiment; and if anything offensive, it will be only to those I am least sorry to offend, the vicious or the ungenerous.

Many will know their own pictures in it, there being not a circumstance but what is true; but I have, for the most part, spared their names, and they may escape being laughed at if they please.

I would have some of them know it was owing to the request of the learned and candid Friend to whom it is inscribed, that I make not as free use of theirs as they have done of mine. However, I shall have this advantage and honor on my side, that whereas, by their proceeding, any abuse may be directed at any man, no injury can possibly be done by mine, since a nameless character can never be found out but by its truth and likeness.

P. SHUT, shut the door, good John! [45] fatigued, I said,
Tie up the knocker, say I'm sick, I'm dead.
The Dog-star rages! nay 'tis past a doubt
All Bedlam [46] or Parnassus is let out:
Fire in each eye, and papers in each hand,

[44] John Arbuthnot, distinguished physician and man of letters, and Pope's close friend
[45] John Searl, Pope's body-servant
[46] London hospital for the insane

They rave, recite, and madden round the land.
What walls can guard me, or what shades can hide?
They pierce my thickets, through my grot they glide;
By land, by water, they renew the charge;
They stop the chariot, and they board the barge.   10
No place is sacred, not the church is free;
Ev'n Sunday shines no Sabbath-day to me;
Then from the Mint [47] walks forth the man of rhyme,
Happy to catch me just at dinner time.
Is there a Parson, much bemused in beer,
A maudlin Poetess, a rhyming Peer,
A clerk foredoomed his father's soul to cross,
Who pens a stanza when he should engross?
Is there who, locked from ink and paper, scrawls
With desperate charcoal round his darkened walls?   20
All fly to Twit'nam,[48] and in humble strain
Apply to me to keep them mad or vain.
Arthur,[49] whose giddy son neglects the laws,
Imputes to me and my damned works the cause:
Poor Cornus [50] sees his frantic wife elope,
And curses Wit and Poetry, and Pope.
Friend to my life (which did not you prolong,
The world had wanted many an idle song)
What drop or nostrum can this plague remove?
Or which must end me, a fool's wrath or love?   30
A dire dilemma! either way I'm sped,
If foes, they write, if friends, they read me dead.
Seized and tied down to judge, how wretched I!
Who can't be silent, and who will not lie.
To laugh were want of goodness and of grace,
And to be grave exceeds all power of face.
I sit with sad civility, I read
With honest anguish and an aching head,
And drop at last, but in unwilling ears,
This saving counsel, "Keep your piece nine years."   40
"Nine years!" cries he, who high in Drury lane,
Lulled by soft zephyrs through the broken pane,
Rhymes ere he wakes, and prints before Term ends,[51]
Obliged by hunger and request of friends:
"The piece, you think, is incorrect? why, take it,
I'm all submission, what you'd have it, make it."
Three things another's modest wishes bound,

---

47 A place in London where debtors could not be arrested. They could not be arrested anywhere on Sundays.

48 Pope's villa at Twickenham, on the Thames near London

49 Arthur Moore, a politician

50 probably Sir Robert Walpole, the prime minister

51 the London season

My friendship, and a Prologue, and ten pound.
  Pitholeon sends to me: "You know his Grace,
I want a patron; ask him for a place."
Pitholeon libeled me—"but here's a letter
Informs you, Sir, 'twas when he knew no better.
Dare you refuse him? Curll [52] invites to dine,
He'll write a *Journal,* or he'll turn divine."
Bless me! a packet.—'Tis a stranger sues,
A Virgin Tragedy, an Orphan Muse.
If I dislike it, "Furies, death and rage!"
If I approve, "Commend it to the stage."
There (thank my stars) my whole commission ends,
The players and I are, luckily, no friends.
Fired that the house reject him, " 'Sdeath, I'll print it,
And shame the fools— Your interest, Sir, with Lintot!" [53]
Lintot, dull rogue, will think your price too much:
"Not, Sir, if you revise it, and retouch."
All my demurs but double his attacks;
At last he whispers, "Do; and we go snacks."
Glad of a quarrel, straight I clap the door;
"Sir, let me see your works and you no more."
  'Tis sung, when Midas' ears began to spring
(Midas, a sacred person and a king),
His very Minister who spied them first,
(Some say his Queen) was forced to speak, or burst.
And is not mine, my friend, a sorer case,
When every coxcomb perks them in my face?
  A. Good friend, forbear! you deal in dangerous things.
I'd never name Queens, Ministers, or Kings;
Keep close to ears, and those let asses prick;
'Tis nothing— P. Nothing? if they bite and kick?
Out with it, *Dunciad!* let the secret pass,
That secret to each fool, that he's an ass:
The truth once told (and wherefore should we lie?)
The Queen of Midas slept, and so may I.
  You think this cruel? take it for a rule,
No creature smarts so little as a fool.
Let peals of laughter, Codrus! round thee break,
Thou unconcerned canst hear the mighty crack:
Pit, box, and gallery in convulsions hurled,
Thou stand'st unshook amidst a bursting world.
Who shames a Scribbler? break one cobweb through,
He spins the slight, self-pleasing thread anew:
Destroy his fib or sophistry in vain!
The creature's at his dirty work again,

50

60

70

80

90

52 a piratical publisher and an enemy of Pope   53 Pope's publisher

Throned in the center of his thin designs,
Proud of a vast extent of flimsy lines.
Whom have I hurt? has Poet yet or Peer,
Lost the arched eyebrow or Parnassian sneer?
And has not Colley [54] still his lord and whore?
His butchers Henley? his freemasons Moore?
Does not one table Bavius still admit?
Still to one Bishop Philips [55] seem a wit?   100
Still Sappho [56]— A. Hold! for God's sake—you'll offend.
No names!—be calm!—learn prudence of a friend.
I too could write, and I am twice as tall;
But foes like these— P. One flatterer's worse than all.
Of all mad creatures, if the learn'd are right,
It is the slaver kills, and not the bite.
A fool quite angry is quite innocent:
Alas! 'tis ten times worse when they repent.
    One dedicates in high heroic prose,
And ridicules beyond a hundred foes;   110
One from all Grub-street will my fame defend,
And, more abusive, calls himself my friend.
This prints my *Letters,* that expects a bribe,
And others roar aloud, "Subscribe, subscribe!"
    There are, who to my person pay their court:
I cough like Horace, and, though lean, am short;
Ammon's great son [57] one shoulder had too high,
Such Ovid's nose, and "Sir! you have an eye—"
Go on, obliging creatures, make me see
All that disgraced my betters met in me.   120
Say for my comfort, languishing in bed,
"Just so immortal Maro [58] held his head:"
And when I die, be sure you let me know
Great Homer died three thousand years ago.
    Why did I write? what sin to me unknown
Dipped me in ink, my parents', or my own?
As yet a child, nor yet a fool to fame,
I lisped in numbers, for the numbers came.
I left no calling for this idle trade,
No duty broke, no father disobeyed.   130
The Muse but served to ease some friend, not wife,
To help me through this long disease, my life,
To second, Arbuthnot! thy art and care,
And teach the being you preserved, to bear.
    A. But why then publish? P. Granville the polite,

54 Colley Cibber, actor,
dramatist, and poet laureate
55 Ambrose Philips, pas-
toral poet

56 Lady Mary Wortley
Montague, well-known lit-
erary woman
57 Alexander the Great

58 Virgil

And knowing Walsh, would tell me I could write;
Well-natured Garth inflamed with early praise,
And Congreve loved, and Swift endured my lays;
The courtly Talbot, Somers, Sheffield, read;
Ev'n mitered Rochester would nod the head,   140
And St. John's self (great Dryden's friends before)
With open arms received one poet more.[59]
Happy my studies, when by these approved!
Happier their author, when by these belov'd!
From these the world will judge of men and books,
Not from the Burnets, Oldmixons, and Cookes.[60]
    Soft were my numbers; who could take offense,
While pure description held the place of sense?
Like gentle Fanny's [61] was my flowery theme,
A painted mistress, or a purling stream.   150
Yet then did Gildon [62] draw his venal quill;
I wished the man a dinner, and sat still.
Yet then did Dennis [62] rave in furious fret;
I never answered,—I was not in debt.
If want provoked, or madness made them print,
I waged no war with Bedlam or the Mint.
    Did some more sober critic come abroad;
If wrong, I smiled; if right, I kissed the rod.
Pains, reading, study, are their just pretense,
And all they want is spirit, taste, and sense.   160
Commas and points they set exactly right,
And 'twere a sin to rob them of their mite.
Yet ne'er one sprig of laurel graced these ribalds,
From slashing Bentleys down to piddling Tibbalds.[63]
Each wight who reads not, and but scans and spells,
Each word-catcher that lives on syllables,
Ev'n such small critics some regard may claim,
Preserved in Milton's or in Shakespeare's name.
Pretty! in amber to observe the forms
Of hairs, or straws, or dirt, or grubs, or worms!   170
The things, we know, are neither rich nor rare,
But wonder how the devil they got there.
    Were others angry: I excused them too;
Well might they rage, I gave them but their due.
A man's true merit 'tis not hard to find;
But each man's secret standard in his mind,
That casting-weight pride adds to emptiness,

59 The men just men-   61 Lord Hervey, men-   of Milton; Lewis Theo-
tioned encouraged Pope in tioned as Sporus below   bald, editor of Shakespeare.
his early work.   62 contemporary critics
    60 authors of secret and   63 Richard Bentley, great
scandalous history (Pope's classical scholar and editor
note)

This, who can gratify? for who can guess?
The bard [64] whom pilfered pastorals renown,
Who turns a Persian tale for half a crown,   180
Just writes to make his barrenness appear,
And strains, from hard-bound brains eight lines a year;
He, who still wanting, though he lives on theft,
Steals much, spends little, yet has nothing left;
And he who now to sense, now nonsense leaning,
Means not, but blunders round about a meaning:
And he whose fustian's so sublimely bad,
It is not poetry, but prose run mad:
All these, my modest satire bade translate,
And owned that nine such poets made a Tate.[65]   190
How did they fume, and stamp, and roar, and chafe!
And swear, not Addison himself was safe.
        Peace to all such! but were there one whose fires
True Genius kindles, and fair Fame inspires;
Bless'd with each talent and each art to please,
And born to write, converse, and live with ease:
Should such a man, too fond to rule alone,
Bear, like the Turk, no brother near the throne;
View him with scornful, yet with jealous eyes,
And hate for arts that caused himself to rise;   200
Damn with faint praise, assent with civil leer,
And without sneering, teach the rest to sneer;
Willing to wound, and yet afraid to strike,
Just hint a fault, and hesitate dislike;
Alike reserved to blame or to commend,
A timorous foe, and a suspicious friend;
Dreading ev'n fools; by flatterers besieged,
And so obliging that he ne'er obliged;
Like Cato, give his little Senate laws,
And sit attentive to his own applause;   210
While Wits and Templars [66] every sentence raise,
And wonder with a foolish face of praise:—
Who but must laugh, if such a man there be?
Who would not weep, if Atticus [67] were he?
        What though my name stood rubric [68] on the walls
Or plastered posts, with claps,[69] in capitals?
Or smoking forth, a hundred hawkers' load,
On wings of winds came flying all abroad?
I sought no homage from the race that write;
I kept, like Asian Monarchs, from their sight: 220
Poems I heeded (now be-rhymed so long)

64 Ambrose Philips   66 law-students   69 posters
65 Nahum   Tate,   poet   67 Addison
laureate at the time   68 in red

No more than thou, great George! a birthday song.
I ne'er with wits or witlings passed my days
To spread about the itch of verse and praise;
Nor like a puppy daggled through the town
To fetch and carry sing-song up and down;
Nor at rehearsals sweat, and mouthed, and cried,
With handkerchief and orange at my side;
But sick of fops, and poetry, and prate,
To Bufo [70] left the whole Castalian state.   230
   Proud as Apollo on his forkèd hill,
Sat full-blown Bufo, puffed by every quill;
Fed with soft dedication all day long,
Horace and he went hand in hand in song.
His library (where busts of poets dead
And a true Pindar stood without a head)
Received of wits an undistinguished race,
Who first his judgment asked, and then a place:
Much they extolled his pictures, much his seat,
And flattered every day, and some days eat: 240
Till grown more frugal in his riper days,
He paid some bards with port, and some with praise;
To some a dry rehearsal was assigned,
And others (harder still) he paid in kind.
Dryden alone (what wonder?) came not nigh;
Dryden alone escaped this judging eye:
But still the great have kindness in reserve;
He helped to bury whom he helped to starve.
May some choice patron bless each gray goose quill!
May every Bavius [71] have his Bufo still!   250
So when a statesman wants a day's defense,
Or Envy holds a whole week's war with Sense,
Or simple Pride for flattery makes demands,
May dunce by dunce be whistled off my hands!
Bless'd be the great! for those they take away,
And those they left me—for they left me Gay; [72]
Left me to see neglected Genius bloom,
Neglected die, and tell it on his tomb:
Of all thy blameless life the sole return
My Verse, and Queensbury weeping o'er thy urn!   260
   Oh, let me live my own, and die so too!
(To live and die is all I have to do)
Maintain a Poet's dignity and ease,
And see what friends, and read what books I please;
Above a Patron, though I condescend

70 probably Lord Hali-   (from the name of a   famous as the author of
fax, a patron of letters   Roman poetaster)   *The Beggars' Opera*
   71 "every poor poet"   72 John Gay, the poet,

Sometimes to call a minister my friend.
I was not born for courts or great affairs;
I pay my debts, believe, and say my prayers;
Can sleep without a poem in my head,
Nor know if Dennis be alive or dead.   270
   Why am I asked what next shall see the light?
Heavens! was I born for nothing but to write?
Has life no joys for me? or (to be grave)
Have I no friend to serve, no soul to save?
"I found him close with Swift"—"Indeed? no doubt"
(Cries prating Balbus), "something will come out."
'Tis all in vain, deny it as I will.
"No, such a Genius never can lie still;"
And then for mine obligingly mistakes
The first lampoon Sir Will or Bubo [73] makes.   280
Poor guiltless I! and can I choose but smile,
When every coxcomb knows me by my style?
   Cursed be the verse, how well soe'er it flow,
That tends to make one worthy man my foe,
Give Virtue scandal, Innocence a fear,
Or from the soft-eyed virgin steal a tear!
But he who hurts a harmless neighbor's peace,
Insults fallen worth, or Beauty in distress,
Who loves a lie, lame Slander helps about,
Who writes a libel, or who copies out: 290
That fop whose pride affects a patron's name,
Yet absent, wounds an author's honest fame;
Who can your merit selfishly approve,
And show the sense of it without the love;
Who has the vanity to call you friend,
Yet wants the honor, injured, to defend;
Who tells whate'er you think, whate'er you say,
And, if he not, must at least betray;
Who to the Dean and silver bell can swear,
And sees at Canons what was never there;   300
Who reads but with a lust to misapply,
Make satire a lampoon, and fiction lie:
A lash like mine no honest man shall dread,
But all such babbling blockheads in his stead.
   Let Sporus [74] tremble— A. What? that thing of silk,
Sporus, that mere white curd of ass's milk?
Satire or sense, alas! can Sporus feel?
Who breaks a butterfly upon a wheel?
   P. Yet let me flap this bug with gilded wings,
This painted child of dirt, that stinks and stings;   310

[73] Sir William Yonge and Bubb Dodington   [74] Lord Hervey

Whose buzz the witty and the fair annoys,
Yet wit ne'er tastes, and beauty ne'er enjoys;
So well-bred spaniels civilly delight
In mumbling of the game they dare not bite.
Eternal smiles his emptiness betray,
As shallow streams run dimpling all the way.
Whether in florid impotence he speaks,
And, as the prompter breathes, the puppet squeaks;
Or at the ear of Eve, familiar toad,
Half froth, half venom, spits himself abroad,   320
In puns, or politics, or tales, or lies,
Or spite, or smut, or rhymes, or blasphemies.
His wit all see-saw between *that* and *this*, ⎫
Now high, now low, now master up, now miss, ⎬
And he himself one vile Antithesis. ⎭
Amphibious thing! that acting either part,
The trifling head or the corrupted heart,
Fop at the toilet, flatterer at the board,
Now trips a lady, and now struts a lord.
Eve's tempter thus the Rabbins have expressed,   330
A cherub's face, a reptile all the rest;
Beauty that shocks you, parts that none will trust,
Wit that can creep, and pride that licks the dust.
    Not Fortune's worshiper, nor Fashion's fool,
Not Lucre's madman, nor Ambition's tool,
Not proud, nor servile;—be one poet's praise,
That if he pleased, he pleased by manly ways:
That flattery, ev'n to Kings, he held a shame,
And thought a lie in verse or prose the same;
That not in fancy's maze he wandered long,   340
But stooped to truth, and moralized his song:
That not for Fame, but Virtue's better end,
He stood the furious foe, the timid friend,
The damning critic, half approving wit,
The coxcomb hit, or fearing to be hit;
Laughed at the loss of friends he never had,
The dull, the proud, the wicked, and the mad;
The distant threats of vengeance on his head,
The blow unfelt, the tear he never shed;
The tale revived, the lie so oft o'erthrown,   350
Th' imputed trash, and dullness not his own;
The morals blackened when the writings 'scape,
The libeled person, and the pictured shape;
Abuse on all he loved, or loved him, spread,
A friend in exile, or a father dead;
The whisper, that to greatness still too near,

Perhaps yet vibrates on his Sovereign's ear:—
Welcome for thee, fair Virtue! all the past;
For thee, fair Virtue! welcome ev'n the last!
   A. But why insult the poor, affront the great?   360
P. A knave's a knave to me in every state:
Alike my scorn, if he succeed or fail,
Sporus at court, or Japhet in a jail;
A hireling scribbler, or a hireling peer,
Knight of the post corrupt, or of the shire;
If on a Pillory, or near a Throne,
He gain his prince's ear, or lose his own.
   Yet soft by nature, more a dupe than wit,
Sappho can tell you how this man was bit;
This dreaded Satirist Dennis will confess   370
Foe to his pride, but friend to his distress:
So humble, he has knocked at Tibbald's door,
Has drunk with Cibber, nay has rhymed for Moore.
Full ten years slandered, did he once reply?
Three thousand suns went down on Welsted's [75] lie.
To please a mistress one aspersed his life;
He lashed him not, but let her be his wife.
Let Budgell [76] charge low Grub-street on his quill,
And write whate'er he pleased, except his will;
Let the two Curlls [77] of town and court, abuse   380
His father, mother, body, soul, and muse.
Yet why? that father held it for a rule,
It was a sin to call our neighbor fool;
That harmless mother thought no wife a whore:
Hear this, and spare his family, James Moore!
Unspotted names, and memorable long,
If there be force in Virtue, or in Song.
   Of gentle blood (part shed in honor's cause,
While yet in Britain honor had applause)
Each parent sprung— A. What fortune, pray?— P. Their own,   390
And better got than Bestia's from the throne.
Born to no pride, inheriting no strife,
Nor marrying discord in a noble wife,
Stranger to civil and religious rage,
The good man walked innoxious through his age.
Nor courts he saw, no suits would ever try,
Nor dared an oath, nor hazarded a lie.
Unlearn'd, he knew no schoolman's subtle art,
No language but the language of the heart.
By nature honest, by experience wise,   400

[75] a hack writer who had slandered Pope   [76] said to have forged a will to his own profit   [77] the publisher and Lord Hervey

Healthy by temperance, and by exercise;
His life, though long, to sickness passed unknown,
His death was instant, and without a groan.
O grant me thus to live, and thus to die!
Who sprung from kings shall know less joy than I.
  O friend! may each domestic bliss be thine!
Be no unpleasing melancholy mine:
Me, let the tender office long engage,
To rock the cradle of reposing Age,
With lenient arts extend a mother's breath,   410
Make Languor smile, and smooth the bed of Death,
Explore the thought, explain the asking eye,
And keep a while one parent from the sky!
On cares like these if length of days attend,
May Heaven, to bless those days, preserve my friend,
Preserve him social, cheerful, and serene,
And just as rich as when he served a Queen.[78]
A. Whether that blessing be denied or given,
Thus far was right;—the rest belongs to Heaven.

THOMAS GRAY (1716–1771)

Gray was born in London on December 26, 1716, the son of a scrivener. He attended Eton, where two of his friends were Richard West (see sonnet on his death), and Horace Walpole, the well-known *littérateur*. From Eton he went to Cambridge, but found the curriculum distasteful, and did not take a degree. Thereafter he traveled on the Continent with Horace Walpole, lived for some two years with his mother at Stoke Poges (the scene of the *Country Churchyard*) and then settled at Cambridge for the rest of his life. He took a degree in law, but never practised; was appointed Professor of Modern History, but was not required to deliver lectures and never did so. He became a profound classicist, and an accurate scholar in so many fields (not including mathematics, which he hated) that he was reputed the most learned man in Europe. He never married. Yet his interests were broader than one might surmise. From the seclusion of his Cambridge rooms he wrote to his friends many charming letters, which show an active and inquiring intellect, and present an engaging picture of the man.

By nature he was extremely retiring, shrinking even from the notoriety which the publication of poems might cause. He was induced to publish the *Elegy* in 1751 only because he feared that an unauthorized version was about to be printed. Other publications were a slender volume in 1753; in 1757 the Pindaric Odes, *The Progress of Poesy* and *The Bard* (printed by Horace Walpole from his press at Strawberry Hill); and in 1768 his ten best poems, carefully corrected. The verse thus hesitatingly offered to the world brought Gray so much fame, in spite of himself, that in 1757 he was offered the laureateship—which

---

[78] Arbuthnot was physician to Queen Anne

he declined as a questionable honor, and one, at any rate, for which he did not care. He died on July 30, 1771, and is buried at Stoke Poges.

The volume of Gray's work is extremely meager. Matthew Arnold thought that his poetic powers were chilled and inhibited by the dominant rationalism of his century, "the age of prose," but it would perhaps be fairer to say, with Professor Phelps, that his sterility was a condition of his severely critical scholar's temperament. He wrote slowly and painfully, and was never satisfied with his product, subjecting it to constant revision. He was eight years writing and revising the *Elegy*. There is not a careless or hasty line in his work. Every phrase is turned until its contours are the most perfect possible. One must not look in his poetry for the effect of spontaneity. It is characterized, instead, by a fastidious sense of form, an exquisite and chiseled beauty.

Gray lived in a period when classic imitation was giving way to a still inarticulate romanticism, and to some extent exhibits in his own work the progress of the new freedom in art. The *Ode on a Distant Prospect of Eton College* is full of eighteenth century personifications and poetic diction; The *Elegy* is sensitive to nature, is suffused with reflective melancholy, and celebrates the humble and obscure; the *Progress of Poetry* in splendid strains expresses the glory of older English verse; *The Bard* is medieval and barbaric in subject-matter, dramatic in conception, impassioned in movement; while *The Fatal Sisters* and *The Descent of Odin* show new influences from the Norse (a literature unknown to the neo-classicists), and a simplicity of diction and treatment that is prophetic. "Such a steady growth," writes Professor Phelps, ". . . shows not only what he learned from the age, but what he taught it." Yet the shift in thought and in technique is incomplete, and the old and the new stand side by side in most of his work.

BIBLIOGRAPHY. Works, ed. by Edmund Gosse, 4 vols. Life, by same, in Eng. Men of Letters ser. Sel., by W. L. Phelps, in Athenæum Press ser., with critical introd. and notes (Ginn).

ODE ON A DISTANT PROSPECT OF ETON COLLEGE

"Ἄνθρωπος· ἱκανὴ πρόφχσις εἰς τὸ δυστυχεῖν.[1]
—Menander.

Ye distant spires, ye antique towers,
　　That crown the watery glade,
Where grateful Science still adores
　　Her Henry's [2] holy Shade;
And ye, that from the stately brow
Of Windsor's heights th' expanse below
Of grove, of lawn, of mead survey,
Whose turf, whose shade, whose flowers among
Wanders the hoary Thames along
　　His silver-winding way.　　　　　　　　10

Ah happy hills, ah pleasing shade,
　　Ah fields beloved in vain,

---

[1] A human being; sufficient cause for misery.　[2] Henry VI, founder of Eton College, 1440

Where once my careless childhood strayed,
   A stranger yet to pain!
I feel the gales, that from ye blow,
A momentary bliss bestow,
   As waving fresh their gladsome wing,
My weary soul they seem to sooth,
And, redolent of joy and youth,
   To breathe a second spring.   20

Say, Father Thames, for thou hast seen
   Full many a sprightly race
Disporting on thy margent green
   The paths of pleasure trace,
Who foremost now delight to cleave
With pliant arm thy glassy wave?
   The captive linnet which enthrall?
What idle progeny succeed
To chase the rolling circle's speed,
   Or urge the flying ball?   30

While some on earnest business bent
   Their murmuring labors ply
'Gainst graver hours, that bring constraint
   To sweeten liberty:
Some bold adventurers disdain
The limits of their little reign,
   And unknown regions dare descry:
Still as they run they look behind,
They hear a voice in every wind,
   And snatch a fearful joy.   40

Gay hope is theirs by fancy fed,
   Less pleasing when possessed;
The tear forgot as soon as shed,
   The sunshine of the breast:
Theirs buxom health of rosy hue,
Wild wit, invention ever-new,
   And lively cheer of vigor born;
The thoughtless day, the easy night,
The spirits pure, the slumbers light,
   That fly th' approach of morn.   50

Alas, regardless of their doom,
   The little victims play!
No sense have they of ills to come,
   Nor care beyond to-day.

Yet see how all around 'em wait
The Ministers of human fate,
  And black Misfortune's baleful train!
Ah, show them where in ambush stand
To seize their prey the murd'rous band!
  Ah, tell them, they are men!   60

These shall the fury Passions tear,
  The vultures of the mind,
Disdainful Anger, pallid Fear,
  And Shame that skulks behind;
Or pining Love shall waste their youth,
Or Jealousy with rankling tooth,
  That inly gnaws the secret heart,
And Envy wan, and faded Care,
Grim-visaged comfortless Despair,
  And Sorrow's piercing dart.   70

Ambition this shall tempt to rise,
  Then whirl the wretch from high,
To bitter Scorn a sacrifice,
  And grinning Infamy.
The stings of Falsehood those shall try,
And hard Unkindness' altered eye,
  That mocks the tear it forced to flow;
And keen Remorse with blood defiled,
And moody Madness laughing wild
  Amid severest woe.   80

Lo, in the vale of years beneath
  A grisly troop are seen,
The painful family of Death,
  More hideous than their Queen:
This racks the joints, this fires the veins,
That every laboring sinew strains,
  Those in the deeper vitals rage:
Lo, Poverty, to fill the band,
That numbs the soul with icy hand,
  And slow-consuming Age.   90

To each his sufferings: all are men,
  Condemned alike to groan;
The tender for another's pain,
  Th' unfeeling for his own.
Yet ah! why should they know their fate?
Since sorrow never comes too late,

And happiness too swiftly flies.
Thought would destroy their paradise.
No more; where ignorance is bliss,
   'Tis folly to be wise.   100

SONNET

ON THE DEATH OF RICHARD WEST [3]

IN vain to me the smiling mornings shine,
  And reddening Phœbus lifts his golden fire:
The birds in vain their amorous descant join;
  Or cheerful fields resume their green attire:
These ears, alas! for other notes repine,
  A different object do these eyes require.
My lonely anguish melts no heart but mine;
  And in my breast the imperfect joys expire.
Yet morning smiles the busy race to cheer,
  And new-born pleasure brings to happier men:
The fields to all their wonted tribute bear;
  To warm their little loves the birds complain;
I fruitless mourn to him that cannot hear,
  And weep the more, because I weep in vain.

ODE ON THE DEATH OF A FAVORITE CAT,

DROWNED IN A TUB OF GOLD FISHES

'TWAS on a lofty vase's side,
Where China's gayest art had dyed
  The azure flowers, that blow;
Demurest of the tabby kind,
The pensive Selima reclined,
  Gazed on the lake below.

Her conscious tail her joy declared;
The fair round face, the snowy beard,
  The velvet of her paws,
Her coat, that with the tortoise vies,   10
Her ears of jet, and emerald eyes,
  She saw; and purred applause.

Still had she gazed; but 'midst the tide
Two angel forms were seen to glide,
  The Genii of the stream:
Their scaly armor's Tyrian hue

3 A dear friend of Gray's, died 1742.

Through richest purple to the view
　Betrayed a golden gleam.

The hapless Nymph with wonder saw;
A whisker first and then a claw,
　With many an ardent wish,
She stretched in vain to reach the prize.
What female heart can gold despise?
　What Cat's averse to fish?

Presumptuous Maid! with looks intent
Again she stretched, again she bent,
　Nor knew the gulf between.
(Malignant Fate sat by, and smiled)
The slippery verge her feet beguiled,
　She tumbled headlong in.

Eight times emerging from the flood
She mewed to every watery God,
　Some speedy aid to send.
No Dolphin came, no Nereid stirred:
Nor cruel Tom, nor Susan heard.
　A favorite has no friend!

From hence, ye Beauties, undeceived,
Know, one false step is ne'er retrieved,
　And be with caution bold.
Not all that tempts your wandering eyes
And heedless hearts, is lawful prize;
　Nor all, that glisters, gold.

ELEGY

WRITTEN IN A COUNTRY CHURCHYARD

THE curfew tolls the knell of parting day,
　The lowing herd wind slowly o'er the lea,
The plowman homeward plods his weary way,
　And leaves the world to darkness and to me.

Now fades the glimmering landscape on the sight,
　And all the air a solemn stillness holds,
Save where the beetle wheels his droning flight,
　And drowsy tinklings lull the distant folds;

Save that from yonder ivy-mantled tower
　The moping owl does to the moon complain

Of such, as wandering near her secret bower,
  Molest her ancient solitary reign.

Beneath those rugged elms, that yew-tree's shade,
  Where heaves the turf in many a moldering heap,
Each in his narrow cell for ever laid,
  The rude forefathers of the hamlet sleep.

The breezy call of incense-breathing Morn,
  The swallow twittering from the straw-built shed,
The cock's shrill clarion, or the echoing horn,
  No more shall rouse them from their lowly bed.   20

For them no more the blazing hearth shall burn,
  Or busy housewife ply her evening care;
No children run to lisp their sire's return,
  Or climb his knees the envied kiss to share.

Oft did the harvest to their sickle yield,
  Their furrow oft the stubborn glebe has broke;
How jocund did they drive their team afield!
  How bowed the woods beneath their sturdy stroke!

Let not Ambition mock their useful toil,
  Their homely joys, and destiny obscure;   30
Nor Grandeur hear with a disdainful smile
  The short and simple annals of the poor.

The boast of heraldry, the pomp of power,
  And all that beauty, all that wealth e'er gave,
Awaits alike th' inevitable hour.
  The paths of glory lead but to the grave.

Nor you, ye Proud, impute to these the fault,
  If Memory o'er their tomb no trophies raise,
Where through the long-drawn aisle and fretted vault
  The pealing anthem swells the note of praise.   40

Can storied urn or animated bust
  Back to its mansion call the fleeting breath?
Can Honor's voice provoke the silent dust,
  Or Flattery sooth the dull cold ear of Death?

Perhaps in this neglected spot is laid
  Some heart once pregnant with celestial fire;

II. 2

In climes [13] beyond the solar road,
Where shaggy forms o'er ice-built mountains roam,
The Muse has broke the twilight-gloom
To cheer the shivering Native's dull abode.
And oft, beneath the odorous shade
Of Chili's boundless forests laid,
She deigns to hear the savage youth repeat   60
In loose numbers wildly sweet
Their feather-cinctured chiefs, and dusky loves.
Her track, where'er the Goddess roves,
Glory pursue, and generous Shame,
Th' unconquerable Mind, and Freedom's holy flame.

II. 3

Woods, that wave o'er Delphi's steep,[14]
Isles, that crown th' Ægean deep,
Fields, that cool Ilissus [15] laves,
Or where Mæander's [16] amber waves
In lingering labyrinths creep,   70
How do your tuneful Echoes languish,
Mute, but to the voice of Anguish?
Where each old poetic Mountain
Inspiration breathed around:
Every shade and hallowed Fountain
Murmured deep a solemn sound:
Till the sad Nine in Greece's evil hour
Left their Parnassus for the Latian plains.
Alike they scorn the pomp of tyrant-power,
And coward Vice, that revels in her chains.   80
When Latium had her lofty spirit lost,
They sought, O Albion! next thy sea-encircled coast.

III. 1

Far from the sun and summer-gale,
In thy green lap was Nature's darling [17] laid,
What time, where lucid Avon strayed,
To Him the mighty Mother did unveil
Her awful face: The dauntless child

[13] Extensive influence of poetic Genius over the remotest and most uncivilized nations; its connection with liberty, and the virtues that naturally attend on it. (Gray)

[14] Progress of Poetry from Greece to Italy, and from Italy to England (Gray)

[15] river flowing through Athens

[16] famous river in Asia Minor

[17] Shakespeare

Stretched forth his little arms, and smiled.
This pencil take (she said) whose colors clear
Richly paint the vernal year: 90
Thine too these golden keys, immortal boy!
This can unlock the gates of Joy;
Of Horror that, and thrilling Fears,
Or ope the sacred source of sympathetic tears.

III. 2

Nor second He,[18] that rode sublime
Upon the seraph-wings of Ecstasy,
The secrets of th' abyss to spy.
He passed the flaming bounds of Place and Time:
The living throne, the sapphire-blaze,
Where Angels tremble, while they gaze,   100
He saw; but blasted with excess of light,
Closed his eyes in endless night.
Behold, where Dryden's less presumptuous car,
Wide o'er the fields of Glory bear
Two coursers of ethereal race,
With necks in thunder clothed, and long-resounding pace.[19]

III. 3

Hark, his hands the lyre explore!
Bright-eyed Fancy hovering o'er
Scatters from her pictured urn
Thoughts that breathe, and words that burn.   110
But ah! 'tis heard no more—
Oh! Lyre divine, what daring Spirit
Wakes thee now? though he inherit
Nor the pride, nor ample pinion,
That the Theban Eagle [20] bear
Sailing with supreme dominion
Through the azure deep of air:
Yet oft before his infant eyes would run
Such forms, as glitter in the Muse's ray
With orient hues, unborrowed of the Sun: 120
Yet shall he mount, and keep his distant way
Beyond the limits of a vulgar fate,
Beneath the Good how far—but far above the Great.

18 Milton   stately march and sound-   rhymes (Gray)
19 Meant to express the   ing energy of Dryden's   20 Pindar

THE BARD

A Pindaric Ode

ADVERTISEMENT

The following Ode is founded on a tradition current in Wales, that Edward
the First, when he completed the conquest of that country,[21] ordered all the
Bards that fell into his hands to be put to death.

I. 1

"Ruin seize thee, ruthless King!
Confusion on thy banners wait,
Though fanned by Conquest's crimson wing
They mock the air with idle state.
Helm, nor hauberk's twisted mail,
Nor even thy virtues, Tyrant, shall avail
To save thy secret soul from nightly fears,
From Cambria's curse, from Cambria's tears!"
Such were the sounds, that o'er the crested pride
Of the first Edward scattered wild dismay,   10
As down the steep of Snowdon's shaggy side
He wound with toilsome march his long array.
Stout Glo'ster stood aghast in speechless trance;
To arms! cried Mortimer, and couched his quivering lance.

I. 2

On a rock, whose haughty brow
Frowns o'er old Conway's foaming flood,
Robed in the sable garb of woe,
With haggard eyes the Poet stood;
(Loose his beard, and hoary hair
Streamed, like a meteor, to the troubled air)   20
And with a Master's hand, and Prophet's fire,
Struck the deep sorrows of his lyre.
"Hark, how each giant-oak, and desert cave,
Sighs to the torrent's awful voice beneath!
O'er thee, O King! their hundred arms they wave,
Revenge on thee in hoarser murmurs breathe;
Vocal no more, since Cambria's fatal day,
To high-born Hoel's harp, or soft Llewellyn's lay.

21 1282–1284

I. 3

"Cold is Cadwallo's tongue,
That hushed the stormy main: 30
Brave Urien sleeps upon his craggy bed:
Mountains, ye mourn in vain
Modred, whose magic song
Made huge Plinlimmon [22] bow his cloud-topped head.
On dreary Arvon's shore they lie,[23]
Smeared with gore, and ghastly pale:
Far, far aloof th' affrighted ravens sail;
The famished eagle screams, and passes by.
Dear lost companions of my tuneful art,
Dear, as the light that visits these sad eyes,   40
Dear, as the ruddy drops that warm my heart,
Ye died amidst your dying country's cries—
No more I weep. They do not sleep.
On yonder cliffs, a grisly band,
I see them sit, they linger yet,
Avengers of their native land:
With me in dreadful harmony they join,
And weave with bloody hands the tissue of thy line.

II. 1

" 'Weave the warp, and weave the woof,
The winding-sheet of Edward's race.   50
Give ample room, and verge enough
The characters of hell to trace.
Mark the year, and mark the night,
When Severn shall re-echo with affright
The shrieks of death, through Berkeley's roofs that ring,
Shrieks of an agonizing King! [24]
She-Wolf of France, with unrelenting fangs,[25]
That tear'st the bowels of thy mangled Mate,
From thee be born, who o'er thy country hangs [26]
The scourge of Heaven. What Terrors round him wait!   60
Amazement in his van, with Flight combined,
And sorrow's faded form, and solitude behind.

II. 2

" 'Mighty Victor, mighty Lord,
Low on his funeral couch he lies!

22 mountain in Wales   24 Edward II., murdered   queen (Gray)
23 The shores of Carnar- in Berkeley Castle, 1327   26 triumphs of Edward
vonshire opposite to the 25 Isabel of France, Ed-   III in France (Gray)
isle of Anglesey (Gray)   ward   II's   adulterous

No pitying heart, no eye, afford
A tear to grace his obsequies.
Is the sable Warrior [27] fled?
Thy son is gone. He rests among the Dead.
The Swarm, that in thy noon-tide beam were born?
Gone to salute the rising Morn. 70
Fair laughs [28] the Morn, and soft the Zephyr blows,
While proudly riding o'er the azure realm
In gallant trim the gilded vessel goes;
Youth on the prow, and Pleasure at the helm;
Regardless of the sweeping Whirlwind's sway,
That, hushed in grim repose, expects his evening prey.

II. 3

" 'Fill high the sparkling bowl,
The rich repast prepare,
Reft of a crown, he yet may share the feast:
Close by the regal chair 80
Fell Thirst and Famine scowl
A baleful smile upon their baffled Guest.
Heard ye the din of battle bray,
Lance to lance, and horse to horse?
Long years of havoc [29] urge their destined course,
And through the kindred squadrons mow their way.
Ye Towers of Julius,[30] London's lasting shame,
With many a foul and midnight murder fed,
Revere his consort's faith, his father's fame,
And spare the meek usurper's [31] holy head. 90
Above, below, the rose of snow,
Twined with her blushing foe, we spread:
The bristled Boar [32] in infant gore
Wallows beneath the thorny shade.
Now, brothers, bending o'er th' accursèd loom
Stamp we our vengeance deep, and ratify his doom.

III. 1

" 'Edward, lo! to sudden fate
(Weave we the woof. The thread is spun)
Half of thy heart we consecrate.
(The web is wove. The work is done.)' 100

27 the Black Prince
28 describes reign of Richard II, whose death by starvation is mentioned in II. 3
29 wars of York and Lancaster, whose red and white rose emblems are alluded to below
30 Tower of London, said to have been founded by Julius Cæsar
31 Henry VI. The consort, Margaret of Anjou; the father, Henry V
32 emblem of Richard III

Stay, O stay! nor thus forlorn
Leave me unblessed, unpitied, here to mourn:
In yon bright track, that fires the western skies,
They melt, they vanish from my eyes.
But oh! what solemn scenes on Snowdon's height
Descending slow their glittering skirts unroll?
Visions of glory, spare my aching sight,
Ye unborn Ages, crowd not on my soul!
No more our long-lost Arthur we bewail.
All-hail, ye genuine Kings,[33] Britannia's Issue, hail!   110

III. 2

"Girt with many a Baron bold
Sublime their starry fronts they rear;
And gorgeous dames, and statesmen old
In bearded majesty, appear.
In the midst a form divine![34]
Her eye proclaims her of the Briton-line;
Her lion-port, her awe-commanding face,
Attempered sweet to virgin grace.
What strings symphonious tremble in the air,
What strains of vocal transport round her play!   120
Hear from the grave, great Taliessin, hear;
They breathe a soul to animate thy clay.
Bright Rapture calls, and soaring, as she sings,
Waves in the eye of Heaven her many-colored wings.

III. 3

"The verse adorn again
Fierce War, and faithful Love,
And Truth severe, by fairy Fiction dressed.
In buskined measures move
Pale Grief, and pleasing Pain,
With Horror, Tyrant of the throbbing breast.   130
A Voice, as of the Cherub-Choir,
Gales from blooming Eden bear;
And distant warblings lessen on my ear,
That lost in long futurity expire.[35]
Fond impious Man, think'st thou, yon sanguine cloud,
Raised by thy breath, has quenched the Orb of day?
To-morrow he repairs the golden flood,
And warms the nations with redoubled ray.

33 the   Tudors,   de-
scended from the Welsh-
man, Owen Tudor

34 Queen Elizabeth
35 The lines above refer,
successively, to Spenser,

Shakespeare, Milton, and
the succession of poets
since Milton's time.

Enough for me: With joy I see
The different doom our Fates assign.   140
Be thine Despair, and sceptered Care,
To triumph, and to die, are mine."
He spoke, and headlong from the mountain's height
Deep in the roaring tide he plunged to endless night.

THE FATAL SISTERS

An Ode (from the Norse Tongue)

PREFACE

In the Eleventh Century Sigurd, Earl of the Orkney Islands, went with a fleet
of ships and a considerable body of troops into Ireland, to the assistance of
Sictryg with the silken beard, who was then making war on his father-in-law
Brian, King of Dublin: the Earl and all his forces were cut to pieces, and
Sictryg was in danger of a total defeat; but the enemy had a greater loss by the
death of Brian, their King, who fell in action. On Christmas day (the day of
the battle), a native of Caithness in Scotland saw at a distance a number of
persons on horseback riding full speed towards a hill, and seeming to enter
into it. Curiosity led him to follow them, till looking through an opening in
the rocks he saw twelve gigantic figures resembling women: they were all employed about a loom; and as they wove, they sung the following dreadful song;
which when they had finished, they tore the web into twelve pieces, and (each
taking her portion) galloped six to the north and as many to the south.

Now the storm begins to lower
(Haste, the loom of Hell prepare),
Iron-sleet of arrowy shower
Hurtles in the darkened air.

Glittering lances are the loom,
Where the dusky warp we strain,
Weaving many a soldier's doom,
Orkney's woe, and Randver's bane.

See the grisly texture grow
('Tis of human entrails made),   10
And the weights, that play below,
Each a gasping Warrior's head.

Shafts for shuttles, dipped in gore,
Shoot the trembling cords along.
Sword, that once a Monarch bore,
Keep the tissue close and strong.

Mista black, terrific Maid,
Sangrida, and Hilda [36] see,

36 Valkyries

Join the wayward work to aid:
'Tis the woof of victory.　　　　　　　20

Ere the ruddy sun be set,
Pikes must shiver, javelins sing,
Blade with clattering buckler meet,
Hauberk crash, and helmet ring.

(Weave the crimson web of war)
Let us go, and let us fly,
Where our friends the conflict share,
Where they triumph, where they die.

As the paths of fate we tread,
Wading through th' ensanguined field:　　30
Gondula, and Geira,[36] spread
O'er the youthful King your shield.

We the reins to slaughter give,
Ours to kill, and ours to spare:
Spite of danger he shall live.
(Weave the crimson web of war.)

They, whom once the desert-beach
Pent within its bleak domain,
Soon their ample sway shall stretch
O'er the plenty of the plain.　　　　　40

Low the dauntless Earl is laid,
Gored with many a gaping wound:
Fate demands a nobler head;
Soon a King shall bite the ground.[37]

Long his loss shall Eirin [38] weep,
Ne'er again his likeness see;
Long her strains in sorrow steep,
Strains of Immortality!

Horror covers all the heath,
Clouds of carnage blot the sun.　　　　50
Sisters, weave the web of death;
Sisters, cease, the work is done.

Hail the task, and hail the hands!
Songs of joy and triumph sing!

36 Valkyries　　　　　37 Brian　　　　　38 Ireland

Between two meeting hills, it bursts a way
Where rocks and woods o'erhang the turbid stream;
There, gathering triple force, rapid and deep, 80
It boils, and wheels, and foams, and thunders through.
　　Nature! great parent! whose unceasing hand
Rolls round the seasons of the changeful year,
How mighty, how majestic are thy works!
With what a pleasing dread they swell the soul,
That sees astonished! and astonished sings!
Ye too, ye winds! that now begin to blow
With boisterous sweep, I raise my voice to you.
Where are your stores, ye powerful beings! say,
Where your aerial magazines, reserved, 90
To swell the brooding terrors of the storm?
In what far-distant region of the sky,
Hushed in deep silence, sleep, ye when 'tis calm?

　·　·　·　·　·　·　·　·　·

　　The keener tempests come: and, fuming dun
From all the livid east or piercing north,
Thick clouds ascend, in whose capacious womb
A vapory deluge lies, to snow congealed.
Heavy they roll their fleecy world along,
And the sky saddens with the gathered storm.
Through the hushed air the whitening shower descends, 100
At first thin-wavering; till at last the flakes
Fall broad and wide and fast, dimming the day
With a continual flow. The cherished fields
Put on their winter-robe of purest white.
'Tis brightness all; save where the new snow melts
Along the mazy current. Low the woods
Bow their hoar head; and, ere the languid sun
Faint from the west emits his evening ray,
Earth's universal face, deep-hid and chill,
Is one wild dazzling waste, that buries wide 110
The works of man. Drooping, the laborer-ox
Stands covered o'er with snow, and then demands
The fruit of all his toil. The fowls of heaven,
Tamed by the cruel season, crowd around
The winnowing store, and claim the little boon
Which Providence assigns them. One alone,
The redbreast, sacred to the household gods,
Wisely regardful of the embroiling sky,
In joyless fields and thorny thickets leaves
His shivering mates, and pays to trusted man 120
His annual visit. Half afraid, he first

Than whom a fiend more fell is nowhere found.
It was, I ween, a lovely spot of ground;
And there a season atween June and May,
Half prankt [2] with spring, with summer half embrowned,
A listless climate made, where, sooth to say,
No living wight could work, ne carèd even for play.

3

Was nought around but images of rest:
Sleep-soothing groves, and quiet lawns between;
And flowery beds that slumbrous influence kest, [3]
From poppies breathed; and beds of pleasant green,
Where never yet was creeping creature seen.
Meantime unnumbered glittering streamlets played,
And hurlèd everywhere their waters sheen;
That, as they bickered through the sunny glade,
Though restless still themselves, a lulling murmur made.

4

Joined to the prattle of the purling rills,
Were heard the lowing herds along the vale,
And flocks loud-bleating from the distant hills,
And vacant shepherds piping in the dale:
And now and then sweet Philomel would wail,
Or stock-doves plain amid the forest deep,
That drowsy rustled to the sighing gale;
And still a coil the grasshopper did keep:
Yet all these sounds yblent [4] inclinèd all to sleep.

5

Full in the passage of the vale, above,
A sable, silent, solemn forest stood,
Where nought but shadowy forms were seen to move,
As Idless fancied in her dreaming mood;
And up the hills, on either side, a wood
Of blackening pines, ay waving to and fro,
Sent forth a sleepy horror through the blood;
And where this valley winded out, below,
The murmuring main was heard, and scarcely heard, to flow.

6

A pleasing land of drowsyhed it was,
Of dreams that wave before the half-shut eye,
And of gay castles in the clouds that pass,
Forever flushing round a summer sky;

2 adorned   3 cast   4 blended

Affrights thy shrinking train,
And rudely rends thy robes;

So long, sure-found beneath the sylvan shed,
Shall Fancy, Friendship, Science, rose-lipped Health,   50
  Thy gentlest influence own,
  And hymn thy fav'rite name!

—*William Collins*

THE PASSIONS

AN ODE FOR MUSIC

WHEN Music, heavenly maid, was young,
While yet in early Greece she sung,
The Passions oft, to hear her shell,
Thronged around her magic cell,
Exulting, trembling, raging, fainting,
Possessed beyond the Muse's painting;
By turns they felt the glowing mind
Disturbed, delighted, raised, refined:
Till once, 't is said, when all were fired,
Filled with fury, rapt, inspired,   10
From the supporting myrtles round
They snatched her instruments of sound;
And as they oft had heard apart
Sweet lessons of her forceful art,
Each—for madness ruled the hour—
Would prove his own expressive power.

First Fear his hand, its skill to try,
  Amid the chords bewildered laid,
And back recoiled, he knew not why,
  Ev'n at the sound himself had made.   20

Next Anger rushed; his eyes, on fire,
  In lightnings owned his secret stings;
In one rude clash he struck the lyre,
  And swept with hurried hand the strings.

With woeful measures wan Despair
  Low sullen sounds his grief beguiled;
A solemn, strange, and mingled air;
  'T was sad by fits, by starts 'twas wild.

But thou, O Hope, with eyes so fair,
  What was thy delightful measure?   30

Still it whispered promised pleasure,
   And bade the lovely scenes at distance hail!
Still would her touch the strain prolong,
   And from the rocks, the woods, the vale,
She called on Echo still through all the song;
   And where her sweetest theme she chose,
A soft responsive voice was heard at every close,
And Hope enchanted smiled, and waved her golden hair.

And longer had she sung,—but with a frown
   Revenge impatient rose;   40
He threw his blood-stained sword in thunder down
   And with a withering look
   The war-denouncing [3] trumpet took,
And blew a blast so loud and dread,
Were ne'er prophetic sounds so full of woe.
   And ever and anon he beat
   The doubling drum with furious heat;
And though sometimes, each dreary pause between,
   Dejected Pity, at his side,
   Her soul-subduing voice applied,   50
Yet still he kept his wild unaltered mien,
While each strained ball of sight seemed bursting from his head.

Thy numbers, Jealousy, to nought were fixed,
   Sad proof of thy distressful state;
Of differing themes the veering song was mixed,
   And now it courted Love, now raving called on Hate.

With eyes upraised, as one inspired,
Pale Melancholy sat retired,
And from her wild sequestered seat,
In notes by distance made more sweet,   60
Poured through the mellow horn her pensive soul:
   And, dashing soft from rocks around,
   Bubbling runnels joined the sound;
Through glades and glooms the mingled measure stole;
   Or o'er some haunted stream with fond delay
   Round an holy calm diffusing,
   Love of peace and lonely musing,
In hollow murmurs died away.

But O how altered was its sprightlier tone,
When Cheerfulness, a nymph of healthiest hue,   70
   Her bow across her shoulder flung,
   Her buskins gemmed with morning dew,

[3] war-announcing

Blew an inspiring air, that dale and thicket rung,
  The hunter's call to faun and dryad known!
  The oak-crowned sisters, and their chaste-eyed queen,[4]
    Satyrs, and sylvan boys, were seen,
    Peeping from forth their alleys green;
Brown Exercise rejoiced to hear,
  And Sport leaped up, and seized his beechen spear.

Last came Joy's ecstatic trial.   80
He, with viny crown advancing,
  First to the lively pipe his hand addressed;
But soon he saw the brisk awakening viol,
    Whose sweet entrancing voice he loved the best.
      They would have thought, who heard the strain,
      They saw in Tempe's vale her native maids,
      Amidst the festal sounding shades,
To some unwearied minstrel dancing,
  While, as his flying fingers kissed the strings,
  Love framed with Mirth a gay fantastic round;   90
  Loose were her tresses, seen, her zone unbound,
    And he, amidst his frolic play,
As if he would the charming air repay,
Shook thousand odors from his dewy wings.

O Music, sphere-descended maid,
Friend of Pleasure, Wisdom's aid,
Why, goddess, why, to us denied,
Lay'st thou thy ancient lyre aside?
As in that loved Athenian bower
You learned an all-commanding power,   100
Thy mimic soul, O nymph endeared,
Can well recall what then it heard.
Where is thy native simple heart,
Devote to Virtue, Fancy, Art?
Arise as in that elder time,
Warm, energic, chaste, sublime!
Thy wonders, in that godlike age,
Fill thy recording sister's page—
'T is said, and I believe the tale,
Thy humblest reed could more prevail,   110
Had more of strength, diviner rage,
Than all which charms this laggard age,
Ev'n all at once together found,
Cecilia's mingled world of sound.[5]

---

4 the wood-nymphs and Diana   5 the organ, said to have been invented by St.   Cecilia (see Dryden's Ode, p. 580)

O bid our vain endeavors cease,
Revive the just designs of Greece,
Return in all thy simple state,
Confirm the tales her sons relate!

—William Collins

ON THE RECEIPT OF MY MOTHER'S PICTURE OUT OF NORFOLK

THE GIFT OF MY COUSIN ANN BODHAM

OH, that those lips had language! Life has passed
With me but roughly since I heard thee last.
Those lips are thine—thy own sweet smile I see,
The same that oft in childhood solaced me;
Voice only fails, else, how distinct they say,
"Grieve not, my child, chase all thy fears away!"
The meek intelligence of those dear eyes
(Bless'd be the art that can immortalize,
The art that baffles time's tyrannic claim
To quench it) here shines on me still the same.   10
    Faithful remembrancer of one so dear,
O welcome guest, though unexpected here!
Who bidd'st me honor with an artless song,
Affectionate, a mother lost so long,
I will obey, not willingly alone,
But gladly, as the precept were her own;
And, while that face renews my filial grief,
Fancy shall weave a charm for my relief—
Shall steep me in Elysian reverie,
A momentary dream, that thou art she.   2c
    My mother! when I learned that thou wast dead,
Say, wast thou conscious of the tears I shed?
Hovered thy spirit o'er thy sorrowing son,
Wretch even then, life's journey just begun?
Perhaps thou gav'st me, though unfelt, a kiss;
Perhaps a tear, if souls can weep in bliss—
Ah, that maternal smile! it answers, "Yes."
I heard the bell tolled on thy burial day,
I saw the hearse that bore thee slow away,
And, turning from my nursery window, drew   30
A long, long sigh, and wept a last adieu!
But was it such?—It was.—Where thou art gone
Adieus and farewells are a sound unknown.
May I but meet thee on that peaceful shore,

The parting word shall pass my lips no more!
Thy maidens, grieved themselves at my concern,
Oft gave me promise of thy quick return.
What ardently I wished I long believed,
And, disappointed still, was still deceived;
By expectation every day beguiled,   40
Dupe of *to-morrow* even from a child.
Thus many a sad to-morrow came and went.
Till, all my stock of infant sorrow spent,
I learned at last submission to my lot;
But, though I less deplored thee, ne'er forgot.
    Where once we dwelt our name is heard no more,
Children not thine have trod my nursery floor;
And where the gardener Robin, day by day,
Drew me to school along the public way,
Delighted with my bauble coach, and wrapped   50
In scarlet mantle warm, and velvet-capped,
'Tis now become a history little known,
That once we called the pastoral house our own.
Short-lived possession! but the record fair
That memory keeps of all thy kindness there,
Still outlives many a storm that has effaced
A thousand other themes less deeply traced.
Thy nightly visits to my chamber made,
That thou might'st know me safe and warmly laid;
Thy morning bounties ere I left my home,   60
The biscuit, or confectionary plum;
The fragrant waters on my cheeks bestowed
By thy own hand, till fresh they shone and glowed;
All this, and more endearing still than all,
Thy constant flow of love, that knew no fall,
Ne'er roughened by those cataracts and brakes
That humor [6] interposed too often makes;
All this still legible in memory's page,
And still to be so, to my latest age,
Adds joy to duty, makes me glad to pay   70
Such honors to thee as my numbers may;
Perhaps a frail memorial, but sincere,
Not scorned in heaven, though little noticed here.
    Could time, his flight reversed, restore the hours,
When, playing with thy vesture's tissued flowers,
The violet, the pink, the jessamine,
I pricked them into paper with a pin
(And thou wast happier than myself the while,

[6] caprice

Would'st softly speak, and stroke my head and smile),
Could those few pleasant days again appear,   80
Might one wish bring them, would I wish them here?
I would not trust my heart—the dear delight
Seems so to be desired, perhaps I might.
But no—what here we call our life is such,
So little to be loved, and thou so much,
That I should ill requite thee to constrain
Thy unbound spirit into bonds again.
Thou, as a gallant bark from Albion's coast
(The storms all weathered and the ocean crossed)
Shoots into port at some well-havened isle,   90
Where spices breathe and brighter seasons smile,
There sits quiescent on the floods that show
Her beauteous form reflected clear below,
While airs impregnated with incense play
Around her, fanning light her streamers gay;
So thou, with sails how swift! hast reached the shore
"Where tempests never beat nor billows roar,"
And thy loved consort on the dangerous tide
Of life long since has anchored by thy side.
But me, scarce hoping to attain that rest,   100
Always from port withheld, always distressed—
Me howling blasts drive devious, tempest-tossed,
Sails ripped, seams opening wide, and compass lost,
And day by day some current's thwarting force
Sets me more distant from a prosperous course.
Yet, oh, the thought that thou art safe, and he!
That thought is joy, arrive what may to me.
My boast is not that I deduce my birth
From loins enthroned, and rulers of the earth;
But higher far my proud pretensions rise—   110
The son of parents passed into the skies.
And now, farewell. Time unrevoked has run
His wonted course, yet what I wished is done.
By contemplation's help, not sought in vain,
I seem to have lived my childhood o'er again;
To have renewed the joys that once were mine,
Without the sin of violating thine:
And, while the wings of fancy still are free,
And I can view this mimic show of thee,
Time has but half succeeded in his theft—   120
Thyself removed, thy power to soothe me left.

—William Cowper

TO MARY [7]

The twentieth year is well-nigh past
Since first our sky was overcast;
Ah, would that this might be the last,
       ·   My Mary!

Thy spirits have a fainter flow,
I see thee daily weaker grow;
'Twas my distress that brought thee low,
             My Mary!

Thy needles, once a shining store,
For my sake restless heretofore,
Now rust disused and shine no more,
             My Mary!   10

For though thou gladly wouldst fulfill
The same kind office for me still,
Thy sight now seconds not thy will,
             My Mary!

But well thou playedst the housewife's part,
And all thy threads with magic art
Have wound themselves about this heart,
             My Mary!   20

Thy indistinct expressions seem
Like language uttered in a dream;
Yet me they charm, whate'er the theme,
             My Mary!

Thy silver locks, once auburn bright,
Are still more lovely in my sight
Than golden beams of orient light,
             My Mary!

For, could I view nor them nor thee,
What sight worth seeing could I see?
The sun would rise in vain for me,   30
             My Mary!

Partakers of thy sad decline,
Thy hands their little force resign;

---

7 Addressed to Mrs. Unwin. Cowper's engagement to her was broken off in 1773, twenty years before the date of the poem, because of the poet's spells of insanity.

Yet, gently pressed, press gently mine,
$\qquad$ My Mary!

And then I feel that still I hold
A richer store ten thousandfold
Than misers fancy in their gold,
$\qquad$ My Mary!   40

Such feebleness of limbs thou prov'st,
That now at every step thou mov'st
Upheld by two, yet still thou lov'st,
$\qquad$ My Mary!

And still to love, though pressed with ill,
In wintry age to feel no chill,
With me is to be lovely still,
$\qquad$ My Mary!

But ah! by constant heed I know,
How oft the sadness that I show   50
Transforms thy smiles to looks of woe,
$\qquad$ My Mary!

And should my future lot be cast
With much resemblance of the past,
Thy worn-out heart will break at last,
$\qquad$ My Mary!
$\qquad$ —*William Cowper*

SAMUEL JOHNSON (1709–1784)

In the passages from Boswell's famous *Life,* below, are vividly presented the personality of Dr. Johnson, his conversation at its best, his contacts with friends and enemies, and the most important happenings of his career. A brief summary of the latter will be sufficient here:

He was born at Lichfield, in Staffordshire, the son of a bookseller; entered Pembroke College, Oxford, but, because of his poverty, left without taking a degree; for a time conducted a school near his native town; then, in 1737, went up to London to earn a living by literary work. After many privations and struggles little short of heroic, he finally attracted attention, and for, roughly, the latter half of his life, was generally recognized as the greatest living man of letters. He had married in 1735 a woman much older than himself, a Mrs. Porter, to whom, however, he was very devoted, and whose death in 1752 he sincerely mourned. Thereafter he resided in different lodgings in London, surrounded by various dependents whom he benevolently supported. For a number of years toward the end of his career he lived as an honored guest in the family of Mr. Thrale, a wealthy brewer. He had as his friends the greatest men of the time in literature and the arts, particularly those in the famous literary *Club* over which he presided as autocrat: men like Burke, Goldsmith, Gibbon the historian, Garrick the actor, Reynolds the painter, and Boswell who wrote his life. In 1762 he was granted by the government a pension of £300 a year. On his death in 1784 he was buried in Westminster Abbey.

The more important of his numerous works are: *London*, 1738, and *The Vanity of Human Wishes*, 1749, two satires in verse; *Life of Savage*, whom he had known during his early struggles in London, 1744; *Irene*, a tragedy, 1749; *The Rambler*, 1750–1752, and *The Idler*, 1758–1760, essay-periodicals; the *Dictionary of the English Language*, imposing product of seven years of scholarly labors, 1755; *Rasselas, Prince of Abyssinia*, a philosophical tale in an Oriental setting, 1759; an Edition of *Shakespeare's Plays*, with valuable comments and a notable preface, 1765; *Journey to the Western Islands of Scotland*, following a tour on foot made with Boswell, 1775; and the *Lives of the Poets*, 1779–1781, biographical and critical introductions to an anthology of English poetry.

Johnson's love of a Latinized vocabulary and a somewhat heavy rhetoric is well known, and is freely illustrated in the selections which follow. This is his literary style. His conversation could be pungent and racy enough, as Boswell's quotations show. Yet even in his writings may be noted a development toward an easier and more informal manner. The later *Rambler* and *Idler* essays are less stilted than the earlier, while many of the *Lives of the Poets* seem like echoes of his own good talk. His critical standards are neo-classical, and yet individual. His sturdy independence of judgment and his abounding good sense join issue often with the accepted dicta of his time, as in his rejection of the classical unities in favor of the freer practice of Shakespeare. Also at work is the "time spirit" of developing Romanticism, much as he would have spurned the imputation.

The more one reads Johnson, the more one admires him for his true wisdom, rarest of human qualities, shining above his own particular set of prejudices and the cramping limitations of his style; it was this, and the revelation constantly in his life of a character essentially noble, in spite of mannerisms petty and sometimes pitiable, that led Macaulay justly to declare that he was both a great and a good man.

BIBLIOGRAPHY. Johnson's periodical writings in Chalmers, *British Essayists*. *Lives of the Poets*, ed. G. B. Hill (Oxford); convenient ed. in World's Classics. Well-chosen selections from Johnson's works by C. G. Osgood (Holt). In addition to Boswell, brief life by Leslie Stephen in Eng. Men of Letters ser. See also famous essay by Macaulay originally written for Encyclopædia Britannica.

THE RAMBLER

NO. 50. SATURDAY, SEPTEMBER 8, 1750

[AGE AND YOUTH]

Credebant hoc grande nefas, et morte piandum,
Si juvenis vetulo non assurexerat, atque
Barbato cuicunque puer, licet ipse videret
Plura domi fraga, et majores glandis acervos.
—JUVENAL [*Satires*, xiii. 54–57]

And had not men the hoary head revered,
And boys paid rev'rence when a man appeared,
Both must have died, though richer skins they wore,
And saw more heaps of acorns in their store.
—Creech

I have always thought it the business of those who turn their speculations upon the living world, to commend the virtues, as well as to expose the faults of their contemporaries, and to confute a false as well as to support a just accusation; not only because it is peculiarly the business of a monitor to keep his own reputation untainted, lest those who can once charge him with partiality, should indulge themselves afterwards in disbelieving him at pleasure; but because he may find real crimes sufficient to give full employment to caution or repentance, without distracting the mind by needless scruples and vain solicitudes.

There are certain fixed and stated reproaches that one part of mankind has in all ages thrown upon another, which are regularly transmitted through continued successions, and which he that has once suffered them is certain to use with the same undistinguishing vehemence, when he has changed his station, and gained the prescriptive right of inflicting on others what he had formerly endured himself.

To these hereditary imputations, of which no man sees the justice, till it becomes his interest to see it, very little regard is to be shown; since it does not appear that they are produced by ratiocination or inquiry, but received implicitly, or caught by a kind of instantaneous contagion, and supported rather by willingness to credit, than ability to prove them.

It has been always the practice of those who are desirous to believe themselves made venerable by length of time, to censure the newcomers into life for want of respect to gray hairs and sage experience, for heady confidence in their own understandings, for hasty conclusions upon partial views, for disregard of counsels which their fathers and grandfathers are ready to afford them, and a rebellious impatience of that subordination to which youth is condemned by nature, as necessary to its security from evils into which it would be otherwise precipitated, by the rashness of patience and the blindness of ignorance.

Every old man complains of the growing depravity of the world, of the petulance and insolence of the rising generation. He recounts the decency and regularity of former times, and celebrates the discipline and sobriety of the age in which his youth was passed; a happy age, which is now no more to be expected, since confusion has broken in upon the world and thrown down all the boundaries of civility and reverence.

It is not sufficiently considered how much he assumes who dares to claim the privilege of complaining; for as every man has, in his own opinion, a full share of the miseries of life, he is inclined to consider all clamorous uneasiness as a proof of impatience rather than of affliction, and to ask, What merit has this man to show, by which he has acquired a right to repine at the distributions of nature? Or, why does he imagine that exemptions should be granted him from the general condition of man? We find ourselves excited rather to captiousness than pity, and instead of being in haste to soothe his complaints by sympathy and tenderness, we inquire whether the pain be proportionate to the lamentation; and whether, supposing the affliction real, it is not the effect of vice and folly, rather than calamity.

The querulousness and indignation which is observed so often to disfigure the last scene of life, naturally leads us to inquiries like these. For surely it will be thought at the first view of things, that if age be thus contemned and ridiculed, insulted and neglected, the crime must at least be equal on either part. They who have had opportunities of establishing their authority over minds ductile and unresisting, they who have been the protectors of helplessness and the instructors of ignorance, and who yet retain in their own hands the power of wealth and the dignity of command, must defeat their influence by their own misconduct, and make use of all those advantages with very little skill, if they cannot secure to themselves an appearance of respect, and ward off open mockery and declared contempt.

The general story of mankind will evince that lawful and settled authority is very seldom resisted when it is well employed. Gross corruption, or evident imbecility, is necessary to the suppression of that reverence with which the majority of mankind look upon their governors, and on those whom they see surrounded by splendor and fortified by power. For though men are drawn by their passions into forgetfulness of invisible rewards and punishments, yet they are easily kept obedient to those who have temporal dominion in their hands, till their veneration is dissipated by such wickedness and folly as can neither be defended nor concealed.

It may, therefore, very reasonably be suspected that the old draw upon themselves the greatest part of those insults which they so much lament, and that age is rarely despised but when it is contemptible. If men imagine that excess of debauchery can be made reverend by time, that knowledge is the consequence of long life, however idly or thoughtlessly employed, that priority of birth will supply the want of steadiness or honesty, can it raise much wonder that their hopes are disappointed, and that they see their posterity rather willing to trust their own eyes in their progress into life, than enlist themselves under guides who have lost their way?

There are, indeed, many truths which time necessarily and certainly teaches, and which might, by those who have learned them from experience, be communicated to their successors at a cheaper rate; but dictates, though liberally enough bestowed, are generally without effect, the teacher gains few proselytes by instruction which his own behavior contradicts; and young men miss the benefit of counsel, because they are not very ready to 10 believe that those who fall below them in practice can much excel them in theory. Thus the progress of knowledge is retarded, the world is kept long in the same state, and every new race is to gain the prudence of their predecessors by committing and redressing the same miscarriages.

To secure to the old that influence which they are willing to claim, and which might so much contribute to the improvement of the arts of life, it is absolutely necessary that they give themselves up to the duties of declining years; and contentedly resign to youth its levity, its pleasures, its frolics, and its fopperies. It is 20 a hopeless endeavor to unite the contrarieties of spring and winter; it is unjust to claim the privileges of age, and retain the playthings of childhood. The young always form magnificent ideas of the wisdom and gravity of men whom they consider as placed at a distance from them in the ranks of existence, and naturally look on those whom they find trifling with long beards, with contempt and indignation, like that which women feel at the effeminacy of men. If dotards will contend with boys in those performances in which boys must always excel them; if they will dress crippled limbs in embroidery, endeavor at gaiety with faltering voices, 30 and darken assemblies of pleasure with the ghastliness of disease, they may well expect those who find their diversions obstructed will hoot them away; and that if they descend to competition with youth, they must bear the insolence of successful rivals.

> Lusisti satis, edisti satis atque bibisti:
> Tempus abire tibi est.—[Horace, Epistles, II. ii, 214–5]

You've had your share of mirth, of meat and drink;
'Tis time to quit the scene—'tis time to think.—ELPHINSTON

Another vice of age, by which the rising generation may be 40 alienated from it, is severity and censoriousness, that gives no allowance to the failings of early life, that expects artfulness [1] from childhood, and constancy from youth, that is peremptory in every command, and inexorable to every failure. There are many who live merely to hinder happiness, and whose descend-

1 skill

ants can only tell of long life, that it produces suspicion, malignity, peevishness, and persecution; and yet even these tyrants can talk of the ingratitude of the age, curse their heirs for impatience, and wonder that young men cannot take pleasure in their father's company.

He that would pass the latter part of life with honor and decency must, when he is young, consider that he shall one day be old; and remember, when he is old, that he has once been young. In youth, he must lay up knowledge for his support, when his powers of acting shall forsake him; and in age forbear to animadvert with rigor on faults which experience only can correct.

NO. 161. TUESDAY, OCTOBER 1, 1751

[THE HISTORY OF A GARRET]

Οἵη γὰρ φύλλων γενέη, τοίηδε καὶ Ἀνδρῶν.—HOMER

Frail as the leaves that quiver on the sprays,
Like them man flourishes, like them decays.

Mr. RAMBLER.

SIR,

You have formerly observed that curiosity often terminates in barren knowledge, and that the mind is prompted to study and inquiry rather by the uneasiness of ignorance than the hope of profit. Nothing can be of less importance to any present interest than the fortune of those who have been long lost in the grave, and from whom nothing now can be hoped or feared. Yet, to rouse the zeal of a true antiquary, little more is necessary than to mention a name which mankind have conspired to forget; he will make his way to remote scenes of action through obscurity and contradiction, as Tully [2] sought amidst bushes and brambles the tomb of Archimedes.[3]

It is not easy to discover how it concerns him that gathers the produce, or receives the rent of an estate, to know through what families the land has passed, who is registered in the Conqueror's survey as its possessor, how often it has been forfeited by treason, or how often sold by prodigality. The power or wealth of the present inhabitants of a country cannot be much increased by an inquiry after the names of those barbarians who destroyed one another twenty centuries ago, in contests for the shelter of woods, or convenience of pasturage. Yet we see that no man can be at rest in the enjoyment of a new purchase till he has learned the history of his grounds from the ancient inhabitants of the

2 Marcus Tullius Cicero, the Roman orator and statesman (B. C. 106–43)
3 Greek mathematician of Syracuse, Sicily (B. C. 287?–212)

parish, and that no nation omits to record the actions of their ancestors, however bloody, savage, and rapacious. The same disposition, as different opportunities call it forth, discovers itself in great or little things. I have always thought it unworthy of a wise man to slumber in total inactivity, only because he happens to have no employment equal to his ambition or genius; it is therefore my custom to apply my attention to the objects before me, and as I cannot think any place wholly unworthy of notice that affords a habitation to a man of letters, I have collected the history and antiquities of the several garrets in which I have resided.

Quantulacunque estis, vos ego magna voco.

How small to others, but how great to me!

Many of these narratives my industry has been able to extend to a considerable length; but the woman with whom I now lodge has lived only eighteen months in the house, and can give no account of its ancient revolutions; the plasterer having, at her entrance, obliterated, by his whitewash, all the smoky memorials which former tenants had left upon the ceiling, and perhaps drawn the veil of oblivion over politicians, philosophers, and poets.

When I first cheapened my lodgings, the landlady told me that she hoped I was not an author, for the lodgers on the first floor had stipulated that the upper rooms should not be occupied by a noisy trade. I very readily promised to give no disturbance to her family, and soon despatched a bargain on the usual terms.

I had not slept many nights in my new apartment before I began to inquire after my predecessors, and found my landlady, whose imagination is filled chiefly with her own affairs, very ready to give me information.

Curiosity, like all other desires, produces pain as well as pleasure. Before she began her narrative, I had heated my head with expectations of adventures and discoveries, of elegance in disguise, and learning in distress; and was somewhat mortified when I heard that the first tenant was a tailor, of whom nothing was remembered but that he complained of his room for want of light; and, after having lodged in it a month, and paid only a week's rent, pawned a piece of cloth which he was trusted to cut out, and was forced to make a precipitate retreat from this quarter of the town.

The next was a young woman newly arrived from the country, who lived for five weeks with great regularity, and became by frequent treats very much the favorite of the family, but at last received visits so frequently from a cousin in Cheapside, that she brought the reputation of the house into danger, and was therefore dismissed with good advice.

The room then stood empty for a fortnight; my landlady began to think that she had judged hardly, and often wished for such another lodger. At last, an elderly man of a grave aspect read the bill, and bargained for the room at the very first price that was asked. He lived in close retirement, seldom went out till evening, and then returned early, sometimes cheerful, and at other times dejected. It was remarkable that whatever he purchased, he never had small money in his pocket; and, though cool and temperate on other occasions, was always vehement and stormy till he received his change. He paid his rent with great exactness, and seldom failed once a week to requite my landlady's civility with a supper. At last, such is the fate of human felicity, the house was alarmed at midnight by the constable, who demanded to search the garrets. My landlady, assuring him that he had mistaken the door, conducted him upstairs, where he found the tools of a coiner; but the tenant had crawled along the roof to an empty house, and escaped; much to the joy of my landlady, who declares him a very honest man, and wonders why anybody should be hanged for making money when such numbers are in want of it. She, however, confesses that she shall, for the future, always question the character of those who take her garret without beating down the price.

The bill was then placed again in the window, and the poor woman was teased for seven weeks by innumerable passengers, who obliged her to climb with them every hour up five stories, and then disliked the prospect, hated the noise of a public street, thought the stairs narrow, objected to a low ceiling, required the walls to be hung with fresher paper, asked questions about the neighborhood, could not think of living so far from their acquaintance, wished the windows had looked to the south rather than the west, told how the door and chimney might have been better disposed, bid her half the price that she asked, or promised to give her earnest the next day, and came no more.

At last, a short meager man, in a tarnished waistcoat, desired to see the garret, and when he had stipulated for two long shelves and a large table, hired it at a low rate. When the affair was completed, he looked round him with great satisfaction, and repeated some words which the woman did not understand. In two days he brought a great box of books, took possession of his room, and lived very inoffensively, except that he frequently disturbed the inhabitants of the next floor by unseasonable noises. He was generally in bed at noon, but from evening to midnight he sometimes talked aloud with great vehemence, sometimes stamped as in rage, sometimes threw down his poker, then clattered his chairs, then sat down in deep thought, and again burst out into loud vociferations; sometimes he would sigh as oppressed with misery, and sometimes shake with convulsive laughter. When he encountered any of the family, he gave way or bowed, but rarely spoke, except that as he went upstairs he often repeated,

'Ος ὑπέρτατα δώματα ναίει

This habitant th' aerial regions boast,

hard words, to which his neighbors listened so often, that they
10 learned them without understanding them. What was his employment she did not venture to ask him, but at last heard a printer's boy inquire for the author.

My landlady was very often advised to beware of this strange man, who, though he was quiet for the present, might perhaps become outrageous in the hot months; but, as she was punctually paid, she could not find any sufficient reason for dismissing him, till one night he convinced her, by setting fire to his curtains, that it was not safe to have an author for her inmate.

She had then for six weeks a succession of tenants, who left
20 the house on Saturday, and, instead of paying their rent, stormed at their landlady. At last she took in two sisters, one of whom had spent her little fortune in procuring remedies for a lingering disease, and was now supported and attended by the other: she climbed with difficulty to the apartment, where she languished eight weeks without impatience, or lamentation, except for the expense and fatigue which her sister suffered, and then calmly and contentedly expired. The sister followed her to the grave, paid the few debts which they had contracted, wiped away the tears of useless sorrow, and, returning to the business of com-
30 mon life, resigned to me the vacant habitation.

Such, Mr. Rambler, are the changes which have happened in the narrow space where my present fortune has fixed my residence. So true it is that amusement and instruction are always at hand for those who have skill and willingness to find them; and, so just is the observation of Juvenal, that a single house will show whatever is done or suffered in the world.

I am, SIR, &c.

THE IDLER

NO. 48. SATURDAY, MARCH 17, 1759

[ON BEING "BUSY"]

THERE is no kind of idleness by which we are so easily seduced as that which dignifies itself by the appearance of business, and, by making the loiterer imagine that he has something to do which must not be neglected, keeps him in perpetual agitation, and hurries him rapidly from place to place.

He that sits still, or reposes himself upon a couch, no more deceives himself than he deceives others; he knows that he is doing nothing, and has no other solace of his insignificance than the resolution, which the lazy hourly make, of changing his mode of life.

To do nothing every man is ashamed: and to do much almost every man is unwilling or afraid. Innumerable expedients have therefore been invented to produce motion without labor, and employment without solicitude. The greater part of those whom the kindness of fortune has left to their own direction, and whom want does not keep chained to the counter or the plow, play throughout life with the shadows of business, and know not at last what they have been doing.

These imitators of action are of all denominations. Some are seen at every auction without intention to purchase; others appear punctually at the Exchange, though they are known there only by their faces. Some are always making parties to visit collections for which they have no taste; and some neglect every pleasure and every duty to hear questions, in which they have no interest, debated in parliament.

These men never appear more ridiculous than in the distress which they imagine themselves to feel from some accidental interruption of those empty pursuits. A tiger newly imprisoned is indeed more formidable, but not more angry, than Jack Tulip withheld from a florist's feast, or Tom Distich hindered from seeing the first representation of a play.

As political affairs are the highest and most extensive of temporal concerns, the mimic of a politician is more busy and important than any other trifler. Monsieur le Noir, a man who, without property or importance in any corner of the earth, has, in the present confusion of the world, declared himself a steady adherent to the French, is made miserable by a wind that keeps back the packet-boat, and still more miserable by every account of a Malouin [4] privateer caught in his cruise; he knows well that nothing can be done or said by him which can produce any effect but that of laughter, that he can neither hasten nor retard good or evil, that his joys and sorrows have scarcely any partakers; yet such is his zeal, and such his curiosity, that he would run barefooted to Gravesend,[5] for the sake of knowing first that the English had lost a tender, and would ride out to meet every

4 from St. Malo, in Brittany
5 in Kent, near mouth of the Thames, where ships from the Continent would come in

mail from the continent if he might be permitted to open it.
Learning is generally confessed to be desirable, and there are
some who fancy themselves always busy in acquiring it. Of
these ambulatory students, one of the most busy is my friend
Tom Restless.[6]

Tom has long had in mind to be a man of knowledge, but he
does not care to spend much time among authors; for he is of
opinion that few books deserve the labor of perusal, that they
give the mind an unfashionable cast, and destroy that freedom
10 of thought and easiness of manners indispensably requisite to
acceptance in the world. Tom has therefore found another way to
wisdom. When he rises he goes into a coffee-house, where he
creeps so near to men whom he takes to be reasoners as to hear
their discourse, and endeavors to remember something which,
when it has been strained through Tom's head, is so near to
nothing, that what it once was cannot be discovered. This he
carries round from friend to friend through a circle of visits, till,
hearing what each says upon the question, he becomes able at
dinner to say a little himself; and, as every great genius relaxes
20 himself among his inferiors, meets with some who wonder how so
young a man can talk so wisely.

At night he has a new feast prepared for his intellects; he always runs to a disputing society, or a speaking club, where he
half hears what, if he had heard the whole, he would but half
understand; goes home well pleased with the consciousness of a
day well spent, lies down full of ideas, and rises in the morning
empty as before.

THE LIVES OF THE POETS

THE METAPHYSICAL POETS

(from the *Life of Cowley*)

WIT,[7] like all other things subject by their nature to the choice
of man, has its changes and fashions, and at different times takes
30 different forms. About the beginning of the seventeenth century
appeared a race of writers that may be termed the metaphysical
poets; [8] of whom, in a criticism on the works of Cowley, it is not
improper to give some account.

The metaphysical poets were men of learning, and to show
their learning was their whole endeavor; but, unluckily resolving

6 said by Johnson to represent one Thomas Tyers, son of the founder of Vauxhall
Gardens, a famous pleasure resort
7 This word is not always used by Dr. Johnson in the same sense, but in general
he employs it as the eighteenth century usually did—for the power, acuteness and
adroitness of the intellect.
8 See introductory sketch on John Donne, above, p. 416.

to show it in rhyme, instead of writing poetry, they only wrote verses, and very often such verses as stood the trial of the finger better than of the ear; for the modulation was so imperfect, that they were only found to be verses by counting the syllables. . . .

Their thoughts are often new, but seldom natural; they are not obvious, but neither are they just; and the reader, far from wondering that he missed them, wonders more frequently by what perverseness of industry they were ever found.

But Wit, abstracted from its effects upon the hearer, may be more rigorously and philosophically considered as a kind of 10 *discordia concors;* a combination of dissimilar images, or discovery of occult resemblances in things apparently unlike. Of wit, thus defined, they have more than enough. The most heterogeneous ideas are yoked by violence together; nature and art are ransacked for illustrations, comparisons, and allusions; their learning instructs, and their subtilty surprises; but the reader commonly thinks his improvement dearly bought, and, though he sometimes admires, is seldom pleased.

From this account of their compositions it will be readily inferred, that they were not successful in representing or moving 20 the affections. As they were wholly employed on something unexpected and surprising, they had no regard to that uniformity of sentiment which enables us to conceive and to excite the pains and the pleasure of other minds: they never inquired what, on any occasion, they should have said or done; but wrote rather as beholders than partakers of human nature; as Beings looking upon good and evil, impassive and at leisure; as Epicurean deities making remarks on the actions of men, and the vicissitudes of life, without interest and without emotion. Their courtship was void of fondness, and their lamentation of sorrow. Their 30 wish was only to say what they hoped had been never said before.

. . . Their attempts were always analytic; they broke every image into fragments: and could no more represent, by their slender conceits and labored particularities, the prospects of nature, or the scenes of life, than he, who dissects a sun-beam with a prism, can exhibit the wide effulgence of a summer noon.

What they wanted however of the sublime, they endeavored to supply by hyperbole; their amplification had no limits; they left not only reason but fancy behind them; and produced combinations of confused magnificence, that not only could not be 40 credited, but could not be imagined.

Yet great labor, directed by great abilities, is never wholly lost: if they frequently threw away their wit upon false conceits,[9]

9 fanciful, extravagant, or ingenious figures of speech, as opposed to those which are harmonious and just, and sincerely derived from the excited poetic imagination and the emotions

they likewise sometimes struck out unexpected truth: if their conceits were far-fetched, they were often worth the carriage. To write on their plan, it was at least necessary to read and think. No man could be born a metaphysical poet, nor assume the dignity of a writer, by descriptions copied from descriptions, by imitations borrowed from imitations, by traditional imagery, and hereditary similes, by readiness of rhyme, and volubility of syllables.

In perusing the works of this race of authors, the mind is exercised either by recollection or inquiry; either something already learned is to be retrieved, or something new is to be examined. If their greatness seldom elevates, their acuteness often surprises; if the imagination is not always gratified, at least the powers of reflection and comparison are employed; and in the mass of materials which ingenious absurdity has thrown together, genuine wit and useful knowledge may be sometimes found, buried perhaps in grossness of expression, but useful to those who know their value; and such as, when they are expanded to perspicuity, and polished to elegance, may give luster to works which have more propriety though less copiousness of sentiment.

This kind of writing, which was, I believe, borrowed from Marini [10] and his followers, had been recommended by the example of Donne, a man of very extensive and various knowledge; and by Jonson, whose manner resembled that of Donne more in the ruggedness of his lines than in the cast of his sentiments.[11]

When their reputation was high, they had undoubtedly more imitators than time has left behind. Their immediate successors, of whom any remembrance can be said to remain, were Suckling, Waller, Denham, Cowley, Cleiveland, and Milton. Denham and Waller sought another way to fame, by improving the harmony of our numbers.[12] Milton tried the metaphysic style only in his lines upon Hobson the Carrier. Cowley adopted it, and excelled his predecessors, having as much sentiment, and more music. Suckling neither improved versification, nor abounded in conceits. The fashionable style remained chiefly with Cowley; Suckling could not reach it, and Milton disdained it.

CRITICAL REMARKS are not easily understood without examples; and I have therefore collected instances of the modes of writing by which this species of poets, for poets they were called

10 Italian poet (1569–1625)
11 The criticism of Ben Jonson is not very penetrating. See above, p. 417.
12 versification. Waller and Suckling are spoken of above, pp. 442–443. John Denham lived 1615–1669, John Cleveland or Cleiveland 1613–1658, Abraham Cowley 1618–1667. The reputation of the latter in his own time was prodigious (he achieved the honor of a burial in Westminster Abbey), but has now sunk almost to nothingness. He is chiefly remembered for his so-called Pindaric Odes, written, because he misunderstood Pindar's versification, in an irregular meter, which he made more or less traditional in English odes.

by themselves and their admirers, was eminently distinguished. As the authors of this race were perhaps more desirous of being admired than understood, they sometimes drew their conceits from recesses of learning not very much frequented by common readers of poetry. Thus Cowley on *Knowledge*:

> The sacred tree midst the fair orchard grew;
> The phœnix Truth did on it rest,
> And built his perfum'd nest,
> That right Porphyrian tree which did true logick shew.
> Each leaf did learned notions give,
> And th' apples were demonstrative:
> So clear their colour and divine,
> The very shade they cast did other lights outshine.

Thus *Donne* shows his medicinal knowledge in some encomiastic verses:

> In every thing there naturally grows
> A Balsamum to keep it fresh and new,
> If 'twere not injur'd by extrinsic blows;
> Your youth and beauty are this balm in you.
> But you, of learning and religion,
> And virtue and such ingredients, have made
> A mithridate, whose operation
> Keeps off, or cures what can be done or said.

Of thoughts so far-fetched, as to be not only unexpected, but unnatural, all their books are full.

The love of different women is, in geographical poetry, compared to travels through different countries:

> Hast thou not found, each woman's breast
> (The land where thou hast travelled)
> Either by savages possest,
> Or wild, and uninhabited?
> What joy could'st take, or what repose,
> In countries so uncivilis'd as those?
> Lust, the scorching dog-star, here
> Rages with immoderate heat;
> Whilst Pride, the rugged Northern Bear,
> In others makes the cold too great.
> And where these are temperate known,
> The soil's all barren sand, or rocky stone.
>
> COWLEY.

The tears of lovers are always of great poetical account; but Donne has extended them into worlds. If the lines are not easily understood, they may be read again.

> On a round ball
> A workman, that hath copies by, can lay

> An Europe, Afric, and an Asia,
> And quickly make that, which was nothing, all.
> So doth each tear,
> Which thee doth wear,
> A globe, yea world, by that impression grow,
> Till thy tears mixt with mine do overflow
> This world, by waters sent from thee my heaven
> dissolved so.

Who but Donne would have thought that a good man is a
telescope?

> Though God be our true glass, through which we see
> All, since the being of all things is he,
> Yet are the trunks, which do to us derive
> Things, in proportion fit, by perspective
> Deeds of good men; for by their living here,
> Virtues, indeed remote, seem to be near.

All that Man has to do is to live and die; the sum of humanity
is comprehended by Donne in the following lines:

> Think in how poor a prison thou didst lie;
> After, enabled but to suck and cry.
> Think, when 'twas grown to most, 'twas a poor inn,
> A province pack'd up in two yards of skin,
> And that usurp'd, or threaten'd with a rage
> Of sicknesses, or their true mother, age.
> But think that death hath now enfranchis'd thee;
> Thou hast thy expansion now, and liberty;
> Think, that a rusty piece discharg'd is flown
> In pieces, and the bullet is his own,
> And freely flies: this to thy soul allow,
> Think thy shell broke, think thy soul hatch'd but now.

They were sometimes indelicate and disgusting. Cowley thus
. . . represents the meditations of a Lover:

> Though in thy thoughts scarce any tracts have been
> So much as of original sin,
> Such charms thy beauty wears as might
> Desires in dying confest saints excite.
> Thou with strange adultery
> Dost in each breast a brothel keep;
> Awake, all men do lust for thee,
> And some enjoy thee when they sleep.
>   COWLEY.

This is yet more indelicate:

> As the sweet sweat of roses in a still,
> As that which from chaf'd musk-cat's pores doth trill,
> As the almighty balm of th' early East;

Such are the sweat-drops of my mistress' breast.
And on her neck her skin such lustre sets,
They seem no sweat-drops, but pearl coronets:
Rank sweaty froth thy mistress' brow defiles.

DONNE.

To the following comparison of a man that travels, and his wife that stays at home, with a pair of compasses, it may be doubted whether absurdity or ingenuity has the better claim:

Our two souls therefore, which are one,
  Though I must go, endure not yet
A breach, but an expansion,   10
  Like gold to airy thinness beat.

If they be two, they are two so
  As stiff twin-compasses are two;
Thy soul the fixt foot, makes no show
  To move, but doth, if th' other do.

And though it in the centre sit,
  Yet when the other far doth roam,
It leans, and hearkens after it,
  And grows erect, as that comes home.

Such wilt thou be to me, who must   20
  Like th' other foot, obliquely run.
Thy firmness makes my circle just,
  And makes me end, where I begun.

DONNE.

In all these examples it is apparent, that whatever is improper or vicious, is produced by a voluntary deviation from nature in pursuit of something new and strange; and that the writers fail to give delight, by their desire of exciting admiration.

[The examples given above are selected from a larger number in Johnson's essay.]

POPE

[The central portion of the essay, which has a unity of its own, is here given. The earlier portion narrates the events of Pope's life and the successive publication of his works; the latter portion is a critique of his poetry.]

The person of Pope is well known not to have been formed by the nicest model. He has, in his account of the *Little Club,* compared himself to a spider, and by another is described as pro- 30
tuberant behind and before. He is said to have been beautiful in his infancy; but he was of a constitution originally feeble and weak; and as bodies of a tender frame are easily distorted, his deformity was probably in part the effect of his application. His stature was so low, that, to bring him to a level with common

tables, it was necessary to raise his seat. But his face was not displeasing, and his eyes were animated and vivid.

By natural deformity, or accidental distortion, his vital functions were so much disordered, that his life was a *long disease*. His most frequent assailant was the headache, which he used to relieve by inhaling the steam of coffee, which he very frequently required.

Most of what can be told concerning his petty peculiarities was communicated by a female domestic of the Earl of Oxford, who
10 knew him perhaps after the middle of life. He was then so weak as to stand in perpetual need of female attendance; extremely sensible of cold, so that he wore a kind of fur doublet, under a shirt of a very coarse warm linen with fine sleeves. When he rose, he was invested in bodice made of stiff canvas, being scarce able to hold himself erect till they were laced, and he then put on a flannel waistcoat. One side was contracted. His legs were so slender, that he enlarged their bulk with three pair of stockings, which were drawn on and off by the maid; for he was not able to dress or undress himself, and neither went to bed nor rose with-
20 out help. His weakness made it very difficult for him to be clean.

His hair had fallen almost all away; and he used to dine sometimes with Lord Oxford, privately, in a velvet cap. His dress of ceremony was black with a tie-wig, and a little sword.

The indulgence and accommodation which his sickness required, had taught him all the unpleasing and unsocial qualities of a valetudinary man. He expected that everything should give way to his ease or humor, as a child, whose parents will not hear her cry, has an unresisted dominion in the nursery.

30   *C'est que l'enfant toujours est homme,*
     C'est que l'homme est toujours enfant.[13]

When he wanted to sleep he *nodded in company;* and once slumbered at his own table while the Prince of Wales was talking of poetry.

The reputation which his friendship gave, procured him many invitations; but he was a very troublesome inmate. He brought no servant, and had so many wants, that a numerous attendance was scarcely able to supply them. Wherever he was, he left no room for another, because he exacted the attention, and employed the activity of the whole family. His errands were so
40 frequent and frivolous, that the footmen in time avoided and neglected him; and the Earl of Oxford discharged some of the servants for their resolute refusal of his messages. The maids, when they had neglected their business, alleged that they had

13 'Tis that the child always is man, the man is always child

been employed by Mr. Pope. One of his constant demands was of coffee in the night, and to the woman that waited on him in his chamber he was very burthensome; but he was careful to recompense her want of sleep; and Lord Oxford's servant declared, that in a house where her business was to answer his call, she would not ask for wages.

He had another fault, easily incident to those who, suffering much pain, think themselves entitled to whatever pleasures they can snatch. He was too indulgent to his appetite; he loved meat highly seasoned and of strong taste; and, at the intervals of the table, amused himself with biscuits and dry conserves. If he sat down to a variety of dishes, he would oppress his stomach with repletion, and though he seemed angry when a dram was offered him, did not forbear to drink it. His friends, who knew the avenues to his heart, pampered him with presents of luxury, which he did not suffer to stand neglected. The death of great men is not always proportioned to the luster of their lives. Hannibal, says Juvenal, did not perish by a javelin or a sword; the slaughters of Cannae [14] were revenged by a ring. The death of Pope was imputed by some of his friends to a silver saucepan, in which it was his delight to heat potted lampreys.

That he loved too well to eat, is certain; but that his sensuality shortened his life will not be hastily concluded, when it is remembered that a conformation so irregular lasted six and fifty years, notwithstanding such pertinacious diligence of study and meditation.

In all his intercourse with mankind, he had great delight in artifice, and endeavored to attain all his purposes by indirect and unsuspected methods. *He hardly drank tea without a stratagem.* If, at the house of his friends, he wanted any accommodation, he was not willing to ask for it in plain terms, but would mention it remotely as something convenient; though, when it was procured, he soon made it appear for whose sake it had been recommended. Thus he teased Lord Orrery till he obtained a screen. He practised his arts on such small occasions, that Lady Bolingbroke used to say, in a French phrase, that *he played the politician about cabbages and turnips.* His unjustifiable impression of the *Patriot King,* [15] as it can be imputed to no particular motive, must have proceeded from his general habit of secrecy and cunning; he caught an opportunity of a sly trick, and pleased himself with the thought of outwitting Bolingbroke.

In familiar or convivial conversation, it does not appear that

14 field of Hannibal's great victory, 216 B. C. Hannibal, when he saw that he was about to be captured, is said to have taken poison, which he kept always with him, concealed in a ring.

15 a political pamphlet by Henry Bolingbroke, Viscount St. John (1678–1751), of which Pope had had a larger edition printed than Bolingbroke had wished

he excelled. He may be said to have resembled Dryden, as being not one that was distinguished by vivacity in company. It is remarkable, that, so near his time, so much should be known of what he has written, and so little of what he has said: traditional memory retains no sallies of raillery, nor sentences of observation; nothing either pointed or solid, either wise or merry. One apophthegm only stands upon record. When an objection raised against his inscription for Shakespeare was defended by the authority of *Patrick*, he replied—*horresco referens* [16]—that *he*
10 *would allow the publisher of a Dictionary to know the meaning of a single word, but not of two words put together.*

He was fretful, and easily displeased, and allowed himself to be capriciously resentful. He would sometimes leave Lord Oxford silently, no one could tell why, and was to be courted back by more letters and messages than the footmen were willing to carry. The table was indeed infested by Lady Mary Wortley,[17] who was the friend of Lady Oxford, and who, knowing his peevishness, could by no intreaties be restrained from contradicting him, till their disputes were sharpened to such asperity, that
20 one or the other quitted the house.

He sometimes condescended to be jocular with servants or inferiors; but by no merriment, either of others or his own, was he ever seen excited to laughter.

Of his domestic character, frugality was a part eminently remarkable. Having determined not to be dependent, he determined not to be in want, and therefore wisely and magnanimously rejected all temptations to expense unsuitable to his fortune. This general care must be universally approved; but it sometimes appeared in petty artifices of parsimony, such as the
30 practise of writing his compositions on the back of letters, as may be seen in the remaining copy of the *Iliad*, by which perhaps in five years five shillings were saved; or in a niggardly reception of his friends, and scantiness of entertainment, as, when he had two guests in his house, he would set at supper a single pint upon the table; and having himself taken two small glasses, would retire, and say, *Gentlemen, I leave you to your wine.* Yet he tells his friends, that *he has a heart for all, a house for all, and, whatever they may think, a fortune for all.*

He sometimes, however, made a splendid dinner, and is said
40 to have wanted no part of the skill or elegance which such performances require. That this magnificence should be often displayed, that obstinate prudence with which he conducted his affairs would not permit; for his revenue, certain and casual,

---

16 I shudder to relate. Patrick was the editor of a Latin dictionary.
17 Lady Mary Wortley Montagu (1690–1762), famous as a wit, letter-writer, and advocate of inoculation against small-pox.

amounted only to about eight hundred pounds a year, of which, however, he declares himself able to assign one hundred to charity.

Of this fortune, which as it arose from public approbation was very honorably obtained, his imagination seems to have been too full: it would be hard to find a man, so well entitled to notice by his wit, that ever delighted so much in talking of his money. In his Letters, and in his Poems, his garden and his grotto, his quincunx [18] and his vines, or some hints of his opulence, are always to be found. The great topic of his ridicule is poverty; the crimes with which he reproaches his antagonists are their debts, their habitation in the Mint,[19] and their want of a dinner. He seems to be of an opinion not very uncommon in the world, that to want money is to want everything.

Next to the pleasure of contemplating his possessions, seems to be that of enumerating the men of high rank with whom he was acquainted, and whose notice he loudly proclaims not to have been obtained by any practices of meanness or servility; a boast which was never denied to be true, and to which very few poets have ever aspired. Pope never set genius to sale; he never flattered those whom he did not love, or praised those whom he did not esteem. Savage [20] however remarked, that he began a little to relax his dignity when he wrote a distich for *his High-ness's dog.*

His admiration of the Great seems to have increased in the advance of life. He passed over peers and statesmen to inscribe his *Iliad* to Congreve,[21] with a magnanimity of which the praise had been complete, had his friend's virtue been equal to his wit. Why he was chosen for so great an honor, it is not now possible to know; there is no trace in literary history of any particular intimacy between them. The name of Congreve appears in the Letters among those of his other friends, but without any observable distinction or consequence.

To his latter works, however, he took care to annex names dignified with titles, but was not very happy in his choice; for, except Lord Bathurst, none of his noble friends were such as that a good man would wish to have his intimacy with them known to posterity: he can derive little honor from the notice of Cobham, Burlington, or Bolingbroke.

Of his social qualities, if an estimate be made from his Letters, an opinion too favorable cannot easily be formed; they exhibit

18 an arrangement of trees, etc., in groups of five (supposed to have a mystical significance). The things of which Pope boasted were on his estate at Twickenham.
19 sanctuary for debtors threatened with arrest. See Pope's *Epistle to Dr. Arbuthnot,* l. 13, and footnote.
20 Richard Savage (1697?-1743), impecunious man of letters, whose *Life* Johnson wrote
21 William Congreve (1670-1729), dramatist and wit

a perpetual and unclouded effulgence of general benevolence,
and particular fondness. There is nothing but liberality, gratitude, constancy, and tenderness. It has been so long said as to
be commonly believed, that the true characters of men may be
found in their Letters, and that he who writes to his friend lays
his heart open before him. But the truth is, that such were the
simple friendships of the *Golden Age,* and are now the friendships only of children. Very few can boast of hearts which they
dare lay open to themselves, and of which, by whatever acci-
10 dent exposed, they do not shun a distinct and continued view;
and, certainly, what we hide from ourselves we do not show to
our friends. There is, indeed, no transaction which offers stronger
temptations to fallacy and sophistication than epistolary intercourse. In the eagerness of conversation the first emotions of the
mind often burst out, before they are considered; in the tumult
of business, interest and passion have their genuine effect; but a
friendly Letter is a calm and deliberate performance, in the cool
of leisure, in the stillness of solitude, and surely no man sits down
to depreciate by design his own character.
20   Friendship has no tendency to secure veracity; for by whom
can a man so much wish to be thought better than he is, as by
him whose kindness he desires to gain or keep? Even in writing
to the world there is less constraint; the author is not confronted
with his reader, and takes his chance of approbation among the
different dispositions of mankind; but a Letter is addressed to a
single mind, of which the prejudices and partialities are known;
and must therefore please, if not by favoring them, by forbear-
ing to oppose them.
      To charge those favorable representations, which men give
30 of their own minds, with the guilt of hypocritical falsehood,
would show more severity than knowledge. The writer commonly believes himself. Almost every man's thoughts, while
they are general, are right; and most hearts are pure, while
temptation is away. It is easy to awaken generous sentiments in
privacy; to despise death when there is no danger; to glow with
benevolence when there is nothing to be given. While such ideas
are formed they are felt, and self-love does not suspect the gleam
of virtue to be the meteor of fancy.
      If the Letters of Pope are considered merely as compositions,
40 they seem to be premeditated and artificial. It is one thing to
write because there is something which the mind wishes to discharge, and another, to solicit the imagination because ceremony
or vanity requires something to be written. Pope confesses his
early Letters to be vitiated with *affectation and ambition:* to
know whether he disentangled himself from these perverters of

epistolary integrity, his book and his life must be set in comparison.

One of his favorite topics is contempt of his own poetry. For this, if it had been real, he would deserve no commendation, and in this he was certainly not sincere; for his high value of himself was sufficiently observed, and of what could he be proud but of his poetry? He writes, he says, when *he has just nothing else to do;* yet Swift complains that he was never at leisure for conversation, because he *had always some poetical scheme in his head.* It was punctually required that his writing-box should be set upon his bed before he rose; and Lord Oxford's domestic related, that, in the dreadful winter of Forty, she was called from her bed by him four times in one night, to supply him with paper, lest he should lose a thought.

He pretends insensibility to censure and criticism, though it was observed by all who knew him that every pamphlet disturbed his quiet, and that his extreme irritability laid him open to perpetual vexation; but he wished to despise his critics, and therefore hoped that he did despise them.

As he happened to live in two reigns when the Court paid little attention to poetry, he nursed in his mind a foolish disesteem of Kings, and proclaims that *he never sees Courts.* Yet a little regard shown him by the Prince of Wales melted his obduracy; and he had not much to say when he was asked by his Royal Highness, *how he could love a Prince while he disliked Kings?*

He very frequently professes contempt of the world, and represents himself as looking on mankind, sometimes with gay indifference, as on emmets of a hillock, below his serious attention; and sometimes with gloomy indignation, as on monsters more worthy of hatred than of pity. These were dispositions apparently counterfeited. How could he despise those whom he lived by pleasing, and on whose approbation his esteem of himself was superstructed? Why should he hate those to whose favor he owed his honor and his ease? Of things that terminate in human life, the world is the proper judge; to despise its sentence, if it were possible, is not just; and if it were just, is not possible. Pope was far enough from this unreasonable temper; he was sufficiently *a fool to Fame,* and his fault was that he pretended to neglect it. His levity and his sullenness were only in his Letters; he passed through common life, sometimes vexed, and sometimes pleased, with the natural emotions of common men.

His scorn of the Great is repeated too often to be real; no man thinks much of that which he despises; and as falsehood is always in danger of inconsistency, he makes it his boast at another time that he lives among them.

It is evident that his own importance swells often in his mind. He is afraid of writing, lest the clerks of the Post-office should know his secrets; he has many enemies; he considers himself as surrounded by universal jealousy; *after many deaths, and many dispersions, two or three of us,* says he, *may still be brought together, not to plot, but to divert ourselves, and the world too, if it pleases;* and they can live together, and *show what friends wits may be, in spite of all the fools in the world.* All this while it was likely that the clerks did not know his hand; he certainly

10 had no more enemies than a public character like his inevitably excites, and with what degree of friendship the wits might live, very few were so much fools as ever to inquire.

Some part of this pretended discontent he learned from Swift, and expresses it, I think, most frequently in his correspondence with him. Swift's resentment was unreasonable, but it was sincere; Pope's was the mere mimicry of his friend, a fictitious part which he began to play before it became him. When he was only twenty-five years old, he related that *a glut of study and retirement had thrown him on the world,* and that there was danger

20 lest *a glut of the world should throw him back upon study and retirement.* To this Swift answered with great propriety, that Pope had not yet either acted or suffered enough in the world to have become weary of it. And, indeed, it must be some very powerful reason that can drive back to solitude him who has once enjoyed the pleasures of society.

In the Letters both of Swift and Pope there appears such narrowness of mind, as makes them insensible of any excellence that has not some affinity with their own, and confines their esteem and approbation to so small a number, that whoever

30 should form his opinion of the age from their representation, would suppose them to have lived amidst ignorance and barbarity, unable to find among their contemporaries either virtue or intelligence, and persecuted by those that could not understand them.

When Pope murmurs at the world, when he professes contempt of fame, when he speaks of riches and poverty, of success and disappointment, with negligent indifference, he certainly does not express his habitual and settled sentiments, but either wilfully disguises his own character, or, what is more likely, in-

40 vests himself with temporary qualities, and sallies out in the colors of the present moment. His hopes and fears, his joys and sorrows, acted strongly upon his mind; and if he differed from others, it was not by carelessness; he was irritable and resentful; his malignity to Philips,[22] whom he had first made

22 Ambrose Philips (1675?–1749), writer of pastorals

ridiculous, and then hated for being angry, continued too long. Of his vain desire to make Bentley [23] contemptible, I never heard any adequate reason. He was sometimes wanton in his attacks; and, before Chandos, Lady Wortley, and Hill, was mean in his retreat.

The virtues which seem to have had most of his affection were liberality and fidelity of friendship, in which it does not appear that he was other than he describes himself. His fortune did not suffer his charity to be splendid and conspicuous; but he assisted Dodsley [24] with a hundred pounds, that he might open a shop; and of the subscription of forty pounds a year that he raised for Savage, twenty were paid by himself. He was accused of loving money, but his love was eagerness to gain, not solicitude to keep it.

In the duties of friendship he was zealous and constant; his early maturity of mind commonly united him with men older than himself, and therefore, without attaining any considerable length of life, he saw many companions of his youth sink into the grave; but it does not appear that he lost a single friend by coldness or by injury; those who loved him once, continued their kindness. His ungrateful mention of Allen in his will, was the effect of his adherence to one whom he had known much longer, and whom he naturally loved with greater fondness. His violation of the trust reposed in him by Bolingbroke could have no motive inconsistent with the warmest affection; he either thought the action so near to indifferent that he forgot it, or so laudable that he expected his friend to approve it.

It was reported, with such confidence as almost to enforce belief, that in the papers intrusted to his executors was found a defamatory Life of Swift, which he had prepared as an instrument of vengeance to be used, if any provocation should be ever given. About this I inquired of the Earl of Marchmont, who assured me that no such piece was among his remains.

The religion in which he lived and died was that of the Church of Rome, to which in his correspondence with Racine he professes himself a sincere adherent. That he was not scrupulously pious in some part of his life, is known by many idle and indecent applications of sentences taken from the Scriptures; a mode of merriment which a good man dreads for its profaneness, and a witty man disdains for its easiness and vulgarity. But to whatever levities he has been betrayed, it does not appear that his principles were ever corrupted, or that he ever lost his belief of

[23] Richard Bentley (1662–1742), distinguished classical scholar
[24] Robert Dodsley (1703–1764), bookseller, man of letters, and editor of *Old English Plays*

Revelation. The positions which he transmitted from Bolingbroke he seems not to have understood, and was pleased with
an interpretation that made them orthodox.

A man of such exalted superiority, and so little moderation,
would naturally have all his delinquencies observed and aggravated: those who could not deny that he was excellent,
would rejoice to find that he was not perfect.

Perhaps it may be imputed to the unwillingness with which the
same man is allowed to possess many advantages, that his learning has been depreciated. He certainly was in his early life a
man of great literary curiosity; and when he wrote his *Essay on
Criticism* had, for his age, a very wide acquaintance with books.
When he entered into the living world, it seems to have happened to him as to many others, that he was less attentive to
dead masters; he studied in the academy of Paracelsus,[25] and
made the universe his favorite volume. He gathered his notions
fresh from reality, not from the copies of authors, but the orig-
inals of Nature. Yet there is no reason to believe that literature
ever lost his esteem; he always professed to love reading; and
Dobson, who spent some time at his house translating his *Essay
on Man*, when I asked him what learning he found him to possess, answered, *More than I expected*. His frequent references
to history, his allusions to various kinds of knowledge, and his
images selected from art and nature, with his observations on
the operations of the mind and the modes of life, show an intelligence perpetually on the wing, excursive, vigorous, and diligent,
eager to pursue knowledge, and attentive to retain it.

From this curiosity arose the desire of traveling, to which he
alludes in his verses to Jervas, and which, though he never
found an opportunity to gratify it, did not leave him till his life
declined.

Of his intellectual character, the constituent and fundamental
principle was Good Sense, a prompt and intuitive perception of
consonance and propriety. He saw immediately, of his own conceptions, what was to be chosen, and what to be rejected; and,
in the works of others, what was to be shunned, and what was
to be copied.

But good sense alone is a sedate and quiescent quality, which
manages its possessions well, but does not increase them; it collects few materials for its own operations, and preserves safety,
but never gains supremacy. Pope had likewise genius; a mind
active, ambitious, and adventurous, always investigating, always
aspiring; in its widest searches still longing to go forward, in its
highest flights still wishing to be higher; always imagining some-

---

25 famous physician, alchemist, and magical adept (1493–1541)

thing greater than it knows, always endeavoring more than it
can do.

To assist these powers, he is said to have had great strength
and exactness of memory. That which he had heard or read was
not easily lost; and he had before him not only what his own
meditation suggested, but what he had found in other writers,
that might be accommodated to his present purpose.

These benefits of nature he improved by incessant and unwearied diligence; he had recourse to every source of intelligence, and lost no opportunity of information; he consulted the
living as well as the dead; he read his compositions to his friends,
and was never content with mediocrity when excellence could be
attained. He considered poetry as the business of his life, and
however he might seem to lament his occupation, he followed it
with constancy; to make verses was his first labor, and to mend
them was his last.

From his attention to poetry he was never diverted. If conversation offered anything that could be improved, he committed
it to paper; if a thought, or perhaps an expression more happy
than was common, rose to his mind, he was careful to write it;
an independent distich was preserved for an opportunity of in-
sertion, and some little fragments have been found containing
lines, or parts of lines, to be wrought upon at some other time.

He was one of those few whose labor is their pleasure: he was
never elevated to negligence, nor wearied to impatience; he never
passed a fault unamended by indifference, nor quitted it by
despair. He labored his works first to gain reputation, and afterwards to keep it.

Of composition there are different methods. Some employ at
once memory and invention, and, with little intermediate use of
the pen, form and polish large masses by continued meditation,
and write their productions only when, in their own opinion,
they have completed them. It is related of Virgil, that his custom
was to pour out a great number of verses in the morning, and
pass the day in retrenching exuberances and correcting inac-
curacies. The method of Pope, as may be collected from his
translation, was to write his first thoughts in his first words, and
gradually to amplify, decorate, rectify, and refine them.

With such faculties, and such dispositions, he excelled every
other writer in *poetical prudence;* he wrote in such a manner as
might expose him to few hazards. He used almost always the
same fabric of verse; and, indeed, by those few essays which he
made of any other, he did not enlarge his reputation. Of this uniformity the certain consequence was readiness and dexterity. By
perpetual practice, language had in his mind a systematical arrangement; having always the same use for words, he had words

so selected and combined as to be ready at his call. This increase of facility he confessed himself to have perceived in the progress of his translation.

But what was yet of more importance, his effusions were always voluntary, and his subjects chosen by himself. His independence secured him from drudging at a task, and laboring upon a barren topic: he never exchanged praise for money, nor opened a shop of condolence or congratulation. His poems, therefore, were scarce ever temporary. He suffered coronations and royal marriages to pass without a song, and derived no opportunities from recent events, nor any popularity from the accidental disposition of his readers. He was never reduced to the necessity of soliciting the sun to shine upon a birthday, of calling the Graces and Virtues to a wedding, or of saying what multitudes have said before him. When he could produce nothing new, he was at liberty to be silent.

His publications were for the same reason never hasty. He is said to have sent nothing to the press till it had lain two years under his inspection: it is at least certain, that he ventured nothing without nice examination. He suffered the tumult of imagination to subside, and the novelties of invention to grow familiar. He knew that the mind is always enamored of its own productions, and did not trust his first fondness. He consulted his friends, and listened with great willingness to criticism; and, what was of more importance, he consulted himself, and let nothing pass against his own judgment.

He professed to have learned his poetry from Dryden, whom, whenever an opportunity was presented, he praised through his whose life with unvaried liberality; and perhaps his character may receive some illustration, if he be compared with his master.

Integrity of understanding and nicety of discernment were not allotted in a less proportion to Dryden than to Pope. The rectitude of Dryden's mind was sufficiently shown by the dismission of his poetical prejudices, and the rejection of unnatural thoughts and rugged numbers. But Dryden never desired to apply all the judgment that he had. He wrote, and professed to write, merely for the people; and when he pleased others, he contented himself. He spent no time in struggles to rouse latent powers; he never attempted to make that better which was already good, nor often to mend what he must have known to be faulty. He wrote, as he tells us, with very little consideration; when occasion or necessity called upon him, he poured out what the present moment happened to supply, and, when once it had passed the press, ejected it from his mind; for when he had no pecuniary interest, he had no further solicitude.

Pope was not content to satisfy; he desired to excel, and therefore always endeavored to do his best: he did not court the candor, but dared the judgment of his reader, and, expecting no indulgence from others, he showed none to himself. He examined lines and words with minute and punctilious observation, and retouched every part with indefatigable diligence, till he had left nothing to be forgiven.

For this reason he kept his pieces very long in his hands, while he considered and reconsidered them. The only poems which can be supposed to have been written with such regard to the times as might hasten their publication, were the two satires of *Thirty-eight;* of which Dodsley told me, that they were brought to him by the author, that they might be fairly copied. "Almost every line," he said, "was then written twice over; I gave him a clean transcript, which he sent some time afterwards to me for the press, with almost every line written twice over a second time."

His declaration, that his care for his works ceased at their publication, was not strictly true. His parental attention never abandoned them; what he found amiss in the first edition, he silently corrected in those that followed. He appears to have revised the *Iliad,* and freed it from some of its imperfections; and the *Essay on Criticism* received many improvements after its first appearance. It will seldom be found that he altered without adding clearness, elegance, or vigor. Pope had perhaps the judgment of Dryden; but Dryden certainly wanted the diligence of Pope.

In acquired knowledge, the superiority must be allowed to Dryden, whose education was more scholastic, and who before he became an author had been allowed more time for study, with better means of information. His mind has a larger range, and he collects his images and illustrations from a more extensive circumference of science. Dryden knew more of man in his general nature, and Pope in his local manners. The notions of Dryden were formed by comprehensive speculation, and those of Pope by minute attention. There is more dignity in the knowledge of Dryden, and more certainty in that of Pope.

Poetry was not the sole praise of either; for both excelled likewise in prose; but Pope did not borrow his prose from his predecessor. The style of Dryden is capricious and varied, that of Pope is cautious and uniform; Dryden obeys the motions of his own mind, Pope constrains his mind to his own rules of composition. Dryden is sometimes vehement and rapid; Pope is always smooth, uniform, and gentle. Dryden's page is a natural field, rising into inequalities, and diversified by the varied exuberance of abundant vegetation; Pope's is a velvet lawn, shaven by the scythe, and leveled by the roller.

Of genius, that power which constitutes a poet; that quality

without which judgment is cold and knowledge is inert; that energy which collects, combines, amplifies, and animates; the superiority must, with some hesitation, be allowed to Dryden. It is not to be inferred that of this poetical vigor Pope had only a little, because Dryden had more; for every other writer since Milton must give place to Pope; and even of Dryden it must be said, that if he has brighter paragraphs, he has not better poems. Dryden's performances were always hasty, either excited by some external occasion, or extorted by domestic necessity; he
10 composed without consideration, and published without correction. What his mind could supply at call, or gather in one excursion, was all that he sought, and all that he gave. The dilatory caution of Pope enabled him to condense his sentiments, to multiply his images, and to accumulate all that study might produce, or chance might supply. If the flights of Dryden therefore are higher, Pope continues longer on the wing. If of Dryden's fire the blaze is brighter, of Pope's the heat is more regular and constant. Dryden often surpasses expectation, and Pope never falls below it. Dryden is read with frequent astonishment, and
20 Pope with perpetual delight.

This parallel will, I hope, when it is well considered, be found just; and if the reader should suspect me, as I suspect myself, of some partial fondness for the memory of Dryden, let him not too hastily condemn me; for meditation and inquiry may, perhaps, show him the reasonableness of my determination.

PREFACE TO SHAKESPEARE

ON THE UNITIES

In the Preface to his edition of Shakespeare (1765), Johnson praises the dramatist for the excellence of his characterization. "His drama is the mirror of life." He criticizes him for his lack of moral purpose, his loose plots, his anachronisms, the coarseness of his comic scenes, his "disproportionate pomp of diction," his unseemly delight in "a quibble." Then follows a discussion of Shakespeare and the classical unities of time, place, and action.

IT will be thought strange that in enumerating the defects of this writer I have not yet mentioned his neglect of the unities, his violation of those laws which have been instituted and established by the joint authority of poets and critics.
30   For his other deviations from the art of writing I resign him to critical justice without making any other demand in his favor than that which must be indulged to all human excellence—that his virtues be rated with his failings; but from the

censure which this irregularity may bring upon him I shall, with due reverence to that learning which I must oppose, adventure to try how I can defend him.

His histories, being neither tragedies nor comedies, are not subject to any of their laws: nothing more is necessary to all the praise which they expect than that the changes of action be so prepared as to be understood, that the incidents be various and affecting, and the characters consistent, natural, and distinct. No other unity is intended, and therefore none is to be sought. 10

In his other works he has well enough preserved the unity of action. He has not, indeed, an intrigue regularly perplexed and regularly unraveled; he does not endeavor to hide his design only to discover it, for this is seldom the order of real events and Shakespeare is the poet of nature: but his plan has commonly, what Aristotle requires, a beginning, a middle, and an end; one event is concatenated with another, and the conclusion follows by easy consequence. There are perhaps some incidents that might be spared, as in other poets there is much talk that only fills up time upon the stage; but the 20 general system makes gradual advances, and the end of the play is the end of expectation.

To the unities of time and place he has shown no regard; and perhaps a nearer view of the principles on which they stand will diminish their value and withdraw from them the veneration which, from the time of Corneille,[26] they have very generally received, by discovering that they have given more trouble to the poet than pleasure to the auditor.

The necessity of observing the unities of time and place arises from the supposed necessity of making the drama cred- 30 ible. The critics hold it impossible that an action of months or years can be possibly believed to pass in three hours, or that the spectator can suppose himself to sit in the theater while ambassadors go and return between distant kings, while armies are levied and towns besieged, while an exile wanders and returns, or till he whom they saw courting his mistress shall lament the untimely fall of his son. The mind revolts from evident falsehood, and fiction loses its force when it departs from the resemblance of reality. From the narrow limitation of time necessarily arises the contraction of place. The 40 spectator, who knows that he saw the first act at Alexandria, cannot suppose that he sees the next at Rome, at a distance to which not the dragons of Medea could in so short a time have transported him; he knows with certainty that he has not changed his place, and he knows that place cannot change

26 Pierre Corneille (1606–1684), French classical dramatist, author of *Le Cid.*

itself—that what was a house cannot become a plain, that what was Thebes can never be Persepolis.

Such is the triumphant language with which a critic exults over the misery of an irregular poet, and exults commonly without resistance or reply. It is time, therefore, to tell him, by the authority of Shakespeare, that he assumes, as an unquestionable principle, a position which, while his breath is forming it into words, his understanding pronounces to be false. It is false that any representation is mistaken for reality, that any dramatic fable in its materiality was ever credible or for a single moment was ever credited.

The objection arising from the impossibility of passing the first hour at Alexandria and the next at Rome, supposes that, when the play opens, the spectator really imagines himself at Alexandria, and believes that his walk to the theater has been a voyage to Egypt and that he lives in the days of Antony and Cleopatra. Surely he that imagines this may imagine more. He that can take the stage at one time for the palace of the Ptolemies, may take it in half an hour for the promontory of Actium. Delusion, if delusion be admitted, has no certain limitation; if the spectator can be once persuaded that his old acquaintance are Alexander and Cæsar, that a room illuminated with candles is the plain of Pharsalia or the bank of Granicus, he is in a state of elevation above the reach of reason or of truth, and from the heights of empyrean poetry may despise the circumscriptions of terrestrial nature. There is no reason why a mind thus wandering in ecstasy should count the clock, or why an hour should not be a century in that calenture of the brain that can make the stage a field.

The truth is that the spectators are always in their senses, and know, from the first act to the last, that the stage is only a stage and that the players are only players. They came to hear a certain number of lines recited with just gesture and elegant modulation. The lines relate to some action, and an action must be in some place; but the different actions that complete a story may be in places very remote from each other; and where is the absurdity of allowing that space to represent first Athens and then Sicily, which was always known to be neither Sicily nor Athens but a modern theater?

By supposition, as place is introduced, time may be extended; the time required by the fable elapses for the most part between the acts, for of so much of the action as is represented the real and poetical duration is the same. If in the first act preparations for war against Mithridates are represented to be made in Rome, the event of the war may without absurdity be represented, in the catastrophe, as happening in Pontus: we know that there is neither war nor preparation for war; we know that we are neither in Rome nor Pontus, that neither Mithridates nor Lucullus are before us. The drama exhibits successive imitations of successive actions; and why may not the second imitation represent an action that happened years after the first, if it be so connected with it that nothing but time can be supposed to intervene? Time is, of all modes of existence, most obsequious to the imagination; a lapse of years is as easily conceived as a passage of hours. In contemplation we easily contract the time of real actions, and therefore willingly permit it to be contracted when we only see their imitation.

It will be asked how the drama moves if it is not credited. It is credited with all the credit due to a drama. It is credited, whenever it moves, as a just picture of a real original, as representing to the auditor what he would himself feel if he were to do or suffer what is there feigned to be suffered or to be done. The reflection that strikes the heart is not that the evils before us are real evils, but that they are evils to which we ourselves may be exposed. If there be any fallacy, it is not that we fancy the players, but that we fancy ourselves, unhappy for a moment; but we rather lament the possibility than suppose the presence of misery, as a mother weeps over her babe when she remembers that death may take it from her. The delight of tragedy proceeds from our consciousness of fiction; if we thought murders and treasons real, they would please no more. . . .

Voltaire expresses his wonder that our author's extravagances are endured by a nation which has seen the tragedy of Cato.[27] Let him be answered that Addison speaks the language of poets, and Shakespeare of men. We find in Cato innumerable beauties which enamor us of its author, but we see nothing that acquaints us with human sentiments or human actions; we place it with the fairest and the noblest progeny which judgment propagates by conjunction with learning, but Othello is the vigorous and vivacious offspring of observation impregnated by genius. Cato affords a splendid exhibition of artificial and fictitious manners, and delivers just and noble sentiments, in diction easy, elevated, and harmonious, but its hopes and fears communicate no vibration to the heart; the composition refers us only to the writer; we pronounce the name of Cato, but we think on Addison.

The work of a correct and regular writer is a garden accurately formed and diligently planted, varied with shades,

---

27 Addison's frigid classical tragedy (see sketch of Addison above)

and scented with flowers: the composition of Shakespeare is a forest, in which oaks extend their branches, and pines tower in the air, interspersed sometimes with weeds and brambles, and sometimes giving shelter to myrtles and to roses; filling the eye with awful pomp, and gratifying the mind with endless diversity. Other poets display cabinets of precious rarities, minutely finished, wrought into shape, and polished into brightness. Shakespeare opens a mine which contains gold and diamonds in unexhaustible plenty, though clouded by incrusta-
10 tions, debased by impurities, and mingled with a mass of meaner materials.

JAMES BOSWELL (1740–1795)

James Boswell, the son of Alexander Boswell (afterwards Lord Auchinleck), a Scotch laird and judge, was born at Edinburgh, and reared as a youth on the family estates in Ayrshire. He attended the University of Edinburgh to prepare himself for the law. He made a tour of the Continent, pursued further studies at Utrecht, was admitted to both the English and the Scottish bar, but never attained much distinction in his profession. He had a passion for cultivating the acquaintance of great men. He had visited and talked with Jean-Jacques Rousseau. At another time, he went to Corsica, met the revolutionary and patriot, Paoli, and thereafter became a staunch supporter of the latter's claims. But the friendship which he most eagerly sought, and which he cultivated with the greatest assiduity, was that with Dr. Samuel Johnson, whom he first met in 1763, when he was twenty-two and Johnson fifty-four. He saw as much of Johnson as possible, got himself elected to the famous Literary Club of which Johnson was autocrat (1773), and of his master's conversation there and elsewhere kept a minute and accurate record, with the intention of writing an intimate biography of the great man. A preliminary to this work was the *Journal of a Tour to the Hebrides with Dr. Johnson* (1785), recording the actions and observations of his hero during a journey undertaken in 1773. Six years after the *Journal* appeared the famous *Life* which made Boswell's reputation, perpetuated Johnson's, and which is universally acknowledged as the greatest biography in the English language.

The book is famous because it presents the complete and living portrait of a great personality with the literary skill of a great writer whose ideal of biography was to let the subject reveal himself. The patience and industry of the biographer, who painstakingly sought out all the information accessible about his hero, who carefully recorded all his conversation, day after day and night after night, are beyond praise; so also is his rigid regard for truth, his presentation of the whole man, without reservations, the noble and heroic parts of him on the one hand, the petty and even disgusting on the other; so also is the art of the writer who presents his materials with dramatic sense, with humor, with pathos when called for, and with constant liveliness. There are dreary stretches in the *Johnson*, but the level of interest is extremely high.

Macaulay detested Boswell, the man. In his celebrated essay on Croker's edition of the *Life* he has, with his customary emphasis, pointed out his toadyism, his pretentiousness, his envy, his vanity, until he arrives at the amazing paradox that the book is great because its author was contemptible. Carlyle, with more justice, retorted that the book itself could not be great unless the man himself had qualities of greatness.

The condensation here attempted presents some of the more interesting passages from the beginning to the end of the *Life*. Since the duller portions are studiously avoided, the impression of the reader will be one of greater brilliance than the book as a whole possesses.

BIBLIOGRAPHY. Boswell's *Life of Johnson*, ed. G. B. Hill, 6 vols., Oxford (standard). The *Life* complete, 2 vols. in one, Oxford. Everyman ed. in 2 vols. (Dutton). Excellent abridgment by C. G. Osgood (Scribner's). C. B. Tinker: *Letters* (Oxford), and *Young Boswell* (Atl. Monthly Press). A monumental limited ed. of the Boswell papers, recently discovered, and now in the possession of Colonel Isham, is in progress (ed. Geoffrey Scott and F. A. Pottle). Macaulay's and Carlyle's essays (famous comments on book and man). New edition of *Journal of a Tour to the Hebrides*, from the MS. recently discovered, restoring Boswell's original text, by F. A. Pottle and C. H. Bennett (Viking Press).

THE LIFE OF SAMUEL JOHNSON, LL.D.

WHAT I consider as the peculiar value of the following work is the quantity it contains of Johnson's conversation, which is universally acknowledged to have been eminently instructive and entertaining. . . . I am fully aware of the objections which may be made to the minuteness on some occasions of my detail of Johnson's conversation, and how happily it is adapted for the petty exercise of ridicule by men of superficial understanding and ludicrous fancy; but I remain firm and confident in my opinion that minute particulars are frequently characteristic and always amusing when they relate to a distinguished man. . . .

To this may be added the sentiments of the very man whose life I am about to exhibit: "The business of the biographer is often to pass over those performances and incidents which produce vulgar greatness; to lead the thoughts into domestic privacies, and display the minute details of daily life, where exterior appendages are cast aside, and men excel each other only by prudence and by virtue." (From Boswell's Introduction.)

Samuel Johnson was born at Lichfield, in Staffordshire, on the 18th of September, N.S., 1709; and his initiation into the Christian Church was not delayed; for his baptism is recorded, in the register of St. Mary's parish in that city, to have been performed on the day of his birth. His father was Michael Johnson, a native of Derbyshire, of obscure extraction, who settled in Lichfield as a bookseller and stationer. His mother was Sarah Ford, descended of an ancient race of substantial yeomanry in Warwickshire.

Young Johnson had the misfortune to be much afflicted with the scrofula, or king's evil, which disfigured a countenance naturally well formed, and hurt his visual nerves so much that he did not see at all with one of his eyes, though its appearance was little different from that of the other. There is amongst his prayers one inscribed *"When my* EYE *was restored to its use,"* which ascertains a defect that many of his friends knew he had, though I never perceived it. I supposed him to be only near-sighted; and indeed I must observe, that in no other
10 respect could I discern any defect in his vision; on the contrary, the force of his attention and perceptive quickness made him see and distinguish all manner of objects, whether of nature or of art, with a nicety that is rarely to be found. It has been said that he contracted this grievous malady from his nurse. His mother yielding to the superstitious notion, which, it is wonderful to think, prevailed so long in this country, as to the virtue of the regal touch; a notion which our kings encouraged, and to which a man of such inquiry and such judgment as Carte could give credit; carried him to London, where
20 he was actually touched by Queen Anne. Mrs. Johnson indeed, as Mr. Hector informed me, acted by the advice of the celebrated physician, Sir John Floyer, then a physician in Lichfield. Johnson used to talk of this very frankly; and Mrs. Piozzi has preserved his very picturesque description of the scene, as it remained upon his fancy. Being asked if he could remember Queen Anne, "He had," he said, "a confused, but somehow a sort of solemn recollection of a lady in diamonds, and a long black hood." This touch, however, was without any effect. I ventured to say to him, in allusion to the political
30 principles in which he was educated, and of which he ever retained some odor, that "his mother had not carried him far enough; she should have taken him to Rome."

1735. In a man whom religious education has secured from licentious indulgences, the passion of love, when once it has seized him, is exceedingly strong; being unimpaired by dissipation, and totally concentrated in one object. This was experienced by Johnson when he became the fervent admirer of Mrs. Porter, after her first husband's death. Miss Porter told me, that when he was first introduced to her mother, his ap-
40 pearance was very forbidding: he was then lean and lank, so that his immense structure of bones was hideously striking to the eye, and the scars of the scrofula were deeply visible. He also wore his hair, which was straight and stiff, and separated behind; and he often had, seemingly, convulsive starts and odd gesticulations, which tended to excite at once surprise and ridicule. Mrs. Porter was so much engaged by his conversa-

tion that she overlooked all these external disadvantages, and said to her daughter, "This is the most sensible man that I ever saw in my life."

Though Mrs. Porter was double the age of Johnson,[1] and her person and manner, as described to me by the late Mr. Garrick, were by no means pleasing to others, she must have had a superiority of understanding and talents, as she certainly inspired him with a more than ordinary passion; and she having signified her willingness to accept of his hand, he went to Lichfield to ask his mother's consent to the marriage, which he could not but be conscious was a very imprudent scheme, both on account of their disparity of years, and her want of fortune. But Mrs. Johnson knew too well the ardor of her son's temper, and was too tender a parent to oppose his inclinations.

I know not for what reason the marriage ceremony was not performed at Birmingham; but a resolution was taken that it should be at Derby, for which place the bride and bridegroom set out on horseback, I suppose in very good humor. But though Mr. Topham Beauclerk used archly to mention Johnson's having told him, with much gravity, "Sir, it was a love marriage on both sides," I have had from my illustrious friend the following curious account of their journey to church upon the nuptial morn:

9th July:— "Sir, she had read the old romances, and had got into her head the fantastical notion that a woman of spirit should use her lover like a dog. So, Sir, at first she told me that I rode too fast, and she could not keep up with me; and, when I rode a little slower, she passed me, and complained that I lagged behind. I was not to be made the slave of caprice; and I resolved to begin as I meant to end. I therefore pushed on briskly, till I was fairly out of her sight. The road lay between two hedges, so I was sure she could not miss it; and I contrived that she should soon come up with me. When she did, I observed her to be in tears."

This, it must be allowed, was a singular beginning of connubial felicity; but there is no doubt that Johnson, though he thus showed a manly firmness, proved a most affectionate and indulgent husband to the last moment of Mrs. Johnson's life.

1736. He now set up a private academy, for which purpose he hired a large house, well situated near his native city. From Mr. Garrick's account he did not appear to have been profoundly reverenced by his pupils. His oddities of manner and uncouth gesticulations could not but be the subject of merriment to them; and, in particular, the young rogues used to

1 born Feb. 4, 1689

listen at the door of his bed-chamber, and peep through the key-hole, that they might turn into ridicule his tumultuous and awkward fondness for Mrs. Johnson, whom he used to name by the familiar appellation of *Tetty* or *Tetsey*, which, like *Betty* or *Betsey*, is provincially used as a contraction for *Elisabeth*, her Christian name, but which to us seems ludicrous, when applied to a woman of her age and appearance. Mr. Garrick described her to me as very fat, with a bosom of more than ordinary protuberance, with swelled cheeks of a florid
10 red, produced by thick painting, and increased by the liberal use of cordials; flaring and fantastic in her dress, and affected both in her speech and her general behavior. I have seen Garrick exhibit her, by his exquisite talent of mimicry, so as to excite the heartiest bursts of laughter; but he, probably, as is the case in all such representations, considerably aggravated the picture.

1744 [AETAT. 35.]—He produced one work this year, fully sufficient to maintain the high reputation which he had acquired. This was *The Life of Richard Savage;* a man of whom
20 it is difficult to speak impartially, without wondering that he was for some time the intimate companion of Johnson: for his character was marked by profligacy, insolence, and ingratitude: yet, as he undoubtedly had a warm and vigorous, though unregulated mind, had seen life in all its varieties, and been much in the company of the statesmen and wits of his time, he could communicate to Johnson an abundant supply of such materials as his philosophical curiosity most eagerly desired; and as Savage's misfortunes and misconduct had reduced him to the lowest state of wretchedness as a writer for bread, his visits
30 to St. John's Gate naturally brought Johnson and him together.

It is melancholy to reflect that Johnson and Savage were sometimes in such extreme indigence that they could not pay for a lodging; so that they have wandered together whole nights in the streets. Yet in these almost incredible scenes of distress, we may suppose that Savage mentioned many of the anecdotes with which Johnson afterwards enriched the life of his unhappy companion, and those of other poets.

He told Sir Joshua Reynolds that one night in particular, when Savage and he walked round St. James's Square for want
40 of a lodging, they were not at all depressed by their situation; but in high spirits and brimful of patriotism, traversed the square for several hours, inveighed against the minister, and "resolved they would *stand by their country.*"

1747 [AETAT. 38.]—The year 1747 is distinguished as the epoch when Johnson's arduous and important work, his Dic-

TIONARY OF THE ENGLISH LANGUAGE, was announced to the world by the publication of its Plan or *Prospectus*.

1748. Dr. Adams found him one day busy at his *Dictionary*, when the following dialogue ensued. ADAMS. "This is a great work, Sir. How are you to get all the etymologies?" JOHNSON. "Why, Sir, here is a shelf with Junius, and Skinner, and others; and there is a Welsh gentleman who has published a collection of Welsh proverbs, who will help me with the Welsh. ADAMS. "But, Sir, how can you do this in three years?" JOHNSON. "Sir, I have no doubt that I can do it in three years." ADAMS. "But the French Academy, which consists of forty members, took forty years to compile their Dictionary." JOHNSON. "Sir, thus it is. This is the proportion. Let me see; forty times forty is sixteen hundred. As three to sixteen hundred, so is the proportion of an Englishman to a Frenchman." With so much ease and pleasantry could he talk of that prodigious labor which he had undertaken to execute.

1752 [AETAT. 43.]—That there should be a suspension of his literary labors during a part of the year 1752 will not seem strange, when it is considered that soon after closing his *Rambler,* he suffered a loss which, there can be no doubt, affected him with the deepest distress. For on the 17th of March, O.S., his wife died.

That his love for his wife was of the most ardent kind, and, during the long period of fifty years, was unimpaired by the lapse of time, is evident from various passages in the series of his *Prayers and Meditations,* published by the Reverend Mr. Strahan, as well as from other memorials, two of which I select as strongly marking the tenderness and sensibility of his mind.

"March 28, 1753. I kept this day as the anniversary of my Tetty's death, with prayers and tears in the morning. In the evening, I prayed for her conditionally, if it were lawful."

"April 23, 1753. I know not whether I do not too much indulge the vain longings of affection; but I hope they intenerate my heart, and that when I die like my Tetty, this affection will be acknowledged in a happy interview, and that in the meantime I am incited by it to piety. I will, however, not deviate too much from common and received methods of devotion."

Her wedding ring, when she became his wife, was after her death preserved by him as long as he lived, with an affectionate care, in a little round wooden box, in the inside of which he pasted a slip of paper, thus inscribed by him in fair characters, as follows:

"Eheu!
Eliz. Johnson,
Nupta Jul. 9° 1736,
Mortua, eheu!
Mart. 17° 1752.*[2]

His acquaintance with Bennet Langton, Esq., of Langton, in
Lincolnshire, another much valued friend, commenced soon
after the conclusion of his *Rambler.* Mr. Langton afterwards
went to pursue his studies at Trinity College, Oxford, where he
10 formed an acquaintance with his fellow student, Mr. Topham
Beauclerk. Johnson, soon after this acquaintance began, passed
a considerable time at Oxford. He at first thought it strange
that Langton should associate so much with one who had
the character of being loose, both in his principles and practice;
but, by degrees, he himself was fascinated, and in a short time
the moral, pious Johnson, and the gay, dissipated Beauclerk,
were companions. "What a coalition!" said Garrick, when he
heard of this: "I shall have my old friend to bail out of the
Round-house." But I can bear testimony that it was a very
20 agreeable association.

One night when Beauclerk and Langton had supped at a
tavern in London, and sat till about three in the morning,
it came into their heads to go and knock up Johnson, and see
if they could prevail on him to join them in a ramble. They
rapped violently at the door of his chambers in the Temple,
till at last he appeared in his shirt, with his little black wig
on the top of his head instead of a nightcap, and a poker in
his hand, imagining, probably, that some ruffians were coming to attack him. When he discovered who they were, and was
30 told their errand, he smiled, and with great good humor agreed
to their proposal: "What, is it you, you dogs! I'll have a frisk
with you." He was soon dressed, and they sallied forth together
into Covent Garden, where the greengrocers and fruiterers
were beginning to arrange their hampers, just come in from the
country. Johnson made some attempts to help them; but the
honest gardeners stared so at his figure and manner, and odd
interference, that he soon saw his services were not relished.
They then repaired to one of the neighboring taverns, and made
a bowl of that liquor called *Bishop*, which Johnson had always
40 liked; while in joyous contempt of sleep, from which he had
been roused, he repeated the festive lines,

"Short, O short then be thy reign,
And give us to the world again!"

2 The Latin words are, in order: alas; married; died; March

They did not stay long, but walked down to the Thames, took a boat, and rowed to Billingsgate. Beauclerk and Johnson were so well pleased with their amusement that they resolved to persevere in dissipation for the rest of the day; but Langton deserted them, being engaged to breakfast with some young ladies. Johnson scolded him for "leaving his social friends, to go and sit with a set of wretched *un-idea'd* girls." Garrick being told of this ramble, said to him smartly, "I heard of your frolic t'other night. You'll be in the Chronicle." Upon which Johnson afterwards observed, "*He* durst not do such a thing. His *wife* would not *let* him!"

1754 [AETAT. 45.]—The *Dictionary*, we may believe, afforded Johnson full occupation this year. As it approached to its conclusion, he probably worked with redoubled vigor, as seamen increase their exertion and alacrity when they have a near prospect of their haven.

Lord Chesterfield, to whom Johnson had paid the high compliment of addressing to his Lordship the *Plan* of his *Dictionary*, had behaved to him in such a manner as to excite his contempt and indignation. He told me that there was never any particular incident which produced a quarrel between Lord Chesterfield and him; but that his Lordship's continued neglect was the reason why he resolved to have no connection with him. When the *Dictionary* was upon the eve of publication, Lord Chesterfield, who, it is said, had flattered himself with expectations that Johnson would dedicate the work to him, attempted, in a courtly manner, to soothe and insinuate himself with the Sage, conscious, as it should seem, of the cold indifference with which he had treated its learned author; and further attempted to conciliate him by writing two papers in *The World* in recommendation of his work; and it must be confessed that they contain some studied compliments, so finely turned, that if there had been no previous offence, it is probable that Johnson would have been highly delighted. Praise, in general, was pleasing to him; but by praise from a man of rank and elegant accomplishments he was peculiarly gratified.

This courtly device failed of its effect. Johnson, who thought that "all was false and hollow," despised the honeyed words, and was even indignant that Chesterfield should for a moment imagine that he could be the dupe of such an artifice. His expression to me concerning Lord Chesterfield upon this occasion was, "Sir, after making great professions, he had for many years taken no notice of me; but when my *Dictionary* was coming out, he fell a scribbling in *The World* about it. Upon which I wrote him a letter expressed in civil terms, but such as might show him that I did not mind what he said or wrote, and that I had done with him."

This is that celebrated letter of which so much has been said, and about which curiosity has been so long excited, without being gratified. I for many years solicited Johnson to favor me with a copy of it, that so excellent a composition might not be lost to posterity. He delayed from time to time to give it me; till at last in 1781, when we were on a visit at Mr. Dilly's, at Southill in Bedfordshire, he was pleased to dictate it to me from memory. He afterwards found among his papers a copy of it, which he had dictated to Mr. Baretti, 10 with its title and corrections, in his own handwriting. This he gave to Mr. Langton, adding that if it were to come into print, he wished it to be from that copy. By Mr. Langton's kindness I am enabled to enrich my work with a perfect transcript of what the world has so long eagerly desired to see.

"TO THE RIGHT HONORABLE THE EARL OF CHESTERFIELD.

"My Lord,   February 7, 1755.

"I have been lately informed, by the proprietor of *The* 20 *World,* that two papers, in which my Dictionary is recommended to the public, were written by your Lordship. To be so distinguished, is an honor, which, being very little accustomed to favors from the great, I know not well how to receive, or in what terms to acknowledge.

"When, upon some slight encouragement, I first visited your Lordship, I was overpowered, like the rest of mankind, by the enchantment of your address; and could not forbear to wish that I might boast myself *Le vainqueur du vainqueur de la terre;* [3]—that I might obtain that regard for which I saw 30 the world contending; but I found my attendance so little encouraged, that neither pride nor modesty would suffer me to continue it. When I had once addressed your Lordship in public, I had exhausted all the art of pleasing which a retired and uncourtly scholar can possess. I had done all that I could; and no man is well pleased to have his all neglected, be it ever so little.

"Seven years, my Lord, have now past, since I waited in your outward rooms, or was repulsed from your door; during which time I have been pushing on my work through difficulties, of which it is useless to complain, and have brought it, 40 at last, to the verge of publication, without one act of assistance, one word of encouragement, or one smile of favor. Such treatment I did not expect, for I never had a Patron before.

3 the conqueror of the conqueror of the earth

"The shepherd in Virgil grew at last acquainted with Love, and found him a native of the rocks.

"Is not a Patron, my Lord, one who looks with unconcern on a man struggling for life in the water, and, when he has reached ground, encumbers him with help? The notice which you have been pleased to take of my labors, had it been early, had been kind; but it has been delayed till I am indifferent, and cannot enjoy it; till I am solitary, and cannot impart it; till I am known, and do not want it. I hope it is no very cynical asperity not to confess obligations where no benefit has been received, or to be unwilling that the Public should consider me as owing that to a Patron, which Providence has enabled me to do for myself.

"Having carried on my work thus far with so little obligation to any favorer of learning, I shall not be disappointed though I should conclude it, if less be possible, with less; for I have been long wakened from that dream of hope, in which I once boasted myself with so much exultation, my Lord, your Lordship's most humble, most obedient servant,

"SAM. JOHNSON."

1755 [AETAT. 46.]—The definitions have always appeared to me such astonishing proofs of acuteness of intellect and precision of language, as indicate a genius of the highest rank. This it is which marks the superior excellence of Johnson's Dictionary over others equally or even more voluminous, and must have made it a work of much greater mental labor than mere lexicons, or word-books, as the Dutch call them. They who will make the experiment of trying how they can define a few words of whatever nature will soon be satisfied of the unquestionable justice of this observation, which I can assure my readers is founded upon much study, and upon communication with more minds than my own.

A few of his definitions must be admitted to be erroneous. Thus, Windward and Leeward, though directly of opposite meaning, are defined identically the same way; as to which inconsiderable specks it is enough to observe that his Preface announces that he was aware there might be many such in so immense a work; nor was he at all disconcerted when an instance was pointed out to him. A lady once asked him how he came to define Pastern the knee of a horse: instead of making an elaborate defence, as she expected, he at once answered, "Ignorance, Madam, pure ignorance." His definition of Net-work [4] has been often quoted with sportive malignity as ob-

4 "Anything reticulated or decussated, at equal distances, with interstices between the intersections." (Johnson's Dictionary.)

scuring a thing in itself very plain. But to these frivolous censures no other answer is necessary than that with which we
are furnished by his own Preface.

"To explain, requires the use of terms less abstruse than
that which is to be explained, and such terms cannot always
be found. For as nothing can be proved but by supposing
something intuitively known, and evident without proof, so
nothing can be defined but by the use of words too plain to
admit of definition. Sometimes easier words are changed into
harder; as, *burial*, into *sepulture* or *interment; dry*, into *desic-*
cative; dryness, into *siccity* or *aridity; fit*, into *paroxysm;* for
the easiest word, whatever it be, can never be translated into
one more easy."

His introducing his own opinions, and even prejudices, under
general definitions of words, while at the same time the original meaning of the words is not explained, as his *Tory, Whig,*
Pension, Oats, Excise, and a few more, cannot be fully defended, and must be placed to the account of capricious and
humorous indulgence.[5] Talking to me upon this subject when
we were at Ashbourne in 1777, he mentioned a still stronger
instance of the predominance of his private feelings in the composition of this work than any now to be found in it. "You
know, Sir, Lord Gower forsook the old Jacobite interest. When
I came to the word *Renegado*, after telling that it meant 'one
who deserts to the enemy, a revolter,' I added, 'Sometimes we
say a GOWER.' Thus it went to the press; but the printer had
more wit than I, and struck it out."

Let it, however, be remembered that this indulgence does
not display itself only in sarcasm towards others, but sometimes in playful allusion to the notions commonly entertained
of his own laborious task. Thus: "*Grub-street*, the name of a
street in London, much inhabited by writers of small histories,
dictionaries, and temporary poems; whence any mean production is called Grub-street."—"*Lexicographer*, a writer of dictionaries, *a harmless drudge.*"

1763 [AETAT. 54.]—This is to me a memorable year; for
in it I had the happiness to obtain the acquaintance of that
extraordinary man whose memoirs I am now writing; an acquaintance which I shall ever esteem as one of the most fortunate circumstances in my life. Though then but two-and-

---

5 *Tory:* One who adheres to the ancient constitution of the state, and the apostolical
hierarchy of the church of England, opposed to a whig. *Whig:* The name of a faction. *Pension:* An allowance made to any one without an equivalent. In England
it is generally understood to mean pay given to a state hireling for treason to his
country. *Oats:* A grain which in England is generally given to horses, but in Scotland supports the people. *Excise:* A hateful tax levied upon commodities, and adjudged not by the common judges of property, but wretches hired by those to whom
excise is paid.

twenty, I had for several years read his works with delight
and instruction, and had the highest reverence for their author,
which had grown up in my fancy into a kind of mysterious
veneration, by figuring to myself a state of solemn elevated
abstraction, in which I supposed him to live in the immense
metropolis of London.

Mr. Thomas Davies the actor, who then kept a bookseller's
shop in Russel Street, Covent Garden, told me that Johnson
was very much his friend, and came frequently to his house,
where he more than once invited me to meet him; but by some 10
unlucky accident or other he was prevented from coming to us.

At last, on Monday the 16th of May, when I was sitting
in Mr. Davies's back-parlor, after having drunk tea with him
and Mrs. Davies, Johnson unexpectedly came into the shop;
and Mr. Davies having perceived him through the glass door
in the room in which we were sitting, advancing towards us,
he announced his awful approach to me, somewhat in the manner of an actor in the part of Horatio when he addresses Hamlet on the appearance of his father's ghost, "Look, my Lord,
it comes." I found that I had a very perfect idea of Johnson's 20
figure from the portrait of him painted by Sir Joshua Reynolds soon after he had published his *Dictionary*, in the attitude of sitting in his easy chair in deep meditation, which
was the first picture his friend did for him, which Sir Joshua
very kindly presented to me, and from which an engraving has
been made for this work. Mr. Davies mentioned my name,
and respectfully introduced me to him. I was much agitated;
and recollecting his prejudice against the Scotch, of which I
had heard much, I said to Davies, "Don't tell where I come
from."—"From Scotland," cried Davies roguishly. "Mr. John- 30
son," said I, "I do indeed come from Scotland, but I cannot
help it." I am willing to flatter myself that I meant this as
light pleasantry to soothe and conciliate him, and not as an
humiliating abasement at the expense of my country. But
however that might be, this speech was somewhat unlucky;
for with that quickness of wit for which he was so remarkable,
he seized the expression "come from Scotland," which I used
in the sense of being of that country; and, as if I had said
that I had come away from it, or left it, retorted, "That, Sir,
I find, is what a very great many of your countrymen cannot 40
help." This stroke stunned me a good deal; and when we had
sat down, I felt myself not a little embarrassed, and apprehensive of what might come next.

A few days afterwards I called on Davies, and asked him
if he thought I might take the liberty of waiting on Mr. Johnson at his chambers in the Temple. He said that I certainly

might, and that Mr. Johnson would take it as a compliment.
So upon Tuesday the 24th of May, I boldly repaired to Johnson. His chambers were on the first floor of No. 1, Inner Temple Lane, and I entered them with an impression given me by
the Reverend Dr. Blair, of Edinburgh, who had been introduced to him not long before, and described his having "found
the Giant in his den;" an expression which, when I came to be
pretty well acquainted with Johnson, I repeated to him, and he
was diverted at this picturesque account of himself.

10   He received me very courteously; but, it must be confessed
that his apartment, and furniture, and morning dress, were
sufficiently uncouth. His brown suit of clothes looked very
rusty; he had on a little old shriveled unpowdered wig, which
was too small for his head; his shirt-neck and knees of his
breeches were loose; his black worsted stockings ill drawn up;
and he had a pair of unbuckled shoes by way of slippers. But
all these slovenly particularities were forgotten the moment
that he began to talk. Some gentlemen whom I do not recollect were sitting with him; and when they went away, I also
20 rose; but he said to me, "Nay, don't go." "Sir," said I, "I am
afraid that I intrude upon you. It is benevolent to allow me
to sit and hear you." He seemed pleased with this compliment, which I sincerely paid him, and answered, "Sir, I am
obliged to any man who visits me."

[On Saturday, June 25] he agreed to meet me in the evening at the Mitre. I called on him, and we went thither at
nine. We had a good supper, and port wine, of which he then
sometimes drank a bottle. The orthodox high-church sound
of the MITRE,—the figure and manner of the celebrated
30 SAMUEL JOHNSON,—the extraordinary power and precision of his conversation, and the pride arising from finding
myself admitted as his companion, produced a variety of sensations, and a pleasing elevation of mind beyond what I had
ever before experienced. I find in my journal the following
minute of our conversation, which, though it will give but a
very faint notion of what passed, is in some degree a valuable
record; and it will be curious in this view, as showing how
habitual to his mind were some opinions which appear in his
works.
40   "Sir, I do not think Gray a first-rate poet. He has not a
bold imagination, nor much command of words. The obscurity
in which he has involved himself will not persuade us that he
is sublime. His *Elegy in a Church-yard* has a happy selection
of images, but I don't like what are called his great things.
His *Ode* which begins,

> 'Ruin seize thee, ruthless King
> Confusion on thy banners wait!'

has been celebrated for its abruptness, and plunging into the subject all at once. But such arts as these have no merit, unless when they are original. We admire them only once; and this abruptness has nothing new in it. We have had it often before. Nay, we have it in the old song of Johnny Armstrong:

> 'Is there ever a man in all Scotland
> From the highest estate to the lowest degree,' &c.

And then, Sir,   10

> 'Yes, there is a man in Westmoreland,
> And Johnny Armstrong they do him call.'

There, now, you plunge at once into the subject. You have no previous narration to lead you to it. The two next lines in that *Ode* are, I think, very good:

> 'Though fann'd by conquest's crimson wing,
> They mock the air with idle state.' "

Here let it be observed that although his opinion of Gray's poetry was widely different from mine, and I believe from that of most men of taste, by whom it is with justice highly 20 admired, there is certainly much absurdity in the clamor which has been raised, as if it had been culpably injurious to the merit of that bard, and had been actuated by envy. Alas! ye little short-sighted critics, could JOHNSON be envious of the talents of any of his contemporaries? That his opinion on this subject was what in private and in public he uniformly expressed, regardless of what others might think, we may wonder, and perhaps regret; but it is shallow and unjust to charge him with expressing what he did not think.

We talked of belief in ghosts. He said, "Sir, I make a dis- 30 tinction between what a man may experience by the mere strength of his imagination, and what imagination cannot possibly produce. Thus, suppose I should think that I saw a form, and heard a voice cry, 'Johnson, you are a very wicked fellow, and unless you repent you will certainly be punished,' my own unworthiness is so deeply impressed upon my mind that I might *imagine* I thus saw and heard, and therefore I should not believe that an external communication had been made to me. But if a form should appear, and a voice should tell me that a particular man had died at a particular place, and a 40 particular hour, a fact which I had no apprehension of, nor any

means of knowing, and this fact, with all its circumstances,
should afterwards be unquestionably proved, I should in that
case, be persuaded that I had supernatural intelligence im-
parted to me.

Here it is proper, once for all, to give a true and fair statement of Johnson's way of thinking upon this question, whether
departed spirits are ever permitted to appear in this world, or
in any way to operate upon human life. He has been ignorantly
misrepresented as weakly credulous upon that subject; and
10 therefore, though I feel an inclination to disdain and treat
with silent contempt so foolish a notion concerning my illustrious friend, yet as I find it has gained ground, it is necessary to refute it. The real fact then is, that Johnson had a very
philosophical mind, and such a rational respect for testimony,
as to make him submit his understanding to what was authentically proved, though he could not comprehend why it was
so. Being thus disposed, he was willing to inquire into the
truth of any relation of supernatural agency, a general belief
of which has prevailed in all nations and ages.

20   As Dr. Oliver Goldsmith will frequently appear in this narrative, I shall endeavor to make my readers in some degree
acquainted with his singular character.

No man had the art of displaying with more advantage as
a writer whatever literary acquisitions he made. *"Nihil quod
tetigit non ornavit."* [6] His mind resembled a fertile, but thin
soil. There was a quick, but not a strong vegetation, of whatever chanced to be thrown upon it. The oak of the forest did
not grow there; but the elegant shrubbery and the fragrant
parterre appeared in gay succession. It has been generally cir-
30 culated and believed that he was a mere fool in conversation;
but, in truth, this has been greatly exaggerated. He had, no
doubt, a more than common share of that hurry of ideas which
we often find in his countrymen, and which sometimes produces a laughable confusion in expressing them. He was very
much what the French call *un étourdi,* [7] and from vanity and
an eager desire of being conspicuous wherever he was, he frequently talked carelessly without knowledge of the subject, or
even without thought.

He boasted to me at this time of the power of his pen in
40 commanding money, which I believe was true in a certain degree, though in the instance he gave he was by no means correct. He told me that he had sold a novel for four hundred
pounds. This was his *Vicar of Wakefield.* But Johnson informed me that he had made the bargain for Goldsmith, and

6 "He touched nothing that he did not adorn"—a line from Johnson's epitaph on
Goldsmith (with a slight change)
7 a rattle-head

the price was sixty pounds. "And, Sir," said he, "a sufficient price too, when it was sold; for then the fame of Goldsmith had not been elevated, as it afterwards was, by his *Traveller;* and the bookseller had such faint hopes of profit by his bargain that he kept the manuscript by him a long time, and did not publish it till after *The Traveller* had appeared. Then, to be sure, it was accidentally worth more money."

Mrs. Piozzi and Sir John Hawkins have strangely misstated the history of Goldsmith's situation and Johnson's friendly interference when this novel was sold. I shall give it authentically from Johnson's own exact narration: "I received one morning a message from poor Goldsmith that he was in great distress, and as it was not in his power to come to me, begging that I would come to him as soon as possible. I sent him a guinea, and promised to come to him directly. I accordingly went as soon as I was dressed, and found that his landlady had arrested him for his rent, at which he was in a violent passion. I perceived that he had already changed my guinea, and had got a bottle of Madeira and a glass before him. I put the cork into the bottle, desired he would be calm, and began to talk to him of the means by which he might be extricated. He then told me that he had a novel ready for the press, which he produced to me. I looked into it, and saw its merit; told the landlady I should soon return, and having gone to a bookseller, sold it for sixty pounds. I brought Goldsmith the money, and he discharged his rent, not without rating his landlady in a high tone for having used him so ill."

My next meeting with Johnson was on Friday the 1st of July, when he and I and Dr. Goldsmith supped together at the Mitre. I was before this time pretty well acquainted with Goldsmith, who was one of the brightest ornaments of the Johnsonian school. Goldsmith's respectful attachment to Johnson was then at its height; for his own literary reputation had not yet distinguished him so much as to excite a vain desire of competition with his great Master. He had increased my admiration of the goodness of Johnson's heart, by incidental remarks in the course of conversation, such as, when I mentioned Mr. Levet, whom he entertained under his roof, "He is poor and honest, which is recommendation enough to Johnson;" and when I wondered that he was very kind to a man of whom I had heard a very bad character, "He is now become miserable, and that insures the protection of Johnson."

He talked very contemptuously of Churchill's poetry, observing that "it had a temporary currency, only from its audacity of abuse, and being filled with living names, and that it would sink into oblivion." I ventured to hint that he was not quite

a fair judge, as Churchill had attacked him violently. JOHN-
SON. "Nay, Sir, I am a very fair judge. He did not attack
me violently till he found I did not like his poetry; and his
attack on me shall not prevent me from continuing to say
what I think of him, from an apprehension that it may be
ascribed to resentment. No, Sir, I called the fellow a blockhead at first, and I will call him a blockhead still. However, I will
acknowledge that I have a better opinion of him now than I
once had; for he has shown more fertility than I expected. To
10 be sure, he is a tree that cannot produce good fruit: he only
bears crabs. But, Sir, a tree that produces a great many crabs
is better than a tree which produces only a few."

On Tuesday the 5th of July, I again visited Johnson. He
told me he had looked into the poems of a pretty voluminous
writer, Mr. (now Dr.) John Ogilvie, one of the Presbyterian
ministers of Scotland, which had lately come out, but could
find no thinking in them. BOSWELL. "Is there not imagination in them, Sir?" JOHNSON. "Why, Sir, there is in them
what *was* imagination, but it is no more imagination in *him,*
20 than sound is sound in the echo. And his diction too is not his
own. We have long ago seen *white-robed innocence* and *flower-
bespangled meads.*"

Talking of London, he observed, "Sir, if you wish to have
a just notion of the magnitude of this city, you must not be
satisfied with seeing its great streets and squares, but must
survey the innumerable little lanes and courts. It is not in the
showy evolutions of buildings, but in the multiplicity of human
habitations which are crowded together, that the wonderful
immensity of London consists."—I have often amused myself
30 with thinking how different a place London is to different people. They whose narrow minds are contracted to the consideration of some one particular pursuit, view it only through that
medium. A politician thinks of it merely as the seat of government in its different departments; a grazier, as a vast market for cattle; a mercantile man, as a place where a prodigious
deal of business is done upon 'Change; a dramatic enthusiast,
as the grand scene of theatrical entertainments; a man of
pleasure, as an assemblage of taverns, and the great emporium
for ladies of easy virtue. But the intellectual man is struck
40 with it as comprehending the whole of human life in all its
variety, the contemplation of which is inexhaustible.

On Wednesday, July 6, he was engaged to sup with me at
my lodgings, in Downing Street, Westminster. But on the preceding night my landlord having behaved very rudely to me
and some company who were with me, I had resolved not to
remain another night in his house. I was exceedingly uneasy

at the awkward appearance I supposed I should make to Johnson and the other gentlemen whom I had invited, not being able to receive them at home, and being obliged to order supper at the Mitre. I went to Johnson in the morning, and talked of it as a serious distress. He laughed, and said, "Consider, Sir, how insignificant this will appear a twelvemonth hence." Were this consideration to be applied to most of the little vexatious incidents of life, by which our quiet is too often disturbed, it would prevent many painful sensations. I have tried it frequently, with good effect. "There is nothing," continued he, "in this mighty misfortune; nay, we shall be better at the Mitre." I told him that I had been at Sir John Fielding's office, complaining of my landlord, and had been informed that though I had taken my lodgings for a year, I might, upon proof of his bad behavior, quit them when I pleased, without being under an obligation to pay rent for any longer time than while I possessed them. The fertility of Johnson's mind could show itself even upon so small a matter as this. "Why, Sir," said he, "I suppose this must be the law, since you have been told so in Bow Street. But, if your landlord could hold you to your bargain, and the lodgings should be yours for a year, you may certainly use them as you think fit. So, Sir, you may quarter two life-guardsmen upon him; or you may send the greatest scoundrel you can find into your apartments; or you may say that you want to make some experiments in natural philosophy, and may burn a large quantity of assafœtida in his house."

I had as my guests this evening at the Mitre tavern Dr. Johnson, Dr. Goldsmith, Mr. Thomas Davies, Mr. Eccles, an Irish gentleman, for whose agreeable company I was obliged to Mr. Davies, and the Reverend Mr. John Ogilvie, who was desirous of being in company with my illustrious friend, while I, in my turn, was proud to have the honor of showing one of my countrymen upon what easy terms Johnson permitted me to live with him.

Goldsmith as usual endeavored with too much eagerness to *shine*, and disputed very warmly with Johnson against the well-known maxim of the British constitution "the king can do no wrong;" affirming that "what was morally false could not be politically true; and as the King might, in the exercise of his regal power, command and cause the doing of what was wrong, it certainly might be said, in sense and in reason, that he could do wrong." JOHNSON. Sir, you are to consider that in our constitution, according to its true principles, the King is the head; he is supreme; he is above everything, and there is no power by which he can be tried. Therefore it is, Sir, that

we hold the King can do no wrong; that whatever may happen to be wrong in government may not be above our reach, by being ascribed to Majesty. Redress is always to be had against oppression by punishing the immediate agents. The King, though he should command, cannot force a judge to condemn a man unjustly; therefore it is the judge whom we prosecute and punish. Political institutions are formed upon the consideration of what will most frequently tend to the good of the whole, although now and then exceptions may occur.
10 Thus it is better in general that a nation should have a supreme legislative power, although it may at times be abused. And then, Sir, there is this consideration, that *if the abuse be enormous, Nature will rise up, and claiming her original rights, overturn a corrupt political system.*" I mark this animated sentence with peculiar pleasure, as a noble instance of that truly dignified spirit of freedom which ever glowed in his heart, though he was charged with slavish tenets by superficial observers because he was at all times indignant against that false patriotism, that pretended love of freedom, that unruly rest-
20 lessness which is inconsistent with the stable authority of any good government.

This generous sentiment, which he uttered with great fervor, struck me exceedingly, and stirred my blood to that pitch of fancied resistance, the possibility of which I am glad to keep in mind, but to which I trust I never shall be forced.

"Great abilities," said he, "are not requisite for an historian; for in historical composition all the greatest powers of the human mind are quiescent. He has facts ready to his hand; so there is no exercise of invention. Imagination is not required
30 in any high degree; only about as much as is used in the lower kinds of poetry. Some penetration, accuracy, and coloring will fit a man for the task, if he can give the application which is necessary.

"Bayle's *Dictionary* is a very useful work for those to consult who love the biographical part of literature, which is what I love most."

Mr. Ogilvie was unlucky enough to choose for the topic of his conversation the praises of his native country. He began with saying that there was very rich land round Edinburgh.
40 Goldsmith, who had studied physic there, contradicted this, very untruly, with a sneering laugh. Disconcerted a little by this, Mr. Ogilvie then took new ground, where, I suppose, he thought himself perfectly safe; for he observed that Scotland had a great many noble wild prospects. JOHNSON. "I believe, Sir, you have a great many. Norway, too, has noble wild prospects; and Lapland is remarkable for prodigious noble

wild prospects. But, Sir, let me tell you, the noblest prospect
which a Scotchman ever sees is the high road that leads him
to England." This unexpected and pointed sally produced a
roar of applause. After all, however, those who admire the
rude grandeur of Nature cannot deny it to Caledonia.

On the 14th we had another evening by ourselves at the
Mitre.

He enlarged very convincingly upon the excellence of rhyme
over blank verse in English poetry. I mentioned to him that
Dr. Adam Smith, in his lectures upon composition when I
studied under him in the College of Glasgow, had maintained
the same opinion strenuously, and I repeated some of his arguments. JOHNSON. "Sir, I was once in company with Smith,
and we did not take to each other; but had I known that he
loved rhyme as much as you tell me he does, I should have
HUGGED him."

Talking of those who denied the truth of Christianity, he
said, "It is always easy to be on the negative side. If a man
were now to deny that there is salt upon the table, you could
not reduce him to an absurdity. Come, let us try this a little
further. I deny that Canada is taken, and I can support my
denial by pretty good arguments. The French are a much
more numerous people than we; and it is not likely that they
would allow us to take it. 'But the ministry have assured us,
in all the formality of *The Gazette*, that it is taken.' Very true.
But the ministry have put us to an enormous expense by the
war in America, and it is their interest to persuade us that
we have got something for our money. 'But the fact is confirmed by thousands of men who were at the taking of it.' Ay,
but these men have still more interest in deceiving us. They
don't want that you should think the French have beat them,
but that they have beat the French. Now suppose you should
go over and find that it is really taken, that would only satisfy
yourself; for when you come home we will not believe you.
We will say you have been bribed. Yet, Sir, notwithstanding
all these plausible objections, we have no doubt that Canada
is really ours. Such is the weight of common testimony. How
much stronger are the evidences of the Christian religion!"

"Idleness is a disease which must be combated; but I would
not advise a rigid adherence to a particular plan of study. I
myself have never persisted in any plan for two days together. A man ought to read just as inclination leads him;
for what he reads as a task will do him little good. A young
man should read five hours in a day, and so may acquire a
great deal of knowledge."

To a man of vigorous intellect and arduous curiosity like

his own, reading without a regular plan may be beneficial; though even such a man must submit to it, if he would attain a full understanding of any of the sciences.

To such a degree of unrestrained frankness had he now accustomed me that in the course of this evening I talked of the numerous reflections which had been thrown out against him on account of his having accepted a pension from his present Majesty.[8] "Why, Sir," said he with a hearty laugh, "it is a mighty foolish noise that they make. I have accepted of a pension as a reward which has been thought due to my literary merit; and now that I have this pension, I am the same man in every respect that I have ever been; I retain the same principles. It is true that I cannot now curse" (smiling) "the House of Hanover; nor would it be decent for me to drink King James's health in the wine that King George gives me money to pay for. But, Sir, I think that the pleasure of cursing the House of Hanover, and drinking King James's health, are amply overbalanced by three hundred pounds a year."

[Tuesday, July 19] Mr. Levet this day showed me Dr. Johnson's library, which was contained in two garrets over his chambers, where Lintot, son of the celebrated bookseller of that name, had formerly his warehouse. I found a number of good books, but very dusty and in great confusion. The floor was strewed with manuscript leaves in Johnson's own handwriting, which I beheld with a degree of veneration, supposing they perhaps might contain portions of *The Rambler* or of *Rasselas*. I observed an apparatus for chemical experiments, of which Johnson was all his life very fond. The place seemed to be very favorable for retirement and meditation. Johnson told me that he went up thither without mentioning it to his servant, when he wanted to study secure from interruption; for he would not allow his servant to say he was not at home when he really was. "A servant's strict regard for truth," said he, "must be weakened by such a practice. A philosopher may know that it is merely a form of denial; but few servants are such nice distinguishers. If I accustom a servant to tell a lie for *me*, have I not reason to apprehend that he will tell many lies for *himself?*" I am, however, satisfied that every servant of any degree of intelligence understands saying his master is not at home not at all as the affirmation of a fact, but as customary words intimating that his master wishes not to be seen; so that there can be no bad effect from it.

On Wednesday, July 20, . . . Mr. Dempster having en-

8 pension granted by George III in 1762

deavored to maintain that intrinsic merit *ought* to make the only distinction amongst mankind. JOHNSON. "Why, Sir, mankind have found that this cannot be. How shall we determine the proportion of intrinsic merit? Were that to be the only distinction amongst mankind, we should soon quarrel about the degrees of it. Were all distinctions abolished, the strongest would not long acquiesce, but would endeavor to obtain a superiority by their bodily strength. But, Sir, as subordination is very necessary for society, and contentions for superiority very dangerous, mankind, that is to say, all civilized nations, have settled it upon a plain invariable principle. A man is born to hereditary rank; or his being appointed to certain offices gives him a certain rank. Subordination tends greatly to human happiness. Were we all upon an equality, we should have no other enjoyment than mere animal pleasure."

I said I considered distinction of rank to be of so much importance in civilized society that if I were asked on the same day to dine with the first Duke in England, and with the first man in Britain for genius, I should hesitate which to prefer. JOHNSON. "To be sure, Sir, if you were to dine only once, and it were never to be known where you dined, you would choose rather to dine with the first man for genius; but to gain most respect you should dine with the first Duke in England. For nine people in ten that you meet with would have a higher opinion of you for having dined with a Duke; and the great genius himself would receive you better because you had been with the great Duke."

He took care to guard himself against any possible suspicion that his settled principles of reverence for rank and respect for wealth were at all owing to mean or interested motives; for he asserted his own independence as a literary man. "No man," said he, "who ever lived by literature, has lived more independently than I have done." He said he had taken longer time than he needed to have done in composing his *Dictionary*. He received our compliments upon that great work with complacency, and told us that the *Academia della Crusca* [9] could scarcely believe that it was done by one man.

[On the next day] at night Mr. Johnson and I supped in a private room at the Turk's Head coffee-house, in the Strand. "I encourage this house," said he; "for the mistress of it is a good civil woman, and has not much business."

"Sir, I love the acquaintance of young people; because, in the first place, I don't like to think myself growing old. In the next place, young acquaintances must last longest, if they

9 the Florentine learned academy

do last; and then, Sir, young men have more virtue than old
men; they have more generous sentiments in every respect.
I love the young dogs of this age: they have more wit and
humor and knowledge of life than we had; but then the dogs
are not so good scholars. Sir, in my early years I read very
hard. It is a sad reflection, but a true one, that I knew almost
as much at eighteen as I do now. My judgment, to be sure,
was not so good; but I had all the facts. I remember very well,
when I was at Oxford, an old gentleman said to me, "Young
10 man, ply your book diligently now, and acquire a stock of
knowledge; for when years come upon you, you will find that
poring upon books will be but an irksome task."

[On] Sunday, July 31, I told him I had been that morning
at a meeting of the people called Quakers, where I had heard
a woman preach. JOHNSON. "Sir, a woman's preaching is
like a dog's walking on his hinder legs. It is not done well;
but you are surprised to find it done at all."

On Tuesday, August 2 (the day of my departure from London having been fixed for the 5th), Dr. Johnson did me the
20 honor to pass a part of the morning with me at my chambers.
He said that he "always felt an inclination to do nothing."
I observed that it was strange to think that the most indolent
man in Britain had written the most laborious work, *The English Dictionary.*

I had now made good my title to be a privileged man, and
was carried by him in the evening to drink tea with Miss
Williams, whom, though under the misfortune of having lost
her sight, I found to be agreeable in conversation, for she had
a variety of literature, and expressed herself well; but her
30 peculiar value was the intimacy in which she had long lived
with Johnson, by which she was well acquainted with his
habits, and knew how to lead him on to talk.

After tea he carried me to what he called his walk, which
was a long narrow paved court in the neighborhood, over-
shadowed by some trees. There we sauntered a considerable
time; and I complained to him that my love of London and
of his company was such that I shrunk almost from the
thought of going away, even to travel, which is generally so
much desired by young men. He roused me by manly and
40 spirited conversation. He advised me, when settled in any place
abroad, to study with an eagerness after knowledge, and to
apply to Greek an hour every day; and when I was moving
about, to read diligently the great book of mankind.

At supper this night [Friday, August 5] he talked of good
eating with uncommon satisfaction. "Some people," said he,
"have a foolish way of not minding, or pretending not to

mind, what they eat. For my part, I mind my belly very studiously, and very carefully; for I look upon it that he who does not mind his belly will hardly mind anything else." He now appeared to me *Jean Bull philosophe*, and he was for the moment not only serious but vehement. Yet I have heard him upon other occasions talk with great contempt of people who were anxious to gratify their palates; and the 206th number of his *Rambler* is a masterly essay against gulosity. His practice, indeed, I must acknowledge, may be considered as casting the balance of his different opinions upon this subject; for I never knew any man who relished good eating more than he did. When at table, he was totally absorbed in the business of the moment; his looks seemed riveted to his plate; nor would he, unless when in very high company, say one word, or even pay the least attention to what was said by others, till he had satisfied his appetite, which was so fierce, and indulged with such intenseness, that while in the act of eating, the veins of his forehead swelled, and generally a strong perspiration was visible. To those whose sensations were delicate this could not but be disgusting; and it was doubtless not very suitable to the character of a philosopher, who should be distinguished by self-command. But it must be owned that Johnson, though he could be rigidly *abstemious*, was not a *temperate* man either in eating or drinking. He could refrain, but he could not use moderately. He told me that he had fasted two days without inconvenience, and that he had never been hungry but once. They who beheld with wonder how much he eat upon all occasions when his dinner was to his taste, could not easily conceive what he must have meant by hunger; and not only was he remarkable for the extraordinary quantity which he eat, but he was, or affected to be, a man of very nice discernment in the science of cookery. He used to descant critically on the dishes which had been at table where he had dined or supped, and to recollect very minutely what he had liked.

1764 [AETAT. 55.]—Soon after his return to London, which was in February, was founded that CLUB which existed long without a name, but at Mr. Garrick's funeral became distinguished by the title of THE LITERARY CLUB. Sir Joshua Reynolds had the merit of being the first proposer of it, to which Johnson acceded, and the original members were Sir Joshua Reynolds, Dr. Johnson, Mr. Edmund Burke, Dr. Nugent, Mr. Beauclerk, Mr. Langton, Dr. Goldsmith, Mr. Chamier, and Sir John Hawkins. They met at the Turk's Head, in Gerard Street, Soho, one evening in every week, at seven, and generally continued their conversation till a pretty late hour. This club has been gradually increased to its present number, thirty-five. After about ten years, instead of supping weekly, it was resolved to dine together once a fortnight during the meeting of Parliament.

Not very long after the institution of our club, Sir Joshua Reynolds was speaking of it to Garrick. "I like it much," said he, "I think I shall be of you." When Sir Joshua mentioned this to Dr. Johnson, he was much displeased with the actor's conceit. *"He'll be of us,"* said Johnson, "how does he know we will *permit* him? The first Duke in England has no right to hold such language." However, when Garrick was regularly proposed some time afterwards, Johnson, though he had taken a momentary offence at his arrogance, warmly and kindly supported him, and he was accordingly elected, was a most agreeable member, and continued to attend our meetings to the time of his death.

The ease and independence to which he had at last attained by royal munificence,[10] increased his natural indolence. In his *Meditations* he thus accuses himself: "GOOD FRIDAY, April 20, 1764.—I have made no reformation; I have lived totally useless, more sensual in thought, and more addicted to wine and meat." And next morning he thus feelingly complains: "My indolence, since my last reception of the sacrament, has sunk into grosser sluggishness, and my dissipation spread into wilder negligence. My thoughts have been clouded with sensuality; and except that that from the beginning of this year I have in some measure forborne excess of strong drink, my appetites have predominated over my reason. A kind of strange oblivion has overspread me, so that I know not what has become of the last year; and perceive that incidents and intelligence pass over me without leaving any impression." He then solemnly says, "This is not the life to which heaven is promised;" and he earnestly resolves an amendment.

It was his custom to observe certain days with a pious abstraction; viz., New Year's Day, the day of his wife's death, Good Friday, Easter Day, and his own birthday. He this year says: "I have now spent fifty-five years in resolving; having, from the earliest time almost that I can remember been forming schemes of a better life, I have done nothing. The need of doing therefore is pressing, since the time of doing is short. O God, grant me to resolve aright, and to keep my resolutions, for Jesus Christ's sake. Amen."

Such a tenderness of conscience, such a fervent desire of improvement, will rarely be found. It is surely not decent in

10 the pension mentioned on p. 846

those who are hardened in indifference to spiritual improvement to treat this pious anxiety of Johnson with contempt.

About this time he was afflicted with a very severe return of the hypochondriac disorder which was ever lurking about him. He was so ill as, notwithstanding his remarkable love of company, to be entirely averse to society, the most fatal symptom of that malady. Dr. Adams told me that as an old friend he was admitted to visit him, and that he found him in a deplorable state, sighing, groaning, talking to himself, and restlessly walking from room to room. He then used this emphatical expression of the misery which he felt: "I would consent to have a limb amputated to recover my spirits."

Talking to himself was, indeed, one of his singularities ever since I knew him. I was certain that he was frequently uttering pious ejaculations; for fragments of the Lord's Prayer have been distinctly overheard. His friend Mr. Thomas Davies, of whom Churchill says, "That Davies hath a very pretty wife," when Dr. Johnson muttered "lead us not into temptation," used with waggish and gallant humor to whisper Mrs. Davies, "You, my dear, are the cause of this."

He had another particularity, of which none of his friends ever ventured to ask an explanation. It appeared to me some superstitious habit which he had contracted early, and from which he had never called upon his reason to disentangle him. This was his anxious care to go out or in at a door or passage by a certain number of steps from a certain point, or at least so as that either his right or his left foot (I am not certain which) should constantly make the first actual movement when he came close to the door or passage. Thus I conjecture: for I have upon innumerable occasions observed him suddenly stop, and then seem to count his steps with a deep earnestness; and when he had neglected or gone wrong in this sort of magical movement, I have seen him go back again, put himself in a proper posture to begin the ceremony, and, having gone through it, break from his abstraction, walk briskly on, and join his companion. A strange instance of something of this nature, even when on horseback, happened when he was in the Isle of Sky. Sir Joshua Reynolds has observed him to go a good way about rather than cross a particular alley in Leicester Fields; but this Sir Joshua imputed to his having had some disagreeable recollection associated with it.

That the most minute singularities which belonged to him, and made very observable parts of his appearance and manner, may not be omitted, it is requisite to mention that while talking or even musing as he sat in his chair, he commonly held

his head to one side towards his right shoulder, and shook it
in a tremulous manner, moving his body backwards and forwards, and rubbing his left knee in the same direction with the
palm of his hand. In the intervals of articulating he made
various sounds with his mouth, sometimes as if ruminating,
or what is called chewing the cud, sometimes giving a half
whistle, sometimes making his tongue play backwards from
the roof of his mouth, as if clucking like a hen, and sometimes
protruding it against his upper gums in front, as if pronounc-
10 ing quickly under his breath *too, too, too:* all this accompanied
sometimes with a thoughtful look, but more frequently with a
smile. Generally when he had concluded a period in the course
of a dispute, by which time he was a good deal exhausted by
violence and vociferation, he used to blow out his breath like a
whale. This I supposed was a relief to his lungs; and seemed in
him to be a contemptuous mode of expression, as if he had made
the arguments of his opponent fly like chaff before the wind.

I am fully aware how very obvious an occasion I here give for
the sneering jocularity of such as have no relish of an exact
20 likeness; which to render complete, he who draws it must not
disdain the slightest strokes. But if witlings should be inclined
to attack on this account, let them have the candor to quote
what I have offered in my defence.

[February 15, 1766] On his favorite subject of subordination, Johnson said, "So far is it from being true that men are
naturally equal, that no two people can be half an hour together but one shall acquire an evident superiority over the
other."

Another evening Dr. Goldsmith and I called on him, with
30 the hope of prevailing on him to sup with us at the Mitre.
We found him indisposed, and resolved not to go abroad.
"Come then," said Goldsmith, "we will not go to the Mitre
to-night, since we cannot have the big man with us." Johnson
then called for a bottle of port, of which Goldsmith and I
partook, while our friend, now a water drinker, sat by us.
GOLDSMITH, "I think, Mr. Johnson, you don't go near the
theatres now. You give yourself no more concern about a new
play than if you had never had anything to do with the stage."
JOHNSON. "Why, Sir, our tastes greatly alter. The lad does not
40 care for the child's rattle, and the old man does not care for
the young man's whore." GOLDSMITH. "Nay, Sir, but your
Muse was not a whore." JOHNSON. "Sir, I do not think she was.
But as we advance in the journey of life, we drop some of
the things which have pleased us; whether it be that we are
fatigued and don't choose to carry so many things any farther,
or that we find other things which we like better." BOSWELL.

"But, Sir, why don't you give us something in some other way?" Goldsmith. "Ay, Sir, we have a claim upon you." Johnson. "No, Sir, I am not obliged to do any more. No man is obliged to do as much as he can do. A man is to have part of his life to himself. If a soldier has fought a good many campaigns, he is not to be blamed if he retires to ease and tranquillity. A physician who has practiced long in a great city, may be excused if he retires to a small town, and takes less practice. Now, Sir, the good I can do by my conversation bears the same proportion to the good I can do by my writings, that the practice of a physician, retired to a small town, does to his practice in a great city." Boswell. "But I wonder, Sir, you have not more pleasure in writing than in not writing." Johnson. "Sir, you *may* wonder."

In February, 1767, there happened one of the most remarkable incidents of Johnson's life, which gratified his monarchical enthusiasm, and which he loved to relate with all its circumstances when requested by his friends. This was his being honored by a private conversation with his Majesty,[11] in the library at the Queen's house. He had frequently visited those splendid rooms and noble collection of books, which he used to say was more numerous and curious than he supposed any person could have made in the time which the King had employed. Mr. Barnard, the librarian, took care that he should have every accommodation that could contribute to his ease and convenience, while indulging his literary taste in that place; so that he had here a very agreeable resource at leisure hours.

His Majesty having been informed of his occasional visits, was pleased to signify a desire that he should be told when Dr. Johnson came next to the library. Accordingly, the next time that Johnson did come, as soon as he was fairly engaged with a book, on which, while he sat by the fire, he seemed quite intent, Mr. Barnard stole round to the apartment where the King was, and in obedience to his Majesty's commands, mentioned that Dr. Johnson was then in the library. His Majesty said he was at leisure, and would go to him; upon which Mr. Barnard took one of the candles that stood on the King's table, and lighted his Majesty through a suite of rooms, till they came to a private door into the library, of which his Majesty had the key. Being entered, Mr. Barnard stepped forward hastily to Dr. Johnson, who was still in a profound study, and whispered him, "Sir, here is the King." Johnson started up, and stood still. His Majesty approached him, and at once was courteously easy.

His Majesty began by observing that he understood he came

11 George III

sometimes to the library; and then mentioning his having heard that the Doctor had been lately at Oxford, asked him if he was not fond of going thither. To which Johnson answered that he was indeed fond of going to Oxford sometimes, but he was likewise glad to come back again.

His Majesty enquired if he was then writing anything. He answered he was not, for he had pretty well told the world what he knew, and must now read to acquire more knowledge. The King, as it should seem with a view to urge him to rely 10 on his own stores as an original writer, and to continue his labors, then said, "I do not think you borrow much from anybody." Johnson said he thought he had already done his part as a writer. "I should have thought so too," said the King, "if you had not written so well." Johnson observed to me, upon this, that "No man could have paid a handsomer compliment; and it was fit for a King to pay. It was decisive." When asked by another friend, at Sir Joshua Reynolds's, whether he made any reply to this high compliment, he answered, "No, Sir. When the King had said it, it was to be so. It was not for me 20 to bandy civilities with my Sovereign." Perhaps no man who had spent his whole life in courts could have shown a more nice and dignified sense of true politeness than Johnson did in this instance.

His Majesty having observed to him that he supposed he must have read a great deal, Johnson answered that he thought more than he read; that he had read a great deal in the early part of his life, but having fallen into ill health, he had not been able to read much, compared with others.

His Majesty expressed a desire to have the literary biog- 30 raphy of this country ably executed, and proposed to Dr. Johnson to undertake it. Johnson signified his readiness to comply with his Majesty's wishes.

During the whole of this interview, Johnson talked to his Majesty with profound respect, but still in his firm, manly manner, with a sonorous voice, and never in that subdued tone which is commonly used at the levee and in the drawing room. After the King withdrew, Johnson showed himself highly pleased with his Majesty's conversation and gracious behavior. He said to Mr. Barnard, "Sir, they may talk of the King as 40 they will; but he is the finest gentleman I have ever seen." And he afterwards observed to Mr. Langton, "Sir, his manners are those of as fine a gentleman as we may suppose Lewis the Fourteenth or Charles the Second."

At Sir Joshua Reynolds's, where a circle of Johnson's friends was collected round him to hear his account of this memorable conversation, Dr. Joseph Warton, in his frank and lively manner, was very active in pressing him to mention the particulars. "Come now, Sir, this is an interesting matter; do favor us with it." Johnson, with great good humor, complied.

He told them, "I found his Majesty wished I should talk, and I made it my business to talk. I find it does a man good to be talked to by his Sovereign. In the first place, a man cannot be in a passion—." Here some question interrupted him, which is to be regretted, as he certainly would have pointed out and illustrated many circumstances of advantage, from being in a situation where the powers of the mind are at once excited to vigorous exertion, and tempered by reverential awe.

During all the time in which Dr. Johnson was employed in relating to the circle at Sir Joshua Reynolds's the particulars of what passed between the King and him, Dr. Goldsmith remained unmoved upon a sofa at some distance, affecting not to join in the least in the eager curiosity of the company. He assigned as a reason for his gloom and seeming inattention that he apprehended Johnson had relinquished his purpose of furnishing him with a Prologue to his play, with the hopes of which he had been flattered; but it was strongly suspected that he was fretting with chagrin and envy at the singular honor Dr. Johnson had lately enjoyed. At length, the frankness and simplicity of his natural character prevailed. He sprung from the sofa, advanced to Johnson, and in a kind of flutter, from imagining himself in the situation which he had just been hearing described, exclaimed, "Well, you acquitted yourself in this conversation better than I should have done; for I should have bowed and stammered through the whole of it."

1769 [AETAT. 60.]—He honored me with his company at dinner on the 16th of October, at my lodgings in Old Bond Street, with Sir Joshua Reynolds, Mr. Garrick, Dr. Goldsmith, Mr. Murphy, Mr. Bickerstaff and Mr. Thomas Davies. Garrick played round him with a fond vivacity, taking hold of the breasts of his coat, and looking up in his face with a lively archness, complimented him on the good health which he seemed then to enjoy; while the sage, shaking his head, beheld him with a gentle complacency. One of the company not being come at the appointed hour, I proposed, as usual upon such occasions, to order dinner to be served; adding, "Ought six people to be kept waiting for one?" "Why, yes," answered Johnson, with a delicate humanity, "if the one will suffer more by your sitting down than the six will do by waiting." Goldsmith, to divert the tedious minutes, strutted about, bragging of his dress, and I believe was seriously vain of it, for his mind was wonderfully prone to such impressions. "Come,

come," said Garrick, "talk no more of that. You are, perhaps, the worst—eh, eh!"—Goldsmith was eagerly attempting to interrupt him, when Garrick went on, laughing ironically, "Nay, you will always *look* like a gentleman; but I am talking of being well or *ill dressed*." "Well, let me tell you," said Goldsmith, "when my tailor brought home my bloom-colored coat, he said, 'Sir, I have a favor to beg of you. When anybody asks you who made your clothes, be pleased to mention John Filby, at the Harrow, in Water Lane." JOHNSON. "Why, Sir, that was because he knew the strange color would attract crowds to gaze at it, and thus they might hear of him, and see how well he could make a coat even of so absurd a color."

[1772] On Monday, April 6, I dined with him at Sir Alexander Macdonald's. Fielding being mentioned, Johnson exclaimed "he was a blockhead;" and upon my expressing my astonishment at so strange an assertion, he said, "What I mean by his being a blockhead is that he was a barren rascal." BOSWELL. "Will you not allow, Sir, that he draws very natural pictures of human life?" JOHNSON. "Why, Sir, it is of very low life. Richardson used to say that had he not known who Fielding was, he should have believed he was an ostler. Sir, there is more knowledge of the heart in one letter of Richardson's than in all *Tom Jones*. I, indeed, never read *Joseph Andrews*." ERSKINE. "Surely, Sir, Richardson is very tedious." JOHNSON. "Why, Sir, if you were to read Richardson for the story, your impatience would be so much fretted that you would hang yourself. But you must read him for the sentiment, and consider the story as only giving occasion to the sentiment." I have already given my opinion of Fielding; but I cannot refrain from repeating here my wonder at Johnson's excessive and unaccountable depreciation of one of the best writers that England has produced. *Tom Jones* has stood the test of public opinion with such success as to have established its great merit both for the story, the sentiments, and the manners, and also the varieties of diction, so as to leave no doubt of its having an animated truth of execution throughout.

He would not allow Scotland to derive any credit from Lord Mansfield; for he was educated in England. "Much," said he, "may be made of a Scotchman, if he be *caught* young."

[1773] On Wednesday, April 21, I dined with him at Mr. Thrale's. A gentleman attacked Garrick for being vain. JOHNSON. "No wonder, Sir, that he is vain; a man who is perpetually flattered in every mode that can be conceived. So many bellows have blown the fire that one wonders he is not by this time become a cinder."

On Tuesday, April 27, Mr. Beauclerk and I called on him in the morning.

He said, "Goldsmith should not be forever attempting to shine in conversation; he has not temper for it, he is so much mortified when he fails. Sir, a game of jokes is composed partly of skill, partly of chance. A man may be beat at times by one who has not the tenth part of his wit. Now Goldsmith's putting himself against another is like a man laying a hundred to one who cannot spare the hundred. It is not worth a man's while. A man should not lay a hundred to one unless he can easily spare it, though he has a hundred chances for him: he can get but a guinea, and he may lose a hundred. Goldsmith is in this state. When he contends, if he gets the better, it is a very little addition to a man of his literary reputation; if he does not get the better, he is miserably vexed."

Johnson's own superlative powers of wit set him above any risk of such uneasiness. Garrick had remarked to me of him, a few days before, "Rabelais and all other wits are nothing compared with him. You may be diverted by them; but Johnson gives you a forcible hug and shakes laughter out of you, whether you will or no."

Goldsmith, however, was often very fortunate in his witty contests, even when he entered the lists with Johnson himself. Sir Joshua Reynolds was in company with them one day when Goldsmith said that he thought he could write a good fable, mentioned the simplicity which that kind of composition requires, and observed that in most fables the animals introduced seldom talk in character. "For instance," said he, "the fable of the little fishes who saw birds fly over their heads, and envying them, petitioned Jupiter to be changed into birds. The skill," continued he, "consists in making them talk like little fishes." While he indulged himself in this fanciful reverie, he observed Johnson shaking his sides and laughing. Upon which he smartly proceeded, "Why, Dr. Johnson, this is not so easy as you seem to think; for if you were to make little fishes talk, they would talk like WHALES."

On Friday, April 30, I dined with him at Mr. Beauclerk's, where were Lord Charlemont, Sir Joshua Reynolds, and some more members of the LITERARY CLUB whom he had obligingly invited to meet me, as I was this evening to be balloted for as a candidate for admission into that distinguished society. Johnson had done me the honor to propose me, and Beauclerk was very zealous for me.

The gentlemen went away to their club, and I was left at Beauclerk's till the fate of my election should be announced to me. I sat in a state of anxiety which even the charming conversation of Lady Di Beauclerk could not entirely dissipate. In a short time I received the agreeable intelligence that I was chosen. I hastened to the place of meeting, and was introduced to such a society as can seldom be found. Mr. Edmund Burke, whom I then saw for the first time, and whose splendid talents had long made me ardently wish for his acquaintance; Dr. Nugent, Mr. Garrick, Dr. Goldsmith, Mr. (afterwards Sir William) Jones, and the company with whom I had dined. Upon my entrance, Johnson placed himself behind a chair, on which he leaned as on a desk or pulpit, and with humorous formality gave me a *Charge,* pointing out the conduct expected from me as a good member of this club.

On Saturday, May 1, we dined by ourselves at our old rendezvous, the Mitre tavern. He was placid, but not much disposed to talk. He observed that "the Irish mix better with the English than the Scotch do; their language is nearer to English; as a proof of which, they succeed very well as players, which Scotchmen do not. Then, Sir, they have not that extreme nationality which we find in the Scotch. I will do you, Boswell, the justice to say that you are the most *unscottified* of your countrymen. You are almost the only instance of a Scotchman that I have known who did not at every other sentence bring in some other Scotchman."

On Friday, May 7, I dined with him . . . at the house of my friends, Messieurs Edward and Charles Dilly, booksellers in the Poultry.

I introduced the subject of toleration. JOHNSON. "Every society has a right to preserve public peace and order, and therefore has a good right to prohibit the propagation of opinions which have a dangerous tendency. To say the *magistrate* has this right is using an inadequate word; it is the *society* for which the magistrate is agent. He may be morally or theologically wrong in restraining the propagation of opinions which he thinks dangerous, but he is politically right." MAYO. "I am of opinion, Sir, that every man is entitled to liberty of conscience in religion; and that the magistrate cannot restrain that right." JOHNSON. "Sir, I agree with you. Every man has a right to liberty of conscience, and with that the magistrate cannot interfere. People confound liberty of thinking with liberty of talking; nay, with liberty of preaching. Every man has a physical right to think as he pleases; for it cannot be discovered how he thinks. He has not a moral right, for he ought to inform himself, and think justly. But, Sir, no member of a society has a right to *teach* any doctrine contrary to what the society holds to be true. The magistrate, I say, may be wrong in what he thinks; but while he thinks himself right, he may

come upon him with a direct proposal, "Sir, will you dine in
company with Jack Wilkes?" he would have flown into a passion, and would probably have answered, "Dine with Jack
Wilkes, Sir! I'd as soon dine with Jack Ketch!" [13] I therefore,
while we were sitting quietly by ourselves at his house in an
evening, took occasion to open my plan thus: "Mr. Dilly, Sir,
sends his respectful compliments to you, and would be happy
if you would do him the honor to dine with him on Wednesday next along with me, as I must soon go to Scotland." JOHN-
SON. "Sir, I am obliged to Mr. Dilly. I will wait upon him." 10
BOSWELL. "Provided, Sir, I suppose, that the company which
he is to have is agreeable to you." JOHNSON. "What do you
mean, Sir? What do you take me for? Do you think I am so
ignorant of the world as to imagine that I am to prescribe to
a gentleman what company he is to have at his table?" Bos-
WELL. "I beg your pardon, Sir, for wishing to prevent you from
meeting people whom you might not like. Perhaps he may
have some of what he calls his patriotic friends with him."
JOHNSON. "Well, Sir, and what then? What care *I* for his
patriotic friends? Poh!" BOSWELL. "I should not be surprised 20
to find Jack Wilkes there." JOHNSON. "And if Jack Wilkes
should be there, what is that to *me*, Sir? My dear friend, let us
have no more of this. I am sorry to be angry with you; but
really it is treating me strangely to talk to me as if I could
not meet any company whatever, occasionally." BOSWELL.
"Pray forgive me, Sir; I meant well. But you shall meet whoever comes, for me." Thus I secured him, and told Dilly that
he would find him very well pleased to be one of his guests
on the day appointed.

Upon the much-expected Wednesday, I called on him about 30
half an hour before dinner, as I often did when we were to
dine out together, to see that he was ready in time, and to accompany him. I found him buffeting his books, as upon a former
occasion, covered with dust, and making no preparation for
going abroad. "How is this, Sir?" said I. "Don't you recollect
that you are to dine at Mr. Dilly's?" JOHNSON. "Sir, I did not
think of going to Dilly's; it went out of my head. I have ordered dinner at home with Mrs. Williams." BOSWELL. "But,
my dear Sir, you know you were engaged to Mr. Dilly, and
I told him so. He will expect you, and will be much disap- 40
pointed if you don't come." JOHNSON. "You must talk to Mrs.
Williams about this."

Here was a sad dilemma. I feared that what I was so confident I had secured would yet be frustrated. He had accustomed himself to show Mrs. Williams such a degree of humane

13 "the hangman"

attention as frequently imposed some restraint upon him; and
I knew that if she should be obstinate, he would not stir. I
hastened downstairs to the blind lady's room, and told her I
was in great uneasiness, for Dr. Johnson had engaged to me
to dine this day at Mr. Dilly's, but that he had told me he
had forgotten his engagement, and had ordered dinner at home.
"Yes, Sir," said she, pretty peevishly, "Dr. Johnson is to dine
at home." "Madam," said I, "his respect for you is such that
I know he will not leave you unless you absolutely desire it.
10 But as you have so much of his company, I hope you will be
good enough to forego it for a day, as Mr. Dilly is a very
worthy man, has frequently had agreeable parties at his house
for Dr. Johnson, and will be vexed if the Doctor neglects him
to-day. And then, Madam, be pleased to consider my situation; I carried the message, and I assured Mr. Dilly that Dr.
Johnson was to come, and no doubt he has made a dinner, and
invited a company, and boasted of the honor he expected to
have. I shall be quite disgraced if the Doctor is not there."
She gradually softened to my solicitations, which were cer-
20 tainly as earnest as most entreaties to ladies upon any occasion, and was graciously pleased to empower me to tell Dr.
Johnson, "That all things considered, she thought he should
certainly go." I flew back to him, still in dust, and careless
of what should be the event, "indifferent in his choice to go
or stay;" but as soon as I had announced to him Mrs. Williams' consent he roared, "Frank, a clean shirt," and was very
soon dressed. When I had him fairly seated in a hackney coach
with me, I exulted as much as a fortune hunter who has got
an heiress into a post-chaise with him to set out for Gretna
30 Green.

When we entered Mr. Dilly's drawing room, he found himself in the midst of a company he did not know. I kept myself
snug and silent, watching how he would conduct himself. I
observed him whispering to Mr. Dilly, "Who is that gentleman, Sir?" "Mr. Arthur Lee." JOHNSON. "Too, too, too," under
his breath, which was one of his habitual mutterings. Mr.
Arthur Lee could not but be very obnoxious to Johnson, for
he was not only a *patriot* but an *American*. He was afterwards
minister from the United States at the court of Madrid. "And
40 who is the gentleman in lace?" "Mr. Wilkes, Sir." This information confounded him still more; he had some difficulty
to restrain himself, and taking up a book, sat down upon a
window seat and read, or at least kept his eye upon it in-
tently for some time, till he composed himself. His feelings, I
dare say, were awkward enough. But he no doubt recollected
his having rated me for supposing that he could be at all dis-

concerted by any company, and he, therefore, resolutely set himself to behave quite as an easy man of the world, who could adapt himself at once to the disposition and manners of those whom he might chance to meet.

The cheering sound of "Dinner is upon the table" dissolved his reverie, and we *all* sat down without any symptom of ill humor. There were present beside Mr. Wilkes and Mr. Arthur Lee, who was an old companion of mine when he studied physic at Edinburgh, Mr. (now Sir John) Miller, Dr. Lettsom, and Mr. Slater the druggist. Mr. Wilkes placed himself next to Dr. Johnson, and behaved to him with so much attention and politeness that he gained upon him insensibly. No man eat more heartily than Johnson, or loved better what was nice and delicate. Mr. Wilkes was very assiduous in helping him to some fine veal. "Pray give me leave, Sir: it is better here— A little of the brown— Some fat, Sir— A little of the stuffing— Some gravy— Let me have the pleasure of giving you some butter— Allow me to recommend a squeeze of this orange;— or the lemon, perhaps, may have more zest."—"Sir, Sir, I am obliged to you, Sir," cried Johnson, bowing, and turning his head to him with a look for some time of "surly virtue," but, in a short while, of complacency.

1777 [Aᴇᴛᴀᴛ. 68.]—[Sunday, September 12] I shall present my readers with a series of what I gathered this evening from the Johnsonian garden.

"Did we not hear so much said of Jack Wilkes, we should think more highly of his conversation. Jack has great variety of talk, Jack is a scholar, and Jack has the manners of a gentleman. But after hearing his name sounded from pole to pole as the phoenix of convivial felicity, we are disappointed in his company. He has always been *at me:* but I would do Jack a kindness rather than not. The contest is now over."

"Colley Cibber once consulted me as to one of his birthday Odes, a long time before it was wanted. I objected very freely to several passages. Cibber lost patience, and would not read his Ode to an end. When we had done with criticism, we walked over to Richardson's, the author of *Clarissa,* and I wondered to find Richardson displeased that I did not treat Cibber with more *respect.* Now, Sir, to talk of *respect* for a *player!*" smiling disdainfully. Bᴏsᴡᴇʟʟ. "There, Sir, you are always heretical; you never will allow merit to a player." Jᴏʜɴsᴏɴ. "Merit, Sir! what merit? Do you respect a rope-dancer, or a ballad-singer?" Bᴏsᴡᴇʟʟ. "No, Sir; but we respect a great player as a man who can conceive lofty sentiments, and can express them gracefully." Jᴏʜɴsᴏɴ. "What, Sir, a fellow who claps a hump on his back, and a lump on his leg, and cries,

'*I am Richard the Third*'? Nay, Sir, a ballad-singer is a higher man, for he does two things; he repeats and he sings: There is both recitation and music in his performance; the player only recites." BOSWELL. "My dear Sir! you may turn anything into ridicule. I allow that a player of farce is not entitled to respect; he does a little thing: but he who can represent exalted characters and touch the noblest passions has very respectable powers; and mankind have agreed in admiring great talents for the stage. We must consider, too, that a great
10 player does what very few are capable to do: his art is a very rare faculty. *Who* can repeat Hamlet's soliloquy, 'To be or not to be,' as Garrick does it? JOHNSON. "Anybody may. Jemmy, there (a boy about eight years old, who was in the room) will do it as well in a week." BOSWELL. "No, no, Sir; and as a proof of the merit of great acting, and of the value which mankind set upon it, Garrick has got a hundred thousand pounds." JOHNSON. "Is getting a hundred thousand pounds a proof of excellence? That has been done by a scoundrel commissary."
20   This was most fallacious reasoning. I was *sure,* for once, that I had the best side of the argument.

On Friday, March 20, [1778], I found him at his own house, sitting with Mrs. Williams, and was informed that the room formerly allotted to me was now appropriated to a charitable purpose; Mrs. Desmoulins, and I think her daughter, and a Miss Carmichael, being all lodged in it. Such was his humanity and such his generosity, that Mrs. Desmoulins herself told me he allowed her half-a-guinea a week. Let it be remembered that this was above a twelfth part of his pension.
30   On Wednesday, April 15, I dined with Dr. Johnson at Mr. Dilly's. . . . From this pleasing subject [Evidence of the Christian Religion], he, I know not how or why, made a sudden transition to one upon which he was a violent aggressor; for he said, "I am willing to love all mankind, *except an American;*" and his inflammable corruption bursting into horrid fire, he "breathed out threatenings and slaughter;" calling them "Rascals—Robbers—Pirates;" and exclaiming he'd "burn and destroy them." Miss Seward, looking at him with mild but steady astonishment, said, "Sir, this is an instance that we are
40 always most violent against those whom we have injured." [14] He was irritated still more by this delicate and keen reproach; and roared out another tremendous volley, which one might fancy could be heard across the Atlantic. During this tempest

14 Johnson had written a pamphlet against the position of the Americans, *Taxation No Tyranny,* and had consistently attacked them in conversation.

I sat in great uneasiness, lamenting his heat of temper; till by degrees, I diverted his attention to other topics.

1781 [AETAT. 72.]—In 1781 Johnson at last completed his *Lives of the Poets,* of which he gives this account: "Some time in March I finished the *Lives of the Poets,* which I wrote in my usual way, dilatorily and hastily, unwilling to work, and working with vigor and haste." In a memorandum previous to this, he says of them: "Written I hope, in such a manner as may tend to the promotion of piety."

This is the work which of all Dr. Johnson's writings will perhaps be read most generally and with most pleasure. Philology and biography were his favorite pursuits, and those who lived most in intimacy with him heard him upon all occasions, when there was a proper opportunity, take delight in expatiating upon the various merits of the English Poets; upon the niceties of their characters and the events of their progress through the world which they contributed to illuminate. His mind was so full of that kind of information, and it was so well arranged in his memory, that in performing what he had undertaken in this way he had little more to do than to put his thoughts upon paper, exhibiting first each Poet's life, and then subjoining a critical examination of his genius and works. But when he began to write, the subject swelled in such a manner that instead of prefaces to each poet of no more than a few pages, as he had originally intended, he produced an ample, rich, and most entertaining view of them in every respect. The booksellers, justly sensible of the great additional value of the copyright, presented him with another hundred pounds, over and above two hundred, for which his agreement was to furnish such prefaces as he thought fit.

On Monday, March 19, I arrived in London, and on Tuesday, the 20th, met him in Fleet Street, walking, or rather indeed moving along; for his peculiar march is thus described in a very just and picturesque manner, in a short Life of him published very soon after his death: "When he walked the streets, what with the constant roll of his head, and the concomitant motion of his body, he appeared to make his way by that motion, independent of his feet." That he was often much stared at while he advanced in this manner, may easily be believed; but it was not safe to make sport of one so robust as he was. Mr. Langton saw him one day, in a fit of absence, by a sudden start drive the load off a porter's back, and walk forward briskly, without being conscious of what he had done. The porter was very angry, but stood still, and eyed the huge figure with much earnestness, till he was satisfied that his wisest course was to be quiet, and take up his burden again.

Our accidental meeting in the street after a long separation was a pleasing surprise to us both. He stepped aside with me into Falcon Court, and made kind inquiries about my family, and as we were in a hurry going different ways, I promised to call on him next day; he said he was engaged to go out in the morning. "Early, Sir?" said I. Johnson. "Why, Sir, a London morning does not go with the sun."

1784 [Aetat. 75.]—[December] Johnson, with that native fortitude which, amidst all his bodily distress and mental sufferings never forsook him, asked Dr. Brocklesby, as a man in whom he had confidence, to tell him plainly whether he could recover. "Give me," said he, "a direct answer." The Doctor having first asked him if he could bear the whole truth, which way soever it might lead, and being answered that he could, declared that, in his opinion, he could not recover without a miracle. "Then," said Johnson, "I will take no more physic, not even my opiates; for I have prayed that I may render up my soul to God unclouded." In this resolution he persevered, and, at the same time, used only the weakest kinds of sustenance. Being pressed by Mr. Windham to take somewhat more generous nourishment, lest too low a diet should have the very effect which he dreaded, by debilitating his mind, he said, "I will take anything but inebriating sustenance."

Having, as has been already mentioned, made his will on the 8th and 9th of December, and settled all his worldly affairs, he languished till Monday, the 13th of that month, when he expired about seven o'clock in the evening, with so little apparent pain that his attendants hardly perceived when his dissolution took place.

A few days before his death, he had asked Sir John Hawkins, as one of his executors, where he should be buried; and on being answered, "Doubtless in Westminster Abbey," seemed to feel a satisfaction, very natural to a poet; and indeed in my opinion very natural to every man of any imagination who has no family sepulchre in which he can be laid with his fathers. Accordingly, upon Monday, December 20, his remains were deposited in that noble and renowned edifice; and over his grave was placed a large blue flagstone, with this inscription:

"SAMUEL JOHNSON, LL.D.
Obiit [15] xiii *die Decembris,*
Anno Domini
m. dcc. lxxxiv.
Aetatis suae lxxv." [16]

---

15 died   16 in the seventy-fifth year of his life

WILLIAM BLAKE (1757–1827)

Blake was born in London, on November 28, 1757, the son of a hosier, and there he lived, except for short periods, till his death in 1827. He was an engraver by trade, and in this capacity made designs for Young's *Night Thoughts,* Blair's *Grave, The Book of Job, The Divine Comedy,* and other works, and decorated and illustrated his own writings. As a draughtsman, his designs are bold, original, and imaginative; mysterious and visionary; and especially in his later work filled with some vast symbolism—qualities that appear as well in much of his literary product. One cannot hope to understand Blake without appreciating this side of him. He could scream with fear when, as a child, he saw God's face at the window; he saw, with as much reality as you or I would see a cloud, a heavenly host before him, and felt he could touch the sky with his finger. Some of his later work, he asserted, was dictated to him by "authors in eternity." Although his outward life contained no violence, he rebelled alike against the authority of the physical senses, the conventions of organized society, and the dominance of the intellect, championing the imagination as a better guide. "To generalize," he said, "is to be an idiot." He thus represents the complete antithesis of the eighteenth century spirit.

Blake's fame as a writer is chiefly based upon his *Poetical Sketches* and his *Songs of Innocence* and of *Experience* (issued 1783, 1789, and 1794, respectively). These delightful poems are thoroughly romantic. They are written from the child's point of view—one of the earliest instances of the return of the child to English literature. They are characterized by the utmost simplicity of manner and diction—sometimes to the point of *naïveté,* but beautiful and impressive, in the best of them, in their unstudied felicity. The abiding mysticism of the man is present here also, but suggested rather than expanded into the systems of his later productions. No one better illustrates that renascence of wonder which is a leading characteristic of Romanticism than the Blake of the earlier poems.

The later products of Blake are the Prophetic Books, such as *Tiriel, Thel,* the *Marriage of Heaven and Hell,* the *Visions of the Daughters of Albion, America, Europe, Urizen, Los, Ahania, The Four Zoas, Milton,* and *Jerusalem.* Written mostly in a kind of irregular verse that anticipates Whitman and others, they are full of a mystic's apocalyptic raptures, of a huge and cloudy symbolism, and of grandiose figurative language. In them are evident the influence of the Old Testament, Ossian, and Swedenborg, but the result is Blake's own. Formerly it was the custom to dismiss them curtly as the unintelligible outpourings of a visionary, perhaps of a madman; but recently much attention has been paid them, and some of their meaning interpreted, and they are bulking large in the present day study of Blake.

Blake's *Poetical Sketches* were printed from type, but the *Songs of Innocence* and *Experience,* and nearly all of his later works were produced by a process of his own discovery which he termed "illuminated printing." In this process the text and surrounding decorations were executed in reverse in a varnish on copper plates, which were then subjected to an acid bath, whereby the letters and designs were made to stand out in relief. From these plates impressions were printed in various colors, which were afterwards hand tinted by the artist. His wife, an uneducated woman, assisted him in his work and bound the sheets. The process was naturally slow and laborious, and very few copies of any work were made. Blake's poetry was thus denied a reading public in his own time, although a choice few appreciated it highly. With the reprinting of his verse in the nineteenth century, he has come into a belated reputation, which has mounted steadily. His significance in his own time is great, but his influence has been exerted only upon succeeding generations.

BIBLIOGRAPHY. *Poetical Works* ed. by John Sampson (Oxford), with careful textual notes. Older ed. with a memoir by W. M. Rossetti (Bell). *Prophetic Writings,* ed. D. J. Sloss and J. P. R. Wallis (Oxford). Biographies by Gilchrist, A. Symons, M. Wilson, and O. Burdett (Eng. Men of Letters ser.). Study by S. F. Damon, *W. Blake, His Philosophy and Symbols* (Houghton Mifflin).

TO WINTER

"O WINTER! bar thine adamantine doors:
The north is thine; there hast thou built thy dark
Deep-founded habitation. Shake not thy roofs,
Nor bend thy pillars with thine iron car."

He hears me not, but o'er the yawning deep
Rides heavy; his storms are unchained, sheathèd
In ribbèd steel; I dare not lift mine eyes,
For he hath reared his scepter o'er the world.

Lo! now the direful monster, whose skin clings
To his strong bones, strides o'er the groaning rocks:
He withers all in silence, and in his hand
Unclothes the earth, and freezes up frail life.

He takes his seat upon the cliffs,—the mariner
Cries in vain. Poor little wretch, that deal'st
With storms!—till heaven smiles, and the monster
Is driv'n yelling to his caves beneath mount Hecla.

SONG

How sweet I roamed from field to field
And tasted all the summer's pride,
Till I the Prince of Love beheld
Who in the sunny beams did glide.

He showed me lilies for my hair,
And blushing roses for my brow;
He led me through his gardens fair
Where all his golden pleasures grow.

With sweet May dews my wings were wet,
And Phœbus fired my vocal rage;

He caught me in his silken net,
And shut me in his golden cage.

He loves to sit and hear me sing,
Then, laughing, sports and plays with me;
Then stretches out my golden wing,
And mocks my loss of liberty.

SONG

My silks and fine array,
My smiles and languished air,
By love are driven away,
And mournful lean Despair
Brings me yew to deck my grave;
Such end true lovers have.

His face is fair as heaven
When springing buds unfold;
Oh why to him was't given,
Whose heart is wintry cold?
His breast is love's all-worshiped tomb,
Where all love's pilgrims come.

Bring me an ax and spade,
Bring me a winding-sheet;
When I my grave have made
Let winds and tempests beat;
Then down I'll lie, as cold as clay.
True love doth pass away!

MAD SONG

The wild winds weep,
And the night is a-cold;
Come hither, Sleep,
And my griefs unfold.
But lo! the morning peeps
Over the eastern steeps,
And the rustling beds of dawn
The earth do scorn.

Lo! to the vault
Of pavèd heaven,
With sorrow fraught
My notes are driven:

They strike the ear of Night,
Make weep the eyes of Day;
They make mad the roaring winds,
And with tempests play.

Like a fiend in a cloud,
With howling woe
After night I do crowd
And with night will go;
I turn my back to the east
From whence comforts have increased;
For light doth seize my brain
With frantic pain.

TO THE MUSES

WHETHER on Ida's shady brow,
Or in the chambers of the East,
The chambers of the sun, that now
From ancient melody have ceased;

Whether in Heaven ye wander fair,
Or the green corners of the earth,
Or the blue regions of the air
Where the melodious winds have birth;

Whether on crystal rocks ye rove,
Beneath the bosom of the sea
Wand'ring in many a coral grove,
Fair Nine, forsaking Poetry!

How have you left the ancient love
That bards of old enjoyed in you!
The languid strings do scarcely move!
The sound is forced, the notes are few!

INTRODUCTION TO SONGS OF INNOCENCE

PIPING down the valleys wild,
Piping songs of pleasant glee,
On a cloud I saw a child,
And he laughing said to me:

"Pipe a song about a Lamb!"
So I piped with merry cheer.

"Piper, pipe that song again;"
So I piped: he wept to hear.

"Drop thy pipe, thy happy pipe;
Sing thy songs of happy cheer:"
So I sang the same again,
While he wept with joy to hear.

"Piper, sit thee down and write
In a book, that all may read."
So he vanished from my sight,
And I plucked a hollow reed,

And I made a rural pen,
And I stained the water clear,
And I wrote my happy songs
Every child may joy to hear.

THE LAMB

LITTLE Lamb, who made thee?
　Dost thou know who made thee?
Gave thee life, and bid thee feed,
By the stream and o'er the mead;
Gave thee clothing of delight,
Softest clothing, woolly, bright;
Gave thee such a tender voice,
Making all the vales rejoice?
　Little Lamb, who made thee?
　Dost thou know who made thee?

　Little Lamb, I'll tell thee,
　Little Lamb, I'll tell thee:
He is callèd by thy name,
For He calls Himself a Lamb.
He is meek, and He is mild;
He became a little child.
I a child, and thou a lamb,
We are callèd by His name.
　Little Lamb, God bless thee!
　Little Lamb, God bless thee!

INFANT JOY

"I HAVE no name:
　I am but two days old."

What shall I call thee?
"I happy am,
Joy is my name."
Sweet joy befall thee!

Pretty Joy!
Sweet Joy, but two days old.
Sweet Joy I call thee:
Thou dost smile,
I sing the while,
Sweet joy befall thee!

THE LITTLE BLACK BOY

My mother bore me in the southern wild,
And I am black, but O! my soul is white;
White as an angel is the English child,
But I am black, as if bereaved of light.

My mother taught me underneath a tree,
And, sitting down before the heat of day,
She took me on her lap and kissèd me,
And, pointing to the east, began to say:

"Look on the rising sun,—there God does live,
And gives His light, and gives His heat away;
And flowers and trees and beasts and men receive
Comfort in morning, joy in the noonday.

"And we are put on earth a little space,
That we may learn to bear the beams of love;
And these black bodies and this sunburnt face
Is but a cloud, and like a shady grove.

"For when our souls have learned the heat to bear,
The cloud will vanish; we shall hear His voice,
Saying: 'Come out from the grove, My love and care,
And round My golden tent like lambs rejoice.'"

Thus did my mother say, and kissèd me;
And thus I say to little English boy.
When I from black and he from white cloud free,
And round the tent of God like lambs we joy,

I'll shade him from the heat, till he can bear
To lean in joy upon our Father's knee;

And then I'll stand and stroke his silver hair,
And be like him, and he will then love me.

A CRADLE SONG

SWEET dreams, form a shade
O'er my lovely infant's head;
Sweet dreams of pleasant streams
By happy, silent, moony beams.

Sweet sleep, with soft down
Weave thy brows an infant crown.
Sweet sleep, Angel mild,
Hover o'er my happy child.

Sweet smiles, in the night
Hover over my delight;
Sweet smiles, mother's smiles,
All the livelong night beguiles.

Sweet moans, dovelike sighs,
Chase not slumber from thy eyes.
Sweet moans, sweeter smiles,
All the dovelike moans beguiles.

Sleep, sleep, happy child,
All creation slept and smiled.
Sleep, sleep, happy sleep,
While o'er thee thy mother weep.

Sweet babe, in thy face
Holy image I can trace.
Sweet babe, once like thee
Thy Maker lay and wept for me,

Wept for me, for thee, for all,
When He was an infant small.
Thou His image ever see,
Heavenly face that smiles on thee.

Smiles on thee, on me, on all;
Who became an infant small.
Infant smiles are His own smiles;
Heaven and earth to peace beguiles.

THE DIVINE IMAGE

To Mercy, Pity, Peace, and Love
All pray in their distress;
And to these virtues of delight
Return their thankfulness.

For Mercy, Pity, Peace, and Love
Is God, our Father dear,
And Mercy, Pity, Peace, and Love
Is man, His child and care.

For Mercy has a human heart,
Pity a human face,
And Love, the human form divine,
And Peace, the human dress.

Then every man, of every clime,
That prays in his distress,
Prays to the human form divine,
Love, Mercy, Pity, Peace.

And all must love the human form,
In heathen, Turk, or Jew;
Where Mercy, Love, and Pity dwell
There God is dwelling too.

THE FLY

LITTLE Fly,
Thy summer's play
My thoughtless hand
Has brushed away.

Am not I
A fly like thee?
Or art not thou
A man like me?

For I dance,
And drink, and sing,
Till some blind hand
Shall brush my wing.

If thought is life
And strength and breath,

And the want
Of thought is death;

Then am I
A happy fly,
If I live
Or if I die.

THE TIGER

TIGER! Tiger! burning bright
In the forests of the night,
What immortal hand or eye
Could frame thy fearful symmetry?

In what distant deeps or skies
Burnt the fire of thine eyes?
On what wings dare he aspire?
What the hand dare seize the fire?

And what shoulder, and what art,
Could twist the sinews of thy heart?
And when thy heart began to beat,
What dread hand? and what dread feet?

What the hammer? what the chain?
In what furnace was thy brain?
What the anvil? what dread grasp
Dare its deadly terrors clasp?

When the stars threw down their spears,
And watered heaven with their tears,
Did he smile his work to see?
Did he who made the Lamb make thee?

Tiger! Tiger! burning bright
In the forests of the night,
What immortal hand or eye
Dare frame thy fearful symmetry?

THE CLOD AND THE PEBBLE

"LOVE seeketh not itself to please,
Nor for itself hath any care,
But for another gives its ease,
And builds a Heaven in Hell's despair."

So sung a little Clod of Clay,
Trodden with the cattle's feet,
But a Pebble of the brook
Warbled out these meters meet:

"Love seeketh only Self to please,
To bind another to its delight,
Joys in another's loss of ease,
And builds a Hell in Heaven's despite."

HOLY THURSDAY

Is this a holy thing to see
In a rich and fruitful land,—
Babes reduced to misery,
Fed with cold and usurous hand?

Is that trembling cry a song?
Can it be a song of joy?
And so many children poor?
It is a land of poverty!

And their sun does never shine,
And their fields are bleak and bare,
And their ways are filled with thorns:
It is eternal winter there.

For where'er the sun does shine,
And where'er the rain does fall,
Babe can never hunger there,
Nor poverty the mind appall.

A POISON TREE

I was angry with my friend:
I told my wrath, my wrath did end.
I was angry with my foe:
I told it not, my wrath did grow.

And I watered it in fears
Night and morning with my tears,
And I sunnèd it with smiles
And with soft, deceitful wiles.

And it grew both day and night
Till it bore an apple bright,

And my foe beheld it shine,
And he knew that it was mine,

And into my garden stole
When the night had veiled the pole:
In the morning, glad, I see
My foe outstretched beneath the tree.

A LITTLE BOY LOST

"Nought loves another as itself,
Nor venerates another so,
Nor is it possible to Thought
A greater than itself to know:

"And, Father, how can I love you
Or any of my brothers more?
I love you like the little bird
That picks up crumbs around the door."

The Priest sat by and heard the child,
In trembling zeal he seized his hair:
He led him by his little coat,
And all admired the priestly care.

And standing on the altar high,
"Lo! what a fiend is here," said he,
"One who sets reason up for judge
Of our most holy Mystery."

The weeping child could not be heard,
The weeping parents wept in vain;
They stripped him to his little shirt,
And bound him in an iron chain;

And burned him in a holy place,
Where many had been burned before;
The weeping parents wept in vain.
Are such things done on Albion's shore?

LONDON

I wander through each chartered street,
Near where the chartered Thames does flow,
And mark in every face I meet
Marks of weakness, marks of woe.

In every cry of every man,
In every infant's cry of fear,
In every voice, in every ban,
The mind-forged manacles I hear:

How the chimney-sweeper's cry
Every blackening church appalls,
And the hapless soldier's sigh
Runs in blood down palace walls.

But most, through midnight streets I hear
How the youthful harlot's curse
Blasts the new-born infant's tear,
And blights with plagues the marriage hearse.

NEVER SEEK TO TELL THY LOVE

NEVER seek to tell thy love,
Love that never told can be;
For the gentle wind does move
Silently, invisibly.

I told my love, I told my love,
I told her all my heart,
Trembling, cold, in ghastly fears.
Ah! she doth depart.

Soon as she was gone from me,
A traveler came by,
Silently, invisibly:
He took her with a sigh.

I SAW A CHAPEL ALL OF GOLD

I SAW a chapel all of gold
That none did dare to enter in,
And many weeping stood without,
Weeping, mourning, worshiping.

I saw a serpent rise between
The white pillars of the door,
And he forced and forced and forced;
Down the golden hinges tore,

And along the pavement sweet,
Set with pearls and rubies bright,

All his shining length he drew;
Till upon the altar white

Vomiting his poison out
On the bread and on the wine.
So I turned into a sty,
And laid me down among the swine.

FROM AUGURIES OF INNOCENCE

To see a world in a grain of sand,
  And a heaven in a wild flower;
Hold infinity in the palm of your hand,
  And eternity in an hour.

A ROBIN redbreast in a cage
Puts all heaven in a rage.
A dove-house filled with doves and pigeons
Shudders hell through all its regions.
A dog starved at his master's gate
Predicts the ruin of the state.
A horse misused upon the road
Calls to heaven for human blood.
Each outcry of the hunted hare
A fibre from the brain does tear.   10
A skylark wounded in the wing,
A cherubim does cease to sing.
The game-cock clipped and armed for fight
Does the rising sun affright.
Every wolf's and lion's howl
Raises from hell a human soul.
The wild deer, wandering here and there,
Keeps the human soul from care.
The lamb misused breeds public strife,
And yet forgives the butcher's knife.   20
The bat that flits at close of eve
Has left the brain that won't believe.
The owl that calls upon the night
Speaks the unbeliever's fright.
He who shall hurt the little wren
Shall never be beloved by men.
He who the ox to wrath has moved
Shall never be by woman loved.
The wanton boy that kills the fly
Shall feel the spider's enmity.   30
He who torments the chafer's sprite

Weaves a bower in endless night.
The caterpillar on the leaf
Repeats to thee thy mother's grief.
Kill not the moth nor butterfly,
For the Last Judgment draweth nigh.
He who shall train the horse to war
Shall never pass the polar bar.
The beggar's dog and widow's cat,
Feed them, and thou wilt grow fat.　　　　40

.　.　.　.　.　.　.　.　.　.

He who mocks the infant's faith
Shall be mocked in age and death;
He who shall teach the child to doubt
The rotting grave shall ne'er get out;
He who respects the infant's faith
Triumphs over hell and death.

.　.　.　.　.　.　.　.　.　.

STANZAS FROM MILTON

AND did those feet in ancient time
　　Walk upon England's mountains green?
And was the holy Lamb of God
　　On England's pleasant pastures seen?

And did the Countenance Divine
　　Shine forth upon our clouded hills?
And was Jerusalem builded here
　　Among these dark Satanic Mills?

Bring me my bow of burning gold!
　　Bring me my arrows of desire!
Bring me my spear! O clouds, unfold!
　　Bring me my chariot of fire!

I will not cease from mental fight,
　　Nor shall my sword sleep in my hand,
Till we have built Jerusalem
　　In England's green and pleasant land.

TO THE EVENING STAR

THOU fair-hair'd angel of the evening,
Now, whilst the sun rests on the mountains, light
Thy bright torch of love; thy radiant crown
Put on, and smile upon our evening bed!
Smile on our loves, and while thou drawest the
Blue curtains of the sky, scatter thy silver dew
On every flower that shuts its sweet eyes
In timely sleep. Let thy west wind sleep on
The lake; speak silence with thy glimmering eyes,
And wash the dusk with silver. Soon, full soon,
Dost thou withdraw; then the wolf rages wide,
And the lion glares thro' the dun forest:
The fleeces of our flocks are cover'd with
Thy sacred dew: protect them with thine influence.

THE LITTLE VAGABOND

DEAR mother, dear mother, the Church is cold,
But the Ale-house is healthy and pleasant and warm;
Besides I can tell where I am used well,
Such usage in Heaven will never do well.

But if at the Church they would give us some ale,
And a pleasant fire our souls to regale,
We'd sing and we'd pray all the livelong day,
Nor ever once wish from the Church to stray.

Then the Parson might preach, and drink, and sing,
And we'd be as happy as birds in the spring;
And modest Dame Lurch, who is always at church,
Would not have bandy children, nor fasting, nor birch.

And God, like a father, rejoicing to see
His children as pleasant and happy as He,
Would have no more quarrel with the Devil or the barrel,
But kiss him, and give him both drink and apparel.

THE GARDEN OF LOVE

I WENT to the Garden of Love,
And saw what I never had seen:

A Chapel was built in the midst,
Where I used to play on the green.

And the gates of this Chapel were shut,
And 'Thou shalt not' writ over the door;
So I turn'd to the Garden of Love
That so many flowers bore;

And I saw it was fillèd with graves,
And tomb-stones where flowers should be;
And priests in black gowns were walking their rounds,
And binding with briars my joys and desires.

THE SCHOOLBOY

I LOVE to rise in a summer morn
When the birds sing on every tree;
The distant huntsman winds his horn,
And the skylark sings with me.
O! what sweet company.

But to go to school in a summer morn,
O! it drives all joy away;
Under a cruel eye outworn,
The little ones spend the day
In sighing and dismay.

Ah! then at times I drooping sit,
And spend many an anxious hour,
Nor in my book can I take delight,
Nor sit in learning's bower,
Worn thro' with the dreary shower.

How can the bird that is born for joy
Sit in a cage and sing?
How can a child, when fears annoy,
But droop his tender wing,
And forget his youthful spring?

O! father and mother, if buds are nipp'd
And blossoms blown away,
And if the tender plants are stripp'd

Of their joy in the springing day,
By sorrow and care's dismay,

How shall the summer arise in joy,
Or the summer fruits appear?
Or how shall we gather what griefs destroy,
Or bless the mellowing year,
When the blasts of winter appear?

MOCK ON, MOCK ON, VOLTAIRE, ROUSSEAU [1]

Mock on, mock on, Voltaire, Rousseau;
Mock on, mock on; 'tis all in vain!
You throw the sand against the wind,
And the wind blows it back again.

And every sand becomes a gem
Reflected in the beams divine;
Blown back they blind the mocking eye,
But still in Israel's paths they shine.

The Atoms of Democritus
And Newton's Particles of Light
Are sands upon the Red Sea shore,
Where Israel's tents do shine so bright.

PROVERBS OF HELL

(FROM *THE MARRIAGE OF HEAVEN AND HELL*)

Unorthodox ideas of good and evil are embodied in these Proverbs. "The moralist sees Heaven and Hell divided by an impassable gulf; to Blake they are complementary. . . . The *Proverbs of Hell* restate in aphoristic form the cardinal doctrines of the 'Devil's party.' They deny the religious sanction of morality by denying the value of the restraint that is practised in obedience to external authority, including the authority of a transcendent deity; and condemn as futile prayer and all religious observances. On the positive side they affirm the value of enthusiasm, and of desire and passion carried to the degree conventionally condemned as excess." (Sloss and Wallis) Energy in all its forms, even in its excesses, becomes the positive virtue, restraint and prudence (like fear and cunning, their offspring), the vice.

---

1 For some account of Rousseau (1712–1778) see introductory sketch for the Eighteenth Century, above. François Marie Arouet, or "Voltaire" (1694–1778) was likewise known as a skeptic. The early scientific explanations of the Greek philosopher Democritus (fl. 4th, 5th cent. B. C.) and the later ones of Sir Isaac Newton (1642–1727) may alike be held out of harmony with Biblical revelation.

In seed time learn; in harvest teach; in winter enjoy.
Drive your cart and your plow over the bones of the dead.
The road of excess leads to the palace of wisdom.
Prudence is a rich, ugly old maid courted by Incapacity.
He who desires but acts not, breeds pestilence.
The cut worm forgives the plow.
Dip him in the river who loves water.
A fool sees not the same tree that a wise man sees.
He whose face gives no light shall never become a star.
10 Eternity is in love with the productions of time.
The busy bee has no time for sorrow.
The hours of folly are measured by the clock; but of wisdom
 no clock can measure.
All wholesóme food is caught without a net or trap.
Bring out number, weight, and measure in a year of dearth.
No bird soars too high if he soars with his own wings.
A dead body revenges not injuries.
The most sublime act is to set another before you.
If the fool would persist in his folly he would become wise.
20 Folly is the cloak of knavery.
Shame is Pride's cloak.
Prisons are built with stones of Law, Brothels with bricks of
 Religion.
The pride of the peacock is the glory of God.
The lust of the goat is the bounty of God.
The wrath of the lion is the wisdom of God.
The nakedness of woman is the work of God.
Excess of sorrow laughs. Excess of joy weeps.
The roaring of lions, the howling of wolves, the raging of the
30 stormy sea, and the destructive sword are portions of eter-
 nity too great for the eye of man.
The fox condemns the trap, not himself.
Joys impregnate; Sorrows bring forth.
Let man wear the fell of the lion, woman the fleece of the sheep.
The bird a nest, the spider a web, man friendship.
The selfish smiling fool and the sullen frowning fool shall be
 both thought wise, that they may be a rod.
What is now proved was once only imagined.
The rat, the mouse, the fox, the rabbit watch the roots; the
40 lion, the tiger, the horse, the elephant watch the fruits.
The cistern contains, the fountain overflows.
One thought fills immensity.
Always be ready to speak your mind, and a base man will
 avoid you.
Everything possible to be believed is an image of truth.

The eagle never lost so much time as when he submitted to learn of the crow.

The fox provides for himself, but God provides for the lion.

Think in the morning. Act in the noon. Eat in the evening. Sleep in the night.

He who has suffered you to impose on him knows you.

As the plow follows words, so God rewards prayers.

The tigers of wrath are wiser than the horses of instruction.

Expect poison from the standing water.

You never know what is enough, unless you know what is more than enough.

Listen to the fool's reproach: it is a kingly title.

The eyes of fire, the nostrils of air, the mouth of water, the beard of earth.

The weak in courage is strong in cunning.

The apple tree never asks the beech how he shall grow, nor the lion the horse how he shall take his prey.

The thankful receiver bears a plentiful harvest.

If others had not been foolish, we should be so.

The soul of sweet delight can never be defiled.

When thou seest an Eagle, thou seest a portion of Genius: lift up thy head!

As the caterpillar chooses the fairest leaves to lay her eggs on, so the priest lays his curse on the fairest joys.

To create a little flower is the labor of ages.

Damn braces. Bless relaxes.

The best wine is the oldest, the best water the newest.

Prayers plow not! Praises weep not!

Joys laugh not! Sorrows weep not!

The head Sublime, the heart Pathos, the genitals Beauty, the hands and feet Proportion.

As the air to a bird or the sea to a fish, so is contempt to the contemptible.

The crow wished everything was black, the owl that everything was white.

Exuberance is Beauty.

If the lion was advised by the fox, he would be cunning.

Improvement makes straight roads, but the crooked roads without Improvement are roads of Genius.

Sooner murder an infant in the cradle than nurse unacted desires.

Where man is not, nature is barren.

Truth can never be told so as to be understood, and not be believed.

Enough or too much.

ROBERT BURNS (1759-1796)

Burns was the son of a Scotch peasant, knew in his youth the bitterest poverty and the hardest kind of physical labor, and remained a tiller of the soil throughout practically all of his short life. He was born at Alloway, near Ayr, in southwestern Scotland, in a clay cottage which his father had built with his own hands. He received little formal schooling, such education as he had being got largely from his father, a superior man in spite of his condition, and from his own surprisingly extensive reading. At fifteen he was doing a man's work on the farm. His father, always unsuccessful, moved from place to place, dying in 1784, whereupon Burns and his brother Gilbert together made efforts equally unsuccessful to wrest a living from the Scotch soil. He decided to give up the attempt and emigrate to Jamaica, and to defray the expenses of the journey published in 1786, at the town of Kilmarnock, a collection of the *Poems, Chiefly in the Scottish Dialect* which he had managed to write during the intervals of his toil behind the plow. The volume, which contained such famous pieces as *The Twa Dogs, The Holy Fair, To a Mouse, To a Daisy,* and *The Cotter's Saturday Night,* created a small sensation, and caused a change in Burns's plans. He was induced to go to Edinburgh to superintend a new edition (pub. 1787), stayed there off and on for more than a year, and was much lionized by the *literati* of the capital—perhaps to his own detriment as poet and man. He returned to his native region, and tried to eke out his farming (this time at Ellisland) with the income derived from an appointment in the Excise (1789), in which his duties were the gauging of wine casks and beer barrels and the prevention of smuggling. In 1791 he gave up the farm and moved to the town of Dumfries, where he tried to live on his pay as exciseman. His open sympathy with the French Revolution and desultory attention to his duties prevented advancement. The post-Edinburgh years were years of gradually failing health and gradually failing powers, yet he wrote in this period the splendid *Tam o' Shanter* (1791), for humor, gusto, and rapidity unsurpassed, and most of the songs which are perhaps now the best loved of his work, contributed in the years from 1787 on to Johnson's *Musical Museum,* and after 1792 to Thomson's *Scottish Airs.* For these songs, nearly 250 in number, Burns refused to take a penny, esteeming it a privilege to write them for the glory of his native land. The best of them are in the vein of the traditional Scottish folk-song. Burns drew freely on older writers, anonymous or known, for incidents, refrains, measures, and phrasing, modifying or amplifying as his genius directed. For some of the best he had apparently no earlier suggestions.

The appetite for conviviality which was one of Burns's worst curses took stronger possession of him in his last years. He drank more and wrote less, and succumbed, in such a way as to rob him of his own self-respect, to his animal instincts which had ever been of the strongest. He was incapable of further producing good work. To him "Death came as a deliverer and a friend."

The achievement of Burns is the achievement of the man who became one of the greatest of our lyric poets in despite of humble birth, depressing hardships, the most galling poverty, and lack of contact with received poetic tradition, fostering culture, and the quick stimulation of a truly responsive audience. Not without predecessors in older Scots poets and in folk-song, he transcended these models by virtue of his own poetic fire, his sincerity, and his sensitiveness to a wide variety of emotions. When he wrote in literary English, he copied eighteenth century models, not always of the best, nor was his touch sure in such traditional English forms as heroic couplet and blank verse, nor is his work other than second-rate when he tried reflective poetry or essayed the grand manner. His first-class work is the lyric and sometimes the narrative in his native dialect, where he speaks with unrestrained simplicity. If his world be perpetually a world of "Scotch drink, Scotch religion, and Scotch manners," as Matthew Arnold sneered, yet man is man, wherever found, and only human sympathy is needed for readers everywhere to realize that the world of Burns is indeed a world, not a province, because it is universal in its applications. It is no wonder that Scotsmen love him above all other poets; it is more of a tribute that for a hundred and fifty years those who speak English the globe around have struggled with his local dialect because they find that he speaks to them. Within his proper domain, his range is wide; he has found, wrote Carlyle, "a tone and words for every mood of man's heart,"—now rollicking humor, now tenderness, now impetuous force, now unaffected pathos.

The tragedy of Burns is the tragedy of the man who could not control his own nature and direct it steadily into that channel of clear poetical activity which meant for him salvation. Pan, his goat-foot father, whom, in the words of W. E. Henley, "he featured so closely, in his great gift of merriment, his joy in life, his puissant appetites, his innate and never-failing humanity," did not bestow on him the restraint of self-discipline. Too often he sunk from the merry friend to the sot. Much distress has also been caused sensitive spirits by the equivocal nature of his relations with women. Jean Armour, who after a somewhat sordid romance became his wife, had previous to their marriage borne him a child; and love-children by other women were the living proofs of his self-indulgent and uncontrolled passions. It is not that countless other men have not done the like, but that mankind expects, rightly or wrongly, more rigorous moral standards of one who is a poet, a *vates*, a seer. Without his numerous amours, we should have lacked the unforgettable songs in which he enshrined his (often temporary) loves; so that the world is the gainer, ironically enough, since they meant the degradation of the man. The Mary Campbell of *Highland Mary* may have been the object of a purer and less sensual love, but she is now largely a myth, and it is impossible to determine if she differed from the rest of Burns's light-o'-loves.

Bibliography. Centenary ed. (standard), 4 vols., ed. W. E. Henley and T. F. Henderson, with brilliant biographical and critical essay by the former. Text and essay reprod. in one vol. Cambridge Poets ed. (Houghton Mifflin). Life by F. B. Snyder (Macmillan); short life by J. C. Shairp in Eng. Men of Letters ser. Carlyle's *Essay on Burns* (the most famous estimate).

ADDRESS TO THE DEIL [1]

O Prince! O Chief of many thronèd powers,
That led th' embattled seraphim to war.
—Milton.

O thou! whatever title suit thee,
Auld Hornie, Satan, Nick, or Clootie,[2]
Wha in yon cavern grim an' sootie,

1 devil   2 hoofs

Closed under hatches,
Spairges [3] about the brunstane cootie, [4]
To scaud poor wretches!

Hear me, auld Hangie, for a wee,
An' let poor damnèd bodies be;
I'm sure sma' pleasure it can gie,
        Ev'n to a deil,   10
To skelp [5] an' scaud poor dogs like me,
        An' hear us squeal.

Great is thy power an' great thy fame;
Far kenned an' noted is thy name;
An', tho' yon lowin heugh's [6] thy hame,
        Thou travels far;
An' faith! thou's neither lag nor lame,
        Nor blate nor scaur. [7]

Whyles ranging like a roarin lion
For prey, a' holes an' corners trying;   20
Whyles on the strong-winged tempest flyin,
        Tirlin [8] the kirks;
Whyles, in the human bosom pryin,
        Unseen thou lurks.

I've heard my reverend graunie say,
In lanely glens ye like to stray;
Or, where auld ruined castles gray
        Nod to the moon,
Ye fright the nightly wanderer's way,
        Wi' eldritch croon. [9]   30

When twilight did my graunie summon
To say her prayers, douce, [10] honest woman!
Aft yont the dyke she's heard you bummin, [11]
        Wi' eerie drone;
Or, rustlin', thro' the boortrees [12] comin,
        Wi' heavy groan.

Ae dreary, windy winter night
The star shot down wi' sklentin light,
Wi' you mysel I gat a fright
        Ayont the lough, [13]   40

---

3 splashes   7 bashful nor scary   11 humming
4 dish   8 unroofing   12 shrub elder
5 slap   9 unearthly moan   13 beyond the lake
6 flaming **pit**   10 sedate

Ye like a rash-buss [14] stood in sight
    Wi' waving sugh.[15]

The cudgel in my nieve [16] did shake,
Each bristled hair stood like a stake,
When wi' an eldritch, stoor [17] "quaick, quaick,"
    Amang the springs,
Awa ye squattered like a drake
    On whistling wings.

Let warlocks grim, an' withered hags,
Tell how wi' you on ragweed nags [18]   50
They skim the muirs an' dizzy crags
    Wi' wicked speed;
And in kirk-yards renew their leagues
    Owre howkit [19] dead.

Thence countra wives, wi' toil an' pain,
May plunge an' plunge the kirn [20] in vain;
For O! the yellow treasure's taen
    By witching skill;
An' dawtit twal-pint hawkie's gane
    As yell's the bill.[21]   60

Thence mystic knots mak great abuse
On young guidmen,[22] fond, keen, an' croose; [23]
When the best wark-lume [24] i' the house,
    By cantraip [25] wit,
Is instant made no worth a louse,
    Just at the bit.[26]

When thowes dissolve the snawy hoord,
An' float the jinglin icy boord,[27]
Then water-kelpies [28] haunt the foord,
    By your direction,   70
An' nighted travelers are allured
    To their destruction.

And aft your moss-traversing spunkies [29]
Decoy the wight that late an' drunk is:
The bleezin, curst, mischievous monkies

14 rush-bush
15 moan
16 fist
17 hoarse
18 *i. e.,* using stems of the ragwort as steeds
19 disinterred
20 churn
21 Petted twelve-pint cow's gone as dry as the bull. The Scotch pint equals two English quarts.
22 husbands
23 cocksure
24 tool
25 magic
26 when needed
27 surface
28 water-demons (usually like horses)
29 will-o-the-wisps

Delude his eyes,
Till in some miry slough he sunk is,
    Ne'er mair to rise.

When masons' mystic word an' grip
In storms an' tempests raise you up,   80
Some cock or cat your rage maun stop,
    Or, strange to tell!
The youngest brother ye wad whip
    Aff straught to hell.

Lang syne, in Eden's bonie yard,
When youthfu' lovers first were paired,
An' all the soul of love they shared,
    The raptured hour,
Sweet on the fragrant flowery swaird,
    In shady bower;   90

Then you, ye auld snick-drawing [30] dog!
Ye cam to Paradise incog,
An' played on man a cursèd brogue, [31]
    (Black be you fa'!)
An' gied the infant warld a shog, [32]
    'Maist ruined a'.

D'ye mind that day, when in a bizz, [33]
Wi' reekit [34] duds, an' reestit gizz, [35]
Ye did present your smoutie phiz
    'Mang better folk,   100
An' sklented [36] on the man of Uzz [37]
    Your spitefu' joke?

An' how ye gat him i' your thrall,
An' brak him out o' house an' hal',
While scabs an' blotches did him gall
    Wi' bitter claw,
An' lowsed his ill-tongued wicked scaul, [38]
    Was warst ava? [39]

But a' your doings to rehearse,
Your wily snares an' fechtin [40] fierce,   110
Sin' that day Michael did you pierce,
    Down to this time,

30 scheming	34 smoky	38 scold
31 trick	35 singed wig	39 of all
32 shake	36 squinted	40 fighting
33 flurry	37 Job	

    Wad ding a Lallan tongue, or Erse,[41]
        In prose or rhyme.

An' now, auld Cloots, I ken ye're thinkin,
A certain Bardie's rantin, drinkin,
Some luckless hour will send him linkin [42]
        To your black pit;
But faith! he'll turn a corner jinkin,[43]
        An' cheat you yet.   120

But fare you weel, auld Nickie-ben!
O wad ye tak a thought an' men'!
Ye aiblins [44] might—I dinna ken—
        Still hae a stake: [45]
I'm wae to think upo' yon den,
        Ev'n for your sake!

THE COTTER'S SATURDAY NIGHT

Inscribed to R. Aiken, Esq.[46]

Let not Ambition mock their useful toil,
   Their homely joys, and destiny obscure;
Nor Grandeur hear, with a disdainful smile,
   The short and simple annals of the poor.

                        —Gray.

My loved, my honored, much respected friend!
   No mercenary bard his homage pays:
With honest pride I scorn each selfish end,
   My dearest meed a friend's esteem and praise:
To you I sing, in simple Scottish lays,
   The lowly train in life's sequestered scene;
   The native feelings strong, the guileless ways;
What Aiken in a cottage would have been;
Ah! tho' his worth unknown, far happier there I ween!

November chill blaws loud wi' angry sugh;   10
   The short'ning winter-day is near a close;
The miry beasts retreating frae the pleugh;
   The black'ning trains o' craws to their repose:
   The toil-worn Cotter frae his labor goes—
This night his weekly moil is at an end,

41 surpass a Lowland
tongue, or Gaelic
42 tripping

43 dodging
44 perhaps
45 something to gain

46 Robert Aiken, Ayr-
shire solicitor and friend
of Burns

Collects his spades, his mattocks, and his hoes,
Hoping the morn in ease and rest to spend,
And weary, o'er the moor, his course does hameward bend.

At length his lonely cot appears in view,
 Beneath the shelter of an agèd tree;   20
Th' expectant wee-things, toddlin, stacher [47] through
 To meet their Dad, wi' flichterin' [48] noise and glee.
His wee bit ingle,[49] blinkin bonilie,
His clean hearth-stane, his thrifty wifie's smile,
 The lisping infant prattling on his knee,
Does a' his weary kiaugh [50] and care beguile,
And makes him quite forget his labor and his toil.

Belyve,[51] the elder bairns come drapping in,
 At service out, amang the farmers roun';
Some ca' [52] the pleugh, some herd, some tentie rin [53] 30
 A cannie [54] errand to a neebor town:
 Their eldest hope, their Jenny, woman grown,
In youthfu' bloom, love sparkling in her e'e,
 Comes hame, perhaps to shew a braw [55] new gown,
Or deposite her sair-won penny-fee,
To help her parents dear, if they in hardship be.

With joy unfeigned brothers and sisters meet,
 And each for other's weelfare kindly spiers: [56]
The social hours, swift-winged, unnoticed fleet;
 Each tells the uncos [57] that he sees or hears;   40
 The parents partial eye their hopeful years;
Anticipation forward points the view.
 The mother, wi' her needle an' her sheers,
Gars [58] auld claes look amaist as weel's the new;
The father mixes a' wi' admonition due.

Their master's an' their mistress's command,
 The younkers a' are warnèd to obey;
And mind their labors wi' an eydent [59] hand,
 And ne'er, tho' out o' sight, to jauk [60] or play:
 "And O! be sure to fear the Lord alway,   50
And mind your duty, duly, morn and night;
 Lest in temptation's path ye gang astray,
Implore His counsel and assisting might:
They never sought in vain that sought the Lord aright."

47 totter   52 drive   57 strange things
48 fluttering   53 careful run   58 makes
49 fireplace   54 quiet   59 diligent
50 anxiety   55 fine   60 dally
51 by-and-by   56 asks

But hark! a rap comes gently to the door;
  Jenny, wha kens the meaning o' the same,
Tells how a neebor lad came o'er the moor,
  To do some errands, and convoy her hame.
  The wily mother sees the conscious flame
Sparkle in Jenny's e'e, and flush her cheek;   60
  With heart-struck anxious care, inquires his name,
While Jenny hafflins ⁶¹ is afraid to speak;
Weel-pleased the mother hears it's nae wild, worthless rake.

With kindly welcome, Jenny brings him ben,⁶²
  A strappin' youth, he takes the mother's eye;
Blithe Jenny sees the visit's no ill taen;
  The father cracks ⁶³ of horses, pleughs, and kye.
  The youngster's artless heart o'erflows wi' joy,
But blate and laithfu',⁶⁴ scarce can weel behave;
  The mother, wi' a woman's wiles, can spy   70
What makes the youth sae bashfu' and sae grave;
Weel-pleased to think her bairn's respected like the lave.⁶⁵

O happy love! where love like this is found;
  O heart-felt raptures! bliss beyond compare!
I've pacèd much this weary mortal round,
  And sage experience bids me this declare:
  "If Heaven a draught of heavenly pleasure spare,
One cordial in this melancholy vale,
  'Tis when a youthful, loving, modest pair
In other's arms breathe out the tender tale   80
Beneath the milk-white thorn that scents the evening gale."

Is there, in human form, that bears a heart,
  A wretch, a villain, lost to love and truth—
That can, with studied, sly, ensnaring art,
  Betray sweet Jenny's unsuspecting youth?
  Curse on his perjured arts, dissembling, smooth!
Are honor, virtue, conscience, all exiled?
  Is there no pity, no relenting ruth,
Points to the parents fondling o'er their child?
Then paints the ruined maid, and their distraction wild? 90

But now the supper crowns their simple board,
  The healsome parritch,⁶⁶ chief o' Scotia's food:
The soupe ⁶⁷ their only hawkie ⁶⁸ does afford,

---

61 half
62 in
63 talks

64 shy and sheepish
65 rest
66 porridge

67 sup (here milk)
68 cow

That 'yont the hallan [69] snugly chows her cood;
  The dame brings forth in complimental mood,
To grace the lad, her weel-hain'd kebbuck, fell; [70]
  And aft he's pressed, and aft he ca's it guid;
The frugal wifie, garrulous, will tell
How 'twas a towmond [71] auld sin' lint [72] was i' the bell.

The cheerfu' supper done, wi' serious face   100
  They round the ingle form a circle wide;
The sire turns o'er, wi' patriarchal grace,
  The big ha'-Bible, ance his father's pride.
  His bonnet rev'rently is laid aside,
His lyart haffets [73] wearing thin and bare;
  Those strains that once did sweet in Zion glide,
He wales [74] a portion with judicious care,
And "Let us worship God!" he says with solemn air.

They chant their artless notes in simple guise,
  They tune their hearts, by far the noblest aim: 110
Perhaps *Dundee's* wild warbling measures rise,
  Or plaintive *Martyrs,* worthy of the name;
  Or noble *Elgin* beets [75] the heavenward flame,
The sweetest far of Scotia's holy lays:
  Compared with these, Italian trills are tame;
The tickled ears no heartfelt raptures raise;
Nae unison hae they with our Creator's praise.

The priest-like father reads the sacred page,
  How Abram was the friend of God on high;
Or Moses bade eternal warfare wage   120
  With Amalek's ungracious progeny;
  Or how the royal bard [76] did groaning lie
Beneath the stroke of Heaven's avenging ire;
  Or Job's pathetic plaint, and wailing cry;
Or rapt Isaiah's wild seraphic fire;
Or other holy seers that tune the sacred lyre.

Perhaps the Christian volume is the theme:
  How guiltless blood for guilty man was shed;
How He who bore in Heaven the second name
  Had not on earth whereon to lay His head;   130
  How His first followers and servants sped;
The precepts sage they wrote to many a land:

---

69 beyond the partition   71 twelvemonth   74 chooses
70 well-saved   cheese,   72 flax   75 fans
pungent   73 gray temples   76 David

How he, who lone in Patmos banishèd,[77]
Saw in the sun a mighty angel stand,
And heard great Bab'lon's doom pronounced by Heaven's com-
      mand.

Then kneeling down to Heaven's Eternal King
   The saint, the father, and the husband prays:
Hope "springs exulting on triumphant wing"[78]
   That thus they all shall meet in future days,
   There ever bask in uncreated rays,   140
No more to sigh or shed the bitter tear,
   Together hymning their Creator's praise,
In such society, yet still more dear;
While circling Time moves round in an eternal sphere.

Compared with this, how poor Religion's pride,
   In all the pomp of method and of art,
When men display to congregations wide
   Devotion's every grace, except the heart.
   The Power, incensed, the pageant will desert,
The pompous strain, the sacerdotal stole;   150
   But haply, in some cottage far apart,
May hear, well pleased, the language of the soul,
And in His Book of Life the inmates poor enroll.

Then homeward all take off their several way;
   The youngling cottagers retire to rest:
The parent-pair their secret homage pay,
   And proffer up to Heaven the warm request,
   That He who stills the raven's clamorous nest,
And decks the lily fair in flowery pride,
   Would, in the way His wisdom sees the best,   160
For them and for their little ones provide;
But chiefly in their hearts with grace divine preside.

From scenes like these old Scotia's grandeur springs,
   That makes her loved at home, revered abroad:
Princes and lords are but the breath of kings,
   "An honest man's the noblest work of God;"[79]
   And certes, in fair Virtue's heavenly road,
The cottage leaves the palace far behind;
   What is a lordling's pomp? a cumbrous load,
Disguising oft the wretch of human kind,   170
Studied in arts of hell, in wickedness refined!

[77] St. John   [79] from Pope's *Essay on Man*
[78] from Pope's *Windsor
Forest*

O Scotia! my dear, my native soil!
    For whom my warmest wish to Heaven is sent!
Long may thy hardy sons of rustic toil
    Be blest with health, and peace, and sweet content!
    And O! may Heaven their simple lives prevent
From luxury's contagion, weak and vile!
    Then, howe'er crowns and coronets be rent,
A virtuous populace may rise the while,
And stand a wall of fire around their much-loved isle.   180

O Thou! who poured the patriotic tide
    That streamed thro' Wallace's undaunted heart,
Who dared to nobly stem tyrannic pride,
    Or nobly die, the second glorious part:
    (The patriot's God, peculiarly Thou art,
His friend, inspirer, guardian, and reward!)
    O never, never Scotia's realm desert;
But still the patriot, and the patriot-bard
In bright succession raise, her ornament and guard!

TO A MOUSE

On Turning Her Up in Her Nest With the Plough, November, 1785

Wee, sleekit,[80] cowrin, tim'rous beastie,
O what a panic's in thy breastie!
Thou need na start awa sae hasty,
    Wi' bickering brattle![81]
I wad be laith to rin an' chase thee
    Wi' murdering pattle![82]

I'm truly sorry man's dominion
Has broken nature's social union,
An' justifies that ill opinion
    Which makes thee startle   10
At me, thy poor earth-born companion,
    An' fellow-mortal!

I doubt na, whyles, but thou may thieve;
What then? poor beastie, thou maun live!
A daimen icker in a thrave[83]
    'S a sma' request;
I'll get a blessin' wi' the lave,[84]
    An' never miss't!

80 sleek   82 plough-staff   24 sheaves
81 hurrying scamper   83 an occasional ear in   84 rest

Thy wee-bit housie, too, in ruin!
Its silly wa's the win's are strewin!   20
An' naething, now, to big [85] a new ane,
     O' foggage green!
An' bleak December's win's ensuin,
     Baith snell [86] an' keen!

Thou saw the fields laid bare an' waste,
An' weary winter comin fast,
An' cozie here, beneath the blast,
     Thou thought to dwell,
Till crash! the cruel coulter past
     Out thro' thy cell.   30

That wee bit heap o' leaves an' stibble
Has cost thee mony a weary nibble!
Now thou's turned out, for a' thy trouble,
     But house or hald,[87]
To thole [88] the winter's sleety dribble,
     An' cranreuch [89] cauld!

But, Mousie, thou art no thy lane,[90]
In proving foresight may be vain:
The best laid schemes o' mice an' men
     Gang aft agley,[91]   40
An' lea'e us nought but grief an' pain
     For promised joy!

Still thou art blest compared wi' me!
The present only toucheth thee:
But och! I backward cast my e'e
     On prospects drear!
An' forward, tho' I canna see,
     I guess an' fear!

TO A MOUNTAIN DAISY

On Turning One Down With the Plough in April, 1786

Wee, modest, crimson-tippèd flow'r,
Thou's met me in an evil hour;
For I maun crush amang the stoure [92]

85 build
86 bitter
87 without house or
   holding

88 endure
89 hoar-frost
90 not alone

91 askew
92 dust

Thy slender stem:
To spare thee now is past my pow'r,
Thou bonie gem.

Alas! it's no thy neebor sweet,
The bonie lark, companion meet,
Bending thee 'mang the dewy weet
　　　Wi' spreckled breast,
When upward springing, blithe, to greet
　　　The purpling east.

Cauld blew the bitter-biting north
Upon thy early, humble birth;
Yet cheerfully thou glinted forth
　　　Amid the storm,
Scarce reared above the parent-earth
　　　Thy tender form.

The flaunting flow'rs our gardens yield
High shelt'ring woods and wa's maun shield,
But thou, beneath the random bield [93]
　　　O' clod or stane,
Adorns the histie [94] stibble-field,
　　　Unseen, alane.

There, in thy scanty mantle clad,
Thy snawy bosom sun-ward spread,
Thou lifts thy unassuming head
　　　In humble guise;
But now the share uptears thy bed,
　　　And low thou lies!

Such is the fate of artless maid,
Sweet flow'ret of the rural shade,
By love's simplicity betrayed,
　　　And guileless trust,
Till she like thee, all soiled, is laid
　　　Low i' the dust.

Such is the fate of simple bard,
On life's rough ocean luckless starred:
Unskillful he to note the card
　　　Of prudent lore,
Till billows rage, and gales blow hard,
　　　And whelm him o'er!

[93] shelter　　　　　　[94] bare

Such fate to suffering worth is giv'n,
Who long with wants and woes has striv'n,
By human pride or cunning driv'n
　　To mis'ry's brink,
Till wrenched of ev'ry stay but Heav'n,
　　He, ruined, sink!

Ev'n thou who mourn'st the Daisy's fate,
That fate is thine—no distant date; 　　　　50
Stern Ruin's ploughshare drives elate
　　Full on thy bloom,
Till crushed beneath the furrow's weight
　　Shall be thy doom!

TO A LOUSE

On Seeing One On a Lady's Bonnet at Church

Ha! wh'are ye gaun, ye crowlin ferlie? [95]
Your impudence protects you sairly;
I canna say but ye strunt rarely,
　　Owre gauze and lace,
Tho' faith! I fear ye dine but sparely
　　On sic a place.

Ye ugly, creepin, blastit wonner,
Detested, shunned by saunt an' sinner,
How dare ye set your fit [96] upon her,
　　Sae fine a lady? 　　　　　　　10
Gae somewhere else, and seek your dinner
　　On some poor body.

Swith, [97] in some beggar's hauffet [98] squattle;
There ye may creep, and sprawl, and sprattle
Wi' ither kindred jumping cattle,
　　In shoals and nations;
Whare horn nor bane [99] ne'er dare unsettle
　　Your thick plantations.

Now haud you there! ye're out o' sight,
Below the fatt'rils,[1] snug an' tight; 　　　　20
Na, faith ye yet! ye'll no be right
　　Till ye've got on it,

95 crawling wonder　　　97 Haste!　　　　99 comb nor poison
96 foot　　　　　　　　98 temple　　　　　1 ribbon-ends

The very tapmost tow'ring height
O' Miss's bonnet.

My sooth! right bauld ye set your nose out,
As plump an' gray as onie grozet; [2]
O for some rank mercurial rozet,[3]
Or fell red smeddum! [4]
I'd gie you sic a hearty dose o't,
Wad dress your droddum! [5]   30

I wad na been surprised to spy
You on an auld wife's flainen toy; [6]
Or aiblins [7] some bit duddie [8] boy,
On's wyliecoat; [9]
But Miss's fine Lunardi! [10] fie,
How daur ye do't?

O Jenny, dinna toss your head,
An' set your beauties a' abread! [11]
Ye little ken what cursèd speed
The blastie's makin!   40
Thae [12] winks and finger-ends, I dread,
Are notice takin!

O wad some Power the giftie gie us
To see oursels as ithers see us!
It wad frae monie a blunder free us,
An' foolish notion:
What airs in dress an' gait wad lea'e us,
An' ev'n devotion!

EPISTLE TO J. LAPRAIK,[13] AN OLD SCOTTISH BARD

APRIL 1, 1785.

WHILE briers an' woodbines budding green,
An' paitricks scraichin [14] loud at e'en,
An' morning poussie whiddin [15] seen,
Inspire my Muse,
This freedom, in an unknown frien',
I pray excuse.

2 gooseberry
3 rosin
4 powder
5 breech
6 flannel cap
7 perhaps

8 ragged
9 undervest
10 a bonnet named after
a balloonist
11 abroad
12 those

13 Ayrshire poet, author
of the song *When I upon
Thy Bosom Lean* (see third
stanza of the *Epistle*)
14 partridges calling
15 hare scudding

On Fasten-een [16] we had a rockin,[17]
To ca' the crack [18] and weave our stockin;
And there was muckle fun and jokin,
   Ye need na doubt;   10
At length we had a hearty yokin [19]
   At "sang about."

There was ae sang, amang the rest,
Aboon them a' it pleased me best,
That some kind husband had addressed
   To some sweet wife:
It thirled [20] the heart-strings thro' the breast,
   A' to the life.

I've scarce heard ought described sae weel,
What gen'rous, manly bosoms feel;   20
Thought I, "Can this be Pope, or Steele,
   Or Beattie's wark?"
They tald me 'twas an odd kind chiel
   About Muirkirk.

It pat me fidgin-fain [21] to hear't,
An' sae about him there I spier't; [22]
Then a' that kent him round declared
   He had ingíne,[23]
That nane excelled it, few cam near't,
   It was sae fine.   30

That, set him to a pint of ale,
An' either douce [24] or merry tale,
Or rhymes an' sangs he'd made himsel,
   Or witty catches,
'Tween Inverness an' Teviotdale,
   He had few matches.

Then up I gat, an' swoor an aith,
Tho' I should pawn my pleugh an' graith,[25]
Or die a cadger pownie's [26] death,
   At some dyke-back,[27]   40
A pint an' gill I'd gie them baith
   To hear your crack.[28]

16 evening before beginning of Lent
17 social meeting
18 have a chat
19 spell
20 thrilled
21 tingle with pleasure
22 inquired
23 genius
24 serious
25 tools
26 peddler's pony's
27 back of a fence
28 talk

But, first an' foremost, I should tell,
Amaist as soon as I could spell,
I to the crambo-jingle [29] fell;
    Tho' rude an' rough,
Yet crooning to a body's sel,
    Does weel eneugh.

I am nae poet, in a sense,
But just a rhymer like by chance,   50
An' hae to learning nae pretense;
    Yet what the matter?
Whene'er my Muse does on me glance,
    I jingle at her.

Your critic-folk may cock their nose,
And say, "How can you e'er propose,
You wha ken hardly verse frae prose,
    To mak a sang?"
But, by your leaves, my learned foes,
    Ye're maybe wrang.   60

What's a' your jargon o' your schools,
Your Latin names for horns an' stools?
If honest Nature made you fools,
    What sairs [30] your grammers?
Ye'd better ta'en up spades and shools,[31]
    Or knappin-hammers.[32]

A set o' dull, conceited hashes [33]
Confuse their brains in college classes,
They gang in stirks,[34] and come out asses,
    Plain truth to speak;   70
An' syne [35] they think to climb Parnassus
    By dint o' Greek!

Gie me ae spark o' Nature's fire,
That's a' the learning I desire;
Then tho' I drudge thro' dub an' mire
    At pleugh or cart,
My Muse, tho' hamely in attire,
    May touch the heart.

O for a spunk o' Allan's glee,
Or Fergusson's,[36] the bauld an' slee,[37]   80

29 rhyming
30 serves
31 shovels
32 hammers for breaking stones
33 fools
34 young bullocks
35 then
36 Allan Ramsay (1686–1758) and Robert Fergusson (1750–1774), Scotch poets
37 clever

Or bright Lapraik's, my friend to be,
    If I can hit it!
That would be lear [38] eneugh for me,
    If I could get it.

Now, sir, if ye hae friends enow,
Tho' real friends, I b'lieve are few,
Yet, if your catalogue be fow,[39]
    I'se no insist;
But gif ye want ae friend that's true,
    I'm on your list.   90

I winna blaw about mysel,
As ill I like my fauts to tell;
But friends, an' folks that wish me well,
    They sometimes roose [40] me;
Tho' I maun own, as monie still
    As far abuse me.

There's ae wee faut they whiles lay to me,
I like the lasses—Gude forgie me!
For mony a plack [41] they wheedle frae me,
    At dance or fair;   100
Maybe some ither thing they gie me
    They weel can spare.

But Mauchline [42] race or Mauchline fair,
I should be proud to meet you there;
We'se gie ae night's discharge to care,
    If we forgather,
An' hae a swap o' rhymin-ware
    Wi' ane anither.

The four-gill chap,[43] we'se gar [44] him clatter,
An' kirsen [45] him wi' reekin [46] water;   110
Syne we'll sit down an' tak our whitter,[47]
    To cheer our heart;
An' faith, we'se be acquainted better
    Before we part.

Awa ye selfish, warly [48] race,
Wha think that havins,[49] sense, an' grace,

38 learning
39 full
40 praise
41 a small coin
42 town near Burns's Mossgiel Farm
43 *i. e.,* light drinker
44 make
45 christen
46 steaming
47 hearty draught
48 worldly
49 good manners

Ev'n love an' friendship should give place
    To catch-the-plack![50]
I dinna like to see your face,
    Nor hear your crack.   120

But ye whom social pleasure charms,
Whose hearts the tide of kindness warms,
Who hold your being on the terms,
    "Each aid the others,"
Come to my bowl, come to my arms,
    My friends, my brothers!

But to conclude my lang epistle,
As my auld pen's worn to the grissle,
Twa lines frae you wad gar me fissle,[51]
    Who am most fervent,   130
While I can either sing or whistle,
    Your friend and servant.

ADDRESS TO THE UNCO GUID

OR THE RIGIDLY RIGHTEOUS

My son, these maxims make a rule,
    And lump them aye thegither:
The rigid righteous is a fool,
    The rigid wise anither;
The cleanest corn that e'er was dight [52]
    May hae some pyles o' caff in; [53]
So ne'er a fellow-creature slight
    For random fits o' daffin.[54]
          —SOLOMON (Eccles. vii, 16).

O YE wha are sae guid yoursel,
    Sae pious and sae holy,
Ye've nought to do but mark and tell
    Your neebor's fauts and folly;
Whase life is like a weel-gaun [55] mill,
    Supplied wi' store o' water;
The heapet happer's [56] ebbing still,
    And still the clap [57] plays clatter!

Hear me, ye venerable core,[58]
    As counsel for poor mortals   10

---

50 hunt-the-coin   53 grains of chaff in it   56 hopper
51 tingle with delight   54 larking   57 clapper
52 winnowed   55 well-going   58 corps

That frequent pass douce [59] Wisdom's door
    For glaikit [60] Folly's portals;
I, for their thoughtless, careless sakes
    Would here propone defenses,—
Their donsie [61] tricks, their black mistakes,
    Their failings and mischances.

Ye see your state wi' theirs compared,
    And shudder at the niffer;[62]
But cast a moment's fair regard—
    What makes the mighty differ?   20
Discount what scant occasion gave,
    That purity ye pride in,
And (what's aft mair than a' the lave [63])
    Your better art o' hidin.

Think, when your castigated pulse
    Gies now and then a wallop,
What ragings must his veins convulse,
    That still eternal gallop!
    Wi' wind and tide fair i' your tail,
    Right on ye scud your sea-way;   30
But in the teeth o' baith to sail,
    It maks an unco [64] leeway.

See Social Life and Glee sit down,
    All joyous and unthinking,
Till, quite transmogrified, they're grown
    Debauchery and Drinking:
O would they stay to calculate
    Th' eternal consequences;
Or—your more dreaded hell to state—
    Damnation of expenses!   40

Ye high, exalted, virtuous dames,
    Tied up in godly laces,
Before ye gie poor Frailty names,
    Suppose a change o' cases;
A dear-loved lad, convenience snug,
    A treacherous inclination—
But, let me whisper i' your lug,[65]
    Ye're aiblins [66] nae temptation.

59 staid   62 exchange   65 ear
60 giddy   63 rest   66 perhaps
61 unlucky   64 uncommon

Then gently scan your brother man,
  Still gentler sister woman;
Tho' they may gang a kennin [67] wrang,
  To step aside is human.
One point must still be greatly dark,
  The moving why they do it;
And just as lamely can ye mark
  How far perhaps they rue it.

Who made the heart, 'tis He alone
  Decidedly can try us;
He knows each chord, its various tone,
  Each spring, its various bias.   60
Then at the balance let's be mute,
  We never can adjust it;
What's done we partly may compute,
  But know not what's resisted.

GREEN GROW THE RASHES, O

There's nought but care on every han',
  In every hour that passes, O:
What signifies the life o' man,
  An' 't were nae for the lasses, O.

Chorus

  Green grow the rashes, O;
  Green grow the rashes, O;
The sweetest hours that e'er I spend,
  Are spent among the lasses, O.

The war'ly race may riches chase,
  An' riches still may fly them, O;
An' tho' at last they catch them fast,
  Their hearts can ne'er enjoy them, O.

But gie me a cannie [68] hour at e'en,
  My arms about my dearie, O,
An' war'ly cares an' war'ly men
  May a' gae tapsalteerie,[69] O!

For you sae douce,[70] ye sneer at this;
  Ye're nought but senseless asses, O;

67 trifle   69 topsy-turvy
68 quiet   70 sedate

The wisest man that warl' e'er saw,
He dearly loved the lasses, O.

Auld Nature swears, the lovely dears
Her noblest work she classes, O:
Her prentice han' she tried on man,
An' then she made the lasses, O.

TAM O' SHANTER

A Tale

Of Brownyis and of Bogillis full is this Buke.
—Gawin Douglas.

When chapman billies [71] leave the street,
And drouthy [72] neebors neebors meet,
As market-days are wearing late,
An' folk begin to tak the gate, [73]
While we sit housing at the nappy, [74]
An' getting fou and unco [75] happy,
We think na on the lang Scots miles,
The mosses, waters, slaps, [76] and styles,
That lie between us and our hame,
Where sits our sulky, sullen dame,   10
Gathering her brows like gathering storm,
Nursing her wrath to keep it warm.
    This truth fand honest Tam o' Shanter,
As he frae Ayr ae night did canter:
(Auld Ayr, wham ne'er a town surpasses
For honest men and bonie lasses).
    O Tam, hadst thou but been sae wise
As taen thy ain wife Kate's advice!
She tauld thee weel thou was a skellum, [77]
A blethering, [78] blustering, drunken blellum; [79]   20
That frae November till October,
Ae market-day thou was nae sober;
That ilka melder [80] wi' the miller
Thou sat as lang as thou had siller;
That every naig was ca'd [81] a shoe on,
The smith and thee gat roaring fou on;
That at the Lord's house, even on Sunday,
Thou drank wi' Kirkton Jean till Monday.

71 peddler fellows
72 thirsty
73 road
74 ale

75 uncommonly
76 gaps in fences
77 good-for-nothing
78 chattering

79 babbler
80 grinding
81 driven (nailed,

She prophesied that, late or soon,
Thou would be found deep drowned in Doon; 30
Or catched wi' warlocks in the mirk [82]
By Alloway's auld haunted kirk.
　Ah! gentle dames, it gars me greet [83]
To think how monie counsels sweet,
How monie lengthened sage advices
The husband frae the wife despises!
　But to our tale: Ae market night,
Tam had got planted unco right,
Fast by an ingle, bleezing finely,
Wi' reaming swats,[84] that drank divinely; 40
And at his elbow, Souter [85] Johnie,
His ancient, trusty, drouthy cronie;
Tam lo'ed him like a very brither;
They had been fou for weeks thegither.
The night drave on wi' sangs and clatter,
And ay the ale was growing better:
The landlady and Tam grew gracious
Wi' secret favors, sweet and precious;
The Souter tauld his queerest stories;
The landlord's laugh was ready chorus: 50
The storm without might rair and rustle,
Tam did na mind the storm a whistle.
　Care, mad to see a man sae happy,
E'en drowned himsel amang the nappy.
As bees flee hame wi' lades o' treasure,
The minutes winged their way wi' pleasure;
Kings may be blest, but Tam was glorious,
O'er a' the ills o' life victorious!
　But pleasures are like poppies spread:
You seize the flow'r, its bloom is shed; 60
Or like the snow falls in the river,
A moment white, then melts for ever;
Or like the borealis race,
That flit ere you can point their place;
Or like the rainbow's lovely form
Evanishing amid the storm.
Nae man can tether time or tide;
The hour approaches Tam maun ride:
That hour, o' night's black arch the keystane,
That dreary hour Tam mounts his beast in; 70
And sic a night he taks the road in,
As ne'er poor sinner was abroad in.

82 dark　　　　　　　84 foaming ale　　　　　85 cobbler
83 makes me weep

The wind blew as 'twad blawn its last;
The rattling showers rose on the blast;
The speedy gleams the darkness swallowed;
Loud, deep, and lang, the thunder bellowed:
That night, a child might understand,
The Deil had business on his hand.
   Weel mounted on his gray mare, Meg,
A better never lifted leg,   80
Tam skelpit [86] on thro' dub [87] and mire,
Despising wind, and rain, and fire;
Whiles holding fast his guid blue bonnet,
Whiles crooning o'er some auld Scots sonnet,
Whiles glow'ring round wi' prudent cares,
Lest bogles catch him unawares:
Kirk-Alloway was drawing nigh,
Whare ghaists and houlets nightly cry.
   By this time he was cross the ford,
Whare in the snaw the chapman smoor'd; [88]   90
And past the birks and meikle stane,[89]
Where drunken Charlie brak's neck-bane;
And thro' the whins,[90] and by the cairn,
Where hunters fand the murdered bairn;
And near the thorn, aboon the well,
Where Mungo's mither hanged hersel.
Before him Doon pours all his floods;
The doubling storm roars thro' the woods;
The lightnings flash from pole to pole;
Near and more near the thunders roll: 100
When, glimmering thro' the groaning trees,
Kirk-Alloway seem'd in a bleeze;
Thro' ilka bore [91] the beams were glancing,
And loud resounded mirth and dancing.
   Inspiring bold John Barleycorn,
What dangers thou canst make us scorn!
Wi' tippenny,[92] we fear nae evil;
Wi' usquabae,[93] we'll face the Devil!
The swats sae reamed in Tammie's noddle,
Fair play, he cared na deils a boddle.[94]   110
But Maggie stood right sair astonished,
Till, by the heel and hand admonished,
She ventured forward on the light;
And, vow! Tam saw an unco sight!
   Warlocks and witches in a dance:

86 hastened
87 puddle
88 peddler smothered
89 birches and big stone
90 furze
91 chink
92 two-penny ale
93 whiskey
94 cared not a farthing
for devils

Nae cotillion brent new [95] frae France,
But hornpipes, jigs, strathspeys, and reels,
Put life and mettle in their heels.
A winnock-bunker [96] in the east,
There sat Auld Nick, in shape o' beast—   12c
A tousie tyke,[97] black, grim, and large!
To gie them music was his charge:
He screwed the pipes and gart them skirl,[98]
Till roof and rafters a' did dirl.[99]
Coffins stood round like open presses,
That shawed the dead in their last dresses;
And by some devilish cantraip [1] sleight
Each in its cauld hand held a light,
By which heroic Tam was able
To note upon the haly table   130
A murderer's banes in gibbet-airns; [2]
Twa span-lang, wee, unchristened bairns;
A thief new-cutted frae a rape
Wi' his last gasp his gab [3] did gape;
Five tomahawks wi' bluid red-rusted;
Five scymitars, wi' murder crusted;
A garter which a babe had strangled;
A knife a father's throat had mangled,
Whom his ain son o' life bereft—
The gray hairs yet stack to the heft;   140
Wi' mair of horrible and awfu',
Which even to name wad be unlawfu'.
    As Tammie glowered, amazed, and curious,
The mirth and fun grew fast and furious:
The piper loud and louder blew,
The dancers quick and quicker flew,
They reeled, they set, they crossed, they cleekit,[4]
Till ilka carlin swat and reekit,[5]
And coost her duddies [6] to the wark,
And linket [7] at it in her sark! [8]   150
    Now Tam, O Tam! had thae been queans,[9]
A' plump and strapping in their teens;
Their sarks, instead o' creeshie flannen,[10]
Been snaw-white seventeen hunder [11] linen!
Thir breeks [12] o' mine, my only pair,
That ance were plush, o' guid blue hair,

I wad hae gi'en them off my hurdies [13]
For ae blink o' the bonie burdies!
But withered beldams, auld and droll,
Rigwoodie [14] hags wad spean [15] a foal,   160
Louping and flinging on a crummock,[16]
I wonder did na turn thy stomach!
But Tam kend what was what fu' brawlie: [17]
There was ae winsome wench and wawlie [18]
That night enlisted in the core,[19]
Lang after kend on Carrick shore
(For monie a beast to dead she shot,
And perished monie a bonie boat,
And shook baith meikle corn and bear,[20]
And kept the country-side in fear).   170
Her cutty sark,[21] o' Paisley harn,[22]
That while a lassie she had worn,
In longitude tho' sorely scanty,
It was her best, and she was vauntie.[23]
Ah! little kend thy reverend grannie
That sark she coft [24] for her wee Nannie
Wi' twa pund Scots ('twas a' her riches)
Wad ever graced a dance of witches!
But here my Muse her wing maun cour;
Sic flights are far beyond her power—   180
To sing how Nannie lap and flang
(A souple jade she was, and strang);
And how Tam stood, like ane bewitched,
And thought his very e'en enriched;
Even Satan glowered, and fidged [25] fu' fain,
And hotched [26] and blew wi' might and main:
Till first ae caper, syne anither,
Tam tint [27] his reason a' thegither,
And roars out, "Weel done, Cutty-sark!"
And in an instant all was dark;   190
And scarcely had he Maggie rallied,
When out the hellish legion sallied.
As bees bizz out wi' angry fyke [28]
When plundering herds assail their byke,[29]
As open pussie's [30] mortal foes
When, pop! she starts before their nose,
As eager runs the market crowd,

13 buttocks
14 ancient
15 wean (through disgust)
16 crooked staff
17 finely
18 plump
19 corps
20 barley
21 short skirt
22 coarse cloth
23 proud
24 bought
25 fidgeted
26 jerked
27 lost
28 fuss
29 hive
30 a hare

When "Catch the thief!" resounds aloud,
So Maggie runs; the witches follow,
Wi' monie an eldritch [31] skriech and hollo.   200
  Ah, Tam! ah, Tam! thou'll get thy fairin! [32]
In hell they'll roast thee like a herrin!
In vain thy Kate awaits thy comin!
Kate soon will be a woefu' woman!
Now do thy speedy utmost, Meg,
And win the key-stane o' the brig: [33]
There at them thou thy tail may toss,
A running stream they dare na cross.
But ere the key-stane she could make,
The fient [34] a tail she had to shake;   210
For Nannie, far before the rest,
Hard upon noble Maggie pressed,
And flew at Tam wi' furious ettle; [35]
But little wist she Maggie's mettle!
Ae spring brought off her master hale,
But left behind her ain gray tail:
The carlin claught [36] her by the rump,
And left poor Maggie scarce a stump.
  Now, wha this tale o' truth shall read,
Each man and mother's son, take heed: 220
Whene'er to drink you are inclined,
Or cutty-sarks run in your mind,
Think! ye may buy the joys o'er dear:
Remember Tam o' Shanter's mare.

OF A' THE AIRTS

Of a' the airts [37] the wind can blaw
  I dearly like the west,
For there the bonie lassie lives,
  The lassie I lo'e best.
There wild woods grow, and rivers row,
  And monie a hill between,
But day and night my fancy's flight
  Is ever wi' my Jean.

I see her in the dewy flowers—
  I see her sweet and fair.
I hear her in the tunefu' birds—
  I hear her charm the air.

31 unearthly
32 reward
33 bridge

34 devil
35 aim
36 witch seized

37 directions

There's not a bonie flower that springs
    By fountain, shaw, or green,
There's not a bonie bird that sings,
    But minds me o' my Jean.

MY HEART'S IN THE HIGHLANDS

Farewell to the Highlands, farewell to the North,
The birthplace of valor, the country of worth!
Wherever I wander, wherever I rove,
The hills of the Highlands for ever I love.

Chorus

My heart's in the Highlands, my heart is not here,
My heart's in the Highlands a-chasing the deer,
A-chasing the wild deer and following the roe—
My heart's in the Highlands, wherever I go!

Farewell to the mountains high cover'd with snow,
Farewell to the straths and green valleys below,
Farewell to the forests and wild-hanging woods,
Farewell to the torrents and loud-pouring floods!

JOHN ANDERSON MY JO

John Anderson my jo,[38] John,
    When we were first acquent,
Your locks were like the raven,
    Your bonie brow was brent; [39]
But now your brow is beld,[40] John,
    Your locks are like the snaw;
But blessings on your frosty pow,[41]
    John Anderson, my jo!

John Anderson my jo, John,
    We clamb the hill thegither,
And monie a cantie [42] day, John,
    We've had wi' ane anither;
Now we maun totter down, John,
    And hand in hand we'll go,
And sleep thegither at the foot,
    John Anderson, my jo!

---

38 sweetheart   40 bald   42 cheerful
39 smooth   41 head

WILLIE BREWED A PECK O' MAUT

O WILLIE brewed a peck o' maut,
　　And Rob and Allan cam to see.
Three blither hearts, that lee-lang [43] night,
　　Ye wad na found in Christendie.

Chorus

We are na fou,[44] we're no that fou,
　　But just a drappie in our e'e.
The cock may craw, the day may daw,
　　And ay we'll taste the barley-bree!

Here are we met, three merry boys,
　　Three merry boys I trow are we;
And monie a night we've merry been,
　　And monie mae we hope to be!

It is the moon, I ken her horn,
　　That's blinkin' in the lift [45] sae hie;
She shines sae bright to wyle us hame,
　　But, by my sooth, she'll wait a wee!

Wha first shall rise to gang awa,
　　A cuckold, coward loun is he!
Wha first beside his chair shall fa',
　　He is the king among us three!

TAM GLEN

My heart is a-breaking, dear tittie,[46]
　　Some counsel unto me come len'.
To anger them a' is a pity,
　　But what will I do wi' Tam Glen?

I'm thinking, wi' sic a braw [47] fellow
　　In poortith [48] I might mak a fen'.[49]
What care I in riches to wallow,
　　If I mauna [50] marry Tam Glen?

There's Lowrie the laird o' Dumeller,
　　"Guid-day to you," brute! he comes ben.[51]

43 live-long	46 sister	49 shift
44 full	47 fine	50 must not
45 sky	48 poverty	51 in

He brags and he blaws o' his siller,
    But when will he dance like Tam Glen?

My minnie [52] does constantly deave [53] me,
    And bids me beware o' young men.
They flatter, she says, to deceive me;
    But wha can think sae o' Tam Glen?

My daddie says, gin I'll forsake him,
    He'd gie me guid hunder marks ten.
But if it's ordained I maun take him,
    O wha will I get but Tam Glen?

Yestreen at the valentines' dealing,
    My heart to my mou gied a sten, [54]
For thrice I drew ane without failing,
    And thrice it was written "Tam Glen."

The last Halloween I was waukin [55]
    My droukit sark-sleeve, [56] as ye ken;
His likeness cam up the house stalkin,
    And the very gray breeks [57] o' Tam Glen!

Come, counsel, dear tittie, don't tarry!
    I'll gie you my bonie black hen,
Gif ye will advise me to marry
    The lad I lo'e dearly, Tam Glen.

AE FOND KISS

AE fond kiss, and then we sever!
Ae farewell, and then for ever!
Deep in heart-wrung tears I'll pledge thee,
Warring sighs and groans I'll wage thee.
Who shall say that Fortune grieves him,
While the star of hope she leaves him?
Me, nae cheerfu' twinkle lights me,
Dark despair around benights me.

I'll ne'er blame my partial fancy:
Naething could resist my Nancy!
But to see her was to love her,
Love but her, and love for ever.

---

52 mother
53 deafen
54 gave a leap

55 watching
56 drenched shirt-sleeve.
One's future husband will

appear to turn the sleeve
as it dries.
57 breeches

Had we never loved sae kindly,
Had we never loved sae blindly,
Never met—or never parted—
We had ne'er been broken-hearted.

Fare-the-weel, thou first and fairest!
Fare-the-weel, thou best and dearest!
Thine be ilka joy and treasure,
Peace, Enjoyment, Love and Pleasure!
Ae fond kiss, and then we sever!
Ae farewell, alas, for ever!
Deep in heart-wrung tears I'll pledge thee,
Warring sighs and groans I'll wage thee.

SWEET AFTON

FLOW gently, sweet Afton, among thy green braes,[58]
Flow gently, I'll sing thee a song in thy praise;
My Mary's asleep by thy murmuring stream,
Flow gently, sweet Afton, disturb not her dream.

Thou stock-dove whose echo resounds thro' the glen,
Ye wild whistling blackbirds in yon thorny den,
Thou green-crested lapwing, thy screaming forbear,
I charge you disturb not my slumbering fair.

How lofty, sweet Afton, thy neighboring hills,
Far marked with the courses of clear winding rills;
There daily I wander as noon rises high,
My flocks and my Mary's sweet cot in my eye.

How pleasant thy banks and green valleys below,
Where wild in the woodlands the primroses blow;
There oft as mild Ev'ning weeps over the lea,
The sweet-scented birk [59] shades my Mary and me.

Thy crystal stream, Afton, how lovely it glides,
And winds by the cot where my Mary resides;
How wanton thy waters her snowy feet lave,
As gathering sweet flowerets she stems thy clear wave.

Flow gently, sweet Afton, among thy green braes,
Flow gently, sweet river, the theme of my lays;
My Mary's asleep by thy murmuring stream,
Flow gently, sweet Afton, disturb not her dream.

58 slopes   59 birch

THE LOVELY LASS OF INVERNESS

THE lovely lass of Inverness,
   Nae joy nor pleasure can she see;
For e'en and morn she cries "Alas!"
   And ay the saut tear blin's her e'e:

"Drumossie [60] moor, Drumossie day,
   A waefu' day it was to me;
For there I lost my father dear,
   My father dear, and brethren three.

"Their winding-sheet the bluidy clay,
   Their graves are growin green to see,
And by them lies the dearest lad
   That ever blest a woman's e'e.

"Now wae to thee, thou cruel lord,
   A bluidy man I trow thou be;
For monie a heart thou hast made sair,
   That ne'er did wrang to thine or thee!"

A RED, RED ROSE

O, MY luve is like a red, red rose
   That's newly sprung in June.
O, my luve is like the melodie
   That's sweetly played in tune.

As fair art thou, my bonie lass,
   So deep in luve am I,
And I will luve thee still, my dear,
   Till a' the seas gang dry.

Till a' the seas gang dry, my dear,
   And the rocks melt wi' the sun:
And I will luve thee still, my dear,
   While the sands o' life shall run.

And fare thee weel, my only luve,
   And fare thee weel a while!
And I will come again, my luve,
   Tho' it were ten thousand mile.

---

60 Culloden, battle in which Highlanders supporting the "Young Pretender," Charles Edward Stuart, were defeated and slaughtered by the Duke of Cumberland, 1746

AULD LANG SYNE

SHOULD auld acquaintance be forgot,
And never brought to mind?
Should auld acquaintance be forgot,
And auld lang syne?

Chorus

For auld lang syne, my dear,
For auld lang syne,
We'll tak a cup o' kindness yet
For auld lang syne!

And surely ye'll be your pint-stowp,[61]
And surely I'll be mine,
And we'll tak a cup o' kindness yet
For auld lang syne.

We twa hae run about the braes,[62]
And pou'd the gowans [63] fine,
But we've wandered monie a weary fit [64]
Sin' auld lang syne.

We twa hae paidled in the burn,[65]
From morning sun till dine,
But seas between us braid hae roared
Sin' auld lang syne.

And there's a hand, my trusty fiere,[66]
And gie's a hand o' thine,
And we'll tak a right guid-willie waught [67]
For auld lang syne!

DUNCAN GRAY

DUNCAN GRAY came here to woo,
(Ha, ha, the wooing o't!)
On blithe Yule night when we were fou,[68]
(Ha, ha, the wooing o't!)
Maggie coost [69] her head fu' heigh,
Looked asklent and unco skeigh,[70]
Gart [71] poor Duncan stand abeigh; [72]
Ha, ha, the wooing o't!

61 cup holding Scotch
pint (two English quarts)
62 hillsides
63 pulled the daisies
64 foot

65 brook
66 comrade
67 draught of good will
68 full
69 cast

70 very skittish
71 made
72 off

Duncan fleeched,[73] and Duncan prayed;
    (Ha, ha, the wooing o't!)
Meg was deaf as Ailsa Craig,[74]
    (Ha, ha, the wooing o't!)
Duncan sighed baith out and in,
Grat [75] his e'en baith bleer't and blin',
Spak o' lowpin o'r a linn— [76]
    Ha, ha, the wooing o't!

Time and Chance are but a tide
    (Ha, ha, the wooing o't!)
Slighted love is sair to bide [77]
    (Ha, ha, the wooing o't!)
"Shall I, like a fool," quoth he,
"For a haughty hizzie die?
She may gae to—France for me!"—
    Ha, ha, the wooing o't!

How it comes, let doctors tell,
    (Ha, ha, the wooing o't!)
Meg grew sick as he grew hale
    (Ha, ha, the wooing o't!)
Something in her bosom wrings,
For relief a sigh she brings,
And O, her e'en they spak sic things!—
    Ha, ha, the wooing o't!

Duncan was a lad o' grace,
    (Ha, ha, the wooing o't!)
Maggie's was a piteous case
    (Ha, ha, the wooing o't!)
Duncan could na be her death,
Swelling pity smoored [78] his wrath;
Now they're crouse and canty [79] baith—
    Ha, ha, the wooing o't!

SCOTS WHA HAE [80]

Scots, wha hae wi' Wallace bled,
Scots, wham Bruce has aften led,
Welcome to your gory bed
    Or to victorie!

73 wheedled
74 a rocky island in the Firth of Clyde
75 wept
76 leaping over a waterfall
77 hard to endure
78 smothered
79 lively and cheerful
80 Bruce is represented as addressing the Scots at the Battle of Bannockburn (1314), where, by defeating Edward II and the English, they secured the independence of Scotland

Now's the day, and now's the hour;
See the front o' battle lour!
See approach proud Edward's power—
Chains and slaverie!

Wha will be a traitor knave?
Wha can fill a coward's grave?
Wha sae base as be a slave?
Let him turn and flee!

Wha for Scotland's king and law
Freedom's sword will strongly draw,
Freeman stand or freeman fa'?
Let him follow me!

By oppression's woes and pains,
By your sons in servile chains,
We will drain our dearest veins,
But they shall be free!

Lay the proud usurpers low!
Tyrants fall in every foe!
Liberty's in every blow!
Let us do or die!

HIGHLAND MARY

YE banks and braes [81] and streams around
Th castle o' Montgomery,
Green be your woods, and fair your flowers,
Your waters never drumlie! [82]
There summer first unfald her robes,
And there the langest tarry;
For there I took the last fareweel
O' my sweet Highland Mary!

How sweetly bloomed the gay green birk, [83]
How rich the hawthorn's blossom,
As underneath their fragrant shade
I clasped her to my bosom!
The golden hours on angel wings
Flew o'er me and my dearie;
For dear to me as light and life
Was my sweet Highland Mary.

81 hillsides   82 muddy   83 birch

Wi' monie a vow and locked embrace
    Our parting was fu' tender;
And, pledging aft to meet again,
    We tore oursels asunder.
But O, fell Death's untimely frost,
    That nipped my flower sae early!
Now green's the sod, and cauld's the clay,
    That wraps my Highland Mary!

O pale, pale now, those rosy lips,
    I aft hae kissed sae fondly;
And closed for ay the sparkling glance
    That dwalt on me sae kindly;
And moldering now in silent dust
    That heart that lo'ed me dearly!
But still within my bosom's core
    Shall live my Highland Mary.

IS THERE FOR HONEST POVERTY

Is there, for honest poverty,
    That hings his head, an' a' that?
The coward slave, we pass him by—
    We dare be poor for a' that!
For a' that, and a' that,
    Our toils obscure, an' a' that,
The rank is but the guinea's stamp,
    The man's the gowd [84] for a' that.

What though on hamely fare we dine,
    Wear hoddin [85] gray, and a' that?
Gie fools their silks, and knaves their wine—
    A man's a man for a' that.
For a' that, and a' that,
    Their tinsel show, and a' that,
The honest man, tho' e'er sae poor,
    Is king o' men for a' that.

Ye see yon birkie [86] ca'd "a lord,"
    Wha struts, an' stares, and a' that?
Tho' hundreds worship at his word,
    He's but a cuif [87] for a' that.
For a' that, and a' that,
    His ribband, star, and a' that,

84 gold   86 fellow   87 fool
85 homespun

The man o' independent mind,
  He looks an' laughs at a' that.

A prince can mak a belted knight,
  A marquis, duke, and a' that;
But an honest man's aboon his might—
  Guid faith he mauna fa' [88] that!
For a' that, and a' that!
  Their dignities, an' a' that,
The pith o' sense, an' pride o' worth,
  Are higher rank than a' that.

Then let us pray that come it may,
  (As come it will for a' that)
That sense and worth o'er a' the earth
  Shall bear the gree [89] an' a' that;
For a' that, and a' that,
  It's comin yet for a' that,
That man to man, the world o'er
  Shall brithers be for a' that.

MARY MORISON

O Mary, at thy window be!
  It is the wished, the trysted hour.
Those smiles and glances let me see,
  That make the miser's treasure poor.
How blithely wad I bide the stoure,[90]
A weary slave frae sun to sun,
  Could I the rich reward secure—
The lovely Mary Morison!

Yestreen, when to the trembling string
  The dance gaed through the lighted ha',
To thee my fancy took its wing,
  I sat, but neither heard or saw:
Tho' this was fair, and that was braw,[91]
And yon the toast of a' the town,
  I sighed and said amang them a':—
"Ye are na Mary Morison!"

O Mary, canst thou wreck his peace
  Wha for thy sake wad gladly die?
Or canst thou break that heart of his
  Whase only faut is loving thee?

[88] must not claim   [90] struggle   [91] handsome
[89] prize

If love for love thou wilt na gie,
  At least be pity to me shown:
  A thought ungentle canna be
The thought o' Mary Morison.

YE FLOWERY BANKS O' BONIE DOON

YE flowery banks o' bonie Doon,
  How can ye blume sae fair?
How can ye chant, ye little birds,
  And I sae fu' o' care?

Thou'll break my heart, thou bonie bird,
  That sings upon the bough;
Thou minds me o' the happy days,
  When my fause luve was true.

Thou'll break my heart, thou bonie bird,
  That sings beside thy mate;
For sae I sat, and sae I sang,
  And wist na o' my fate.

Aft hae I roved by bonie Doon
  To see the woodbine twine,
And ilka bird sang o' its luve,
  And sae did I o' mine.

Wi' lightsome heart I pu'd a rose
  Frae aff its thorny tree,
And my fause luver staw [92] my rose,
  But left the thorn wi' me.

O, WERT THOU IN THE CAULD BLAST

O, WERT thou in the cauld blast
  On yonder lea, on yonder lea,
My plaidie to the angry airt, [93]
  I'd shelter thee, I'd shelter thee.
Or did Misfortune's bitter storms
  Around thee blaw, around thee blaw,
Thy bield [94] should be my bosom,
  To share it a', to share it a'.

Or were I in the wildest waste,
  Sae black and bare, sae black and bare,

---

92 stole   93 direction of the wind   94 shelter

The desert were a paradise,
    If thou wert there, if thou wert there.
Or were I monarch of the globe,
    Wi' thee to reign, wi' thee to reign,
The brightest jewel in my crown
    Wad be my queen, wad be my queen.

ODE, SACRED TO THE MEMORY OF MRS. OSWALD OF AUCHENCRUIVE [1]

DWELLER in yon dungeon dark,
Hangman of creation, mark!
Who in widow-weeds appears,
Laden with unhonored years,
Noosing with care a bursting purse,
Bated with many a deadly curse?

STROPHE

View the wither'd beldam's face:
Can thy keen inspection trace
Aught of Humanity's sweet, melting grace?
Note that eye, 'tis rheum o'erflows—   10
Pity's flood there never rose.
See those hands, ne'er stretch'd to save,
Hands that took, but never gave.
Keeper of Mammon's iron chest,
Lo, there she goes, unpitied and unblest,
She goes, but not to realms of everlasting rest!

ANTISTROPHE

Plunderer of Armies! lift thine eyes
    (A while forbear, ye torturing fiends),
Seest thou whose step, unwilling, hither bends?
No fallen angel, hurl'd from upper skies!   20
    'Tis thy trusty, quondam Mate,
    Doom'd to share thy fiery fate:
    She, tardy, hell-ward plies.

---

1 A rich woman, who died in December, 1788, following by four years her husband,
who had been, among other things, an army contractor (hence "plunderer of armies").
Burns, on a stormy night in January, 1789, had been forced out of an inn where
he had taken up his rest by her "funeral pageantry" as the body was on its way to
Ayrshire from London, where she had died.

Epode

And are they of no more avail,
Ten thousand glittering pounds a-year?
In other words can Mammon fail,
    Omnipotent as he is here?
O bitter mockery of the pompous bier!
While down the wretched vital part is driven,
The cave-lodg'd beggar, with a conscience clear,   30
Expires in rags, unknown, and goes to Heaven.

THE JOLLY BEGGARS [2]
A CANTATA

Recitativo

When lyart [3] leaves bestrow the yird,
Or, wavering like the bauckie-bird,[4]
    Bedim cauld Boreas' blast;
When hailstanes drive wi' bitter skyte,[5]
And infant frosts begin to bite,
    In hoary cranreuch [6] drest;
Ae night at e'en a merry core [7]
    O' randie, gangrel bodies,[8]
In Poosie-Nansie's held the splore,[9]
    To drink their orra duddies; [10]   10
        Wi' quaffing and laughing,
            They ranted an' they sang;
        Wi' jumping an' thumping,
            The vera girdle [11] rang.

First, niest the fire, in auld red rags
Ane sat, weel brac'd wi' mealy bags
    And knapsack a' in order;
His doxy [12] lay within his arm;
Wi' usquebae [13] an' blankets warm,
    She blinket on her sodger.   20
An' ay he gies the tozie [14] drab
    The tither skelpin [15] kiss,
While she held up her greedy gab

2 Suggested by a chance visit, in company with two friends, to the "doss-house" (a disreputable inn) of Poosie Nansie (see l. 9) in Mauchline.

3 gray	6 frost	9 carousal
4 bat	7 gathering (corps)	10 spare rags
5 violent shower	8 lawless, vagrant folk	
11 round metal used in cooking oatcakes.		12 woman
13 whiskey	14 tipsy	15 spanking

Just like an aumous [16] dish:
　Ilk smack still did crack still
　　Like onie cadger's whup;
　Then, swaggering an' staggering,
　　He roar'd this ditty up:—

AIR (Tune: *Soldiers' Joy*)

I am a son of Mars, who have been in many wars,
　And show my cuts and scars wherever I come:　　　30
This here was for a wench, and that other in a trench
　When welcoming the French at the sound of the drum.
　　　　Lal de daudle, etc.

My prenticeship I past, where my leader breath'd his last,
　When the bloody die was cast on the heights of Abrám; [17]
And I servèd out my trade when the gallant game was play'd,
　And the Moro [18] low was laid at the sound of the drum.

I lastly was with Curtis among the floating batt'ries, [19]
　And here I left for witness an arm and a limb;
Yet let my country need me, with Eliott [20] to head me　　　40
　I'd clatter on my stumps at the sound of the drum.

And now, tho' I must beg with a wooden arm and leg
　And many a tatter'd rag hanging over my bum,
I'm as happy with my wallet, my bottle, and my callet [21]
　As when I us'd in scarlet to follow a drum.

What tho' with hoary locks I must stand the winter shocks,
　Beneath the woods and rocks oftentimes for a home?
When the tother bag I sell, and the tother bottle tell,
　I could meet a troop of Hell at the sound of a drum.
　　　　Lal de daudle, etc.　　　50

RECITATIVO

He ended; and the kebars sheuk [22]
　Aboon the chorus roar;
While frighted rattons backward leuk, [23]
　An' seek the benmost bore: [24]
A fairy fiddler frae the neuk, [25]

16 alms
17 or Abraham, at Quebec, scene of Wolfe's victory over Montcalm, 1759.
18 fort at Santiago de Cuba, stormed by the British, 1762
19 before Gibraltar, destroyed by Admiral Curtis, 1782
20 He defended Gibraltar, 1787　　22 rafters shook　　24 inmost chink
21 wench　　23 rats look back　　25 nook

He skirl'd out *Encore!*
But up arose the martial chuck,
An' laid the loud uproar:—

AIR (Tune: *Sodger Laddie*)

I once was a maid, tho' I cannot tell when,
And still my delight is in proper young men.   60
Some one of a troop of dragoons was my daddie:
No wonder I'm fond of a sodger laddie!
     Sing, lal de dal, etc.

The first of my loves was a swaggering blade:
To rattle the thundering drum was his trade;
His leg was so tight, and his cheek was so ruddy,
Transported I was with my sodger laddie.

But the godly old chaplain left him in the lurch;
The sword I forsook for the sake of the church;
He riskèd the soul, and I ventur'd the body: 70
'Twas then I prov'd false to my sodger laddie.

Full soon I grew sick of my sanctified sot;
The regiment at large for a husband I got;
From the gilded spontoon [26] to the fife I was ready:
I askèd no more but a sodger laddie.

But the Peace it reduc'd me to beg in despair,
Till I met my old boy in a Cunningham Fair;
His rags regimental they flutter'd so gaudy:
My heart it rejoic'd at a sodger laddie.

And now I have liv'd—I know not how long!   80
But still I can join in a cup and a song;
And while with both hands I can hold the glass steady,
Here's to thee, my hero, my sodger laddie!
     Sing, lal de dal, etc.

RECITATIVO

Poor Merry-Andrew in the neuk,
   Sat guzzling wi' a tinkler-hizzie,[27]
They mind't na wha the chorus teuk,
   Between themselves they were sae busy.
   At length with drink and courting dizzy,

---

26 halberd   27 tinker wench (hussy)

He stoiter'd [28] up an' made a face;
   Then turn'd, an' laid a smack on Grizzie,
Syne [29] tun'd his pipes wi' grave grimace:—

AIR (Tune: *Auld Sir Symon*)

Sir Wisdom's a fool when he's fou; [30]
   Sir Knave is a fool in a session; [31]
He's there but a prentice I trow,
   But I am a fool by profession.

My grannie she bought me a beuk,[32]
   An' I held awa to the school;
I fear I my talent misteuk,
   But what will ye hae of a fool?   100

For drink I wad venture my neck;
   A hizzie's the half of my craft;
But what could ye other expect
   Of ane that's avowedly daft?

I ance was tyed up like a stirk,[33]
   For civilly swearing and quaffing;
I ance was abus'd i' the kirk,
   For towsing [34] a lass i' my daffin.[35]

Poor Andrew that tumbles for sport,
   Let naebody name wi' a jeer: 110
There's even, I'm tauld, i' the Court
   A tumbler ca'd the Premier.

Observ'd ye yon reverend lad
   Mak faces to tickle the mob?
He rails at our mountebank squad—
   It's rivalship just i' the job.

And now my conclusion I'll tell,
   For faith! I'm confoundedly dry;
The chiel that's a fool for himsel,
   Guid Lord! he's far dafter than I.   120

RECITATIVO

Then niest outspak a raucle carlin,[36]
Wha kent [37] fu' weel to cleek the sterlin,[38]

28 staggered   32 book   36 sturdy beldam
29 then   33 young bullock or heifer   37 knew
30 drunk   34 tousling   38 snatch the sterling (money)
31 of court   35 larking, fun

For monie a pursie she had hookèd,
An' had in monie a well been doukèd.
Her love had been a Highland laddie,
But weary fa' the waefu' woodie! [39]
Wi' sighs and sobs she thus began
To wail her braw [40] John Highlandman:—

AIR (Tune: *O An' Ye Were Dead, Guidman*)

A Highland lad my love was born,
The Lalland [41] laws he held in scorn,   130
But he still was faithfu' to his clan,
My gallant, braw John Highlandman.

CHORUS

Sing hey my braw John Highlandman!
Sing ho my braw John Highlandman!
There's not a lad in a' the lan'
Was match for my John Highlandman!

With his philibeg,[42] an' tartan plaid,
An' guid claymore [43] down by his side,
The ladies' hearts he did trepan,
My gallant, braw John Highlandman.   140

We rangèd a' from Tweed to Spey,
An' liv'd like lords an' ladies gay,
For a Lalland face he fearèd none,
My gallant, braw John Highlandman.

They banish'd him beyond the sea,
But ere the bud was on the tree,
Adown my cheeks the pearls ran,
Embracing my John Highlandman.

But, Och! they catch'd him at the last,
And bound him in a dungeon fast.   150
My curse upon them every one—
They've hang'd my braw John Highlandman!

And now a widow I must mourn
The pleasures that will ne'er return;
No comfort but a hearty can
When I think on John Highlandman.

39 rope   **41** Lowland   **43** sword
40 gaily dressed   **42** kilt

RECITATIVO

A pigmy scraper on a fiddle,
Wha us'd to trystes [44] an' fairs to driddle,[45]
Her strappin limb an' gawsie [46] middle
       (He reach'd nae higher)
Had hol'd his heartie like a riddle,
       An' blawn't on fire.

Wi' hand on hainch and upward e'e,
He croon'd his gamut, one, two, three,
Then in an *arioso* key
       The wee Apollo
Set off wi' *allegretto* glee
       His *giga* solo:—

AIR (Tune: *Whistle Owre the Lave O't*)

Let me ryke up to dight [47] that tear;
An' go wi' me an' be my dear,
An' then your every care an' fear
       My whistle owre the lave [48] o't.

CHORUS

I am a fiddler to my trade,
An' a' the tunes that e'er I play'd,
The sweetest still to wife or maid
       Was *Whistle Owre the Lave O't.*

At kirns [49] an' weddins we'se be there,
An' O, sae nicely's we will fare!
We'll bowse about till Daddie Care
       Sing *Whistle Owre the Lave O't.*

Sae merrily the banes we'll pyke,[50]
An' sun oursels about the dyke;
An' at our leisure, when we like,
       We'll—whistle owre the lave o't!

But bless me wi' your heav'n o' charms,
An' while I kittle hair on thairms,[51]
Hunger, cauld, an' a' sic harms
       May whistle owre the lave o't.

160

170

180

44 cattle markets   47 reach up to wipe   50 bones we'll pick
45 toddle   48 rest, remainder, others   51 tickle (horse) hair on (cat) gut
46 buxom   49 churns

RECITATIVO

Her charms had struck a sturdy caird [52]
  As weel as poor gut-scraper;
He taks the fiddler by the beard,
  An' draws a roosty rapier;
He swoor by a' was swearing worth
  To speet him like a pliver,[53]
Unless he would from that time forth
  Relinquish her for ever.

Wi' ghastly e'e poor Tweedle-Dee
  Upon his hunkers [54] bended,
An pray'd for grace wi' ruefu' face,
  An' sae the quarrel ended.
But tho' his little heart did grieve
  When round the tinkler prest her,
He feign'd to snirtle [55] in his sleeve
  When thus the caird address'd her:—

AIR (Tune: *Clot the Cauldron*)

My bonie lass, I work in brass,
  A tinkler is my station;
I've travell'd round all Christian ground
  In this my occupation;
I've taen the gold, an' been enrolled
  In many a noble squadron;
But vain they search'd when off I march'd
  To go and clout [56] the cauldron.

Despise that shrimp, that wither'd imp,
  With a' his noise and cap'rin,
An' take a share wi' those that bear
  The budget [57] and the apron!
And by that stowp, my faith an' houpe!
  And by that dear Kilbaigie! [58]
If e'er ye want, or meet wi' scant,
  May I ne'er weet my craigie! [59]

RECITATIVO

The caird prevail'd: th'unblushing fair
  In his embraces sunk,

190

200

210

220

52 tinker
53 plover
54 hams

55 snicker
56 mend
57 tinker's bag of tools

58 a kind of whiskey
59 throat

Partly wi' love o'ercome sae sair,
    An' partly she was drunk.
Sir Violino, with an air
    That show'd a man o' spunk,
Wish'd unison between the pair,
    An' made the bottle clunk
            To their health that night.

But hurchin [60] Cupid shot a shaft,   230
    That play'd a dame a shavie: [61]
The fiddler rak'd her fore and aft
    Behint the chicken cavie; [62]
Her lord, a wight of Homer's craft,[63]
    Tho' limpin' wi' the spavie,[64]
He hirpl'd up, an' lap [65] like daft,
    An shor'd them "Dainty Davie" [66]
            O' boot that night.

He was a care-defying blade
    As ever Bacchus listed!   240
Tho' Fortune sair upon him laid,
    His heart, she ever miss'd it.
He had no wish but—to be glad,
    Nor want but—when he thirsted,
He hated nought but—to be sad;
    An' thus the Muse suggested
            His sang that night.

AIR (Tune: *For A' That, an' A' That*)
I am a Bard, of no regard
Wi' gentle folks an' a' that,
But Homer-like the glowrin' byke,[67]   250
    Frae town to town I draw that.

CHORUS

For a' that, an' a' that,
    An' twice as muckle's a' that,
I've lost but ane, I've twa behin',
    I've wife eneugh for a' that.[68]

60 urchin   61 trick   62 coop
63 "Homer is allowed to be the oldest ballad singer on record." (Burns)
64 spavin   66 a piece of obscene slang
65 hobbled up and leapt   67 staring crowd
68 The ballad singer means, that after he has passed over one of his women to the
fiddler, he still has two left.

I never drank the Muses' stank,[69]
Castalia's burn, an' a' that;
But there it streams, an' richly reams—
My Helicon I ca' that.[70]

Great love I bear to a' the fair,   260
Their humble slave an' a' that;
But lordly will, I hold it still
A mortal sin to thraw [71] that.

In raptures sweet this hour we meet
Wi' mutual love an' a' that;
But for how lang the flie may stang,[72]
Let inclination law that!

Their tricks an' craft hae put me daft,
They've taen me in, an' a' that;
But clear your decks, an' here's the Sex!   270
I like the jads for a' that.

Chorus

For a' that, an' a' that,
An' twice as muckle's a' that,
My dearest bluid, to do them guid,
They're welcome till't for a' that!

Recitativo

So sung the Bard, and Nansie's wa's
Shook with a thunder of applause,
Re-echo'd from each mouth!
They toom'd their pocks,[78] they pawn'd their duds,
They scarcely left to coor their fuds,[74]   280
To quench their lowin [75] drouth.
Then owre again the jovial thrang
The Poet did request
To lowse his pack, an' wale [76] a sang,
A ballad o' the best:
He rising, rejoicing
Between his twa Deborahs,
Looks round him, an' found them
Impatient for the chorus:—

69 pool   70 i. e., whiskey is his Muses' fount, the source of his inspiration
71 thwart   73 emptied their pockets   75 burning
72 sting   74 cover their tails   76 choose

AIR (Tune: *Jolly Mortals, Fill Your Glasses*)

See the smoking bowl before us!   *290*
  Mark our jovial ragged ring!
Round and round take up the chorus,
  And in raptures let us sing.

CHORUS

A fig for those by law protected!
  Liberty's a glorious feast!
Courts for cowards were erected,
  Churches built to please the priest!

What is title? what is treasure?
  What is reputation's care?
If we lead a life of pleasure,   *300*
  'Tis no matter how or where!

With the ready trick and fable,
  Round we wander all the day;
And at night, in barn or stable,
  Hug our doxies on the hay.

Does the train-attended carriage
  Thro' the country lighter rove?
Does the sober bed of marriage
  Witness brighter scenes of love?

Life is all a variorum,   *310*
  We regard not how it goes;
Let them cant about decorum
  Who have character to lose.

Here's to budgets, bags, and wallets!
  Here's to all the wandering train!
Here's our ragged brats and callets!
  One and all, cry out, Amen!

CHORUS

A fig for those by law protected!
  Liberty's a glorious feast!
Courts for cowards were erected,   *320*
  Churches built to please the priest!

HOLY WILLIE'S PRAYER [77]

"And send the godly in a pet to pray."—POPE.

O THOU that in the Heavens does dwell,
Wha, as it pleases best Thysel,
Sends ane to heaven an' ten to Hell,
    A' for Thy glory,
And no for onie guid or ill
    They've done before Thee!

I bless and praise Thy matchless might,
When thousands Thou hast left in night,
That I am here before Thy sight,
    For gifts an' grace   10
A burning and a shining light
    To a' this place.

What was I, or my generation,
That I should get sic exaltation?
I, wha deserv'd most just damnation
    For broken laws
Sax thousand years ere my creation,
    Thro' Adam's cause!

When from my mither's womb I fell,
Thou might hae plung'd me deep in hell   20
To gnash my gooms, and weep, and wail
    In burning lakes,
Whare damnèd devils roar and yell,
    Chain'd to their stakes.

Yet I am here, a chosen sample,
To show Thy grace is great and ample:
I'm here a pillar o' Thy temple,
    Strong as a rock,
A guide, a buckler, and example
    To a' Thy flock!   30

77 "Holy Willie was a rather oldish bachelor elder [said to have been a certain William Fisher] in the parish of Mauchline, and much and justly famed for that polemical chattering which ends in tippling orthodoxy, and for that spiritualized bawdry which refines to liquorish devotion. In a sessional process [church trial] with a gentleman in Mauchline—a Mr. Gavin Hamilton [Burns's landlord and friend] —Holy Willie and his priest, Father Auld, after full hearing in the Presbytery of Ayr, came off but second best, owing partly to the oratorical powers of Mr. Robert Aiken, Mr. Hamilton's counsel; but chiefly to Mr. Hamilton's being one of the most irreproachable and truly respectable characters in the country. On losing his process, the muse overheard him at his devotions, as follows." (Burns)

But yet, O Lord! confess I must:
At times I'm fash'd [78] wi' fleshly lust;
An' sometimes, too, in warldly trust,
          Vile self gets in;
But Thou remembers we are dust,
          Defil'd wi' sin.

O Lord! yestreen, Thou kens, wi' Meg—
Thy pardon I sincerely beg—
O! may't ne'er be a living plague
          To my dishonor!   40
An' I'll ne'er lift a lawless leg
          Again upon her.

Besides, I farther maun [79] allow,
Wi' Leezie's lass, three times, I trow—
But Lord, that Friday I was fou,[80]
          When I cam near her,
Or else, Thou kens, Thy servant true
          Wad never steer her.

Maybe Thou lets this fleshly thorn
Buffet Thy servant e'en and morn,   50
Lest he owre proud and high should turn,
          That he's sae gifted;
If sae, Thy han' maun e'en be borne
          Until Thou lift it.

Lord, bless Thy chosen in this place,
For here Thou hast a chosen race!
But God confound their stubborn face
          An' blast their name,
Wha bring Thy elders to disgrace
          An' open shame.   60

Lord, mind Gau'n Hamilton's deserts;
He drinks, an' swears, an' plays at cartes,
Yet has sae monie takin arts
          Wi' great and sma',
Frae God's ain priest the people's hearts
          He steals awa.

An' when we chasten'd him therefore,
Thou kens how he bred sic a splore,[81]
And set the warld in a roar,

O' laughing at us: 70
Curse Thou his basket and his store,
Kail an' potatoes!

Lord, hear my earnest cry and pray'r,
Against that Presbyt'ry of Ayr;
Thy strong right hand, Lord, make it bare
Upo' their heads!
Lord visit them, an' dinna spare
For their misdeeds!

O Lord, my God! that glib-tongu'd Aiken,
My vera heart and flesh are quakin   80
To think how we stood sweatin, shakin,
An' pish'd wi' dread,
While he, wi' hingin lip an' snakin,[82]
Held up his head.

Lord, in Thy day o' vengeance try him!
Lord, visit them wha did employ him!
And pass not in Thy mercy by them,
Nor hear their pray'r,
But for Thy people's sake destroy them,
An' dinna spare.   90

But, Lord, remember me and mine
Wi' mercies temporal and divine,
That I for grace an' gear may shine,
Excell'd by nane;
And a' the glory shall be Thine—
Amen, Amen!

82 sneering

INDEX

Authors and literary groups and periods in capitals, titles in italics, first lines in Roman. First line only given where title is identical.

INDEX TO THE ENGLISH LITERARY MAP

(Inside front cover)

The first number is the meridian (west from Greenwich, except where the letter *E* is added); the second number is the parallel. Project the respective meridian and parallel; the place will be found near the intersection of the two lines.